Library of
Davidson College

KNOWLEDGE, CULTURE AND VALUE

Knowledge, Culture And Value

Papers Presented in Plenary Sessions, Panel Discussions
and Sectional Meetings
OF
WORLD PHILOSOPHY CONFERENCE
[*Golden Jubilee Session of The Indian Philosophical Congress*]
(*December* 28, 1975 *to January* 3, 1976)

Edited by
R. C. PANDEYA : S. R. BHATT

MOTILAL BANARSIDASS
Delhi :: Varanasi :: Patna

MOTILAL BANARSIDASS
Indological Publishers & Booksellers
Head Office : BUNGALOW ROAD, JAWAHAR NAGAR, DELHI-7
Branches : 1. CHOWK, VARANASI-1 (U. P.)
2. ASHOK RAJPATH, PATNA-4 (BIHAR)

100
W927k

©The Indian Philosophical Congress

ISBN 0 8426 0850 8

First Edition : Delhi, 1976

Price : Rs. 125.00

85-17004

Printed in India
BY SHANTILAL JAIN, AT SHRI JAINENDRA PRESS, A-45, PHASE-I, INDUSTRIAL
AREA, NARAINA, NEW DELHI-28 AND PUBLISHED BY SUNDARLAL JAIN FOR
MOTILAL BANARSIDASS, BUNGALOW ROAD, JAWAHAR NAGAR, DELHI-7

CONTENTS

PART I

EDITORS' NOTE ix

Plenary Session I : Knowledge and Truth

1. KNOWLEDGE AND TRUTH — T. R. V. Murti — 1
2. TRUTH AND OBJECTIVITY — A. K. Chatterjee — 9
3. KNOWLEDGE AND TRUTH — P. F. Strawson — 17
4. KNOWLEDGE AND TRUTH — Dharmendra Kumar — 19
5. CHISHOLM ON KNOWING AND BELIEVING — Shibajiban Bhattacharya — 31
6. KNOWLEDGE AND TRUTH — Rajendra Prasad Pandey — 37

Plenary Session II : Science, Technology and Value

7. AN APPROACH TO THE PROBLEM OF INDUCTION — Pranab Kumar Sen — 41
8. SCIENCE, TECHNOLOGY AND VALUE — Donald H. Bishop — 51
9. SCIENCE, TECHNOLOGY AND VALUE — Basant Kumar Lal — 53
10. TRANSCULTURAL VALUE-PRESUPPOSITIONS OF SCIENCE — W. Steinkraus — 63

Plenary Session III : Vidyā and Avidyā

11. VIDYĀ AND AVIDYĀ — T. M. P. Mahadevan — 69
12. CHINKS IN THE ARMOUR OF AVIDYĀ — Richard De Smet — 77
13. AVIDYĀ AND ITS RELATION TO VIDYĀ — D. P. Sen — 85
14. A NOTE ON VIDYĀ AND AVIDYĀ — S. R. Bhatt — 93
15. VIDYĀ AND AVIDYĀ — K. P. Mishra — 97

Plenary Session IV : Language, Culture and Man

16. LANGUAGE, CULTURE AND MAN   N. Mishra   103
17. LANGUAGE, CULTURE AND MAN   H. D. Lewis   113
18. LANGUAGE, CULTURE AND MAN   Pritibhushan Chatterji   115
19. LANGUAGE, CULTURE AND MAN   Roop Rekha Verma   127
20. MEANING, CRITERIA AND PURPOSE   Rajendra Prasad   129

Plenary Session V : Commitment and Action

21. COMMITMENT AND ACTION   P. T. Raju   143
22. COMMITMENT AND ACTION   S. S. Barlingay   159
23. COMMITMENT   Archie J. Bahm   169
24. COMMITMENT AND ACTION   Kewal Krishan Mittal   179
25. EXPLANATION AND DESCRIPTION OF ACTION- A PHILOSOPHICAL DEFENSE OF FREUD   Mrinal Miri   185

Plenary Session VI   Theory and Praxis

26. THEORY AND PRAXIS-A PLEA FOR A COMPLETE HUMAN BEING   S. N. Ganguly   205
27. THEORY AND PRAXIS   Evryalo Cannabrava   219
28. THEORY AND PRACTICE   Ram Jee Singh   223
29. THE VITAL CIRCLE : THEORY AND PRAXIS   R. Panikkar   233

Panel Discussion I : Buddhism and Vedānta

30. THE MĀDHYAMIKA AND ADVAITISM   R. K. Tripathi   239
31. THE BASIC IN INDIAN PHILOSOPHY   G. N. Joshi   247

Panel Discussion II   Myths and Symbols

32. MYTH AND SYMBOL   N. S. S. Raman   255

33.	SYMBOLS AND THEIR USERS	R. C. Gandhi	261
34.	MYTH AND SYMBOL	Margaret Chatterjee	271

SPECIAL LECTURE

35.	SCIENCE AND RELIGION, AND THEIR COMPLEMENTARY NATURE	Andre Mercier	277

PART II

1.	MORALITY AND CULTURE	N. K. Devaraja	287
2.	MORALITY, TEMPORALITY AND IMMORTALITY	J. A. Yajnik	297
3.	SOME DISTINGUISHING FEATURES OF MORAL JUDGMENTS	Ved Prakash Verma	305
4.	DISINTERESTED ACTION	Sanat Kumar Sen	315
5.	ETHICAL RELATIVITY AND CULTURAL RELATIVITY : AN ANALYSIS AND EVALUATION	Donald H. Bishop	323
6.	DHARMA AND THE OPEN SOCIETY	Austin B. Creel	331
7.	SOME REFLECTIONS ON SOCIAL DIMENSION OF RENUNCIATION IN ADVAITA VEDANTA	Kapil N. Tiwari	337
8.	THE SPIRITUAL LIFE AS ETHICAL SENSITIVITY	W. E Stein Kraus	345
9.	SCIENCE, RELIGION AND MAN	Santosh C. Sengupta	353
10.	RELIGION, SCIENCE AND MAN	L. K. Aravkar	373
11.	RELIGION AND SCIENCE AS DEFINITION OF HUMANITY	Howard L. Parsons	383
12.	SOME PHILOSOPHICAL IMPLICATIONS OF MODERN PHYSICAL SCIENCE	J. R. Puri	395
13.	RELIGION, SCIENCE AND MAN	Tu Li	401
14.	MAN IN RELATION TO SCIENCE, RELIGION AND PHILOSOPHY	Y. Masih	411
15.	PHILOSOPHY, RELIGION AND TRUTH	P. B. Vidyarthi	421
16.	TO SPEAK CLEARLY	K. K. Banerjee	435
17.	LANGUAGE, THOUGHT AND REALITY (SOME ASPECTS OF INDIAN THOUGHT)	R. R. Dravid	447

18.	HEIDEGGER ON LANGUAGE (THE ROLE OF THE POET AND THINKER)	Thomas A. Fay	455
19.	EPITEMOLOGICAL LANGUAGE VIS-A-VIS 'KNOWN OBJECT'	K. Bagchi	461
20.	CAN ONE PARTICIPATE IN THE VEDANTIC GNOSIS (JÑĀNA) THROUGH THOUGHT ALONE?	J.G. Arapura	475
21.	CONSCIOUSNESS—THE VEDĀNTIC PREDICAMENT	Debabrata Sinha	487
22.	ARE THESE LOGICALLY UNANSWERABLE QUESTIONS?	Mihirvikash Chakravarti	499
23.	ANOTHER LOOK AT BUDDHA-HUME "CONNECTION"	Bina Gupta	509
24.	AUROBINDO AND WHITEHEAD: A QUEST FOR GENERAL IDEAS	A. K. Sarkar	517
25.	LANGUAGE, THOUGHT, REALITY	Thomas J. Sheehan	525
26.	REFLECTIVE INQUIRY AND LANGUAGE	Lewis E. Hahn	533
27.	THE UNCONVENTIONAL CHARACTER OF MYTHICAL—SYMBOLIC LANGUAGE	Caterina N. Conio	539
28.	STATEMENTS ABOUT THE FUTURE AND THE LAW OF EXCLUDED MIDDLE	D.Y. Deshpande	547
29.	TARKA AS CONTRAFACTUAL CONDITIONAL	V.K. Bharadwaja	559
30.	COMMON SENSE AND PHILOSOPHICAL PARADOX	Shashi Bharadwaja	563
31.	KNOWLEDGE PREDICATES	B.S. Sanyal	574
32.	SEEING AND TASTING AFTER IMAGES	S. Chandra	583
33.	THE PROBLEM OF FOUNDATIONS: HUSSERL	Gopal Chandra Khan	595
34.	EDUCATION AND HUMAN DEVELOPMENT	Chand Mal Sharma	607

35.	CAN HUMAN NATURE BE CHANGED THROUGH THE EDUCATION PROCESS THE CONFUCIAN VIEW	*Tsung I. Dow*	609
36.	SRI AUROBINDO ON EDUCATION AND HUMAN DEVELOPMENT	*Pramod Kumar Koyal*	617
37.	PHILOSOPHY AND EDUCATION FOR DEVELOPMENT	*J. de Marneffe*	623
38.	THE PROCESS OF UNIVERSALIZATION IN POETIC CREATION	*Nagendra*	633
39.	WITTGENSTEIN ON PUZZLEMENT AND EXPLANATION IN AESTHETICS	*V. P. Sharma*	641
40.	ON FAMILY RESEMBLANCES AND AESTHETIC DISCOURSE	*N.J. Mantasfakis*	649
41.	AN ANALYTICAL NOTE ON ABANINDRANATH'S AESTHETICS	*S.C. Nandi*	673

EDITORS' NOTE

Having completed fifty years of its active existence the Indian Philosophical Congress is celebrating its Golden Jubilee in the form of World Philosophy Conference, sponsored by the International Federation of Philosophical Societies and hosted by the University of Delhi.

The central theme for deliberation in the Conference is *Knowledge, Culture and Value* which is therefore the title of the present Volume. Pursuit of knowledge and attainment thereof is natural to and inevitable for Man; however, it is not 'knowing' for the sake of mere knowing but also for the betterment of 'living' and hence it engenders a culture-pattern and a scheme of values strived for by the Mankind. The delegates in the conference are to discuss how modern knowledge can be related to a country's cultural tradition and cherished human values with a view to deriving benefit for the country's economic and social development.

The present volume consists of the papers presented in the different Plenary Sessions, Panel Discussions, Special Lectures and Sectional Meetings. The papers presented in the Sectional Meetings constitute its second part. Some of the scholars who are to participate in the Plenary Sessions and Panel Discussions have not sent their papers in advance and therefore we could not print them here. Prof. Daya Krishna is a speaker in the Plenary Session V but due to oversight his name is left out in the programme. Owing to limitation of space we regret our inability to accommodate all the papers presented in the different sections. However, we have published their abstracts separately. In the present volume we have endeavoured to make our selection representative. In the choice of the papers we have been guided by a panel of experts to whom our thanks are due. Mr. K. N. Namboothiri and Miss Amarjeet Kaur deserve our thanks for help in reading proofs. We are also thankful to messrs Motilal Banarsidass for undertaking its publication.

Delhi
December 21, 1975.

R. C. P.
S. R. B.

PART I

1
KNOWLEDGE AND TRUTH

T.R.V. Murti

The framing of the topic poses a preliminary question. It presupposes that we know knowledge or can know it. For how else, it may be asked, can we ascertain whether it is true or not, whether it conforms to its deliverance of the content or otherwise. When and how, if at all, do we become aware of knowledge? We do not admittedly know knowledge either simultaneously when we perceive an object, or subsequently by a separate act of knowing. We also have no memory of knowledge, not having perceived it in the first instance. When we perceive the table or the tree, it is the table or the tree that we perceive, and not the knowledge and table together or even their distinction. In normal empirical perception, the datum does not appear as distinctly distinguished from the perceiving consciousness, there being no need to separate the two. Nor is it possible to do so. For when I see a patch of colour, I am conscious of the patch of colour only and not at once conscious of my perception of it or any distinction from it. These two, the colour and my perception of it, cannot obviously be given together. Nor is it true that immediately after the occurrence of a perception, in the second and subsequent moments, there is consciousness of the previous act of perception—the so-called introspection of old time psychology or the *anuvyavasāya* of the *Nyāya*. It is even thought that such introspection intervenes automatically. There is no experiential basis for this introspection. It is not that every act of perception is *ipso facto* followed by a back-stroke of the consciousness of itself. Should not this introspection itself be followed by another which apprehends it as introspection and still by another and so forth indefinitely? There is no evidence of this un-ending series, and a person's life-time will be consumed in one single act of perception.

Moreover, the disembodied act of perceiving, contentless and diaphanous as it is, cannot be an object of thought, for it does not arrest attention, being the act of attention itself. As being invariable and uniform, it eludes our grasp. How then do we become aware of knowledge, for even to speak of it is in some measure to be conscious of it ? One way in which we could become conscious of our involvement is the experience of *the same objective content* in two different ways or stages, first *as believed to be true* and subsequently *as disbelieved*, or at least the belief from which has been withdrawn. Without one and the same object appearing in two different stages or modes of apprehension, we may not become aware of our act of attending to it. In the transition of our attitude, as we pass from belief in the reality of the object to disbelief in its reality, we are indirectly aware of our act of attention. If the objective content were to differ in the two stages or if it were a unitary unanalysable fact, reflection cannot result. Only when what we took to be one thing really turns out to be another on closer inspection, do we scratch our head and become self-conscious. Did I perceive it after all or was I day-dreaming ? What was it that I actually perceived ? Some such misgivings and searchings of the heart, as it were, describe the attitude of self-reflection. As long as a machine is running smooth and in order, we have no occasion to become inquisitive about its inner structure and functioning. Only as a breakdown happens, we begin to inquire about the economy of each part in the whole and the functioning of the entire mechanism. This is an interesting but somewhat intricate and intriguing topic for investigation. And this is not the place to undertake a fuller analysis of the context of illusion. I may state my conclusion briefly that the consciousness of the false engenders reflection; it makes us turn back upon ourselves.

Knowledge and Truth involve each other. We cannot be conscious or be aware of knowledge as such without a previous belief and a subsequent disbelief or at least a re-confirmation of the content. Re-confirmation must be understood as annulment of a previous disbelief. Without the consciousness of the false or at least its suggestion, we cannot affirm anything as true. To speak of the true is to distinguish it from the false. If every thing which passes for knowledge were true without exception, or if every thing were false without exception, we cannot call any particular knowledge true or false.

II

Knowledge is a cognitive experience, and it has to be distinguished from types of non-cognitive experience, such as willing and feeling as exemplified by volitional acts or emotional states as pleasure, anger or lust. What is peculiar about the cognitive attitude is that we want to "see" or "take in" things as they are, as they obtain in reality; we do not want to add or modify or distort the given, and to the extent we do this, it is not knowledge.

The notions of truth and falsity imply that knowledge is a mode of consciousness which is, or should be, determined solely by the object (jñānaṁ tu pramāṇa-janyam, pramāṇaṁ ca yathābhūtavastuviṣayam, ato jñānam kartum akartum anyathā vā kartum aśakyam, *kevalaṁ vastu-tantraṁ eva tat*, na codanā-tantraṁ nāpi puruṣa-tantram". Śaṅkara's Bhāṣya on Br. Sūt. I. i. 4; "na vastu-yāthātmyajñānam puruṣabuddhyapekṣam, kiṁ tarhi, *vastutantram* eva tat." ibid, I.i.2.). Consciousness or the subject cognizing must merely reveal or discover the object, neither adding anything to it nor distorting it. To be discovered, the object of knowledge should exist prior to and independent of the knowing; it must be an accomplished fact—a *siddha-vastu*—one that is not brought into being through the knowing. If it were simultaneous with knowledge or were created by it, how can any knowledge be true or false ? The perception of the "rope-snake" would not be an illusion and would not be recognised as such any time, if the rope (the real) were not taken as existing both during and *before* the illusion; it must be something absolutely independent of our knowing of it. The "rope-snake", however, has no existence independent of our knowing, and is totally exhausted in that relationship (*dṛśyatvāt mithyā*). Once this is granted that the object of knowledge should exist prior to it, we cannot also assign any period or limit to its priority. For, to do any such thing we have to reach a stage when consciousness alone existed and the object was ushered into existence later on, presumably by the former. It is evident that such consciousness is not knowledge; it is willing. However far back we may trace our knowledge it will always presuppose the object as prior to it. This priority is not primarily temporal, but only signifies the accomplished character of the object.

Similar considerations require that the object of knowledge should not be subject to the accidental conditions of the percipient. To take the example of perspectives. If a certain object were to be known from a certain position at a certain time and by a certain person only, we cannot call that object real, nor that knowledge true. For, we have no means of deciding whether the object is not our creation or a joint product of the conditions of the percipient and those of the object. Thus the object of knowledge cannot be uniquely particular; it must be universal, free from all conditions and accidents. And if this were pushed further it would mean that strictly speaking, only Pure Being can be said to be the object *par excellence*.

Not only is the object to be independent of our knowing, but we have also to regard the object as not being required to be known by any person or mind. When we know an object we need not at once be conscious of this very knowing. For, the object, which alone should determine the nature of consciousness in knowledge, says nothing about its present knownness or its past un-knownness.

The above contentions about the ideal of knowledge run counter to the commonly received principle of idealism that the object is mind-dependent in some way or the other. But all arguments of idealism (e.g. those advanced by *Vijñānavāda*, Berkeley or Hegel) rely upon feeling and willing and mis-apply them to knowledge. The knowledge-absolutist agrees with the realist and with Kant, as against the idealist, that the object of knowledge is or should be independent of the knowing-consciousness. There is profound disagreement, however, with realism in another respect. The realist uncritically takes what is ordinarily given as pure knowledge. No actual knowledge (in the empirical way) is completely free from non-cognitive factors such as imagination, construction, bias and prejudice etc. Such states appear as knowledge, are taken to be knowledge, but are actually illusion or erroneous perception. It is a necessary demand that we should purify and disassociate knowledge from other factors which are non-cognitive, but which masquerade as knowledge. The 'rope-snake' for example is mistaken as knowledge; what we seem to perceive is not given or known; it is a creation or projection of our imagination or fantasy, although not apprehended as such in the state of illusion.

Thus knowledge as such is invariably true, and Truth is *known* only, not felt or willed. It is only metaphorically that we speak of the truth of a feeling or willing, not literally.

III

It is a very widely held notion that Truth can obtain only between propositions, or that it is a function of propositions. For, it may be said in justification of this position, that how else can we ascertain and know anything as true ? It is only thought as expressed in language and having a structure (i.e. several elements in a recognisable and ordered configuration) that we can consider and be aware of it as true or truth. As for the question, with what is the proposition to be aligned or compared, two answers might be given : one is that the proposition may be related with other propositions, thus forming a coherent system of propositions; the other alternative is that the proposition may be compared with the object and its correspondence with the latter may be ascertained.

In the first case, what we arrive at is only consistency or logical truth. We only draw implications and more implications and still further implications. There is nothing to justify or validate the original proposition or body of propositions with which we have started. Given these propositions or presuppositions, we can correctly draw the consequences that flow from them. This is eminently the procedure of formal logic. Even a lie may be consistently bolstered up by other lies and these by some others, the whole procedure being sustained by our ingenuity and inventiveness. Such truth is not concerned with conformity of thought with the real, unless we granted the *assumption* that ultimately Thought and Reality are identical. The Real is nothing but systematic or coherent thought. This is what Hegel says. His whole dialectic is a good example of this. The super-structure raised by him should not be taken as in any way validating the assumption, but only as a sustained drawing out of the implications of the assumption. All knowledge is reduced to one mode, that of thought or reason. There is no given or independent fact, nor direct, immediate perception. This does offend our sense of Truth as discovery of what exists independent of our knowing act.

The other theory is that our knowledge conforms or corresponds, point by point, item by item, to the real given to us in perception or direct acquaintance. Where there is one-one Correspondence between the two, there is Truth (*Tadvati tatprakārakaṁ jñānam*). Some merit in this theory may be accepted; there is recognition of the independence of the real. The difficulty, however, is how can we ascertain that what appears in knowledge is a true transcript of what obtains in reality. We do not, *ex hypothesi*, have the original also before us in knowledge. It may be said primarily the real is given to us in perception as "this", as the subject of a judgment, and thought only elaborates it (*sarvaṁ jñānaṁ dharmiṇy abhrāntam, prakāre tu saṁśayaḥ*). The persistent question is how we can assert that what appears in knowledge and given expression in language is identical with what we perceived as given reality. It might be said that knowledge which leads to successful activity in our empirical ventures should be taken as valid or true (*saphala-pravṛtti-janakatva*). The criterion of truth is now not correspondence of knowledge and object, but that which leads to successful or uncontradicted activity, i.e. what works in practice. Even a postulate or assumption may work. Here there is no question of absolute truth, but what is useful or leads to desirable results. This may well vary with regard to different spheres of our interest. This is Truth according to commonsense and science.

The philosophical question still awaits an answer. It may well be that whatever appears in knowledge as thought-elaboration and finds expression in linguistic forms may not be identical with the real. The possibility of discrepancy and deviation is still there. When we look at a building from a distance or from a particular angle, we may get only a perspective. There could be an infinite number of such perspectives, and each one may be useful, no doubt. No one perspective or a combination of them can claim to be absolutely correct.

The only way to be sure of absolute truth is to get into the skin of the thing as it were, by becoming identical with it. Here knowledge and its object coincide. This is intuition *par excellence*. There is no possibility of discrepancy or falsity here, because we are not looking at the thing externally, mediately, from a distance or through the mediation of categories, or in a biassed or prejudiced way. We know the thing not by representation, but by being it, as it were. Knowledge and the thing known become one. There is, however, a drawback. When we have the intuition we are not at once aware of it as intuition of the real. It is indeed a paradox : we have the truth when we are identical with the real, but cannot be reflectively aware that we know the truth; and when we reflectively make the assertion, we are already away from it. Our assertion may be a falsification or a distortion of the real, and is therefore only appearance. To avoid this predicament, the Advaita Vedānta takes recourse to negation. By consciously and systematically negating all thought-elaboration and linguistic expression in every form, we arrive at Ultimate Truth or Reality (*adhyāropāpavādābhyāṁ niṣprapañcam brahma prapadyate*).

The presupposition behind this is that thought, and this applies to language also, falsifies reality and by the negation of this falsification or appearance, we alight upon the absolutely real. For a discovery of the real, the appearance is negated. This is possible only if the appearance were in some sense related to the real. All appearance is appearance *of the real*, (is indicative, if not constitutive of the real), and by removal of the appearance we realise the presence of the real as underlying it. A further consequence of this view is that we have recourse to two levels or orders of things, the real and its appearance.

Suppose for instance we hold the view that language and thought are closed circles, that they are arbitrary conventions, and although we may express one set of terms in other terms, simple or complex, there is nothing behind or beyond these linguistic expressions, like a transcendent reality. Modern linguistic philosophy holds that language is a game or sets of games, and we cannot get out of the linguistic to anything non-linguistic called the real. The quest for absolute truth or real is meaningless. The world is what it is. The problem of Truth or any other philosophical problem is solved by dissolving it, by showing that there is no problem at all. This leads to an unmitigated relativism and indifference towards the great issues of life. This view has to be discarded on this score. The statement that all language is a game is itself not a game, but a veritable statement. There is thus a deep inconsistency in linguistic philosophy.

The stand of the *Mādhyamika* (Śūnyavāda), as understood

by the orthodox schools, is not much different. There may be the Real, but thought and language are no indication or guide to it. There is falsification, and everything is false, but it is not a falsification of the real. Negation of the false does not at once mean the apprehension of the real behind it, as held by the *Advaita Vedānta*. We can only refute this stand attributed to the *Mādhyamika* by showing that in all our experience there is no mere falsity, which is not at once the falsification of an underlying ground. The very impossibility of the false otherwise is the argument.

I have considered in brief some of the principal points of view on Knowledge and Truth. One point clearly emerges out of this. It is not possible to formulate a neutral or universally acceptable position, for any position presupposes or is but an expression of a particular metaphysical stand. This is the nature of all philosophy.

Benaras Hindu University.

2
TRUTH AND OBJECTIVITY

A.K. Chatterjee

Any attempt to chart out the difficult terrain of the cluster of cognitive concepts would naturally situate the notion of truth at the very centre of such a topography. The questions "what is it to know something?", "How is knowing distinguishable from not-knowing?", "Could I be mistaken when I say I know something?"—these and a host of similar questions all seem to revolve, directly or deviously, round the notion of truth. Let us take the simplest-looking question "What is it to know something?", and try to disentangle the different strands in its texture. First, in saying 'A knows that P' it is implied that A has a positive or affirmative attitude towards P, that is to say, A believes in the truth of P. Of course 'A knows that P' is not to be equated with 'A believes that P'; in the latter case no claim is made of the truth of P, and such a truth-claim might be withheld from a belief-sentence without resulting in any oddity. A belief might easily be mistaken, and the truth-value of P does not enter into truth-value of the intensional function 'A believes that P'.

Knowing P thus presupposes believing P without being identical with it. They differ essentially in the fact that belief is primarily a state of mind. It might claim truth and objective reference, but this claim and this reference might be mistaken, without the mental state of belief itself being affected by the mistake. One might have a false belief but it is a belief nonetheless. Knowledge on the other hand would seem to stand or fall with its ability to substantiate its truth-claim. If a piece of knowledge is mistaken, it is understood as not having been knowledge at all in the first instance. A belief-sentence generates intensional functions while knowledge can continue to revolve round extensional compounds. Belief is subjective in a sense in which knowledge is not. Cases of knowledge are all governed by the all-or-none principle—one either knows categorically or does not know at all—and do not require the employment of modal operators.

Could we add truth to P, and say that knowledge amounts to having a true belief? This subterfuge would not do; one might believe that P, and as a matter of fact P turns out to be in agreement with states of affairs, but that would not be a sufficient condition for saying 'A knows that P'. A must be in a position to justify his reliance on the truth of P, he must be able to adduce evidence relevant to his belief, so that the truth of P be not merely a fortuitous phenomenon. In a game of dice, A might believe that a deuce would come, and as a matter of fact it does come out, so that A has now a true belief, yet he cannot claim any knowledge of it, since he cannot explain why a two-spot should have come out. Truth of a proposition is a necessary, but not a sufficient condition, for making any claim to know. 'A knows that P' implies that P is a true proposition, but from the mere fact that P happens to be true we cannot conclude that A has the claim to know it. A must further have reasons to justify why he thinks P is true. Of course one need not always be aware of these reasons which therefore are not always explicitly spelt out. But the point is that in claiming to know it is suggested that the reasons are there and that they may be called upon when challenged. A lucky guess is not knowledge. It is this warrant of certitude that assimilates knowing to other performative utterances like promising. To know is to be able to certify.

In any case truth would seem to be pivotal to the claim to know. Something cannot be knowledge if it lacks in truth. Any analysis and valuation of the knowledge-situation would thus entail an explication of the notion of truth. What is truth? Here two distinct but overlapping questions are involved : What does truth consist in, and how do we verify something as true? I call them the meaning-question and the criterion-question respectively. What then is the meaning of truth? Usually truth is supposed to be exclusively a prerogative of propositions. A proposition is, by definition, what is either true or false, if modal complications are avoided. Knowledge then can claim truth only when it is propositionalized, i.e. expressed in propositions. 'Knowing that' is the paradigm of all knowledge, and for the purposes of this paper we will not be concerned with the other type of knowledge viz. 'knowing how'. It might even be argued that one could not really speak, in the proper sense of the term, of 'knowing how' unless it involved 'knowing that', that a mere practical ability or a technical skill does not really amount to knowledge if it does not ensue out of some modicum of theoretical understanding.

Our difficulties just begin when truth is characterized as propositional. Is it a property that certain propositions have and others lack? In that case we could read off its truth simply by inspecting a proposition taken by itself. But apart from logical truth which is indeed a class apart, no empirical proposition wears its truth on the surface, as it were. In order to claim that a given proposition is true, we have to transcend the proposition itself as a solitary thought, and somehow measure it against something lying beyond it. Truth is something relational and pertains to a proposition only as understood in relation to something else. A furious debate has raged precisely about what this 'something else' could mean. One school of thought has insisted that a proposition is made true only by being related to other propositions, or rather to a system of propositions, so that in our quest for truth we do not require any pernicious comparison between propositions and a putative objective reality. The question of truth now reduces itself to one of internal consistency. There are weighty reasons behind this line of thinking, endorsed by some of the greatest figures in classical philosophy. Kant, for instance, held that the objective world is a construction out of the synthesis of the manifold of representations. What saves it from subjectivity is paradoxically still more subjectivity, that is to say, intra-subjectivity. A real object is what is common to many subjects. Falsity is exposed, sooner or later, as giving rise to an inconsistency. The source of falsity is to be located in a free floating proposition, which is unceremoniously expelled from the systematic structure of the whole as not being acceptable to it. The best example of this type of structure is provided by an axiomatic system, as developed in mathematics and logic, where the addition of any formula, not belonging to the system, leads to a contradiction. In technical jargon such a set is called a maximal set. A system that is all-comprehensive and excludes nothing could be shown to be inconsistent. The criterion of truth in such a system is immanent in the system itself. And the justification for this sort of conception of truth is the presumed impossibility of getting outside all thought and language in order to secure a direct and unmediated disclosure of the external world. Whatever we could know and say about the world would perforce have to be propositionalized, so that a proposition could be corrected only by the totality of current knowledge. i.e. the system of all other propositions available to us. A non-propositional encounter with things would be an inarticulate 'Aha'-experience, and such expletives are totally unsuited for making any proposition either true or false.

This simple equation of truth with consistency founders however on its utter insufficiency to yield objectivity. No amount of piling up of propositions could ever result in contact with facts, in a truth about the world. Our purchase on reality is irretrievably lost and we move round and round a nightmarish circle of propositions, without ever managing to say a single thing about objects. The system could certainly be logically consistent but absence of contradiction, though necessary, is never a sufficient condition of truth, except in a Pickwickian sense of the term. This queer situation is illustrated time and again in the history of foundations of mathematics. Euclid, the father of axiomatic geometry, did not distinguish between truths of fact and truths of reason. A geometrical theorem was at once a piece of information about things and a part of a deductive system. The grave difficulty about the dubious postulate of parallels led to the complete separation of the two, and the truth of a theorem became simply its integration into a system. Theorems incompatible with one another could both be true, provided that they were related to different systems. Truth is now entirely divorced from the propositions themselves and is found only in the logical link which unites them. Which system of geometry then describes the actual world? The question simply does not arise; each geometry is an abstract deductive structure, true in its own terms, but there is no question of absolute truth. One might contend that mathematics is purely a formal discipline and, as such, does not engage itself in questions of fact, but the whole point is that if truth is reduced to mere consistency the very distinction between the two kinds of truth lapses. There is no way to distinguish between formal and material truth if all that is available to us is internal consistency. A system might well be consistent, and yet fail to decide about its applicability.

A more recent example is the famous axiom of choice (AC), probably the most discussed axiom of mathematics second only to Euclid's axiom of parallels introduced more than two thousand years ago. It was first explicitly stated by Zermelo in 1908, though need for it had been noted by Peano twenty years earlier. Whether the Zermelo-Freenkel system (ZF) is consistent or not is as yet not known. Goedel's Incompleteness Theorem may be readily adapted to show that consistency of ZF cannot be proved within ZF, but Goedal showed in 1938 that *if* ZF is consistent then it remains consistent if AC is introduced as an additional axiom. We can have as much confidence in AC as in the remaining axioms of set theory. But it took a further twenty-five years to show that AC is in fact a new axiom, not derived from ZF. Independence of AC was established by Cohen in 1963. But the whole situation remains extremely murky. If ZF is consistent with or without AC, which of the two systems is the *true* one? One simply does not know.

Consistency then cannot be taken as a sufficient condition of truth. For explicating truth we have to get behind the circle of propositions, and seek to check them against something non-propositional, i.e. reality itself. We have to speak of the truth of a proposition as its correspondence—however much we hate ourselves for it—to an objective state of affairs. The paradigm of knowledge must be a direct perception of the world, and is expressed in sense-data statements. Truth consists in the fact that a proposition corresponds directly to what it reports. This is essentially Locke's version of the theory but systematically worked out, with a great deal of sophistication, in the Tractatus. Recently correspondence theory has been given a great boost by Tarski's semantic conception of truth. Truth, for Tarski is a property ascribable to sentences, but it is a semantic property, not a grammatical property of them. He neatly sidesteps the invocation of the concept of a fact, as being vague and metaphysical. He therefore states the truth-conditions of sentences as a series of equivalences. To give his own example : "The sentence 'snow is white' is true if, and only if, snow is white". This may be abbreviated into "'P' if, and only if, P", since the predicate 'is true' is redundant, à la Ramsey. The whole difficulty here is in construing the nature of the equivalence which gives the truth-condition of a sentence. Equivalence is a relation that obtains between propositions and so, if the second occurrence of the letter 'P' in the formula is already understood as a proposition, we are reverting back to a variation of coherence theory. We are still moving within the sphere of propositions and the contact with reality cannot be secured. If, on the other hand, the second P stands for a fact, the equivalence itself breaks down; a proposition and a fact cannot be equivalent. A fact, unlike a proposition, is neither true nor false; it just is, and has no truth-value. There are other difficulties too. If the second P is in object-language, and somehow manages to report what the case is, the first P, being within quotes, is in meta-language, and must be a name of the sentence P. But a thing and its name can never be equivalent. If the quotation marks are ignored then the formula is reduced to a tautology and, being trivialized, cannot serve as an explication of the notion of truth. Any form of correspondence theory seems to suffer from this sort of unclarity; one end of the correspondence-relation, viz. a fact or a state of affairs, remains obscure, and we do not really know what it is to which a proposition is supposed to correspond in order to be true.

No theory of truth then succeeds in yielding objectivity, which should be of the very essence of truth. What I propose here, is not to suggest a theory of truth, but rather what seems to me to be a presupposition of any theory. Before any proposition could acquire truth, it appears that there should be a point of contact between the proposition and an objective reality. The contact itself is not propositionalized, without inviting an infinite regress. How this contact comes about is a mystery. The picture theory of language claimed to provide an explanation of this but the theory is now long discredited, and was disowned by its author himself. But whatever be the explanation of the nature of the purchase that a proposition has on reality, this is the minimum condition that would have to be fulfilled in order that a proposition becomes true. It seems that we have to go back to Russell, and speak of some sort of acquaintance with reality, something being given to direct awareness. This is the prius of all knowledge and, consequently, of all truth. This immediate acquaintance is itself not describable as true—it is in this regard that empiricism is sadly led astray—since what is given has not yet been propositionalized. It is just bare givenness, what the Advaitin calls the 'isness' (sattā) of things. Propositional knowledge intervenes subsequently, so that the pure given is overlaid by all sorts of accretions. The question of truth arises only in this later emergence, the Being of the Advaitins being neither true nor false. But without this minimal, pre-propositional, direct acquaintance with being, there would have been no objectivity, and therefore no truth. The Advaitin therefore says that being is given in every act of knowledge (sarva-pratyaya-vedya). It is not implied that the filling in of the content of being is its falsification, as the Advaitin claims. I am not suggesting a veiled form of māyāvāda invidiously, but allowing the question of subsequent speculative formulations of the nature of being to remain open. In any case there could be no truth without some sort of givenness, whatever be the character of what is given.

Benaras Hindu University

KNOWLEDGE AND TRUTH

P.F. Strawson

In Western Philosophy discussion of truth tends to merge, on the one hand, with discussion of language and meaning, on the other hand, with discussion of knowledge and belief. There are good reasons for both associations. The former is dominant at present; but it is the latter which is the theme of this Session and of this paper.

One way of making clear the conceptual connexions involved is to indicate the sources of some traditional philosophical debates and tensions and to sketch the lines on which the tensions should be resolved. This is the way proposed here. In particular, an attempt is made to show how a correspondence view of truth and a foundationalist view of empirical knowledge—though both have their contributions to make—need to be complemented with insights associated with coherence theories of truth. The task is one of steering a middle way between mutually opposed and ultimately self-destructive exaggerations of different aspects of the truth.

4
KNOWLEDGE AND TRUTH
Dharmendra Kumar

The verb 'to know' is followed by several different kinds of expressions. Philosophers have been largely concerned with the case in which this verb is followed by 'that' which is then followed by a sentence expressing a proposition. Sometimes the word 'that' may be absent as in 'I know you are innocent', but this makes no more difference to the meaning than the omission of 'them' in a conditional sentence. One may speak of this case of knowledge as knowledge of a proposition as distinguished from knowledge of a thing or object, knowledge of a skill, etc. The verb and its cognates used in the propositional context indicated here may be said to be epistemic terms which express a certain relationship (or possibly several relationships with some differences) between a person and a proposition. An obvious feature of the epistemic verb 'to know', which distinguishes it from other familiar epistemic verbs like 'to believe', is that every knowledge-proposition, that is, a proposition to the effect that a certain person knows that P (where 'P' is a sentence expressing a proposition), entails the proposition that P. This is sometimes expressed by saying that knowledge entails truth. Several verbs of English besides 'to know' share the feature that a sentence of the form 'X Vs that P' entails that P. Among these verbs are 'to see', 'to notice', 'to realise', 'to remember' and even non-epistemic verbs like 'to prove'. The verb 'to know' is particularly important, being in a sense the most general of these epistemic verbs. The analysis of the concept of truth may thus be viewed as a part of an adequate analysis of the concept of propositional knowledge. The concept of truth is important in the analysis of epistemic concepts in general, for even an epistemic phrase like 'believes that P' can meaningfully occur only after an expression denoting someone who has the concept of a proposition and therewith the concept of truth with or without acquaintance with the word 'true' or any word synonymous with it. An infant, a parrot, possibly a dog can hardly be said to believe a proposition, even if it shares with grown up human beings certain responses, the utterance of certain indicative sentences.

I

The coherence and pragmatic theories of truth have now been discarded by most philosophers. But the correspondence theory has seemed to Ramsey's followers to be equally wrong. In his contribution to the Aristotelian Society symposium on Truth in 1950 Strawson viewed Austin's plea for refining the correspondence theory as basically misguided. "The correspondence theory requires, not purification, but elimination", he said. (*Truth*, George Pitcher, ed. 1964, p. 32). Strawson's attack on the correspondence theory of truth in this paper seems to be a consequence of his failure to notice certain things some of which he seems to notice in his reply to Warnock without acknowledging any change in his views. While attacking the correspondence theory Strawson distinguishes his view from Ramsey's. "It will be clear that, in common with Mr. Austin, I reject the thesis that the phrase 'is true" is logically superfluous, together with the thesis that to say that a proposition is true is just to assert it" (p. 46). He admits that 'true' and 'not true' "have jobs of their own to do" (p. 46) He may thus seem to differ considerably from Ramsey who said, "it is evident that 'It is true that Caesar was murdered' means no more than that Caesar was murdered", that the phrase 'it is true that' is one which we generally "use for emphasis or for stylistic reasons, or to indicate the position occupied by the statement in our argument" (p. 16). But the difference between Ramsey and Strawson is really verbal. Unlike Ramsey, Strawson engages in a detailed study of the contexts in which the phrase 'is true' is employed in ordinary discourse, and says that we use it for confirming, granting, conceding, expressing agreement, etc. rather than for saying something about a statement. He says, for instance, that "we may state (in the way of corroboration, agreement, granting, etc.) that X is Y by saying "It is indeed" or "that is true." (p-45). He says that in these contexts 'true' and 'not true' "are functioning as abbreviatory statement-devices" like "yes", etc. (p. 45) He says explicitly that his rejection of the view of logical superfluity of 'is true' and of the view that to say that a proposition is true is just to assert it "does not entail acceptance of Mr. Austin's thesis that in using 'true' we are making an assertion about a statement" (p. 46). "Nor does it entail the rejection of the thesis...that to say that an assertion is true is not to make any further *assertion* at all." (p. 46). It is clear that what Strawson means by denying the logical superfluity of 'is true' is that the use of a sentence containing this phrase is what Austin calls "purely performatory" (p. 31) and Ramsey calls "stylistic", etc. Strawson not only accuses Austin of "the failure to distinguish between the task of elucidating the nature of a certain type of communication (the empirically informative) from the problem of the actual functioning of the word "true" within the frame-work of that type of communication" (p. 53); he also finds it "difficult to see how Mr. Austin could accommodate" what he describes as "the generally concessive employment of "It is true that p......" (p. 46). But in reply to Warnock who argues that the phrase 'is true' is used to make a statement *about* a statement and that its role in expressing agreement, etc. depends on its use in making such a statement, Strawson straightaway accepts Warnock's thesis "that someone who says that a certain statement is true thereby makes a statement about a statement" (p. 68) and calls it "the undisputed thesis". This seems clearly to be a change from Strawson's earlier position, but he does nothing to acknowledge this. One may think Strawson possibly uses "statement about a statement" in a weak sense which may be consistent with the view expressed in his contribution to the Aristotelian Society symposium. He says that "we had better allow that in a paraphrase of a predication of 'is true' of a statement, something is said about that statement if that statement is referred to in the paraphrase, even though it is not a subject of predication there" (p. 77). He rightly observes that the rule of substituting 'P' for a sentence in which 'is true' is predicated of the statement that P" is but a clue to a general method of elucidating the predication of 'is true', a method which has far greater flexibility than "the rule itself suggests at first (p. 77). As an example, he says that 'A's statement that X is eligible is true' may, "entirely in the spirit of the Ramsey-like method" be paraphrased as "As A stated, X is eligible" (p. 78). He points out that one who utters the latter words is ordinarily "saying something about A's statement" (p. 78). Similarly "for 'what he said about the house is true' we might have "The house is as he said it was" (p. 79). Thus he contends "that the requirements of the undisputed thesis do not favour an Austinian account of the sense of predications of 'is true' rather than a Ramsey-like account" (p. 81) Strawson springs a surprise by going on to say that "a Ramsey and an Austin give a common answer to one question", that "they are at one on what it is for a (made) statement to be *true* "and that" Austin additionally offers a (partial) account of what it is for a (true) statement to be *made*." (p. 82) But if that be so, how can the correspondence theory or Austin's version of it need to be eliminated rather than to be refined ? The view taken in reply to Warnock seems clearly to be inconsistent with the earlier denunciation of the correspondence theory.

Strawson's conversion to the view of the identity of Austin's answer with Ramsey's answer to the basic question of the theory of truth seems to show less understanding of the correspondence theory than his earlier view as a critic of this theory. The basic question of the theory of truth is : what is it for a proposition to be true ? It is unfortunate that both Austin and Strawson discard the term 'proposition' traditionally used by philosophers and logicians in favour of 'statement' taken from ordinary discourse in spite of the latter's unsuitability for philosophical purposes in view of (1) the ambiguity between the act of stating and that which is stated, and (2) the implication of the proposition having been stated by someone. In one sense of 'sense' or 'meaning' it is, of course, wrong to say that a proposition is the sense or meaning of an indicative sentence, as some philosophers were careless enough to say. But this mistake can be easily corrected and the term can be defined so as to conform to its traditional use as denoting the bearer of truth-value. According to the correspondence theory of truth, a proposition's being true consists in its correspondence with the facts or in a fact corresponding to it, or something like it. This is, of course, a truism, as it should be. It is not trivial, however, thanks to the rival theories. According to the usual versions of the theory there are as many types of facts as there are types of propositions : empirical, mathematical, logical, possibly ethical, theological, etc. There is in any case need for refinement so as to explicitly rule out inflating the universe with negative, conjunctive, disjunctive and existential facts.

Strawson fails to appreciate the merit of Austin's choice of the stronger question : what is it for anything to be a true statement ? Austin's answer to this stronger question clarifies the nature of the relation of correspondence between the statement or the proposition and the fact. It shows that propositions and facts are individuated together by linguistic conventions, that to understand a proposition is usually to know what fact corresponds to it if the proposition is true. This approach escapes Pitcher's puzzlement over "correspondence-as-correlation" and "correspondence-as-congruity" (pp. 9-11).

The possibility of eliminating, for ordinary purposes, the word 'true' from an English sentence by paraphrasing in the manner suggested by Ramsey and Strawson follows from the correspondence theory itself, and it shows the coherence theory and the pragmatic theory to be wrong. Even a sentence like 'the statement that the present king of France is bald is neither true nor false', which Strawson has occasion to use, may be capable of being paraphrased so as to drop the words 'true' and 'false'. What the correspondence theory denies is not the identity of truth-conditions (or logical equivalence) of (1) the proposition that P (briefly, tp) and (2) the proposition ascribing truth to tp (briefly, tpT); it only denies identity of these propositions. Austin gave arguments for denying the identity supposed by Ramsey, and Strawson countered one of these arguments in the symposium paper. How can Austin's view of what it is for a proposition to be true be the same as Ramsey's ?

One of the arguments given by Austin to show the non-identity of tp and tpT is based on the fact that in many countries two different trials are held, one for libel and another for crime. "If Mr. Q writes on a notice board 'Mr. W is a burglar', then a trial is held to decide whether Mr. Q's published statement that Mr. W is a burglar is a libel: finding Mr. Q's statement was true (in substance and in fact)'. Thereupon a second trial is held, to decide whether Mr. W is a burglar, in which Mr. Q's statement is no longer under consideration: verdict 'Mr. W is a burglar'. It is an arduous business to hold a second trial: why is it done if the verdict is the same as the previous finding ?" (p. 26) Austin does notice that "there are many legal and personal reasons for holding two trials" (.26n), but

he insists that the issue being tried is not the same. " (p. 26).
It is indeed true that the questions considered in the two trials
are not the same, and the two trials would usually be held in
different courts. But the questions are not (1) whether the
proposition that W is a burglar is true, and (2) whether W is
a burglar. If these were really the questions at issue, there
would be no need for two trials. For on Austin's own admission, "Whenever tstS (the statement that S) is true then tstST
(the statement ascribing truth to tstS) is also true and conversely,
and that whenever tstS is false tstST is also false and conversely."
(p. 26). The wording of the verdict notwithstanding, the basic
question before a court is whether the evidence produced conforms to the norms laid down by law for awarding a certain kind
of penalty. Great philosophers do sometimes give very poor
arguments. This argument is no worse than the howlers
Moore himself later noticed in his *Principia Ethica*.

There are good reasons for distinguishing the identity of
propositions from the identity of their truth-conditions in certain
cases. There are good reasons for so using the term 'proposition'
and even the term 'statement' as to allow one to speak of logically true and logically false propositions and statements, besides
ordinary empirical propositions. Strawson admits inconsistent
statements although, according to him, nothing at all is said when
one is guilty of inconsistency. If thus logically true and logically
false propositions are admitted, there is good reason for admitting
more than one logically true and more than one logically false
propositions. It is not plausible to say that 'It is raining now
or it is not raining now' and 'If anything is red or yellow then
it is either blue or not blue' express the same proposition,
although their truth-conditions are the same, both being true
under all circumstances. Strawson himself seems clearly to be
opposed "to treating all logically equivalent propositions as
identical" (p. 82n). In some cases two logically equivalent
propositions may be distinguished on the ground that it is conceivable that one may believe one of these propositions without
believing the other even when one considers both the propositions. This is possible for some logically true and some logically
false propositions. But this will not do for distinguishing tpT
from tp. In view of Strawson's emphasis on the role of 'is true'
in expressing agreement, in confirming, conceding, etc. in an

earlier paper in *Analysis*, Austin asked : "but what of the case where......I say nothing but '*look and see*' that your statement is true ?" (p. 31). Strawson was quick to reply that "the man who looks and sees that the statement that there is a cat on the mat is true, sees no more and no less than the man who looks and sees that there is a cat on the mat" (p. 48). Anyone capable of seeing that P must have the concept of truth. If tp is different from tpT ,anyone who considers both the propositions and sees that P would also see that this proposition is true, though the impossibility of seeing that P without considering tpT and thus without seeing that tpT is not obvious.

The strongest of Austin's arguments is based on the premise that no statement or proposition can refer to itself (p. 25). Certain paradoxes, among other things, strongly support this premise. Strawson himself admits that "few statements are about themselves" (p. 77n.). Austin's argument may be constructed as follows: tpT is different from tp, for if (1) it is not different as the logical superfluity view requires, and yet (2) it is really a proposition about a proposition, then tpT is about itself or refers to itself, which is an absurdity. While Strawson did not seem to treat sentences containing 'is true' as expressing propositions about propositions at all, the above argument could not be effective against Strawson without being conjoined with reasons for treating tpT as a proposition about a proposition. Strawson's acceptance of "the undisputed thesis" later does not make such reasons dispensable, as the import of the undisputed thesis is not altogether clear. Once it is admitted that a proposition need not be identical with a proposition logically equivalent to it, every proposition about a proposition should be regarded as different from the latter proposition. But is tpT about tp in the strict sense of 'about' ?

This question calls for a criterion for determining second-order propositions or propositions about propositions. The verbal expression is not a reliable guide. 'Something may be both red and round ' expresses what may also be expressed by the sentence : The proposition that something is both round and round is consistent. This latter sentence seems to express a second-order proposition. A singular proposition ascribes something to an object or a relation to a set of objects. Objects of any domain are thus classified by applying predicates.

It is undeniable that propositions can also be classified in various ways. First-order propositions can certainly be classified as true or false. There is then no reason for denying tpT the status of a second-order proposition, and then there seems no reason for viewing it as identical with tp.

This line of reasoning can be extended to show the untenability of an objection raised by Strawson against the correspondence theory of truth. He says that Austin's account of truth "encourages the assimilation of facts to things" (p. 35). "An expression used referringly has a different logical role from an expression used describingly" (p. 36), as he observes. He is also right in saying that "stating is different from referring, and different from describing" (p. 36). But the objects referred to may be of various sorts. They may be particular material objects or empirical universals or numbers or propositions of any order. The correspondence theory of truth demands "something in the world *which makes the* statement true.... or *to which* the statement corresponds when it is true" (p. 37), he says, and he thinks "it is evident that the demand that there should be such a relatum (for a true statement) is logically absurd : a logically fundamental type-mistake." (p. 37). The core of his objection is that while a statement does state a fact, "the fact it states is not in the world". (p. 37) But what is to be regarded as being in the world or what the world is to be regarded as consisting of admits of a variety of answers, each of which would serve to bring out some point of philosophical interest. To say that the world consists of things or particulars is, among other things, to emphasise (1) that a universe A cannot be identical with a universe B if one of them has a particular which the other does not have (2) that universes A and B cannot have different universals if they have the same particulars, (3) that two universes may well have the same universals and yet have different particulars. To say, on the other hand, as Wittgenstein said in the *Tractatus*, that the world consists of the totality of facts and not of the totality of things, is to elucidate the concept of knowledge of the world among other things. The model of a classroom or a basket of apples does not do justice to the philosopher's conception of the world.

The use of the word 'fact' is, in any case, not essential to the correspondence theory of truth. Any theory of truth may be said to be a version of the correspondence theory, if it (1) takes propositions rather than linguistic entities to be the bearers of truth-value, (2) is incompatible with the coherence and pragmatic theories of truth, and (3) affirms the non-identity of tpT and tp and thus brings out the use of the predication 'is true' in expressing the relation between thought (not "language," as Austin said unwittingly) and reality.

II

There is a large number of epistemic expressions in English, each suitable for characterising the epistemic relationship between a person and a proposition, taking into account the person's epistemic situation as a whole. Any of the words 'conscious', 'aware', 'think', 'believe' 'sure', 'certain', 'know', etc. followed by 'that' is used in a way which is different from the use of any other. As the basic and most general of the truth-entailing epistemic verbs, 'to know' has a logic derived from these basic features. The truth entailed by knowing is not something ascribable to the person who knows. What can be ascribed to the person is a strong attitude of acceptance which knowing the proposition must entail. Knowing that P, therefore, entails being sure, and not merely believing, that P. For similar reasons, knowing and being sure must be ascribable to a person independently of many circumstances including his state of consciousness. Being sure, as entailed by knowing, is thus to have a disposition rather than a fleeting state of consciousness. The verb 'to know' has, therefore, no use in the continuous tense or in the imperative mood ordinarily, though philosophers have talked of acts of knowing. It is wrongly thought sometimes that a person may know in his heart of hearts that P and even admit this in a state of hypnosis or narcosis without being sure or even believing that P. A person may be unconsciously sure of something he consciously does not even believe. One may sincerely claim to be an atheist and yet consistently pray in distressing situations. In the dispositional sense in which one knows that P while he sincerely denies that P, one is also sure that P.

Since knowing that P entails that P, pursuit of (propositional) knowledge is obviously pursuit of truth. But pursuit of truth may be more significantly said to be pursuit of knowledge. For pursuit of truth cannot be a matter of a hunch each time. The verb 'to know' would not be very significant if knowing that P simply meant the truth of the belief that P. Pursuit of truth has to be systematic seeking of evidence and its evaluation which knowing that P involves. That is why perhaps every developed language has an expression fairly close to 'to know that P'. The truth of propositions we are ordinarily concerned with is neither inaccessible nor just at hand. Access to truth does not satisfy the model of access to the top of the building. One cannot think of a situation in which the evidence available to a human being for a proposition's truth would be logically inconsistent with the proposition being false, although one can often be quite certain of its truth. Even if for every proposition we are concerned with, there could be a finite body of evidence entailing the proposition, one could well go wrong in thinking of a given body of evidence as entailing a proposition which it did not entail. While the logical possibility of failure in getting at truth must thus be admitted in every case, it does not imply the unlikelihood of success, much less its impossibility. This situation also indicates how the coherence theory and the pragmatic theory could have greater appeal for some philosophers than the correspondence theory which makes knowledge an ideal uncertain of attainment.

In view of the requirement of truth, knowing that P naturally requires stronger evidence than certainty that P. But a person's claim to know that P may not only fail on account of his evidence being not good enough; it may fail in a stronger sense in view of the 'evidence' being too good to be evidence. It is wrong to say that the reports of one's sense-data including pains and aches are learned verbal responses but basically like screams rather than propositions. They are certainly propositions which are true or false. But the concept of knowing that P is geared to the logical gap between the proposition and the evidence at the disposal of a thinker. It makes no sense to speak of knowing a proposition about one's own sense-data, but not just because knowing that P entails that P. The absurdity is no less true of any other epistemic verb. It makes no more sense to speak of somebody believing (or not believing) a proposition about one's own sense-data. A sentence of the form 'X Vs that P' where 'to V' is an epistemic verb and 'P' expresses a proposition about the sense-data of x, would either express an inconsistent proposition or one indistinguishable from the proposition that P. Such a sentence would be inadmissible in ordinary discourse. One may, however, thoroughly revise the use of the verbs concerned and consistently speak of believing and knowing propositions about one's own sense-data. But little will be gained by this exercise which will make these verbs rather indeterminate like the Bengali verb which covers not only eating, drinking and smoking but also kissing.

University of Delhi

5
CHISHOLM ON KNOWING AND BELIEVING

Sibajiban Bhattacharya

I shall examine here two theories of knowing and believing which Chisholm has presented in his two books, *Perceiving* and *Theory of Knowledge*. I shall note some points of difference between these two versions, and discuss their respective merits and demerits. (1) In *Perceiving* Chisholm has argued that temporal references should be incorporated in the definitions of epistemic terms. "For, there are times when, as we would ordinarily say, the available evidence may favour some proposition which is false; at such times a false proposition is more worthy of one's belief than is a true proposition. Thus it may be true that a man is going to win a lottery and yet unreasonable for him to believe he is. But once the drawings are announced, the belief may no longer be unreasonable. The example indicates *that our definitions should contain* temporal references. For a proposition may be evident at one date and unreasonable at another. The phrase 'at t' could be inserted in our definitions: a proposition would then be said to be evident at a time t provided only that its contradictory is unreasonable at t; and so on. But, for simplicity, I shall not make these temporal references explicit" (p .6; my italics).

In *Theory of Knowledge*, however, Chisholm makes temporal references explicit in the definition of 'know that'. "S knows at t that h is true, provided : (1) S believes h at t; (2) h is true; and (3) h is evident at t for S." (p. 23).

Now we examine whether Chisholm's argument is valid. He argues from the fact that it is desirable and even necessary to incorporate temporal reference in the definition of 'evident' and 'believe', that it is desirable and necessary to do the same in the definition of knowledge. But this argument is unconvincing, for even his own definition of knowledge ascribes a non-temporal sense to 'know'. Although it is true that "there are times when, as we would ordinarily say, the available evidence may favour some false proposition", still no one can ever be said to *know*, even in Chisholm's sense of the term, a false proposition. The temporal reference built in 'h is evident at t for S' and 'S believes h at t' gets *cancelled* by 'h is true' in his definition. Although it is quite possible that a false proposition is evident at a particular time to some one, and also that he believes at t^1 that a particular proposition is true, but may not do so at another time, say $t2$, still these fluctuations in attitudes cannot affect knowledge. It is quite possible that one does not know that h is true; but if one knows, 'his intellect may be in "a state of repose" ' (quoted in *Theory of Knowledge*, p .13). Although Chisholm does not accept this as a definition of knowledge, still his definition has this (desirable) consequence. One can *come to know* that h is true, at a certain time; one cannot *know at a particular time.* One can change, revise, modify and even give up one's belief, one *cannot do* any of these things with *knowledge.* Thus the three conjuncts in the definient function at cross purposes with each other; while (1) and (3) *require* incorporation of temporal reference, (2) cancels it, so that the definiendum 'S knows that h is true' cannot have any temporal reference incorporated in it.

(2) Moreover, the definition of knowledge as given in *Theory of Knowledge* (quoted above) is logically defective, because it contains a redundant conjunct in the definiens. This becomes clear when we note what Chisholm says to bring in and 'solve' Gettier's problem. He says, "If we countenance the possibility that some propositions are both evident and false.. then it would be necessary to add a qualification to our definition of 'know' "(ibid, fn). Thus he explicitly states that in the definition given above 'the possibility that some propositions are both evident and false' is *not* 'countenanced'. But this only means that every proposition which is evident is true, so that the conjunct (2) in the definiens logically follows from (3), and is, therefore redundant.

This shows that in this definition in *Theory of Knowledge* Chisholm does not accept the position of *Perceiving*, where he has argued that "there are times when, *as we would ordinarily say,* the available evidence may favour some proposition which is false". The definition of knowledge in *Perceiving* is, therefore, logically proper, and does not contain any redundant conjunct. Chisholm holds two opposite theories with regard to the possibility that some propositions "are both evident and false" in the two definitions given in his two books, yet he offers the same type of definition in both. This has the consequence of making the definition in *Theory of Knowledge* logically defective.

(3) About the relation of knowing to believing, Chisholm says : "But even if there is a sense of 'believe' or 'accept' in which *knowing* entails *believing* or *accepting*, we must not think of knowing as being, in any sense, a 'species of' believing or accepting. A man can be said to believe firmly, or reluctantly, or hesitatingly, but no one can be said to *know* firmly, or reluctantly, or hesitatingly.... The relation of knowing to believing, in the present sense of 'believe', is not that of falcon to bird : or of airdale to dog; it is more like that of arriving to travelling. *Arriving* entails *travelling*—a man cannot arrive unless he has travelled—but arriving is not a species of travelling" (*Perceiving*, pp. 17-18).

If, however, we examine the *definitions* of knowing which Chisholm has given, we find that, contrary to what Chisholm says here, these definitions turn knowing into a *species* of believing. If the relation of knowing to believing 'is more like that of arriving to travelling', then knowing cannot be defined as believing *and* doing something more—arriving cannot be travelling and doing something more. The method of defining by describing properties or predicates by a *conjunction* of terms or sentences stating general properties and special properties, is defining by *genus and differentia*. Thus to define 'man' as 'both rational *and* living' is to turn man into *a species* of living beings. This becomes clear if we notice *how exactly* knowing entails believing. We cannot say 'X has travelled' follows from 'X has arrived' by *simplification*; but 'X believes that p' follows from 'X knows that P' by simplification on the definitions which Chisholm himself has offered , just as 'X is a living being' follows from 'X is a man' by simplification. Moreover, what Chisholm himself says in *Theory of Knowledge* about the *approach* to the question of defining knowledge, makes it clear that in this book he himself considers knowing as a species of believing. "One approach to the question, which Plato himself suggests, is to assume, first, that if one man knows and another man has true opinion, but does not know, then the first man has everything that the second man has and something else as well. Then, having made this assumption, we ask: What is that which, *when added to true opinion*, yields knowledge?" (*Theory of Knowledge*, p. 5; my italics). It is clear the arriving cannot be defined as travelling *plus* something, and if on the contrary we do suppose that it *can be so defined*, then arriving becomes a species of travelling. It will be inconsistent to suppose that by adding a differentia to a generic property we do not get the defining property of *the species*. If the problem of defining knowing is formulated as that of finding out what must be added to believing truly, then knowledge is necessarily regarded as a 'species' or 'kind' of true belief.

(4) Chisholm holds two opposite positions on the question of the propriety of the expression 'ought to believe' in his two books, yet offers the same type of *definition of knowledge* I now examine how far his position is consistent in his two books.

In *Perceiving* he says; "when it is said, then, that people *ought to believe* what is evident, and that they *ought not to believe* what is unreasonable, 'ought' has its practical sense. But when it is said that they *ought to believe* what is true and that they ought not to believe what is false, 'ought' has its absolute use. Our locution 'h is more worthy of belief than i' is to be taken in its practical sense" (p. 8; my italics). Chisholm uses the locution 'h is more worthy of belief than i' synonymously with 'h *ought to be believed* more than i' in the practical sense of 'ought' and he uses 'more worthy of belief' as a primitive in the set of epistemic terms he defines in his book. In his *Theory of Knowledge*, however, Chisholm holds the opposite view. "But 'duty' as we ordinarily understand the term, is in connection with actions, or possible actions, that are within the agent's power and for which he can be held responsible if he performs them....But are beliefs actions or possible actions, that are within anyone's power? And can a man be held responsible for what he believes, or fails to believe? We often speak of what a man *ought to know* but *seldom, if ever*, of what a *man ought to believe*" (p. 12; my italics).

Before we examine the bearing of this theory on Chisholm's *definition of knowledge*, we note here that Chisholm's argument against using 'ought to believe' as presented here is wholly misleading. Chisholm regards the expression 'ought to believe' as improper, whereas he regards 'ought to know' as proper. Yet his argument applies to knowledge with equal if not more force as to belief. If 'ought to believe' is improper because beliefs 'are not actions or possible actions' which are within the agent's power, then 'ought to know' is equally improper because Knowledge is definitely not an action or a possible action which is within the agent's power. If a belief is not an action, knowledge, too, is not. On this ground 'ought to believe' and 'ought to know' should be regarded as equally improper. The reason why 'ought to believe' is 'seldom, if ever, used', whereas 'ought to know' is a proper expression, has to be sought and found in a *difference*, not similarity, between knowing and believing.

Now we examine whether the definitions of knowledge which Chisholm has offered can explain the use of 'ought to know'. We, first, study the definiton *in Perceiving*.

D^1. "S knows that h is true" means; (1) S accepts h; (ii) S has adequate evidence for h; and (iii) h is true. (p. 16).

What will 'S ought to know that h is true' mean on this definition? Apparently, it may mean one of the following three things :—

(A) (i) S ought to accept h; (ii) S has adequate evidence for h; and (iii) h is true,

(B) (i) S accepts h; (ii) S ought to have adequate evidence for h; and (iii) h is true,

(C) (i) S ought to accept h; (ii) S ought to have adequate evidence for h; (iii) h is true, which is a combination of (A) and (B).

Of these three, (B) and (C) are ruled out on Chisholm's interpretation of 'adequate evidence'. The 'evident', according to Chisholm, 'is more worthy of belief than is the unreasonable' (p. 6) and as we have already seen that this means that the evident is what ought to be believed (in the practical sense of 'ought'), so that if anything 'ought to be evident' then this would be that "which ought to be 'ought to be believed !'" which is absurd. Moreover (B) has the consequence that 'S accepts h' follows from 'S ought to know that h is true' which means that a man ought to know only what he already accepts. This is not a desirable consequence. Both (B) and (C) involving 'ought to be evident' are ruled out as possible interpretations of 'ought to know'. As the *conjunction* of (i), (ii) and (iii) of D^1 cannot be said to be a duty which S can possibly perform, (A) becomes the only meaning of 'S ought to know that h is true'. There is no difficulty in accepting this, for, as Chisholm points out 'accept' means the same as 'believe' in the appropriate sense (p. 17), 'S ought to accept h' means the same as 'S ought to believe that h'; and Chisholm, in this book, accepts this locution as proper and even fundamental. But to accept (A) as the proper interpretation of 'ought to know' is to concede that the 'ought' has relevance for knowledge only insofar as it is relevant to belief involved in knowledge. To prescribe that it is someone's duty to *know* that h is simply to prescribe that it is his *duty to believe it* insofar as believing that h is an element in knowing that h. But in his *Theory of Knowledge* Chisholm *rejects* this locution as improper, yet gives the same definition of knowledge :—

D2. S knows at t that h is true, provided : (i) S believes h at t; (2) h is true; and (3) h is evident at t for S.
(p. 23).

Now if we accept this definition of knowledge, *and* also reject 'ought to believe' as an improper expression, then there is *no way of* interpreting 'S ought to know that h is true'. It is not clear whether we can at all have the locution 'S ought to know *at t* that h is true' instead of 'S ought to know that h is true'. In any case, if the adequacy of a definition of knowledge is to be tested by its success in eliminating 'know' from 'ought'-contexts also, then obviously Chisholm's definition in this book is inadequate.

University of Burdwan

6
KNOWLEDGE AND TRUTH

Rajendra Prasad Pandey

1. In philosophy there are only eternal problems, paradoxes, but no corresponding eternal solutions. Perhaps therein lies the peculiarity of philosophical investigation—it is not so much a quest into determining and clarifying whatever we know and understand, but more a quest into those dark corners in our knowledge and understanding which constantly threaten our security in knowing and understanding. These dark corners are the habitat of the problems and paradoxes as old as philosophy itself.

2. The basic problem concerning 'Knowledge and Truth' is one such problem—the problem, namely, how to understand the inevitable conjunction between the two? The inevitable conjunction not only provides that the meaning of the one requires to be related to the meaning of the other so as to be properly understood, but also for the same reason it provides that the meaning of the one is obscured by the meaning of the other insofar as they do not mean one and the same thing. Hence the problem, really a paradox : Indeed *we know* (there are the truths known) and yet *do we know* (how about obscurities arising from within knowledge-phenomenon) ? Consider in this light the Kantian problem of 'Synthetic *a priori*'.

3. This ever present paradox in our knowledge situation, however, is the most important guarantee of the reality of our 'seeking-to-know.', indeed of ourselves as the knowers. Man has to *acquire* knowledge and he has to be constantly engaged in acquiring it, for truth is neither automatically revealed to him nor has he the reason to be sure that the whole truth is ever revealed or even that there is anything like the whole truth, whatever that be. There is no question of raising doubts as to the objectivity of what is true; but doubts naturally arise as to *how* man comes to identify and determine *that* (objectivity) in terms of his knowledge—knowledge which involves, essential elements of subjectivity. Consider Socratic paradox pertaining to this 'how' : 'A man cannot seek to know that (truth)

which he already knows, for if he knows the truth there is no need to seek to know it; nor can he seek to know that (truth) which he does not know, for how can one even begin to seek that of which he has no idea !" (Plato: *Meno*).

4. The most modern attempt to resolve this paradox has been that of some modern analysts—*in fact*, though, they succeed only in reiterating it. Consider these three views: (i) 'to know' is a capacity verb (Ryle); (ii) 'I know' commonly has a 'performative' rather than a 'descriptive' use (Austin); and (iii) if something is known, it is true and one is sure, has even the right to be sure, that it is true (Ayer). Obviously these views are not necessarily mutually exclusive; even if one is reluctant to resort to the parable of 'elephant and blind men' to account for the difference of these standpoints, he would nevertheless note that *essentially* in all of them the same thing is asserted, namely, that there is a strict logical relation between 'Knowledge' and 'Truth', that the one implies the other in its assertion. To be able to give the conditions of truth means also knowing it and *vice versa*. And to admit this means that the Socratic paradox is explained away !

5. But, then, what reasons we have to believe that the same conditions, the same objectivity governs both 'Knowledge' and 'Truth'—even as concepts in ordinary language ? The analyst must show that these conditions are given in the *use* of these concepts. But their 'use' shows something else: 'knowledge' has a corresponding basic verb form 'to know'; there is no such corresponding verb form, even a derived one, for 'truth'. Therefore 'knowledge' and 'truth' cannot *mean* exactly the same thing—the conditions determining them as such may not be exactly the same. Hence the paradox: In a consistent epistemology they ('knowledge' and 'truth') must signify the same objectivity and yet insofar as they are signifying concepts of objectivity they may not mean exactly the same thing. Assertions of truth necessarily imply the assertions of knowledge; and yet what *is* there in Truth to correspond with seeking-to-know ? Or should we regard all knowledge instantaneous realisation and all Truth immanent revelation ? Even as 'operative truth' (performative, capacitative or non-necessary conditional truth) *truth* must presuppose outside itself that *seeking-to-know* which renders that (truth) possible as a historical

achievement. Did we ever leave Socratic paradox even for a moment?

6. Like most of other analysts' contentions, the above views too suffer from the fallacy of logical simplification and transparency. Logically simplified and transparent things are no more the 'original' things—the reality or Truth—with which philosophy concerns itself. Logic robs them of their variegated richness, though at the same time assuring *us* that it is perfectly just, right and correct in doing so, that we have achieved 'truth' as well as 'knowledge' within the single 'logical space'. Consider the assertion in *Tractatus* : facts and propositions are in the same logical space. We are in Plato's cave with no openings provided.

7. *Conclusion*: The paradox remains—precisely because logic fails us and we are able to see through its trap, can we still resort to the old wonder and remain lovers of wisdom. Love of wisdom is eternal 'seeking-to-know' an eternal confrontation with problems and paradoxes, which we enjoy in the attitude of wonder :—How at all the historical, temporal can grapple with the eternal ! The philosopher remains basically a 'seeker'; he rejoices being with problems and paradoxes.

Viswa-Bharati

Plenary Session II

SCIENCE, TECHNOLOGY AND VALUE
    President : D. D. Vadekar
    Secretary : Chettimatham

Main Speakers:
    (1) P. K. Sen
    (2) Donald H. Bishop
    (3) B. K. Lal
    (4) W. Steinkraus
    (5) A. Kosing

AN APPROACH TO THE PROBLEM OF INDUCTION

Pranab Kumar Sen

1. I take induction to be an assertion of a contingent universal proposition on the basis of an examination of some, but not all, particular instances which fall under it. Accordingly, I take the following to be a preliminary formulation of the problem of induction : Is it possible to assert a contingent universal proposition on the basis of an examination of some, but not all, particular instances which fall under it ?

2. It is necessary to distinguish, at the outset, the genuine problem of induction, which is *logical*, from another problem which is merely psychological, and with which it may be confused.

When we ask, "Is it possible to assert a universal proposition etc. ?", we might ask simply whether it is *psychologically* possible to do so; i.e., whether it is ever possible to come to believe that the universal is true without ascertaining the truth of each of the singular propositions falling under it. The answer to *this* question is obviously in the affirmative; if not for any other reason, for the simple reason that our beliefs are not always based on adequate evidence. But, if the problem of induction consisted just in this question, it would probably cease to have any philosophical importance. At any rate, it would have been easy to solve it.

So, what is known as *the* problem of induction is different from this question. It is not a psychological question at all, it is a question of logic : Is it *logically permissible* to assert a universal without ascertaining the truth of all particulars falling under it ?

3. Let us make this logical question a bit more precise. The question is really concerning the possibility of *justifying*, logically, the process of induction, i.e. the process of asserting a universal on the basis of an examination of only some instances of this universal ? In a slightly different way of putting the same question : Could such a process be ever regarded as rational ?

4. David Hume, who is usually credited with the discovery, at least with the first clear formulation, of the problem of induction, addressed himself to both the psychological and the logical questions. To the psychological question he gave an affirmation answer, but his answer to the logical question was in the negative. He concluded that, while belief in universal truths is psychologically inevitable, and also biologically indispensable, this belief can never be sustained by reason. We shall try to show that, if we do not expect something really impossible of the process of induction, it is as reasonable as the process of deduction with which it is almost always unfavourably compared.

5. Before we proceed further with our discussion, it is necessary to clarify, I think, one point regarding the formulation of the problem of induction. We have formulated the problem as one of justifying the transition from particulars to universals. But a distinction is sometimes made between two kinds of induction : (i) from particular to universal, and (ii) from particular to particular. Some logicians, particularly John Stuart Mill, were also of the opinion that induction of the latter kind (sometimes called 'eduction') was more basic. (See his *A System of Logic*, Book II, Chapter III, Section 3.) But, actually, the *logical* problem involved in the latter kind of induction is not in any way different from that involved in the former. The reason for this is that the transition from a set of particulars of one kind to a new particular of the same kind is justified *if and only if* a transition from these particulars to *any* particular of the same kind is justified; and to say that a transition to *any* particular of a kind is justified is to say that a transition to the universal itself is justified. We shall illustrate this point by help of one simple example :

We find in some particular cases that a piece of copper conducts electricity. From these particular cases we can infer either (i) that a hitherto unexamined piece of copper conducts electricity, or (ii) that all pieces of copper do so. Now the inference that the new piece of copper conducts electricity is reasonable (i.e. justified) *if and only if* the inference that *any* piece of copper would conduct electricity is justified. But the inference that any piece of copper would conduct electricity is really the same as the inference that all pieces of copper would do so.

John Stuart Mill, who emphasised the relative importance of inference from particular to particular also realised this point. (See his *A System of Logic*, Book II, Chapter III, Section 5). But this is incompatible with one view which has been very often held about the relative probability of the universal and corresponding particular propositions. It has been held that an evidence which makes a universal proposition probable to the degree m, makes the corresponding particular probable to the degree $m+n$, when $n>0$. But if by probability we do not mean the *antecedent* or *a priori* probability, but empirical probability relative to empirical evidence, then this is surely a mistake.

6. I shall now try to define a certain approach to the problem of induction, to indicate a way in which a solution to the problem may be found. It should be pointed at the outset that I am not offering any actual solution.

Various attempts have hitherto been made to solve the problem. The general impression among philosophers seems to be that none of these attempts have succeeded. I shall not however make any comments on these attempts, neither shall I try to relate explicitly my approach to the problem to any of them. Instead, I shall devote the time to a clarification of the problem of induction as I see it, for it may be that the difficulty which is posed by the problem is largely due to a misconstrual of the problem itself—a misconstrual which this clarification may remove.

With a view to clarifying the problem of induction, I shall construct and consider an analogous problem for *deductive inference*. That is, I shall first

(i) state what could be called the Problem of Deduction, and then

(ii) show how this problem is tackled by us.

7. The analogous problem of deduction is: Are we justified in making a deductive inference, while the fact remains that we very often do so?

The very first thing, and a very important thing at that, which we must note is that we do not construe the question to be a question about deductive inference *as such*. For we do not suppose that either *all* deductive inferences are justified, or *no* deductive inference is justified. We think, actually, that *some* deductive inferences are justified (can be justified or valid), while some others are not.

Let us consider next how we proceed to justify a deductive inference.

A typical method of justifying a given deductive inference is the so called method of natural deduction. This method of justifying a deductive inference is a method of proving its validity, and it consists in *actually deducing* the conclusion from the premise (or premises) by help of a number of rules of inference. Let us consider one example of the application of this method.

We want to justify (i.e. prove the validity of) the following inference :

Philosophers are clever and thoughtful.
Some philosophers are rationalists.
Therefore, some thoughtful people are rationalists. In obvious symbolism the argument is formulated as follows:

1. $(x) ((Px \supset (Cx. Tx))$
2. $(Ex) (Px. Rx)$ ∴ $(Ex) (Tx. Rx)$

And we proceed to justify this inference in the following manner :

3. $Pw. Rw$ 2,   EI
4. $Pw \supset (Cw. Tw)$ 1,   UI
5. Pw 3,   Simp.
6. $Cw. Tw$ 4,   5, M.P.
7. $Tw. Cw$ 6,   Com.
8. Tw 7,   Simp.
9. $Rw. Pw$ 3,   Com.
10. Rw 9,   Simp.
11. $Tw. Rw$ 8,   10, Conj.
12. $(Ex) (Tx. Rx)$ 11, EG

What have we done to prove that the given inference is valid ? We have accepted that there are some rules of inference which are such that if a conclusion is derived from the premises (strictly) in accordance with them, then the inference is valid; and, then, have actually derived the conclusion of the inference in question from its premises in accordance with these rules. And what we have done in this particular case is also what we do in all others. The very method of natural deduction consists in accepting some rules of inference (as valid) and deriving the conclusion of the inference, to be justified, from its premise (or premises).

8. The important philosophical question which arises at this point is : What is the justification for the *rules* themselves ?

There are at least four distinguishable ways in which one may try to answer this question. I shall consider each of them briefly.

(i) The first one may be called *deductivism*. According to this, the rules are to be justified by other rules from which they could be deduced. But it is clear that *all* rules of derivation (or justification) cannot be justified in this way.

(ii) We may call the second *conventionalism*. According to this, the justification of the rules consists in the fact that they are accepted just as a matter of convention. This is also unsatisfactory because it ultimately leads to the view that the decision that a particular inference is valid is arbitrary in the last analysis.

(iii) The next view, which we shall call *formalism*, might be regarded as a sophisticated, and perhaps a slightly modified, version of conventionalism. According to this view, the question of justification or proving validity does not make sense without any reference to a *system*. An inference which is justified in one particular system may not be justified in another. But the system in which the justification for the inference in question is given is itself *defined* in terms of (by reference to) the rules which are used for the purpose of this justification. Thus 'justification' or 'proving validity' is really *defined* in terms of these rules in the system; and therein lies the justification of these rules.

This view, as I have already said, does not appear to me to be fundamentally different from conventionalism. For the question which is immediately raised by this view is why we accept the system at all; and this question cannot be answered on this view in a way which could enable us to avoid the charge of ultimate arbitrariness in our decisions regarding validity. To bring out this point, we imagine a system in which the following schema is accepted as a rule of derivation:

$$\therefore \quad \begin{array}{c} P \\ \wr P \end{array}$$

Are we prepared to accept this system? Obviously we are not. And the grounds on which this system will be rejected are, in the last analysis, non-formalistic; the fundamental reason for rejection being that this system is *counter-intuitive*, i.e. in conflict with our intuitive judgments of validity and invalidity. (Compare A.N. Prior, "The Runabout Inference-Ticket", *Analysis*, Vol. 21, 1960).

This brings us to the last view regarding the kind of justification for the rules by which we justify particular inferences.

9. (iv) This last view I shall call *intuitionism*. According to it, the rules of justification are ultimately justified by our basic logical intuitions. As we reflect on the rules, we *see*, and see *immediately* that any inference made in accordance with them must be valid. If we like, we may say that they are established by *intuitive induction*.

This view has indeed gone out of fashion. But we accept this view for it appears to us that all other views would either lead to infinite regress (e.g. deductivism) or have the inevitable consequence that our judgments of validity are, in the last analysis, arbitrary (e.g. conventionalism and formalism).

10. What, then, is our solution of the problem which we have called the 'problem of deduction'? Our solution is this: Some deductive inferences are justified (i.e. valid), and they can be justifying by deriving, actually, their conclusion from their premises in accordance with some rules of inference, which are accepted on the ground that they are intuitively evident.

Now we shall see whether a similar solution to the problem of induction is possible.

11. In order to work out a solution of the problem on this line, we should *first* discourage, once for all, the general form in which the problem is almost invariably posed: Is it possible to justify an inductive inference? As if, either *all* induction is justified, or *no* induction is: But we have pointed out, in the case of deduction, that the fact is that some deductive inferences *are*, while others are *not* justified. And exactly the same is the case with induction. It is unreasonable altogether to accept this 'all or none' formula in the case of induction also. So the form in which the question ought to be posed is: Is there *any* inductive inference which is justified? And *if* there is any, *how* is it justified?

12. There is nothing in an inductive inference *as such* which makes it either necessarily justified or necessarily unjustified. The distinction between the justified and the unjustified cuts across the distinction between the deductive and the inductive.

But some philosophers have actually maintained that there is something in the inductive inference as such which makes it necessarily unjustified. So we shall spend some time in arguing that this is a mistake. (Actually, it is this mistake which tends to perpetuate the problem of induction).

It has been maintained that *no* inductive inference can be justified because, in an inductive inference, we assert a universal proposition on the basis of only *some* particular instances, and, as such, we can never be *absolutely* certain about the truth of the universal. It is always (logically) possible that what has been found to hold true of some particular instances will not hold true of others, and consequently of all. In view of this possibility, an inductive inference can never be quite (and, so, rationally) justified.

But this only brings out that every inductive inference has the following characteristics :

(i) The conclusion of an inductive inference is never necessarily true; and

(ii) it does not follow necessarily from the premise or premises.

We need not take the first seriously at all, for the conclusion in a deductive inference may also be contingent. We should not take the second seriously either, for it only means that the premise in an inductive inference does not provide a conclusive evidence for the conclusion. And this is no objection to induction at all; for induction *is* problematic. The premise in an inductive inference cannot be said to make the conclusion *true*, it only makes it *probable*.

13. We may consider at this point, a bit more closely, the general conception of justification. An inference is justified (or is justifiable) if and only if it is possible to sustain the claim which is made in that inference. So, in deciding whether or not an inference of a particular kind can be justified, we are to be clear about the claim (or the kind of claim) which is made by any inference of that kind. Now, a *deductive* inference claims that if the premise or premises are true then the conclusion *must* be true. (This is sometimes expressed by an

explicit use of the words "must", "necessarily", etc. in the formulation of the conclusion). So, a deductive inference is justified if and only if this claim can be sustained. Thus, we show that a deductive inference is unjustifiable (i.e. invalid) by showing that it is quite possible that all the premises are true, but the conclusion is false. But the claim which is made in an inductive inference is very different. The claim which is made here is that if the premise or premises are true then it is *probable* that the conclusion is also true (or, for short, the conclusion is probable). So, an inductive inference is justified if and only if *this* claim could be sustained. Thus, to maintain that no inductive inference is ever justified is to maintain that the premise or premises in an inductive inference can never make the conclusion probable; or, to be more precise, the fact that some thing is true in some cases can never make it probable that it is also true in others. But this is certainly absurd.

The only question which we are thus entitled to ask about induction is : Does the premise of an inductive inference ever make the conclusion probable ? And the only sensible answer to the question is : It does on some occasions, and it does not on others.

14. In our solution to what we called the problem of deduction we started with the observation that some deductions are valid while others are not. Then, in the next step, we argued that the deductions which are valid can be shown to be so (can be justified, in other words) by help of a number of intuitively evident rules of derivation. We have already taken the corresponding first step in the solution to the problem of induction. We are now to take the second step. That is, we shall have to show now that there *are* intuitively evident rules of *probabilification*, or as it is also called of *confirmation*. But can we do this ? I think we can. There are *at least some* rules of confirmation which are, I believe, quite intuitively evident. Only to give an example of the kind of rule which I have in mind, I shall very briefly mention here what is called the Nicod Criterion. By defining a positive instance, as well as a negative instance, for generalisations of a certain kind, it provides us with a criterion of confirmation and disconfirmation for generalisations of that kind.

15. According to Jean Nicod's double rule of confirmation and disconfirmation, a universal proposition of the form "All F are G" is confirmed by an object which is both an F and a G, and is disconfirmed by an object which is an F, but not a G. (See Jean Nicod, *Foundations of Geometry and Induction*, p. 219). This does seem to be intuitively evident, and to formulate one of our basic insights about confirmation and disconfirmation. I say this in spite of the fact that this criterion has been rejected by many, because I believe that the grounds on which it has been rejected are not valid, and are far from being intuitive. The Nicod Criterion has been rejected mainly on the grounds that (i) its acceptance leads to some paradoxical consequences, and that (ii) it is applicable to only a limited variety of cases where an evidence is supposed to confirm or disconfirm a hypothesis. So far as the first is concerned I have tried to argue elsewhere (in "Approaches to the Paradox of Confirmation", *Ajatus*, 1972) that the paradoxes are not due to any defect in Nicod's Criterion, but either to Hempel's Equivalence Condition or to an uncritical use of the Law of Contraposition. The second ground on which the critetrion has been rejected, viz. its limited applicability, does not really entitle one to reject the criterion itself; it only entitles one to reject the claim that it is the *only* criterion of confirmation or that it is a criterion which can be applied to all cases of confirmation. But this is not a claim which I intend to make, even though my researches have convinced me that it has a much wider application than it is usually supposed to have. I have mentioned it as only *one* example of an intuitively evident rule of confirmation. There are, I think, many other examples.

16. An explicit formulation of these rules (both rules of qualitative confirmation, like the Nicod Criterion, for deciding *whether or not* a generalisation is confirmed by some given evidence, and rules of quantitative confirmation determining the degree of confirmation provided by an evidence to a generalisation), is showing interconnections between them, and deriving from them further rules of confirmation, constitute what is called the Logic of Confirmation. Thus what I contend is that a solution to the problem of induction consists *precisely* in the development of this logic. Since such a logic is gradually being developed for some time, the problem of induction is also being gradually

solved. It is true that the problem has not been *completely* solved as yet, for we have not yet been able to work out a system of rules which has a thoroughly intuitive grounding and is adequate for all kinds of confirmation contexts. But this, I think, is true also of what I have called the Problem of Deduction.

Jadavpur University

8
SCIENCE, TECHNOLOGY AND VALUE

Donald H. Bishop

It is often pointed out that we live in a new age of science and technology and this is true. It is often assumed that this has resulted in a new set of values. This, I believe, is false. What has happened is that science and technology have simply created a new content for values to be worked out in. The setting has changed; values have not.

An example of this is the concept of neighbor. There is general agreement as to what being a good neighbor involves or what a good neighbor is. It is also generally agreed that neighborliness, being friendly rather than hostile to those around us, is desirable or a value. What science and technology have done is not to change the concept of neighbor or decrease its value, but simply to extend the range of neighborliness or broaden the setting in which the concept of neighbor is applied.

Science and technology have brought the world closer together than ever before. Persons living in one part of the globe have become much more aware of people living on the other side of the world. They can conceive of them and act toward them as if they were neighbors just as much as the people living immediately adjacent to them. Science and technology, then, have provided mankind with the means of applying values on a world scale while before they could be only locally or regionally.

This reminds us that science and technology are only means. In themselves they are neutral. How they will be used or the ends they will be used for will depend on man himself, more specifically, man's will. The German philosopher Immanuel Kant declared that the only absolute good is a good will. Science and technology underline this today. If man wills to use science and technology for peaceful and good ends, he can achieve a world of plenty and prosperity for all. If he uses them for evil ends, he can literally destroy himself because of the magnitude of possible destructive power the new science and technology have made available.

In the end science and technology cannot be separated from values or morality. This means that the philosopher of science must be concerned not only about the concepts but the uses of science as well. Nor can the scientist and technologist remain aloof from the uses to which their discoveries and inventions are put. The moral implications of science must be taken into account by philosopher, scientist and technologist alike.

Washington State University

9
SCIENCE, TECHNOLOGY AND VALUE
Basant Kumar Lal
I

What precisely is the relationship between Science and Technology on the one hand, and Values on the other ? Is it a fact that advancement of science and technology leads to a collapse of values ? This problem has engaged the attention of many a contemporary thinker, but almost always the problem centres round 'science and values', and tends to overlook both the importance of technology and its difference from science. In fact, science and technology are not concerned with values exactly in the same way, and this difference may prove to be very vital for any attempt to determine whether science and technology in any way lead to a collapse of values.

II

The modern man lives in a world of science and in a technological wonderland. Consequently he tends to overlook the difference between the two. It is a fact that every technology (of course in the modern sense of the term) presupposes a science, and that achievements of science inevitably lead to the development of new techniques and thereby to the growth of technology. Even so, there is a basic difference between 'a purely scientific attitude' and a 'technological temper' which must be appreciated in order to understand their relationship with values.

Both science and technology are parts of our cultural heritage. Science represents a systematic knowledge of nature and technology contains the application of that knowledge. Both science and technology are admired because they give us a power over nature, but science is valued as a means of *knowing* the world and technology provides ways for *changing* the world in accordance with one's needs or desires.

This distinction appears to be commonplace, but it is not so, as it has far-reaching implications. The goal of science is 'pursuit of truth', but the goal of technology is more or less a utilitarian and empirical goal—a goal that is attainable in the immediate future. A purely scientific adventure initiated by nothing else but a longing for the knowledge of truth, may be completely oblivious of and indifferent to the ends to which the results of science may ultimately be put. On the other hand, technology invariably is conscious of the end which it seeks to attain. There is so to say an intrinsic connection between the means that technology employs and the end that it pursues. As such, technological ends are instrumental and immediate and not ultimate. That is why it is said that technology is closer to the practical needs of life than science which is generally interested in a sincere pursuit of truth.

III

On account of this difference between science and technology the values that emerge from a purely scientific attitude and those that emanate from a technological way of life tend to differ. Of course in actual life the two kinds of values are not easily distinguishable, because the influences of science and technology on life tend to overlap. The word 'value' here is being used in its most comprehensive sense standing for the worth that emerges as a result of the strict adherence to a particular way of life. As such, it includes social and moral values and also such other values which give meaning and significance to life.

If the word 'value' is understood in this way, it may be urged, more or less in opposition to what is being suggested here, that values that emerge from science and technology are basically similar, because they are this-worldly and positivistic. It may again be pointed out in favour of this contention that these two are not distinguished from each other even by the traditionalist who condemns them both as contributing towards the erosion of values. But, this over-simplified way of looking at science and technology does not realise that failure to make a distinction between the two may become a source of confusion.

As it has been said, the real aim of a purely scientific action is 'pursuit of truth'. Therefore, if any other aim begins to influence scientific pursuit it vitiates it to that extent. If a scientist, for example, gives up his scientific pursuit for certain moral considerations, he does not remain scientific to that extent. In theory, therefore, the only scientific value is 'pursuit of truth', and apparently there is no scope here of any conflict between this value and value of any other kind. Of course it is possible that this 'pursuit of truth' itself becomes ultimate value, and is pushed so far that it comes in conflict with moral and religious values. The way of science very often becomes the way of life for those who are engaged in it, and as such, it may come in conflict with any such endeavour that does not give to the 'pursuit of truth' that value which science gives to it. That is why it is said that science does not lead to elimination of values; on the other hand, the conflict that is seen there is between the values emanating from science and those emanating from ordinary behaviour.

The relationship of technology with value is much more direct. As we have seen, technology always has an empirical goal. Therefore, the usefulness of technology is always apparent—at least much more apparent than that of science. That shows that technology cannot develop unless goals are fixed and clearly held. But then, it is quite possible that the goals that are held are held on account of certain moral or social considerations. Thus, technology becomes related to values in a very direct manner. This can be illustrated in a very simple way. Let us suppose that a particular society or a nation fixes up a particular goal and tries to develop a technology for its realisation. But, another society or a nation which has a different goal in view may create obstacles for the former. Such conflicts are either political or moral or social, that is to say, such conflicts are not between technologies, but between values resulting from different technologies, and at times, such a conflict may become so acute as to limit the growth and development of technology itself.

IV

At this point one may raise a doubt and say that this distinction may not be relevant to the present-day science and technology. It is only when technology is understood in its widest possible sense that it becomes related to values in a different way from that of science. But, the present-day technology is a technology in a special way; it is scientific technology. Indeed there was a particular technology for the ancient man whose sole profession was hunting; likewise, agriculture-technology which replaced hunting-technology was a technology in its own right. But, today whenever we talk of technology, we mean a technology which is through and through rooted in science and which takes its origin in scientific discoveries and inventions. As such, one may point out that in the present-day context it is neither necessary nor desirable to assert that values emanating from science and those emanating from technology are not necessarily similar.

It may be urged against this assertion that the present-day technology is not actually scientific technology, it may be called *Industrial Technology*. The distinction between the two is very significant for the problem of values in the present times.

Since the first world-war Governments and industries have become big employers of scientists. Scientists themselves are inclined to take up such jobs not only because these jobs give them a security but also because these jobs carry very handsome remunerations. The result is that scientists begin to cater to the demands of the industries. They are no longer free spirits, they no longer take to scientific research in the spirit of free adventure purely for the sake of the knowledge of truth, their only function is to provide the basis for a useful technology, by employing which industries will have monetary gains and economic power. This impact of industrial technology has taken away from the scientist his autonomy, his control over the goals and methods of research and does not leave any scope for the realisation of his research-potential. That is how a distinction is made between a university science and industrial science. The former is science proper because its main goal is pursuit of scientific truth, and the rewards are recognition and honour. On the other hand, in industrial science science becomes a handmaid of industrial demands, and is thus ruled over by technology. The goals and the rewards are both basically economic. Thus the present-day technology is not really scientific technology, but industrial technology,. That is why it seeks to utilise even science for economic gains and political power. This is very clearly evident in all the developing countries like India. Even in highly developed countries which can (and even do) afford the luxury of purely scientific research industrial technology by far outweighs and takes a precedence over research oriented science.

V

Keeping in mind these distinctions let us now consider the question whether advancement in science and technology leads to erosion of values. Obviously, this is a contemporary question and it is being raised in complete awareness of the fact that these days science and technology have become the 'order of the day'. An impatient modern-minded radical may at once brush aside the question by asserting that there has not been any collapse of values in the present times. But, that is a problem that cannot be solved merely by argumentation and to the full satisfaction of the rival parties. Therefore it is rationally expedient to listen to the arguments that those who say so advance in support of their contention.

Normally, such a view is expressed by three types of people: (a) the traditionalists who somehow believe in the ultimacy of some trans-empirical or spiritual values, (b) some existentialists and (c) and those ultra-moderns who have somehow come to develop a feeling of despair as a result of over-indulgence in the modern ways of life. Curiously enough the line of argument adopted in all the three cases happens to be more or less similar. They all assert that a life based on science and technology leads to a sort of dehumanisation of man's existence, which, in its turn, causes a collapse of values. Let us try to follow the line of this argument.

Indeed these people do not say anything about what science and technology do in their own fields, but they feel that they have a tremendous impact on our everyday existence—on our economies and on our social and political lives. The result is that "today it is taken as a matter of course that human life is the supply of mass-needs by rationalised production with the aid of technical advances" (Jaspers, *Man in the Modern Age*, p. 37). If we try to discern the effects of science and technology on the present-day human life we clearly notice that it has led to (a) a new basis for production, (b) to a better organisation of enterprises, (c) to a world-wide improvement in the means of transport and communication, and (d) as result of all this to the fact that our elementary needs are supplied with an efficiency unknown to history. Even in countries where the efficiency is not that great, it is not due to the failure of science and technology, but due to some fault in the procurement and distribution system.

The upshot of all this is that the necessities of life come to us in a mechanical way, more or less as a matter of course. As such, they lack the aroma of that which is produced by personal effort and cause no sense of affection. A continued and repeated indulgence in such a mechanistic way of life reduces even man to a function, and he comes to regard even himself as a cog in the machine—as a function of the mechanical apparatus of life. This is, what is called, the dehumanisation of man. This causes the individual to lose the sense of personal participation; even his recreations and enjoyments are mechanically regularised.

Now, it is argued that this dehumanisation of man's life uproots all values. If an individual is reduced to a mere function he loses his sense of individuality, and thereby is released from the obligation to conform to traditional standards and established values. These people take great pains to demonstrate by taking examples from everyday life that the modern man caught in the cobweb of science and technology has himself become a machine, and as such, has neither time nor the vitality to think even about himself, much less about values.

VI

One may perhaps say against this argument that it suffers from over-statements and exaggerations. But, exaggerations do not try to make the false true, they merely give to something more than what is due to it. Therefore it has to be accepted that the argument as outlined above does contain *some* elements of truth. It has to be accepted then that established values *are* losing ground and that technological advancement *does* contribute something to this gradual erosion of traditionally accepted values.

It is at this point that the distinction between science and technology becomes very relevant. If we reflect upon this argument we shall find that it is not science that is reducing man's life to the status of a machine, but it is being done as a result of the impact of the present-day technology—the industrial technology. This process started immediately as technology began to utilise scientific achievements for practical ends, it grew along with the growth of industrialisation, and today it is in full swing.

The scientist himself is acutely aware of this. So long as he remains confined to his own sphere and works in the spirit of a true scientist, he has a control over his research material. But the moment the scientist begins to work in accordance with the dictates of his master—the Industries (private or public), he begins to lose control over his own materials. Gradually even he (qua a scientist) begins to feel isolated. His creativity is not only threatened but, at times, even throttled. Consequently, even he begins to suffer from self-estrangement and despair. Thus the scientist himself discovers that he is in a state of bondage, imprisoned by a demon of his own creation.

How does this state of affairs bring about an erosion of values? This technology-oriented bondage encourages activities of the impulses. It creates in man a longing for having greater and greater means of comfort, and this urge ever remains unsatisfied. Consequently the modern man is always after the satisfaction of his individual impulses. He does not have either the time or the impulse to think about others entirely on his own. Even the diversions that he seeks are invariably for self-satisfaction or for escaping the boredom resulting from the continuous indulgence in the same type of activities. This is clearly evident in the life of an average city-dweller, who has had a taste of technologically determined ways of life. For example, if he wants to have a TV set, he will remain restless till he acquires it; and after a while, he will not even sit at the TV for days together and will even be disgusted with the children using it. That is how he becomes indifferent to values. Values are valued only when existence offers a continuous attraction and interest. In a life of despair and anguish, in a life of fleeting attitudes and hurry, values fail to get a foot-hold.

VII

But, let us pause to reflect on the situation once again. Is it really a fact that values have been thrown overboard ? And, is it really a fact that one of the factors responsible for this is technological advancement ?

These questions can very well be answered both with a 'yes' and a 'no'. It is a fact that some of the old and traditional values are being steadily eroded, and this also is a fact that the life that technological influences have made available to us does play a part in the erosion of *these* values. But, *values as such* have not collapsed. New values, radically different from the old ones, have emerged. In developing countries like India, where tradition continues to have a stronghold, these radically new values are viewed with suspicion and even with horror because they are completely incompatible with the traditional values. Even so, even in India, these values are making their appearances (at times even prominently) at least in the lives of those 'moderns' who have taken to the positivistic ways of life determined by the present day scientific and technological development.

The startling novelty of these new values constrains one to think that the concept of value itself is undergoing a change. It is as a result of the impact of science and technology on life that it is being realised that clinging to anything fixed and static is dogmatism. Even values must be changing. The scientific insistence on dynamism is made a model even in the realm of values. Now, nothing is regarded as true or as good for ever. This leads to the feeling that old values have outlived their utility. It is true that even the most modern of them all retains something of the old after giving to it a modern garb, but he also believes that it is inherent in the nature of values themselves to grow and change. The traditionalists view at it with awe because it takes away from them the security of their conservative habitat. They used to give to values both an objectivity and an absoluteness, values, according to them, used to be something established, fixed and inviolable. Today values are given objectivity only in a limited way. Values are objective, but they are not absolute; they are relative to the time and age and also to the society in which they are held. They are objective only in the sense that they are not subjective, i.e., they do not vary from individual to individual, but are held by particular groups and societies, and even when they are held, the belief that they may give place to another set of values persists.

What are the new values that have emerged in the scientific and technological society of the present day? Two of the most prominent values that have come to stay in the modern society and which have been directly determined by a technological life are *Modernity* and *Speed*. Both of these presuppose the inevitability of change, and as such none of them can be determined rigidly and finally. We can say neither that 'this' is the final phase of modernity, or that 'this' is the zenith of speed. What is considered to be modern today may appear to be stale and out-of-date tomorrow. Likewise there is no way of making the speed of life uniform. Let us try to understand the nature of these two values in a more concrete way.

Modernity stands for that process of change towards social, economic and political life which had developed in western countries in the seventeenth century and which has come to flower in the twentieth century. In principle, modernity denotes "the process in which clusters of old social, economic and psychological commitments are eroded and broken and people become available for new patterns of socialisation and behaviour" (Eisenstadt, *Modernization, Protest and Change*, p. 2). This shows that modernity has both a negative and a positive import. Negatively it shows scant respect for old and traditional values. Positively, it stands for a positivistic attitude which relies almost entirely on a scientific attitude of life including a fancy for what technological achievements have placed at the disposal of man. Modernity understood in this way is one of the most important values that the modern man holds and cherishes. That is why spiritual ideas no longer appear to him as valuable, that is why anything that gives vitality to his life, anything that enhances his claim to be modern appears to him as valuable.

The word 'speed' denotes dynamism. Science and technology have steadily been conquering both space and time. One can listen to what is happening thousands of miles away just by switching on an instrument; every part of the earth has come closer to every other part. Most of the things that man could do in hours, he can now do within a fraction of a minute. (Paradoxically) this has not given to him a leisure but a speed to his life's activities. He very soon becomes disgusted with any activity that consumes time, no proceedings can keep his interest sustained for long. He is always in search of new enterprises, fresh adventures and diversions of activities. Nobody now prefers to travel by slow-moving vehicles, nobody now has the time nor the aptitude to sit for the whole night and enjoy musical concerts. New devices for giving speed even to ordinary activities like cooking, knitting, baking, calculating etc. are being preferred and employed even by those who cannot normally afford to have them. The modern man is always busy—almost in a hurry, and he loves to be so. Whatever gives a 'quick' solution to his problem, whatever gives 'speed' to his life's activity is considered valuable. The traditionalist treading along his well-trodden path fails to cope with this speed and begins to clamour that this new speed of life's activities has ruined his old pathway of values.

Patna University

10
TRANSCULTURAL VALUE-PRESUPPOSITIONS OF SCIENCE

W. Steinkraus

No one would seriously argue that the fundamental laws of natural science are limited by culture or circumstances. But there are some scientists who are not at all sure that there are standards of moral value which have similar universal scope. A merely empirical study of behaviour patterns throughout the world does not readily confirm the existence of such norms. Yet it may be argued that the sciences themselves, social as well as natural, are impossible as reliable bodies of truth without the acceptance and practice of certain ethical presuppositions.

The epistemological, logical, and metaphysical presuppositional structures necessary to the scientific enterprise have been explored for centuries, beginning with Aristotle, coming up through Bacon and Kant to Whitehead in our own century. Even now there are continuing debates about the kind of logic or epistemology scientists must take for granted.[1] The broader sciences claim to have unearthed the primitive sources for the world's evolving value practices and standards, but even that enterprise assumes moral structures. Is a theory of the evolution of morals possible if there is not first some use made of basic value standards?

We need not linger long over such obvious value assumptions all scientists seem to make, for example, that scientific knowledge itself is valuable, that more rather than less science is desirable, or that the more effort spent in science, the better human life will be. In this paper we are concerned with the moral presuppositions which are preconditions of reliable science. Are there indeed such moral prerequisites? If it can be shown that there are, we may find in those norms a basis for better world understanding and a basic humanity which unites North and South, East and West.

I propose that there are at least three such moral presuppositions.

1. The first principle of moral value is the principle of integrity or basic honesty. If practising scientists anywhere are not honest or suffer lapses in integrity, there can be no science. Strangely, there are some scientists who conduct their studies honestly trying to show that moral universals such as honesty, are impossible. Now honesty means several things for a scientist. The first is simply truth-telling, reporting the facts accurately as defined by the selected area of investigation. It further means that the scientist will not withhold evidence that does not fit his desired scheme, that he will not weigh the evidence in a favorable way, that he will not rearrange or tamper with the data in order to yield a pre-established outcome, and that he will not rush to interpretation of flimsy data, as Percival Lowell did when he claimed there were canals on Mars.

Jacques Monod, whose skill as a geneticist is not paralleled by much philosophical wisdom, nevertheless recognizes this ethical presupposition of all scientific knowledge. He argues that "the very definition of 'true' knowledge reposes in the final analysis upon an ethical postulate," and he concludes that "the ethic of knowledge that created the modern world is the only ethic compatible with it, the only one capable, once understood and accepted, of guiding its evolution."[2] That, at the very least, is honesty.

2. But honesty has a corollary and that is conscientious avoidance of personal or other bias. When a scientist knows he might be prejudiced in his fact-finding ventures, he must compensate for it and strive rigorously to be unbiassed about his discoveries and their interpretation. The ethical obligation to avoid bias varies with the degree of exactness of the particular science. Natural scientists do not have to spend as much time immunizing their methods "against the virus of human subjectivity", as do others. The lesser sciences struggle almost excessively to exclude the personal equation. For example, in order to avoid subjectivism, psychologists have a phobia about the introspective method, notes Köhler, which "hardly befits the scientific mind."[3] Even nationalistic bias operates,[4] and there is evidence too of political bias, as in the infamous Lysenko case some years ago.[5]

3. A third value presupposition is the principle of cooper-

ation. No scientist can further his work if he does not rely on past investigations, share his present findings, and maintain communication with colleagues elsewhere. As sciences get less exact and further away from easily duplicable verification procedures, cooperation becomes all the more important. One is rightly suspicious of large claims by single archaeological investigators like Erich von Daeniken, whose work cannot easily be checked out by others. Co-workers are needed to confirm or deny findings. And they are obligated to report investigative misconduct to the scientific community when they find it.[6]

When such cooperation becomes international, it leads to the breakdown of secretive and paranoid nationalistic loyalties. International cooperation is utterly crucial in sciences like meteorology, astrophysics, and epidemiology. It is also essential when there is disagreement. Gerard Piel once noted that scientists seldom speak with a single voice even about scientific questions, and added: "As scientists, however, they are obliged to resolve such differences."[7] Note the word "obliged".

Now these three value presuppositions have the character of hypothetical imperatives. If one is to be a scientist, he is obligated to be honest, to avoid bias, and to cooperate. Failure to do so destroys science. But it may be objected that science is *Wertfrei*, that these presuppositions are part of its logic, not value questions at all. Thus, Wolfgang Köhler prefers the word "requiredness" in his discussion.[8] But we argue that these are still primarily moral questions because scientists are held personally accountable for deviations from them. A person guilty of dishonesty is discredited, and what is more, all his previous work is called into question.[9] The work of a whole institution over generations may be jeopardized or ruined by the unfaithfulness of a single scientist to his calling.

It may also be objected that such presuppositions reflect bourgeois bias and a false ideology. But that criticism cannot be voiced if we do not assume that the person announcing it has based his objection on honestly reported findings. Truth-telling, the avoidance of prejudice, and a cooperative spirit are in fact meaningful terms world-wide. If they are not such and do not have an unconditional claim on scientists, how are we to find out that they are not,—without using them? And if they are so ineluctable, perhaps they can provide a minimal basis for transcultural understanding and break down childish ideological barriers and destructive international hostilities.

NOTES

1. See for example Henry Margenau's *The Nature of Physical Reality* (N.Y.: McGraw Hill, 1950) who disapproves of Carnap's view. And see Rudolf Carnap's *Philosophical Foundations of Physics* (N.Y.: Basic Books, 1966). For a sample view differing from both of these, see Errol Harris's *Nature, Mind & Modern Science* (N.Y.: Macmillan, 1954)

2. Jacques Monod, *Chance and Necessity*, tr. Wainhouse (N.Y.: Knopf, 1971), 173 and 177.

3. Wolfgang Köhler, *The Place of Value in a World of Facts*. (N.Y.: Mentor, 1966), p. 47.

4. See the case of archeological discoveries at Glozel, France in the 1920's. After foreign investigators examined the data, they declared it a hoax, but in 1927 a French commission supported the original findings "with French honor saved at home but with the site discredited abroad." Happily, the techniques of thermoluminescence dating used in 1974 confirmed the early findings but no one before that date really had any right to accept the results. (See account in *Scientific American*, February 1975, pp. 41-42)

5. In the mid-fifties, Lysenko's botanical views were held in esteem in the USSR. Later his views were repudiated as being out of gear with socio-political theory.

6. In June of 1974, co-workers at the Parapsychology laboratory in Durham, N.C., discovered deception on the part of the Director of the Institute for Parapsychology and exposed him. See below.

7. Gerard Piel, in a review, *New York Times*, May 2, 1965, pp. 44f.

8. Köhler, *op. cit.*, Chapter II. He notes: "Certainly in science we are not very clear about requiredness although our work is utterly imbued with it." (p. 39)

9. Such was the case with the Director of the Parapsychology Institute, who resigned on June 12, 1974, when it was discovered that he had altered data. His superior, J. B. Rhine asserted that it was an isolated case of fraud but conceded that it now became necessary to suspend all judgment on the person's previous work until it could be independently reduplicated. (*Scientific American*, Sept., 1974, pp. 72)

State University College of New York, Oswego.

Plenary Session III

VIDYĀ AND AVIDYĀ

President : T. M. P. Mahadevan

Secretary : K. P. Mishra

Main Speakers
- (1) De Smet
- (2) Karl Potter
- (3) D. P. Sen
- (4) Eliot Deutch
- (5) S. R. Bhatt

11
VIDYĀ AND AVIDYĀ

T. M. P. Mahadevan

*vidyāṁ cā'vidyāṁ ca yas-tad-vedobhayaṁ saha |
avidyayā mṛtyuṁ tīrtvā vidyayāmṛtam aśnute ||*

—*Īśāvāsya-upaniṣad*, 11.

*vidyāvidye tato na staḥ cinmātrajyotiṣo mama |
nityavijñānarūpasya jñānājñāne na me sadā. ||*

—*Upadeśa-sāhasrī*, xiii. 2 & 5

A distinction is made in the *Upaniṣads* between two kinds of knowledge, the higher (*parā*) and the lower (*aparā*). The lower knowledge consists of all the empirical sciences and acts as also of such sacred knowledge as relates to things that perish and enjoyments that are contingent. It is to be noted that even the four *Vedas* are included in the category of lower knowledge. A great scholar, Nārada, in spite of his encyclopaedic learning, both secular and sacred, finds himself weighed down by sorrow, and so seeks enlightenment from a sage, Sanatkumāra. The sage asks him to state his credentials. Nārada responds by reeling off a long list of the arts and the sciences he has mastered. The sage characterizes the knowledge that is represented by all these disciplines as mere name (*nāma eva*), and declares that that alone is the supreme knowledge which reveals the imperishable Reality (*akṣara*). This higher knowledge is described as that whereby what has not been heard of becomes heard of, what has not been thought of becomes thought of, what has not been understood becomes understood. This is further explained as the knowledge of the ground which is more than and inclusive of the knowledge of various expressions or manifestations of the ground. "Just as by one lump of clay all that is made of clay may be known, the modification being only a name depending on a word—

the truth being that it is just clay : so is that teaching."[1] Compared with the knowledge of the ultimate ground which is the absolute Self, the lower knowledge is nescience or false knowledge (*avidyā*). "Widely contrasted and leading in different ways", says the *Kaṭha-upaniṣad*, "are these two—nescience (avidyā) and what is known as knowledge (*vidyā*)."[2] Like darkness and light, they are opposed to each other, and result respectively in bondage and release, what are referred to as the pleasing (*preyas*) and the good (*śreyas*). It is the knowledge of the non-dual Self that is the means to the supreme good, whereas nescience, its opposite, is the cause of bondage. In the *Śvetāśvatara-upaniṣad*, it is declared : "In the imperishable, infinite, supreme *Brahman* are the two, knowledge and nescience, placed hidden. Perishable, indeed, is nescience, while knowledge, verily, is immortal. And, he who controls knowledge and nescience is another (i.e. he is distinct from either)."[3] Here, it is taught (i) that nescience, (*avidyā*) is the cause of bondage consisting in transmigration (*saṁsāra*), (ii) that knowledge (*vidyā*) is the means to release (*mokṣa*) which is immortality (*amṛtam*) and (iii) that the Self which regulates both knowledge and nescience is distinct from them because it is the witness thereof.

Let us consider the implications of the upaniṣadic teaching regarding knowledge and nescience as indicated by the representative texts we have cited, along with their contexts.

Knowledge or consciousness, in the empirical sense, is a characteristic of the mind. Through the channels of knowledge, such as perception and inference, it is the mind that 'knows' the objects. For any piece of objective knowledge, what serves as the instrument is a cognitive mode (*vṛtti*) of the mind. But such modes of the mind cannot become reflexive and know themselves. We do know our minds. How do we know them ? When I say, for instance, "I did not notice the thing that is in front of me, because my mind was away," what is it that is aware of the mind being away ? It cannot be a mental mode; it must be an awareness which is non-mental.

1. *Chāndogya*, VI, 1. 4.
2. *Kaṭha*, II, 4.
3. *Śvetāśvatara*, v, 1.

The cognition of the form, say, "this is a pot", is, obviously, the result of a mental mode. But, I am not only aware of the pot, I am also aware of the awareness of the pot. This awareness of awareness—is this a mental mode? It cannot be, because one mental mode cannot become the object of another mental mode. When I apprehend another object, say, a table, there is involved another mental mode. But, my awareness of the awareness of the table is the same. Table-cognition differs it is true, from pot-cognition. But, the consciousness which illumines these cognitions is the same. When I say, "I do not know what you say", I seem to know that I do not know. How do I know that I do not know? This problem is not to be confused with the problem of how to know what one knows not. This latter is the problem of induction, the problem of ampliation.[4] Our concern is not this. Our problem is : how does one know *that* one does not know? This awareness of non-knowledge, again, is not mental. In dream, there are no 'physical' objects. A world is created out of mental impressions which involves, as in the waking state, the distinction between subject experiencing and objects experienced without there being any basis for such distinction. The elephant that is seen in dream is no elephant. The king that rides on it is no king. That consciousness which reveals them is neither the one nor the other. In dream, it is the identical consciousness that becomes subject as well as object. Commenting on a text of the *Bṛhadāraṇyaka-upaniṣad* which relates to dream experience, Śaṅkara observes : "With this his own lustre as object, and revealing it by his own light, as the unattached subject or witness possessing constant vision, he dreams." An analysis of the dream state exhibits the light that is the self, the eternal witness, unrelated to anything and distinct from the body and such organs as the eye, is realized as it is, revealing everything. In deep dreamless sleep, no objects are experienced, and there is no subject experiencing either. Is sleep, then, a night of nothingness, an utter lapse of consciousness? The answer is : no. The mind has ceased to be, but not consciousness. Otherwise, the recollection on waking

---

4. See *The Psychology of Knowing*, ed, by Joseph R. Royce and Wm. W. Rozeboom (Gorden and Greach, New York, 1972), p. 118.

up from sleep, in the form "I slept happily; I did not know anything" would be unintelligible. If there were no experience in sleep, it would not be recollected subsequently. There was experience in sleep; only, there was no duality. And so, it is unlike the other states of experience. Although there is no duality in sleep, the cause thereof, i.e. ignorance, persists. If this is removed, then the eternal non-dual consciousness will be realized.

How is the Self which is non-dual Pure Consciousness to be realized? It is through Self-knowledge. Self-knowledge, here, does not mean the Self as knowledge, but knowledge of the Self. This knowledge of the Self is the last mental mode known as *akhaṇḍākāra-vṛtti* where there is no trace of impurity, which is like unto the Infinite. It removes the obstacle that stands in the way of the disclosure of the Self, and removes itself. The function of the final mode of the mind is not on a par with the cognitive modes that reveal objects. In the case of an empirical object, the cognition mode has to pervade it and occasion therein a reflection of consciousness. This dose not happen in the case of the final mode which has the Self for its object. The Self is self-luminous, and does not require to be illumined. All that the final mode does is to remove the veil which is nescience (*avidyā*), and thus leave alone the Self which is self-revealed. The knowledge that lets the Self stand self-revealed is *parāvidyā* (higher knowledge).

Knowledge—even empirical knowledge—is not an act, although we sometimes use such an expression as 'cognitive act'. It is true that both knowledge and action relate to the mind. But while action is what the agent does and is dependent on his will, knowledge must be conditioned by its object. Action depends on the agent (*kartṛ-tantra*); knowledge depends on its content (*vastu-tantra*). For instance, it depends on a man's will whether he decides to go to a particular place or not, and if he decides to go, how to get there. It is not so with knowledge. If what is in front of me is a pillar and I mistake it for a man standing, that would not be knowledge. Knowledge should conform to its object; it cannot be arbitrarily constituted by an act of will.

We have shown that knowledge is not action, although action may precede it. In a book, *A Threefold Lord*, Herbert

Dingle offers the following explanation for the distinction between experience and voluntary action : "By experience I mean that of which we are aware, that which is given to us, so to speak without our having designed it and independently of any wish of our own.... Voluntary action, on the other hand, is what we chose to do and could avoid doing if we would. Of course, the two things are often associated with one another. I might choose to look at the sky to see the stars, but my choice here is merely that of opening my eyes and turning in a certain direction : What I then experience is not of my contrivance". If this is so even in the matter of the knowledge of empirical objects, it is clear that knowledge of the Self is not of the nature of an act. Self-awareness is the plenary experience; it is not willed activity.

The reason why Self-knowledge is not attained through action is as follows : The Self is eternal and infinite : it cannot be gained through action which can only effect what is phenomenal and finite. The Self is what is eternally accomplished; and so, it is not what is to be accomplished by action. All action is a means only to the non-eternal. Action, indeed, is but of four types : What generates (*utpādyam*), what leads to attainment (*āpyam*), what purifies (*saṁskāryam*), and what transforms (*vikāryam*). Other than these, there is nothing special about actions. The Self is unborn, immortal, immutable, unmoving, firm, constant, and ever pure. Hence, there is nothing that action can do in regard to the Self.

But, has action—that form of it which is unmotivated by selfish desire—no place in the disciplines that lead to Self-knowledge ? The answer is this : the competence to tread the path of knowledge is gained only when one's mind has become pure. For the purification of the mind, the means is *karmayoga*, the performance of one's duties without attachment to results. In the case of the ordinary man, his actions and knowledge are the outcome of his narrow egoistic impulses. These he has to get over first. They are referred to as *mṛtyu*, death, in the *Īśāvāsya-upaniṣad* (11) which prescribes a method of overcoming it. The method is the performance of obligatory duties. This is also *avidyā* (nescience). But, this will enable

---

5. See Śaṅkara's commentary on *Muṇḍaka-upaniṣad*, I. ii, 12.

one to get rid of the egoistic impulse. Thus, through *avidyā*, i.e. *karma*, one overcomes *mṛtyu* (death).

Higher than the performance of obligatory duties is meditation on deities. This is called *vidyā*; but it is not knowledge of the Self; it is *upāsanā*. Meditation is a mental act. When a person meditates on a deity, he assigns to it a form and takes it to represent the deity. What distinguishes meditation from fitful thinking is that in it one directs towards the object a continuous flow of thoughts. It serves to keep away from the mind distracting and dissipating thoughts. Also, one attains, through constant meditation of a deity, identification therewith. To that extent one becomes rid of limitations that are incidental to the ego which one imagines one is. Becoming one with the deity meditated upon is what the *Īśāvāsya* text calls 'immortality' (*amṛtam*). One attains immutability through *vidyā*, i.e. meditation. Thus, the *Īśāvāsya* :

avidyayā mṛtyuṁ tīrtvā vidyayā' mṛtam aśnute

'Overcoming death through *avidyā* (i.e. *karma*), one attains immortality through *vidyā* (i.e. meditation).'

Even meditation on the supreme attributeless *Brahman* is not knowledge, although, it is true, it may lead to *Brahman*-realisation. *Nirguṇa-upāsanā*, as it is called, is compared to a delusion which culminates in a fruitful result (*saṁvādi-bhrama*). Both the light of a lamp and the light of a gem may be mistaken for a gem. Both are delusions. But the man, who mistakes the lamp-light for the gem and approaches the place whence the light comes, gains nothing, whereas the person, who mistakes the light of the gem for the gem itself, obtains the precious stone. Both of them have delusive cognition, but unlike the former, the latter finds his cognition come true. One mistakes steam for smoke and infers the existence of fire. He hastens to the place where he thinks there is fire, and as chance would have it, he finds fire there. The existence of fire does not make his inference valid; but still it serves the purpose of him who was in search of fire. A person, thinking that the Godāvarī is the Gaṅgā, bathes in that river or sprinkles its water on his head. Mistaking the Godāvarī for the Gaṅgā is no doubt a delusion; but still the sprinkling of the sacred water purifies the man, and makes him holy. It is declared in the sacred texts that if a person utters the name of the Lord at the moment of his death, he attains heaven. A dying man may take the Lord's name even without intention. Yet it is proclaimed that he reaches heaven. All these are cases of *saṁvādibhrama*, or delusions that come true. The path of meditation may be likened unto these. The meditator has not the knowledge of *Brahman* to start with. He begins his journey in ignorance, but he ends it in knowledge.

Knowledge, as we have seen, does not reveal the Self or *Brahman* in the way it does empirical objects. All that it does is to remove the barrier in the form of nescience. It leads to Self-realisation by the negative mode of excluding what is not the Self, as 'not this, not this'. When the not-self has been removed, what remains is the non-dual Self. Even the notion that the Self is to be known is the result of nescience. When *vidyā* (knowledge) has destroyed *avidyā* (nescience), the one eternal Self alone shines. To the sage who has realised the Self there are no *vidyā* and *avidyā*, no *jñāna* and *ajñāna*. In the *Upadeśa-sāhasrī*, Śaṅkara expresses the plenary experience of the sage thus :

"To me who am the light of pure consciousness, there are no knowledge and nescience.

"To me who am of the nature of eternal awareness, there are no knowledge and ignorance."

University of Madras.

12
CHINKS IN THE ARMOUR OF AVIDYĀ

Richard De Smet,

Scripture declares that the *Ātman*, although eternally unchanging and uniform, reveals itself in a gradual series of beings and so appears in forms of various dignity and power.
(*Vedānta Sūtra Bhāṣya*, 2, 1, 14)

There is the story of that horseman who, at night and in a thick fog, rode unknowingly across a frozen lake. On reaching the other side he found an inn where exhausted he went to sleep for a long time. When he woke up, the sun was high in the sky and had melted the ice into scummy water. On seeing this the man got so frightened that he collapsed.

And there is the story of Modern Man who started so confidently on his journey towards progress only to find himself today in the midst of a disintegrating world, his values shattered and his self struck with existentialistic despair.

Would the Vedāntin be right after all? Is the scientific world of our reliance a mere crust of ice upon an abyss of nothingness? Are all the advances of modern knowledge nothing but waves upon waves of sheer nescience?

But modern man easily brushes aside such questions as absurd and such parables as irrelevant. For even though our progress is no unmixed blessing and our science is quite shortsighted, the tree of modern knowledge is vigorous and its fruits are mostly nutritious or curative. And if we turn to Śaṅkara, the Vedāntin, his pessimism may be doubted for he often confirmed the capacity of secular knowledge to achieve man's goals within its own domain, simply condemning its pretension to deal equally well with metaphysical questions regarding the metempirical nature of reality and man's supreme goal. His calling it *avidyā* (or rather *a-Vidyā*) only did away with this pretension and set it down as totally inferior to *Vidyā*, the saving knowledge grounded on the testimony of the Upaniṣads.

Yet, *a-Vidyā* does not easily accept to climb down and to acknowledge *Vidyā*'s claim to sovereignty. Especially in its modern expansion it is well-armoured and combative. Instruments of observation and refined methods of experimentation give it access to the inner structures of biological life and physical reality. The psychical itself is open to its investigation. And there seems to be no limit to the illumining power of its purely rational enquiry. It stands strong and well-entrenched whereas religions, metaphysics, mysticism and revelational wisdoms, including Vedānta, appear disabled and disspirited.

However, to my mind, this is a false prospect arisen from a condition of cold war between *a-Vidyā* and *Vidyā*. So long as we oppose them to each other in either-or fashion, they appear as irreconcilable foes and the strength of the one seems to imply the weakness of the other. But if for warlike opposition we substitute peaceful dialogue we shall discover beyond their undeniable heterogeneity a surprising amount of mutuality, complementarity and concurrence, *Vidyā* permeating *a-Vidyā* and the latter providing helps towards the advent of *Vidyā*. There will appear chinks in the armour of *a-Vidyā*, not only as points of weakness but as apertures shining with the bright presence of *Vidyā* in the very texture of *a-Vidyā*. In discerning them we shall be guided mainly by Śaṅkarācārya.

At the outset, let us recall his two important definitions of *Sat* and *a-Sat* (Being and non-Being), on the one hand, and of *Vidyā* and *a-Vidyā*, on the other hand. The first is found in his *Gītā-Bhāṣya*, 2, 16 in the course of his transcendental analysis of any affirmation of the type, 'this is a pot', (*san ghaṭaḥ, iti*). Although concerned with a single substratum, such affirmation is always twofold (*dve buddhī*) since it bears simultaneously upon 'existent' (*sat*) and upon a concrete object such as a pot (*ghaṭa*). Now, whereas in its second respect it varies and can fail, in its first respect it is constant and unfailing (*tayoḥ buddhyoḥ ghaṭādibuddhiḥ vyabhicarati, na tu sadbuddhiḥ*). Hence, the definition : "*Sat* is that, the affirmation of which is constant" (*yadviṣayā buddhiḥ na vyabhicarati, tat sat*) and "*asat* is that, the affirmation of which is inconstant" (*yadviṣayā buddhiḥ vyabhicarati, tat asat*). *Sat* is thus defined here in Platonic fashion as the absolutely permanent, that which never falls under the scope of negation but is, on the contrary, affiirmed in some way in every judgment. As such, it can only be the absolute Being and, since it is the fixed Pole of the affirming intellect, it must be its innermost A-priori and supreme *Ātman*, namely, the self-effulgent Light (*svayaṃ jyoti*) of pure Consciousness (*Cin-mātra*), the radical Subject (*Viṣayin*) and transcendent Witness (*Sākṣin*). The variables associated with it, whether empirical objects, subjects or acts of cognition, constitute the sphere of the non-permanent, hence, of non-Being, *a-Sat*. This sphere comprises the whole changing universe, the subject-matter of all mundane knowledge both ordinary and scientific. What opposes it to *Sat* is not unaffirmability (for it is affirmable) but only its changeableness. Thus *Sat* and *a-Sat* are not contradictories (like *Sat* and *Asat*, the utterly non-existent and impossible) but contraries. More precisely, they stand, says Śaṅkara, in the relation of cause and effect. For just as a pot can never be apprehended apart from (*vyatirekeṇa*) its immanent substrate, clay, so also the changeable can never be affirmed apart from the unchangeable *Sat*; and how to interpret this dependence in affirmability otherwise than as the total dependence of the effect on its immanent cause and ontological support?

What happens now in the judgment? Since we cannot affirm its subject (*viśeṣya*), namely, the pot or any such object, independently of the existential predicate (*viśeṣaṇa*), we super-impose it upon *Sat* and vice-versa. Thus it takes on as it were the properties of *Sat*, its beingness, constancy, solidity, inde-pendence, etc., and in turn *Sat* becomes endowed as it were with the properties of *a-Sat*, its plurality, changeability, materiality, etc. Potness or any other kind of name-and-form (*nāma-rūpa*) seem to be the differentiating predicates (*viśeṣaṇa*) of *Sat* while they are only external adjuncts (*upādhi*) superimposed on it and masking it. This leads us straight to Śaṅkara's definition of *a-Vidyā*.

First, the illusions and errors of ordinary experience provide him with the general notion of superimposition (*adhyāsa*) as "the apparent presentation of the attributes of one thing in another thing" (*anyasyānyadharmāvabhāsatā*: *Ved. Sūt. Bh.*, 1, 1.1) Then, he applies it to the case of the judgment which exhibits a "mutual superimposition of the Self and the non-Self" (*ātmā-nātmanoritaretar-ādhyāsaṃ* : *ibid.*) This superimposition, located in the judicative assertion and "thus defined, wise men consider to be *a-Vidyā*, and the ascertainment of the proper nature of the Real (*vastusvarūpa*) by discriminating it from the un-Real, they call *Vidyā*" (*ibid.*) Therefore, the *a-Vidyā* which Śaṅkara wishes to dissipate is a case apart from the trivial errors of perception, etc. and this I have meant to convey through my use of capital letters. It is not a limited and contingent accident of perception but a pervading feature of all human knowledge short of *Vidyā*. "In this world," says Śaṅkara, "it is the natural (*naisargika*) procedure," innate to our undiscriminative mode of knowing. It can thus be identified with it so that we should label as *a-Vidyā* all ordinary knowledge, all scientific achievements and even the Upaniṣads in the discursivity of their text though not in their meaning (cf. *Muṇḍaka Up. Bhāṣya*, 1,1,4-6).

Discursive, undiscriminated knowledge, although it is *a-Vidyā* in the special sense of Śaṅkara's definition, is not *avidyā* in the ordinary sense of error. Indeed, "it results from *pramāṇas* (means of procuring valid knowledge) and the object of the *pramāṇas* is reality as it exists" (*yathābhūtavastuviṣayam* : *Ved. S. Bh.* 1,1,4). It may not penetrate down to the radical difference between *Sat* and *a-Sat* and perceive its reals (*sat*) as un-Real (*a-Sat*) but its constant horizon is *sattā*, reality, *astitva*, 'is-ness'. "Between Brahman and the world, there is at least one characteristic in common : *sattā*" (*ibid.*, 2,1,8). The awakening to the true Self will reveal that this commonness is due to the sovereign causality of this Self within the universe of its effects but, in the mean time, it gives ontological weight and truth-value to discursive knowledge. "Before the awakening to the true Self, every cognition is real in regard to its own object" (*Chānd. Up. Bh.*, 8.5.4.)

This is why *a-Vidyā* is not simply dismissed as if it were sheer absurdity (*Avidyā*) like the nonsensical stanza quoted by Śaṅkara :

"Having bathed in the water of a mirage,
Crowned with sky-flowers,
This son of a barren woman goes
Armed with a bow made of a hare's horn."
(*Taittirīya Up. Bh.*, 2.1.)

It actually constitutes the field throughout which Śaṅkara exercises his discriminating analysis under the guidance of upaniṣadic *Vidyā*. Being naturally pervaded (*vyāpta*) by

Vidyā, illumined by pure Consciousness, it is made cognitive by its light and reflects it in all its partial truths. "The light of Consciousness is the illuminer of the mind (*manaso avabhāsakam*) because it is its controller (*niyantṛtvāt*), being the source of its light. The inner *Ātman* being the innermost of all objects, the mind cannot move towards it. Rather the mind itself is able to think only when it is illumined by the light of Consciousness residing inside it. Hence, knowers of *Brahman* declare that the mind with all its functions is made into thought (*matam*), made into a cognizing subject (*viṣayīkṛtam*), as pervaded by (*vyāptam*) this inner *Ātman*" (*Kena Up. Bh.*, 1,6.)

Due to this kind of osmosis between *Vidyā* and *a-Vidyā*, the latter provides the principle of contradiction so often appealed to by Śaṅkara, the principle of the *cogito ergo sum* owing to which the Self is never unknown to exist though its nature remains undiscerned and which is brandished by Śaṅkara as his main weapon against Buddhist *anātmavāda* (denial of all self), the principle of retortion by which he ridicules self-stultifying statements, the principle of the self-validity (*svataḥprāmāṇya*) of knowledge, the prohibition of infinite regress (*anavasthā*) in hierarchical chains of causes or middle terms, and other principles of reason. These are all at work in the vast field of human knowledge circumscribed as *a-Vidyā*.

Again, due to the same osmosis, *a-Vidyā* unfolds itself as propelled by an intellectual dynamism, a desire for knowing (*jijñāsā*), which spurs it on from lesser to greater realities and opens it up beyond its own limited reach to the achievement procured by *Vidyā*. *Jijñāsā*, indeed, is a constitutive teleology whose ultimate aim is *Brahman*, the absolute *Sat*, to be apprehended as *Ātman* in a most comprehensive intuition (*avagatiparyanta* : *Ved. Sūt. Bh.*, 1,1,1.) It impels the mind within the horizon of *sattā* from sense-perception to rational disquisition, from the apprehension of external forms to the disclosure of the whole hierarchy of internal and universal forms (*ibid.*, 1,1,11 quoting *Aitareya Āraṇyaka*, II, 3,2,1), from effects to the ascending series of their more and more internal causes or *ātmans* (*Kaṭh. Up. Bh.*, 1,3, 10-11), from the ephemeral to the longer-lasting, etc.

In this teleological search, *a-Vidyā* is costantly evaluative. The lowest judgment is already an act of transcending the sense data in terms of being. The in-built norm—due to the presence of *Vidyā*—of intellectual valuation is ontic permanence (*avyabhicāritva*), uncontradictedness (*abādhitatva*). In the measure in which a thing appears to be durable, it is accepted as satisfying *jijñāsā*; in the measure in which it appears transitory, it is transcended and *jijñāsā* seeks beyond it for its total fulfilment. This is an unceasing process of discrimination (*viveka*) which is found to be at work, though often fallibly, in every man even before he eventually turns for help to the upaniṣads. Indeed, Śaṅkara states that the first prerequisite for upaniṣadic schooling is "discrimination between eternal and non-eternal reality" (*nityānityavastuviveka* : *Ved. Sūt. Bh.*, 1,1,1). Man's endowment of *viveka* gives him a privileged status among living beings and makes him alone directly capable of liberation from transiency and *a-Vidyā* (cf. *Taitt. Bh.*, 2,1). It can be educated and become effective to turn his natural *jijñāsā* into that "desire for liberation" (*mumukṣatva*) which is the fourth qualification required for Vedāntic schooling. This is not a new desire but only the explicit and proper focusing of the human *jijñāsā* which will not relent its drive till it is satiated in the blissful grasp of the Infinite (*Chānd. Up. Bh.*, 7, 23-24). Its effect is to make man so disposed that he is ready to seek beyond the limits of his own intellectual acquisitions and put his faith in such a verbal testimony as the upaniṣadic *śruti* which promises perfect liberation. It is thus from within *a-Vidyā* and through the very dynamism which animates it that he aspires definitely towards *Vidyā*.

It is also due to the infinite dynamism immanent iu *a-Vidyā* that man has discovered the degrees of being and the possibility of a Maximum. This is imbedded in language which uses words on various levels of meaning. Detached words have a one-level, primary meaning (*mukhyārtha*), which their definition circumscribes, but when used contextually, in sentences, they put on different-level, secondary meanings (*lakṣyārtha*). Some words, like being, bliss, knowledge, etc., whose definition does not debar infinity, can even take on a supreme meaning (*paramārtha*) and serve the need of indicating the absolute goal of intellectual dynamism.

Śaṅkara made excellent use of this feature of speech, especially in his exegesis of the "great sayings" of *Taitt. Up.*, 2,1 :

"Brahman is Reality, Knowledge, Infinite" (*satyaṃ jñānam anantam Brahma*) and *Chānd. Up.*, 6,8-16 : "That thou art" (*tat-tvam-asi*). The truth-meaning of such statements pertains to *Vidyā* but through their sentential structure they still belong to *a-Vidyā* according to Śaṅkara. They bridge the gap between the two. While unable, of course, to express directly and comprehensively the ineffable *Brahman*, they yet manage to indicate it correctly as definitions of its proper essence (*svarūpa-lakṣaṇa*) because of the *paramārtha* of their terms. Through them, says Śaṅkara, "that (Brahman) is indicated (or defined) but not expressed" (*tallakṣyate na tūcyate* : *Taitt. Up. Bh.*, 2,1). His exegesis remains apophatic and thus bears the mark of *a-Vidyā*.

The whole thrust of Śaṅkara's teaching is to exalt *Vidyā* and make us pass beyond *a-Vidyā* but he is ever aware of the kinship between *a-Vidyā* and *Vidyā* which remains hidden to the man of *a-Vidyā*. Witness again his theory of the one Seer of the two sights, the one transitory and the other eternal : "through this unfailing, eternal sight which is his essence and is called the self-effulgent light, the Seer of sight always sees the other, transitory sight whether in dream as impression or in the waking state as idea" (*Bṛh. Ār. Up. Bh.*, 1,4,10) "It is only as nhabited by the energy of Brahman that the eye and other aculties have the power of seeing and so forth" (*ibid.*, 4,4,18). "Man discerns only through the Ātman which is of the nature of consciousness and is altogether distinct from the aggregate (of the senses, etc.) just as it is by fire that a metal burns" (*Kat. Up. Bh.*, 4.3). The immanence of the absolute Witness (*Sākṣin*) grounds the whole efflorescence of *a-Vidyā* on *Vidyā* itself, giving it a derived effulgence, an induced dynamism and an infinite capacity to use with discernment the various *pramāṇas* and explore the nature of all things in this vast universe.

This active curiosity of *a-Vidyā*, its hope (*āśā* : *Chānd. Up. Bh.*, 7,14,1) of penetrating to the very essence of things (for truth is *vastu-tantra*, depending on things themselves) lead it to metaphysical questions. But it is prone to answer them erroneously or, at least, to trust as final its inadequate insights, because it spontaneously superimposes on the still unknown its memory of the already known. This is why it is in need of a radical conversion by which it will cease to trust itself and begin to rely on the *Śruti* under the guidance of an expert Vedāntin guru. Once converted, the man of *a-Vidyā* will be led along the path of interiority blazed by the "great sayings" to the innermost Ātman which is the Ground of *a-Vidyā* and along the path of transcendence to the absolute *Sat* of which all *a-Sat* is but a reflection and an *upādhi*, including his own finite self (cf. *Upadeśa Sāhasrī*, 18, 27-39).

Scriptural *Vidyā* cancels *a-Vidyā* insofar as the latter is erroneous in its pretensions of independence, self-sufficiency, perfect reliability and metaphysical finality. But insofar as *a-Vidyā* is accurate within the limits of its own *pramāṇas*, admits the inadequacy and revisability of its own achievements and obeys the teleology of a dynamism which opens it to the possibility of becoming healed and perfected by a *pramāṇa* superior to its own, it is not exactly abolished but fulfilled by *Vidyā*.

I have tried to show something which is only a side object of Śaṅkara's teaching, namely, the hidden kinship of *a-Vidyā* with *Vidyā*. But it is not to be belittled for, as he says, "it is from (the relative reality of) the objects (known by *a-Vidyā*), such as breath and so forth that is obtained the discriminative knowledge of that which is True Reality in the supreme sense of the term" (*prāṇa-viṣayāt-paramārtha-satya-vijñānābhimānāt*: *Chānd. Up. Bh.*, 7, 17, 1).

University of Poona

13
AVIDYĀ AND ITS RELATION TO VIDYĀ
D. P. Sen

Avidyā in Indian philosophy is a pervasive word. Almost every system of Indian philosophy, whether Vedic or non-Vedic, makes an extensive use of this word in its theory of knowledge and metaphysics. The word *avidyā* like the corresponding positive word *vidyā* has a long history which may be traced back to the Vedas. Thus, in the Atharva-Veda it has been stated that *vidyā*, *avidyā* and whatever else is fit for being instructed entered the body of Brahman along with the Ṛks, Sāma and Yajus.[1] In the Chāndogya Upaniṣad we read, "Both perform the sacrificial act, he who knows and he who does not know. But there is a difference between *vidyā* and *a-vidyā*. For what is performed with *vidyā*, with faith and with upaniṣad, that is most efficacious,".[2] Again in the Bṛhadāraṇyaka we find that a man, when dying, shakes off his body and his *avidyā*.[3] In the passages referred to above the word *avidyā* seems to have been used in the sense of personal ignorance and the word vidyā in the sense of true knowledge. Both are in that sense more or less subjective. But even in the context of the upaniṣadic teaching these two concepts are often used in a more objective and independent sense. Thus, in the Īśa upaniṣad we read "Into a blind darkness they enter who are devoted to *avidyā*, and into greater darkness, as it were, those who are devoted to *vidyā* alone"[4]. Consider again the verses of the Kaṭha upaniṣad where *vidyā* and *avidyā* are conceived as mutually opposed and divergent, and those who dwell within the bounds of *avidyā* are compared with blind men being helplessly guided by the blind.[5] In all these verses the word *avidyā*, or its counterword *vidyā*, has a richer connotation, implying much more than subjective ignorance or knowledge. In later upaniṣads the concept of *avidyā* came to acquire a new dimension, and also the new name, *Māyā*. In the Śvetāśvatara upaniṣad *Māyā* as universal or cosmic ignorance is identified with *Prakṛti*, the root cause of the phenomenal world[6]. Thus, *avidyā*, which originally stands for subjective ignorance comes to assume the role of the creative power behind the world of our experience.

When we come to the age of the systems, (in this paper we shall confine our discussion within the orthodox systems only), we find that the concept of *avidyā* happens to be a key concept in most of the philosophies. It is, of course, variously defined and variously named in the systems. In the Nyāya, for example, it is called *mithyājñāna*, the Sāṅkhya points it under the names, *ajñāna, aviveka* and also *avidyā*, while Vedānta calls it variously as *māyā, avidyā* and *ajñāna*. Its manifold nature, which accounts for its various names given in different philosophical systems, has been beautifully summed up by Udayana, the great Naiyāyika, in one of the verses of his Nyāya-Kusumāñjali : "This unseen potency a power of the Lord is called *māyā*, because it is not clear to our reason, *prakṛti*, because it is the root-cause (of the world) and *avidyā*, because it is opposed to true knowledge.."[7].

With regard to the nature of *avidyā* it may be said that it is no mere absence of knowledge. On this point all the systems are closely agreed. Analysing the nature of *avidyā* in his commentary on the Yoga-sūtras, Vyāsa, the commentator, observes that "it (*avidyā*) is neither a source of valid knowledge, nor its absence, but a piece of knowledge which is opposed to true knowledge"[8]. Derivatively the word is analogous to the word *a-mitra* (non-friend), which denotes neither a friend nor simply the absence of a friend, but one who is unfriendly and, therefore, an enemy.[9] The Yoga-sūtra specifies four types of *avidyā*, namely (1) acceptance of the non-eternal as eternal, (2) taking the impure as pure, (3) taking what is painful as pleasing, and (4) confusing the not-self with the self. Thus defined, *avidyā* is itself a source of affliction and is the root-cause of all other sources of affliction, that is bondage.

But though a positive state of consciousness, *avidyā* is in the yoga view no more than a subjective state. It is interesting to follow how this subjective function gradually develops into a significant objective principle in the hands of the philosophers of the Advaita School. The Advaitin defines *ajñāna*, that is *avidyā*, as "something which appears to be existent, is not definable as either real or unreal, is made of the three *guṇas*, and is opposed to knowledge"[10]. As a positive entity it is directly intuited by the *Sākṣin*, i.e. the over-subjective consciousness, in such experiences as "I am ignorant" or "I had a very sound sleep, I did not know anything." The Advaitin employs a host of arguments to prove that *ajñāna* is an object of immediate knowledge, like our internal states of happiness etc.

Perceptual experience or direct intuition is not, however, the only evidence on which the theory of positive ignorance rests. The Advaitins also appeal to scriptural testimony as a proof of their thesis. Śruti texts like "it (ignorance) is the power of God concealed behind its own *guṇas*"[11] constitute such proof.

The Advaitin is not particularly eager to prove the existence of positive ignorance by any process of inference, for, inference is a rational or logical process, whereas, the concept of ignorance as propounded by him is a non-rational or a-logical one. If it were permeable by reason *avidyā* would lose its character and turn into its opposite i.e. *vidyā*.[12] Still for the satisfaction of those who have some weakness for inference as a mode of proof the Advaitin has devised an ingenious piece of inference[13]. The gist of the inference may be put thus : Every knowledge which is produced by a pramāṇa presupposes something other than its own antecedent negation, which has the same object and the same locus and is at the same time removable by it, as darkness is removable by light. That something is *avidyā*. We do not intend to go further into the details of this intricate inference.

It is doubtful whether Śaṁkara ever regarded *māyā* or *avidyā* as the material or stuff of the world. He does indeed hold that Brahman which is one, Infinite and undivided appears as many in name and form through *avidyā*. But the theory that *avidyā* is the creative power of Brahman having the twofold functions of concealment and projection seems to be a later development in Advaitism.

The post-Śaṁkarite Vedāntins have indulged in various kinds of speculations about the causal status of *avidyā*. Some, for example Vācaspati, have argued that as Brahman appears as the world through the instrumentality of ignorance *avidyā* is just an auxiliary cause in creation[14]. Others, like Sarvajnātman, hold the view that as pure *Brahman* by itself cannot be a cause of anything, it is through *māyā* that it appears as the cause. Hence *māyā* happens to be the *dvāra-kāraṇa*[15]. Others again are of the opinion that both *Brahman* and *māyā* are to be taken as the material causes of the world, *Brahman* as the stuff which appears as, and maya as the stuff which changes into the world.[16] Such divergences in interpretation originate from the diversity of the śruti-texts describing both *Brahman* and *māyā* as the cause of the world. Thus, for example, the text of the Taittirīya upaniṣad "that from which all these beings originate, that by which they are held in existence after origination and that into which they dissolve when destroyed" describes the Brahman as the world-cause. Again the Śvetāśvatara text—" "know *māyā* to be the primal cause" affirms the causality of *māyā*. Such apparent contradictions in the Upaniṣadic texts have led the philosophers of the Advaita school to formulate different views by way of resolving the contradiction.

Is *Avidyā* identical with *māyā*, or is there any sort of difference between the two? This question too has been variously answered in Advaitism. According to some, *avidyā* and *māyā* represent the subjective and objective sides respectively of one and the same fundamental fact of experience[15]. Others again hold that *māyā* as the cosmic ignorance is the magical power of God, whereas *avidyā* as individual ignorance pertains to the finite *jīvas*.[16] It has also been argued in this context that *māyā* as the limiting adjunct (*upādhi*) of God has a preponderance of pure Sattva in its structure, while *avidyā* which is the limiting adjunct of the finite *jīva* has a preponderance of impure sattva.

One important conclusion which follows from the above account of *avidyā* is that there are two grades of knowledge or *vidyā*,—the higher and the lower. Thus, in the Muṇḍaka Upaniṣad we read "there are two *vidyās, parā* and *aparā*,— so it has been said by those who have known the Brahman". The higher knowledge is that by which the supreme self is realised. All other knowledge, including the Vedas and the ancillary sciences such as grammar, astronomy, rhetoric etc. falls within the sphere of lower knowledge.

At this point it needs to be mentioned that self-knowledge or *mokṣa* is not any new state of the self which is produced by *parā vidyā*. The self is eternally pure and eternally free. It only appears to be in bondage due to the veil of *avidyā*. The function of *vidyā* is just to remove the veil, to destroy the *ajñāna* so that the self may reveal itself. Hence, in Advaitism knowledge as a function of mind i.e. *antaḥkaraṇa* has been conceived as something which dispels or destroys ignorance. *Pramā* has, therefore, been defined as that which removes the ignorance concealing its object.[17] According to one school of Advaitism (i.e. the Vivaraṇa school) the final knowledge which results in self-realisation is a perceptual function (*a-parokṣa vṛtti*) of the mind produced by the hearing of such scriptural sentences as "that thou art". According to the philosophers of this school, in special circumstances even words are competent to produce an immediate knowledge. The mental state (*vṛtti*) produced by the uttered statement "that thou art" destroys the enveloping *ajñāna* which conceals the true nature of the self. Vācaspati Miśra, however, does not subscribe to this view. He holds that verbal knowledge in no circumstance can be immediate. The mind, he says, becomes a direct instrument of self-realisation when purified by reasoning and meditation[18]. Vācaspati's view on this point seems to agree with the standpoint's of Nyāya-Vaiśeṣika and Sāṅkhya-Pātañjala schools. That the pure and concentrated mind becomes an instrument to true knowledge is admitted on all hands.[20]

Is *Vidyā* opposed to *a-vidyā*, as light to darkness ? It is an intriguing question, for in the upaniṣads we find two trends of thought one of which would say 'yes' and the other would say 'no' to it. As an instance of the first, we may refer to the Kaṭha upaniṣad where we read "far apart are these, opposite, divergent, the one that is known as the ignorance and the other the knowledge"[21]. This view is confirmed by philosophers is general and seems to be in agreement with commonsense too. Śaṁkara's Vedānta, as we have indicated, subscribes to this view. The other view is strongly suggested by the seer of the Īśa Upaniṣad[22] when he says, "Into a blind darkness they enter who follow after the ignorance, they as if into a greater darkness who devote themselves to knowledge alone, other verily, it is said, is that which comes by the knowledge, other that which comes by the ignorance; this is the lore we have received from the wise who revealed that to our understanding. He who knows that as both in one, the knowledge and the ignorance, by the ignorance crosses beyond death and by the knowledge enjoys immortality". Literally understood these verses clearly recommend simultaneous pursuit of both knowledge and ignorance. In any case they do not suggest any opposition between the two. The expression "by the ignorance crosses beyond death" seems puzzling, because it clashes with the commonly accepted notion of *avidyā*. No less puzzling is the expression "they as if into a greater darkness who devote themselves to knowledge alone", as it is plainly contrary to the universally accepted idea of *vidyā*. Śaṁkara in explaining these verses takes the word avidyā in the sense of action or karma, and *Vidyā* in the sense of worship or meditation of gods. Again, the word 'death' has been taken by Śaṁkara in the sense of ordinary knowledge and work, and 'immortality' in the sense of godliness,—*devatva*, and not *mokṣa* or liberation.[23] Thus interpreted the verses do not appear to conflict with Śaṁkara's way of thinking. As the words *vidyā* and *avidyā* in these verses do not mean knowledge and ignorance, but worship of gods and sacrificial acts, the pursuit of the two together becomes not only intelligible, but also desirable. For, according to Śaṁkara though *jñāna* and *karma*, that is, *vidyā* and *avidyā* are diametrically opposed to each other, sacrificial acts and worship of Gods being but two modes of *Karma* are not only not opposed, but also, in a sense complementary.

It is not difficult to see that for the sake of consistency with his own position Śaṁkara has imposed a forced interpretation on the text cited above. As against Śaṁkara Sri Aurobindo maintains that there is no essential opposition between *vidyā* and *avidyā*. They are only two aspects of the same power of the Lord. To him *vidyā* means the consciousness of unity and *avidyā* means the consciousness of multiplicity. *Avidyā* is necessary to *vidyā*, since without multiplicity, the unity of the Lord would be no better than a 'void of non-existence' or a 'blank repose' of self-absorption. *Vidyā*, similarly is necessary to *avidyā* for the consciousness of the many without a vision of their essential one-ness would plunge us into error and delusion. "The perfection of man, therefore, is the full manifestation of the Divine in the individual through the supreme accord between *vidyā* and *avidyā*"[24]

It is not possible to deal with the relative merits of the two views within the compass of this short paper. Sri Aurobindo's view is strikingly original and illuminating in many ways. But it is not always easy to follow his logic, particularly his account of the origin of ignorance. Of course, Sri Aurobindo has no fancy for logic. He has assigned a low grade to logical thinking. Logic cannot solve all our problems.

In order that we may be able to deal with the problem of the relation of *vidyā* and *avidyā*, we should first attempt to fix the meanings of these two terms. In course of our brief survey of their history we have seen that their meanings have changed significantly with the growth and development of the philosophical systems. If we take them in their original subjective sense, that is, as states of individual mind or consciousness, then perhaps there will be no contradiction in supposing that they are mutually opposed and yet, complementary to each other. Knowledge and ignorance, *vidyā* and *avidyā* in this sense are relative terms, differing not in kind but in degree only. We may then arrange our knowledge in a scale as higher and lower, and in every area of the scale the higher knowledge which falsifies the lower is to be regarded as *vidyā*, and the lower knowledge which is corrected or expanded by the higher is to be called *avidyā* in relation to the higher. Parā *vidyā* is the highest term in the scale,—the goal of philosophic contemplation and spiritual aspiration. As, however the evolution of spiritual life is a progressive advancement from ignorance to knowledge, that is, from comparative ignorance to comparative knowledge, ignorance is fulfilled in knowledge, and is in this sense, complementary to knowledge. But they are also opposed to each other, for the progress of knowledge means rejection of ignorance, while to be in ignorance is to be shut out from knowledge. Nothing short of *parā vidyā* can liberate the soul from the bondage of worldly life, and so every term in the scale of knowledge below the highest is a sort of *avidyā*. The soul's pilgrimage to *vidyā*, then, lies through the realm of *avidyā*. This view of the relation between *vidyā* and *avidyā* accords well with the Sāṁkhya-Yoga position which regards knowledge and ignorance as functions of the *Buddhi*,—knowledge as the function of *sāttvika*, and ignorance as the function of *tāmasika Buddhi*.

As the Sattva element in *Buddhi* increases *ajñāna* gradually disappears yielding place to *jñāna*. This view may also be found to be in conformity with the vedāntic theory of *Kramamukti*, that is, the theory of liberation by gradual steps, set forth in the upaniṣads.

University of Burdwan

REFERENCES.

1. Atharva-1-4-10 (Maṇḍala 23)
2. Chāndogya I.1.10
3. Bṛhadāraṇyaka IV-4-3
4. Īśa Upaniṣad—9
5. Kaṭha Up. I-2—4-5
6. Śvetāśvatara Up. IV. 10
7. Nyāya-Kusumāñjali, Verse I. 21
8. Vyāsa's Commentary on Yoga Sūtra II. 5
9. -do-
10. Vedānta-Sāra by Sadānanda Yogīndra
11. Śvetāśvatara Up. I. 3
12. Bṛhadāraṇyaka-Bhāṣya—Vārttika Verse—0.181
13. Vivaraṇa of Prakāśātman p. 13 (Vijaynagar Ed.)
14. Siddhāntaleśa-saṁgraha—I. 4
15. S. Radhakrishnan. Indian Philosophy Vol-II p. 588
16. -do- p. 589
17. Muṇḍaka Upaniṣad 1-1-4
18. Advaita-Siddhi (The section on pramā), and Advaita-ratna-rakṣaṇa
19. Vedānta-Paribhāṣā—Prayojana-paricchedaḥ.
20. Vide Nyāya-Sūtra IV.2.38, Yoga-Sūtra II.11 Sāṁkhya-Kārikā-23
21. Kaṭha Upaniṣad I.2.4., Sri Aurobindo's translation.
22. Īśa Upaniṣad—9-11 (Sri Aurobindo's translation)
23. Śaṁkara's Commentary on Īśa Upaniṣad—9-11
24. Sri Aurobindo on Īśa Up. 9-11-

A NOTE ON VIDYĀ AND AVIDYĀ

S.R. Bhatt

This is just a note and not a fully developed paper on the analysis of the concepts of *vidyā* and *avidyā* which play a predominant role in the Vedāntic thought, though they are also available in the Buddhist, Jain and Sāṁkhya traditions.

The history of Indian philosophical thought witnesses several uses of the terms *vidyā* and *avidyā*. Sometimes they occur jointly and sometimes singly, and their meaning has altered considerably in both the cases. Ordinarily, the word *vidyā* means knowledge or a discipline of knowledge but in the *Vedāntic* tradition it stands for absolute or unconditional knowledge of the ultimate reality. That is why a prefix *parā* is usually added to it. This renders it free from ambiguity as in the form of *parāvidyā* it unequivocally means 'unconditional knowledge of the ultimate reality.' The word *avidyā* has also been used differently. Apart from its usual epistemological sense as a synonym of māyā it is understood to be a metaphysical principle. In the epistemological sense it has the negative meaning of ajñāna (absence of knowledge) as also the positive meaning of conditional knowledge of the empirical reality. In the latter sense the prefix '*aparā*' is generally added to it. Whenever it is used along with *vidyā* jointly or singly in the same context, it seems to have always been used in the sense of conditional knowledge.

The distinction between *vidyā* and *avidyā* (or, *parāvidyā* and *aparāvidyā*) seems to be a logical corollary of the doctrine of two-fold standpoints about reality viz., *pāramārthika* (absolute) and *vyāvahārika* (empirical). Such a distinction has been a keynote of the Vedāntic thought. Knowledge concerning the *pāramārthika* is *vidyā* and concerning the *vyāvahārika* is *avidyā*.

When the vedāntic thinkers define *vidyā* as the unconditional knowledge of the *pāramārthika sat* they mean that it is the embodiment of the ultimate truth (*satyasya satyam*). It is a knowledge which is true for all times (*trikālābādhita satya*) as contrasted with that which is true-at-a-time. (*Kālika satya*). This property is by virtue of its being regarded as unfalsifiable (*bādharahita*). It is sui generis (*anadhigata*) and hence unacquired through experience. Since it is transempirical it is not amenable to empirical verification. In fact it needs no verification as it is self-validating (*svayam prakāśa*). The *pāramārthika sat* is impartite and unitary (*niṣkala*) and therefore *vidyā* also is said to be non-synthetic (*akhaṇḍārtha*). All statements of *vidyā* are only prakāṣa (pure experience) free from *vimarśa* (ratiocination and conceptualisation). That is why Śaṅkara has characterised them as *vastutantra* and defined *vidyā* as *vastu svarūpāvadhāraṇam*. In other words, it does not purport to describe the reality but leads to the realisation of identity with it (*Brahmavidbrahmaiva bhavati*).

Avidyā, on the other hand, is a knowledge which apprehends relations only (saṁsargāvagāhi). It is necessarily relational. Not only that it is also a conditional knowledge. Both in its origin and validity it is dependent upon certain conditions. Under certain conditions it becomes true and under changed conditions it becomes false. In this sense the upanisads describe it as *asatyam* or just *satyam* as contrasted with *satyasya satyam*. This means it is subject to verification and its truth or falsity is contingent upon confirmation or confutation. This is due to its being empirical and synthetic (*sakhaṇḍārtha*) in character. All empirical knowledge is *avidyā* which is not really true but is believed to be true. That is why Śaṅkara has characterised it as *puruṣatantra*. Here we do not have just *prakāśa* but *vimarśa* is also intermingled in it. It is *mithyā* i.e., an intermixture. In it always there is an imposition (adhyāsa) of conceptual categories upon pure experience (*saṁvedana*) and this renders it subject to built-in falsification (*atasmintadbuddhi*) This falsification is inherent in the very process of knowing and hence Śaṅkara describes it as natural and inevitable (*naisargika*). This *mithyātva* has also been referred to as *sadasadvilakaṣaṇa* as it is an intermixture of *sat* and *asat*. It is not pure *sat* because it cannot be absolutely validated. It is not *asat* also because it cannot be completely confuted as it has a basis in experience and hence a reality of some kind. Though given in experience and hence not false there is no guarantee of its being true. Owing to this peculiar character it is said to be *anirvācya*. Since it is neither absolutely true nor absolutely false, no absolute assertion with respect to its truth or falsity can ever be made.

From the above analysis it becomes quite evident that *avidyā* stands for all empirical knowledge and has only provisional validity. It does not purport to give us knowledge of the reality, but only a guidance in our worldly conduct (*lokavyavahāra*). *Vidyā*, on the other hand, signifies that knowledge which is unconditionally true, whose illustrations are the identity statements like *Aham brahmāsmi Tattvamasi* etc. They have ultimate validity as they imply identification with rather than a description of the reality. They are true by virtue of their *akhaṇḍārthatva* and this consists in pure experience free from all conceptualisation (*nāmadheyam*) and verbalisation (*vācārambhaṇam*).

As regards the interrelation between *vidyā* and *avidyā* there seem to be two broad possibilities. They may be regarded to differ either in degree or in kind. In case of a difference in degree they may be complementary to each other or they may have includer-included relationship. In case of a difference in kind they may be incompatibles and contradictory. In the early period since *vidyā* and *avidyā* were regarded to have their distinct spheres of operation both were regarded to be true in their own way and none was treated as contradicting the other. But when it was argued that the empirical standpoint is false or illusory *avidyā* came to acquire a negative meaning and was regarded as being contradicted (*bādhita*) by *vidyā*.

To conclude, it can be discussed as to what is the purpose and significance of drawing this distinction between *vidyā* and *avidyā*. Of course, an acceptance of the validity of this distinction presupposes the Advaita Vedāntic metaphysics. What it aims at conveying is the idea that conceptual apparatus has a distinct sphere of operation which is the field of experience whereas the absolute reality defies all rational and linguistic account. Our intellect has only practical serviceability and is inadequate to deal with the absolute reality.

University of Delhi

15
VIDYĀ AND AVIDYĀ
K. P. Mishra

In Indian philosophical literature, especially in the Vedāntic texts, the word *vidyā* or *trayīvidyā, avidyā, parāvidyā, aparāvidyā* and *brahmavidyā* or *ātmavidyā* are important concepts, as in finding out their meanings, one finds out answers to many metaphysical and epistemological problems. A close study of the meaning of these concepts points out that *vidyā, avidyā* and *aparāvidyā* form one class and *brahmavidyā* and *parāvidyā* another one. These two are contradictory classes, not *vidyā* and *avidyā*, though *prima facie*, they may appear to be so. They are rather so related that *avidyā* includes *vidyā* or *trayīvidyā* as a genus includes its species. Iś a upaniṣad declares that those who worship *avidyā* enter into blinding darkness; but into greater darkness than that enter they who are engaged in *vidyā*. Taking one to be inclusive of the other, more attention has been paid in discussing the formal features of *avidyā* than of *vidyā*, though a list of different subjects included in the *vidyā* has been given in a number of upaniṣads. A knowledge of these different subjects does not give one liberation (*paraṁ Śreyaḥ, parama puruṣārtha*), does not enable one to go beyond the ocean of unhappiness. According to Chāndogya, Nārada was a knower of all the *vidyās* but still he was unhappy. He approached Sanat Kumāra to be initiated into the *brahmavidyā* as only *brahma vidyā* gives one supreme and lasting happiness.

Thus *avidyā* is not absence of knowledge as it includes all sorts of knowledge, lists of which have been given by the upaniṣads. The negative prefix '*A*' here is to point out the fundamental difference of *avidyā* from *brahmavidyā* for which sometimes the word *vidyā* is used. The object of knowledge is the *adhiṣhāna*, which creates the occasion for knowledge. It conceals the real nature of the object (*āvaraṇa*) and also creates other things in its place (*vikṣepa* or *asatkhyāpana*). All the *vidyās* are included in *avidyā* as they share its presuppositions. These conditions and presuppositions etc., have been accepted by human beings since time immemorial (*anādi bhāvarūpam*) on practical grounds (*vyavahāra* or *sāmvṛti*) as they satisfy their various interests and purposes. *Brahmavidyā* is a critique, both of the conditions and pre-suppositions and also of the various interests and purposes, satisfaction of which is linked up as a consequent with the acceptance of the conditions and pre-suppositions. In Kaṭha, Naciketā rejects all of them saying *api sarvaṁ jīvitam alpameva*. *Brahmavidyā* is an attempt to substitute one set of conditions by another set (*atra brahma samaśnute*) and also an attempt to unravel the fundamental desires of all human beings (*Amṛta*). The new set of rules are acceptable on the ground that they are capable of satisfying those fundamental desires which are not the *eṣaṇās* but the desire to become immortal which indeed is the supreme bliss (*athaiṣa eva parama ānandaḥ*).

Knowledge implies the knower, the known and the relation between the two (*tripuṭī*). It not only covers external objects but also subjective facts, ideas, volitions, emotions and the like. A belief comes up in an object distinct from the knowing of it. With the belief in objectivity, difference is ushered in. This differentiation into 'I' (*asmad*) and 'You' (*yuṣmad*) and superimposition of one upon the other is the stuff of all ignorance. One should know a thing as it is, not as it is not. Criticizing the notions we have of knowledge, *brahmavidyā* points out that prevalent criteria of knowledge do not let us know the things as they are, as it is based upon the mutual superimposition (*adhyāsa*) of the Self which is pure consciousness and non-self. Self-identification with the body, mind, senses, etc. are pre-requisites for the knowing activity as one accepts the senses as his own, has to take the body as himself, etc. in this activity. The world of multiplicity (*prapañca*) is conceived as different series of three, like time, space and causation (*trayam*). The objects are taken to be related by way of cause and effect. Knowledge is based on all these conditions. Though these conditions and presuppositions are positive and beginningless, they would go when other conditions and presuppositions are accepted (*yad vijñānaṁ vilīyate*).

Brahman transcends the three divisions of time (*trikālātpara*.) He is partless (*akalaḥ*). He is other than virtue and vice, right and unright, cause and effect and past and future. He is infinite, unitary and undifferentiated (*avyākṛta*). Brahman is identical with the soul (*ātman*). He is the non-dual pure consciousness. *Brahmavidyā* thus points out what there is to know. Not ordinary sources of knowledge, but only *aparokṣānubhūti* enables one to know this reality, the *adhiṣṭhāna*, or the world-ground, which creates the occasion both for *avidyā* and *vidyā*. In itself it is indeterminate (*anirvacanīya*), unconditional and unsullied. In order to express this truth, upaniṣads adopt the negative mode of instruction : *Athāta ādeśaḥ:neti neti* : This absolute is the realm of ultimate truth (*paramārtha satya*).

Utkal University

Plenary Session IV

LANGUAGE, CULTURE AND MAN

President : S. Vahiduddin
Secretary : Roop Rekha Verma

Main Speakers :
(1) Nityananda Mishra
(2) H. D. Lewis
(3) P. B. Chatterjee
(4) Rajendra Prasad

LANGUAGE, CULTURE AND MAN

N. Mishra

Man at the present moment is facing what may be called the human crisis. Man is set against man. The nations are divided into hostile camps and are making frantic efforts to equip themselves with arms and ammunitions of almost unimaginable destructive power. Despite conferences and pacts suspicion lingers and no party wants to run the risk of being caught napping. But at the same time people also realize, though only half-heartedly, that the result of a full-scale war at the present moment will not be victory or defeat for any side. It is bound to be man's suicide and total annihilation. Thus man is at the crossroads and at a fix as to what he should do. This has set him thinking. He has become somewhat self-introspective and has been reminded of the Socratic 'Know thyself' and the Upaniṣadic *Ātmānaṁ Viddhi*. Perhaps he realizes that he does not know himself sufficiently well and the crisis he is in is due to his own ignorance of himself. Hence in the present philosophical climate of analysis and clarification it is but necessary that the philosopher turns his attention towards a proper analysis of the concept of man.

It should also be noted that it is man's special privilege that he speaks a language and has a culture. For all we know we cannot say that any other species of living beings has the ability to speak a language and build a culture. Language and culture seem to be characteristic of human existence and it is expected that an analysis of the concepts of language and culture will throw light on the nature of man.

What I intend to do therefore, is to analyse the nature of language and culture and to see what they tell about the nature of man. And I start with language.

It is a commonplace that we have to use language for communication with others. But we use language for our own thinking as well. As a matter of fact we are able to communicate only because we are able to think. When I communicate something to you, I think what I communicate. But in communicating I also intend that you should understand what I think. When there is no such intention, language is used for mere thinking. Now, thinking by means of language is perhaps found in human beings only. It is no doubt true that the lower animals also think, but their thinking is different from verbal thinking.

Thinking, which is different from perceiving, involves cognition of the absent. A being who cannot transcend the given and can be conscious of only things which are present, is not a thinking being at all. It is not true that the lower animals remain completely tied to the mere present. They can remember the past and expect the future. A cat has been chased by a barking dog several times and the cat has been able to escape on each occasion. The cat hears the bark again without seeing the dog. And the cat immediately runs away or hides itself. This is surely a case of thoughtful and intelligent behaviour. Of course, the cat has not done its thinking first and then acted in accordance with its thinking. Rather, it has done its thinking in and through its action. In this thinking the barking of the dog is the perceptual cue which signifies the coming of the dog. The former is the sign and the latter is the significate. The thinking of the cat is a case of what may be called sign-thinking.

Human beings are surely capable of sign-thinking, but they are capable of a different kind of thinking as well. Human thinking can be possible even without perceptual cues. Such autonomous thinking by man is dependent on his ability to use symbols which are different from signs.

In order to differentiate clearly between sign-thinking and symbol-thinking we had better differentiate between signs and symbols. Signs are not consciously devised by anyone; they just happen in nature. But symbols are consciously devised by man. So, whatever can be easily produced by man can be a symbol. A man can easily produce a sound, a mark, a gesture, a diagram, a picture etc. So these things can become symbols. But they cannot be symbols by themselves. A sound, in order to be a symbol, has to be linked with something other than itself. When the sound 'cat' is linked with the animal cat through ostensive definitions, it becomes a symbol for cat. The animal cat cannot be a symbol, because the animal cat cannot be produced by man. A house does not become a symbol, because a house cannot be produced by man at once. Thus symbol-relation is not reversible whereas sign-relation is. The sound 'cat' is a symbol of cat, but cat is not a symbol of the sound 'cat'. But barking is a sign of dog and dog also is a sign of barking.

Just as signs in order to be signs have to be empirically linked with the things signified, so also symbols, in order to be symbols, have to be empirically linked with the things symbolized. But in the case of symbols once the link has been established, its empirical origin becomes insignificant, and it takes the character of a rule. Only when this happens, the symbol becomes a symbol in the full sense. Of all symbols the words are by far the most important, because they can be produced easily at once and can be used in various combinations. Hence the unique importance of the words in language. And it is this word-using capacity of man that distinguishes him the most from the lower animals.

But what does this word-using capacity of man reveal about his nature? It reveals that man is an autonomous thinker. He can freely create symbols and can think with them independently of any perceptual signal. Both in his own thinking for himself and in his communication with others man uses symbols with an understanding which even the most accomplished sign-cognizant is not capable of. And this type of understanding is operative not only in one who communicates but also in one who is communicated to. I cannot communicate with one who is fast asleep, nor can I communicate with one who does not take my utterances as symbols. It is only between users of language that communication can be possible. Language is a monopoly of the free creative spirits.

A symbol can be effective in communication only if it affects both parties of communication in an identical way; that is, if it has identical meaning for both parties. If I exclaim 'Fire !' in order to apprise Jones of the danger from the adjacent burning house, I shall be communicating with him, if I shall myself be taking the word 'fire' as a symbol of danger. Communication is both made and received in semantically identical way. And this can be possible if the person communicating does not, from the semantic point of view, only communicate to somebody else, but also to himself. In communication the communicator acquires the role of the communicated also. So the language-using individual must be a self-conditioning indivudual who can simultaneously take the role of another individual as well. We are all very familiar with the phenomenon of talking to oneself. In self-talking the talker is not merely thinking for himself; he is also addressing himself in the same way as he addresses others. This creating of another within one's own self is the prerogative of man. No wonder this talking to oneself has been noticed only in man and not in other animals.

Thus we see that the use of language is the special prerogative of man and it is fully dependent on his creative ability. We shall now take up the concept of culture.

'Culture' has been defined by Sir Edward Tylor as "that complex whole which includes knowledge, belief, art, morals, law, custom and any other capabilities and habits acquired by man as a member of society"[1]. Theodosius Dobzhansky defines culture as "the sum total of habits, customs, language, techniques of doing things, in general, all that people do or think as a result of having been so taught"[2]. He says further, "Cultures are not transmitted by genes in the sex cells;...... culture is acquired by every person individually from his parents, siblings, teachers, friends, neighbours, books, radio broadcasts, and so on"[3]. Thus it is quite evident that culture is a social affair, but it is not merely social. Many lower animals such as ants, bees, monkeys, etc. develop social relationships with the members of their kinds, but they do not have any culture. Sub-human societies are cultureless. Language is a characteristic feature of culture and it is through language that culture is transmitted from generation to generation. It is true that birds and mammals can and do interact by means of their cries and sounds, but their interaction does not come up to the level of linguistic communication.

1. Primitive Culture, (London, 1891).
2. Heredity and the Nature of Man, (London, 1965) P. 141.
3. Ibid.

But then how are language and culture related to each other? According to the thesis of linguistic relativity advocated by the American linguist-anthropologist Benjamin Lee Whorf thought and culture not only reflect linguistic forms and categories but are determined by them. He says, "......... the background of linguistic system (in other words, the grammar) of each language is not merely a reproducing instrument of voicing ideas, but is rather itself the shaper of ideas, the program and guide for the individual's mental activity, for his analysis of impressions, for his synthesis of his mental stock in trade. Formation of ideas is not an independent process, strictly rational in the old sense, but it is part of a particular grammar and differs, from slightly to greatly, between grammars"[1]. What is implied is that the grammatical features of a language determine or mould the ways of thinking and behaving of the speakers of that language. He illustrates his view by pointing out that the absence of tenses in the Hopi language gives rise to a historical and timeless outlook in the Hopi people who regard the past, the present and the future as continuous, cumulative and unchanging[2].

But the Whorfian hypothesis does not appear to be convincing. It is surely not the case that in any society language comes first and then in accordance with the grammatical structure of that language the culture of that society is built and shaped. Rather, it is the peculiarities of the culture of a society that give rise to the peculiarities of the language of that society. Joshua A. Fishman points out that the Eskimo language has many words for different kinds of snow, but English has only 'snow' and 'ice'[3]. He also says that as against the English term 'horse' Arabic has a large number of terms for different kinds of horse[4]. These linguistic differences in Eskimo and Arabic are obviously due to the cultural peculiarities of the Eskimos and the Arabs respectively. The Eskimos are more interested in snow and the Arabs in horses than are most English

1. Quoted by Joshua A. Fishman in his article 'A Systematization of the Whorfian Hypothesis' in *Communication and Culture* edited by Alfred G. Smith (Holt, Rinehart and Winston; New York, 1966), P. 509-10
2. *Ibid*, pp. 510-11.
3. *Ibid*., p. 506.
4. *Ibid*.

speakers. Thus it appears that it is language which is determined by culture.

But this controversy as to whether language determines culture or culture determines language does not seem to be true to the facts of the case. Man could not have developed language first and then in the light of that language built a culture. How can a language develop without a cultural background? Language is a social phenomenon and it is governed by rules which are inter-personally operative. Even the understanding of a simple word 'table' requires a complex cultural *milieu*. Words do not drop from heaven ready for use, but evolve through inter-personal sharing of ideas and co-operative behaviour. They are the results of much cultural contact between person and person.

But then could there be a culture without a background of language? Culture is transmitted from generation to generation not through genes but through language. Exchange of ideas and co-operative behaviour, so necessary for culture, are dependent on linguistic communication. Language and culture then are interdependent and any attempt to make either of them the determiner of the other appears to be misleading. They have arisen simultaneously and have grown interactively together.

Ludwig Wittgenstein has very well pointed out that language is a kind of behaviour and it is a game like other games. In fact the linguistic games and the non-linguistic games are often found intimately blended together. He says, "I shall also call the whole, consisting of language and the actions into which it is woven, the 'language-game'[1]. For him playing a language-game is very much the same as living a 'form of life'[2]. And obviously a form of life is nothing else but a culture.

What does this organic complex of language and culture indicate of the nature of man? Is man a creature of his language and culture? Well, it is a commonplace that there are various languages and cultures in the world and no man speaks all the languages and shares all the cultures. A child is born and brought up in a particular culture and learns to speak the

---

1. *Philosophical Investigations*, section 7.
2. *Ibid.*, section 23.

language of that culture. In course of time it acquires a personality that bears the impress of that language and culture. The personality of an illiterate person born and brought up in a very interior village of India is surely very different from that of a highly educated English or Chinese scientist. And the mental set-up of a multimillionare tycoon of the U.S.A. is surely very different from that of a Buddhist monk of Japan. It has been well said that 'The East is East and the West is West and the twain shall never meet.' Professor F.S.C. Northrop in his book *The Meeting of East and West* has said that the western man is theoretical or rational and the eastern man is aesthetic or empirical. Many people regard the eastern man as spiritual and the western man materialistic, the eastern man as introvert and inactive and the western man extrovert and active.

Even if these personalistic differences between the eastern man and the western man are true, they are surely cultural, not genetic. Theodosius Dobzhansky writes, "........all human beings who are not congenital idiots can acquire at least rudiments not merely of a culture, but of any culture. Most of us use a fork and a spoon instead of chopsticks because we were taught to use them, not because our genes are different from those of the inhabitants of China and Japan. To repeat again, there are no genes for Chinese, or American, or Hottentot culture or language"[1].

It may be argued here that even though human beings belonging to different societies are biologically alike, they are very different in their mental constitution. And it is on account of the differences in the mental constitution of human beings that different languages and cultures have come into being. Now, it is surely true that persons in different societies have different languages and cultures. But these linguistic and cultural differences are not due to any difference of mental constitution which should not be confused with mental accomplishment. What the mind accomplishes is dependent not only on its constitution, but also on the environmental context. And it is the contextual differences which account for the differences of accomplishment either linguistic or cultural. Even so, language and culture are no superimpositions on man,

---

1. *Ibid.*, p. 143.

nor is man a creature of language and culture. They are the offsprings of his own creative genius working in relation to some specific environment. The lower animals may share with men the same environment, but they lack the mental constitution necessary for accomplishing any language or culture.

We shall now look into some specific aspects of culture such as science, myth, art, religion etc. in order to see what they tell about the nature of man. One thing that can be said all at once about these cultural phenomena is that they are all results of man's endeavour to fulfil his basic needs and requirements. It is true that these phenomena differ in contents from age to age and from society to society. Differences are to be found not only in myth, art and religion, but also in scientific theories. Man, though a creative being, is beset with privations and wants. And it is his privations and wants which goad him to proceed on his cultural quests. God[1] does not need to undertake any cultural quest, not because he already possesses a culture, but because he does not need any, for he has no privations and wants. He does not need to adjust himself with an alien environment, for he is full, complete and perfect. Where perfection reigns, there can hardly be any scope for culture.

But then man's needs and aspirations are of different sorts. If he has his physical and biological needs, he has his spiritual needs too. So he not only performs bodily actions, but also tries to know and enjoy. As a result he has given rise to material culture, myth, science, art, religion, magic, rituals, morals, etc. Behind each of these human creations there lurks some specific human need which is either cognitive or emotional or conative, or of any mixed psychological type. If science satisfies the cognitive need, art the emotional, morals the volitional, religion satisfies a psychologically mixed variety of need.

But alas ! man has to fulfil his needs and aspirations in his own characteristic way. God's relation with the world is direct and immediate and he does not need to adjust himself with it. The case of man is different. He cannot have straight

---

1. In this article I have assumed that God exists. And by 'God' I mean an all-perfect, omniscient and all-pervading being.

and direct dealings with the world. For communicating ideas to others he has to take the help of a language; for apprehending the world he has to create myths or has to frame scientific theories; for aesthetic enjoyment he has to take recourse to artistic creations such as poetry, music and painting; for getting mental peace he has to be religious. All these phenomena of language, myth, science, art and religion are symbolic in the sense that they allude to things beyond themselves. John Beattie in his book *Other Cultures*[1] says that the cultural activities are both instrumental and expressive. They are instrumental inasmuch as they are the means for realizing some ends or purposes. And they are expressive because they express or say something. And because what they say is not sayable straightway, they have to be symbolic. This symbolism of culture is both necessary and important. It is necessary because what a symbol symbolizes is too abstract to be grasped straightway, and it is important because the symbolized is something very valuable. A cultivator ploughs his field and sows seeds in it for accomplishing a good harvest. These activities of the cultivator are purely instrumental. But when the same cultivator sacrifices a goat at the altar of the rain-god for a gift of rain, his action though believed to be instrumental is really expressive. The cultivator's sacrifice of the goat is not only a concrete symbolic expression of his belief in an abstract reality, but it also symbolizes his utmost regard for that reality as a bestower of good things. It is true that with the advancement of science and technology the practice of symbolic activities of the type referred to above is bound to wane. But man *qua* man can never attain the ideal of apprehending and dealing with the world in the direct, immediate way. Perhaps he is condemned to be symbolic in a deeper way. Decline or disappearance of symbolism in some fields at some levels is surely possible. But total disappearance of all symbolism at all levels is not the destiny of man. Ernst Cassirer says, "........products of culture—language, scientific knowledge, myth, art, religion— become parts of a single problem-complex : they become multiple efforts, all directed toward the one goal of transforming the passive world of mere *impressions*, in which the

1. Cohen & West, London, 1964.

spirit seems at first imprisoned, into a world that is pure *expression* of human spirit"[1].

But then man need not decry or bemoan his symbolic fate. In order to get rid of all symbolism man has to be either a beast or a God. And the choice either way is hardly worth making, for both God and the beast are non-creative beings. God does not need to create, for he is full and complete. The beast, though incomplete, cannot create, for it cannot liberate itself from the hold of the given. The capacity to create symbols of different types and of different levels is the monopoly of man. And it is on account of this creative capacity that man has been able to possess both language and culture. And he is not the worse for that. The creation and possession of language and culture by man must be a matter of much envy by both God and the beast, if, of course, they are capable of any envy at all.

Some people think that differences of languages and cultures imply that human beings are divided into different species. But they are mistaken because they regard man's accomplishment as his basic nature. The truth is that at the source of all languages and cultures lies the creative power of man which makes all men of all times and places kindred in heart and soul. Those who are panicky of the present human crisis are mindful only of the differences of languages and cultures. But man is man not because he has created this or that particular language or culture, but because he has the competence of creating languages and cultures. And this creative competence is the common characteristic of all men. We have also seen that man in his cultural quests shows his deep concern for what is valuable. He is thus not only a creator, but also a reckoner of values. Only if man realizes this truth and behaves accordingly, he can get out of the crisis he is in. The sages have not for nothing said 'Know thyself : *Ātmānaṁ Viddhi*.

Bhagalpur University

---

1. 'The Concept of Symbolic Form' in Thomas M. Olshewsky edited *Problems in the Philosophy of Language*. (Holt, Rinehart and Winston Inc., New York, 1969) p. 37.

LANGUAGE, CULTURE AND MAN

H. D. Lewis

The importance of the study of language, as reflected in the history of philosophy down the ages has to be noted and recognised. This point should be related to different levels at which our cultural background affects our philosophical outlook. At the same time the study of language is ancillary to other considerations, and the important point to be made will be that philosophy must be regarded as a special way of looking at what we find the world to be like. There is no foolproof method, either of analysis or of language study, nor can we argue the world into existence—or out of existence. A philosopher is always reluctant to say that argument must stop, but Wittgenstein seems to have been quite right in saying that we must stop somewhere. "The way of looking" in philosophy is however very special, and it is the subtlety of this that is reflected in much of the preoccupation with linguistic studies in philosophy. The mistakes of crude forms of realism and intuitionism can be accounted for in the same way. There are ultimates in philosophy, but the appeal to them needs to be very cautious indeed. This theme will be illustrated briefly by reference to the problem of the self and identity.

King's College, University of London.

LANGUAGE, CULTURE AND MAN

Pritibhushan Chatterji

Man alone is a talking animal. The ability to talk or to use language is a peculiarly human phenomenon. We do not find the use of language at the infra-human level. But at the human level linguistic behaviour is universal—there is no tribe or race without some form of language. No accumulation or transmission of culture is possible apart from some language. No individual can develop and express his mind without the help of a language. It is obvious that language is closely related to culture and individual mind. In the present paper we propose to explore the relation of language to culture and man.

But what is language? Language is a system of phonetic symbols which are used for expressing thoughts and feelings. It involves an unconscious selection of certain phonetic stations or sound units. It is a structured system of communication and it is used in common by the members of a particular group to describe, classify and catalogue diverse experiences. In short "language is a system of conventional spoken or written symbols by means of which human beings, as members of a social group and participants in its culture, communicate."[1] Sapir, an acknowledged authority in the field of Linguistics, defines language "as a purely human and non-instinctive method of communicating ideas, emotions and desires by means of a system of voluntarily produced symbols."[2] These symbols are produced by the so-called organs of speech and are in the first instance auditory. They have no instinctive basis.

Language, though a symbolic substitute for experience, never stands apart from it, but all through remains closely linked with it. With the help of language we can analyse our experience into theoretically separable diverse elements and effectuate their intergrading. As related to experience, language becomes a medium for the expression of meanings and references.

The linguistic symbols also give vent to the varying attitudes of the speaker to the diverse objects of the world around him. Language enables an individual to go beyond the immediately given and to think of the past and the future. The linguistic symbols may go back to previous experiences wherefrom they derive their existence and may also point to the future and may be anticipatory in character. But language is not a pure referential organization like the mathematical symbols. The ideal of pure and perfect reference may not be attained by linguistic symbols.

Language is not an inherited skill and there is a non-genetic transmission of language; and yet in a sense there is an innate capacity for language. There is a controversy on this point and authorities in Linguistics are divided into two groups, empiricists and rationalists, former holding that languages are learnt and the latter holding that there is an innate linguistic skill. Perhaps the two views may be reconciled and we may follow Chomsky in this matter. Children are not born with an innate tendency to learn any language rather than another. They pick up the language of the community in which they are born and 'live, move and have their being'. Thus far the empiricists are right. But it is also noticed that every child has a 'creative command' of the language he learns by virtue of which he can construct and understand sentences he has never learned before. This leads Chomsky to presume that every child has an innate knowledge of the principles of what he calls 'universal grammar'. Apart from this hypothesis it cannot be explained how on hearing a *limited* number of utterances in a particular language a child can construct sentences (not learnt before) in accordance with the grammatical rules governing that particular language This shows the truth of the rationalistic theory. In fact, it is better to make a distinction in this connection between *language* (in the singular) and *languages* (in the plural)—the former referring to an innate or inborn linguistic skill or set of capabilities and the latter to particular structures built on these capabilities.[3]

II

To understand the nature of language more fully we should study its functions. Various functions are performed by language. The primary function of language is communication. When we experience reality, we have a tendency to express our experience symbolically and to communicate the same to our fellowmen. We then take the help of language. So language may be regarded as the proper instrument for 'vocal actualization' of our experience and also as an instrument for communication. Moreover language functions not merely as a device for reporting and communicating experience but also as an instrument for defining experience for the experiencer. As Whorf remarks, "We dissect nature along lines laid down by our native language."[4]

It may be pointed out in this connection that sociologists and social psychologists are today taking special interest in mass communication and in this field language is of great aid. Through the diverse means of mass communication media like propaganda and advertising we try to carry on social control and in such media language plays an important role. As Lasswell points out, The study of diffusion and restriction processes (in society) calls for a general theory of language as a factor in power.... When men want power, they act according to their expectation of how to maximize power. Hence *symbols (words and images)* affect power as they affect expectations of power."[5] Thus by applying linguistic studies to the specific areas of mass communication we may determine the effect of a given message upon the hearer or receiver of that message. A new kind of applied linguistics (which may be given the name 'linguistic engineering') may be developed and this may help us in solving many social problems, specially those relating to communication.

Another important function of language is the creation of rapport among the members using the same language. It is through the use of the same language that an individual can feel unity with other members of the same social group, imbibe the same social spirit and interpret the social surroundings in the same way. The social ideal is communicated to an individual (specially in his childhood) by other members of the community through the medium of language. Thus language is a great helper in socialization of an individual and in social interpretation. Sapir explains the social function of language thus : "Language is a guide to 'social reality'.

Though language is not ordinarily thought of as of essential interest to the students of social science, it powerfully conditions all our thinking about social problems and processes. Human beings do not live in the objective world alone, nor alone in the world of social activity as ordinarily understood, but are very much at the mercy of the particular language which has become the medium of expression for their society."[6]

III

But the most important function that language serves is in the sphere of cultural accumulation and historical transmission. The word 'culture' is derived from Latin 'colo', meaning 'to cultivate'. It means something cultivated or ripened and is opposed to the raw and the crude. In the narrower sense the term 'culture' refers to some kind of refinement which is born of education and enlightenment (*e.g.*, fine arts). But in Anthropology and Sociology it is generally used in a wider sense to imply the way of life of its members, the manifestations of social habits, the collection of ideas and habits which the members of a community learn, share and transmit from generation to generation. "Culture", as Tylor defines it, "is that complex whole which includes knowledge, belief, art, morals, law, custom, and any other capabilities and habits acquired by man as a member of society."[7] Culture is, in short, the *total* heritage borne by a society.

From this brief description of culture it is obvious that language is the chief carrier of cultural values. It is through language that the members of a community can exchange their thoughts and feelings, that the ideas and ideals of one generation can be transmitted to another, that the present may be related to the past and the future. There are some lower animals that lead a social life and yet they have no culture; and the most important reason why they have no sustained culture is that they have no language. Indeed, the young of the human species can be initiated into the knowledge of their predecessors with the aid of language. Any normal human being can learn about the experience of any other through the medium of language. Thus language confers on man the unlimited capacity for developing and transmitting culture. The culture of any civilised community with its vast stores of knowledge is inconceivable without some verbalised form or other. Indeed, the role of language as a culture-preserving medium is too patent to deserve any detailed discussion. As Bright rightly remarks : "One may imagine handicrafts being taught by one generation to another without the use of language but social legal, religious, political or economic institutions are another matter. It is hard to imagine that a community of deaf-mutes (if they were deprived of such speech-surrogates as writing) could carry on human social life." [8]

In this connection we may refer to an interesting question : Should we speak of language *and* culture or language *in* culture ? If we take the term in a wide or generic sense, language becomes a part of culture and we should then speak of language *in* culture. But the term 'culture' is also used in a narrower sense as a convenient 'shorthand term' for certain particular aspects of culture, and we may then speak of language *and* culture (provided, of course, the aspects of culture referred to *do not* include language). The phrase 'language *and* culture' would then be comparable to phrases like 'technology *and* culture', 'music *and* culture' and so on. On this matter Hymes comments : "What makes the slipping back and forth between the two uses of 'culture' a rather vicious habit is the fact that the generality and prestige of the first use may be implicitly carried over into the second. Then the implicit parentheis of 'X and (other aspects of) culture' is erased, and the X relegated to a periphery, the burden of proving a relevance to the central term being its own."[9] The controversy centering round the relative aptness of the phrases 'language *and* culture' and 'language *in* culture' thus loses much of its edge if we remain careful about the exact sense in which we are using the term 'culture' in a particular case. Anyway, that language has a cultural nature and that it has an important status as a cultural 'marker' cannot be denied, and as cultural markers linguistic facts are, as Carroll remarks, "far more reliable than other cultural markers, such as tools used by a culture, or its style of architecture. Tools and styles of architecture are much more readily borrowed than certain aspects of language."[10]

The foregoing discussion has made it clear that language plays a large and significant role in the acquisition, maintenance, development and spread of culture. But in this context certain misunderstandings and exaggerations should be guarded against.

In the first place, it should be noted that there is no causal relation between culture and language. Culture is an 'inventory of experience' and language is the medium of expressing that experience, and the one need not be causally related to the other. Language and Culture help each other—the richer a language, the greater is the scope of culture to expand and develop itself and the more developed a culture, the more it enriches the language or languages through which it finds expression.

Secondly, a culture need not stick to one language for its expression, nor again a particular language should be the carrier of one type of culture. A particular culture may be expressed through different languages, while different cultures may have one linguistic medium of expression. As Sapir says, "Totally unrelated languages share in one culture, closely related languages—even a single language—belong to distinct culture spheres."[11]

Thirdly, languages may differ widely from each other, and to the extent they differ, they may stand in the way of cross-cultural understanding and communication. That linguistic differences may create some such difficulty cannot be denied; but they do not constitute any insuperable difficulty. No culture is so completely self-contained and unique as to preclude the influences of, and communication with, other cultures. Cultures, in spite of their differences, have important resemblances and language-differences cannot debar inter-cultural communication. As Hoijer remarks, "It is easy to exaggerate linguistic differences....and the consequent barriers to inter-cultural understanding....Intercultural communication, however wide the difference between cultures may be, is not impossible."[12]

IV

If language embodies the culture of a community and helps its development and expansion, it also contributes to the growth of the individuality of man. Language helps an individual in understanding the outer world, in formulating his opinion about men and things and in communicating his views. In fact, the linguistic behaviour of an individual is an index to his personality. How the linguistic behaviour of an individual serves as an indicator of his personality is well expressed thus : "The fundamental quality of one's voices, the phonetic patterns of speech, the speed and relative smoothness of articulation, the length and build of the sentences, the character and range of the vocabulary, the stylistic consistency of the words used, the readiness with which words respond to the requirements of the social environment, in particular the suitability of one's language to the language habits of the person addressed—all these are so many complex indicators of personality."[13] In short, the different dimensions of verbal behaviour are all pertinent to the study of personality. It may be noted here that the credit for microcultural analysis of communication goes to Sapir, Boas and some psychologists associated with them. Today a new science called Psycholinguistics is shaping itself and is able to throw much light on the personality of an individual from the study of his linguistic behaviour. Psycholinguistics is "chiefly concerned with the way in which the speaker of a language encodes his behaviour into linguistic responses, depending on the structure of his language, and as a hearer, decodes linguistically coded messages into further behaviour."[14]

The study of linguistic behaviour has also got a diagnostic value. It enables the psychologist to find out the causes of an individual's maladjusted behaviour. As Sapir says,".... linguistic forms and historical processes have the greatest possible diagnostic value for the understanding of some of the more difficult and elusive problems in the psychology of thought.."[15] He also suggests that speech should be regarded as a series of levels which should be analysed separately. To quote his own words,"....if we make a level-to-level analysis of the speech of an individual and if we carefully see each of these in its social perspective, we obtain a valuable lever for psychiatric work."[16]

V

It may be asked in this connection : Does language give freedom to man, or does it keep him in bondage or slavery ?

It is difficult to give a clear-cut answer. The possession of linguistic capacity gives freedom to man in various ways. It gives him freedom from the limitations of the 'here' and the 'now', freedom from hazards, freedom from facing similar problems over and over again, and so on. As man is endowed with the capacity for language, he can remember the past and imagine the future, and thus he can overcome the limitations of the present. But a lower animal hardly possesses the linguistic capacity necessary for memory and imagination, and so, unlike man, an animal is tied to the present. In this respect man has a distinct advantage over lower animals. Endowed as he is with linguistic capabilities, he may with the help of his memory adjust himself to a situation which is like the one he experienced before, or with the help of imagination to a situation which has just been described to him even though it was never experienced by him before. Thus language confers on man freedom of understanding and freedom of adjusting in his own way.

But language is also slavery. Man is under the thumb of a kind of linguistic determinism. He is bound to perceive the world around him through a screen of linguistic stereotypes—through a set of categories which has been created by his language. These categories rule man's life and experience, and colour his perceptions, beliefs and opinions. As Green says, "In a very real sense, man does not live in a world of men at all, threatening or otherwise, but in a world of believers, atheists, heretics, communists, capitalists, organized labor, princes of privilege, and friendly and unfriendly nations."[17]

Whether a man would be considerate and kindhearted or would be inhuman and oppressive is determined by his interpretation of the world in linguistic terms. Like lower animals, man also experiences emotion; but his emotion is coloured and modified by his language. The verbal concepts of man express emotions and characterize and heighten them. An individual does not live among his fellow-men merely as a man amongst men—but he interprets their behaviour, establishes various relations with them and develops various attitudes towards them; and all these become possible due to man's linguistic capacity. Thus the diverse human relations and attitudes are constructed by language and an individual becomes subject to such constructions.

Language also creates different linguistic groups and these linguistic differences may create mental barriers which we can undo only with great difficulty. Much of our inter-group conflict is due to *our own* way of interpreting our fellow-men and our surrounding situations, and needless to say, in our interpretations we are tied to the patterns of the language we use.

Language also enslaves us in another way. We are prisoners of the connotation of some of our verbal concepts. We may here refer to an example given by Whorf. An investigator belonging to a fire-insurance company found that where gasoline drums are stored, great care is exercised by employees not to throw cigarette stubs. On the other hand, cigarette butts are likely to be carelessly tossed about where *empty* drums are piled. But the so called empty drums are more dangerous, as they contain explosive vapour. The word 'empty' is interpreted as 'free from hazard' and not as 'null and void, *not* containing anything'. Hence the employees do not take sufficient precaution in regard to 'empty' drums which though not containing gasoline contain explosive vapour. Thus the employees here are 'prisoners' of one kind of interpretation.[18]

VI

Philosophers have a vested interest in language and the problem of communication, and a common field is traversed by Linguistics, Philosophy, Sociology and Psychology. Most of the problems relate to meaning, and Psychology holds the key to the problem of meaning. Hence every philosopher interested in language should be acquainted with the psychological approach to language. A philosopher should also take into account the contributions of Social Sciences specially where a study of cross-cultural data is involved. A linguistic study, when properly carried out, raises various issues in exoliguistics and gradually leads to the development of a linguistic *Weltanschauung*. This type of *Weltanschauung* is concerned with the way in which a language system organises human experience and it comes closer to a philosophical world-view. Thus a joint venture of Linguistics, Philosophy, Social Sciences and

Psychology is called for, and this joint venture alone can throw light on man and his culture.

Two groups of thinkers—the Analytical philosphers and the Existentialists—have in recent times shown special interest in the problem of language. There are, however, some differences in their approaches. The Analyst is mainly interested in analysing the internal structures, syntax and meaning of language, in the significance or reference of words and sentences and in the conditions that make them true. On the other hand, the Existentialist is interested in language as a human or existential phenomenon. He pays greater attention to the spoken word, the 'talk' , the voice and gestures of speakers than to the internal structure of a sentence and its object of reference. An existentialist studies language insofar as the speaker is in being-with-others. "There are at least two ways", points out Macquarrie, "in which language is inseparably linked to personal existence. First, all language is someone's language. Language does not spring up in a vacuum, it proceeds from *homo loquens*....Second, all language is addressed to someone."[20] And an existentialist studies language from these two perspectives.

In the last analysis the two approaches—the Analytical and the Existential—are not opposed to each other; rather they are complementary. The Analyst and the Existentialist are both conscious of the importance of language as a human phenomenon and of the possibility of its misapplication and misinterpretation, and they both offer guidance for the proper use of language.

A philosopher is not a cold theoretician. To whichever school he may belong, no philosopher worth his profession can avoid his responsibility to interpret culture and to devise ways and means for inter-cultural understanding. He should take greater interest in the broad problems of human communication as they affect society and individuals. He is to be a communication generalist and has to develop the art of communication engineering. As a communication generalist he is to take an increasing interest in social and inter-personal relations and for this purpose he is to see how healthy inter-lingual relations can be established. A philosopher should therefore plan and execute more of such programmes as will focus our attention on the various inter-relations of cultural, psychological and linguistic factors.

REFERENCES

1. *Encyclopaedia Britannica*, Vol. 13: Article on 'Language'.
2. Edward Sapir, *Language* : *An Introduction to the Study of Speech* p. 8.
3. *International Encyclopaedia of Social Sciences*, Art. on 'Language'.
4. B. L. Whorf, *Collected Papers on Metalinguistics*, p. 5.
5. Lasswell et. al., *Language of politics* : *studies in Quantitative semantics*, pp. 18-19.
6. D. G. Mandelbaum (Ed.), *Selected Writings of Edward Sapir in language, culture and personality*, p. 162.
7. E. B. Tylor, *Primitive Culture*, p. 1.
8. *International Encyclopaedia of Social Sciences*, Art. on Language.
9. Dell Hymes (Ed.), *Language in Culture and Society*, General Introduction, pp. xxvi & xxvii.
10. J. B. Carroll, *The Study of Language*, p. 112.
11. Sapir, *Language*, p. 213.
12. Harry Hoijer (Ed.), *Language in Culture*, p. 94.
13. *Encyclopaedia of Social Sciences*, Vo.. IX, Art. on 'Language'.
14. Carroll, *op. cit*, P. 111.
15. Sapir, *Language*, Preface, p. V.
16. Sapir, 'Speech as a Personality Trait' in *American Journal of Sociology*, Vol. 32, p. 905.
17. A. W. Green, *Sociology*, p. 81.
18. J. B. Carroll (Ed.), *Language, Thought and Reality* : Selected writings of Benjamin Lee Whorf, p. 135.
19. The term 'exolinguistics' is coined by Carroll. The prefix 'ex' suggests that "one is dealing with something which stems out of linguistics, but which is not indentical with linguistics." (*The Study of Language* p. 29).
20. John Macquarrie, *Existentialism*, pp. 110-111.

Calcutta University.

LANGUAGE, CULTURE AND MAN

Roop Rekha Verma

The theme uses three notions, each of them being itself a subject of very rich and vast disciplines. Some connections between these three notions—'Man', 'Language' and 'Culture'—are obvious. At least two of them, viz, 'Man' and 'Culture', are too vague and elusive to be neatly defined.

'Man' is variously defined as a rational animal, as a tool making animal, as a laughing animal, and so on. Perhaps no particular difinition can claim to be *the right* definition of man. This concept seems to be one of those vague concepts for which a definition has to *stipulate* a choice over a range of available hazy meanings.

Without claiming it to be a definition—or at least the only correct definition—it may be said that man, although not necessarily cultured, is potentially a culture-creating and culture-dependent being. Culture is the mental medium in which man lives and breathes, just as air is the physical medium in which he sustains his existence.

Language, in the form of a systematic network of symbols, is the most wonderful, useful and complex product of culture.

What we call 'culture' is a huge system of many smaller systems of culture-units, and language is one of such culture-units or cultural subsystems. As such, language is the most influential and basic culture-units; it affects almost all the other cultural manifestations.

The contribution of comparative linguistics to the study of culture-history is well-known.

Man is unique in his capacity to create and use language as a system of symbols.

Hence the intimate connection between man, language and culture.

Language, the most rudimentary of the three, raises many intricate problems, one of them being that of the universals of language.

Many philosophers have compared culture—universals with language-universals, and some have argued the latter's case on the basis of the former.

It seems that if there are culture-universals, there must be language-universals, but not vice versa. That is, the possibility of language-universals does not entail that of culture-universals.

A Linguistic element, and so a language-universal, need not be dependent upon, or even correlative of, a cultural trait or fact.

The reality, that is the continuum of experience, is cut up and reassembled in different ways by different languages.

And to a great extent the choice may be dictated by the cultural perspectives of the society or the community.

(Although, many cultural perspectives themselves may, in their turn, be determined by the linguistic angles by which a community shapes their experience. This is apart from the fact that a linguistic perspective is itself a cultural perspective, since a language is a culture-unit.)

The language-universals, it seems, are to be found in the logical framework of a language, not in the descriptive or even grammatical schemes.

But, even there, not every element gives a language-universal.

Only some basic logical operations seem to be universal, and they seem to be free of cultural variation and cultural construction. This goes against the Sapir-Whort thesis.

A logical operation is introduced by a logical law. The latter 'introduces' or 'governs' a logical operation in much the same way as a theory introduces its concepts. But the sort of operational meanings given to theoretical constructs are not available for logical constants.

Logical operations are certain ways of handling concepts and sentences.

They are also the basic ways of inducting pre-conceptualized reality into conceptual framework.

Hence they also determine the basic forms of our questioning and answering. And these most basic forms of our questioning and answering are not determined by culture peculiarities but by the bare necessities of communication and thinking themselves common to and independent of all cultures.

Lucknow University.

20
MEANING, CRITERIA AND PURPOSES
Rajendra Prasad

Although it would be unfair to say that pre-twentieth century philosophers were not aware of the distinction between the meaning of an expression and the criteria of its application, the degree in which the philosophical importance of the distinction has been emphasized in the third quarter of the twentieth century is certainly distinctive of it. This distinction has not only been acknowledged to be of great importance for the general theory of meaning and language, but has also been used to justify some very specific theses. In this paper I shall examine one attempt of the latter variety.

A number of philosophers, led by R. M. Hare, claim to have discovered in the meaning—criteria distinction a sure basis for the (irreducible) duality of descriptive and evaluative languages. This discovery, if genuine, would be of paramount importance to those who accept as well as to those who deny the duality, since it would justify the former's right to affirm it, and disprove the latter's right to deny it.

Those who use the meaning-criteria distinction to justify the duality make the specific point that the meaning of a descriptive term is, whereas that of an evaluative term is not, identical with the criterion or criteria of its application. Since the distinction is logical, if descriptive and evaluative languages differ in this respect, then they have to be regarded as logically different.

Let us call those who hold that descriptive and evaluative languages are logically different linguistic dualists, or, simply, dualists, and those who hold that they are not, linguistic monists, or, simply, monists. The dualist asserts that there is no clear, stable, logical bridge between descriptions and evaluations. That is, no description entails an evaluation, and no evaluation entails a description. Given a specific description, one cannot pass on to a specific evaluation, unless there is another evaluation already linked up with the given description. This means that between a description and an evaluation there has to be placed another evaluation to work as the bridge, otherwise one can hope to pass on to the latter only by jumping over the gulf at his own risk. There always lies a great amount of uncertainty when one attempts to jump even over a very narrow gulf. There is no guarantee that he will not fall into it. The difficulties in passing from an evaluation to a description are similar.

To illustrate what has been said very abstractly above, let us take an example. Suppose I offer a description of the pen I am writing with as follows : 'This pen is not very costly, is leak-proof, does not scratch the paper it writes on, has a nib with extrafine point, and gives a regular flow of ink.' According to the dualist, this statement by itself does not entail any evaluative judgment about the pen. From it I cannot infer either 'It is a good pen', or 'It is a bad pen'. I can dot hat only if I am provided with an evaluative bridge in the form of another evaluation, say, 'All pens which are.... are good (or bad)'.

The above is indeed a very crude presentation of the dualist thesis. Almost all dualists have presented their views fortified with very impressive logical sophistications and refinements, but still the above description, though too short, gives the gist of dualism without any serious disfigurement.

Assuming that it is a fact that there is no logical bridge between the two, one can legitimately ask for an explanation of this fact. One standard explanation, as available in recent literature, is that the logical role performed by a description is different from that performed by an evaluation. But it does not stop further questioning. In fact it generates a more serious question, namely, what is the justification for saying that they perform different roles? It is here that some philosophers make use of the meaning-criteria distinction. They seem to hold that since in the case of one meaning and criteria are identical and in the case of the other they are not, the two must be performing different roles, and hence even if structurally or morphologically they look alike, they must be considered to be logically different.

I do not want to question the dualistic position that descriptions and evaluations perform logically different roles, though I would like to state and explain this fact in a manner different from that in which the received theories do.¹ But I do want to question the claim that descriptions and evaluations are logically different because of their different fates with the meaning-criteria distinction. I want to maintain that there are at least some descriptive terms whose meaning is not identical with the criteria of their application, and therefore the distinction between descriptions and evaluations cannot be maintained on the ground that the meaning of an evaluative term is not, while that of a descriptive term is, identical with the criteria of its application.

I feel inclined to believe that the stronger thesis, asserting the non-identity of meaning and criteria for all, or most of, descriptive terms, can also be made plausible. But since even the weaker thesis that the non-identity is true of at least some descriptive terms is sufficient to refute the dualist's argument, I shall not attempt to vindicate the former here.

I shall first present, as fairly as possible, the dualist's position on the meaning-criteria distinction as applicable to evaluate terms. I shall then take some descriptive terms and show that at least in this respect there is no difference between them and any evaluative term. In the end I shall state very briefly and rather dogmatically my own position about the nature of the descriptive-evaluative duality.

Let us assume that the word 'good' is used to commend and not to describe the object to which it is applied. That is, when I say that this is a good pen what I do by calling it good is not to describe it as not very costly, leak-proof, etc., but to express commendation or admiration for it. Further, I call it a good pen *because* it has certain properties, e.g., it is not very costly, is leak-proof, does not scratch the paper on which I write with it, gives a regular flow of ink, etc., etc. These are the properties which, according to me, a pen must have in order to be good. They are the criteria of a good pen; their presence in a pen makes it a good pen. Thus the criteria consist of the good-making properties. The good-making properties may differ from one thing to another, from one culture to another, from one person to another, or even for the same person at different periods of his life. But although the criteria of goodness differ, the meaning of goodness does not. In all cases to say that something is good is to commend it. Whether

I apply 'good' to a pen, a pocket-knife, or a person, I always mean to commend the object I call good.

A good pen has so many properties besides its goodness but I cannot define it as that which has these other properties, since, if I do, a dualist may remind me of committing the naturalistic fallacy, or a fallacy very similar to the latter. He may even interpret what Moore named the naturalistic fallacy, in a slightly non-Moorean manner, as a fallacy arising out of the identification of the meaning of an evaluative term with some or all of the criteria of its application. For example, since 'good' does not mean 'being pleasurable', though being pleasurable may be the criterion, or at least of one of the criteria, entitling an experience to be called good, defining 'good' as 'pleasurable' is fallacious as it involves identification of meaning with the (or a) criterion. In some such way from the facts to which Moore wants to draw our attention by his discussion of the naturalistic fallacy an argument may be derived for defending the importance of the meaning-criteria distinction for 'good', or for any evaluative term whatsoever.

I can *understand* someone else's calling a pen a good pen even without knowing what are his criteria of a good pen. I can do it if I know that calling a thing good means commending it. From his commendations I can know what are the things he considers good, though without further investigation I may not know on what basis he commends what he commends. It is for this reason that the meaning of 'good' cannot be given by means of any demonstration or ostensive definition. I can demonstrate or explain by an ostensive definition some of the properties of a pen on account of which it is called a good pen, but this will only mean explaining its criteria, its good-making properties, and not the meaning of 'good' as applied to it.

If one knows what commending, choosing, preferring, favouring, etc., mean, I can *explain* to him what 'good' means in one simple lesson, but the criteria of goodness cannot be taught in one lesson, since different kinds of things are good on account of possessing different kinds of properties. This is possible only because the meaning of 'good' is not the same as the criteria of its application. Had the two been identical, either it would not have been possible to teach its meaning in one lesson, or it would have been possible to teach in one lesson even the criteria of its application to all types of things.

In fact it is *not necessary to teach* the criteria of 'good' in order to teach what it means. I can teach one its meaning if he knows what choosing, commending, etc., mean, without teaching him what properties a thing of a certain type must have in order to be called good. If I know that he is willing to commend or choose a certain kind of pen, I can tell him that he can call that pen a good pen, even without knowing what properties of the pen constituted his reasons for commending or choosing that pen. If he commends the pen, I can definitely say that he thinks it is a good pen (perhaps unknowingly because he did not know the meaning of 'good' before I taught him), though his thinking that it is a good pen is not a criterion of a good pen. Similarly, it is possible in principle to teach him the criteria of a good pen without teaching him the meaning of 'good'. Assuming that he does not already know what 'good' means, I can tell him that when a pen has the properties a, b, c, it is a good pen, without telling him what does it mean to call it a good pen. He then might think that 'good' means 'having the properties a, b, c,' which will be a mistake because many good things are good without possessing the properties, a, b, c, or that 'good' is a descriptive term such that 'a good pen' simply means a pen which has the properties a, b, c. In either case he acquires a new competence to distinguish between good and bad pens, like the one he already had, e.g., to distinguish between red and black pens, without commending the pens with the properties a, b, c. For such a person 'good' has ceased to perform the function of expressing commendation which it normally performs in language, and thus has lost its normal meaning, even though he knows the criteria for applying it to at least one class of things, i.e. pens.

In the case of descriptive terms, the situation is very different. Here the distinction between meaning and criteria does not hold good. The meaning of a descriptive term is the same as the set of its criteria. Take the word 'red' for example. The meaning of 'red' can best be *taught* by exhibiting examples of red things, and by exhibiting many different kinds of them, e.g. red ties, red roses, red lips, etc., so that the learner may know that things are red not in virtue of their size, shape, smell, etc., but only in virtue of their colour. This shows that the meaning of 'red' cannot be taught just in one lesson, and it cannot be taught without teaching when it can correctly be applied to things. In fact, we know what it means to call a thing red only by knowing what being coloured red is. That is, the property of being coloured red, the possession of which by a thing is the criterion for applying 'red' to it, is also the meaning of 'red'. To say that this pen is red-coloured means to say that this pen has the property of being coloured red. Here we do not have two things, meaning and criterion, 'red' and some 'red-making' property or properties. To be red means to have the specific property of redness, whereas to be good means being an object of commendation, and the criteria of goodness depends upon what kind of thing it is which is called good. Since certain properties of a good thing constitute the criteria of its goodness, its good-making properties, it is not possible that two things are exactly alike except that one is good and the other is not, because if they are exactly alike, then they are also alike in having similar good-making properties and when they have them, both must be good. It is not possible that a thing has the good-making properties and is not good. If it satisfies the criteria of being good, then it must be good. But two things can be exactly alike except that one is red and the other is not, because no set of the properties of a thing can be called its red-making properties. Of two artificial roses both can have the properties a, b, c, and still it is possible that one of them is red and the other is not. It is not the set of a, b, c, which makes the red one red; it is red because of having the property of being red. When we say that it is red, we just *mean* that it has the property of being red-coloured. On the other hand, if we call a thing good we mean to commend it, and if we refer to some of its properties, we refer to them as the reasons, or criteria, for calling it good. This is why we cannot teach the meaning of 'good' by exhibiting good things even of the same variety. If we exhibit several good pens, we shall be drawing the attention of the audience only to the criteria of a good pen, and not to its meaning. The meaning of 'good' is not located in any good thing. Had goodness been a property like redness, it would have been possible to give an ostensive definition of 'good', and then its meaning and criterion would have become non-different. But that would mean that it has ceased to be an evaluative word as it cannot then, like 'red', express commendation.

Teaching or learning the *meaning* of 'red' necessarily involves reference to the red colour, and teaching or learning what is it to be red necessarily involves reference to the meaning of 'red'. In fact these are not two processes, but just one. If I do not know what it is to be red I do not know the meaning of 'red' and vice-versa. I cannot teach or learn one without teaching or learning the other.

I have presented in the preceding paragraphs, in as favourable a light as possible, the dualist's theory that the meaning of an evaluative, unlike that of a descriptive, term is not identical with the criterion or criteria of its application. I might have done some reconstruction therein, but my main intention behind my presentation (or reconstruction) has been to make the contours of the theory distinctly visible, and not to make it unduly vulnerable, or vulnerable at wrong points. I shall now proceed to examine how far it is logically defensible to use the satisfaction or non-satisfaction of the meaning-criteria distinction as a ground for the duality of evaluative and descriptive languages.

In stead of making a direct attack on his theory I shall first comment on the dualist's basic approach to the meaning-criteria problem. It seems to me that it is his basic approach, rather than any particular insight or error, which has led him to hold such a theory. He seems to have assumed, without proper examination, as unquestionably true that the things which are the objects of our evaluations first have, or are first thought by us to have, some evaluatively neutral properties and it is later on that we add to them an evaluative meaning by commending them by means of our evaluations. It seems as if we first simply boiled the soup unspiced, and later on fried it with whatever spice we or our society considered appropriate. It is these so-called neutral properties which the dualist calls the criteria, the good-making properties, and the appended spice of evaluation the meaning. There is nothing absolutely wrong in describing the evaluative situation in terms of criteria and meaning, but he makes the separation between them too inflexible. We do evaluate things on account of their possessing, or rather our thinking that they possess, certain properties which constitute the criteria for the application of the evaluative term we apply to them. But criteria and meaning are not related to each other as boiling the soup and frying it are related to each other. The two, the evaluative meaning, i.e., the notion of commending, choosing, etc., and the notion of properties attributed, or the recognition and identification of these properties, which figure as the criteria, grow and evolve together. We consider, e.g., the properties of being juicy, sweet, fresh and pleasant in smell as the criteria of a good mango since we have found mangoes with these properties satisfying our needs and tastes in a much better way than others having a different set of properties. Our evaluation of mangoes as good or bad and our fixing of the criteria of their goodness or badness have evolved together in the course of our conceptual evolution.

It is therefore incorrect for the dualist to emphasize so much the meaning-criteria distinction in the case of evaluative terms. If I have to teach the meaning of 'good' to a learner, though my teaching may involve reference to such concepts as those of choosing, commending, etc., I cannot teach him its meaning unless I give some examples of good things. In fact, quite often an intelligent learner would ask for the mention of good-making properties. Similarly, if I simply narrate the good-making properties of a thing to a learner who belongs to the same social and cultural milieu to which I belong, he will immediately evaluate it as good without waiting for me to call it good or express commendation for it. When a salesman tells an Indian that the mangoes in the corner basket are sweet, juicy, fresh and fragrant, he does not have to add that they are good.

I am not completely denying the conceptual distinction between meaning and criteria; I am only suggesting that as relevant to evaluative language it is not as rigid as the dualist thinks it is. But my objection against him is not simply that he has been unrealistic in his emphasis on its rigidity. I want rather to assert that even if his claim about the non-identity of the meaning and criteria of evaluative terms is justified, he is not justified in using it as a ground for differentiating between evaluative and descriptive languages, because, as I shall show in what follows, the meaning of some descriptive terms is also in no way less non-identical with their criteria than is the meaning of an evaluative term with its criteria.

One common feature of evaluative and descriptive expressions which is quite often not only missed but even denied of evaluative expressions is their referring function. It is commonsensically obvious that value-words refer to certain properties. When I call a pen a good pen I do have in mind some properties of the pen which I refer to in calling it good. Reference to properties by a value-word is essential, and in no way less essential than it is in the case of a descriptive word, if it is to function successfully. We evaluate a thing as possessing certain properties, and not infrequently we have to withdraw or modify the evaluation if some of the references made are not true. Further, an expression, no matter whether it is evaluative or descriptive, does not have to refer to the same property in all contexts in order to earn its right to be an expression with a referring character. Perhaps it is the mistaken assumption to the contrary, coupled with the innocent and true belief that value-words do not refer to the same properties in all of their uses, which has motivated several philosophers to deny their referring function. Since most of them also assume that descriptive expressions refer to the same things or properties in all contexts, or at least maintain, in comparison with evaluative terms, a better constancy or uniformity in their referring behaviour, they find it convenient to say on this very ground that evaluative expressions are logically different from descriptive expressions. All these assumptions are mistaken since both of them perform referring functions and both perform them with varying degrees of uniformity. This does not mean that the meaning of an evaluative expression, or even that of a descriptive expression, can be conclusively explicated in terms of what it refers to, since the meaning of no expression can be so explicated.[2]

I have referred to the above common feature of evaluative and descriptive expressions hoping that it will help us to see the meaning-criteria controversy in the proper light.

The properties which constitute the criteria of the application of a word to a thing are the properties it refers to, and since a word can refer to different properties in different contexts, the criteria of its application can also differ in different contexts.

Let us take the word 'red' which is taken by any as a paradigmatic example of a word always referring to the same property. Firstly, it cannot be said to have no variation in its referring behaviour, since it does refer to different shades of redness, or to different degrees of concentration of the red colour. Secondly, even the criteria of its application to different things are not identical. We apply the word 'red' to, say, apples, lips, blood, and *sarees*, and though we mean the same colour by it in all the four cases, the criteria for applying it to all of them are not the same. The criteria for calling a lip red are very different from those for calling an apple red. If the former are taken to be the correct criteria, no apple can ever be said to be red. It is clear then that even in the case of 'red' its meaning and criteria are not identical. Here again meaning and criteria have evolved together, and not that the meaning of 'red' is like a flavouring added to the otherwise neutral colours of red apples or red lips.

It is not difficult to find many more examples of descriptive terms to which the meaning-criteria distinction applies in the same way as it does to evaluative terms. Take our familiar word 'pen'. The criteria which a thing must fulfil in order to be called a pen have changed, say, in Indian society, tremendously in the present century, but still we understand the same thing by calling a thing a pen.

One may object to my arguments on the ground that I have chosen such simple terms as 'red', 'pen', etc., which may not be accepted as incontrovertible examples of descriptive expressions, or that their logic may not be illustrative of the logic of more complicated descriptions. There may be some force in this objection, but my apology, if one is needed, is that in using such examples, I have only followed the practice prevalent among a large number of recent dualists. Several of them have used such terms as obvious examples of descriptive expressions. This does not mean, however, that my analysis of descriptions can at best be true only of such simple descriptive terms as 'red', 'pen', etc.

Whichever expression is considered to be a *bona fide* descriptive term, no matter how it is structured and whether it is simple or complex, whenever we use it to describe anything, there is always a purpose, a point of view, embedded in the description. This purpose, broadly speaking, is to facilitate the recognition or identification of the object described. Unless one understands that this is the main purpose, or the point, of an expression uttered to him with the intention of functioning as a description, he will not understand it in the manner of a description and therefore it will not then perform to him any descriptive role. The meaning of a description cannot be realized if the purpose behind it is not properly understood.

The criteria which determine whether or not a certain description is applicable to an object (or a situation) consist of such features of the object which are relevant to the fulfilment of the describer's purpose in giving the description. For example, if I describe the *social status* of lower class farmers under the prime ministership of Lal Bahadur Shastri, those features of the then farmers' life which will help the recognition (or identification) of such facts as whether or not they were socially respected, etc., will be relevant to the fulfilment of the purpose of my description. If whatever I assert or imply through it accords with those features, then alone it would be considered a fitting description, otherwise not. It is these features therefore which would constitute the criteria of its fittingness. A person who knows what these features are knows what its criteria are, but if he does not know its purpose, he will fail to understand its meaning. Suppose he (wrongly) thinks that my purpose is to point to their economic felicity. Suppose further that during Shastri's prime ministership they were socially respected but not financially better than in earlier times. Then he may (mis)comment on my description by saying that though it truly depicts their social status, it fails to show in the proper light their economic conditions. He thus misses the point of the description even when he knows the criteria which the farmers must satisfy in order to be rightly described in the way I have described them.

It is clear now that the meaning-criteria distinction cannot provide a conclusive reason for the descriptive-evaluative dichotomy because, if it is valid, it applies not only to evaluative but also to descriptive expressions. From this it does not follow, however, that there is no point in, or other method of, distinguishing between them. As I have already suggested while talking of the general purpose embedded in the use of descriptive expressions, the safest method, or at least one of the safest methods, according to me, to explain their differing behaviours is to explain them in terms of the differing purposes for which they are primarily and ordinarily used. In fact to me it seems to be the best method, or at least one of the best methods, for explaining the logic of any expression.[3] But since I have done it elsewhere,[4] I shall not exhibit in detail how one is to carry out such a programme to clarify the descriptive-evaluative distinction. I shall content myself with making only some very brief remarks.

The primary purpose in the use of a descriptive expression ordinarily (or generally) is to help the recipient in recognising or identifying the object described, whereas that in the use of an evaluative expression ordinarily (or generally) is to help him in making up his mind as to what sort of conduct or attitude he should consider appropriate to adopt towards the object of evaluation, and in fact adopt if the necessary and sufficient conditions for his being able to do so have been fulfilled. An evaluative expression is primarily and ordinarily intended to function as an attempt at persuasion, while a descriptive one is primarily and ordinarily intended to function as an aid to recognition or identification. It would however be wrong to consider their dichotomy as exhaustive and mutually exclustive. Several expressions function neither evaluatively nor descriptively, and several function both evaluatively and descriptively. Do I make a value-judgment or simply offer a neutral description when I say of a bus that it is a chartered bus ? The decision will not be easier to arrive at if I called it hired or reserved.

REFERENCES:

1. See my 'A Persuasion Theory of Moral Language', in *Contemporary Indian Philosophy*, 2nd Series, ed. by Lewis and Chatterjee, George Allen and Unwin, 1975, pp. 155-176.

2. See my 'Evaluative, Factual and Referring Expressions', *The Viswa-Bharati Journal of Philosophy*, Vol. V, no. 1, August 1968, pp. 72-82.

3. See my 'A Functional Analysis of Language' in *Current Trends in Indian Philosophy*, ed. by Murty and Rao, Andhra University Press, 1972, pp. 230-242.

4. For a detailed statement of my position see my 'A Persuasion Theory of Moral Language' (already referred to).

Professor of Philosophy
Indian Institute of Technology
Kanpur.

Plenary Session V

COMMITMENT AND ACTION

President : P. T. Raju
Secretary : Mrinal Miri

Main Speakers :

(1) S. S. Barlingay
(2) Archie J. Bahm
(3) K. K. Mittal
*(4) K. J. Shah

21

COMMITMENT AND ACTION

P. T. Raju

I

The topic 'Commitment and Action' is of direct human, social, and political significance. Commitment and action have very close connection. Mahatma Gandhi was a man of honest commitment and every action he did was, to the best of his understanding, the result of his intellectual, moral, and religious commitments. None of the forms can now be entirely dissociated from political and social commitments—a truth which, I think, Jawharlal Nehru also saw clearly. It needs a monk, an honest *sanyāsin*, of the highest level of spiritual development to dissociate the spiritual from the rest; a man of the world of action cannot attain the required loneliness (*kevalatva, kaivalya*) for the dissociation.

II

What are the nature and conditions of commitment and action? And what is the relation between the latter two? The answers to the questions require conceptual and hermeneutical analysis. There are many kinds of commitment and many kinds of action. First, we may take up the idea of commitment for our discussion.

A judge commits a person to prison, a commander commits a battalion to a dangerous task. This commitment may correspond, one may say, to what the Mīmāmsakas call *niyoga* and *codanā*. In their terminology, *dharma* is the action and the implied potencies that follow, viz., the prisoner's abiding in his cell and the battalion's carrying out the command. The word "commit" is used here in the context of being committed" as applying to the prisoner and the battalion, not to the judge and the commander. It will apply to the judge as committing himself to carrying out the enacted law and to the commander as committing himself to winning the war for his country. Morality is primarily concerned with this kind of commitment and secondarily with the former type. In moral discussions, we are concerned mainly with the "commitment of oneself by oneself" to a cause, an ideal, and action leading to its realisation.

When I am committed to a cause and the implied activity, I identify myself with that cause and that activity. I am full of them (with them) in their potential and actual forms. In experience, we are more identical with our activity than with qualities like white and black except when they constitute character resulting in conduct. For instance, "truthful" and "sympathetic" are generally called qualities—as though they are like white and black—but they constitute a man's character. The propositions "I am sympathetic" and "I have sympathy" sound natural and identical in meaning; but not the propositions "I am running" and "I have running" or even "I have the act of running." The latter expressions sound absurd in English. Sanskrit idiom is an exception. But the Sanskrit grammarian philosophers would interpret "have" in a different way. For instance, the Naiyāyikas call the relation *samavāya* (inherence), which is often constitutive, but only often. One feels, therefore, that the general attitude of the Mīmāṁsā is right, viz., nouns and verbs, or substantives and actions, are more important than qualities, and that what we call merit (*dharma*) is a potency, but not a quality like color.

Now, the idea of identification as the essence of commitment needs further explanation. "I commit myself to this cause" may also be expressed as "I identify myself with this cause." My whole personality is involved in the ideal even before it is realised. Willing the realisation is an aspect of this identification. Now, commitment implies also the possibility of my dis-identification or dis-involvement. Where this freedom to dis-identification is not present, there is no question of committing oneself. The possibility and the freedom of detaching oneself from identification are necessary conditions of commitment. Otherwise, we shall have to say that the magnet commits itself to attracting iron. Again, so long and so far as I identify myself with a cause, the cause, whether an idea or actuality, becomes part and parcel of my personality. For instance, one identifies oneself with one's family—compare the family feuds of medieval times for the name and prestige of one's family—but when one cannot fulfil the conditions implied by this identification, one feels self-alienated. Wherever this eeling is absent, we may suspect hypocrisy.

III

The forms of commitment can be many : ontological commitment or metaphysical commitment, epistemological commitment, sociological and cultural commitment, ethical commitment, and political commitment.

Ontological commitment, which is identification with something which is other than one's pure self, or the "I am", or pure spirit, has not generally been recognised by thinkers as a commitment. There is first the Cartesian *cogito*, which is the "I am" involved in "I think." But this "I am" is neither male nor female, neither young nor old. Only when thus isolated and differentiated, does the Cartesian certainty apply to it. The "I" am this or that", on the other hand, may be false and is open to doubt. The isolation of the "I am" from the body is not fashionable with a number of present-day philosophers, particularly in the West. But with regard to the body, there are two kinds of experiences : "I am the body" as in "I am six feet tall" and "I have the body" as in "My body is aching." The latter expression indeed implies the distinction between the "I" and the body. But the former, "I am the body", does not stand further examination. Every part of my body can be made an object of my "I"; and we cannot answer how this objectivity of the body is possible if the "I" and the body are identical. Again, we cannot, for instance, substitute "I am aching" for "My body is aching" and vice versa.

This identification with my body and the necessity not to violate the laws of the body are born with me. So far as my ordinary knowledge goes, I have not *voluntarily* accepted the commitment to obey the laws implied by this identification. But all higher religions tell us that for the sake of salvation one has to detach oneself from this identification and commitment and some religions such as Hinduism, Buddhism, and Jainism tell us that we *voluntarily* accept this commitment through desire for rebirth and enjoyment of the senses. I call this ontological commitment because man's phenomenal being as this or that person is a result of this commitment. It is somewhat like the *involuntary* commitment to observing the laws of a society by a person born into that society. However, the analogy should not be pressed too far.

The second, viz., *epistemological commitment* lies in all epistemological assertions like "That is a rose" and "That is red." When I make an assertion like "That is a rose," I commit myself to accepting the existence of the object, the red rose, not only for myself but also for every one else. I make my own cognised or experienced object (or I claim it) to be part and parcel of the objective world, part and parcel of a world common to all other percipients, and I commit myself to the acceptance of an objective world also. The Stoics called this assertion "consent," —which is very significant—thereby implying a kind of responsibility for making the assertion. Even in epistemologically pure intellectual activity like arithmetic, the student giving a solution to a problem takes the responsibility for doing so. His claim to being right, i.e., to being objective, to following the right arithmetical laws is judged of course by his teacher. If the student is found wrong, to have committed an error, the teacher does not give him the credit; and the student not only does, but also has to change his commitment, his consent to the answer he has arrived at. In epistemology also there can be self-alienation or what Bosanquet calls an epistemological vertigo. If I am convinced that "S is P" and assert it, but all others say that "S is not P", and again, if P implies Q and I find that "S is not Q", but cannot still see a proper reason for forfeiting "S is P", I shall have epistemological vertigo. For then I am obliged to swallow both "S is P" and "S is not P". My intellectual (epistemological) self is shaken up without regaining its integrity, which I regain when the solution is found. To think earnestly is for regaining one's integrity; the following action led up to by the result of thinking is meant for regaining it. This is identification with truth and reality.

IV

The *ethical or moral commitment*—if we ignore the distinction made by Hegel between morality and ethics—is the third form of commitment and is usually the one which philosophers have in mind when the topic of commitment is broached. This form includes in a general way cultural, social, and political commitments. There are many who do not care to think about what we have called ontological commitment because it is not within the easy reach of our ordinary consciousness; and there can be many, even philosophers, who may not see the importance of treating cognitive assertions as commitments for the simple reason that ethical actions or any actions—the pragmatists and instrumentalists of America, the Marxists, quite a few Mīmāṁsakas, particularly Prabhākara, and some Buddhists do not follow such philosophers—may or may not result from cognitions. Or as Nietzsche said, we can live with untruth, both knowingly and unknowingly, and there need be no commitment to truth alone and no action need follow from it. But almost all are concerned with ethical commitment, identification with an ethical ideal, let it be that of the Superman (*übermensch*). For unless this identification is a hypocritical lie, there is bound to be a psychological and spiritual vertigo, which is the same as self-alienation, a sense of not being myself, a loss of personality and its integrality.

First, ethical commitment may be voluntary or involuntary. Man is born into a set of mores and into a political set up or constitution. He is born also into a traditionally developed group of cultural forms like manners and etiquette, and into a religion. Most men follow them without much thinking and questioning. Theirs is involuntary acceptance and identification in the beginning, but later it may become voluntary also. But there are others, although born into such forms, reflect on them later, and discard some of them as unsuitable for the changed times and as even invalid and unjust. Such people are at first committed to every form, but later free themselves from some of them, and commit themselves to new forms. All religious, social, and political reformers, many of them becoming martyrs—scientific reformers like Galileo have also to be mentioned in this context—belong to this class of great men. Although during their own time they may have been condemned as irreligious and unethical, later history extolled them as great religious and ethical leaders. Mahatma Gandhi and Martin Luther King are two of contemporary examples.

Man's inability to fix what exactly is absolutely valid in ethics and religion makes it difficult for ethical and religious commitments to be absolute. There are many religious and many ethical codes. Like Pyrrho of ancient Greece and Sañjaya of ancient India one may find it difficult to give absolute assent to any one religion or ethical code, not to speak of committing oneself to it. The contemporary tendency to evade the question: What exactly is the right in the life of man ? and concentrate on the question : Whatever be the right, if there is something right, what is meant by "Is it right to follow the right ?" and "What is the linguistic meaning of this question ?" and so on, which is a mere hypothetical, conceptual, and linguistic analysis is a sign of the philosophical fatigue in the search for what actually is the right, *Ṛta, Dharma*. But in the world of facts and actions, man cannot be satisfied with an analysis of meanings of words and sentences. Hence the need for the traditionally accepted religious and ethical codes, and hence also the need for religious and social reformers. Nobody has been able to give a universally acceptable definition of religion. Is it essentially the relation to God of man in his loneliness (Whitehead) ? Or is it the invidividual's relation to society as the most important creature of God ? To which of the two am I to give primary importance and commit myself in thought, word, and deed ? Similarly, what ultimately is the ethical ideal to which I am to commit myself ? Job, for instance after infliction could not get the answer and in the end resigned himself to "God alone knows it" and committed himself to the commandments without asking for their Whys, Hows, and Whats. Similarly, the *Bhagavadgītā* tells us that ultimately the ethical ideal is to commit oneself (identify oneself) with the ways of the Cosmic Person (*Viśvarūpa* or *Virāṭ*) and be an instrument in his processes. This reminds us of the Stoic ideal of identifying oneself with the Logos. In the history of Western thought, the Socratic ideal of "knowing one's true self" ended in the idea of identification with the Logos of the Stoics. We find this identification in Hegel also. But who has given a scientific, rational, practicable definition of the Logos or *Viśvarūpa* (Cosmic Person) ? Yet it works in us as, for instance, in our dissatisfaction with the established justice in a society as not being just enough. Hence the distinctions *jus naturale, jus gentium,* and *jus civile*.

But wherefrom do we derive the highest standard of justice? Not certainly from mere emotions and sentiments. Otherwise, we have to accept that emotions and sentiments have their deeper roots in the Logos itself. When one realises the defects of the legal justice of his society, can he and should he commit himself to that legal justice absolutely? Hegel had to say—to give some concreteness to his ideal, the Absolute Idea—that the highest moral and ethical law, his Absolute itself, finds its embodiment in the state, i.e., the political structure and its laws (for him, the German state of his time). But has any political structure been perfect? There has been a gradual change, often for the better, but occasionally for the worse, in the political structures of countries. Hence, absolute commitment to any one form of the structure and laws of the state is not possible and perhaps not to be recommended also.

V

In spiritual or religious life, one's commitment to what one considers to be his right relation individually (in his loneliness) to the Supreme Spirit is on the whole absolute. But his commitment to the structure of society as the field of divine service cannot be absolute, for it has to be transcended by his individual relation to the Supreme Spirit. He does not carry his society with him after death. And his relation to society cannot be precisely fixed except in the general sense of humanitarian and social service, but not in the sense of serving a political or social structure and its laws as they exist at a particular time. The answer to what form of social service and to what ways and means one ought to commit oneself remains fluid; and commitment remains an act of the will to do the right and the good without defining their concrete forms.

Concrete forms of the right and the good are found in concrete social relationships, of which political relationships, the inter-relationships of the citizens of a state as derived from its written or unwritten constitution and the laws derived from that constitution, all of which are enforceable, are the most tangible. Politics is said to be a branch of ethics, but it leaves a wider margin of freedom for the individual's commitment than morality and is more amenable to change. Uniformity of commitment to political laws—in spite of legal power—is much less observable than uniformity of commitment to moral laws. Not only is there a great variety of political parties and their ideologies, but also there is a real possibility and even necessity of changes in the political structure. There can, therefore, be no absolute commitment, a commitment without reservations, to any one transient ideology or political structure. In such human situations there can be no absolute commitment to commitment, like Royce's ideal of loyalty to loyalty, whatever be the object or objective of the second loyalty. The same has to be said about that part of social ethos, like manners and etiquette, that falls outside the forms of the legally established political constitution.

VI

We have now come down to the idea of commitment to commitment. How can there be mere commitment to commitment? Like loyalty to loyalty and Kant's willing the pure will, is it not empty? What am I to commit myself to then? And why should I commit myself to anything, ideal or policy, if it is in need of constant change in this mundane world? Is not the human world also really in constant change, politically and culturally? How can I commit myself to anything if it itself is subject to constant change? Did not Heraclitus tell us that we could not step into the same river twice? We need answers to these questions.

Commitment is the work of the will; it is a self-repetitive act of identifying myself with something, an ideal, cause, or policy. It is my self-repetitive act of "to be" something in particular as in the will to be an honest follower of a religion, creed, or policy. In the case of action, it is my self-repetitive act of "to do". There can be no activity if it is not self-repetitive, but absolutely instantaneous. Otherwise, it cannot get a pattern; we cannot give it any name. Even in apparently simple activities like walking and running, there is some continuity of the same act. In complex activities like cooking, thinking and lecturing, there are action-continuities within action-continuities, pattern within patterns, all together obtaining an overall pattern which we call by a simple name, but which has a complex content. For instance, cooking consists of cleaning a vessel, placing it on the oven, pouring water into it, then pouring corn or rice into it, and boiling the whole till it is ready. "Till it is ready," i.e., ready for my eating indicates that some actions have a purpose which, if rightly done, must have a termination that is fixed in advance. Others like walking or taking a walk also have a termination, but the end is not fixed as it is fixed in cooking. I may continue walking indefinitely as long as I like, but cannot continue cooking indefinitely as the food will then be overboiled. Thus action, in its analysis, involves my self as willing, my self in movement, a motive, an intention—which indicates generally the purpose I wish to achieve—and along with the whole activity the continuity and identity throughout of my self. This is the identification of my self with the whole activity. When I am performing an action, I do not differentiate myself from the activity. The truth of this identification was noticed in different degrees by Aristotle, the Buddhist Vijñānavādins, and even contemporary Merleaeu Ponty. This identification applies *mutatis mutandis* even to perception and thinking. Unless one is lost in thought, one is not thinking well. Similarly, unless one is lost in perception, does not attend to anything, not even to himself, but to the object, one does not perceive well. In ordinary perception this absolute attention lasts at least for a second or so; otherwise, what we perceive will be hazy. The differentiation of the self from thinking, perceiving and acting is a later experience. The identification of the self with these acts is what we call commitment in act or actual commitment.

It is the continuity and integrality involved in commitment that will be at stake, if a person does not commit himself to anything. Can one commit oneself to an absolute non-commitment? The answer can be both Yes and No, depending on how one interprets Pyrrho and Sañjaya in their final answer that they doubted whether they doubted. But they kept back their own self-certainty, self-assertion, or commitment to preserve their self in tact—which, from another point of view, Yang-chu the fore-runner of Lao Tzu seems to have done, viz., existential self-affirmation, for which Schweitzer extols him.

The moral and spiritual value of all commitment lies in the preservation of one's continuity and integrality. Absolute non-commital with reference to everything including one's existence is not possible, although, in contemporary philosophy, there can be thinkers like Bertrand Russell who say that they doubt whether they exist. One of my students, who was perhaps wrongly influenced by some contemporary social psychologists and by some misunderstanding of George Herbert Mead, said that he did not know that he existed until society told him that he existed. Such philosophers and psychologists may shake Descartes from his rest in his grave. Now, one's continuity and integrality are preserved in the moral and political spheres by the formation of a stable character—here one may compare the *Gītā* concepts of *vyavasāyātmikā buddhi* (resolute or steady rational consciousness) and *sthitaprajña* (a man of settled rational life) and relate them to our context—from which corresponding conduct, necessarily consisting of action (*karmas*), does and must issue forth. Remember that some Mīmāṁsakas went so far as to say that action (*karma*) not performed with hands is no moral action, thereby implying that thought and speech are not moral actions in the proper sense of the term. But we may say that in the moral sphere all action—including thought and speech—that has an effect on other persons is action. Even inaction like not helping a man in distress, even when one can help him, is wrong action. Otherwise, we take only the legal sense of the term "action;" for instance, to think evil is not legally punishable. Again, in the spiritual sphere one's own personality also has to be included when we consider effects of actions on persons. However, this subject of the Conference seems to be concerned mainly with morals and politics.

In the two areas of morals and politics, there can be no commitment without resulting in corresponding actions and there can be no non-commitment without detriment to the integrality of the self. Mere verbal commitment without intellectual and practical commitment is what we may call hypocrisy, weakness of the will, imposture and so on. But in the case of earnest and sincere personalities, deviation from commitment, generally when the deviation is forced on them, leads to various degrees of moral and spiritual vertigo, which is the same as moral and spiritual self-alienation, and may result in psychological troubles. You may take the cases of convinced philosophers of the spirit forced to accept the communist indoctrination and vice versa or men of one religion being forced to accept another. Sometimes such persons may resort to atonement through fast unto death. Here obtain the difficult choices to be made between death and acceptance of what is considered to be unworthy and immoral, and also pricks of conscience.

The example of Antigone is generally mentioned as a confrontation with a difficult choice between alternatives leading to a crisis in life. The examples of martyrs—religious, moral, and political—also come under the same class. The guide in such a choice, if the commitment is a true one, lies in the answer to the question : Which alternative preserves the integrality of my self without producing a moral and spiritual vertigo, self-alienation leading to the suppression and repression of a part of myself, necessitated by the need for forgetting the unwanted and undesirable part of my ethical life ? Leaving Freud aside, what I mean is the necessity of knowing the deeper significance of the Socratic and Upaniṣadic exhortation, "Know thyself" and the ontological exhortation "Be thyself", not only in the metaphysical and epistemological contexts, but also in the moral and political. It brings out also the import of the *pratyabhijñā* (self-recognition) of Kāśmīra Śaivism in its moral context also, viz., the ability to recognize the identity and integrality of one's self in its activities of immediate and distant past without the need for cutting out of one's memory any part of one's past. The importance given by this school to memory as time and personal history (autobiography) and as the self present in them, but rejected by the Nyāya school, can be properly appreciated in this context, viz., the need for the recognition of the identity, continuity, and integrality of one's self not only in its ontological aspects (or with reference to salvation) but also in the spheres of morals and action, of time and history. Some of these aspects of the problem may not have been touched by thinkers like Vasugupta and Abhinavagupta; but they are all involved there. This self-recognition becomes foggy, incomplete and pierced by anxiety, if one's activities do not follow from one's commitment, need concealment in the subconscious and the unconscious, and to that extent render the self impure, ignorant, fractured, disturbed and distorted in depths.

But concealment is not the same as destruction. Again apart from considerations of abnormal psychology, what is concealed becomes part of the unconscious potencies of our being, a part of what the Advaita calls the causal or seed body (*kāraṇa-śarīra*), about which there need be no absolute mystification. The Advaita concept of the causal body and the Buddhist concept of Ālayavijñāna (storehouse-consciousness) are analogical in that they constitute the basic foundations of the structure of potencies—instincts, drives, ideosyncrasies etc.—of the individual. Even according to the Mīmāṁsā, all activities become potencies (*śaktis*) and lie dormant at the base of the individual's being. That is why even in the Vedāntic thought, mundane *puruṣa* (person) is called "constituted by *karmas* (actions) in their potential state" (*karmamaya puruṣa*) and Rāmānuja, although he does not accept Ajñāna (Unconscious, Ignorance, Nescience) as a positive and distinct category, equates it to *karma* (action potency). (This equation used to puzzle me for a long time.)

Both the good and evil potencies—which the Mīmāṁsā and some other Indian philosophies treat as actions transformed into potencies, but which others say are the results of actions—cannot be destroyed by suppression and repression, but by working them out, exhausting them (Jainism). Otherwise, they distort man's personality, and if we accept that the universe is one of interlocked persons and material objects, his universe even. It is this constant distortion of man and his universe including nature and society that gave rise to the idea of the world of man being ruled by God and the Devil, God struggling to straighten, and the Devil trying to distort our personality.

VII

This commitment and the resulting actions in conduct are essential for the continuity and integrality of self and personality in the moral sphere including the social and political. If commitment is natural, then what we call the "Ought" is also natural. It is not fashionable now, after G.E. Moore's attack on the naturalism of the tertiary qualities, to accept the naturalism of the "Ought". His attack may be interpreted to mean that there is nothing in the objective world to support the theory that moral laws and moral qualities are really objective, that they are there in objective nature. Here one may demand the definition of "natural", which can be universally accepted. Even if one does not demand it, if we accept different levels of Being such as matter, life, mind, and spirit; say that the highest level cannot be reached without moral purity and perfection; and maintain that the process of attainment lies in positively relating the lower to the higher levels; *then the moral "Ought"— and so moral qualities—are as natural as the primary and secondary qualities. They are the formative forces, potencies, constituting the strand which we in general call the "Ought", which itself is a part of nisus towards fulfilment and realisation.* There is real justification for the ancient Greek and the ancient Indian identification (or non-distinction) of the laws of physical nature and the laws of morality. No one will rationally say that the activities and qualities or potencies pertaining to the transformation of inorganic matter to living or organic matter (life) are not natural. Then why should we treat the qualities and activities or forces that transform mind intos pirit and are called moral qualities as non-natural or merely deontic ? If there is truth in the evolutionist doctrine of the nisus transforming matter into life, mind, and spirit;— compare S. Alexander and Lloyd Morgan, we can read this into Bergson's doctrine of matter again becoming alive and one with the *elan vital*—then at the level of man moral qualities as potencies and drives—recall again the Mīmāṁsā doctrine of *Dharma* as a potency (*śakti*), but not as an inert quality—must be treated as natural. They belong to the very structure of the universe with its interconnected and inter-penetrating levels of Being. They do not remain natural merely at the levels of the spontaneous processes of natural evolution and suddenly cease to be natural the moment man's free choice becomes involved in the upward push.

If the moral oughts are natural—they are the laws obtaining vertically between the lower and the higher levels of Being, they are dynamic potencies, not static qualities—, not mere interjections and exclamations, then man can avoid them only at the cost of losing his integrity, moral and spiritual. The oughts are the demands for commitments, and commands for the necessary activities. *They involve self-direction or what we call will; they involve self-control in the direction of the ideal to which one commits oneself,* and self-assimilation to one's continuity and integrality involved in one's re-cognition and re-collection (*pratyabhijñā*) of oneself. Otherwise, one distorts one's self-experience of "I am that I am" or simply "I am." To will is the same as to throw oneself entirely into an act after collecting and re-collecting oneself, which in simple terms is called self-control, which in turn means complete self-involvement and withdrawal of one's self from hostile desires preventing the act. *There is no will without self-control. We may say also that, if meditation is concentration of the whole conscious self in an idea or object, willing is the concentration of the whole self in an act.*

In the field of practical politics, absolute commitment even in the span of a single generation is not always possible. Politics and policy are associated, and policy is not an eternal creed or ideal, but a way towards attaining the ideal or a method for attaining it in a changing medium. This way or method develops into an art or technique called the art or technique of government. It is said that the aim of all government is to have no need for government. On this point Lao Tzu and William James, though removed by many centuries, are at one. But when the method of government develops into a technique, the ideal is lost sight of—here we find "art for art's sake" and "technique for technique's sake" dominating—vested interests grow strong within the forms of the technique, government becomes corrupt, and people long for a change. For instance, there can be nothing wrong with monarchy but only so long as the monarch acted up to the principle that the king is akin to God and Father (*nāviṣṇuḥ pṛthvīpatiḥ*). But like the Devil quoting from the Bible, the ideal was interpreted in favour of wicked kings. The art of being a king became the art whereby the king conducted his affairs for maintaining himself in power and pleasure. Similar abuses led to the failures and changes in feudalism, and may lead to abuses and failures of even democracy and socialism if the men in power become too self-centered to keep the ideal of government in sight.

Their commitment has changed or they are not really committed to what they profess.

In the mundane world with human imperfection never disappearing, policy is always the best plan to achieve the ideal of general welfare, but a plan that has to be transformed and transvalued in face of the changing situations brought about by the inherent defective human material and media. But commitment to a plan and to the actions implied, without losing sight of the ideal, will have to be said to be a moral imperative, to follow which, as Manu would say, is an important element of *Dharma* or *Ṛta*, the Law sustaining the state and the world.

Some Literature

John Finley Scott : *Internalization of Norms, A Sociological Theory of Moral Commitment* (1971. Prentice-Hall Inc., Englewood Cliffs)

P. T. Raju : "Activism in Indian Thought" (*Annals of The Bhandarkar Oriental Research Institute* Poona Vl. XXXIX, Parts III and IV 1938)

Alfonso Pinkney : *The Committed* (1968. College and University Press, New Haven, Conn.)

Myles Brand : *The Nature of Human Action* (1970. University of Pittsburgh,)

Richard Taylor : *Action and Purpose* (1966. Prentice-Hall, Inc., Englewood Cliffs, N.J.)

Anthony Kenny : *Action, Emotion, and Will* (1964. Routledge and Kegan Paul, London)

Robert Twigg : *Reason and Commitment* (1973. Cambridge University Press, Cambridge, England)

Sir Malcolm Knox : *Action* (George Allen and Unwin Ltd., London, 1968)

Relevant concepts in the Mīmāṁsā and the Nyāya should be thoughtfully studied and assimilated. They throw much light on corresponding western concepts.

The College of Wooster,
Wooster, Ohio.

COMMITMENT AND ACTION
S. S. Barlingay

In this paper I propose to discuss the following questions. (1) What is commitment? (2) What is the field of its operation? (3) Does commitment impel any action? (4) What is an action? and (5) Does action necessarily presuppose any commitment?

Let us see how we use the word *commitment*. The following examples may be considered—

(1) I am committed to this action.
(2) I am committed to him.
(3) This is the committed judiciary.
(4) The Governor of Reserve Bank is committed to pay the bearer the sum equal to the one assured on the currency note.
(5) Is there any ontological commitment in holding this view?
(6) What he wanted to say, he has now committed to writing.
(7) He committed suicide.

It may be granted that in the above sentences the word commit is not used in one sense. Perhaps the common element in all these sentences is the idea of 'binding'. But the binding need not be of the same kind. Let us try to explicate the intended meaning of the sentences.

When I say I am committed to this action, what is perhaps meant is that I am obliged to do this (action). Does it mean that it is my duty to do this action? Yes, but can I decide at some later stage to withhold my earlier decision or decide on a contrary action? Perhaps my commitment to certain action may be due to certain agreement with some one else and if the other party breaks the terms of contract my commitment may also cease. Such commitments are *bilateral* and do not have any meaning in unilateral contexts. Treaties between two countries are of this kind. In such cases one commitment is bound up with another commitment on the other side and vice-versa. But I may be committed to a certain action unilaterally also. When Indira Gandhi announced ceasefire unilaterally in the recent war with Pakistan, she was committed to this kind of unilateral decision. That is, she was obliged not to ask our armies to open fire on the Pakistan armies *without* some provocation from them. But if there had been provocation from the Pakistan side then she would have been justified in disregarding or ignoring her commitment. One can then say that although Indira Gandhi was committed to a certain decision it was only contingent. Is there any action to which one is necessarily committed? Can one say that man is necessarily committed to a certain action? Can one say that man is bound to certain principles or values? Kant, for example, would say that man is bound by the Categorical Imperative'. Perhaps yes, but this would be so only if he decides *to act*. Is he necessarily committed to action? This may lead to another question—What is action? But for the time being, we shall leave the question open. When I say 'I am committed to him' perhaps, I mean that I have promised him something, and now I have to keep my promise. Lord Krishna, for example, had his sympathies with the Pāṇḍavas. But he was committed to Duryodhana that he would not fight.

When one talks of committed judiciary one does not of course, mean that the members of the judiciary have promised something to the Parliament. It only means that the members of the judiciary would not act against the *party in power* (1) as they have the same ideology and/or (2) as the judiciary is completely controlled by the party in power.

The Number 4, is similar to 2. But if the currency notes are demonetized the promise would have no value and although it may be a break of promise it may have no *moral* repercussion.

The sentences 5 and 6 behave in altogether different way. The six and the seven are unimportant for us. The sixth merely means that what he wanted to say he has *reduced to* writing. Similarly the 7th uses the word commit in the sense of 'act', 'make', and is not of much consequence for the present paper. The sentence (5) on the other hand means that a certain view *presupposes* certain philosophic position and this position requires that certain kinds of objects *exist*. But it is possible that all presuppositions need not be ontological presuppositions. For example, when I say, all Greeks are men and all men are mortal, imply that all Greeks are mortals, I am presupposing some logical presupposition like $[(p \supset q) \cdot (q \supset r)] \supset (p \supset r)$. It is in this sense again that the law of contradiction is *presupposed* in logical thinking whether or not we can say that we are committed to the law of contradiction when we are doing logical thinking.

In short, we can say that when we use the word commitment we use it in the sense of 'binding.' But this 'binding' is of two types at least. When the word is used in moral and social senses it sometimes means responsibility and when it is used in the context of logic and ontology it means presupposition. Of course, this distinction may not be watertight and it may mean presupposition even when the word commitment is used in moral and social senses. Let us restrict ourselves to moral and social sense.

Let me now ask what action is. We do use some such expressions as X is *active* and Y is *inactive*. In this sense, action suggests some kind of *doing*. However, although in such contexts one uses the substantive, 'action or the gerund 'doing', in the philosophic grammar action or doing is only a verb and can be properly described by the verb '*to do*'. Von Wright says that to act is to bring about change. This is certainly true, but to bring about is to act, *to do*. So '*do*'-verbs are to be regarded as a unique category. Perhaps, primary verbs may belong to different groups such as '*to be*', '*to do*', '*to intend*', '*to expect*' etc. One ancient Sanskrit grammarian seems to have said that all verbs can be classified in only two classes, *to be* and *to do*. I wonder whether we would not have to expand the list by adding to the list verbs like *to expect, to intend* etc. But for the time being we shall restrict ourselves only to *to be* and *to do*. However, it will be significant to say that in some sense verbs like do, (intend, expect etc.) can be expressed in terms of the verb '*to be*', for in some sense this verb to do etc., does suggest a state of affair, though it may be argued that the use of the verb *to be* may mean something different in each case. In our language grammar we have two voices, *active* and *passive*. The sentence 'I do this' can be expressed in passive voice by 'it is done by me'. I feel that reduction of a sentence from active voice to passive voice suggests some kind of translation of the '*do*'-verb into '*be*'-verb. When I reduce *I do this* to *it is done by me*, what I really mean is a certain state of affairs—it is the case that it is done by me,—my doing this is a case. This is not suggested explicitly when I say, 'I do this'.

This of course, poses a problem. When can the word *to do* be properly used? It will be agreed that *to run*, is a '*do*' verb. Let us consider the following examples.

(1) This train is running in time.
(2) This horse is running at the maximum speed.
(3) This boy is running fast.

(I am purposly using the verb *to run* in the present continuous. For I do not want to suggest any tendency).

In all these three sentences although the same verb is used it should be generally agreed that the three uses of the verb, 'to run' are significantly different. When we say the train is running in time, we do not suggest that the train is the real subject in the sense that it does something. If the train is to run it must be run by *someone*. Even if it is run by some distant control ultimately the doer of the action will not be the train but some person. The analysis which holds good for the train does not hold good in the context of *horse*. When the train runs what we can properly say is that it moves. In the case of a horse when it runs it certainly moves. But it is something more. The horse can move of its own accord and when the horse moves one cannot simply say that it is simply 'flowing' just as water flows according to the law of gravitation. Again, there is a difference between running of a horse and running of a boy. Of course the difference cannot always be brought out distinctly. Both the cases may be subject to some conditioning. Further, one could argue that the horse's behaviour may be voluntary and one could also say that some kind of involuntary behaviour might be experienced in the case of a boy. All these are, of course possibilities. But acceptance of these possibilities give us two varieties of action—

(1) Voluntary and (2) Involuntary. Voluntary action is the one which is controlled by the agent. But mere controlling of the action is not enough. Even instinctive action is so controlled. A hungry animal for example, runs after food. It is in some sense, an action—the agent's action—and is controlled by the agent. But it could be a blind action. Thus it would

be proper to make a distinction between a blind but purposive action which is instinctive and the conscious purposive action. In fact, whether the action is done instinctively or with some conscious purpose behaviouristically there is no difference. The only difference is that when an action is done on conscious purpose the agent is aware of what he does. A purposive action other than the instinctive, thus, seems to be a self-conscious action. In the case of animals such self-conscious action may be present; but most probably its sole objective may be negative. A horse may resist when his master wants it to go. This resistance on the part of the horse may be intentional. But we do not know whether the horse will willfully run to achieve a certain objective—a certain goal. When an animal does something, I feel it is primarily an instinctive activity. I am not interested in establishing the thesis that an animal behaviour is only instinctive. I have taken this instance only to point out that human action can be purposive. Again, I use the word *can* in order to point out that it need not always be purposive. If, as Keats says "my heart aches and a drowsy numbness pains", neither the aching of my heart nor the pain generated by drowsy numbness can be regarded as my action. There are several such movements of my body like the throbbing of my heart which are definitely involuntary. None of these can be regarded as an action.

In the strict sense of the term then, it is only the voluntary 'movement' of man which can be regarded as an action. It means if we have to locate the concept of action, we would have to locate it in the human world, i.e., we will have to say that the concept of action is an anthropocentric concept. Of course, there may be several other anthropocentric concepts and all these may be related to one another either directly or through the agent. These concepts may be expressed by such verbs as, *to know, to do, to desire, to expect, to decide, to resolve, to promise* and so on. One important aspect of such verbs is that they can be primarily use only with the subject *I*. That is, they cannot be significantly used unless—I am conscious of myself. This is not the case when we use such verbs as rotate and revolve. Thus when the earth rotates round itself or when it revolves round the sun we do not say that it is *acting*. We only say that it is *moving*. The verb to *move* and its synonyms do not suggest a concern with self-consciousness. Although every action is a movement, every movement is not an action. The Vaiśeṣika category of karma is usually translated as action. But it should have been translated as movement only.

At this stage it may be useful to distinguish between acting on some incentive and acting on account of some binding. Free competition in the economic sphere can largely be explained as a product of acting on incentive. Although an action is always an individual action, there is a greater universality involved in the action on account of binding. Of such actions, one could make rules, although they could be broken. But they are broken because it is not possible for us to *separate* pure action based on binding and the pure action based on incentive. But it could be asserted that when a man acts on account of some incentive he is as it were *judging* a certain situation and is acting more or less on his judgment. Thus a man who acts on some incentive may be desirous of something, may be interested in something. He may calculate in a utilitarian manner and think of *karmaphala*. It may be interesting to point out here that even in such 'pure' situations some kind of *binding* may creep in. The actions become *bound* to him and he begins to think that he is *responsible* for his acts. I may just mention here that *responsibility* is also a species of binding and may ultimately develop into some kind of commitment. There is another way also that man's interest may be intimately related to this action. One cannot, for example, overlook the possibility of a *fixed idea*, which may not, in fact, be purely due to sense of duty, or guilt, but may be due to some unconscious interest, although one might believe that it was due to some sense of duty. In such cases, too, one could perhaps say that one had some kind of unconscious commitment.

What is the relation between *action* and commitment? Does action presuppose any commitment? What are the sources of commitment? We do use expressions such as "I am committed to this"; "This is my commitment". Perhaps expansion of some of the ideas which I mentioned earlier may help us in understanding these problems. Suppose, for example, I desire something. Say, I desire to have a television set. If I have sufficient amount of money to buy a television set, I may go to a shop and buy one. Did I buy it because I was committed to buying it? My desire and voluntary striving to fulfil that desire—are they concerned with commitment? I expect a friend to come. I wait for him. Is waiting my commitment? A friend of mine is suffering from kidney-trouble. Am I committed to help him financially? Is my commitment over as soon as I send him some amount? Suppose he needs a kidney, am I committed to give him my kidney? When I ask a question, "Am I committed to give him a kidney?" am I saying, is it my duty to give him my kidney? In what way is this commitment connected with either obligation or duty? Earlier I have asked the question, whether there is commitment when I wait for my friend, perhaps one is likely to answer that there is no commitment. But does not this case appear to be similar to the one where I ask "whether I am committed to a friend who wants a kidney". Perhaps, the question may be generally connected with a bigger question, whether our social customs or traditions are bound with the question of commitment. It appears to me that human actions have to be classified into two kinds, (1) directed to oneself and (2) directed to others. Perhaps commitment is operative where one's action is in relation to others. This may also be the source of morality, obligation and duty. I see a person drowning in a river. If I can swim, I would jump into the river to save him and not wait for anyone. If I do not know how to swim, I will atleast shout and try to find someone who would be able to save him. A child is born. The question is why should the mother feed it? One can perhaps say that it is on account of the selfish interest of the mother that she feeds the child. It is because I get pleasure in saving a person, that I try to save a drowning person. But such an explanation appears rather farfetched. A simple explanation seems to be that we have a primary motivation to help others. Such a motivation presupposes that I owe something to others. Ordinarily, the verb 'owe' takes two objects. It requires another person to whom I owe and it also requires something which I owe. For example, I can say, I owe Rs. 10/- to X. But when we are talking of the primary motivation, we cannot really know, what we owe. For, this object of owing is not strictly determined, specified. We only know that some kind of relation of owing exists between me and someone else. Further it is not just the case that I alone owe someone; this feeling seems to be universal; everyone else owes me and I owe everyone else. When the concept of owing is universalised, we get a proposition 'everyone owes everyone else', and such a proposition does not require two objects. I think, such a concept of owing is at the back of commitments. Sometimes it develops into commitment and when it is still stronger it develops into obligation and duties. There seems to be a family tree of owing, commitment, obligation and duty.

Is not one committed to oneself? What about the actions which are not directed to others and which are directed solely to oneself, which are done for one's own sake? Shall I say that such actions are not instance of commitment?

Earlier I have taken an instance of a drowing person and I said if I did not know how to swim I would shout for help. Why do I not jump in the river even if I am not a swimmer? The answer is because I would myself be drowned. Thus, I have already given my preference. I would certainly prize my life more than anyone else's. This means that in the sense I am committed to others, I am also committed to myself. Absense of such commitment would either lead to suicide or self-alienation or some kind of multiple personality. However, too much commitment to self is likely to create an imbalance in the other directed commitments. In fact, too much self-commitment leads to possession or *owning*. It may perhaps be said that owning may be explained as too much owing to oneself. I may conclude that whether my commitments are self-directed or other-directed they have their origin in the primitive concept or motivation of *owning*.

It appears to me that the problem of social values is very intimately connected with the problem of commitment. By being born in this country, I am *bound* to our constitution. I cannot, e.g., say that I am not a citizen of this country. If I have to go abroad I cannot do so without a pass-port from my government and the visa of the other government. If a war breaks out between my country and some other country and if I am in the other beligerent country I shall either be interned by that country's government or I shall be sent back to my own country. These are all cases of accepting certain social or political values. As a matter of fact acceptance of a social order seems to be a part of the child's learning and education. The child shows reverence to parents, he shows reverance to law and order. He shows respect for friendship. All these arise primarily though indirectly, from the sense of owing. Even if one rebels against the existing order this "acceptance" cannot be completely eliminated. In fact it appears to me that what we call social values are merely the generalization of the social customs that prevail over a long stretch of time and which are accepted by the people. Social values are just the products of such *acceptance*. It may of course be said that this is an over simplification of what happens in the society. The social dynamism may be more complex than what is said above. But what is said above is definitely an element in social dynamism. Many times values and things are confused. Sometimes valuable things may be regarded as values and sometimes these 'qualities' which make them valuable are regarded as values. It is this second alternative which is in my mind when I talk of values and if I ask myself what is that quality which makes the thing valuable, I would have to say that it is merely 'acceptance' which makes the things and actions valuable. It may be said that when a reformer or a rebel rebels against the old values he is not accepting the old values. It means that the universality of the old values is challanged. This means that at this point, the old values are not universally accepted. But the rebel or the reformer certainly has some other code of conduct in his mind and it is the acceptance of this code which makes him fight the old values. He thinks that the society should not accept the old code of conduct, but rather accept the new one. Thus in the very process of rejecting the old code of the society one is accepting some other code of conduct. Of course, accepting and rejecting certain code of conduct is only relative. It could also be the case that barring rebels the other people who follow certain code of conduct prescribed by the society, need not actually accept it entirely or in parts. For, acceptance is, and could be, imposed on the 'individuals'. One will have, thus, to draw a distinction between conforming to the social rules or the code of conduct and accepting the social rules or the code of conduct. Conforming to the social rules is due to certain social process. Acceptance has some individual or personal bias. Acceptance of a social code is to *make* it our own. Although, in society certain values are originally accepted the individuals in the society only try to conform to them. And in most cases where the conflict is not imminent, one merely follows the 'social routine' without ever bothering about the same. It will be clear that when an individual consciously and legitimately accepts the social values there may be a commitment, whereas, where he simply conforms to the social values and rules there is no commitment. Most things in the society thus proceed without commitment.

Earlier I have said that action presupposes self-consciousness. Such an action is bound to be individual. But an individual is a part and parcel of society. He may surrender himself to society either partly or wholly and this may perhaps be regarded as his commitment to society. In a society where individual has to surrender completely to the society, individual actions may be looked at merely as a state of affair from the point of view of society. This would be cosmocentric point of view in miniature. In such a society there would be individual commitment to society, but not the commitment of society towards an individual.

However, commitment appears to me to be primarily a relation between two or more individuals and society in this sense would be merely a function of individuals. So when we talk of the commitment of society towards an individual, we understand the concept of society only loosely as only a group of individuals. But if we regard society as some rigid system then man's actions would be nothing but movements determined by the system. Whether this is possible and desirable or not is a different matter but a thought of this pattern would be a shift from anthropocentric to cosmo-centric point of view. But even if such a shift is not designed at the level of society, the concepts of action, commitment, consequence and responsibility become significant only between two points, the point of birth and the point of death. That is why philosophers continuously strive to translate *action* in terms of *movement*. The author of Bhagavadgītā also has brought this out by saying :

"Oh ! you have ability to act, but not the ability to control its consequences. So (while 'acting') do not keep in mind the concepts like action and its consequences. And you may not take recourse to inaction (or bad action) either."

University of Poona.

COMMITMENT
Archie J. Bahm

Commitment and action interdepend. Committing is acting, and acting (i.e., as a person) is committing. Each act of commitment is both an act and a commitment. The commitment of any act is both a commitment and an act. A person cannot commit without acting, and cannot act without committing.

Both commitment and action are categories of personality. Without either, personality ceases to exist. Space permits treatment of only one of the two categories. I have chosen commitment. (For a treatment of "action," see my *Metaphysics, An Introduction*, especially Chs. 8, 9, 15, 18, 30, 36. Barnes and Noble Books, N. Y., 1974.)

Commitment will be treated at three levels : (1) General nature of commitment. (2) Kinds of commitment. (3) Particular commitments.

GENERAL NATURE OF COMMITMENT

Commitment and Committing

Commitment (noun) and committing (verb) interdepend. Distinction may be made between an act of committing (which may be momentary), a process of committing (which may take some time, whether short or long), and a state or condition of having been committed (which may be temporary or permanent, and with or without further committing, e.g. ,recommitting or continuingly committing). Commitment involves committing; otherwise the commitment ceases, unless one can somehow be committed with being committing. Committing involves commitment to continue, unless one can somehow be committed to the momentariness of a particular moment, i.e., exists as a merely momentary commitment.

Whether, and for how long, a person can be committed without committing is a complicated question, the answer to which involves further questions about the nature of self (or personality), of intention (or will), that in turn involve us in questions about the nature and role of substance, potentiality, time, causation, degrees, and others that cannot be explored here.

This problem is complicated further by the fact that one may commit himself negatively, i.e., both to the non-existence of something (temporarily, as in fasting, or permanently, as in murder or suicide), and to non-commitment (temporarily, as in sleep, or permanently, as in a yogic quest for *nirvāṇa*). Paradoxes of commitment to non-commitment, and how to overcome them, must not detain us here. (See my *Bhagavad Gītā, The Wisdom of Krishna*, pp. 7-16. Somaiya Publications, Bombay, 1970). Seeming paradoxes of commitment to further committing, including commitment to change, in which the committer both remains somewhat the same and becomes somewhat different, disappear as one understands the dialectical nature of living processes. (See *Metaphysics, An Introduction*, Chs. 34-37; *Polarity, Dialectic, and Organicity*, Ch. 18).

A person who commits himself to accept life with whatever problems it brings, thereby commits himself to adventure, to both uncertainty and a quest for security, to following the argument wherever it may lead, and to prospects of survival or extinction, and to living "for better and for worse" whether with or without marriage.

Commitment and Self

No completely uncommitted self exists. No commitment exists unless a self commits. To be a self is to be committed. To be a commitment is to be a commitment of a self. Neither exists without the other.

When a person commits his self in acting, does he commit his self wholly or partially? Does he commit his whole self or only a part of his self? Does he commit his self to the whole of the act or to only a part of the act? If the act has consequences, some of which are not known, can one commit his self to all such consequences, to only some part of the consequences, or even to only those which appear to be known? When one is unclear about the consequences, is he also unclear about his commitment? If one is unclear about his self, is he thereby also unclear about how, and how much, his self commits itself? Are there degrees of commitment? Are commitments irrevocable or may one be committed to openness to modify his commitment, to tentativity, to termination, or to reversibility of his commitment? Not only do a self and its commitments interdepend, but the complexity, dynamicity, variability, uncertainty, and terminability of a self and of its commitments interdepend.

How, and how much, a self commits itself depends upon how it conceives itself. I cannot review here the multiplicity of different conceptions that have been proposed. Such multiplicity itself suggests the great variability of self-conceptions. Is a self an illusion (as with Advaitins, Sāmkhyans, Theravādins, Mechanistic Materialists), a soul separable from the body (as with Christian and Jain Dualists), inclusive of the body (as with Taoists and Pragmatists), a social product (as with George Herbert Mead), or a particular manifestation of divinity (as with the Sufis)? Is self a momentary existence (as with Theravāda and Whitehead), or a temporary being evolving for a lifetime (as with Emergentists and Pragmatists)?

I propose a theory of self as resulting from both biological, social, and cultural factors, in which self-conceptions originate in awareness of functioning in different circumstances, physical, biological, psychological and social. One learns to understand his self as both agent and patient, both remaining and changing, and both individual and social. (See "Self as Multi-Dimensional," *Research Journal of Philosophy and Social Sciences*, Vol. II, No. 2, 1966, pp. 1-8). Differing circumstances require him to behave in different ways, and he learns to try out, pragmatically, different conceptions of his self as appear needed in each. Thus one may at times oppose his self to his body, identify his self with his body, his clothes, his tools, car, home, land, bank account, and with his parents, children, siblings, clan, village, state, nation, race, or mankind as a whole. He may identify himself with all sentient beings, or with universe as a whole. My view is that a self may rightly identify itself with all of these varying levels of existence at times with profit (enjoyment), but he may also have reason for not doing so.

My point here is that, since a self and its commitment interdepend, a self which at times commits itself as merely momentary, or as for an hour when giving a lecture, or for a life time as in marriage, or as a race in racist wars, or as a nationalist in serving his country, or as mankind in living everybody, thereby varies in the magnitude of his commitments. In each of these varieties, the problems recur of whole versus partial commitment, of certainty or uncertainty of one's conceptions and of consequences, and of the intensity of his intention or will, in such self-commitment.

Commitment and Value

Valuings and committings interdepend. Although some intrinsic value, as enjoyments, such as pleasant sensations, may occur without conscious commitment, once such values occur, their nature is such that they motivate commitment to seek them more. Intrinsic value is associated with desire, either as feeling of satisfaction, feeling of desireousness, such as zest or gusto, or feeling of contentment, undisturbed by desire. (See "Four Kinds of Intrinsic Value," *Darshana International*, Vol. V, No. 3, July, 1965, pp. 22-31.) Desiring involves committing, at least in some degree. When one feels satisfied, is he not committing himself to the enjoyment of such a feeling? When one feels desireous, does he not commit himself to such desiring? And when one feels contented, does he not commit himself to his feeling of contentment?

Likewise intrinsic evils, as when we suffer feelings of unpleasantness, frustration, apathy, or disturbance, are experienced as something to be eliminated, diminished or prevented; and our commitment to their elimination, diminution, or prevention is spontaneous. Commitment, when enjoyed, itself exists as intrinsic value. Thus do values and commitment interdepend.

But also instrumental values, the means to ends, not only interdepend with instrinsic values, but also conduce commitment to use them whenever their value becomes apparent. Instrumental evils, means to intrinsic evils, likewise conduce commitment to eliminate, diminish, or prevent them whenever their evil becomes apparent.

Self and commitment interdepend. Value and commitment interdepend. Self and value interdepend. (See "Self as Value," *Darshana International*, Vol. V., No. 4, Oct., 1964, pp. 34-39).

Commitment and Obligation

Obligation, or oughtness, and commitment interdepend. Oughtness is the power which an apparently greater good has over an apparently lesser good, or an apparently lesser evil has over an apparently greater evil, in compelling our choices. (See my *Ethics as a Behavioral Science*, Ch. 6. Charles C Thomas, Springfield, Ill., 1970). Accepting such compulsion is one kind of commitment.

Distinction needs to be made between conditional and actual oughts. An actual ought is a feeling of obligation one has at present, a feeling of compulsion to act because goods and/or evils are actually at stake. A conditional ought is something which would feel compelled to act upon if and when all of the necessary conditions occur. Most laws function as parts of conditional oughts, some of which never function as part of a person's actual oughts. But one may nevertheless become preconditioned to feelings of compulsion in the presence of laws. Habits, mores, and institutions embodied in a self tend to function as latent commitments, even when not participating in actual committings.

Commitment and Society

Commitment and society interdepend. Society consists of commitments, because it consists of persons committed to living together. Since persons are essentially social, persons and societies interdepend. So commitment to being a person involves some commitment to being social. Groups differ greatly regarding numbers of members and kinds of functions, just as a self may vary in the range of levels of being with which it feels identified. So groups are constituted by many different kinds of commitment, because they are constituted by persons with different kinds of commitment. Not only are a mother and child naturally committed to each other, but people also create artificial commitments, known as companies or corporations, and contracts for loans, leases, services, and employment. Without commitments, society would cease. Without society persons would cease. Without persons, personal commitments would cease. Society and commitment interdepend.

Commitment and Other Categories

Time does not permit exploring all of the categories of personality. But commitment interdepends with all of them. Awareness, for example, and consciousness, perception, memory, anticipation, intention, inference, thinking, language, problems, purpose, hope, fear, love, waking, sleeping, all may be seen to interdepend with commitment.

KINDS OF COMMITMENT

If commitment is a category, or universal condition, of both personality and society, then an adequate treatment of all kinds of commitment would require a survey of all of the kinds associated with both persons and groups. That endless task is avoided here by selecting some samples of the kinds of functions, ways of functioning, fields of functioning, objects and objectives of functioning, methods of functioning, and attitudes used in functioning.

Some functions are bodily, so, unless a person is ignorant of his own physiological nature, he normally is committed to serving his digestive, circulatory, muscular, skeletan, nervous, and reproductive systems. Some functions are psychological, so a person normally commits himself to desiring, wanting, wishing, willing, intending, loving, hating, fearing, hoping, and to effort, work, play, and rest. Some are social, so a person tend to associate, to cooperate, to reciprocate.

Ways of functioning include accepting, rejecting, approving, disapproving, admiring, despising, assenting, dissenting, assisting, hindering, urging, resisting, creating, destroying, preserving, consuming, believing, doubting, insisting, tolerating enjoying, suffering.

Fields of functioning include the disciplines, the sciences the arts, and the occupations : economic, political, social, educational, recreational, military, agricultural, transportational, medical, geological, geographical, mathematical, physical, chemical, biological, physiological, religious, ethical, aesthetic, artistic, musical, dramatic, athletic, culenary.

Objects and objectives of functioning include whatever things one is committed to deal with, problems one is committed to solve, goals or objectives one is committed to achieve, from baking bread to living out his life.

Methods of commitment may be childish or mature, scientific or emotional, disciplined or muddled, rigid or flexible, habitual or innovative. Methods of commitment involve commitment to methods. Nothing is more revealing of the nature of one's commitments than his methodologies.

Attitudes toward commitments may range from frivolous to unrelenting, from mild assent to intense insistence, from uncertainty to conviction, from distrust to confidence. Attitudes toward commitments involve commitments to attitudes.

PARTICULAR COMMITMENTS

Although I have committed my self to a life of commitment, not until being invited to participate in the present session did try to examine the nature of commitment. Now that I see commitment as a category of personality, and thus as present in all kinds of personality functions, it is easy to survey some of my particular commitments. I am committed to continuing, to live, to explore, to improve to benefit, to do as I ought, and to accept what I cannot change, including an end to my life. As essentially social, I have commitments to my family, my neighbourhood, my city, my state, my nation, and to mankind, and to my university, my college and my department, and to my profession and its numerous professional associations.

Particular societies to which I have commitments include : The New Mexico-West Texas Philosophical Society, The Southwestern Philosophical Society, The American Philosophical Association, The Inter-American Philosophical Society, and The International Federation of Philosophical Societies, to say nothing of more specialized societies pertaining to metaphysics, aesthetics, value theory, logic, philosophy of science, philosophy of religion, and philosophy of education.

Regarding each, I may ask, how much am I committed and in what ways? If I am committed to its welfare, does payment of dues, presenting papers, and serving as an officer fulfil my duties? Or does each, now existing in a world swarming with crises of many kinds, have responsibilities not being born because I fail to urge its attention to both needs, which it may help to meet, and opportunities for trying to meet them, and feelings of responsibility for so trying? At the XVth World Congress of Philosophy in Varna, Bulgaria, I presented a paper: "Ought Our World Congress Concern Itself With World Morality?" and urged the establishment of a standing committee of F.I.S.P. A committee on general policy, "Commission de la Politique Generale," was appointed. I trust that some report of its work will become available during this Congress. But I am convinced that its achievements will not have been, and will not become, enough to have much influence in serving our crucial needs (rescuing us from prospects of human anihilation).

My commitments motivate me to urge others to consider and accept some commitments regarding world government, world religion, world philosophy.

Suicidal war threatens mankind because diversity of interests, including diversity of mores and of philosophies, prevent the kind of cooperation needed to eliminate war. Just as there are limits to population growth, limits to available natural resources, so also there are limits to philosophical diversity and limits to demoralization.

Lack of world government is due, in part, to lack of a world religion, which is due in part to lack of a world philosophy. Religion unites; religions divide. The world is suffering from too many religions and not enough religion. Philosophy aims to comprehend all wholesomely. The world is suffering from too many philosophies and not enough philosophy, I urge commitment to world government, world religion, and world philosophy.

How? I do not know? A world dictator could do this for us. I hope that we never have such a dictator. One way is enough for philosophers to want a genuine world philosophy to join in efforts to achieve it. A world society of world philosophers is needed. A world philosophical think-tank, or institute, should be associated with the United Nations University, perhaps. There is an International Institute of Philosophy consisting of some of the world's elite philosophers. But it functions as a feudal holding company, an exclusive, self-elected house of lords which shows no sign of becoming more democratic in its methods or more widespread geographically in its representation. We need a World Institute of Philosophy consisting of philosophers willing to be responsible for mankind's philosophical and religious shortcomings. New Delhi is the locus of one responsible group called "Concerned Philosophers for Social Action," which published an inaugural issue of its new journal, *Philosophy and social Action*, about a year ago. But its commitment to Third World philosophies brands it as biased in one direction as the International Institute of Philosophy is biased in another direction. The world has been, and continues to be, organized into special-interest groups. As long as the achievement of a genuine world philosophy remains in the hands of special-interest groups, the date of its birth remains remote.

Why should we not, as philosophers, commit ourselves to a *philosophical* approach to a world philosophy? Why not join in a quest with a genuine willingness to follow the argument wherever it may lead, even if it leads us to give up some of our own vested interests, including those of our special-interest groups?

COMMITMENT AND ACTION
Kewal Krishan Mittal

I thankfully appreciate my commitment to the act of participation in the discussion on 'Commitment and Action' by the executive committee of the Indian Philosophical Congress. On being invited by the general secretary, Dr. R. C. Pandeya, on behalf of the said committee, I gladly accepted the obligation. But suppose, instead of doing the same I had pleaded my diffidence to Prof. Pandeya on the ground that this commitment went against another commitment of mine i.e. to the code of conduct involving the etiquette of not joining the issue with professors so senior as the ones who could as well have been my teachers as I am required to do while participating in this discussion. He like a good friend, Philosopher and guide, might have tried to pursuade me in a manner something as follows :—

"Placed as you are in the responsible position of a person holding a responsible post in the University of Delhi, that is hosting the golden jubilee session of the Indian Philosophical Congress, and serving as a joint-secretary of the Congress itself, it ill behoves you to run away from your natural normal duty. Your taking refuge under a supposed commitment to etiquette is an excuse that cannot be accepted. You need not be afraid of loosing in discussion, for, it is meritorious to go down doing one's duty than to indulge in that which does not pertain to one's own work. A wiseman is unperturbed by the thought of victory as well as defeat. Moreover, as far as you are concerned, you would be a gainer in both ways—if you win glory and fame shall greet you and if you loose you would be happy in the thought that by participating in the discussion you did what should have rightly been done. Defeat in a discussion or debate is not the end of one's career, one does survive many-rather-all such debates. If you meet with an end as a debator you can emerge as an author whose propoundings may as well be discussed by others. You, in essence, are unassailable, even though you may fail in the performance of many a task. Do ye perform your action disinterestedly for, to act alone is your right and never to covet its result.

"Furthermore, you think not that you can desist from such a task, as the one before you, forever. Your own nature— your training and temperament, your having philosophising as your job as well as a hobby—will drag you out for the same. Now, if you think that the persons ready to enter into discussion with you are formidable enough for you to meet their challenge, I lay before you all the various positions that can be maintained on 'Commitment and action' and also show it to you that none of them is, in fact, unassailable". After taking me through a wonderful experience of listening to all the pros and cons of the question, he might have exhorted me in the words "Be ye just formally instrumental in doing the thing that has already been done, namely the assailing of the various positions that your adversaries in discussion might occupy". Finally, he might have asked me to enter the area through a very personal appeal saying, "you be commited to me—as a friend and colleague—and leaving aside all other considerations do my bidding, i.e. the needful, I will take care of all your blemishes, if any".

Those of you who are acquainted with the reasoning that goes into the dialogue between Śrī Kṛṣṇa and Arjuna in the Bhagavad Gītā might have already discerned the purpose of my drawing freely from that 'Song Celestial'. That purpose needs to be laid down explicitly not only for the benefit of those who have not yet grasped the same but also for the sake of a proper progress of the points that I want to make in the discussion. My contention is that whatsoever be the kind of action may it be as stupendous as that which Arjuna faced or a most ordinary one as the action that is before me—wherever and whenever we come to think of the commitment or commitments connected with it we cannot escape considerations that call for having a Philosophy of life.

Not only is every action preceded by a commitment but also by its result it gives rise to fresh commitments issuing forth into further actions and reactions. No action can be concerned as taking place in isolation from other action or 'packages of actions' i.e. commitments. If an action, performed in fulfilment of a commitment does relieve us of a certain tension, it also results in further tension insofor as it generates further commitments. This does create a formidable problem that we meet so frequently in the entire process of commitment—action—commitment. Identifying this process as the phenomenal world or *Saṁsāra* the ancient Indian philosophers were grappling with the problem of 'Commitment and Action' itself when they were concerning themselves with the problem of *Saṁsāra*. When they accepted the phenomenal world as beginning less or *anādi* all they meant was this that we were born with certain commitments to act in certain ways and aquired fresh commitments to act in certain other ways as a result of the actions that we performed. This is what is the meaning of rebirth or *Punarjanma* through *Karma* i.e. Action. They, however, did not accept that the *Saṁsāra* was endless or *ananta* insofar as they held out the possibility for an individual to be free finally of all commitments and actions. The question hinged on the status, nature or character of the self as the real doer of action, the fulfiller of commitments or of his being so only apparently. There are systems of thought, say for example, the Advaita Vedānta, the Sāṁkhya and the Jainism, which hold that the doership as vested in the self is only apparent, in the ultimate analysis and freedom of the self from the bondage of *Karma* consists in the realizing of the self its real status as that of a knower—knowing not construed as an activity—and never as that of a doer. It is true that they differ significantly. If Advaita Vedānta regards 'Commitment and Action' as pertaining to the sphere of Mystery (*Māyā*) and the Sāṁkhya considers them as the self differentiation, or the game of predominance of one or other, of the three constitutive qualities—*Sattva, Rajas* and *Tamas*—of *Prakṛti* or Nature apart from the *Puruṣa* or Man, then Jainism gives an account in which the *Jīva* or the living-being, the self does appear to come in contact with a real non-living (*Ajīva*) material force called *Karma* (the actions as well as the packages of actions) that affects the *Jīva* in eight of its aspects in as many as 148 ways. The *Karma*, according to this elaborate scheme of the Jainas, obscures vision or faith as well as knowledge of the *Jīva*, arouses feelings in it, infatuates it, adds to or substracts from its name and fame i.e. brings praise or blame to it, aligns it to or disaligns it from a group or groups, increases or decreases the longevity of its life i.e. affects its mental and physical health in one way or the other, and obstructs its efforts to come out of the rut of 'Commitment action-commitments'. Yet they hold that, in the final analysis, the relation between *Karma* and *Jīva* is like that between dirt or dust and a cloth which can be brushed off or washed away—of course not very easily.

Another system of thought, namely Buddhism, with its emphasis on change (Pāli : *Aniccā*, Sanskrit, Anityatā), non-substantiality (Pāli, Anattā. Sanskrit, *Anātmavāda*) and dependent origination (Pāli; *Paṭiccā*, Sanskrit : *Pratītya Samutpāda*) of all phenomena does tell us, in one of its formulations i.e. the mādhyamika school, that the 'doer, deed and the done-upon' or 'commitments and actions' do not make any sense. They are devoid of reality, non-reality, both or neither i.e. *Śūnya*. When suchness (*Tathatā*) of such a characterless character of the world of phenomena (Saṁsāra) is realized the final release (*Nirvāṇa*) is there from all actions and commitments.

I am well aware of the fact that most of us are not interested in any final freedom from all actions and commitments, and many never were. I have made a mention of some centuries old schools of Philosophy with the belief that they still serve as howsoever distant light-houses and guide-posts for those few who care to look upto them with sympathy and understanding. Besides, each one of them, conscious of the differing interests and capabilities of different individuals have prescriptions for all according to their needs.

We are, perhaps, interested today much more in such social and political commitments that seem to guide or misguide our present day actions and those that result from them. Commitments we have of all sorts. Many of them are picked up in the process of socialization. These are by and large beyond our control. Some others are such that are drilled in us through the modern techniques of propaganda and indoctrination by agencies like political parties, state and the church. Very few commitments are such that are acquired consciously, through serious thought i.e. those as serve our convictions for which we are ready to act in a spirit of dedication and genuine concern.

The first of these three kinds of commitments can hardly be distinguished from superstitions and we hardly ever think about them. They are habitually acted upon. We do think about the second kind, occasionally, but our thinking about them amounts to a mere rationalisation and that too through a borrowed reasoning. The third kind of commitments dominate very few lives and since most of us lead our lives as guided and controlled by the first two kinds our living is not authentic, it is either steeped in ignorance or marred by hypocrisy. Those saints and heroes who have not only convictions but also courage of convictions are rare among us and it is their and their commitments and actions alone that deserve to be lauded, appreciated and emulated. Not freedom from them but a willing involvement in them is to be welcomed, lived and enjoyed. It is in this context, that we can understand the commitment of a *Bodhisattva* who undertakes the alleviation of the suffering of the countless number of creatures by himself going through the pain of a great number of births and deaths; and the wish of Swami Vivekananda, which in his own words is : "May I be born again and again, and suffer thousands of miseries so that I may worship the only God that exists, the only God I believe in, the Sum-total of all souls—and, above all, my God the wicked, my God the miserable, my God the poor of all races, of all species, ...". (The complete works of Swami Vivekananda; Vol. V page 136).

University of Delhi.

EXPLANATION AND DESCRIPTION OF ACTION : A PHILOSOPHICAL DEFENSE OF FREUD.

Mrinal Miri

Let me begin with some quotations :

"What did Freud do ? Not just suggest a set of causes for the data, the neurotic symptoms and the rest, but tell us for the first time what the data were"[1]

"....if the prestige of causal explanations makes us rush past the ascriptions of purpose in order to concentrate attention on Freud's causal explanation of the neurotic patient's inability to recognise his symptoms for what they are, and to control and to alter his behaviour we shall miss a whole dimension in Freud's achievement. For an essential part of Freud's achievement lies not in his explanations of abnormal behaviour but in his redescription of such behaviour".[2]

"His (Freud's) recognition of purpose is logically independent of his causal explanation. But when Freud refers to the patient's behaviour unconsciously motivated he compresses the two parts of his explanation into one".[3]

Implicit in these statements is the idea that Freud's description of neurotic behaviour can be divorced from his explanation of it in such a way that the validity and correctness of the former may be seen to be quite independent of the validity and correctness of the latter : We may accept the description and reject the explanation alogether. This dichotomy between description and explanation in Freud's work is, I think, a

---

1. MacIntyre, *The Unconscious* p. 62.
2. Ibid P. 61
3. Ibid P. 63

spurious one. Of any genuine description it must be possible to ask whether it is a correct description. In other words there must always be criteria of correctness for any genuine description. Of any putative description where there are no obvious criteria of correctness, it must be doubted whether it is a genuine description at all. In Freud's case the criteria of correctness of his redescription of abnormal behaviour are embodied in his explanatory theory. His "explanation of abnormal behaviour" and his "redescription of such behaviour" cannot thus be divorced from one another in the way that the statements quoted above seem to do.

Much of the confusion here, I think, arises from an inadequate appreciation of the fact that psycho-analysis, at any rate in Freud's hands, is a science of *interpretation*. Explanation here consists in spelling out meanings—meanings of bits of actions, patterns of behaviour, dreams, thought processes etc., whose surface meanings are obscure. The interpretations (redescriptions) that psycho-analysis offers flow from certain fundamental assumptions about the workings of the human psyche. And these assumptions are essentially causal. Empty a Freudian description of a piece of neurotic behaviour of all its explanatory content : What you will have left is something more like poetic imagery and *not* really description in the ordinary sense of the term. Take the following : "Wilt thou (sleep) upon the high and giddy mast/Seal up the ship-boy's eyes, and rock his brains/In cradle of the rude imperious surge". This is an image and it does not involve explanation of any sort, and, deeply moving as it is, the question of truth or falsehood does not arise with respect to it. The explanatory content of a piece of psycho-analytic description of neurotic behaviour, on the other hand, marks it off from mere imagery of this kind, and turns it into a statement whose truth or falsehood can be assessed.

I

Let us take one of the ways in which the kind of distinction implicit in the passages quoted above is sought to be made. MacIntyre says, "The concept of wish-fulfilment which we have seen to be so important in Freud's theoretical structure is not a genuinely causal concept". The idea is that if this were true, then wish-fulfilment could not be regarded as a genuinely explanatory concept. Some of the things that MacIntyre says (e.g., "an essential part of Freud's achievement lies not in his explanations of abnormal behaviour but in his redescription of such behaviour") would seem to ignore the very important consideration that there may be varieties of explanations. I think here the assumption is that explanation in terms of causation is the only genuine mode of explanation. This may indeed be true, but it is not true obviously; and if it is true, its truth therefore needs to be shown. Take the notion of desire, I don't think anybody would like to deny that to say that a certain action is done out of a particular desire is also very often to explain it. Yet it seems a very strong case could be made out for saying that desire is not a causal notion, that is, for the view that to explain an action in terms of a desire is not necessarily to assign a cause to it. However, fortunately, for my present purpose I do not have to enter into this controversy. Freud not only describes neurotic behaviour in terms of wish-fulfilment, he also explains it in these terms: and his explanation consists precisely in treating wish-fulfilment as a causal notion.

What I wish therefore to do is to try to show that the position that the notion of wish-fulfilment cannot be a genuinely causal notion is not a tenable one. Indeed, I will not argue for the extreme position that wishes are necessarily causes. This is not necessary for my purpose. All I need to show is that there is nothing logically wrong in the supposition that wishes *can be* causes.

I assume the kind of argument MacIntyre has in mind is similar to arguments produced in support of the thesis that desires cannot be causes of actions. The main thrust of these arguments is that there is a conceptual connexion between desires and actions, and that this rules out the possibility of their being causally connected.

The thesis is a vague one; but I suppose, in its most clear and plausible form, it is this : the causal theorist is wrong because he will be forced to admit, under logical pressure, that there is no intellectual access to a desire *except* as the cause of the action which is supposed to be its effect. If this were true, there would seem to be here a clinching argument against the causal theorist. But whether or not this is true, the point, I think, is specific to the notion of *desire*. It is rather surprising that in the entire controversy terms such as desire, intention, purpose, motive, wish are treated as equivalent. I want to say that the notion of wish, at least, as far as this particular controversy goes, is quite different from that of desire.

There is certainly a conceptual connexion between a wish and its object, but this connexion cannot prevent the possibility of their being a causal connexion (a) between a wish and the realization of its object, and (b) between a wish and the action (if any) directed towards the achievement of its object. Perhaps the whole idea of (b) is dubious, because, so it might be said, when a wish is backed up by action directed towards its fulfilment, then it is no longer a mere wish, it becomes a desire; so there can't in fact be the kind of connexion (causal or otherwise) envisaged in (b). I do not want to go into the plausibility or otherwise of this kind of objection. Fortunately, my purpose will be served even if point (a) alone is granted. A wish is not in fact causally connected with the realization of its object (i.e., a wish is not by itself the cause of its fulfilment), but there is no logical incoherence in suggesting that it might be. As Pears says, "fairy stories, which treat wishes as causes and describe a wish simply as concentrated willing that such and such should happen, may be incredible but they are not conceptually incoherent". Having made this point, however, Pears does not go on to discuss the nature of wishing any more. But, I think, a proper understanding of Freud's talk of neurotic behaviour as wish fulfilment crucially depends on a deeper appreciation of this point. Freud's statement that, say, neurotic behaviour or dream is wish fulfilment is usually taken to mean that neurotic behaviour or dreaming is action of some kind *directed* somehow *towards* the fulfilment of a wish. Taken in this way the statement is immediately in danger of succumbing to considerations which, as I pointed out, might be brought to bear upon (b) above. Besides, how can anybody soberly believe that lunging systematically at lamp-posts, for instance, is action directed towards fulfilling the wish to kill one's father? No, the statement must be taken to mean just what it says—

namely, that neurotic behaviour or dreaming (*embodies* in a symbolic way) *the* fulfilment of a wish, *the* attainment of its object. Once we see the statement in this light the analogy between the logic of wishing in fairy tales and in Freudian psychology becomes clear. The differences, of course, are enormous. But the crucial thing is: in both wish is a genuinely causal notion; and there is no conceptual incoherence committed by either on this account.

I wish to come back to this point *via* a consideration of a much more fundamental objection to Freudian theory embodied in the following remark of Wittgenstein: "The majority of dreams Freud considers have to be regarded as camouflaged wish fulfilments and in that case they simply don't fulfil the wish". There are two quite different theses embodied in this remark—but the two are conflated; and while one of them is valid, the other is quite false. The two theses can be brought out by alternately emphasizing two words in the quoted sentence: (i) "camouflage" and (ii) "fulfil".

To take the second emphasized word first, since in neurotic behaviour as in dreaming wishes *ex-hypothesi* are not fulfilled in reality, they cannot be said really to be fulfilled at all. This point is incontestable and has really nothing to do with dreams being "camouflaged" fulfilment of wishes; for no dream-fulfilment whether direct or camouflaged of a wish can be the real fulfilment of the wish. No wish except the wish to have a dream of a certain kind can be fulfilled by a dream. What can be allowed at the most, therefore, is that in dreams there can only be dream-fulfilment of wishes and in neurotic behaviour, there can be only "neurotic" fulfilment of wishes. But Freud would really have had no quarrel with this tautology. His theory does not require a thesis which is stronger than this. What it does emphasize, however, is that between the wish and its dream-fulfilment, there is a causal connexion. It is, therefore, the other element of the remark which must be taken seriously in the context of Freudian theory. What this element does is to question the most inalienable character of Freudian theory, namely, that it is a theory of interpretation. A science of interpretation is based on the following fundamental assumptions: (i) that its subject matter has meaning, sense or significance; (ii) that this meaning is for a subject of experience,

(iii) that it is only obscurely, obliquely present in the subject matter, and (iv) that it has to be unearthed, made clear through interpretation. Assumption (iii) is what seems to be questioned by Wittgenstein's remark : it seems to deny that dreams cannot have a meaning which is somehow hidden from their surface. It is, of course, not known whether Wittgenstein would have cared to extend his remark about dreams to other cases. But, I think, it is quite clear that, thus extended, the remark would be obviously invalid. It must then be taken to be specific to dreams. But there does not seem to be any argument at all to show that dreams must be a special case. What has gone wrong, I think, is that the two theses have been conflated, the two theses, namely, (i) that dreams cannot be camouflaged fulfilment of wishes and (ii) that they cannot *really* fulfil wishes; and the truth of (ii) is taken to be the same as the truth of (i). But from the logical fact that wishes cannot in reality be fulfilled in dreams, it does not follow that there cannot be dream-fulfilment of wishes. Once this point—and the truth of this is all that Freudian theory requires—then there must be a further argument to show that there cannot be "camouflaged" dream-fulfilment of wishes. But no such argument seems available.[4]

Now granted that there can be fulfilment (direct or camouflaged) of wishes in dreams—to repeat the question we have already asked and partially answered—how can there be a causal connexion between wish and its dream-fulfilment?

---

4. One argument perhaps may be this : If it is possible for there to be camouflaged dream-fulfilment of wishes, it must be possible for there to be camouflaged fulfilment of wishes in reality as well, and this, however, is not the case. But is it so? The idea of camouflage, as far as the present argument goes, comes to no more than this : There is a situation which is truly describable as the fulfilment of a wish of mine, but this description, for some reason, is not available to me at the time. For example I have never had *bhang* in my life, although I have always wished to; and unbeknown to me what I have in my friend's house under the description "sweet" is really bhang. The situation is thus describable as the fulfilment of my wish to have *bhang*, although this description is not available to me at the time. It might be said that the non-availability of the description here is owing to my *ignorance*, while in neurotic behaviour, as in dreams, it is due to, one might say, self-deception. But this point is really not at issue, as far as Wittgenstein's remark goes.

The important thing to note is that dreaming is not something which the subject does in *order to* fulfil a wish of his. In other words alternative (b) that I mentioned above is ruled out. The dream represents—one might even say—it *is* a state of affairs which is describable as *the* fulfilment (one must of course add "in dream") of the dreamer's wish. The relationship between the wish and its fulfilment is of the same logical order as that of a wish and its fulfilment in the fairy tale. Both are causal. The only difference is that while the former is a genuine causal relationship, the latter is not. But it might be thought that there is another crucial difference and this is that while in the fairy tale the object of the wish is realized in the objective, interpersonal world (no doubt of the fairy tale) in a wish-fulfilment dream the object is realized only in the dreamer's own private world. But this difference while undoubtedly it is a real one, is really collapsible into the first. The second difference springs from the fact that the causal relationship in the fairy tale is only an imaginary one and that this relationship in dreaming is a genuine one (a justifiable one). A genuine cause-effect relationship between a wish and the realisation of its object can exist only in the subject's own private world, and, no doubt, when this is the case, the subject's private world in which the wish is fulfilled takes on some of the characteristics of the interpersonal public world. It is quite easy to see that this happens in dreaming, because of the analogy between dreaming and hallucination. The same is true of neurotic behaviour although at first sight, it may seem difficult to make out. The space of the dream-world is a private space : It is unrelated to the space of the inter-subjective public world. But neurotic behaviour takes place in this common space. How can then neurotic behaviour be regarded as embodying the fulfilment of a wish in a private world ? One thing that is certain is that neurotic behaviour cannot be regarded as the fulfilment of a wish in the *public* world. But, I think, the following can be said. Neurotic behaviour and all the elements of the common world to which it seems to be connected are bound together by meanings which are derived from the particular experiences of the patient, and are peculiar to him. These meanings are different from the meanings which constitute the world of common objects. It is not simply that neurotic behaviour and the elements of the public world which are connected with it have a symbolic significance in the way in which "concrete imagination" in poetry has a symbolic significance; but although they are elements in the common world they get detached from the network of common meanings and come together in a new nexus of meanings which are the patient's own. And this detachment is not something that is voluntary—within the patient's control. It is something that happens, as it were, in spite of himself. This is what gives it somewhat of the character of objectivity which is not unlike the "objectivity of a dream world". The patient, in more than a metaphorical sense, *lives* in this world of which his own neurotic behaviour is a central part. The latter, as it were, gets detached from the real world and forms the nucleus of the neurotic's private world.

II

So far we have considered one of the ways in which it might be sought to drive a wedge between explanation and description in Freud's psychology, namely, by treating wish-fulfilment as a descriptive, non-causal notion. If wishes could not be regarded as causes then Freudian theory would not be an explanatory theory at all : There would be in it, owing to conceptual confusion an illusion of explanation but no real explanation. And the thesis about separation of description from explanation would be a thesis about separating the illusion from the reality. But, if, as I have shown, wishes can be the causes of the realisation of their objects, and if it is a fact, as it is one, that Freud did proceed from this assumption, then would it still be possible to separate explanation and description in Freud ? Yes, so it might be said, for we could replace Freud's explanation by some other (s) either without any loss or even with some positive gain, while Freud's descriptions could be retained just as they are. This seems to be the argument of the following passage from MacIntyre's book :

..While Freud illuminatingly describes a good deal of behaviour as unconsciously motivated and describes too how the recall of events and situations of which we had become unconscious may have a therapeutic role, he wishes to justify not just the adverb or the adjective but also the substantive form; the unconscious. Yet from the supposition of such an entity what consequences flow that could not otherwise be predicted. Freud's hypothesis as to the infantile origin of adult traits and disorder can all be formulated without reference to it..[5]

Let me take this sentence : "Yet from the supposition of an entity (e.g., an unconscious wish which is causally charged) what consequences flow that could not otherwise be predicted". Well, Freud never claimed the power of prediction for psychoanalysis : "So long as we trace the development from the final outcome backwards, the chain of events appears continuous, and we feel we have gained an insight which is completely satisfactory or even exhaustive. But if we proceed the reverse way, if we start from the premises infered from the analysis and try to follow these up to the final result, then we no longer get the impression of an inevitable sequence of events which could not have been otherwise determined. We notice at once that there might have been another result, and that we might have been just as well able to understand and explain the latter" And, while the "chain of causation can always be recognised with certainty if we follow the line of analysis... to predict it along the line of synthesis is impossible".[6]

For Freud, perhaps, that he was not claiming the powers of prediction for his science, was a reluctant admission; but nevertheless it contained a profound insight into a truth about the sciences of man, the truth, namely, that prediction, in the sense that it is understood in the physical sciences is not possible in the sciences of man. And this, in spite of the fact that sciences of man are, like the physical sciences, concerned with giving *causal* explanations of what they study.

I suppose now MacIntyre's question can be reformulated as follows : If Freud was not interested in prediction any way, what difference does it make to our understanding of the data,

---

5. MacIntyre—The Unconscious, pp 71-72.
6. "The Psycho-genesis of a Case of Homosexuality in a Woman" Standard Edition XVIII, p. 167 and P. 268.

which, as MacIntyre says, were re-described illuminatingly by
Freud, whether or not we accept also his *explanations* of the data ?
MacIntyre's suggestion is that we would be much better off
scientifically, if, instead of accepting Freud's hypothesis of
repressed wishes, we talked only in terms of, say, brain-
processes.

I shall come to this suggestion of MacIntyre's presently.
But let us first examine the view that we can retain Freudian
description of neurotic behaviour, while at the same time altogether rejecting the Freudian *explanation* of it. Let us first
grant (without much conviction) that all genuine explanation
must tell a causal story. Now if my argument of the previous
section is correct, it follows that reference to wishes can legitimately occur in a causal story told in the explanation of a piece
of neurotic behaviour. A difficulty, however, is created now
by the fact that these wishes (which are part of the causal
story) must be regarded as unconscious, or as residing, in the
Unconscious. This difficulty can be circumvented—so seems
MacIntyre's view—on the one hand, by focussing our attention
on the fact that wishes perform a descriptive role and, on the
other hand, by ignoring the possibility that wishes can be
causes as well.

Let us pursue this suggestion. Take the distinction between
latent and manifest contents of dreams which is so crucial for
Freud. The manifest content of a dream is what might be
called our ordinary, pre-Freudian description of it; the latent
content is the Freudian *re*-description of the manifest content.
We must note, however, that the redescription does not *replace*[7]
our ordinary description, rather it interprets the latter, gives it
its "correct" meaning, constitutes a "translation" of it. Now
MacIntyre's suggestion is that we can divest this redescription
of all reference to unconscious causal processes, and retain it
as a valid contribution to our understanding of dreams. Is
this possible ? It might be possible if it were the case that the
Freudian "rules of translation" from the manifest to the latent
content did not involve any references to the *origin* of the manifest content—of the individual images and experiences that

---

7. Occasionally MacIntyre talks as though Freudian description *replaces* our ordinary pre-Freudian description.

make up the latter. Unfortunately, however, this is not so. Even in the case of those elements in the manifest content of a dream, (which Freud calls symbols) which have a sort of fixed meaning independently of the dreamer, an investigation of their "proper" meaning in the context of a particular dream must ask questions about their origin *in the dreamer*. As Freud puts it, "Often enough a symbol has to be interpreted in its proper meaning and not symbolically". (ID p. 352). And to interpret it in its "proper" meaning is to embark upon an enquiry into its origin in the mental processes of the dreamer. This is, of course, all the more true of elements in the manifest content other than "symbols". Let us take one of the simplest of all dreams analysed in *The Interpretation of Dreams* : "A child of under four years old reported having dreamt that *he had seen a big dish with a big joint of roast meat and vegetables on it. All at once the joint has been eaten up whole and without being cut up. He had not seen the person who ate it.*" The latent content of this dream is as follows : The unknown person of the dream is the child himself, and the dream represents the fulfilment of his own wish for rich food. But how is this interpretation arrived at? Only through a genetic, a causal enquiry whose aim is to identify the wish. In this particular case, the enquiry reveals the following : "By Doctor's orders he (the child) has been put on a milk diet for the past few days. On the evening of the dream-day, he had been naughty, and as a punishment he had been sent to bed without supper. He had been through this hunger-cure once before and had been very brave about it. He knew he would get nothing, but would not allow himself to show by so much as a single word that he was hungry. Education had already begun to have an effect on him". (Ibid p. 268). It is clear that what fixes the meaning of the dream for Freud is its explanation in terms of the *causal* power of a wish. How can then the kind of separation—envisaged by MacIntyre—between the latent content of a dream and a reference to causal processes in the mind be achieved? Obviously, the dream can be interpreted in other, non-Freudian, ways; e.g., in terms of anxiety, future promise of food and so on, but what gives legitimacy to the Freudian redescription is precisely the availability of an explanation in terms of the causality of a particular wish. MacIntyre's prescription about separation, therefore, amounts to this : Retain Freud's redescription, but at the same time, remove the very ground on which such redescription is based.

Let us return now to neurotic behaviour. MacIntyre's own example is as follows : "The patient performs an obsessional ritual, say, before going to sleep. Jugs, clocks, everything that might fall or make a noise must be removed from the room. When all is done then the room once again must be inspected to make sure that nothing has been left undone. Pre-Freudians we say that this unaccountable behaviour is such that the patient is unable to sleep and so to have a normal life. Freud points out that the patient performs the ritual in order not to sleep. The ritual expresses the patient's fearful avoidance of sleep. Then he accounts for this attitude of the patient by a causal explanation in terms of what the patient experienced when as a child she woke in the dark and when she was taken into her parent's bed. (pp 61-62).

Now there is not really much that is specifically Freudian in MacIntyre's suggested "description". "The patient performs the ritual in order not to sleep. The ritual expresses the patient's fəarful avoidance of sleep." Such a description may well form part of a larger description of the case which is clearly non-Freudian. Thus, we might say that the patient is possessed by a devil which is afraid of sleep and thus invents excuses for not sleeping. Such a description sees purpose in the ritual and nicely accommodates MacIntyre's suggested redescription, and yet Freudianism can hardly have anything to do with it. A Freudian redescription of the case will no doubt recognise a purpose in the ritual, but will inevitably go further in connecting all the elements of the pattern of neurotic behaviour with one another and with the patient's past experiences—both immediate and remote—in such a way as inexorably to point to an explanation in terms of the workings of a wish formed as a result of childhood experiences. The redescription, in other words, is the result of a causal enquiry the object of which is an unconscious wish. To retain the Freudian description, and, at the same time to reject his explanation, would be something like accepting the description of a case of death, as a cast of murder, while at the same time, rejecting any explanation of the case in terms of deliberate killing by one or more other human beings.

Here we must note a distinction between wish-fulfilment in neurotic behaviour and wish-fulfilment in fairy tales (see p.188 above). In a fairy tale the situation which is describable as the fulfilment of a wish, can be so described even though the wish itself had nothing *causally* to do with the coming into being of that situation. Thus instead of the wish bringing the situation about, it might have been God or a kind spirit. However, the wish-fulfilment meaning underlying neurotic behaviour can be there at all, because the behaviour can be explained as having resulted from the operations of the wish. One reason for this may be that the connexion between the wish-fulfilling situation and the wish in a fairy tale can be established without any enquiry into the origin of the former, whereas neurotic behaviour gets its Freudian meaning at all only by virtue of its *origin* in the wish which it represents as fulfilled. In Freud the semantic and the genetic enquiry go necessarily hand in hand; the meaning of neurotic behaviour is determined by its origin. A consideration of any case history in Freud will make this point abundantly clear. Take an actual case of obsessional neurosis discussed by Freud : A young girl of 19 suffered from two nightly obsessions : she must have silence at night and must exclude all possibility of noise, *and* she must arrange her bed in one particular way. The latter obsession consisted of making sure that the bolster at the head of the bed did not touch the back of the wooden bedstead. Also the pillow must lie across the bolster exactly in a diagonal position and in no other; she would then place her head exactly in the middle of the diamond, lengthwise.

Analysis revealed that the ritual expressed the fulfilment of the girl's wish to separate the parents and prevent intercourse from occurring. The bolster "meant" her mother and the upright back of the bedstead her "father". Now the elements in the ritual could have acquired such meanings for the patient only through a (causal) chain of association of ideas (meanings) which linked them eventually with the elements of the wish. In spelling out the meanings of the ritual, one will have to tell a causal story in terms of association of ideas which will terminate in the wish itself.

To conclude this part of my argument, MacIntyre's suggested "Freudian" description of the neurotic ritual of his example is not Freudian at all, except in a trivial sense. It can become Freudian only by being expanded in a particular way. And this will consist in filling in details whose justification will depend on the possibility of telling a certain causal story. This Freudian redescription of neurotic behaviour is similar to the historian's redescription of historical events : To say that the independence of India was the triumph of Indian nationalism is to imply the truth of a certain causal story about Indian *Independence*. For the event(s) described as independence of India to have this meaning (i.e., "triumph of Indian nationalism"), a certain causal (genetic) explanation of these events must be true.

An objection at this point might be that if Freudian redescription of neurotic behaviour involves the truth of the Freudian explanation of such behaviour, then wouldn't Freud be really arguing in a circle? The description would be justified in terms of the explanation; but also the explanation in terms of the description. But, of course, this is really not so. As I pointed out a little earlier, in Freud the causal and the semantic enquiry go hand in hand. The possibility of a certain description points to a certain explanation and the possibility of a certain explanation points to a certain description. But there can be no doubt that the primary enquiry is the causal enquiry. The objection would have a degree of plausibility if it were the case, as MacIntyre sometimes seems to believe, that Freudian redescription of neurotic behaviour *replaces* (displaces) our ordinary description of such behaviour. For then, it would be reasonable to suppose that Freud, from the start, presents the data in such a way as to presuppose the truth of his explanation of the data. The truth, however, is that Freud does not dispense with our ordinary description of neurotic behaviour; rather he arrives at a redescription of such behaviour by means of pursuing a certain conception of their causal explanation.

A difficulty here may be presented by the writings of present-day Freudians who however reject the primacy of some of Freud's explanatory notions, e.g., the oedipus complex. Take Eric Fromm's brilliant little essay, "The Oedipus Complex"; Comments on the Case of Little Hans" (in *The Crisis of Psychoanalysis*, Penguin Books, 1970.) Fromm's procedure here may seem such that he accepts Freud's redescription of the data *in toto*, and yet gives a psychoanalytic explanation of these data in terms which are radically different from Freud's. If this were so, my argument so far would be invalidated, and there would be support for MacIntyre's view that we can accept Freud's redescription of neurotic behaviour while, at the same time, rejecting his explanation of it. However, even a slightly careful reading of Fromm's essay will show that he shifts the emphases in Freud's redescription in such a way that the result is a description which is quite other than the one that Freud meant. And of course it is this that suggests for Fromm an explanation in terms other than the oedipal wish.

Now to MacIntyre's suggestion that we would be scientifically much better off, if instead of Freud's own explanation of the data as redescribed by him, we accepted an explanation of them in terms of neuro-physiological processes. I think it is clear in view of our discussion above that the only way in which this suggestion could be made to seem plausible is by accepting the so-called identity-thesis in relation at least to unconscious wishes. For only then, it would seem, we could retain Freudian description (in terms of wish-fulfilment), and yet have an explanation in terms of brain-processes. Apart from the quite serious difficulties of the Identity-theory which have been pointed out fairly frequently in recent philosophical discussions, there is one difficulty which seems crucial in the present case. This may be presented as follows: Among the claims made by the Identity-theory is the one that mental concepts are to be analysed causally. To take an example, the notion of a sensation, say, of pain, is that of something which is the cause of a characteristic kind of behaviour which is called "pain behaviour". This something is (may be) contingently identical with a brain process. An important point to remember here is that the brain process which is taken to be identical with the sensation gets its name ("Pain") from the behaviour that it characteristically causes. This would presumably be true of all mental processes which are conscious. But there is a crucial difference in the case of at least *some* unconscious mental processes. Take the notion of a repressed wish which is supposed to be the cause of neurotic behaviour. Now, neurotic behaviour is not characteristic, typical, of behaviour which is the effect of the the operations of a wish. It is because it is so different that the need for interpretation arises. Suppose then before a description of neurotic behaviour in terms of wish-fulfilment becomes available we trace the chain of neurophysiological causes of such behaviour and are able to identify the originating cause. This cause, however, will not be identifiable as a wish prior to our identification of the behaviour itself as wish-fulfilment. But if our arguments above are correct, the latter identification is possible at all only through a causal enquiry of quite another sort, namely, the sort that psychoanalysis pursues. The upshot of all this is as follows : A neurophysiological explanation of neurotic behaviour may indeed be possible, but if we want to retain Freudian description of neurotic behaviour, the primary causal enquiry must be the Freudian one. Independently of this latter enquiry, there would be no way of identifying the originating neurophysiological process (es) as the repressed wish.

Let us now look for a moment at MacIntyre's contention that he finds Freud's redescription of neurotic behaviour *illuminating*, although he would, at the same time, like to reject Freud's explanation of it. From our discussion so far it would seem to follow that one account of the illuminating character of Freud's redescription is to be found in the fact that his redescription contains an explanation of neurotic behaviour which is such that it gives us new insights into the workings of the human psyche. If this is right, then denuded of its explanatory content "Freudian" description would perhaps also lose its illuminating character. But perhaps we have misunderstood MacIntyre all along. May be for him, it is enough, for a description of a piece of neurotic behaviour to count as Freudian, that it sees purpose in the behaviour and the agent is unconscious of this purpose. Freudian description would then be illuminating in that it sees purpose in behaviour which to pre-Freudians appeared purposeless. Such a minimal characterisation of Freudian description might also escape difficulties, about causal explanation, for it may well be that mere recognition of purpose in a piece of behaviour need not commit one to any kind of causal explanation of it. There is however, a crucial difficulty in this argument; and this has to do with the fact that Freudian description is not the only one which sees purpose in neurotic behaviour. Some pre-

Freudian descriptions of neurotic behaviour, say, in terms of possession by an evil spirit, or punishment by God, also see neurotic behaviour as essentially goal directed; and it may at least sometimes be part of such descriptions that the subject is *unconscious* of the purpose behind his behaviour. For Freudian description to be illuminating, as opposed to these other descriptions which also see purpose in neurotic behaviour, the *way* it sees purpose must therefore be different. And it is my contention that this difference cannot be specified without also enlarging the description in a way which will clearly link it up with Freud's explanatory scheme. Take MacIntyre's own example of obsessive ritual which I quoted above. His suggested description of the case—"fearful avoidance of a sleep"—while it sees purpose in the ritual, is not really particularly Freudian just as it stands. Nor is it in any clear sense illuminating. The behaviour now cries out for explanation, and without any explanation forthcoming it is at least as baffling as it was under any pre-Freudian description. And what will enrich the description in order for it to attain a recognisably Freudian character will have to be an explanation of the kind that Freud provides. The illumination that Freudian description carries seems therefore to reside precisely in the explanatory content of the latter.

I have not here, of course, argued for the inviolability of the Freudian doctrine. All that I have tried to defend is its *integrity*. The doctrine, in my opinion, cannot be *divided up* in the way that MacIntyre and some others have suggested.

N.E. University, Shilong.

Plenary Session VI

THEORY AND PRAXIS

President : B. L. Atreya
Secretary : P. K. Sundaram

Main Speakers :
  (1) S. N. Ganguly
  (2) Evryalo Cannabrava
  (3) Ramjee Singh
  (4) R. Panikkar
  (5) D. P. Chattopadhyaya

THEORY AND PRAXIS
(A plea for a complete human being)
S. N. Ganguly

"The resolution of *theoretical* contradictions is possible only through *practical* means, only through the practical energy of man. Their resolution is by no means, therefore, the task only of the understanding, but is a *real* task of life, a task which Philosophy was unable to accomplish precisely because it saw there a purely theoretical problem". K. Marx (*Economic & Philosophical Manuscripts*, 1844)

"Our life gains what is called 'value' in those of its aspects which represent eternal humanity in knowledge, in sympathy, in deeds, in character and creative works....civilization is to express Man's *dharma* and not merely his cleverness, power and possession." *Religion of Man*, Rabindranath Tagore.

Introduction : The above lines,—though they come from thinkers of rather different temperament, background and historical situation—indicate firmly and clearly that man is a 'praxis-being'. It is in and through man's nature that change is turned into creative transformation, a purposive 'transsubstantiation'[1] as Sartre says; and the goal is 'expression of essence', a completeness, a totalization or, in short, *becoming universal*. In what follows I shall try to show that *praxis* is not opposed to *theory*, both are the essential ingredients of human development; a development which is not mere growth but a journey towards *completeness*—a journey which has been ruthlessly thwarted by a separation between theory and praxis. The textual orientation and bias of the paper will presuppose on the part of the readers some acquaintance with the writings of Marx, Sartre and those of liberal or radical thinkers in the field of sociology and social psychology like C. Wright Mills, Eric Fromm or Gouldner, etc—that is writers who have been intensely involved with reestablishing a link between reason and human freedom and pointing to the increasing rate of self-alienation in contemporary competitive society. Throughout this paper I have positively tried to analyse the relationship between theory and praxis as a counterimage of the extremely mechanical image of man which culminated in B. F. Skinner's book, *Beyond Freedom and Dignity*, a fear C. Wright Mills exposed long ago in his reference to "Cheerful Robots" (*The Sociological Imagination*, U.S.A., 1967). Though I have reacted considerably in my formulation within this background, nevertheless the actual mode of reflection is quite general in its structure and conclusions.

Contemporary civilization very definitely indicates that the role of theory has overshot its mark. Instead of exploring and building a path of unfettered development of a so-called 'theoretical, contemplative or rational man' and evolving a corresponding life-style of 'absolute knowledge'[2], the contemporary inheritors of the ideal of a 'contemplative man' have landed themselves into several *impasses*, theoretical as well as practical. As a point of departure, I shall mention only two out of them in this paper. The over-emphasis and over-reliance on 'pure theory' motivated by an unnatural demand for clarity and precision, as opposed to adequacy and effectiveness, has engendered the phenomenon of a 'puzzled man' rather than a 'problematic man'. The two impasses I shall mention shortly, are not only interesting in that they are representative of our age but reveal almost a profound moral implication in the context of an increasing frustration and alienation. The one is language-predicament expressed as *meaning-obsession* and the other is action-paralysis leading to the paradox of a 'theory of efficiency' or a *discipline of praxiology*.

The former is well-known in the history of philosophy as 'the problem of synonymy'. After a lot of philosophical storm Professor Quine very ably brought out the impotency of the problem in his famous paper on "Two dogmas of empiricism", in his books *From a Logical Point of View*. According to a contemporary writer :

> Quine seeks to bring out the interrelationships between the concepts of analyticity, necessity and synonymy. He argues that these concepts, although

definable in terms of each other, are not definable except in terms of each other ; that is, they form an intensional circle. This intensional circle he concludes to be vicious, arguing that it means that the terms under discussion cannot be given any *clear meaning* apart from each other, and hence can have no clearly specifiable meaning.[3]

The chequered career of the concept of 'meaningfulness' coming through positivism and analytic school can be seen to be hitting a blind alley in Quine's formulation given above if we realize that like any key classificatory concept the concept of meaning is dependent on a more intuitive, primitive concept of synonymy; if and when synonymy itself presents an insoluble problem the concept of meaning cannot stand on its own any more. The 'vicious intensional circle' weakens the formal demands of 'independence' and 'adequacy' of communication as a 'coding-decoding operation'. The contemporary obsession with the problem of meaning with a large number of philosophers can best be understood as a desire to distinguish between 'interference' and 'information', between 'significant' and 'insignificant' elements in our discourse, as a prerequisite to the *scientific use of language*. But Quine demonstrated that at the root lies a more primitive problem of 'synonymy' before constructing or using any language L where 'analytic' & 'synthetic', 'necessary' & 'contingent' sentences can be demarcated or defined. In short meaning is to be understood within a wider model of synonymy as far as L is concerned. What happens to synonymy ? Let me quote the views of a contemporary linguist on the matter :

> It would be idle to discuss the role of synonymity statements in grammar and semantics unless it could be shown that, in principle, it is feasible to formulate procedures which will make the construction of synonymity statements for L possible. But procedures of this kind cannot be formulated independently of the adoption of some specific concept of 'linguistic knowledge'; for we cannot, ultimately, say what will count as evidence for or against a given

synonymity statement unless we are clear about where the boundary between the linguistic and the non-linguistic lies.[4]

Historically, we can say that significant communication depended on a rigorous formulation of the problem of meaning, the problem of meaning on the concept of synonymy; and again, synonymy, in its turn, on the very distinction (of course in a formalized way) between 'language' and 'non-language'. How obviously we are only widening the 'vicious intensional circle', pointed out by Quine. The author quoted above unfortunately suggests the same fateful line of building a formalized 'will—o'-the-wisp'. He says in the concluding lines of the book that the discussion of the entire book is "merely preliminary to an investigation which opens up the possibility of replacing 'synonymy' by a more *precisely defined set of equivalences*, and thus providing a more *adequate conceptual framework* for the *analysis of natural languages*"[5]. The above lines express more a despair and the outline of a trap for further precision, and less a determined measure of redemption of the natural language. If we have to cross such an arabesque of 'formal staircase' before effectively using a natural language, is not it time that we finally cried halt to this 'game playing' and realize language as a concrete, historical project of human community?

As for the other interesting paradox I shall only barely touch the problem. Theory and practice in its process of separation led us to the absurd situation of discovering and seriously indulging in a new discipline of "Theory of Practice" or "praxiology". In other words, our shameless fetish for theory forces us, as it were, in the face of severest odds, to hope that a failure in efficiency of acts can best be redressed by evolving a 'theory of efficient action'. Such a science was conceived by Kotarbinski[6] and christened as "Praxiology". Kotarbinski worked on this new theory since 1910. Kotarbinski, of course, was not a lonely genius in the field but ably followed in the line of thinkers likes Charles B. Dunoyer, the Spanish engineer Meliton Martin, the French philosopher Alfred Espinas and so on. This dependence, almost pathological, on 'improvement of theories of x' and 'theory for improvement of theory of x' and so on, made us completely blind toward a simpler human solution, natural and more concrete on that account, through conjoining theory with practice and *vice versa*. I have, for very obvious reasons, taken these two illustrations from philosophical literature,—one representing 'theory of natural language', the other 'theory of efficient action'—to drive home the dangerous obstinacy of philosophers not to see truth in the context of a total human nature or in the context of 'man-nature continuum'. It is precisely for this reason that we hopelessly move into theoretical ruts oblivious of life and change. By reconsideration of praxis as a defining characteristic of human reason we can see ourselves as architects of our own future—a reminder that man is both a *Homo Sapiens* and *Homo Faber*. This is why I have inserted the sub-title *a plea for a complete human being*.

Nature of Praxis : It is necessary at the very beginning to understand that when I am talking of praxis, I am not referring to or describing a new 'Philosophy of action' or merely suggesting the truism that practice or/and action are necessary ingredients of man's knowledge or other so-called mental conducts. To indulge in any one of such things will amount to committing the same error that has repeatedly been done in history by contrasting theory and practice or sometimes even treating them as opposed aspects of our life. My perspective in the present paper, I submit, is the widest possible. I firmly believe, and have tried to show accordingly in the sequel, that a proper understanding of Praxis, especially after Marx, is possible or tenable only by a reconsideration or/and rectification of the prevalent image of man. It is only such a comprehensive understanding of praxis that will redeem knowledge finally from philosophy and thereby help us *interpret* the world by changing it. A brief resume of the role of theory in relation to practice or act will also be helpful as a preliminary to seeing more clearly the reason and consequences of the historical process of gradually separating theory and practice to perpetuate the present image of a 'rational man', by steadily ascribing a superior role to contemplation or pure theory.

In 1802 Schelling eulogized the role of theory traditionally associated with the greatness of philosophy as follows :

> It is by studying a strictly theoretical philosophy that we become most immediately acquainted with

ideas, and only ideas provide action with energy and ethical significance.⁷

True knowledge, in order to orient action, must necessarily be firmly and uncompromisingly theoretical. The word "theory" came from the Greek word "theoria" having a religious origin. *Theoria* is looking on at sacred events. From this the philosophical shift was to mean by it 'Contemplation of the Cosmos'. This connotation emphasized or possibly presupposed a distinction between a being beyond change and becoming which came under the realm of *doxa*. Thus somehow theory came to be associated more with a stable structure beyond the changing world. A contemplative life also was supposed to be a life incorporating the characteristics of a stable, harmonious structure found or discovered in the Cosmos. A contemplative or theoretical life was thus from the time of the Greek thinkers a life not swayed too much by *history* or *change*. It was no wonder that life gradually dropped from such an anti-historical approach and let theory prosper with a world of concepts and law-governed structures. In short, a contrast between eternal structure and temporal structure is the ontological root of a demarcation between theory and practice as the tradition in the West goes. In the Indian tradition such a distinction was maintained, but 'laws' always played an inferior role (I am not talking of the laws or order like *Ṛta* or Law of Karma) or at least less respectedth an 'revelation of truth' or being *per se*. Intellect was subordinated to some form of experience or encounter (*sākṣātkāra*). Thus though we developed a contradiction between theory and practice (hypocrisy or double standard) in the context of social action, the separation of theory and practice or purging intellect from interest and action did not develop in the manner it did in the West. In the name of 'pure theory' Husserl, in recent times, tried to evolve a life of theory through a criticism of the over-objectivity of the sciences. However, one does not have to journey too far in history to see that human reason was glorified as 'theory bereft of practice'. In other words, theory and practice were always regarded as distinct and the latter as always inferior to the former, giving rise finally to the hierarchical attitude to the 'brains' and 'muscles' of society.

Knowledge and comprehension, whether of ourselves or others or even nature, were relegated to the domain of theory as a conceptual frame or repetitive use of symbols, (though sometimes leading to consequential action). Action and practice were thus mere *consequences* of ideas rather than generators of ideas. This is why the concept of *Praxis* cannot be treated identically or on a par with either practice or action in their current usage. As we understand the term practice today, it reflects more a set conformist behaviour not necessarily connected with a definite historical goal. Action, on the other hand, has been the preoccupation of most of the modern philosophers, both for its relation with 'free will' controversy (with a juristic overtone) and its relation with explanatory hypotheses of social sciences. The very basic characteristic of action, accepted in almost all quarters of philosophical and legalistic thinking, is regarded as bodily or personalistic acts controllable by agent. Praxis on the other hand as understood by and since Marx, is more a creative behaviour of man having a definite goal and in a dialectical relationship with our thought and consciousness. Moreover, praxis is more related with our species-being than our individual being. This also means or atleast implies, that praxis is connected with historicity of our existence. Marx wrote in his manuscripts of 1844 : "Thought and being are distinct, but at the same time they form a unity." Man as a praxis-being forges this unity and initiates a process of creativity and freedom. It is this unity in man that reveals the true nature of praxis. I have used the term 'praxis-being' often in the above; what is really meant by the term is that praxis is human nature in its totality and cannot be opposed to his theoretical activity—because consciousness of theoretical activity is as much a part of human nature or natural man. According to Predrag Vranicki, "practice" is, "the basis of humanity, the philosophical characteristic of man."[8] Vranicki then proceeds to analyze practice as an all-embracing (and, therefore, inclusive of man's theoretical self) concept where essence is expressed in three different ways : (a) the sensuous-concrete (b) the theoretical-abstract and (c) the emotional-experiencing. Thus :

> ..concept of practice embraces the sensuous and the theoretical——it is inadequate to oppose theory and

practice, as if they were two which should be a unity; practice itself understood as a fundamental function of man, contains both in itself.[9]

In the rest of this section I shall try briefly to suggest in barest outline, the nature and development of this all-embracing characteristic of praxis.

Man is an animal born in nature with a set of needs. So he is both natural and labour-using. Man's use of labour on nature towards fulfilment of his needs is different from other animals because his consciousness enables him to enter into relatively stable relationship with nature and other beings and be aware of these *relations* as relations. But, "for the animals, its relation to others does not exist as a relation."[10] It is this interrelationship on a concrete plane that makes man's being, from the very beginning, both natural and social; and 'species-being' signifies this universality as essential to man. But then the relations are not given *absolute* into which men *passively* entere; it is also man's nature to transform these relations. Nature makes man as much as man makes nature[11]. Natural man and human nature, therefore, are one and the same thing. Praxis, then, are those kinds of acts which help maintain this unity and hence reveal the creative essence of man. Since the transformation and integration of existing and newly created relations, though necessary, are dependent on a fairly determinate structure, we can as well say that praxis emanates in consonance with (and thereby acquires significance) a certain structure within and outside man. The levels of structure, in terms of universality, may be *generic, species-specific* and *Individual*. In objective terms the same reality can be seen as biological, anthropological and historical-psychological. But whatever the natural level of these structures, at each level there is a bi-polarity in that the structure displays a *competence-pattern* and a *performance-pattern*. Perhaps by widening the Chomskyan model one can sum up all these characteristics under one heading by defining man as a 'learning animal', operating with an 'action-interaction-reaction' model. Praxis through such a model operates in three different ways : (1) through language, (2) through community and (3) through nature. Theory according to such a view of human development is certainly included in practice. Therefore, to succumb to the existing practice of alienating theory from practice is to give up the image of a natural, creative man. At the same time it is patent in our everyday experience and conduct that such alienation has been a powerful trend dominating our thought and action. The analysis of the nature and consequences of this alienation between theory and praxis will occupy us in the following section.

Alienation between theory and praxis : What I have tried to show so far is that man as a praxis-being is embedded in man as a learning animal, i.e., a structured being with competence and performance. The structure also makes man a *universal being* and *necessarily* so. Through his performance man enjoys and engenders his universality but his competence imparts a sort of necessity to his universality. In short, man's freedom is freedom *of necessity* rather than *from necessity*; the entire controversy on free will, therefore, is obviously due to a failure to take a natural view of man or human view of nature. The kind of universality we are talking of here is certainly not a spiritual principle of man's self-transcendence; it is merely a concrete principle of man's communicative nature and hence, motive and method of such a natural extension is and can only be his having a set of basic needs. Earlier we have talked of man being a 'learning animal', of man as a 'structured being'; needs add a definite sensuous and historical content to this structure. Needs are never timeless because dependent on a specific space-time continuum for evolving a method of fulfilment. Through his needs man carries his past through his present into a projected future. Man's creativity and freedom are thus not independent principles of perfection but a natural development of his *essence*, incorporating his history, a history which is not superimposed on him from the outside but something in which he participates actively from the very beginning through his *natural* propensities. In this sense praxis is the major principle which bestows human identity to us. When we separate theory from praxis we are actually driving a wedge between human nature and natural man and thereby generate one or several abstract principles (conceptually worked out leaving no or very little room for 'sense-activity' or need-based intervention) of human identity. Consequently human praxis is substituted by *ideologically determined acts* (I am using the term 'ideology' in the sense used by Marx as a rationalizing frame for class interests).

At this point I shall make a classification between 'primary praxis' and 'secondary praxis' depending on the fulfilment of 'basic needs' or 'non-basic needs' respectively. When for historical reasons secondary praxis is severed from primary praxis (but not *vice versa*) and transformed into apparently unrelated, self-sufficient acts, there occurs a corresponding substitution of priority, that is human identity is subordinated or even totally denied in favour of a class identity. In this substituted structure need becomes subordinate to greed, acquisitiveness, ownership etc. Under such strain man ceases to be a praxis-being and indulges for non-natural purposes, merely in ideological[12] acts displaying a historically determined class identity. In order to conceal, cover up or mystify such alienation knowledge and reason are identified with *pure theory*. Such a mode of human reason, cut off from nature and community, works against our own freedom and historically has, as a matter of fact, generated the so-called image of a 'rational man' in contrast to what I have elsewhere described as a 'reasonable man'[13], the latter obviously signifying a useful execution of theory in and through practice relevant to man's *nature* and *needs*.

Conclusion : We started in the *introduction* with two paradigm cases of bankruptcy of human reason, at least so I thought, if and when a cleavage between knowledge and human praxis is idealized as the true and most efficient method of learning and theorizing. The various forms of alienation threatening our society born out of this suicidal and identity destroying practice are pretty well-known today through the concerted concern of the sensitive sociologists, psycho-analysts and social psychologists. Apart from creating a stiff dichotomy between intellectuals and manual workers through this separation of theory from practice and making knowledge praxis-independent, the contemporary society is maintaining and nurturing the most de-humanizing trend of self-alienation by separating our intellectual from moral behaviour. Convictions are scrupulously kept apart from commitments. In the present society a seeker of objective truth must preserve his 'ethical neutrality'.

Mental paralysis is admired as composure; gross moral lapses go by the name of 'ethical neutrality'. An intellectual *qua* intellectual must not be a partisan to any issue. A batch of ballistic experts are *primarily experts* and as such will study the effect of napalm on his fellow-beings without the slightest commitment, moral or otherwise, to the cruelty involved in burning babies with such a monstrous weapon. A scientist today is not held responsible for letting some incapable human beings use 'asphyxiation bomb' on his own species, because *qua* scientist he is only interested in knowledge and not in how that knowledge is being put into practice. An intellectual must take off his uniform before reacting as a 'total man'. This is what C.P. Snow has called "Contracting out" or Adam Smith upheld as "minding one's business". When we start taking serious note of all this human decadence and distortion all around us (and even this straightforward awareness takes a lot of struggle in our consciousness) we tend to be more perceptive to the other (but more human) alternative of looking at knowledge as a part of man's praxis, knowledge as a unified front *for learning and human development*.

Knowledge and Praxis

Knowledge is not, as we have been prone to believe, a passive reception of information, ideas and experiences which we call *data* to be arranged, stored and organized *internally* and then finally expressed as an abstract set of symbols. Knowledge, on the other hand, is a human encounter of reality in concrete terms and will always be on that account no less an active struggle against ignorance and obfuscation initiating a historical process of dialectical *participation* with reality in order to *see* as well as *deal with* the constraints laid in the path of our development as *complete human beings*. The traditional Indian concept of constraints to knowledge as *Āvaraṇa* and *Prakṣepa* is helpful in this context. The former conceals and the latter mystifies by projection. The ideological acts or 'praxis—substitutes' (which include philosophy, science, sociology, psychology, and the whole range of theoretical disciplines as well as the vocational or creative pursuits like arts and crafts) whether of ourselves or our adversaries constantly engender and enforce the two processes of concealment and mystification which must be fought to set the paces of human liberation and this is the meaning of knowledge. It is, therefore, not by making *new theories* or adopting a fresh *philosophy of man* that we shall know but, as Marx suggested, by transcending philosophy altogether and adopting revolutionary practice instead. According to Marx : "The coincidence of the changing of circumstances and of human activity or self-changing can only be grasped and rationally understood as revolutionary *practice.*"[14] Philosophy is incapable of performing this because there we start with an alienation between theory and practice (see the first quotation in the beginning of this paper). In society knowledge and ignorance are residing side by side; but theirs is not a peaceful co-existence, it is a bitter struggle. As philosophers we have to go beyond mere interpretation to fight the dehumanizing process of concealment and mystification launched in the name of understanding and knowledge bereft of creative practice so that knowledge can finally amount to a recovery of human nature not alienated from, but in harmony with nature. Even science, Marx hoped, will one day be a "single science", because, "science is only *genuine* science when it proceeds from sense-experience, in the two forms of *sense* perception and *sensuous* need, that is, only when it proceeds from nature."[16] Knowledge and human relevance are inseparable and thus it is a scientific preparedness to fight for human freedom through historical mist, haze and oppression in order to regain or and realize our true human identity constantly expressing itself *in our language through our community within nature.* Knowledge, in short, in the view upheld here, is a process of becoming *complete man* instead of cramping our potential into a one-dimensional mould of either "utility" or "wisdom".

NOTES AND REFERENCES

1. J. P. Sartre, *Problem of Method*, Methuen & Co. Ltd., (tr. Hazel Barnes) U.K., 1963.
2. Jurgen Habermas, *Knowledge and human Interests* (paper back), Beacon Press, U.S.A., 1972. pp 301-302
3. L. M. Broughton, "Quine and Two Dogmas of Empiricism" in *International Logic Review*, Vol. 5, no. I, 1974, pp 41-50 (p. 41)
4. Roy Harris, *Synonymy and Linguistic Analysis*, Basil Blackwell, Oxford 1973. p. 146

5. *ibid.*, p. 159 (emphases mine)

6. Henryk Skolimowski, *Polish Analytical Philosophy*, Routledge & Kegan Paul, London 1967. pp 116-130. It is interesting to read the exact words used by Skolimowski :

"Until the twentieth century there was no *general* theory of efficient action which would embrace *all* human activities regardless of the kind of activity ...It is rather peculiar that no department of learning was reserved for the theoretical reflection upon practical activities from the point of view of their efficiency or efficacy....The science of efficient action, whatever the field of activity, physical or mental, and whatever the scale of activity, a oneminute performance or a gigantic undertaking, has received the name of *Praxiology*." (p. 116)

7. Quoted in Jurgen Habermas, *op. cit*, p. 301

8. "On the Problem of Practice", in *Praxis*, year 1965, no. 1. pp. 41-48 (p. 42) Vranicki uses "practice" as identical with praxis.

9. *ibid.*, p. 44

10. K. Marx, *German Ideology*. Quoted in T.B. Bottomore & Maxmilian Rubel. ed. *Selected writings in Sociology and Social Philosophy*. a Pelican book. U.K. 1956 p. 86

11. This nature-man continuum is beautifully brought out by Marx in the following lines: "The universality of man appears in practice in the universality which makes the whole of nature into his inorganic body : (1) as a direct means of life; and equally (2) as the material object and instrument of his life-activity. Nature is the inorganic body of man; that is to say nature, excluding the human body itself". T.B. Bottomore, ed & tr., *Karl Marx* (early writings), paper back. Mc Graw-Hill Book Company, U.S.A. 1963. p. 126 Significantly enough the great humanist thinker in contemporary India Rabindranath Tagore viewed external nature in a similar manner. He wrote in his famous book *Religion of Man* : "Our physical body has its comprehensive reality in the physical world, which may be truly called our universal body, without which our individual body would miss its function." George Allen & Unwin, London 1931 p. 147

12. An ideological act is nothing other than severing secondary praxis from primary praxis and hypostatizing the former as history-independent and constitutive of human essence in its entirety. Even non-basic need like love, sympathy etc. are distorted into charity, domination etc.

13. S. N. Ganguly, "Reasonableness versus rationality : a reinterpretation of freedom", a paper read in the seminar organized by The Centre for Social Science Studies, Calcutta, in June 1974.

14. T. B. Bottomore & Maxmilian Rubel ed., *Op. cit.*, p. 83

15. *ibid.* p. 87

Viswa Bharati

THEORY AND PRAXIS

Evryalo   Cannabrava

   The concept of civilisation is associated to a set of techniques, since the workmanship in arts and crafts up to binary operations of electronic computation. This assemblage of techniques is *called* technology. Technology, however, has other connotations. It is a word imbued with entropic *variety* of meanings. It is true, however, that *technology* is not linked to scientific applications. The relations between technology and science are shallow or intricate. The connotative richness of a word, like technology, may convey, in the long run, a multifarious gathering of meanings.

   Between these meanings, there are some that carry distortions instead of clarified form. Technology, of course, is not confined to scientific applications, although it could be extended to embrace scientific techniques. But technology is not an assessorial complement of science, it is not a sort of implement for scientific devices. It is always challenging science in a kind of rivalry or competition. Science forecasts, technology accomplishes. What technology performs is not vinculated to theoretics, that is, to the speculation part of science. Science surmises, building up hypothesis which are not true or false.

   A technologist like von Braun is not a scientist, has not contributed a new theory or envisaged a new outlook in the domain of scientific theoretics. He is solely and proudly a programmer of creativity and invention, which are not scientifically predictable, but are technologically fulfilled. An astronomer, like Fred Hoyle, in his bestseller "The Nature of Universe" published in 1955, has predicted that men will put in orbit the first artificial satellite in a hundred years. It was, however, two years later, in 1957, that Russian technologists put in orbit the first Sputnik, correcting technologically the astronomical error commited by Hoyle.

There is a relevant difference between technological progress and scientific evolution. Technological progress is not determined by scientific predictions, because technological progress is a consequence of praxiological models for human activities. Scientific evolution is the result of theoretical models for natural phenomena. Discoveries and inventions are not the outcome of scientific or mathematical knowledge. If it was so, then, as remarked once by Hilbert, the discovery of relativity theory would be gratifying to young students in mathematical Gottingen instead of Einstein. The reason is, as asserted by Hilbert, that those students than were much more at home with four-dimensional geometry than Einstein did. But the question is that Einstein worked out the four-dimensional space-time structures for the relativity theory.

There are technical aspects of science that philosophers must be aware of. But to know scientific technicalities is philosophically relevant when the philosopher is prone to forget them, whenever he takes philosophical decisions. Philosophy, therefore, is not a science, but an art. An art of substituting solutions for problems. A very subtle art indeed, which is invigorated by creative activity and by critical reflexion. There is a philosophical way of approach which separates out the relevant questions of technology from the irrelevant ones. Theoretical questions belong to science. But praxiological questions are philosophically important insofar as they are connected with optimisation criteria, based in informal rigour and relative control.

Informal rigour and relative control are technological devices. Both of them, rigour and control, were at the basis of any human activity as an efficient tool for the survival of human species. But informal rigour and relative control enlivened the Rupestrian designs, found on or among rocks, in the paleolithic caverns of Lascaux and Altamira. It is a proof that men, before art, science and religion were discovered, was inspired by visual imagery with all the aesthetic connotations. Visual imagery created visual thinking, in Rudolf Arnhein's interpretations. Visual thinking, from the other side, is praxis and not theory.

Praxis, not theory, is a technological tool for inferences, based on experience, for subjective logic and for building up a system of beliefs. But theory too is visualisation in an abstract sense, a selective aptitude for inspective knowledge, an endowment for analysis, underlied by creative imagery. Creative imagery is a praxiological model for free and open inventiveness. Inventiveness is an aptitude for envisaging the image of form, whenever it remains concealed by distortions and metamorphosis.

The image of form could be eroded or enhanced by noises in the self-organizer systems. That is why form might be informative in the sense of concrete or abstract form. Mental images too are abstract or concrete: they are concrete as intersensorially organised at its very grounds. They are abstract insofar as they are the outcome of conscious mental activity. Visual thinking is informative, saturated by noises, as a self-organizer system. A theoretical model of visual thinking cannot fulfil the requirements of *positive* knowledge. In this interpretation we must appeal to a psycho-dynamic version of natural and spontaneous thinking.

The artificial thinking, in contrast to the natural thinking, is subdued by mechanical procedures symbolically codified. What is symbolically codified becomes artificial language, in its aloofness from the vital sources of natural language. The hypothesis, now emphasised, is that the cognitive style of natural thinking could be reconstructed as a praxiological model for linguistic activity. But, now, must be added that praxiological models for human activities, which are not reducible to theoretical terms, could be optimised in accordance with rules and criteria for theoretical formalisation. This meeting of praxiological models with theoretical models must be performed in agreement with the technological operator. The technological operator, based on informal rigour and relative control, must conciliate the antithetical terms of theory and praxis not at the basis of apriori knowledge, but at the basis of action.

Brazil

THEORY AND PRACTICE

Ram Jee Singh

I

Theory has various meanings in ordinary usage and in science and philosophy. It may be contrasted with *practice* as unverified speculation. It may signify some hypothesis. In its best use, as the *Encyclopaedia Britannica* (Vol. XXII, p. 69) says, it signifies "a systematic account of some field of study, derived from a set of general propositions", called as *postulates* or *principles*. The *Oxford English Dictionary* (Vol. XIII, p 278) gives *seven* different meanings. Runnes in his "*Dictionary of Philosophy* regards 'theory' as the "hypothetical universal aspect of anything". The Soviet (A) *Dictionary of Philosophy* (ed. Rosenthal Yudin), agrees with Runnes because 'theory' signifies as "unverified suppositional knowledge". For Plato, 'theory' signifies a 'contemplated truth' but for Aristotle, it means "pure knowledge as opposed to practical." It may signify an obstruction from 'practice' or the principle from which the practice proceeds.

'Practice' means 'an action or 'an act of practicising', that has its goal within itself. In its simple sense, 'practice' means the 'action of doing something, performance, execution, working, operation method of action etc. It also signifies 'habitual doing', doing of something repeatedly', 'an exercise,' 'the carrying on some profession or occupation', 'trickery or artifice', 'action of scheming', or planning etc. (*The Oxford English Dictionary*, Vol. XIII, pp 1218-19.).

II

The question of relationship between theory and practice can be discussed from various angles. On the empirical level, some of our 'practices' are measured and calculated while others are not and there are definite tests for deciding whether a particular action is measured or not. On the philosophic level, the different schools of philosophy give different types of answers which can be categorised broadly under four heads:—

(a) The *Dualism of Theory and Practice* :—According to this view, theory and practice are regarded as absolutely different and distinct. Theory is pure thought, while practice is the act of the person. But this answer is blatantly tautological, when it asserts that *theory is theory* and *practice is practice.*

(b) *The Monism of Theory and Practice* :—Unlike the above view, the monistic approach emphasised the identity of *thought* and *action*. Those who identify *thought* with the Ultimate Reality, for them theory is regarded as more foundational. But those who regard it as the by-product of the Elan Vital like Bergson, theory becomes identical with the *vital force* and so on. But this monistic answer is either *false* or *self-contradictory*. It is *false* if it maintains that practice is calculated, measured or preplanned, or that all kinds of theorising are useful and serviceable to the whole of mankind. It is *self-contradictory* because it treats theory and practice as identical which is manifestly wrong. They are two distinct terms with different meanings. So 'theory' cannot mean 'practice' nor 'practice' can signify 'theory'.

(c) *The Doctrine of Relativity of Theory and Practice* :—According to this view, either theory is regarded as of supreme importance and all our practices should be subjected to the test of theory or practice is more important than theory because "theory starts with practice, and reaches the theoretical place via practice and then has to return to practice" and so on. Both these views are one-sided and hence only half-truths.

(d) *Mutual Relevance of Theory and Practice* :—According to this view theory influences practice and practice gives direction to our theory. This view is more satisfactory. The explanation follows hereafter.

III

The distinction between theory and practice is sought to be obliterated by pointing towards the practical character of all so-called theoretical activity. It is held that theory serves the purpose of practice. Theory arises out of a practical situation and is also an instrument to solve some practical problems. But it is true that much of higher and abstract thinking is free from any practical situation, like philosophising. Even when we think of some practical problems, the essence of thinking or theorising is fundamentally different from that of practice. This means that in spite of mutual relevance between theory and practice, they are essentially distinct. Theory is theory, and practice is practice.

Heidegger rejects this dichotomy of theory and practice but he does not also believe in false reductionism of one to the other. He rejects both the monistic and the dualistic approaches. He would derive both theory and practice from the common primitive human existence. Man is as much concerned with theory as with practice, because both originate in the essential constitution of man. On the one hand he is a *subject*, on the other hand he is a *person*. When a theory is formulated, it is a universal affair, when a practice is performed, it is an individual thing. Theory is essentially universal, practice is individual. Theory is thought, which discloses *Being* or *Essence*. Practice is action, which gives us real existence. Thus theory and practice, though they are essentially different, are yet factually interwoven, although in the time-structure, theory is backward looking, while practice is forward looking.

IV

To Socrates, knowledge was virtue, in other words, theory and practice were identical. In identifying theory with practice or wisdom with virtue, his intention was to show that without thought there would be absolute chaos. Without reflection man would forget his spirituality—the essence of his real being. But the problem is that majority of us are un-Socratic beings. The business of thinking should not overreach itself. "The flair of Hamlet's for abstract thinking is perpetually liable to make him momentarily indifferent to the concrete world about him". (*Shakespearean Tragedy*, H. B. Charlton, Cambridge 1949, p 93). Hamlet's tragedy was because his way of thinking frustrated the object of thought. In other words, it is due to the talk of harmony between thought, feeling and action-power of his personality. Will Durant says (*Philosophy and the Social Problems*

p. 7) "speculation..develops sensitivity of perception and destroys decision of action. Thought adventuring in a labyrinth of analysis, discovers behind society the individual." Maladjustment of theory and practice is the result of immense increase in man's knowledge and his consequent helplessness in the field of action. Mechanised action ignores spiritual and ethical aspects of man. It is, therefore, that the eyes of the common people turn towards Buddha and Aristotle, who emphasise maximum cooperation of knowledge with action, theory with practice. The *Gītā* also speaks of synthesis between the Sāṅkhya and Yoga, i.e. theory and practice. The Sāṅkhya is incomplete without the Yoga. The Gītā gives us not only metaphysics (*Brahmavidyā*) but also a discipline (*Yoga-śāstra*) not only metaphysical theories, but also spiritual dynamics. (*Bhagvadgītā*, III 3 cf. *Mahābhārata* (Śānti-Parva, 240.6). Wisdom is not incompatible with action. So Gītā says—"Not by abstention from work nor by mere renunciation does a man obtain perfection"—III. 4. While life remains, action is unavoidable. Thinking is an act; living is an act and these acts cause many effects.

IV

According to Marxism, "the theoretical conclusions of the communists are in no way based on ideas or principles that have been invented or discovered, by this or that would-be-universal-reform, but they merely express actual relations springing from an existing class-struggle from a historical movement." (Marx-Engels, *Selected Works*, Vol. I p. 44). "Without a sense of theory among the Westerners the scientific socialism would never have entered their flesh and blood as much as is the case"—(Marx-Engels Vol. I, p. 590). "An ever clearer insight into all theoretical questions is necessary to free from the influence of traditional inherited world outlook" (Ibid p 591)." The significance of the theory is that there is understanding of the line of march, the conditions and then ultimate goal general—results of the proleterian movement". (*Communist Manifesto*, pp. 64-65).

It is a fact that sometimes the noblest and the loftiest ideas find no realisation in life. Hence, the problem of relation between theory and practice is very important. Any "contempt of theory is evidently the most certain way to think naturalistically and therefore incorrectly." (Engles, F., *Dialectics of Nature*, p. 81). A nation that wants to climb the pinnacles of science cannot possibly manage without theoretical thought (*Dialectics*, pp. 60-61); because theory is people's experience generalised in their consciousness, the sum total of their knowledge of the objective world. The development of theoretical investigations enabled people to penetrate deeply into the essence of natural phenomena and to create a constantly changing scientific picture of the world. The success of practice or practical activity largely depends on our precise knowledge with regard to the law gaining the motion in those phenomena of reality which we wish to change. (P. V. Kopnin, "Thought and Action" *Proceedings of Indian Philosophical Congress*, 1957, p 111.) Thought is a special form of human activity in which object is only reflected in the conscious mind. Theorising is a purposeful spiritual process by means of which we acquire knowledge of an accurate and adequate reflection of the reality in the form of abstractions and not as sensual concrete images. In theory, we deviate from the immediacy of the object. However, this does not mean that theory does not enable us to obtain knowledge of concreteness in all its complexity. Every scientific theory does not directly originate from immediate requirements of practice, they can also arise from the interior logic, like Theory of Reflexes in Physiology. Theory of Relativity in Physics, theory of Quantum Mechanics etc. But this cannot justify absolute independence of thought from the requirements of practice. The independence of thought is only relative because theory is ultimately rooted in practice. It is true that there are certain progressive ideas and theories in the world, for whose practical implementation, conditions have not yet matured. However, the ability of human thought is the gnostic basis for its errors. Man is only actually free when he acts on the basis of the law which he has come to know. Knowledge is the necessary prerequisite for the attainment of freedom. But the laws of internal logic are also ultimately based on practical action. Even scientific foresight and development of society in terms of material and moral culture is impossible if it detaches itself from the immediate practice of today. It seems that truth of thought lies within the sphere of practical activity, because thought springs up from the requirement of practical human activities and this is the criterion for truth of our knowledge. Practice not merely converts theories into true and false but also serves as a basis for their further development. Practice proves the objective truth of thought but sometimes it is incapable of fully conforming or disapproving all the existing theoretical constructions. Of course one cannot check every thought with the results of action, for the progress of scientific knowledge would be impeded. We can determine the truth of our ideas by establishing their conformity or non-conformity with other scientific principles. Theoretical knowledge is necessary for attainment o freedom, but knowledge alone is not sufficient. What is necessary is an energetic activity of the people, their determination to resist evils and injustices. Great social changes always come as a result of the practical revolutionary activity of the people. The best and the noblest ideas remain merely ideas if they are not assimilated by the masses of the people, and people do not act in conformity with the ideas. (Kopnin-Ibid., p. 121).

V

Thus our whole life is a process of action. We live by action and without action there is no life, there is no experience, there is no thinking. Thus "thought is action" (J. Krishna Murti, *The First and the Last Freedom*, London : Victor Golloncz 1956, p. 50). Our life is a sum of actions or a process of actions. Consciousness is action. Action creates the actor and the actor comes into being when there is some result in action. Thus action, actor and result is a unitary process. But the problem is whether an action is brought by an idea or does action come first and then we build idea around it. If the idea comes first, then action merely confirms to an idea, and therefore it is no longer action but imitation (J. Krishna Murti Ibid, p. 52). In this way action is the handmaid of an idea. Ideas and mere ideas overburden the society with idealism. Not withstanding, this practical difficulty in accepting this position, there is theoretical difficulty also : Can ideas ever produce action or do thoughts merely mould and therefore limit action ? If action is produced by an idea then there is no freedom for man. If the idea is supposed to shape action, then action can never bring about freedom from miseries because before idea is put into action, we have first to discover how the idea came into being. Idea is the outcome of a thought process which is the result of S-R phenomena. It is the response of memory, which is always conditioned being in the past.

But can there be action without ideation ? Spontaneous action or uncontrolled action is like that or action when the idea ceases. But the idea ceases according to Krishnamurti only when there is love. Love is not conditioned. We cannot think of love, it is not an experience. Therefore, there is no gap between love and action, as there is between idea and action. As long as we cling to ideas, we are in a state in which there can be no experiencing at all. It is only when the mind is free from idea that there can be experiencing.

VI

Thinking established its superiority over action at the dawn of the history of philosophy, for it claimed the privilege of being concerned with 'reality', whereas the process of action was relegated to the sphere of 'appearance'. To them thinking is an instrument and not merely an ornament. Things are what they are experienced. But experience does not exist independently of nature, it is just an outcome of the interaction of an organism and its environment (*A Philosophy of Living*, Shriniwas G. Sathay, Asia Publishing House 1963, p. 34) Now, since experience is itself considered in terms of interaction of events, there is no room left for dualism of any sort between body and mind, thought and action. Everything can be viewed under the category of interaction of events. For an empiricist there can be no such thing as thinking, because it is not itself a sensation or an impression. According to Dewey, we think when habits break down and we are compelled to find effective means for guiding our actions. Kantian ethics divorced conation from action. Dewey on the other hand combies theory and practice (Ibid., p. 40). For him morality is to be determined not by motive alone, nor by consequences alone but by

Theory and practice are like *form* and *content*, not opposed to *foreseen and intended consequences* which meet the needs of the situation. According to Dewey, thinking arises in action but he does not go on to establish that thinking is impossible unless we presuppose action and the ultimate test of truth lies in its dependence upon the rightness of action. His view of the origin of thinking is too objective to be of much help in action. He overlooks the fact that in the formation of habits there is already involved some amount of thinking. It is therefore circular to explain thinking as arising from conflict of habits. According to Dewey, everything is determined by interaction of events. But this amounts to saying that man is not free to choose, hence morality becomes impossible. Hence we can conclude that Dewey's notion of interactionism between theory and practice is not a reliable guide either to thinking or to action.

VII

Unreasonable activity and inactive mind are things that can both be found in life. The divorce of thought from practice is detrimental for both. Such practical people as the Russian communists are deeply concerned about philosophy. A man's creed matters. We cannot destroy the social disease if we do not know how to repudiate the fallacies of the system. It is why philosophy is a compulsory subject in the curriculum of all schools and colleges in the Soviet Union. True, "no creed comes into existence as a mere development of thought and out of all relations to social needs yet once a creed is born it has an activity and force of its own". (*A Text Book of Marxist Philosophy*, Ed. John Lewis, Agra : Lakshmi Narain Agrawal, 1946, Introduction p. 26). They agree with Chesterton that "we think that for a general, about to fight an enemy, it is important to know the enemy's numbers, but still more important to know is the enemy's philosophy" (Ibid p. 25). There has been no revolution without a renaissance. "The time of big theories was the time of big results" (Ibid p. 26). Those who belittle philosophy are mediocrities, opportunists and vacillating. Philosophical tendencies are always closely related to the sociopolitical movements of the day. Totalitarianism in thought leads to absolutism in practice. "Sound theory is only the eye of practice and practice is blind without it." (Ibid p. 27).

each other but related into one. There is a union or fusion. But as Mao-Tse-tung says "If we have a correct theory, but merely prate about it, pegionhole it, and do not put it into practice then that theory, however good, has no significance. Knowledge starts with practice, reaches the theoretical place via practice and then has to return to practice." He further says that the "actual function of knowledge is a leap from rational knowledge to revolutionary knowledge. (*Philosophy and Social Action*, Jan. 1973, p. 85). History shows that separation of theory and practice has led to the stagnation in science and technology. Theories have emerged as a result of requirements created by practical problems. Even before the Taj was built it was conceived in the mind of some great architect. On the other hand, practice also determines the aim and direction and tasks of theories. This is proved by the history of science and human civilization. Random thinking is different from problem-solving thinking. Thinking, as Stebbing says, is a strenuous task. So theory to be theory must come as a basis for practice or else it is a mere intellectual pastime. According to the advocates of speculative thinking practice would debase the dignity of thought but this is wrong. In fact practice lends theory clarity of purpose and objectivity.

Hence, we can conclude that the relation between theory and practice is not one-sided. Theory is not mere registration of results yielded by practice, it also influences practice in a far-reaching manner. The basic function of theories is to determine the direction of society. The results arrived at through practice become theory which finds application in the practical actions of the people. Thus mutual influence or interaction goes on. Theory and practice form one indissoluble unity; they do not exist without each other, on the other hand, they constantly influence each other. Practice is the basis of these interactions. "Theory is directly woven into the language of real life" (*Soviet Dictionary of Philosophy*, p. 449). Gandhi also said "we need not be afraid of ideals or of reducing them to practice even to the uttermost". (*Speeches and Writings of Mahatma Gandhi*, Fourth ed., G. A. Nateson & Co., Madras p. 355). To him, "new facts should be made to suit the principle, instead of changing the principle to suit existing facts." (*Young India*, 26.1.22).   Bhagolpur University

THE VITAL CIRCLE : THEORY AND PRAXIS

R. Panikkar

The price Man has paid in the last four millennia for his increasingly individualized awareness of the world outside and within himself has been not only an augmented estrangement from the divine and the cosmic, but also an ever-swelling chasm between theory, the work of the mind, and praxis, human action in the world. We seem to be nearing the close of at least a second full round on an ontological spiral and becoming acutely aware that if the first cycle could be called *Nature*, and the second *Culture*, then, we are now slowly entering a third, post-cultural, era.

Whatever this may be on such an overall and universal scale, I would like to show that 1) the theory-praxis problem is one of many similar paradoxes; (2) the problem arises because it is approached in a dialectical way; and (3) the question may open up for us a more encompassing insight into reality.

You will not find if you do not seek. Yet you would not seek if you had not already found.

You will not love a thing if you do not somehow know it. Yet you could not know if you did not love beforehand.

You cannot understand if you do not pre-understand. But pre-understanding is already a kind of understanding. The hermeneutical circle is well known.

You would not believe if you did not know that you have to believe. Yet you would not know that you have to believe if you did not believe. How can one believe in God, for instance, if one does not know at least what God means and that he exists?

This same fundamental situation is also manifested in the relation between theory and praxis. A theory which is not based on genuine involvement and does not lead to action is hardly a real theory. On the other hand, every action presupposes a theory and leads to yet another theory. There is no true contemplation without action. Every true contemplation is the fruit of an action and leads to further action. Nor is action authentic without contemplation. Every action is the fruit of a prior insight and it subsequently opens up new vistas.

The entire history of Man is full of such paradoxical situation. If these are pushed to the extreme, we find ourselves in a vicious circle without exit.

But there is an alternative : a vital circle. My hypothesis is two fold- :

Negatively : These types of relations appear paradoxical because they are approached in a dialectical way : i.e. as relations governed by the principle of non-contradiction and thus reducible to the classical *sic et non* formula. To have considered them solely in dialectical terms has not only divided reality and real processes into almost irreconcilable halves, but also implies a rather restricted epistemological and ontological assumption, namely that our mind is *only* dialectically structured and that reality has the same structure as our mind. I submit that this does not need to be the case : the human spirit does not need to function only dialectically, nor does reality need to be only dialectical.

To begin with, if the approach is not dialectical there is no difficulty in admitting the existence of two antagonistic principles: Theory and Praxis, Reason and Will, Knowing and Believing, Loving and Understanding. These, like Body and Soul, Life and Death, God and Man do not need to be dialectically opposed. In fact there are no longer oppositions the moment we stop considering them dialectically. Understanding is not reached by dialectics alone.

Let us take our case : Praxis is not human praxis if it is not a fully human act. And there is no human act as such without a minimum of consciousness and self-consciousness, so that praxis is praxis only if theory is one of its elements. Analogously, the other way round. There is no theory as a real act of the human intellect if disconnected from all that Man is. And Man is by being in the world, which implies actions and interactions with the human environment and cosmic surroundings. Thus praxis is an ingredient of theory.

Positively : Such paradoxes reveal what I call the vital circle that characterizes reality on all levels. The impasses which our mind finds should lead us to consider that perhaps what needs examination is the nature of the claim of our mind to be the only criterion of reality.

Our image of the vital circle could perhaps be justified like this : Any ultimate problem is ultimate precisely because it allows no room outside its own premises in which to approach it. We may deny to a particular question the atribute of being ultimate—like saying that the question about the 'last' star in an astronomical universe makes no sense. But if we allow the question we cannot contradict it in the answer—like saying that there is 'empty space' 'beyond' the 'last star'. (Either it is not the 'last' or if it is the 'last' there is nothing beyond). To have put dialectical thinking outside the problem it wants to solve—as if such thinking were as absolute and, or a pure given—, is the philosophical flow in such an approach. From this point of view, the notion of ideology is a necessity. Ideology is, then, the ultimate carrier of meaningfulness in any sociologically given situation. But, it is no longer a necessity to let the ideologies themselves also follow dialectical laws. If we say that a galaxy is the entire universe, we cannot then construct a theory of galaxies by following the intragalactic behaviour of one of them.

In other words, the *radical relativity* of all that there is demands that we approach real problems so that the polarities found in reality—such as the between praxis and theory—are not converted into ontological dualism (38).

How to do this ? First of all : by becoming aware of the problem. Secondly : by conquering a wholistic consciousness, a new innocence as it were, a more encompassing synthesis in which the subject-object dichotomies are overcome, and, last but not least, by allowing 'philosophical congresses' and human conventions to put together our human efforts for a more truly universal wisdom.

University of California

Panel Discussion I

BUDDHISM AND VEDĀNTA

Chairman : T. R. V. Murti

Participants :

(1) R. K. Tripathi
(2) G. N. Joshi
(3) R. C. Pandeya
(4) Hajime Nakamura

THE MĀDHYAMIKA AND ADVAITISM

R. K. Tripathi

It seems to us that every system of philosophy, whatever be its approach, not only claims to give us truth but also gives some criterion of truth and falsity implicitly or explicitly. What is necessary is that the criterion should not be wholly a priori and arbitrary but something already known in experience, otherwise it will be not only useless but also unintelligible. In this regard, Indian systems of philosophy have the merit of keeping close to experience. In this paper we propose to bring out the relation between the Mādhyamika and the Vedānta by analysing their views on truth and falsity.

I

The terms truth and falsity are used in various contexts. This makes it obligatory for every one to decide and declare in which sense he has chosen to use these terms. We may distinguish three different senses in which these terms are used. Firstly, the term true is sometimes used in the sense of correspondence between a statement or a belief and a fact. If the statement or the belief corresponds to a fact then it is said to be true otherwise it is false. If some one says that the Bank is closed today, then this statement will be true if the Bank is closed and false if it is not closed. Similarly if someone says that the Bank is not closed today, then the statement will be true if the Bank is not closed today and false if it is closed.

There is another situation in which the terms truth and falsity are used. This happens in the context of perceptual experience. When something is perceived as a snake and then as a rope, the first perception is negated by the second and we say that the snake is false and the rope is real. Here we are not concerned with a statement and fact but with two perceptions, one of them superseding the other; we are concernned here with the reality or unreality of an object given in perception. The incompatibility is between two perceptions and not between a statement and a fact. Here something is mistaken for something else or something appears as something else, and the appearance (snake) is said to be false when reality (rope) is known.

In the third kind of situation in which the terms truth and falsity are used, we have two statements having logical contradiction or self-inconsistency. It is based purely on the law of contradiction as the incompatibility here is neither between thought and fact nor between two perceptions but between two thoughts. For example, if it is said that a thing is real and unreal at the same time or is permanent and changing at the same time, it will be regarded as a self-contradiction. Such views or statements nullify each other and if one is taken as true the other becomes false and vice-versa. Both cannot be true.

So there is falsity in three different contexts; either when there is discordance between a view or statement and a fact, or when there is incompatibility between two perceptions, or when there is self-contradiction between two views. We are here not going to dwell upon the first kind of falsity as the Mādhyamika and the Vedānta seem to be concerned with the last two only. We will try to see why the Mādhyamika accepts the one and the Vedānta the other view and which of the two choices is really justifiable and tenable.

II

The Mādhyamika, it seems to us, does not accept falsity as incompatibility between thought and fact nor as incompatibility between two perceptions. He confines himself only to thought or views and regards inconsistency as falsity. All thought is classified under four categories (*Catuṣkoṭi*) that are formally exclusive and exhaustive. Then each view is examined and it is shown that each view has self-contradictory implications and is therefore false. No reference is made here either to any fact or any perception; only logical contradiction is taken to be enough. A view is false not because another view is true but because it is self-inconsistent, and all views are self-inconsistent and hence false. So it is concluded that the *tattva* is beyond all thought and speech. The Mādhyamika rejects only views of reality and not reality itself, because he is not a nihilist as he rejects nihilism itself as a view. He makes also a distinction between *samvṛti* and *paramārtha*. He insists on the negation of appearance for the realisation of tattva (*prajñā*). He is an absolutist.

Now the first question that arises is whether the Mādhyamika is right in confining himself merely to thought and to logical inconsistency? Is thought supposed to give us reality and can formal inconsistency give us falsity. In life mere logic (except in formal sciences like mathematics and logic) does not decide the question of truth and falsity as logic is purely formal; reality is always given in some experience. Let us concede that each view when analysed leads to self-contradiction. How then does it follow that self-contradiction is inapplicable to reality and gives falsity? It is true that two self-contradictory views cannot be simultaneously held, but why is it so? It is because reality does not permit it. It does not at all matter if we remain inconsistent in thought and do not have anything to do with reality. But if we have to deal with reality we cannot afford to be self-inconsistent. In other words if thought and reality are separated, inconsistency in thought becomes irrelevant and inconsequential. Self-contradiction in thought is intolerable because reality makes it impossible.

How does the Mādhyamika come to know that self-contradiction is the sign of falsity? Does he know the *tattava* before examining thought and finding it self-contradictory? If so, how does he know the *tattva*? And if he knows reality already how does it become necessary to examine thought and to reject it? If he does not know reality already, how does he know that self-contradiction is repulsive to reality? It may well be that contradiction is the very nature of reality. And if inconsistency is the mark of falsity can we say that consistency is the mark of reality? But in that case one cannot go beyond thought as the Mādhyamika wants to do, because consistency being just a formal characteristic is found only in thought. If something beyond thought is accepted, one may ask: how do you know that there is something beyond thought? How do you even make a distinction between thought and reality? Does the Mādhyamika accept any other *pramāṇa* like *śruti*? Obviously not.

Then can thought itself in any way show a kind of self-transcendence suggesting something beyond itself? How does it do it? Self-transcendence of thought can be shown only if a distinction between thought and perception or some immediate experience is admitted as was done by Kant. The Mādhyamika does not do it. In order to declare thought as false, at least the possibility of reality reflecting itself in thought is to be admitted. If even the possibility is not there then thought is simply irrelevant and empty and not false. Unless some possible relation between thought and reality is there, the two fall apart from each other and thought cannot be given even an appearance of reality.

III

It is because of the above difficulties that the Vedāntin does not accept merely logical error or inconsistency as the mark of falsity. He chooses to depend on perceptual experience to discover the distinction between truth and falsity. It is in perceptual experience that reality is universally believed to be given, Perception may be mistaken or wrong but the mistake here is not logical but experiential. The snake is false not because there is any logical inconsistency in accepting it as real but because the experience of the snake is nullified or superseded (*bādhita*) by the experience of the rope. The correction is not merely logical or formal; there is a kind of experiential immediacy here not to be found in thought. It may be said that there is no difference between perception and thought except of degree. But that would be a wrong position. First of all, the distinction is universally accepted. Secondly, there is a kind of immediacy in perception but not in thought and that makes for a qualitative difference between the two. Finally, if a distinction between perception as some thing in which reality is given and thought as something in which nothing is given is not made then it will not be possible to make a distinction between knowledge and imagination or pure thought. It is wrong to suggest that thought becomes objective when it is consistent, because consistency is purely formal having nothing to do with reality.

It seems to us that the Mādhyamika like Hegel takes all experience to be thought. There is no consideration given to experiences like perception and sleep. If all experience is just thought, then it is obligatory for the Mādhyamika to show how at all distinction is made between perception and thought ? If there is nothing but thought then there will be neither a way of nor an urge for going beyond thought. So the Vedāntin seems to be right in taking perceptual experience as the source of our awareness of the distinction between truth and falsity.

There are other advantages also in starting with perceptual experience as our model. It gives us not only the nature of falsity but also the nature of reality. If the false is what is *bādhita* or cancelled by superior experience then reality is what is never cancelled (*trikālābādhita*). And then it becomes our duty to find out whether there is or not something which is neither cancelled nor cancellable at any time. And if there is something like that, it would be real. If however there is nothing like that then there will be no reality. Vedānta discovers and gets it confirmed by *śruti* that self or *Ātmā* as pure consciousness is neither cancelled or cancellable as all cancellation presupposes it; the self is *trikālābādhita* never cancelled in all the three times.

IV

So the Mādhyamika has two options : either all experience is reduced to thought or some experience which is not just thought is accepted. If all experience is thought and thought does not have even a tangential relation to reality, then it cannot be called false; it may be irrelevant but not false. Mere logical inconsistency is not falsity. Of two absolutely unrelated realms, thought and reality, one cannot be called false and the other real. That would require prior knowledge of reality and would oblige us to show the relation between the two. That reality is known in immediate experience requires us to admit that we know what an immediate experience is, otherwise the statement will be unintelligible. That would mean that everything is not reducible to thought. So the Mādhyamika has to admit immediate experience like perception as distinguished from thought. And if he does so, it will be obligatory for him to consider perceptual experience and to analyse it to see what can be learnt about truth and falsity, because it is in perception that reality is said to be given. Mere thought, unless it is shown that it is related to reality, can give us neither the idea of truth nor of falsity; in thought we can have only consistency or inconsistency. It is for this reason that the Mādhyamika is not able to give even an instance of falsity; he cannot point out in what sense the world is false.

The Mādhyamika makes a distinction between *vyavahāra* and *paramārtha* and holds that it is only by negating *samvṛti* that we get the *paramārtha*. That is why it is said that there is no difference whatsoever between *samsāra* and nirvāṇa as *nirvāṇa* is nothing but knowing the *samsāra* truly. It is further heldth at *samvṛti* covers or conceals reality. If so, can we say that the *tattva* (reality) is the gound of appearance (*samvṛti*)? The Mādhyamika would demur to say even this, because he does not want to say anything about the *tattva*. If he says as the Vedāntin does, that reality is the ground of appearance, then there is no difference between the two. But to be able to say this one has to depend on perceptual experience and not on mere thought. If however the *tattva* is not said to be the ground of appearance then it would be either because there is no *tattva* or because it is not related to appearance. Either position is damaging to the Mādhyamika. In the first case, appearance itself will be reality and in the second, there will be dualism of appearance and reality and there will be no need to negate appearance.

The Brahman of Vedānta has three special features: it is the ground of the universe (*adhiṣṭhāna*), it is one with our true self (*Ātmā*) and it is *saccidānanda*. None of these is explicitly admitted by the Mādhyamika. If the *Śūnya* is not taken to be the ground of the universe, *avidyā* or illusion cannot be made adequately intelligible. If the *Śūnya* is not taken to be our very self there can be nothing to explain the immediacy of *tattva* or *prajñā*. And if the *Śūnya* is infinite, then it has to be *ānanda* also, because *ānanda* is nothing but absolute infinitude (*yo vai bhumā tat sukham*).

It seems to us therefore that the two extreme views regarding Vedānta and Śūnyavāda, namely that the two are one and that the two are completely different are false. We can only say that the Vedāntic view is implicit in Śūnyavāda and that it has to be made explicit. It can be made explicit only if Śūnyavāda admits the above three features. And for that, the

Mādhyamika will have to abandon its purely logical or dialecitcal approach and will have to start with perceptual illusion as the Vedānta does. Though the Mādhyamika does not accept the Upaniṣads, it does depend upon the Buddhist tradition and so the acceptance of tradition is common to both. And if the acceptance of tradition is dogmatism, both are equally dogmatic.

Hegel and Bradley in the West try to arrive at some kind of absolutism purely on the basis of reason or logic. But neither Hegel nor Bradley is able to point out whether and how the Absolute can be realised, and their Absolute remains purely an obect of thought or imagination. Some people see too much in Bradley's doctrine of sentient experience or feeling and try to draw it near Advaitism. But they fail to see that Bradley's Absolute being infinite cannot be realised by our finite intellect. The Mādhyamika differs from Hegel and Bradley inasmuch as he does not make appearances the asset of the Absolute, but at the same time he fails to point out any experience in which we have any contact with the Absolute. In other words the the emphasis of the Mādhyamika is only on transcendence and not on immanence while Advaitism emphasises both.

Banaras Hindu University

THE BASIC IN INDIAN PHILOSOPHY

G. N. Joshi

Indian Philosophy is rich both in content and variety. All kinds of philosophical approaches ranging from Materialism and Atheism to Pantheism and Transcendentalism are seen in Indian Philosophy. Every philosophical view and systeme has its own peculiar metaphysics and epistemology. There are incongruent metaphysical ideas contained in the various systems, and the systems also emphasize different aspects of the process of knowledge. The *Āstika* and *Nāstika darśanas* differ in their metaphysical perspectives and sometimes hold polar views also. Vedānta and Buddhism hold entirely opposite views; the one emphasizes permanence, unity and monism, while the other stresses change, diversity and unreality. Vedānta firmly believes in the turth of a positive Reality described as *Brahman* and *Ātman*, while Buddhism asserts that ultimate reality is Nothingness, Void, Emptiness, and it denies the existence of *Ātman* as an enduring entity. Vedānta undermines the importance of the world and phenomenal existence as unreal (*mithyā*), and extols the supreme significance of the Brahman (*Ātman*) as the ultimate, eternal and permanent existence. Buddhism also denies reality to the ever-changing world as an enduring thing, and considers it to be illusory, without asserting anything unchanging, enduring and permanent behind it. Vedānta erects its system on the rock-foundation of the eternal and unchanging Brahman, while Buddhism stands on the evershifting sands of the momentary reality. But both, Vedānta and Buddhism, agree in holding that the empirical world has only phenomenal, changing and transitory existence, and it does not enjoy the status and significance as ultimate reality.

The empirical world and material and phenomenal existence are looked upon as only partially real, not only by Vedānta and Buddhism, but even by other systems such as the Sāṁkhya,

Jainism, Nyāya-Vaiśeṣika and other systems except the Cārvāka.

It is a peculiarity of the Indian view-point that almost every philosophical system and school gives littlei mportance to the life of the world and to nature, believing that the visible, tangible and phenomenal reality is not the final and perfected existence. The phenomenal existence has only partial reality and it amounts to be a phantom, a shifting shadow, and so possesses only deceptive and elusive significance. The world is only a passing show, a transitory place, for camping for the eternal pilgrimage of the immortal self. The worldly life is not accepted as enduring and capable of giving to man lasting satisfaction and enduring peace and tranquillity.

It is quite true that change is inherent in the very constitution and nature of the physical world and social life of man. Buddhism has rightly emphasized the changing nature of the world and generalised from the incessant change the momentariness of the entire reality. Change is a matter of actual experience of each sensible being, and life is characterised by the capacity for change and movement. Buddhism has rightly asserted that change, visible and invisible, is the essence of reality, and anything like endurance and permanence is a fiction of the human mind, and hence imaginary, unreal and illusory. Buddhism asserts a thoroughgoing change and nothing else. But it cannot be all.

Other systems like Vedānta, Sāṁkhya, Jainism, Nyāya-Vaiśeṣika, Mīmāṁsā etc. do not completely reject change, but assert that change is partially real, but there is another and superior kind of reality which is not governed and affected by change. They assert the existence of an enduring, unchanging, intransitory, permanent, immutable and eternal something, designated in diverse ways by different words. Almost every system considers a state of experience characterised by peace, contentment, tranquillity, equipoise, equanimity, imperturbability, stability, insensitivity to all kinds of pleasurable and painful experiences, and blessedness as ideal, and aim at realising it. It will be found that an experience of a kind of deconditioned, unlimited, unpurturbed, free, undetermined, peaceful and delightful consciousness is the aim of the most of the sys tems expressed directly or indirectly, in different words, such as

The Basic in Indian Philosophy

Mokṣa, Mukti, Kaivalya, Apavarga, Niḥśreyasa, Nirvāṇa, Liberation, Salvation, Freedom etc. All the systems look upon the life of man in the world as utterly imperfect, miserable and incapable of yielding enduring delight, peace, satisfaction and a sense of fulfilment. They use their own metaphysical positions to underrate and condemn man's life of sense and mind in the world, and extol and prescribe the value of a transcendental kind of life. All of them believe that the ultimate reality is one and the same for all, though it is interpreted in different ways by different schools. The real knowledge of the ultimate reality develops in man a kind of consciousness which is described above. The state of consciousness of the perfect man is of a universal kind, and its contents are beyond determination and description. It is truly said by many that there can and must be only one and one Reality for all, though it appears in infinitely diverse ways to many people, who too describe it in several different words. The Annapūrṇopaniṣad says "What is void (*Śūnya*) to the Nihilists, is the Brahman to the believers in the Brahman, the same is the *Vijñānam* of the Vijñānavids, that very is the *Puruṣa* of the Sāṁkhyas, and God of the believers in the Yoga; it is also the Śiva of the believers in Śaiva traditions; it is the Time of the believers in Time alone, and it is both one and many, qualified and unqualified, at one and the same time. "This ultimate Being is the principle of all schools and it can be known by every one *in one's own experience alone.*" (3: 19-21). Thus, as it is pointed out very eloquently in this passage, the ultimate reality or Being is *one* and only one, and must be the same for all, though it is described in different words. It is indeterminable in character and hence transcends and eludes all possible description based on the mental conception and intellectual categorisation. All mental and intellectual (conceptual) thinking becomes inapplicable to it; hence it is said that the mind is incapable of grasping and expressing it, because it is wider than the human mind. What is true of the ultimate reality or Being is equally true of its experience or state of consciousness which beholds it. In fact at the highest stage the dichotomy of Being and thought, Reality and Consciousness or Object and Subject disappears, and the two are discovered to be identical. Therefore the experience of the perfect man, which may be said to be one of Mokṣa or Nirvāṇa, also can and should be *one and the same*, since any attempt to describe or express it in definite words and language will prove to be an attempt to determine the indeterminable, limit the illimitable, conceive the inconceivable and to describe the indescribable.

It is a special contribution of the Indian philosophers who advocate that by Yoga man can attain to the supreme state of consciousness, which relieves man from all his bondages. The Yoga has devised a new therapy by which it analyses the process of working of the mind, and it points out the way of freeing the self from the domination and influence of the Mind. The human mind has its own faculties of working such as perception, imagination, abstraction, conception, relation, memory, comparison, attachment to objects of experience, feeling pleasure, pain, aversion etc. The Indian philosophers do not trust the mind as an adequate instrument or agent of knowing the ultimate reality. Though the mind is very important and necessary for knowing everything it is not sufficient also for knowing the essence of reality. The mind has a tendency to distort and misrepresent the objects of knowledge, and to produce attachment and other passions, and finally cause afflictions to the Citta. Indian philosophers do not accept Mind as the final authority of knowledge. Unfortunately the human mind has serious limitations. It is highly flexible and plastic and it has a tendency to identify itself with its objects. It can be contaminated by the objects of its contemplation and it can conceal behind it the real self of man. As S. N. Dasgupta has said "It is, rather, the mind, and its activities by which the true nature of the spirit seems to be obscured so that the mind usurps the rightful place of the spirit." (Hindu Mysticism P. 69). Indian philosophers have always been sceptical about the functions of the human mind, and have maintained that the mind plays the main mischief in creating a belief that the perceptual (phenomenal) world is real. The Tejobindūpaniṣad says that the root cause of all our illusions and misunderstanding is the mind; all our volitions, sufferings, passions, anger, sorrow, the sense of time, multiplicity and diversity are all due to the mind only. It is the mind that is the entire world, and the mind alone is the greatest enemy. The mind alone is the greatest evil (5: 97-100). The mind obscures the steady consciousness of the self which is the real nature of man, and it makes man run after unessential and transitory things which are inherently incapable of yielding enduring peace, satisfaction and happiness to man. The mind makes confusion between itself and self and misleads man in his pursuits. Dasgupta says "All mental operations involve this confusion by which they usurp the place of the principle of pure consciousness so that it is only the mind and the mental operations of thought, feeling, willing, which seem to be existing, while the ultimate principle of consciousness is lost sight of" (Ibid, 68-69). The Yoga system has rightly realised the functions of the mind and therefore it insists on stopping the entire working of mind (*Citta vṛttinirodha*), and tries to dissociate the mind from all its objects. For that it prescribes a code of *Yamas* and *Niyamas*, which are measures that control the activities of the mind, and help the mind to withdraw its support to effect complete dissociation from the objects of the world, and thus it saves the mind from its involvement in the experiences and enjoyment of the worldly objects. This practice results into disinterestedness (*Vairāgya*) and asceticism (*Sannyāsa*), which is emphasized not only by Vedānta and Buddhism, but by all seekers of *Mokṣa*.

Thus it will be seen that the practice of Yoga is *basic* to Vedānta and Buddhism and other systems, athough they hold diametrically opposite metaphysical views. Dasgupta has said that philosophy came to the Indian sages *much later* than the actual practice of the liberation of the true self from the bondage of the association with all our socalled psychical states, ideas, feelings, emotions, images and concepts. (Ibid, p. 66). If philosophy is considered to be a rational explanation of man's all experiences, such a fundamental intuitive experience of unity, undifferentiated universal consciousness, peace, satisfaction, imperturbability, tranquillity, equanimity and happiness must be accepted as *basic* to all philosophers who have advocated the doctrine of liberation, *Mokṣa* or *Nirvāṇa*. All these systems have advocated the practice of major moral virtues such as Universal friendship (*Maitrī*), Compassion (*Karuṇā*), Cheerfulness (*Muditā*), and Detachment (*upekṣā*). Thus it will be seen that inspite of great opposition in their metaphysical views they are agreed on the basic truth of their intuitive unitive experience. They advocate the *same Yoga* or science of self-control, for attaining the highest and noblest state of consciousness, which is one of absolute freedoms in which there is complete absence of every kind of limitation, determination and which is nothing but eternal, all-pervading unconditioned consciousness, which is beyond the apprehension of the mind and intellect and incapable of linguistic description. *Nirvāṇa* appears to be negative unlike *Mokṣa*, but it is apparent. Both *Nirvāṇa* and *Mokṣa* are states of consciousness which are beyond description as their conceptualisation is impossible. But the final state of liberation is essentially a state of *Experience* and nothing but experience, and can be understood by itself alone, it alone can be and is *its own measure (Svānubhūtyekamānam)*. It is to be understood in its own terms. It is a state of perfection and complete fulfilment from which nothing lacks. The *Nirvāṇa* is described to be the kind of happiness (*Sukharāja*) in Sekoddeśa Ṭīkā. The final state of perfection and liberation is a basic and native fact of one's being of which mentalisation and intellectualisation is impossible and meaningless. It is to be felt by oneself in oneself.

It will thus be seen that inspite of all the divergent metaphysical views the spiritually oriented Indian philosophers and their schools have assumed a universal intuitive experience of undifferentiated, unconditioned and eternal consciousness and are united on following the path of Yoga and a code of universal morality for the attainment of this basic state of being.

Fergusson College,
University of Poona

Panel Discussion II

MYTHS AND SYMBOLS

Chairman : P. T. Raju

Participants :
- (1) N. S. S. Raman
- (2) R. C. Gandhi
- (3) Margaret Chatterjee
- (4) Peter Henrici

MYTH AND SYMBOL

N. S. S. Raman

During the last fifty years the relation of myth and symbol to religious experience has exercised the mind of thinkers, both theologians and philosophers all over the world. In an age of reason and science characterized by a kind of scepticism and partial disillusionment, it is but natural that we should try to understand and rediscover if, possible, the essence of traditional religion. The disillusionment with modernity is not to be understood in mere platitudes as expressed by the statement: "Ideas, logic, order, truth, reason,,—we give them all up to the nothingness of death. You do not know to what length our hatred of logic can make us go". In fact (as P. B. Medawar has commented somewhat icily)[1], many a tidy literary reputation has been built upon exploiting it. The significance of the symbol and myth to civilization has not been fully grasped, though the excessive emphasis on logic and reason has almost killed man's creative spirit. It appears that some thinkers have veered round to the view that if religion is to be understood at all, it cannot be through the revival of rational theology or of the logical foundations of faith or even by an analysis of religious statements, but through the variety of forms of expression which the human mind has been able to create—myth, metaphor, simile, parable, fable, allegory, ritual etc. All these properly constitute the realm of 'culture' (used in a somewhat wider sense than that of the sociologist or the anthropologist). At least these constitute a major part of human culture, the rational and the logical being but aspects of man's nature. Yet philosophy seems to stress the latter more than the former. Theology under the influence of philosophy has also fallen into the same state. In Indian philosophy, the Vedānta, which is by no means 'modern', has tended to ignore the mythical, the symbolic and the emotive in man's quest for self-expression.

Students of philosophy are well-acquainted with the controversies regarding demythologization. Since the days of transcendental idealism in Europe, the tendency had been strong to interpret religion in rational terms; but this has only served to deprive religion of its most important character. In religions like Hinduism, for example, in the absence of dogma and doctrine, mythology has come to play a significant role in religious experience along with ritual. This is true also of Buddhism, where inspite of atheism and over all scepticism, religion has survived because of a mythology built around the Buddha. If mythology and ritual are taken away from Hinduism and Buddhism the whole religious edifice falls to the ground.

It is true that philosophers should not take refuge in myth or metaphor, when philosophical thoughts are expressible in simple propositional forms. Some of these so-called myths may just be illustrative metaphors as in the case of many of Plato's so-called 'myths', a brilliant study of which was made by Stewart many years ago. Such illustrative myths are of course translatable in simpler forms of expression. I do not mean that myths should be capable of being logically analysed if they are to be made intelligible at all. Under the impact of religion, philosophers had learned to use language beautifully, and made liberal use of metaphor, myths, allegories etc., but under the influence of science the ideal of a proper philosophical expression is that it should be simple, precise and straightforward in its meaning. R. G. Collingwood has remarked that "the philosopher must go to school with the poets, in order to learn the use of language." I would amplify this statement: the philosophers must go to school also with religious men (not theologians) in order to learn to use language "in their way as a means of exploring one's own mind and bringing into light what is doubtful and obscure in it. This, as the poets know, implies skill in metaphor and simile, readiness to find new meanings in old words, ability in case of need to invent new words and phrases, which shall be understood as soon as they are heard and briefly a disposition to improvise and create, to treat language as something not fixed and rigid, but infinitely flexible and full of life."[2] The ancients did not care so much for logical form as we do to-day. They did not hesitate, like the Upaniṣadic thinkers, to use poetry, if necessary, to express their thoughts. Using poetry as a medium of philosophical expression would be unthinkable and even laughed at in the present day. Indeed the use of myths is regarded as very archaic. In our search for clarity we have allowed the literary affinities of philosophy gradually to fade away.

Indeed art and poetry have been called the "germinating centres of language"[3]. Religious consciousness finds poetry and myth quite expressive; thus the language of the Bible, of the Vedas or of other religious texts is neither scientific nor logical nor even metaphysical. Here one is guided more by what Pascal called the 'logic of the heart' than by reason. The ancient man thought less in logical or scientific terms, and more in terms of the symbolic and the mythical, and these find their expression not only in a recited religious text, but also in non-religious poetry of nature, myth, art, architecture and even music. The Vedas would be incomplete without the *Sāma Veda*. The question here is whether philosophy is a worldview (a Weltanschauung) or a system of concepts or a 'theory' of reality. In the Anglo-Saxon world, old forms of metaphysics are overthrown by the application of the principles of formal logic and by linguistic analysis. The significance of the symbolic in philosophy is nowhere so much conspicuous as in Indian philosophy (except perhaps in German philosophy influenced by the romantic movement). Hegel appropriately describes the symbolic as 'Alphabet des Weltgeistes'. Under the influence of Western thought Indian philosophy has fallen into the habit of regarding philosophy as ontology, as metaphysics, as ethics, as logic, as epistemology, as a criticism of science, and so on.

The task of philosophy therefore is to preserve its ancient heritage of the symbolic, as we find it in philosophical poetry, in dialogue, in art and in mythology. It is the task of philosophy also to bring into limelight the depth of this symbolism, and to make its meaning as clear as possible. Philosophers like Karl Jaspers have regarded the function of metaphysics as the investigation into the symbolic (as the 'reading of what Jaspers calls 'ciphers'). In the interpretation of the symbolic and the mythical, we cannot apply the principles of propositional logic. Who can for instance subject the great sayings of the Upaniṣads regarding Brahman (which have an aphoristic character), to linguistic analysis? What kind of analysis can bring into the forefront the force and depth of Naciketā's dialogue with death? This means that the tendency to classify philosophical ideas through 'isms' must also be given up, at least with reference to ancient thought. Such labelling is a product of the post-renaissance European mind, when philosophy was regarded either as consisting of so many different systems as the philosophers themselves, or as theories about the universe, or as criticisms of science. The various schools of the Vedānta, by applying logical criteria, and by applying rigorous rules of interpretation failed, in my opinion, to penetrate into the real meaning of the Upaniṣads and of the Bhagavad-Gītā. This may be the reason that in spite of the spate of the commentaries written on the above, there is a wide difference of opinion amongst the Vedāntins. This only shows that it is difficult to grasp the meaning of the symbolic by logic, however acute it may be. The symbol has really no ground on which it can stand; its meaning must be understood solely by a kind of experience similar to the artistic, though not identical with it. The appeal of the symbolic is partly and not entirely emotive like that of the artistic.

The myth as the expression of the symbolic has manifested itself more in religious experience. Indeed, in ancient culture, the distinction between philosophy and religion is very thin. In Indian thought there is hardly any distinction between the two. The myth (as one aspect of the symbolic) is used both by philosophy and by religion, though it has come to be more associated with the latter. This is so because philosophy is more identified with a systematic pursuit in accordance with the principles of logic. In the direct experience of religious consciousness, application of the philosophical categories of thought would make little sense. Hence the myth as we find in religious texts has a direct appeal. Philosophy is by nature interpretative and categorial whereas religion is based on personal faith. But in the ancient world such distinctions are superfluous, as the religious world-view was a philosophical world-view and vice-versa. The symbolic in its various aspects, particularly that of the myth, is inseparable from religious experience. As to how deep-rooted the mythical is in religious experience, is best illustrated by reference to Zen Buddhism, where the objects of discourse logically and even in terms of ordinary language are unintelligible, but to one who has been initiated into the fold, become clear and unquestionable.

In most cases of symbolism, the objects of the mythical symbol are vague and unrecognizable or inexpressible in words, like the ultimate reality of the Upaniṣads. But they become clear to the authentic religious experience. This is the reason why we should not try to reduce myths to historical facts. If we do, they lose their force. This would be particularly true of the socalled miracles, which sustain most religions of the world. They are not to be explained by the ordinary laws of reason; causal laws are almost inapplicable to such events. For this reason they are also not to be reduced to historical facts. But religious experience is built upon them, and without them religion would lose its force. So also the myths around the prophets and religious leaders are not built around only historical facts; applying a historical or empirical criterion to examine such myths may not lead us anywhere. Yet some persons have spent years in patient resesearch trying to find out if the myths correspond to historical facts. In the task of philosophical interpretation and criticism, the students of philosophy have to examine the great works of the past, in order not only to appreciate their literary worth, but to arrive at an understanding of their underlying thoughts which they cover with metaphors, allegories and myths. They may not always be successful in this task. A correct perspective for the study of symbolism in general and myths in particular will help in appreciation of ideas.

References
1. *The Art of the Soluble*, p. 80.
2. *An Essay on Philosophical Method*, Oxford, 1953, p. 214
3. Karl Jaspers : *Von du Wahrheit*, Munich, 1947, p. 917. He calls it *"Keimstatte" der Sprache*

Banaras Hindu University

33

SYMBOLS AND THEIR USERS

R. C. Gandhi

I

Suppose I am looking at an artefact, say a fountain pen. Insofar as I identify it at all as a fountain pen, my thought of the fountain pen, my contemplation of it, would have what I would like to call a minimal logical environment. I shall explain what I mean by this. My thought of the fountain pen, my contemplation of it, would be set in a context of notions and thoughts and ideas about what fountain pens are, what they are for—their use and function. The central contemplation of the artefact and this minimum context of thoughts—explicit or implicit—would be logically, and not associatively, connected. This context is what I call a logical environment. The fountain pen would also of course undeniably have an associative environment.

It is not only artefacts which, as objects of contemplation, exhibit a logical environment and, in this sense, point beyond their particularity. If I am looking at a tree, contemplating it, my thought must necessarily, whether explicity or implicitly, move around the tree in a context of thoughts and ideas and notions connected with plant life, its contrast with animal life, and so on. In this way the tree would point beyond itself. Any object of contemplation whatever—and it need not be a material or sense-perceptible object—would, in virtue of the fact that it is a certain *kind* of object, oblige thought to move beyond its particularity in a logical environment of notions and ideas connected with the character of the object. In this way, it would appear, all objects of contemplation point beyond themselves. But it is not *this* fact which makes an object a symbol. Nor does an object become a symbol in virtue of its associative power to compel thought to move in an environment of ideas and thoughts and images 'associated' with the object in diverse ways.

So what is a symbol, a symbolic object ? It is not an object of a particular kind in the way in which a plant or a rock are objects of particular kinds. Any object whatever can be used, regarded, seen as, etc. a symbol in some framework of thought or other—even a private (altough not logically private) framework of thought. A fountain pen can symbolize literature, the power and phenomenon of writing. A rock can be a symbol of stability or barrenness, a cat of cynicism and a dog of unquestioning loyalty, and so on. But what is the manner of 'pointing beyond itself' in virtue of which an object becomes a symbol ? I see a piece of rock. Associatively my contemplation of it may suggest the thought of stability or barrenness. But it is not in *this* way that the piece of rock can function for me as a symbol of stability or barrenness. Definitionally, the piece of rock could involve me in thinking about—literally-the hardness and stability of certain types of substances, the barrenness—in the literal sense of lack of vegetative growth on them—of such substances. But suppose, aided in the above ways to think about stability and hardness and barrenness, I contemplate *these* objects, these abstract objects, and permit my thought to move in *their* logical and associative environments. I would conceivably find myself contemplating the stability and hardness and barrenness of individuals, nations, attitudes, and what not. Now *these* thoughts would not definitionally or associatively lead me back to contemplate the piece of rock which was the focal-point of this whole movement of thought. But from these new thoughts I could—not definitionally or associatively—but *illustratively* go back to the piece of rock. When I have made this reverse illustrative movement back to the piece of rock, I can see that piece of rock (or any rock thereafter) as *symbolizing* the hardness and stability and barrenness of individuals, nations, attitudes, and what not. The piece of rock would suffer a profound imaginative transfiguration. I would see it as embodying these new thoughts, symbolizing them. My contemplation of the rock having developed in this symbol-generating way, I could say or think the following things : "Our nation is a house built not on a rock but on sand". (Notice here the parallel symbolizations of *house* and *sand*). "His hatred is unyielding, it is like a rock". "No ideas grow in my mind anymore, it is a piece of rock".

Symbols and Their Users

The thought of rock becomes available to me in these ways for symbolic (metaphorical) use—and so does consequently, the *word* "rock".

Take another example. The thought of a ship would definitionally and associatively yield the thought of being transported safely from shore to shore. If I now contemplate the thought of transportation from insecurity to security, which would be available to me in the logical and associative environment of the thought of safe transportation from shore to shore, I could illustratively return to the thought of a ship. And thereafter I could think of a ship symbolizing a religion, an ideology, a way of life, whatever. The *word* "ship" would similarly become available to me for symbolic-metaphorical use. I could say the words or think the thought "To escape the sorrows of the world, let us get on the ship of Buddhism", or whatever.

The manner of my return to the thought of a ship in the above example, and to the thought of a piece of rock in the earlier example, being modes of imaginative retrieval of these objects of contemplation and not merely associative thinkings of them, I could say the following : "The piece of rock (for example) is only grossly apparently, and not really, *merely* associatively generative of the general ideas of stability and barrenness. So it can be seen by me as not merely associated with, but *correlated* with, these general ideas. It is in this way that it symbolizes them for me, and could symbolize them to others in the same way". This way of explicating the symbolic character of non-linguistic objects is very closely analogous to the way in which, in the next section, I seek to explicate the symbolic character of bits of language.

(2)

Consider now the following question : "In what way do words, and other bits of language, acquire a symbolic character?" Take the word "tree". Obviously, if I were to think of this word, I would find myself moving in an associative environment (I am assuming that I am familiar with the word "tree") of thoughts and images and memories, etc., of trees and forests and so on. But it is not in virtue of *this* fact that the word "tree" has a symbolic character. A hot walk down a treeless avenue would also associatively yield thoughts of trees. But we would not want to say that a hot walk down a treeless avenue was symbolic in character—at any rate we would not want to say that it was symbolic in character in the way in which the word "tree" was symbolic in character. The word "tree" would also have—to borrow a phrase from J. L. Austin—a "perlocutionary" environment of thoughts about what effects its use could produce in the minds of people. If, walking in a desert, I shouted "tree", my utterance would very probably cause my companion to anticipate some respite from the heat, and so on. But it is not the perlocutionary effect-producing-power of the word "tree" that constitutes its symbolic character. Now the word "tree" also possesses what might be called—to use another phrase of Austin's—an "illocutionary" environment. In thinking of the word "tree" I would inevitably think, explicitly or implicitly, the thought that I could use the word—embedded in a suitable sentence to *indicate* the existence of a tree to someone, to *refer* to a tree in conversation with someone, to *describe* a tree, and so on. What is it to do these things —indicate, refer, describe, etc? Suppose I address the following words to you "There is a shady *neem* tree in the courtyard of my house". Would you think, in normal circumstances, that I was trying to *get* you to believe that there was a shady *neem* tree in the courtyard of my house ? Admittedly the completely unqualified, indicative, declarative, definitive, character of my utterance has the appearance of my actually confronting you with the shady *neem* tree in my house—the appearance of my actually *showing* you this tree. But this is manifestly only appearance, not reality. We both know this and know that we both know this. So my utterance—because of the completely open character of the pretence of "showing "involved in it—comes under the description of being an act of only grossly obviously appearing to be, but not really being, an act of showing you the *neem* tree in the courtyard of my house. You would interpret my utterance as an *invitation* to you to think that there was a shady *neem* tree in the courtyard of my house—as an act of *symbolically showing you the shady neem tree in the courtyard of my house*. It is in this way that the word "tree", or any other word, suitably embedded in a sentence, can be seen as a symbolic entity, a symbol.

There is a more straightforward way of exhibiting, making clear, the symbolic character of a word. Suppose I utter the word "tree" "to myself", as one says, sitting in my room from where no tree can be seen. Wouldn't I be constrained to regard my utterance as a completely give-away way of putting it to myself that I was confronted by a tree, contemplating it, thinking about it, etc? Having seen this I would readily interpret my utterance (strictly, I think I would here have to imagine that I had issued the utterance to an imagined audience, or that an imagined speaker had issued it to me) as an imaginative invitation to me to contemplate a tree, think about it, etc., i.e. as a symbolic way of getting, or trying to get, me to do these things. The above explication of the symbolic character of the word "tree" could, with suitable supplementation, apply to the case when I do not *utter* the word "tree", but merely *think* of the word.

If my explication of the symbolic character of words has been sound, the symbolic character of complex units of language could be similarly explicated. The symbolic character of an indicative utterance—I have already hinted at this—would consist in its being an act of symbolically—i.e. "not really" causally efficaciously-showing to an audience that something was the case. The symbolic character of an imperative utterance would consist in its being an act of "not really" (i.e. only appearing to be and that too in a completely give-away way) getting, or trying to get, an audience to do something. And the symbolic character of an interrogative utterance would consist in its being an act of "not really" (in the above sense) getting an audience to complete an utterance initiated by a speaker.

Of course pieces of language have an associative and "perlocutionery" environment. But to see the symbolic character of language is to see the deliberate and open frustration of the capacity of these environments, and also an exploitation of these capacities, in the employment of language. Just as seeing the symbolic character of non-linguistic objects involves an excursion into their associative environment and a consequent retrieval of these objects in a profoundly imaginatively transformed manner. There is here an analogy between my accounts of the symbolic character of non-linguistic and linguistic objects; but I would not press this analogy too far.

Before concluding this section, I would like very briefly to indicate my dissatisfaction with two proposals about what constitutes the meaning (i.e. at least the symbolic character) of linguistic expressions. In the *Tractatus* Wittgenstein suggested that the symbolic character of language consisted in the relationship of structural reduplication that obtained between the configuration of the parts of language and the configuration of the parts of what it symbolized. Now the configuration of the elements of one human face is a structural reduplication of the configuration of the elements of another human face, but this does not make one face a symbol of the other. Consider now the more recent attempt to explicate the meaning (i.e. at least the symbolic character) of a linguistic expression in terms of the notion of the "rules of use" of the expression. Now it seems to me that such "rules of use" can only be—and this has been said, for instance, by Ryle—linguistic fiats, prohibitions, instructions, etc., whose symbolic character as bits of language stands as much in need of explication as the symbolic character of the linguistic expression they purport to explicate.

(3)

Consider the words "I", "You", and "He". What is the symbolic character of these words? Clearly they are words, and they must have a symbolic character, they must *mean* something. But here one feels uncomfortable. One wants to say that these words do not stand for anything, that their meaning consists in their function, their use. One wants to say—and this has been said—that the essential function of the word "I" is that of introducing a speaker to his audience. And that the function of the word "You" is to identify one's audience, and to refer to him. And that the function of the word "he" is to identify, refer to, etc, a third person. Now this is all right as far as it goes. But consider the following question "What is the function of the symbol 'I' in soliloquy?"

One might say that soliloquy is imaginative communication and that my use of the symbol "I" is soliloquy is that of imaginatively introducing myself to any imagined audience. In order to examine the correctness and adequacy of this response, let us look at another question. Suppose I were to ask you the question "Who am I ?" You might think I was completely mad in asking this question. But suppose that tolerance prevails and that you persist in reflecting about my question. You might, with a slight tone of exasperation, say "You are my friend". But suppose I persist and ask the following question, "But who is this person of whom you say that he is your friend ?" You might now, in a physicalist mood, say the following: "The person sitting in front of me". Suppose I persist and ask "Who is the person sitting in front of you ?" I think you would very likely simply say "You !". I might then, in a spirit of resignation, say "I see, you mean I am myself". I think you would agree with me here, and not even think that I was indulging in philosophical eccentricity. Now clearly in saying "I am myself" I am not introducing myself to you. So the "introduction" theory of the symbol "I" breaks down here. Consider now the role of the *thought* "I, myself" in soliloquy. Here I would not be under pressure to say that in thinking the thought "I, myself" I was imaginatively introducing myself to an imagined audience. What would I be doing ? I would be thinking of myself as myself—this is what thinking the thought "I, myself" or the thought "I" comes to. But what is it to think the thought "I" in this manner ? I believe that the thinking of the thought "I, myself", or, more simply, the thought "I", involves the performance of a complex and fundamental imaginative act. It is not the imaginative act of introducing myself to an imagined audience. It is the imaginative act of imagining that a speaker had addressed me, non-referentially picked me out. I must explain what I mean by the phrase "non-referentially picked me out". When you address me, initiate communicative relationship with me, you do not, *in* addressing me, refer to me. You could refer to me in conversation with me only if communicative contact were already established between us. You cannot, *in* establishing communicative contact with me, refer to me. And yet you undeniably identify me. You put me in possession of the thought "He means me". This is what I mean by non-referential identification of a hearer by a speaker in an act of addressing. Now when I think the thought "I" I imagine that a speaker non-referentially identifies me. And insofar as non-referential identification involves no reference to me, it cannot involve, on the part of the speaker, any thought what *sort* of creature I am, i.e. any predicative thought about me, although in other contexts he may of course think of me in this way. *In* addressing me, a speaker must think of me as myself, a unique but bare particular. So in thinking the thought "I" I imagine that I am being non-referentially, non-predicatively, thought of. I imagine that I am being regarded, quite simply, as myself. So I cannot imagine, in thinking the thought "I", that the symbol "I" is the name of anything at all. I might try to say that "I" names, *means*, "myself". But the notions of "I" and "myself" are not different notions. Paradoxically, the symbol "I" symbolises itself. This would be one way of interpreting the tautological thought "I, myself", of which I have been trying to give an account above. This is a strange situation. When I enter most intimately into myself, to use Hume's language, I find that the thought "I, myself" is what does most justice to my hankering after a deep and final self-acquaintance. And yet this self-acquaintance turns out to be thoroughly imaginative in character. It turns out to be an imaginative act in which I am regarded as myself in imaginative communication—i.e. in imaginative symbolic activity. The symbol "I" seems to symbolise the most fundamental symbolic activity, the act of addressing, the act of initiating symbolic activity.

A similar, apparently disturbing conclusion, can be reached regarding the symbol "You". The primordial use of the word "You" is in an act of addressing, in an act of establishing communicative contact. I have only to use the word "You" in relation to you in order to secure a communicative relationship with you. And if, in response to my vocative use of the word "You" in relation to you, you were to ask "Who do you mean?", I would, in the last analysis, simply say "You", thereby again simply addressing you: i.e. non-referentially, non-predicatively, identifying you, thinking of you quite simply as you. The symbol "You" also appears to symbolize the foundational symbolic activity of initiating symbolic activity, i.e. an act of addressing.

What about the symbol "He"? Now insofar as I think of a man as a third "person", i.e. think of him as a personal subject, I must imaginatively cast him as the object of an act of addressing, i.e. as the object of non-referential, non-predicative, thinking. Thus insofar as I think of him as him, a unique but bare particular, I must employ the symbol "he" or "him" again as symbolising symbolic activity itself, i.e. the act of addressing. In saying all this I do not wish to imply that we *are* bare particulars, that we have no attributes at all. What I wish to assert is that the self-imposed illusion that we are quite simply ourselves, unique but bare particulars, lies at the heart of our communicative mode of life. It is precisely this self-imposed illusion which enables us also to think of ourselves predicatively. Because, given the availability of the concepts "I", "you" and "he", the function of these symbolas that of introducing oneself, identifying another, referring to yet another, etc. becomes possible. The association of attributes with ourselves, and the ascription of attributes to ourselves, becomes possible. If what I have been saying above is at all sound, then in their most fundamental character, although not in all respects, the symbols "I", "You", "He" do not succeed in moving beyond the realm of symbolization. It would follow from this that we cannot say that these symbols stand for any *thing*, any *object*, whatsoever, (Can't it be said that "I", "You", "He", stand for the unique non-attributive beings we imaginatively see ourselves as, when we most intimately enter the thought of "ourselves"? But seen as non-attributive beings, we are not beings of any sort: we are "I", "You", and "He". So "I", "You", and "He", if they stand for anything at all, stand for themselves. And this is a baffling conclusion. Of course, the proper names "Peter", "John", "James", can stand for persons with attributes. But the predicative notion of a person becomes available to us because of the original, non-predicative character of the nations of "I", "You", and "He"). The self-imposed illusion—an indispensable illusion which lies at the heart of communicative activity, is the thought that we are unique but bare particulars, essentially capable only of being non-predicatively thought about: i.e. that we are souls. Were

I sufficiently clear about the nature of myths, I would have sought to introduce the topic of myths by elaborating upon this theme of the imaginative necessity of regarding ourselves as souls. But I do not see my way clearly here. I shall conclude merely by saying that an attempt to understand the symbolic character of personal pronouns must inevitably lead one to consider the myth of a soul.

Delhi University

MYTH AND SYMBOL

Margaret Chatterjee

Some reflections on demythologisation in an Indian context

My comments on myth and symbol take off from some preliminary remarks made by me in the course of a paper entitled "Does the analysis of religious language rest on a mistake?" published in *Religious Studies* (London) in December last year. I may be forgiven for repeating these take-off points in order to get what I have to say going. The issue concerns the relation between the historical and the mythical in religious traditions. In the historic religions, in addition to certain objects and gestures seen as symbolic we have the phenomenon of *events* seen as having a symbolic significance. God's mighty acts are symbols of his powers. The events on the Mount of Transfiguration, the rent veil in the temple, indeed the Resurrection itself—are all symbol-laden. This rootedness in the actual provides an empirical anchorage under the umbrella of historicity and the historic religions have in fact usually set great store by their freedom from myth and legend.

Reflecting on why Bultmann raises little if any interest in India I located the following possible answers: (1) the non-historic religions have no problem of sorting out the historical from the mythical. This is the case even in Buddhism which happens to have a historic founder figure. (2) the need to demythologise is felt only when myths no longer live. When myths are part of a culture-pattern re-enacted through the calendar-year of festivals, the need is different, e.g., it may be needed to preserve the myth apart from its historical accrescences (say, caste), or to utilise myth for new social purposes. Only when a myth is already dead or dying does the question of removing the traces arise. There are also in third world countries interesting instances of new myths being grafted on to old ones.

'Demythologisation' no doubt is a technical term used by Bultmann within the context of a particular type of theologising. It must not be confused with the Comtian secular conception of a 'coming of age' which enjoins the complete rejection of myth and legend, the complete rejection in fact, of numinosity in any form. Three sets of special circumstances which attend Christian theological reconstruction can be singled out:— (1) Thanks to the prestige of the sciences efforts to find a rational basis for faith have been on the increase. (2) New translations of the scriptures and related documents have opened out questions of hermeneutics in a more radical way than nineteenth century theologians like Schleiermacher could anticipate. (3) The branch of theology known as Christology is rooted in the belief in the 'contemporaneity' of Christ. This makes a constant reinterpretation, a constant plumbing of the depths and reaching out to the heights not only desirable but obligatory for the Christian in his changing situation from day to day. Of these factors the only one that we can find parallels to in Hinduism is the first, that is to say, we could describe for want of a better term, as the thrust towards modernization. The paper explores whether we can find in the thinking of some of the great thinkers in India in the nineteenth and twentieth centuries *an analogue* to the sort of re-thinking done by some of the Christian theologians.

We find that the criticism of myth and the re-casting of myth was the work of (i) literary men (ii) reformers. The contributions of Rabindranath Tagore, Bankim Chandra Chatterjee, Raja Rammohun Roy, Swami Vivekananda and Mahatma Gandhi are briefly pinpointed in this regard. It seems clear that myths are capable of reinterpretation from age to age. Reformist Hindu thought shows two special characteristics relevant to our theme:— (a) the infusing of myth with nationalist sentiment (b) the attempt to rethink *dharma* shorn of at least part of its mythic context. Both of these were by no means academic exercises, but had important practical consequences in the country. It could also be said, perhaps, that in almost all these cases (the Brahmos being the main exception) significant moves were made towards bridging the gap between 'popular' religion and the higher reaches of philosophico-religious thought, a gap which had hitherto been taken to be an inalienable characteristic of Indian religious life.

Delhi University

SPECIAL LECTURE

By

Andre Mercier

SCIENCE AND RELIGION, AND THEIR COMPLEMENTARY NATURE

Andre Mercier

Grossly speaking, there are the following opinions availing among contemporary philosophers.

There are such, like Bertrand Russell (cf. his *History of Western Philosophy*), who consider philosophy as being a kind of no man's land situated between religion and science, whereby both science and religion eat their way through philosophy and hence destroy and reduce the kind of thought exercised in philosophy to less and less.

There are also such as think, especially according to Marxism, that there should be no such thing as religion (since it is but an opium for the people), so that only science concerns philosophy and hence (they say) philosophy has in the long run to become "scientific".

There are also such, like Mahadevan as a representative of Advaita, for whom philosophy, indeed also somehow between science and religion, expands over the borders of these two enterprises and hence integrates them more and more so, that finally both religion and science will dissolve into philosophy. This list is not exhaustive. I shall not dwell here on the evidence, that in these views, neither art nor morals—also enterprises comparable with science and religion—are given any attention by such representatives of various currents of thought, although in my opinion art and morals ought to be taken into account in a comprehensive argument. But it will simplify the argument if they are left out of the consideration. Therefore I confine myself here to the relation, which I believe exists, between philosophy, science and religion.

I have just quoted three opinions and I confess that their characterization has happened in a most cursive way, so I would understand such contentions as would claim, that they are over-simplifications of the intentions of individual authors or schools.

Also, it will be said, such a simple classification cannot be made, for the multiplicity of schools and opinions renders the situation much more complicated than that.

On the one hand, I could agree with such criticism. On the other hand, let me recall that simple presentations, even oversimplifications have the advantage of showing more acutely either the good aspects or the bad ones of opinions which somehow can be envisaged under the specific points of view in question.

When I consider the first one, I ask myself, in case it were true that philosophy is being eaten at both ends, how it can be then, that there is still so much philosophical substance to be consumed after two and a half thousand years. For there is no doubt that there are in our days an astonishing number of philosophers who do find subject matters for reflexion and, among them, quite a spirit of creativeness. I have once met a logician who declared that science is a finite piece of knowledge. Yet very few people utter such opinions at all. Now, on the contrary, philosophy is perhaps by definition—whatever its right definition may be—an infinite source which on account of its infinity will never be reduced to such a tiny bit of material, that the procedure of its assumed consumption will appear to be at an end. But even if that were the case, I am not so happy at looking at the image given, for to my mind, to simply put philosophy between the two will-be-greedy enterprises like science and religion is not a true picture of the facts. Indeed, is not philosophy rather a kind of reflexion which stands on a level different from both scientific research and the contemplation and adoration of the Divine? In any case, it is not, I believe, any encyclopaedic knowledge measurable by its content: hence the picture of being eaten or invaded does not apply.

There are for instance specific activities called either philosophy of science or philosophy of religion, whereas 'science of philosophy' or 'religion of philosophy' do not make any sense, unless philosophy were made to (b) science—in which case we are led to the second view to be discussed in a moment—or philosophy were made to (a) religion, which seems contradictory since, for sure, philosophy should in the mind of all those who consider themselves philosophers be at least a critical enterprise, whereas religion is non-critical (meaning that it is not an activity of the critical mind) because the activity of any kind of criticism assumes a subject who acts somehow critically upon, or towards, objects or at least interacts with these objects by keeping sufficient independence from them to allow for judgements to be passed, whereas the foundation and formulation of religion do not rely upon judgements passed by the subject, on the contrary, in religion—from the contemplative character assumed by the mystic source at its very origin—judgements, if at all comparable with the first modality of judgement, are being passed upon the subject by a capital Being encompassing all plural beings, which means that no criticism can be incorporated in its workings. Hence, if anything of the nature of a critique is developed around religion, then it becomes not religion itself, but e.g. history of religion, or something like a theory of religion as might be developed in so-called comparative religion, or, at its highest, precisely philosophy of religion, and that shows again that philosophy cannot just be put at the disposal of, either religion, or, again, science. For that reason, I would reject the whole medieval tradition of Western philosophy which made philosophy ancillary to religion: I believe that it was disastrous to the activity of the mind to maintain such an opinion. Perhaps—I venture to say—even Bertrand Russell has fallen into the trap of that historical fact though he himself was a great opponent of the Catholic Church. Yet he had a deep feeling for mysticism as can be recognized from his writings, especially on the foundation of mathematics.

The same contention would apply to any attempt to make philosophy ancillary to science.

I should like here to insist upon the fact that, for me, a will-be religion which were devoid of mystic at its very root, would not be a religion at all, it would be nothing but ideology.

Such authors, who, it seems to me, do not recognize the authenticity of religion as a cognitive manifestation of the mind, do not either sufficiently emphasize or even assume that philosophy is apt to exercise a corrective influence on religion: this is different from, being ancillary to it. So, as a first contention, I would reject an opinion which would, so to speak, put in some way or other philosophy between the tungs of science and religion.

The second view, according to which there is no sense in

any religious activity other than falsifying the right aspirations of man and/or society, whereas science is an authentic, even the only authentic step of the mind towards an ever greater knowledge, seems to me to be delusive, because firstly it is not true that religion, if rightly comprehended, is illusive; secondly there are more steps than just science, which cannot be reduced to science proper and which also lead, in their own way, the human mind towards authentic knowledge. I have dwelt on these matters at length in books and papers, so I shall not repeat my arguments here. I beg at this point simply my audience to keep it in mind and I shall confine myself to disputing the rightfulness of a view according to which all activity of the mind, including philosophy, has to be scientific if it is to lead to authentic knowledge. Especially, I feel unable to give any sense to a phrase like 'scientific philosophy'. For instance, Adam Schaff, in a yet unpublished paper to appear in *Philosophers on their Own Work* claims that philosophy has to become scientific in order to be acceptable, following a procedure of 'generalization' from principles known in the various specific sciences, thus becoming a kind of science which, he claims, is however itself no more a specific or, as he puts it, a particular science. I must confess that firstly, I do not understand how that generalization actually works or could work; secondly that I do not believe philosophy to be any generalization of anything already accepted, and thirdly that philosophy is not just the result of a process of transcending an already established or recognized subject-matter. Philosophy is totally different in nature from the kind of activity called science. It is not a 'knowledge' of any kind accumulating itself in ever more numerous books on our shelves, for how could it then e.g. reflect especially upon knowledge itself.

By the way, there are scholars who would like to consider religion as obtaining if science and especially the logical structure applying to science and religion be transcended in a way such that a 'limit' between science and religion would be traversed. In a conception like that, science would be left behind and it would let by and by religion take over the activity of the mind. Also that view seems to me a wrong picture of the difference between science and religion as well as of their mutual relation. Indeed, if religion would just obtain by a procedure of transcendence like that, how could the mind, i.e. the subject, do else than keep its power of judgement and remain the judging subject; in other words, how could the subject renounce being what it was at the beginning of the procedure? It is a hopeless way to try to continuously leave science and win religion instead. Furthermore, to correct this by saying that the procedure of transcendence is not to be assumed continuous but should be conceived as a jump over a barrier, is also fallacious for, if there is a barrier, a limit establishing a hyatus, then the two enterprises are in one way completely distinct, like two countries where two different languages are spoken or two different laws apply, and their relation is not established by a one way transcendance: much rather they allow for a choice between two approaches which may or may not admit of an alternative to be, eventually, made more precise. Moreover, if-as I however do not believe—science were to yield to religion, it would so to speak make science obsolete when religion obtains—a view which, I know, is shared by many religious minded people, especially among a certain form of protestantism. One could accordingly, so to speak, be a scientist on week-days and a religious man on Sundays. But if religion were to be the better and science the worse enterprise, all days in the future should then become sundays and we would not use the nights between week-days and Sundays to let the procedure of traversing apply forth and back. Are not both eventualities evidently ridiculous? Furthermore, the double procedure would make religion obsolete when science obtains,—again an opinion which, I think, is an untenable as the converse one.

I shall finally try to explain in a moment that it is neither correct to distinguish science from religion by shifting in between anything like philosophy, nor to have them just disconnected either by a dimensionless limit or by a more or less broad no man's land endowed with no apprehensible existence. I shall at the same time also try to demonstrate that science and religion do not either make each other obsolete or contradict each other.

Incidentally, if from both science and religion each would make the other obsolete under specific circumstances, then both would have to be considered obsolete not only under such circumstances but at all, since they have in their own way each a universal significance, and this would eliminate them both from the field of an actually authentic activity of the mind. Who would believe that?

Perhaps the adepts of some kind of Advaita Vedānta believed it.

Indeed, from the point of view of Advaita, there is no dualism, —which, in a popular manner, could be interpreted by saying that there is not the distinction between science (as the objective mode of cognition) and religion (as the mode of participation into the cognition of the Divine), for—as e.g. a representative like Mahadevan would, I believe, put it,—philosophy might be used to designate that enterprise of the mind which itself would swallow by and by both science on the one hand and religion on the other. This sounds like the opposite of what is described in B. Russell's view. This, it seems, can be interpreted as an apriori accomplished liberation from the appertenence of the individual either to the activities of science: or to those of religion.

It is not my intention to dwell on Advaita, especially since it is not at all my field and he who really knows what it means would soon show that I am a mere amateur. Here again, it was meant as a paradigmatic simplification. However, some criticism may be uttered against a view which first recognizes science and religion as facts and then wants or declares them to be suspended or eliminated by a philosophic attitude like the one of non-dualism. For it requires, as Gabriel Marcel has put it, at least a 'second reflexion' which of course any individual is free to accept as the only one by which he intends to dwell, but which by no means suppresses in any final manner the first kinds of reflecion manifested in science or in religion. It is, in my opinion, an artificial, or if you please a non-compulsory way to eliminate or at least to avoid a thing which is there. It answers neither the question as to why these two modes are practised, nor the question whether they are compatible or alternative to each other, etc. It simply evades the problem. Yet problems should be eluded neither by principle, nor by convenience.

Moreover, I do not agree that philosophy, or a particular philosophical attitude, can suppress, or swallow, or make obsolete either religion, or science, or both. Activities like these, which cannot be denied and which have real consequences for man, cannot be just disposed of like that. They are meaningful, they are not illusory, they even make many people happy, or unhappy according to circumstances, they contribute to man's integration into the totality of the world. Even Gabriel Marcel, who nearly or seemingly discarded science by declaring that all its concepts have the character of artificiality—whereby the artifice is to be positively, and not negatively understood, viz. as construct—was careful enough to acknowledge the doings of science as meaningful, though he preferred the way of religion, and as near as possible to mystics within the Catholic faith, for his own guidance.

In a paper published in *Religious Studies*, I have been bold enough to trace the seemingly paradoxical character of religion back to the attempt made by the supporters of religion (of any religion) to artificially connect the fundamentals of the religious attitude precisely with the fundamentals of the scientific attitude, these two attitudes being however totaly complementary (but not incompatible, please). Here, the word artificially means : by the invention of doctrinary elements which are borrowed from an alien modality of thought. Rather than using the denomination of attitudes, I have decided to call them modalities, as I have explained in my published works. The word modality should not be understood in that connexion as it is in Aristotle's logic. I use it in a most comphrehensive sense.

Indeed, I have explained several times that cognition can be exercised along two fundamental modalities.

One modality is the one of judging. Within this *judicatory* modality, one does not restrict judgements to the mere utterance of propositions assumed to deliver a value of truth as do most analysts and logicians. By judgement, I mean the establishment of any value implying truth, or the beautiful, or the good (or any combination of these like injustice) by a subject acting within a concrete field of action. There are three fundamental modes of judgement: the objective judgement of science (and of science alone), the subjective judgement of art (and of art alone) and the communicative mode of morals (and of morals alone) allowing for the disclosure of the three cardinal values just quoted. Since I have repeatedly explained the difference between these three modes, established their authenticity, shown their specific outcomings and led them back to the original situation of man facing the task of cognition, a few words will suffice.

Man's primordial situation which makes out of him what I have called *homo inquietus* is that of discovering by painful evidence his isolation from everything else than his immediate existence. This is what makes him a subject facing objects, in their plurality and diversity as well as in their unity, the reality of which he deeply feels before he does anything about it. Being isolated, he experiences the need to re-establish a link with that reality.

Fundamentally, he can choose between two principal attitudes to do so: one is by judging, the other by refusing judgement and replacing it by the acceptance of being judged himself. These two modalities or attitudes I have given the names of the modality of judgement and the modality of contemplation.

Why call the first one like that needs so to speak no comment. The word judgement is popular enough, whereas what contemplation renders is less easy to conceive. *Templum* means originally the area surrounded by a line (drawn in sand or materialized by an enclosure), within which everything is sacred, and wihtout which sacredness is not at hand. Owing to the sacredness of the area of the temple, people ought to purify themselves before getting in, the purification ruse being physical or spiritual. *Contemplation* is therefore the attitude of being together with what is sacred, of even submitting one's self to the sacred.

Now there are such as deny that there is anything sacred. They have no experience of it. One even meets such people e.g. among scientists, though most great scientists including contemporaries have an experience of the sacred and deplore the phenomenon of the gradual loss, since antiquity, of the feeling for the sacred—as is by the way described in one of my books.

The sacredness of all Being, of the reality of everything, is for me one of the *prime evidences* with which knowledge has to reckon. So—to my mind—the whole of the universe is a huge temple, and I feel due to try to keep pure within its unlimited realm. But this sacredness need not necessarily be always taken into account. Science qua science does not take it into account, whereas contemplation qua contemplation does so fundamentally.

Now, the only mode of cognition valid along the contemplative modality is that called mystic. In mystic contemplation, it is the subject which is being judged by the capital Being which encompasses everything. The capital Being is under circumstances called God, especially when its personification is assumed Yet, the easier modes to handle are the ones where the subject himself passes judgements upon objects, and along that judicatory modality the objective mode peculiar to science is the wider spread and was nearly always the most popular on account of its easy testability either by everyday experience or by experiment requiring some skill. Thus the temptation arose to apply the objective mode or at least to assume the judicatory modality or attitude valid even along the other, alternative modality, i.e. for the subject to pass judgements even though actually judgements are passed upon him. This is paradoxical. It leads to utterances known as dogmas, to behaviours known as rites and the like, all things typical of religions which always contain whole codes of such atterances, rules of behaviour etc. veiling the original ottitude which is contemplation and nothing but contemplation.

This is what makes religion a business not free from ambiguities, even from contradictions, blunders and other deficiencies. It contributes to persuade people who only notice these incongruities to reject religion and to condemn it as delusion. Theology ought to find sufficient reasons to explain these deficiencies, but it has at times sought rather to justify them. I am afraid, that could not satisfy those who are philosophically minded.

From what I have said follows, to my mind, that science and religion are not contradictory, only the attempt to make religion work like an objective enterprise leads to such deficiencies. The non-contradictoriness between the two is linked with the fact that the pertinence of each of them is distinct: one is objective, the other not, the latter is contemplative in nature, the former not. Pythagoras, it is true, invented—it is at least reported so—the term 'theory' to designate a procedure which is closely related to the contemplation of the Divine. In French, the word *theorie* is up to our days also used to designate a procession of people, e.g. marching towards an altar or a shrine. That conception, I believe, results from the certainty people in antiquity had of the sacred nature of all research of the valuable connexions between beings. But we should rather not compare the scientific and the religious enterprises. It is better to say that the scientific an dthe *mystic* enterprises do not exclude each other, they complement each other. Complementarity does not mean exclusion, on the contrary, there is a competition involved by which one adds to the other and reciprocally. But the simultaneous assumption of both attitudes is not a matter of course and should never follow a procedure by which one is submitted to criteria specific of the other. It is not an easy matter, either it requires a sense of harmony between the two if they are to respond to each other satisfactorily. This mutual response has a very simple name, viz. *responsibility*. Hence responsibility is not a problem for morals or ethics, though it may imply morals together with other steps like science and mystics. Also the problem of responsibility has retained my attention at length and repeatedly. I think that if philosophers would take the trouble to forget about received views and to try to put the concepts in a better reciprocity than has been done up to now rather than to try to explain them in their isolation as is so much the fashion especially in analytical work, they would gain in insight and come nearer to an understanding of, e.g. the relation between so tremendously important concepts as science and religion.

University of Berne, Switzerland.

PART II

I

MORALITY AND CULTURE

N.K. Devaraja

The question, how, if at all, is morality or moral life related to culture ? may be answered differently by different thinkers depending on their respective conceptions of morality and culture. Thus the term culture may be so defined as to exclude not only morality but also religion from its range. This would happen if cultural life is conceived as consisting in the pursuit and enjoyment of aesthetic values and in the observance of rules and manners appropiate to civilized living. The relationship between morality and religion is equally uncertain : quite a few religious traditions conceive the religious goal to be beyond good and evil, i.e. to transcend the sphere of action characterized by moral conflict. It is not possible here to raise and discuss the many controversial issues regarding the meaning of the terms morality, religion and culture and their existential bearing on one another. What I propose to do within the limits of this short paper is to set forth my own views on the inter-relationship between the modes and directions of life indicated by the terms morality and culture. Religion may be alluded only to the extent to which it has a bearing on the moral and the cultural life of man.

Cultural life, as conceived by the present writer, consists in the pursuit and/or enjoyment of the values that affect the quality of human personality, or the quality of man's spiritual being. The values in question should be distinguished from the utilitarian values which latter contribute mainly to man's survival and his effective existence in natural and technological environment. Another important distinction between the two sorts of values may be drawn by saying that while the utilitarian values have reference to competitive goods, the spiritual or cultural values are, generally speaking, non-competitive. Thus while my aspiration to be wealthy and to hold a position of power or prestige is likely to put me in conflict with other aspirants to the same or similar gains or benefits, my desire to pursue knowledge or moral excellence does not generate any comparable conflicts. It is only when I seek the prestige or recognition or fame attending the acceptance of my views that I find myself in conflict with other workers in the field. Recognition and fame or prestige and influence, may however, be looked upon as values directly or indirectly connected with utilitarian benefits leading to comfortable living in the world. Here it may be noted that genuine and earnest workers in the field of knowledge are generally free from the disturbing sentiments of jealousy and envy.

In the third place the production and/or enjoyment of cultural values involves an element of awareness which is pleasurable and to some extent shareable. Thus competent or properly trained persons find a common source of contemplative enjoyment in a work of art or thought or in a virtuous deed.

It should not be supposed that the cultural values have no relation whatever with utilities or utilitarian values. While literary taste is not equitable with the possession of literary masterpieces, the cultivation of the former obviously depends on access to the latter. In our money economy a person needs to be economically secure and well to do in order to be able to buy books, paintings and musical instruments. A certain charm of manner is to some extent incompatible with the harshness of the struggle for existence. And a large part of active virtuous life, such as that of a Gandhi, has to occupy itself with the realm of utilities where justice is sought to be secured and injustice to be eliminated. Still, the distinction between the utilitarian values that contribute mainly to the actor's comfortable living and the spiritual values that tend to enrich and ennoble or qualitatively improve his personality, remains.

Culture, we are saying, is what affects the quality of my spiritual being. One important aspect of my spiritual growth or progress is the enrichment of my conscious life. This enrichment is effected through education, i.e. through the cultivation of the arts and the sciences. Left to himself, even in the modern environment, the individual is likely to learn but little about the history of mankind comprising not only political history but also social and economic history and the history of the arts and the sciences. Nor can one, by himself, learn much about the geography of the world and the dimensions of the astronomical universe : we inherit through education the vast treasure of aesthetic awarness and scientific knowledge that have accumulated slowly by virtue of the creative labours of hundreds of gifted individuals. Here it may be noted that most of the religions do not seem to attach importance to the acquisition of the aforesaid types of awareness and knowledge. Quite a few religions of the world have been frequently hostile to the cultivation of the arts and/or sciences. Thus, Christianity remained prejudiced against science during the past several centuries and Islam was unfriendly to such arts as sculpture and drama. This may imply that there is some sort of antagonism between culture and religion. Likewise, one may see a conflict between the pursuit of culture and the pursuit of moral excellence.

According to us, however, the perception of the antagonism or incompatibility between culture on the one hand, and morality and religion on the other is due to faulty conceptions of the latter. Morality and religion, rightly conceived, are aids to cultural life; they also constitute important aspects of that life. This point can be brought home only by a deeper analysis of the nature of man as the creator and enjoyer of the diverse types of values.

Man is essencially a value-pursuing being. He seeks constantly to create and enjoy values. These activities are carried on with varying degrees of awareness and conscious effort. Pursuit of values in the form of activity directed towards the realization of objectives or ends beneficial to the organisms seems to be characteristic of living beings as a whole. This is the reason why biological and physiological phenomena lend themselves to be explained with reference to their utility for the organism. Freud has shown that even the so-called neurosis aims ultimately to enable the patient to rid himself of the tension of repressed wishes. As a conscious being man seeks either to produce utilities leading to comfortable existence or to create and enjoy spiritual values contributing mainly to the enrichment and qualitative growth of the human personality.

We shall now attempt to investigate the inter-relation between the aforesaid two aspects of the cultural life of man, i.e. between the enrichment and qualitative improvement of man's cognitive life through varied experiences relating to the visible phenomena. During the course of his active, utilitarian life man is brought into contact with innumerable objects and their varied functional manifestations. However, these contacts and experiences can become the source of enriched psychical life only to the extent to which the person concerned is able to take, so to say, a sort of disinterested interest in them. A distinction should be drawn between the comforts yielded by objects and situations and the sense of enriched being produced by the same. Such sense, we are suggesting, is promoted only when a person takes a detached, aesthetic view of things. Such a view implies one thing more, viz. the sense of meaningful connexion among things and situations, the meaningfulness in question being of a non-utilitarian type. Speaking from the view-point of cognition, a distinction may be drawn between unconnected items of information and scientific or systematic knowledge. The latter alone may be said to contribute to the enrichment of man's spiritual personality.

The pursuit of systematic connexion among pieces of information is science; scientific quest, properly so called, however, is not possible without a measure of detachment. A like distinction obtains between sporadic encounters with the beautiful on the one hand and systematic pursuit of beauty through the creation and enjoyment of the arts including literature on the other. In this connexion another equally important fact about the cultivation and enrichment of spiritual life may be noted: such a life involves not only the impulse and the effort to disclose or establish systematic connexions but also to cultivate the attitude of detached contemplation towards experience as distinguished from sporadic acts of detached observation and reaction. A rich spiritual life, according to us, is not possible without such attitude towards the utilitarian order of values.

The attitude of detachment towards what is merely useful is the mark of the aristocratic man. Traditionally, the aristocrat has been the person belonging to the ruling or the rich class. However, a member of the bourgeois class may be altogether bereft of the aristocratic temper; a miserly man, however rich, cannot claim the aristocratic virtues. A real aristocrat can afford to be indifferent to what are considered to be the petty utilitarian concerns. But the traditional aristocrat cares a good deal for the larger concerns affectng his position and prestige in society. The spiritual aristocrat, on the contrary, is indifferent to utilitarian concerns because he has cultivated a taste for the higher order of values, aesthetic, intellectual, moral and or religious. The greater the person and the intenser the quest for truth or beauty or goodness or holiness in his life, the greater is his indifference to the values that are merely utilitarian. In the life of such a man detachment towards the lower, utilitarian order of values is due to the attraction felt by him towards the higher spiritual values.

Thus understood the attitude of detachment should not be taken to be a negative one. The attitude in question stands not for the negation of life but for the negation of life tied merely to the needs and satisfactions of animal existence. Here it may be noted that the so-called civilized life does not necessarily imply the transcendence of the utilitarian order of values. The spiritual quality of a man's life is not materially affected by the mere fact that he satisfies his animal needs in relatively more complicated ways with greater sophistication, subtlety and refinement. The amenities of civilisation contribute to greater comfort and luxury, and to greater complexity of life and behaviour; but they do not necessarily and automatically improve the quality of man's spiritual being. A modern ruler or diplomat may be as revengeful and cunning as his counterpart in a less developed society; only the behaviour and the manoeuverings of the former would be more complex, subtler and outwardly more refined than those of the latter.

Practically all the spiritual qualities of man, i.e. the qualities that improve his spiritual being, are rooted in the sense of detachment. Indeed, the capacity for detachment is what places man above the order of the animal world. The energies of the sub-human species of living beings are generally exhausted in their pursuit of the means of subsistence and their struggle for survival against their enemies. Man differs from them in his capacity to rise above those needs and to save time and energy for looking around him in a spirit of detachment or detached wonder. The sense of wonder, which, characterizes the child, the artist and the philosopher alike, is indeed one of the important expressions or byproducts of the spirit of detachment. Our aesthetic and intellectual values owe their incidence largely to our sentiment of wonder, and the delight accompanying the creation or contemplation of these values is attainable only by those who are capable of standing aside from utilitarian involvements.

Another manifestation of the spirit of detachment is the sense of justice which lies at the basis of our moral consciousness. A man residing purely in the world of utility is essentially a selfish person. In order to be able to see the justice of another person's claim as against one's own, it is necessary that the concerned individual should be capable of looking and going beyond the circle of his own selfish interests. Having gone beyond that circle the person concerned finds it possible to have an objective view of the situation and to connect the claims of other persons with their deserts. In general, justice consists in balancing the claims of different actors against the creative effort and labour put by them severally in the production of the utilities or values being considered for distribution. As already stated no person who lacks the capacity or inclination to look beyond the order of utilitarian values can aspire to have a spiritually or culturally rich personality. On the other hand the man who is endowed with the aforesaid capacity and has also cultivated the inclination to live in and enjoy the non-utilitarian orders of values is bound to develop the sense of moral propriety. Ultimately, the prevalence of the moral order in a society is a necessary pre-condition of active production and enjoyment of all types of values including the utilitarian ones.

The above account of the moral attitude may lead one to think that the so-called moral values are merely the instruments that facilitate the production (and distribution) of other values. Such a conclusion is implied in the utilitarian or teleological theories of ethics. What these theories fail to explain is the intuitive perception that the practice of virtue is an end in itself and that virtue is its own reward. The truth is that the aristocratic virtue of disdainful indifference towards petty utilitarian affairs is one of the important marks of the superior man; another mark of such a man is his concern to extend protection to the weak and to punish those who seek to exploit or mis-appropriate the labour, property or achievements of others. It is noteworthy that the aforesaid qualities of the superior man have been traditionally ascribed to the saviour or the Avatāra in the Indian tradition. This goes to show how the power to rise above the utilitarian order and to save others from being absorbed and crushed within that order is regarded as a mark of excellence by mankind.

The attitude of detachment towards utilitarian values exists in its most developed form in the religious person, the traditional saint or sannyāsī. The personality of the saint is marked by the total absence of struggle and tensions that characterize the lives of the worldly persons involved in anxious pursuit of finite or perishable goods of diverse kinds. The artist and the philosopher, as also the man of justice or morality, may still retain limited attachment to utilities and the values, such as power and influence, indirectly related to the comforts and amenities of worldly life. Although the saint too continues to have needs associated with bodily existence, he is mentally unattached not only to such mundane values as wealth, position, fame and the like but also to the will to continued existence, the *āśrava* known as *bhāva* in Buddhist literature. This does not imply that the saint harbours any desire for self-extinction. However, a real saint need not be and ought not to be indifferent to the troubles and miseries of creatures suffering from want and privation, ill-luck and disease, injustice and ignorance. A real saint, while behaving as a true stoic and a Sthitaprajña with respect to his own afflictions and misfortunes, acts as a compassionate Saviour and Bodhisatta in relation to other living beings. As a Sthitaprajña, or one who is endeavouring to reach the ideal of the Sthitaprajña, the saint comes to incarnate in his behaviour the true aristocracy of the spirit which refuses to be disturbed by the vicissitudes of historical existence, his own and even that of nations and of mankind; however, as embodiment of compassion he is moved to meaningful action at the sight of suffering and injustice of all kinds. Probably completely moral life is not possible without the religious spirit as described above. It seems that a virtuous life of heroic dimensions tends to merge into religious life. Such a life involves absolute commitment to the ideal or cause of justice, and is possible only for one who slowly prepares himself to stake all his claims to mundane gains and comforts.

Insofar as worldly possessions and the privileges of leisure gained by virtue of those possessions are indispensable or necessary for the pursuit of the arts and the sciences, it seems that there is an element of conflict between that pursuit and the pursuit of moral and religious excellence. The conflict, however, relates more to the active part of the two kinds of life than to the attitudes of the persons involved in those pursuits. Relatively speaking the moral and religious persons are more visibly associated with the realm of action and fulfil themselves by acts of service and compassion. The artist, the scientist and the philosopher, on the contrary, need more leisure and solitude to cultivate and use their respective talents. In the earlier stages the religious man, too, needs to prepare himself silently for the life of renunciation coupled with compassionate action. But in general true religious spirit need not involve a conflict between the attainment of spiritual excellence and the exercise of love and compassion.

Ancient Indian thinkers did not visualize any conflict between the pursuit of knowledge involving reflection and contemplation and the life of active service to living beings in general and the fellow humans in particular. This is particularly true of the Mahāyāna Buddhist conception of religious life. According to the Mahāyāna scriptures a Bodhisattva has to pass through several stages of spiritual discipline called the *bhūmis*. In the *Mahāvastu* the first *bhūmi* is called *Durārohā* (difficult to enter). In this *bhūmi* Bodhisattva cultivates 'charity, compassion, indefatigable energy, humility, study of all the branches of learning, heroism, renunciation of the world, and fortitudes. From this it is clear that there is no necessary conflict between the pursuit of knowledge and the practice of compassion in the life of the religious person. Referring to the conduct of the Bodhisattva in the third *bhūmi* called *puṣpamaṇḍitā* it is stated that he 'confers happiness on all creatures without any selfish motive. He also loves learning so much that he is prepared to make the greatest sacrifices only to bear a single instructive verse or stanza.' In the seventh *bhūmi* called Durjayā (difficult to conquer), we are told, the Bodhisattva, learns everything about gold, silver, gems and precious stones, and acquires all knowledge that may be useful to mankind. Mahāyāna Buddhism, it seems, did not favour the life of retirement into a cave for the Bodhisattva. Both Hīnayāna and Mahāyāna Buddhism recommended the practice of *Brahma vihāras* which is possible only in relation to other human beings.

In the above account of the religious man I have not made any reference to any set of doctrinal beliefs. The reason is that I attach more importance to religious values reflected in saintly conduct than to sets of beliefs invoked in support of those values. According to us, as according to Indian tradition in general, one of the important tests of the soundness of a religio-philosophical doctrine is that it encourages and promotes the right sort of attitudes, conduct, and values. While there are no rigorous deductive procedures available for arriving at value-conceptions, it is noteworthy that some common values or value attitudes have been recommended by different cultural traditions on the basis of their divergent religio-philosophical assumptions. In other cases such assumptions may lead and have led in the past to divergent and even conflicting recommendations in regard to ethico-religious life and conduct. On the whole, it seems, there has been greater unanimity among moral teachers than among the teachers of religion, insofar as the latter's teachings concern matters unrelated to moral life.

REFERENCES

1. Har Dayal, *The Bodhisattva Doctrine in Buddhist Sanskrit literature,* (Delhi, Motilal Banarsidass, 1970), p. 273
2. Ibid, p. 274
3. Ibid, p. 275

Banaras Hindu University, Varanasi.

MORALITY, TEMPORALITY AND IMMORTALITY

J.A.Yajnik

This paper aims at pointing out that as morality has necessarily to do with temporality and as immortality is necessarily atemporal, it cannot plausibly be maintained that immortality of the soul is a postulate of morality regarded as an end in itself. This main argument of the paper is completed through the three sections into which the paper is divided.

Section I attempts to bring out the temporal nature of morality by pointing out that the reality of time is one of the postulates of morality. It has also been pointed out here that the acceptance of the reality of time and objective validity of moral judgment does not logically necessitate the denial of the timeless Ultimate Reality.

Section II attempts to analyse the concept of immortality with a view to bring out its atemporal character. Section III is concerned with the critical consideration of the Kantian argument for the immortality of the soul as a postulate of morality. An attempt has been made here to show that the argument is based on a confusion between immortality of the soul and continuity of the temporal existence of the empirical ego, and fails even to show that the belief in man's survival after death is a postulate of morality which is based only on the doctrine of duty for the sake of duty.

The paper has been concluded with a passing remark concerning a fundamental difference between the morality completely independent of religion and the one based upon religion.

I. *Morality and Temporality*

Moral excellence or moral degradation is made possible through a definite change in a character of a moral agent. A being whose character does not admit of being morally changed is either below the level of morality or beyond it. This means that the possibility of change in the character of the moral agent is a prerequisite of any talk about moral endeavours. And as change is a temporal process, morality is necessarily time-bound. Moral progress and moral degradation are necessarily temporal processes. A philosophy which denies reality to change or temporality can hardly escape the charge of undermining morality. There is a point in the objection against Śaṅkarācārya that his advaitism leaves no room for morality. The fact that Śaṅkarācārya can meet the objection only through his doctrine of trividhasattā makes it evidently clear that morality is significant only at the level of vyāvahārika sattā. That is to say, we can speak of morality only with respect to changing empirical ego which passes through the cycle of saṁsāra in accordance with its moral desert. The liberated soul with a clearance certificate regarding all his moral accounts enters into or realizes the divine life of eternity and goes forever beyond all temporal processes including those of moral changes. Morality and temporality thus remain inseparable. Any soul is either within the limits of both or is beyond both.

It is hardly necessary to point out that the fact that morality has to do with temporality does not mean that there is a mathematically exact relationship between the amount of time consumed and the degree of moral elevation or degradation achieved. As the essential being of the moral agent is beyond time, it has a capacity to conquer time through the intensity of will. It is thus possible that a moral change which would normally take many years of effort may be brought about within a few moments. This, however, does not affect the fundamentally temporal character of morality because the capacity to conquer time in this sense is itself temporal. Thus the reference to moments or years, (i.e., to some period of time) is a must for understanding any moral change. And where there is no possibility of any kind of moral change, we are not within the sphere of morality.

The fact that reality of time is a necessary postulate of moral life has been very clearly brought out by Rashdall in his 'The Theory of Good and Evil'. He has rightly maintained that the belief in the objective validity of moral judgments logically necessitates the admission of the reality of time. Rashdall however, seems to have been mistaken in holding that the admission of the reality of time amounts to the denial of the doctrine of timeless Reality; and the admission of a timeless Reality amounts to the denial of the reality of time, and consequently, the objective validity of moral judgments. He has therefore maintained: "The doctrine of a timeless Reality makes the world's history unmeaningful and all human effort vain. The Buddhists, whose creed is often patronized by our modern believers in a timeless Absolute, at least have the merit of admitting that corollary of their system, however much inconsistency and contradiction there may be in the anti-social ascetic's effort to escape from effort."[1] Rashdall has thus failed to see that time can be real without being Ultimate Reality. It is not logically impossible to hold both that the Ultimate Reality or even the Ultimate nature of human self is beyond time and that the temporal and moral distinctions are objectively valid for human beings, empirical egos in the cycle of saṁsāra. Just as the yellowness of gold does not speak anything against the whiteness of silver, the timelessness of Ultimate Reality does not in the least affect the soundness of temporal moral progress made by any moral agent. Rousseau said that man is born free and finds himself in chains. In a similar vein it is true to say that the human self which is essentially beyond time finds itself in the stream of time, the ocean of saṁsāra. Whether it goes deeper and deeper into this ocean or is finally enabled to cross it is largely determined by its moral efforts. This means that moral efforts which are necessarily temporal do not become vain on account of the timelessness of Ultimate Reality. On the contrary they become most meaningful only on account of that.

II. *Temporality and Immortality*

Temporality and immortality are poles apart. As temporality is a differential characteristic of mortality, immortality has to be completely beyond temporality. [The popular conception of immortality as persistence of existence of a being through everpassing time is self-contradictory. The contradiction involved here is this: As the number of moments in the time series is infinite we can never say, without being involved in a contradiction, that a particular being will continue to exist for *all moments to come* because owing to the infinite stretchability of time-series, *all moments to come* can never actually come. This means that this conception regards immortality as that which it cannot be by this very conception. Such ascription of a self-negating characteristic cannot be avoided in any attempt to conceive immortality in terms of temporality. Thus we see that any interpretation of immortality in terms of temporality must necessarily lack logical tenability.

The recognition of the fact that immortality is not to be interpreted in terms of temporality helps us only negatively. That is, it only enables us to know what immortality is not. This is by no means a small advantage because the cognitive value of cleaning up of confusion in our language and thought can hardly be exaggerated especially with reference to philosophizing.

It is very difficult, if not impossible, for our intellect and language to conceive and express the positive content of immortality. This is so because our thought and language can be at their best only when dealing with temporal modes. The fact of our inability to deal very successfully with eternal modes of existence has been well depicted in the Upaniṣadic saying: 'from which speech returns together with mind unable to reach it'. (Yatovāco nivartante aprāpya manasā saha). However, it is a matter of great philosophical fortune that the thought and language which returns from the experience of eternity or immortality do not remain completely silent because it is against their very nature. We have thus numerous examples from all over the world describing, of course in an analogical way, the mystical experiences of immortality. As a representative of these we shall quote a passage from Eckhart:

> It ranks so high that it communes with God face to face as he is. (It)....is unconscious of yesterday or the day before and of tomorrow and the day after for in eternity there is no yesterday, nor any tomorrow, but only Now.[2]

Interpretation of immortality as 'Eternal Now' sounds paradoxical. This paradoxical character of the interpretation speaks for two points about our language and logic: 1) we) cannot help taking analogies from our temporal experiences even while describing things atemporal; and (ii) we cannot help judging from the standard of our logic which always tries to keep away from contradictions, without perhaps ever being fully successful. In the light of these two points it is not at all difficult to admit that the description of immortality in terms of 'Eternal Now' brings out very clearly the atemporal character of immortality.

III. *Kant's argument for Immortality as a postulate of Morality*

We have seen that reality of time is a necessary postulate of morality and that temporality and immortality are poles asunder. This means that the postulation of immortality of the soul is not logically necessitated by a moral theory which regards goodwill, not as good for the attainment of immortality but, as good without qualification. This will be brought out by a critical consideration of the Kantian argument for the immortality of the soul as a postulate of morality. His argument is as under:

> ....the perfect accordance of the will with the moral law is *holiness*, a perfection of which no rational being of the sensible world is capable at any moment of his existence. Since, nevertheless, it is required as practically necessary, it can only be found in a *progress in infinitum* towards that perfect accordance ....this endless progress is only possible on the supposition of an *endless* duration of the *existence* and personality of the same rational being (which is called the immortality of the soul).[3]

If the wordings of the above argument are taken into account in the light of what we have said regarding the atemporal character of immortality, it becomes evidently clear that the argument rests on a confusion between immortality of the soul and the continuity of the temporal existence of the empirical ego. Really speaking, the argument is only for rebirth or man's survival after death in the 'sensible world' itself. 'Progress in infinitum' and 'endless duration' refer to nothing but unending cycle of saṁsāra.

Even as an argument for rebirth the Kantian argument is vitiated by the following difficulties :—

(i) As it has been pointed out by C.D.Broad, "Kant's premises are really inconsistent with each other. One premise is that moral perfection must be attainable or it could not be our duty to seek it. The other premise is that it is attainable only after an unending time. And this is surely equivalent to saying that it is not attainable at all."[4]

(ii) It follows from the above criticism that Kant is required to admit that the moral law commands the impossible and the command therefore is irrational, and the irrational command cannot be accepted as the categorical imperative. Hence the justification of S.Korner's observation that "we do not recognize the command to achieve holiness as a law which we can possibly choose to satisfy."[5]

(iii) Kant "held that it was better to base the belief on immortality upon the moral disposition rather than to base the moral disposition on a hope for future rewards".[6] Now, if the above mentioned criticism is correct, it must be admitted that Kant has failed to show how the belief in future life or the so-called immortality of the soul can be based on autonomous moral disposition. This means that Kant's acceptance of the immortality, and also of God, as a postulate of morality definitely jeopardizes the autonomy of moral disposition and evidences an unconscious slip into "heteronomy of the will" which has been considered by Kant as "the source of all spurious principles of morality".[7]

We thus see that Kant's argument not only fails to touch immortality but it also fails to substantiate even the belief in man's survival after death as a postulate of morality. This means that the philosopher who regards moral law as absolutely categorical imperative and stands for the pure autonomy of will cannot consistently admit any postulate of morality except that of the freedom of will.

Our denial of immortality of the Soul as a postulate of morality simply means that no one is justified in saying that, 'I can be moral, only if I am immortal'. One is, however, fully justified in saying that 'I should be moral in order that I may attain immortality'. In this case morality is not regarded as an end in itself but as a means to a religious goal. Belief in rebirth, immortality of the soul and the existence of God can be justified only from the point of view of our religious or mystical consciousness. Moral consciousness which asserts its complete independence from religious consciousness and takes pride in being autonomous must consistently give up all hopes regarding the continuity of moral progress even after death as well as regarding the realization of the summum bonum conceived as the conjuction of perfect happiness with the perfection of virtue (i.e., holiness.) [8] This means that the moral theory which refuses to base itself upon religious or mystical experience has to be satisfied with purely humanistic ethics.

Gujarat University, Ahmedabad

REFERENCES

1. Rashdall, *The Theory of Good and Evil*. Vol.II. (Second Edition, Oxford, 1948). p.245.
2. *Meister Eckhart*, (Trans. by R.B. Rlakney, New York, Harper & Brothers, 1941). Sermon 12, p.153.
3. Abbott, T.K., (Trans). *Kant's Critique of Practical Reason and Other Works on the Theory of Ethics*. (Sixth Edition, Longmans, 1954). p. 218-19.
4. Broad, C.D., *Five Types of Ethical Theory*.(Routledge & Kegan Paul, 1956). p.140.
5. Korner, S., *Kant*. (Penguin Books, 1955) p.166.
6. The reference is to be found in L.W. Beck's *A Commentary on Kant's Critique of Practical Reason*. (The University of Chicago Press, 1961). p. 265.
7. Abbott, T.K., *Op.cit*. p.59.
8. This conception of the *Summum bonum* has been described by L.W. Beck as "the maximal conception". Kant's argument for the immortality is based upon this maximal conception of the *Summum bonum*—see L.W. Beck, *op. cit*. pp.268-70.

3

SOME DISTINGUISHING FEATURES OF MORAL JUDGMENTS

Ved Prakash Varma

What makes a judgment moral or what are the features which distinguish it from all other judgments is one of the most important questions concerning contemporary moral philosophy. This paper is an attempt to assess critically some of the important answers given to the above question by the proponents of major meta-ethical theories, such as naturalism, non-naturalism, emotivism and prescriptivism. If we carefully examine and analyse the views and arguments put forward by the exponents of these various meta-ethical theories regarding the function and justification of moral judgments, we can reasonably conclude that these judgments are marked by the following five features which, taken together, distinguish them from descriptive statements, purely emotive utterances and non-moral value judgments.

(1) Moral judgments do say something about the objects judged—they evaluate (that is, praise or blame) these objects. The objects of these judgments are necessarily human beings, their motives, intentions, or actions. This evaluation of the objects is based on their natural qualities which constitute the criteria for testing the truth or falsity of these judgments. The descriptive meaning of moral judgments lies in these criteria which vary from case to case and which provide us with reasons for justifying these judgments.

(2) Moral judgments, like factual statements, are universalizable—that is, they must be applied to all similar cases in similar situations. In other words, like descriptive statements, these judgments, are subject to the principle of universalizability which is explained by R.M. Hare as follows: "If I call a thing red, I am committed to calling anything else like it red. And if I call a thing a good X, I am committed to calling any X like it good....Moral judgments are universali-

zable in just the same way as descriptive judgments are universalizable—namely, the way which follows from the fact that both moral expressions and descriptive expressions have descriptive meaning; but in the case of moral judgments the universal rules which determine this descriptive meaning are not mere meaning—rules, but moral principles of substance— I have been maintaining that the meaning of the word "ought" and other moral words is such that a person who uses them commits himself thereby to a universal rule. This is the thesis of universalizability".[1] Thus principle of universalizability draws our attention to the important fact that, like factual statements, ethical judgments too are impartial and cannot be governed by arbitrary choices or personal likes and dislikes of anybody. It also enables us to justify these judgments by rational arguments which are not usually required or expected in the case of purely emotive utterances expressing mere personal likes and dislikes.

(3) Moral judgments, unlike descriptive statements, do express the speaker's favourable or unfavourable attitudes regarding the objects judged. This expression of attitudes is different from the expression of mere personal likes and dislikes, because, unlike the latter, it is subject to rational justification, and in this sense can be said to be objective. This indeed, is the affective element of moral judgments, and it clearly distinguishes them from factual or descriptive statements which are usually neutral in the sense that they merely describe certain facts.

(4) Ethical judgements have the element of prescriptivity— that is, they entail imperatives and thus guide choices or actions. A person who sincerely assents to a moral judgment thereby commits himself to perform or to refrain from performing the same action in similar circumstances if it is in his power to do so. If he assents to a moral judgment and yet does not act himself according to it in similar situations in spite of being able to do so, then either he does not in fact assent to this judgment or he is not sincere in assenting to it. Thus by sincerely assenting to a moral judgment the speaker not only guides choices of other persons, but also commits himself to do or not to do certain action in similar circumstances provided it is in his power to do or to refrain from doing

that action. This element of prescriptivity also distinguishes moral judgments from factual statements which merely describe some facts without guiding choices or actions in their usual contexts.

(5) Moral judgments are overriding in the sense that we attach far greater importance to them than to other kinds of judgments. Morally praising or blaming someone's character or conduct is considered to be a far more serious matter than a mere description of certain facts or the expression of personal likes and dislikes. When we make a moral judgment about somebody's character or conduct, we want others to share our view concerning such a moral appraisal, but this does not necessarily happen in the case of factual statements, subjective judgments of taste and non-moral value judgments. Thus, ethical judgments for us have a special status which other kinds of judgments do not seem to have, and this fact can also be said to be one of the important distinguishing features of moral judgments. These, in short, are five salient features which, taken together, clearly distinguish ethical judgments from descriptive statements, purely emotive utterances or expressions of personal likes and dislikes, and non-moral judgments.

Now it must be emphasized here that although all these five features are found in a moral judgment, none of them exclusively belongs to these judgments alone. Each of these features is shared by other kinds of judgments as well. For example, features (1) and (2) are shared by factual statements which convey some information concerning the objects judged in virtue of certain criteria and which are universalizable. Similarly, features (3) and (4) are shared by emotive utterances and imperatives respectively, because emotive utterances express the speaker's attitudes and imperatives tell someone to do or not to do some action. Finally, feature (5) may be shared by legal judgments which sometimes an individual or a group of individuals may regard as of supreme importance. Thus, none of the five characteristics stated above can be said to be an exclusive property of ethical judgments, though all these characteristics, taken together, clearly distinguish them from all other judgments.

In fact, the presence, of all these five features in ethical judgments renders them unique and irreducible to any kind of non-moral statements and expressions. For instance, features (1) and (2) distinguish these judgments from purely emotive utterances, expressions of personal likes and dislikes, and imperatives. This is because, unlike moral judgments, emotive utterances, expressions of taste, and imperatives are not subject to rational justification and the principle of universalizability. On the other hand, features (3) and (4) clearly mark moral judgments off from descriptive statements, because the former, unlike the latter, do express favourable or unfavourable attitudes of the speaker and also guide choices or actions. As we have previously observed, ethical judgments do not merely describe certain facts while descriptive statements are made primarily with a view to conveying some factual information concerning certain state of affairs. Thus, descriptive statements usually lack emotive element and normative character which are indispensable features of moral judgments. Finally, the presence of feature (5) clearly distinguishes these judgments from purely subjective statements and non-moral value judgments which are not usually held to be overriding and of supreme importance. We certainly regard moral judgments as having far greater importance than non-moral value judgments and expressions of personal likes and dislikes which, we hold, must be overridden by ethical judgments if they conflict with these judgments. We usually allow and tolerate radical differences concerning subjective statements and non-moral value judgments, but this cannot be said with regard to ethical judgments which for us are too serious to be taken so lightly. We can thus conclude from the foregoing considerations that all the five characteristics of ethical judgments, taken jointly, mark them off from all non-moral statements, expressions or judgments.

Now the important question to be considered here is which, if any, of the four major meta-ethical theories, referred to in the beginning of this paper, accounts most satisfactorily for the nature, function and justification of moral judgments. It is necessary to examine briefly and critically the merits and demerits of each of these meta-ethical theories before we give any definite answer to the above question. Let us first consider naturalism which reduces moral judgments to factual or empirical statements. According to this theory, these judgements can be wholly identified with or can be defined in terms of some kind of naturalistic statements. Thus, for naturalists, there is no logical gap between ethical judgments and descriptive statements, because the former can be deduced from the latter. All hedonists, utilitarians, evolutionists, subjectivists, and some other descriptivists subscribe to this doctrine in some sense or the other.

The basic defect of this theory lies in the fact that it completely rejects the autonomy of ethics as a distinct subject and overlooks the normative character or evaluative element of moral judgments. According to this doctrine, ethical judgments are as factual and neutral as descriptive or empirical statements. This, however, does not seem to be plausible, as we have seen, moral judgments are essentially normative and do express favourable or unfavourable attitudes of the speaker. Thus, naturalists entirely ignore features (3) and (4), and lay too much emphasis on features (1) and (2). This is why they fail to account satisfactorily for the nature and function of moral judgments. In fact, it is because of naturalists' total denial of the autonomy of moral judgments and their rejection of the normative character or evaluative element of these judgments that non-naturalists and non-cognitivists alike have completely abandoned ethical naturalism.

Contrary to naturalists, G.E. Moore, W.D. Ross, C.D. Broad and H.A. Prichard, who are known as non-naturalists, claim to defend the autonomy of ethical judgments by regarding them as unique and irreducible to any other kind of statements—natural, theological or metaphysical. According to these non-naturalists, moral terms, such as "good", "right", "ought" etc. refer to what they call "non-natural" properties or relations. It is because of referring to these "non-natural" properties or relations that, for non-naturalists, moral judgments are unique and irreducible to any other kind of statements. Unlike natural qualities and relations, these "non-natural" properties and relations can be directly apprehended by intuition alone and are not the objects of our empirical observation. This is because, according to non-naturalists, these properties and relations do not exist by themselves in space and time. It is necessary to mention in this connection that the impact of Moore's well-known notion of the naturalistic fallacy has been extremely fatal to all kinds of naturalistic ethical theories.

But, like naturalism, this theory is also unable to explain the nature and function of moral judgments. In the first place, its basic assumption that moral terms refer to non-natural qualities or relations appears to be untenable, for we have no experience of such qualities or relations, and the non-naturalists themselves have failed to explain satisfactorily their precise nature. These so-called non-natural properties or relations have therefore become mysterious entities which are wholly beyond our comprehension. Secondly, non-naturalists attach a great importance to "intuition" which, if it exists at all, is only a subjective faculty and therefore is not open to any objective tests or criteria. We have no reliable method to test the validity of conflicting intuitions, consequently disagreement about moral issues can never be satisfactorily resolved. Thus, non-naturalism, if true, leads us ultimately to complete subjectivism, because if rightness or wrongness of actions can be apprehended only by intuition which is a wholly subjective faculty not open to any reliable objective tests or criteria, then moral judgments are as subjective as our statements of personal likes and dislikes. This implication of non-naturalism is not only very serious and fatal to this theory, but it is also very strange, for non-naturalists claim to be objectivists and reject all forms of subjectivism. Thirdly, non-naturalism also completely overlooks the normative character or evaluative element of moral judgments by regarding them as fundamentally descriptive. If moral judgments refer to or describe some non-natural properties or relations, they cannot be said to be fundamentally different from factual or descriptive statements. The only difference between empirical statements and moral judgments, according to non-naturalists, is that while the former describe "natural" qualities or relations, the latter refer only to "non-natural" ones. Thus, non-naturalism is vulnerable to the same objection that was urged against naturalism—that is, it, like naturalism, entirely ignores the evaluative element or normative character of ethical judgments by laying exclusive emphasis on their features (1) and (2) at the cost of their other essential features. These, in brief, are some of the serious objections to non-naturalism, and all these objections, taken together, conclusively prove this doctrine to be untenable.

Now it is clear that the failure of both naturalism and non-naturalism is the result of their wholly descriptivist approach to moral judgments. Both these doctrines completely overlook the evaluative element or normative character of ethical judgments by regarding them as mere descriptions of natural or non-natural qualities and relations. This, indeed, is the basic drawback which renders both these theories to be unplausible. In fact, it is for this reason that most of the contemporary moral philosophers have now abandoned this descriptivist approach to ethical judgments. Contrary to both naturalists and non-naturalists, these philosophers regard moral judgments as wholly or primarily non-cognitive. According to the emotivists, like A.J. Ayer and C.L. Stevenson, the primary meaning of these judgments is emotive, for they express and evoke feelings or emotions. Being thus mere expressions and evocations of feelings, these judgments are neither true nor false, and are also not open to rational justification. This purely emotivist approach to ethical judgment was a reaction against the descriptivist theories, and therefore it went to another extreme by equating these judgments with mere ejaculations or exclamations. Thus, the emotivist theory overemphasizes feature (3) to the exclusion of all other essential features of moral judgment, and therefore fails to give a satisfactory account of their nature and function. This is why contemporary moral philosophers do not subscribe to this theory which, they hold, is as one-sided as the descriptivist theories.

The last major meta-ethical doctrine, which aims at explaining the nature and function of moral judgments, is known as prescriptivism propounded by R.M. Hare. According to him, ethical judgments are primarily prescriptive in the sense that they entail imperatives and thus guide our actions or choices, but at the same time they are also secondarily descriptive and therefore are subject to the principle of universalizability as well as rational justification. These judgments are distinct from descriptive statements on the one hand and expressions of feelings or emotions on the other. Their primary function is not to describe some facts or to express and arouse certain feelings but to evaluate our actions or to guide our choices. On Hare's view, ethical judgments can also be justified by rational arguments, because, like factual statements, they are subject to the principle of universalizability which, roughly speaking, states that, to be consistent and impartial we must apply our moral judgments to all similar cases in similar circumstances. This, according to him, is a logical principle in the sense that universalizability is a part of the very meaning of moral terms—that is to say, ethical judgments must be universalized to avoid self-contradiction. It is now clear that Hare does not regard moral judgments as primarily emotive. He contends that these judgments do have descriptive meaning in the sense that they refer to certain natural qualities or characteristics of the object judged. It is these characteristics which constitute the criteria for judging or evaluating the object concerned. Since these criteria necessarily change from case to case, the descriptive meaning of moral judgments is only secondary. Their primary function is prescriptive or evaluative for it remains the same in all cases. It is this primary evaluative function which distinguishes moral judgments from descriptive statements that, in their normal use, merely convey to us some factual information about the object concerned.

Hare's prescriptivism is certainly an important improvement upon the emotive theory which identifies moral judgments with mere expressions and evocations of feelings or emotions. His position is considerably strengthened by the fact that he regards ethical judgments as neither purely descriptive nor wholly emotive but as primarily prescriptive or evaluative. He seems to have adopted a middle course between the two extremes of complete descriptivism and pure emotivism. Hare's theory appears to take into account all the important five features of moral judgments mentioned in the beginning of this paper, and therefore seems to be more convincing and satisfactory than other meta-ethical doctrines which we have so far considered. It can, however, be argued against his prescriptivism that prescriptivity is not a defining characteristic of all ethical judgments, because some moral judgments are not prescriptive. Hare himself admits this.

fact when, in a footnote, he remarks : "It must be emphasized that it is not a part of my thesis that moral words are used prescriptively in all contexts; and it makes sense to call them 'moral' even when they are not so used." It is thus clear that prescriptivity is not an indispensable feature of all ethical judgments. But, despite this difficulty, Hare's prescriptivism accounts for the nature and function of moral judgments far more satisfactorily than other meta-ethical doctrines do.

From the foregoing discussion of major meta-ethical theories it is clear that moral judgments are distinct from descriptive statements and emotive expressions. But now it is necessary to point out here that these judgments are distinct from judgements of non-moral value as well. It is true that all value judgments, whether moral or non-moral, are necessarily concerned with the act of evaluation which is beyond the scope of factual statements. In other words, these judgments unlike descriptive statements, estimate the worth or value of something instead of merely describing it. But, in spite of this common characteristic, there are at least two important factors which clearly distinguish moral judgments from non-moral value judgments. The first obvious distinction between these two types of value judgments is concerned with the kind of the objects judged. Non-moral value judgments evaluate all objects—whether human or non-human; but, as previously observed, ethical judgments are confined to normal human beings, their motives, intentions and some voluntary actions performed by them as members of society. This means that the scope of ethical judgments is much narrower than that of non-moral value judgments, because the former do not evaluate non-human or material objects while the latter do.

Another important distinction between ethical judgments and non-moral value judgments lies in the fact that we, as members of society, exhibit serious concern for and attach supreme importance to the former rather than the latter. When, for instance, we say that some material object is good or a certain picture is beautiful, we are not so much concerned to see others sharing our view as we are when we judge an action to be morally right or wrong, or a human being to be good or bad. This shows that we can be indifferent to what others say about the value of material objects but not to what they say regarding moral goodness of human beings or rightness of their actions. This gives to moral judgments a special status which non-moral value judgments do not possess. Thus, feature (5) of moral judgments clearly distinguishes them from non-moral value judgments.

University of Delhi, Delhi

---

1. R.M. Hare, "Freedom and Reason", pp. 15, 30.

4

DISINTERESTED ACTION

Sanat Kumar Sen

The concept of disinterested action (*niṣkāma karma*) may well be said to be the key concept of the theory of action as preached in the *Bhagavadgītā*. The aim of this paper is to attempt an analysis and interpretation of this concept.

By 'action' here is meant voluntary action, i.e. behaviour that is subject to conscious control. It includes activities such as eating, drinking, walking, talking, playing, singing etc. Even breathing is not excluded; for it also can be consciously varied or stopped for a while.

Action, in this sense, is a necessity of life. It is a *sine qua non* for maintenance of bodily existence. Total inaction is impossible, because it is beyond human power. For example, it is hardly possible for a man to decide to stop breathing and carry out his determination by suspending intake of breath and exhalation altogether. Here nature would have its own way over the obstinacy of man. Death by resolute voluntary fasting has been heard of. But has anybody ever known any case of death by total abstention from drinking? There is a limit to human resoluteness over demands of nature[1]. Moreover, even if we grant for argument's sake that total actionlessness is possible, that would mean the end of physical existence—death[2]. Therefore, it is not a matter of choice whether to do action at all or not. Actions have to be done somehow or other.

Action also includes internal behaviour such as conscious wishing, wanting, deciding, attending, thinking etc. Even deliberate silence is action, for this too requires conscious effort. But all unconscious behaviour is excluded. So also are reflex acts, acts under hypnosis, sleep-walking etc. The functioning of the internal organs of the body like the stomach, lungs, heart, the ductless glands etc. are of course excluded. These activities are not amenable to direct or deliberate conscious regulation, even though changes in the moods or modes of consciousness such as anger, fear elation, dejection etc. have pronounced effects on them.

What is 'disinterestedness' in respect of actions ? Is it the same as 'desirelessness' ? Can actions be done without desire? Can one, for example, take food without any desire for it? Yes. We may eat, not to satisfy hunger or the desire for food, but for such reasons as keeping a request, conformity to social norms, avoiding embarrassment etc. In such cases, there is no desire for food. But is there no desire at all ? If that were so, eating in such cases would not be conscious or voluntary action at all but automatic behaviour. I submit that voluntary action is always action with some desire or other. A totally aimless or purposeless human action is inconceivable, because it does not make sense. The concept of aim, purpose or desire is essential to the concept of action. I therefore conclude that action, in the sense in which we have taken it, cannot be totally desireless. Hence, 'disinterested action' does not mean 'desireless action'. *Kāma* is literally translated as 'desire', and 'desireless action' is the literal translation of *niṣkāma karma*. But such rendering could possibly mislead, inasmuch as it suggests that action totally devoid of desire or purpose is action still. 'Desire' is a term of very wide meaning and application. It at least means a pro-attitude towards some end—a wish for something, and it is in this sense that it is taken here.

The way or attitude that is recommended in the Gītā in respect of voluntary actions is couched in such expression as 'non-attached' (*āsakta*)[3], 'fixed in yoga' (*yogastha*)[4] 'renouncement of the results of actions' (*karmaphalatyāga*)[5] etc. One precept that has been harped again and again is that of offering of all actions to the supreme Lord[6] or that of taking complete refuge in Him[7]. I think that the concept of disinterested action is allied to and continuous with these concepts and it is in terms of or in the light of these that its explication and development has to be sought.

Verse II. 47 of the *Gītā* says: "You have a right to action only, never to its results; do not be the cause of results of actions; do not be attached to inactivity." What is meant by 'results of an action'? What is 'not having a right to the results'? What again is 'being the cause of results'? It seems that an understanding of these concepts is essential for understanding disinterested action.

In one sense, by 'results of an action' is meant the intended consequences of it. An action is said to succeed if the desired consequences follow from it. But there is no absolute guarantee that any action would succeed; for the results aimed at depend on various factors, not on the action alone. One such cause is Fate or unknown factors, over which we have no control. In spite of all human care and effort, an action may fail to achieve its purpose on account of certain unknown, unexpected or inexplicable causes. Therefore it has been said that one does not have any 'right' to the results. The reason is that the results are never wholly within the means of any human being. Since they exceed one's control, one cannot assure or guarantee them. What one cannot guarantee one does not have a right to. One can only perform actions, to which there may be a right. Results may be wanted or hoped for but cannot be ensured, and hence there is no right to them.

When an action succeeds, it produces pleasure or satisfaction in the doer; and when it fails, dissatisfaction or disappointment ensues. It is needless to say that there is a natural tendency in man to seek pleasure and avoid pain. Praise, profit, victory etc. are generally pleasing and their opposites, viz. blame, loss, defeat etc., are generally unpleasant. Pleasure or happiness and reduction, cessation or avoidance of pain as well as states of affairs leading to them may also be said to be the results of action. When an action is motivated by these things, i.e. when a person acts with such specific purposes, he is said to be the 'cause' of the results of the action. Pleasure or pain, gain or loss etc. may befall a man without his specific seeking. But they may also be aimed at and thus determine his actions. In such cases where a person is motivated by the results of actions he is bound by or responsible for them. Such motivated actions have a self-perpetuating tendency. Motives persist and actions multiply, involving man inevitably in strife, struggle and discord. Here is the root cause of suffering, of chains of pleasure-pain and of the cycle of births and deaths. These constitute what is called *karmabandha*—bondage or entanglement by actions. That is why it is said that one should not become the cause of results of actions.

But is it at all possible to act and yet avoid being the cause of the results ? If desire necessarily accompanies actions—and desire is the desire for results—how can they help being the cause of the results? Voluntary actions are always goal-directed; the goal is the achievement of some purpose; and the purpose in the end may well be said to be happiness or painlessness, in whatever form it may be. There seems, therefore, to be no way of being active and yet avoiding pleasure-pain or suffering. All actions seem to be actions with interests. A businessman is interested in profit or avoidance of loss, a lawyer in successful practice, a fighting soldier in victory, an examinee in passing the examination and so on. Can there be disinterested action then?

Disinterestedness lies not so much in desirelessness or purposelessness as in non-attachment. It is not mere desire or goal-directedness that is harmful but desire with attachment. If attachment can be overcome, then perhaps one can do actions for specific results and yet not be bound by them. But what is attachment?

I find it convenient to explain attachment by reference to *rāga* and *dveṣa*—interest and aversion. Interest dwells on pleasure[8]. It is the thirst, greed or eagerness for pleasure or its means. It depends upon previous experience of pleasure, which leaves impressions on the mind. Interest may not always be conscious. It exists as a natural tendency or disposition towards pleasures of the senses and its objects. As interest is related to pleasure, so aversion is related to pain. Aversion can be there only if there has already been the experience of pain. It is dislike for, antipathy to, or hostility towards pain and its objects. It also is a very natural propensity.

I think that it is interest and aversion that constitute attachment (*saṅga* or *āsakti*), so that one who is or has become free from atttachment is also free from interest and aversion, even though he may have wishes or desires and may not be insensitive to pleasure-pain.

One who acts without attachment to result is not in any way troubled by them. His mental poise is not disturbed one way or another, whether, results be favourable or unfavourable. For he has no passion for, is not addicted to, results. He is neither impatient for anything, nor intolerant with anything. He is ever contented, whatever the result. He truly is skilful in action. The skill is reflected in a serene equality which rises above the dualities of success-failure, praise-blame, pleasure-pain. victory-defeat etc. Such skilfulness in action and equanimity in all circumstances is called *yoga* in the Gītā. It is the *yoga* of disinterested action—also called the *yoga* of the intelligent will (*buddhiyoga*).

The ideal of *karmayoga* is grand. But the practice of it is not at all easy. For it requires complete control over the senses and the mind, and mastery over the emotions. We, however, are not so much concerned with the grandness of the ideal or the difficulty of achieving it as with its intelligibility. The *karmayogī* is not one who spends his life meditating in seclusion for realisation of subtle metaphysical entities or occult truths. He is a very active man in the midst of whirlpool of affairs. But he is not in the whirlpool, for he is completely detached. But why should a man who has such detachment be very active ? It might rather seem that he would be as little active as possible, if at all. If all attachment to results are excluded, would there remain any motive still to spur action ? The argument that some actions are inevitable for continuance of physical existence itself is not tenable either. For what is the point in sustaining the physical body? Or, even if we grant this argument for argument's sake, the difficulty persists all the same. The *karmayogī* is not a selfish man who acts merely for the sake of maintenance of his own body. He is a man with a wide heart, working selflessly for general welfare. But why should one work for general good sacrificing one's own interests ?

I do not think that a satisfactory answer to this problem is possible until we can see that the ideal of action is integrally connected, or at a higher stage fused, with the ideal of knowledge. The ideal karmayogī is also a supremely wise man (*jñāni*). He knows that his real self is not a petty limited thing which clashes with other selves. He sees the unity of selves and is equal-visioned. He knows the ultimate root of all suffering. His ways of action are in perfect harmony with his metaphysical knowledge of faith.

When this knowledge dawns, a person realises that he has not only no right to the results of actions, but not even to actions themselves either. They ultimately are not his actions. It is sheer haughtiness and delusion to think "I am the doer"[11] It is rather nearer to the truth to think that actions are spun out according to the laws of nature (not gross physical nature although). But the perfect *karmayogī* realises that there is one supreme Master of everything—the supreme Lord, who also is the innermost self of beings.[12] The ideal worker regards himself as an instrument in the hands of the Lord and fulfils divine purpose through actions. It is the spirit in which actions are done that is important. Outwardly, the actions of the wise man need not necessarily differ from those of the unwise. But the spirit of attitude is different[13]. Acts of self-denial and service to mankind are seen by the wise as means of self-purification[14] leading to highest knowledge[15] and as fulfilment of divine purpose. Works then are done as offering to or worship of the Lord[16]. Work done in this spirit does not cause further misery but in the end leads to the end of all suffering, which is the ultimate goal.

The revelation or understanding that an all-comprehensive higher purpose is working in the universe has its appropriate emotive aspect. This is called *bhakti* or Devotion. It is expressed in deep love and reverence towards the object of devotion as also in accordant conative attitudes and actions. Thus goes with the ideal of action intellectual and emotive excellence also. Such an integration or synthesis of action, emotion and knowledge is spoken of in the Gītā, with varying emphasis on different aspects according to context, their embodiment being projected in the personality of Śrī Kṛṣṇa.

Disinterested action, I think, is possible under the nexus or realisation of some such ideal. One can accept the ideal and subscribe to intelligent unselfish action or do the poposite, viz. reject them both. One can argue about the whole thing and advance alternative theories or interpretations. But I do not think *definitive* argument is possible here. For myself, I find the philosophy of *niṣkāma karma* uniquely appealing both from the theoretical and practical points of view. No wonder that commentaries on the Gītā, dating back from ancient times, still continue to pour in !

NOTES

1. Vide *Gītā*, XVIII. 11 : "Indeed, embodied beings cannot renounce all actions. ...
2. Vide *Gītā*, III. 8 : "...Even the maintenance of physical life cannot be effected without action."
3. *Gītā* III. 19 : "Therefore without attachment perform ever the action that is to be done...
4. *Gītā* II. 48 : "Fixed in Yoga, do thy actions..."
5. Vide *Gītā* XII. 11-12.
6. *Gītā* IX. 27 : "Whatever you do...make it an offering unto Me." Also III. 30, V. 10, XII. 6 etc.
7. *Gītā* XII. 8 : "On Me respose all thy mind and all thy understanding..." XVIII. 57 : "...Be always in heart and consciousness with Me." XVIII. 62 : "In Him take refuge in every way of thy being..." XVIII. 66 : "Abandon all *dharmas* and take refuge in Me alone..." XI.55, XVIII. 65 etc.
8. Vide *Yoga-sūtra*, II.7.
9. *Gītā* VI. 29-30,32 : "The man in Yoga sees the self in all beings and all beings in the self and is equal-visioned everywhere... He sees Me everywhere and seas all in Me...He sees with equality everything in the image of the self whether it be grief or it be happiness....."
10. *Gītā* V. 8-9 : "The man who knows the truth thinks, 'I am doing nothing';...He holds that it is only the senses acting upon the objects of the senses."
11. *Gītā* III.27 : "While the actions are being entirely done by the modes of Nature, one who is bewildered by egoism thinks 'I am the doer".
12. *Gītā* IX. 18 : " I am the path and the goal, the upholder, the witness, the refuge, the benign friend—the origin, destruction and the eternal resting-place of all apparent existence." Gītā XV.15 : "I am lodged in the heart of all... ." Also XVIII. 61.
13. *Gītā* III. 25-26 . "As the ignorant act with attachment, he who knows should act without attachment, for the people. He should not confuse the understanding of the ignorant who are attached to actions; he should set them to all actions, doing them himself with knowledge and in Yoga".

14. *Gītā* V. 11 ; "The Yogins do actions,...abandoning attachment, for self-purification."

15. *Gītā* IV. 33 : "Knowledge is that in which all this action culminates..."

16. *Gītā* XVIII. 46 : "He from whom all beings originate (or all efforts flow), by whom all this universe is pervaded, by worshipping Him by his actions, a man reaches perfection."

University of North Bengal

5
ETHICAL RELATIVITY AND CULTURAL RELATIVITY, AN ANALYSIS AND EVALUATION

Donald H. Bishop

I.

Ethical relativity is the view that there are universal or universally accepted standards or norms. There are no moral rules which apply to all persons as such. What is considered moral at one time and place is not at another. The good is dependent on, relative to, determined by circumstances. All moral standards are subjective. What one individual considers good another person may deem the opposite. Moral judgments are purely individual. Morality is a matter of personal opinion.

Ethical relativity is based on several assumptions. One is individual variation. No two people are alike. There is no common human nature. Thus what is good for one individual may not be for another and each person decides for himself what is good for him. Values are determined by emotions. Moral judgments are simply expressions of attitudes or feeling Feelings vary between individuals; thus their moral standards will too.

The relativist emphasizes differences between individual much more than similarities. He assumes that right or wrong is determined or known through experience. Again, since the experiences of individuals vary, their ethical norms will too. The relativist assumes a particularistic metaphysics and a process view of reality. Reality is constantly changing and only particulars exist. His is an empirical and particularistic epistemology also. We can only know material things and there are no knowable universals.

Ethical universalism, on the other hand, is the view that there are basic moral principles, laws or norms which are universally and always true. There are certain ideals for moral standards which are eternal and immutable. There is but one constantly true and valid moral code. It does not vary in time and location. There is a single moral standard equally applicable to all persons at all times and places.

The ethical universalist admits the concept of the apriori. Values exist apriori and are discovered, not created by man. They are known through reason or perhaps intuition. They are not dependent on whim, fancy or feelings. Experience demonstrates, not verifies, these apriori moral truths.

The universalist emphasizes the distinction between what is actually right and a particular person's or group's opinion of right and wrong. He accepts a metaphysical monism and idealism. It may be of the Platonic variety which insists on the reality of universal "forms." Reality is one, a unity, a whole. Similarities far outweigh differences in number and significance. The universalist may be a theological monist in that he presupposes a single God, author or vindicator of a single, universal moral code.

In epistemology the universalist tends toward absolutism. Truth, like reality, is characterized by permanence. Unchanging truths exist which persons discover by going beyond appearances and feelings which are momentary or fleeting. Moreover, there is a common human nature in which all men share and which transcends individual differences or dissimilarities.

The cultural relativist emphasizes the diversity of cultures. Cultures or societies vary in mores, practices, outlook and beliefs. Moreover, there is variation within a particular culture from one time to another. Each society and age has its own patterns of life which are valid for itself but not for others.

When ethical and cultural relativism are combined we come up with a number of assertions. There are no common ethical or cultural standards. Each society and age has its own distinct mores and practices. There are no cross-cultural universals of any type. Moral beliefs and actions are socially or culturally determined and thus inevitably vary from society to society. Man is determined by his environment. Culture is a product of man's interaction with his environment. Since environment varies, or is not constant, cultures will vary as will moral codes.

II

Thus far I have simply described the concept of ethical and cultural relativity and its opposite, universalism or objectivity. It might be of value to insert a historical note at this point. Ethical relativity is not a new or recent phenomenon. We find it in classical Greek times in the tenets of the Sophist. What is new is the extent to which it is found in the twentieth century. This can be accounted for by a number of factors— the preeminence of behaviourism in psychology, the revolt against nineteenth century absolutisms in philosophy and the expanded activities of early twentieth century anthropologists due to the increased facility of travel which led to extensive research and data on many cultures or societies throughout the world.

One might point to several positive results of twentieth century ethical and cultural relativity. A major one is that it has helped western man to overcome his ethnocentrism (to the extent that he has). There does seem to be a universal propensity for persons to think of their own culture or society as best, their own pattern of life as most suitable, their own moral code as superior. There seems to be a natural tendency to believe that one's own ways ought to be emulated by everyone for they are inherently or obviously superior and one cannot understand why others do not realize this. The superior-inferior distinction seems quite widespread. Cultural and ethical relativity forthrightly punctured the ballon of Western cultural superiority or of self-righteousness or rightness and has rendered a valuable service in doing so. It has led us to be more self critical and certainly such criticism is sorely needed.

A second contribution of relativism has been its stimulating of individuality and non-conformity in thought and life styles. It has accelerated the revolt against nineteenth century orthodox philosophical absolutisms of various types. It has reinforced democracy which is based on the premise of individuality. It has broken down rigid social patterns and made possible desirable changes in social thought and practices. By resisting dogmatism and conformity, relativity has released individual creativity in thought and expression and socity has benefited greately as a result.

A third and recent value of relativism is its questioning of our western sacrosanct belief in inevitable progress. Western man has accepted linear social view which enabled him to hold that western society has been advancing constantly through the centuries and has reached a level of progress and modernity never achieved previously. Western man has reached a peak of civilization never known anywhere or at any time. Recent events have led some westerners to question this assumption. Is a society characterized by violence, wars, depressions, impersonalness, self-deception, competitiveness the ultimate in human excellence? Perhaps other societies which exhibit other traits, values and methods are far superior to the western one. Perhaps they are the civilized and the modern west the barbarian. Relativity has led us to examine both our supposed superiority and our criteria of progress. Are the measures of social excellence or advance western man uses the most, valid after all?

On the other hand there are a number of important criticisms of cultural and ethical relativity which must be taken into account. Anthropologists have overlooked similarities and focused almost exclusively on differences. They have made evaluations of a non-empirical type based on empirical evidence. It is erroneous, for example, to conclude that men are different because they use different tools, stone in one culture and metal in another. Thirdly, anthropologists have assumed that the exception disproves the rule. If an isolated society is found somewhere which practices cannibalism then one cannot validly claim cannibalism is wrong even though it is found nowhere else.

This brings up an error committed by cultural and ethical relativists alike, namely the relating of the is and the ought. Both fall prey to the so-called naturalistic fallacy. When we see people in a given society engaged in a particular practice, we cannot validly conclude that it is therefore right or good. The 'ought' or the 'right' is not determined by the 'is.'

In regard to individual differences it is true that people vary externally. There are short people, tall people, etc.;

there are white-skinned, dark-skinned people etc. But because people are unlike physically does not mean that they are different emotionally, attitudinally, etc. External variation is no basis for internal variation. Further it might be questioned whether differences are much in terms of degree than type, also whether differences are superficial in nature while man's similarities are much more significant.

The relativist also may be as dogmatic as those he opposes. To claim that "all is relative" whether ethically or culturally, is to make as absolute type a claim as is the opposite that "there is only one standard." The relativist assumes that no universal generalization is possible or valid, yet his statement that all is relative is itself an absolute type universal. The relativist, then, is inevitably involved in contradiction.

Relativism may be criticized from a pragmatic standpoint also. In its present status it has gone too far. It has overstressed individuality. It has been turned into an excuse philosophy by many. To say that everything is relative and dependent on environment is to present to oneself a rationalization for doing whatever one pleases, for evading responsibility for what one does, for not taking into account those around us and their wishes and needs. Relativism carried to its logical end would result in social anarchy or no society at all. There has to be a minimum of agreement in belief and practice if a society is to hold together and endure.

While relativity may rightly lead to a questioning of social progress, in its extreme form it leads to a denial of any social and moral progress, whatever. This runs contrary to the facts first of all. It is also an invalid denial of human rationality or persons as rational beings with a capacity to discern between the better and the wrose, the lower and the higher, the true and the false. Relativity leads to a denial of any grades of being or man's ability to make distinctions, and this is contrary to the fact.

III.

There is one criticism of relativism which it seems to me has not been emphasized enough and which I would like to consider in some detail. It is the charge that relativists have failed to take into account sufficiently the means/ends disjunction. This is a basic distinction which has a number of significant implications. When applied to the notion of cultural and ethical relativity it provides a method for not becoming an extremist or avoiding the extremes of relativism and absolutism. It enables us to claim that different cultures are but different means to similar ends. Every society devises particular ways of meeting common human needs or coping with common problems. Those ways will depend on a number of factors such as geography, knowledge level, history, degree of influence of custom or tradition. Similarly, within a culture what individuals need is pretty much the same; the ways individuals satisfy their needs will vary.

This view acknowledges that societies or the means are man-created but ends are not. They are natural or inherent. Means are of the category of the extrinsic or external; ends are intrinsic and internal. The means are superficial or less significant. The ends are much more genuine, significant or of greater worth. It is obvious that such a viewpoint presupposes a communality or identity of needs, ideals, goals or values. The psychic and social needs of individuals are pretty much the same everywhere. What varies is the way needs are met, goals reached or ideals applied. Differences or means will be determined by the context. The ideal is constant; how it is applied will depend or vary with the situation.

Such a view would assume a metaphysical position which declares that ends are ontological or grounded in being *per se* while means are empirical. Ends are of the category of the universal, means of the particular. Ends are apriori; means are a posteriori. Ends are monistic; means are pluralistic. Ends are absolute; means are relative. Distinguishing between means and ends makes room for individuality and communality, for differences and similarities, the new as well as the old. It does justice to man as a rational being as it has a place for insight and choice.

IV

It seems to me that the means/ends distinction is very significant for our contemporary situation. A central question today is whether we are to have a monolithic or pluralistic world. Actually it need not be an either/or choice. Technology has brought man closer together than ever before. It has made mankind a unit. Does this mean we must have a world in which everything is alike ? The answer is no. It is possible to have unity in diversity. The concept of a pluralistic world is not a contradiction as long as we keep the means/ends distinction in mind. Mankind can, in fact does, have communality of ends, needs, goals. The need for food, shelter and clothing is basic and the goal of an adequacy of such is universal. Psychic needs are likewise the same everywhere, the need to be accepted, to be part of a larger group, to be wanted and respected. The aesthetic sensibility is universal. A sense of morality is universal. There are, then, cross-cultural ethical and social values which all persons seek. The means or ways they are realized may vary and such variation will give delight and novelty to our world. There may be a conformity of ends but there can be non-conformity of means. Let each society, culture or country devise the means, ways or institutions its people feel are best for achieving the ends they have in common with their fellowmen.

Washington State University, Washington.

6

DHARMA AND THE OPEN SOCIETY

Austin B. Creel

In various ways India has evidenced a commitment to the "open society," meaning by this term primarily the presence of freedom of choice throughout society.[1] This openness to what may also be termed a component of modernization poses attendant problems of integrating new patterns and values with the traditional heritage which greatly (and deliberately) restricted such choice during one's life in the world.[2] For Hindus, as the majority community in India, a cardinal feature of the traditional world view, which is widely reaffirmed as of contemporary relevance, is the idea of *dharma*. But as the West has learned, in connection with the problems identified by Walter Lippman as the "acids of modernity," social change in the direction of an open society may mean the erosion or the displacement or even the repudiation of various ideas and patterns of traditional culture.[3] It is, of course, widely agreed that many details of what once was deemed *sanātana dharma* are outmoded; our concern here is rather with the concept of *dharma*.

Dharma historically has been associated with a stable (or "closed") society, lacking important features of the modern ethos. The ideal of an open society contrasts in important ways with the intellectual and social heritage expressed in the concept of *dharma*, and the assumptions involved in the idea of *dharma* are at variance with some modern aspirations. What are these contrasts and variations, and do they represent conflicts of sufficient moment to suggest the incompatibility of *dharma* and the open society ? Is dharma, historically an accompaniment of a stable society, defective *vis-a-vis* the open society advocated (and avidly sought after) today ? The "infirmities" of *dharma* to be examined here involve both its historical associations and its conceptual framework.

The most pervasive contrast between ancient and modern approaches lies in the attitudes toward stability and change, expressed in a number of ways. *Dharma* in the past connoted prescribed social roles; one's social placement was given by inheritance. Mobility was rejected in theory and impeded in practice. Of course, change did occur in the society structured around the *dharma*, but this was unintended and viewed negatively, as deviation from the authoritative pattern handed down in the past.[4] One's aspirations and goals in worldly life were limited and inherited. The open society of today and tomorrow, however, postulates the right and the possibility of persons departing from given social roles, with social positions dependent upon their own attainments. Development and change are viewed positively. Goals and aspirations should be virtually limitless. The Fundamental Rights stated in Part III of the Indian Constitution clearly express this determination to provide for all citizens access to all the resources of society. Again and again in the modern period the right and the opportunity of choice are highlighted.

Of obvious relevance are the differing approaches to the priorities assigned to individuals and to groups. *Dharma* as a social reality focused on the group, as the locus of norms and values, with an attendant restriction of initiative for the individual.[5] As Dayal Saran Verma says, "The individual has not to decide about himself; he does not make a choice. *He* is given to himself; *he* does not realize himself."[6] Today there is great stress on the individual with a repudiation of group constraints felt to be arbitrarily imposed by birth or even by previous social participation. Freedom of choice is considered fundamental, for as Wilfred Cantwell Smith notes, ,'Modernity . . . lies not in what one chooses but in the fact of being able to choose."[7]

The recognition of individuals as separate from traditional groupings and of their right to be treated accordingly is reflected also in the endorsement of the secular state. It is apparently conceded today that there cannot be one *dharma*, viewed religiously, for all. Some seem to shy away from *dharma*, with its Hindu connotations, for fear of fostering communalism. Others take a more ecumenical approach, identifying *dharma* primarily as "religion,"[8] and speak of Hindu *Dharma*, Muslim *Dharma*, Christian *Dharma*, etc., rather than of an embracing *dharma*, for deviations from which there might be prescribed social sanctions which have theological justification. The secular state has forceful sanctions to back its laws and regulations, to be sure, but theological justifications are thought to be unavailable and unnecessary. In this special sense a question is raised as to whether *dharma* can be meaningful in the secular or multi-religious society to which India is committed.

In still another sense, *dharma* involved a comprehensive ordering of life. That endowment may in some respects facilitate modern social planning (as opposed to the legacy of a *laissez-faire* ideology), In the past it was affirmed and accepted that deviation from *dharma* was viewed negatively and prohibited as far as possible by supportive social arrangements and potent sanctions. In today's outlook, it is thought that deviation from traditional *dharma* will bring progress, which is positively valued, in the form of social and economic improvements. "Development" becomes a rallying cry, perhaps almost the *summum bonum*.

The contrast between the assumptions of a stable society and the commitment to progress is pervasive. The modern framework does not merely seek to change existing institutions; rather, it embodies the expectation of continuing, ceaseless change. *Dharma* with the ideas of structure and comprehensive order seems incongruent. *Dharma* intends and promises to *preserve*; the open society endeavors to *create*. *Dharma* was said to be given in scripture and tradition (*sadā-cāra*). Today the past is seen as an inadequate or even defective source, but no compensatory sources of norms for personal and group life appear to arrest the tendency to drift along unexamined channels lured by the talismans of development and progress. The rigidities of the past are frequently contrasted with "modern need."

Some question only the details of the patterns of *dharma* in the past, asserting an ideal of continuing relevance, but the very conceptual formulation of *dharma* sees out of step with a modern world view.[9] Stability was conceivable because there was believed to be an embracing order in the cosmos. Not only are past postulations of that order rejected today, but there is also skepticism about the existence of such order, combined with a manifest inability to comprehend or describe meaningfully such universal patterns that might exist. A.K. Saran questions whether such "postulates" are possible in a dynamic, industrial society "in which change is ubiquitous and conflict central."[10] Moreover, some modern voices question whether the very search for structure is not subversive to the emergence of the open society. M.K. Haldar, in an issue of *Seminar* on "Our Changing Values", says, "Value in the sense of free choice from among alternatives seems to be completely out of place in the concept of *dharma* as it is or was understood by the Indians of today or of the past one thousand years or so. Indeed, the Indians' excessive preoccupation with *dharma* may well work to blunt their appreciation of what the value of human choice may be all about."[11]

Writers who speak of the old *dharma* as outmoded tend to speak of a new *dharma* rather than of a principle or principles of *dharma*. *Dharma* is, of course, said to be eternal (sanātana) as well as changing, introducing some puzzlement. Is changeableness consistent with the perfection connoted by eternality ? A metaphysic of process would still not readily establish the character of this structure of the universe which ought to be the norm of human action, but it would address itself to one feature of the contemporary outlook. What seems needed in the fluidity of the twentieth century is not a plan for moving from one old pattern to another new pattern, not direction for a season of change but guidance through a process characterized by ceaseless change. Assumptions here are very different than those of the tradition of *dharma*. However appealing the notion of structure as antidote to the manifest chaos and pain of change, there does not seem to be a way to utilize *dharma* in this situation, except, of course, in a reactionary fashion to oppose change entirely. In the midst of the problems of order and authority in modern life and the many centrifugal forces which operate, *dharma* at first glance seems a welcome corrective, recalling duties and requirements in existence prior to our willing and valuing. When one looks more closely, however, for the detailed role of *dharma*, it seems empty, a comforting proclamation but one essentially archaic since it is inconsistent with what are thought to be the virtues of the modern world.

Hindu society in the past did a remarkable job of providing for stability, as expressed in and structured around *dharma*. One might contemplate a continued role, beyond the present sequences of change, upon the arresting of development and change at a particular stage and the emerging of a new *dharma*. There are various obvious difficulties with this, although in some sense there would be a precedent for maintaining such a new stasis, but that would be alien to the open society. It would also suggest no role for the ideal of *dharma* in developing the good society, only a conservative role in maintaining a social pattern otherwise delineated. Again, *dharma* can preserve; can it create? Can change be assimilated into the very essence of the meaning of *dharma*?

It is too early to say—in India or elsewhere, for the problems are global—what the outcome of rampant change will be on traditional modes of thought. Many extol *dharma* as of continuing and special relevance, but there are at least the foregoing obstacles and impediments. If *dharma* can offer principles of guidance through the process of change characteristic of modern society, this has not yet been demonstrated by Hindu thinkers. Generally *dharma* is affirmed, but it is not specified just what the modern content of *dharma* would be or how it would operate in relation to specific insistent problems posed by the open society. One seems to have to turn elsewhere to deal with such matters. Hindu wrestling with problems of cultural reintegration may serve to neutralize the acids of modernity, with great benefit thereby offered also to various other cultural traditions. But noting the formidable divergences of *dharma* and the open society, we may recall Walter Lippman's quoting of Aristophanes to characterize the modern world, "Whirl is King, having driven out Zeus,"[13] and suggest a tentative paraphrase, "Modernization is king, having driven out *dharma*".

University of Florida, Gainesville, U.S.A.

NOTES

1. The term "open society," as used by such writers as Henri

Bergson (*The Two Sources of Morality and Religion* [New York : Henry Holt, 1935]) and Karl R. Popper (*The Open Society and its Enemies* [London : Routledge & Kegan Paul, 1945]), has some connotations beyond the very general usage here. For our purposes freedom of choice is the central ingredient in modernity; other aspects lie beyond the present compass.

2. The situation of a *saṃnyāsin*, of course, was quite different; see Louis Dumont "World Renunciation in Indian Religions," *Contributions to Indian Sociology* (Apr. 1960): 47, 62.

3. *A Preface to Morals* (New York : Macmillan, 1934) pp. 51-67 *et passim*.

4. See Austin B. Creel, "Dharma as an Ethical Category Relating to Freedom and Responsibility, "*Philosophy East and West* 22 (Apr. 1972): 160.

5. R.N. Dandekar, "Hindu Intellectuals Under Recent Impacts of Modern Culture", in *Proceedings of the 11th International Congress of the International Association for the History of Religions* (Leiden : E.J. Brill, 1968), 1:77. See also Irawati Karve, *Hindu Society: An Interpretation* (Poona : Deccan College, 1969), p. 9.

6. "Modernity, Social Reconstruction and Ethics of Knowledge, *Inter-discipline* 6 (1969) : 152.

7. *Modernisation of a Traditional Society* (Bombay : Allied Publishing House, 1965), p. 21.

8. Surendranath Dasgupta points out, however, that the tendency to equate *dharma* with religion is misguided; see *Hindu Mysticism* (New York: Frederiek Ungar Publishing, 1927, 1959), p. 8.

9. See M.A. Venkata Rao, "The Ideal of the Open Society," *Aryan path* 24 (1953) : 206.

10. "Emotional Integration of India,'. in *Seminar on Social Integration in India : Report* (Agra : Agra University, Institute of Social Sciences, 1961), p. 30.

11. "A World of Make-believe," *Seminar*, no. 64 (1964), p. 22.

12. See Austin B. Creel, "The Reexamination of *Dharma* in Hindu Ethics," *Philosophyt East and West* 25 (Apr. 1975) : 163.

13. *A Preface to Morals, p*: 1.

SOME REFLECTIONS ON SOCIAL DIMENSION OF RENUNCIATION IN ADVAITA VEDĀNTA

Kapil N. Tiwari

This study on the philosophico-religious category of Renunciation (*Saṁnyāsa*) in its social dimension is an attempt to clarify some of the divergences that have marked the interpretation of the Vedāntic thought in this respect in our time. It is unfortunate that not much work has been done to explore the social dimension of Renunciation, although there is no dearth of writing on the metaphysical aspect of it. I believe that a positive world philosophy oriented towards a constructive action theory can be fully in accord with the Vedāntic concept of renunciation, perhaps in fact, be even drawn from it. In actual fact, we find the explanation of that potentiality has been achieved only exceptionally rather than in rule. The reason why the renunciation theory has not flourished as a common philosophy—the inadequacy of this theory is partially right but to blame the theory itself is not justified. To act positively on the basis of a positive ethics or philosophy of action would be easier for the generality of mankind than to base one's positive action on sheer freedom. To this extent, the renunciation theory may not have acted as a sufficient impulsion to accomplish all the positive things that we have come today to expect from philosophy. But the nature and characteristics of Renunciation in Advaita Vedānta and the analysis of hypothesis involved in greater details, as brought out in the present inquiry, has made the author aware of its social aspect in harmony with Indian spiritual tradition.

Definition of Renunciation

Renunciation as such cannot be defined independently by itself. Such an approach to renunciation is not advaitic. This may very well be the key difference between the Advaitic standpoint and any other including perhaps the Buddhistic. In fact, it is nothing of itself. It is only an extension of knowledge (*jñāna*) into the realm of practical living. It is life being grasped by knowledge, leaving no other alternative. This is true of individual life as well as the life of society as a whole. At the same time it also acts as only means to the realization of what has been given through theoretical fore-knowledge. In fact, some scholars have interpreted this phenomenon without proper regard to this point. Indian philosophy in general and Advaita Vedānta in particular, therefore has resulted in simplifications, which are moreover, inferred from a limited body of data. Conclusions based on such study need further revision and construction.

In the light of the above observation, I am inclined to suggest that the pattern of renunciation in the Vedānta has a different implication from what has been suggested by some of its critics. In its most characteristic sense, renunciation would indicate an enlightened attitude having no superficial concern with the world as it forces itself mechanically and blindly upon us, for what characterizes the superficial structure of the world is its wrongness which once realized, transforms the nature of the universe so radically (to the extent of its disappearance, as if) that the world becomes an arena for the discharge of motiveless activity at the religious plane, free from all anxieties born of egoism and self-aggrandizement. The present definition implies three elements :

(a) Renunciation aims at the denial and transcendence of the Universe when the latter is approached independently of any Reality behind it. This is the world at its surface and therefore does not fascinate the Indian mind;

(b) The superficial structure of the universe is not denied dogmatically. Behind it is the strong support of *Śruti*, (revelation) based on the proper understanding of a religious cosmology; and thirdly,

(c) Renunciation unfolds the meaning of existence by eliminating egoism which constitutes human conditioning and keeps a man divided from the rest of universe. It aims at a complete eradication of all obstacles, stemming from the so-called gulf between the object and subject as if they were independent and autonomous.

These characteristics differ slightly in various traditions but the underlying rationale of renunciation remains unaffected. It stands primarily for self-culture which is a pre-requisite for the social culture, finally culminating in the realization of the harmonious whole where all the conflicts completely disappear and the man becomes virtuous by nature.

The central problem here therefore is whether such a man of self-knowledge (who is a renunciant) can contribute to social activism based on positive this-wordly conduct ? Are not there directions in the doctrine of renunciation itself which could be profitably reshaped and re-interpreted to serve as a positive foundation for a harmonious functioning of society ? Needless to say this question has provoked a host of controversies which by and large are understandable as reflecting the fact that the traditional religious values based on salvation are hard to combine with this-worldliness, as ordinarily understood. Let me say at the outset that I value all these controversies as they have stimulated many scholars for re-interpretation of Indian thought and many thoughtful Indians for re-appraisal of their own religious tradition but to say that the Vedāntic spirit of renunciation was irrelevant to 'inner worldly life conduct' and value orientations seems rather to represent a hypothetical projection on the Vedānta. My contention here is that it is possible to show that the Vedāntic philosophy of renunciation is not a major obstacle to the ideal of commitment as one of the mechanisms of the sacralization process but that in fact it is helpful to it. It is, however, a fact that in the Vedāntic tradition the individual is not a datum of society but from the point of view of the cosmic order he is not totally free from society. The individual, in other words, fulfils two roles and both these roles are complementary to each other. As a part of the cosmic order, he is instrumental to it and as being essentially *Brahman* he is free from it. These two trends of thought seem to be mutually exclusive but I want to suggest that the doctrine of renunciation which attempts a reconciliation between the two aspects, enriches itself by participating in the cosmos order without being overthrown by it. What I want to suggest here is that the cosmic ideal of renunciation (representing the cosmic order linked with *Dharma*) and the acosmic ideal (representing *Mokṣa*) are not contradictory life-orientations but complementary to each other. To be in the world is to be bound to the cosmic order, its obligations and commitments and to realize Brahmanhood is again to participate in *Brahman* as a free individual.

Perhaps I should further explain the above possibilities by highlighting the spirit of renunciation as a sanctifying principle in every sphere of life. The Vedānta does not lose sight of the differences between the pragmatic truth and the metaphysical validity of that pragmatic truth. The pragmatic truth must be brought forward in order to serve the collectivity in a spirit of renunciation. A direction towards the fulfilment of this ideal is again made metaphysically valid by denying the 'objective' status of the collectivity and bringing it at par with oneself. Whether this spiritual recipe for the pragmatic truth is likely to materialize or not is another matter. But what is to be noted carefully is that renunciation is a way of purifying the commitment without undermining it. It should rather mean here a life of 'disinterested interestedness' only so far as it turns our mind from appropriating the results of our actions, rather than actions themselves. This attitude does not minimize the importance of responsibility which I think remains at its maximum. What is central to the ideal of commitment, according to the Vedāntic ideal of renunciation is not only disregard of the fruits and consequences of actions but also the conception of being a *kartā* (doer) and *bhoktā* (enjoyer). In this wider sense, it takes as its essential basis the pure activities. The course of pure activity is endangered only when it lacks the ideal of renunciation and is utilized for selfish ends. Renunciation, therefore, eliminates anxieties, doubts and dispondency which dominate over natural activity. Only in this sense, I have called renunciation as an enlightened attitude.

Two objections might be raised here. Firstly, how shall I explain the question of *Karma-saṁnyāsa* (renunciation of action) and secondly the delusion of earthly achievement which is associated with the principle of renunciation and 'do-nothing' kind of attitude of the renunciants. We should not forget here that the Vedānta does not take the word *Karma-samnyāsa* in an ordinary sense. In its philosophical meaning, it stands for spontaneous and automatic action without any strain or struggle due to the realization of the cosmic consciousness outside of which nothing remains. The desire for non-performance of action will be a state of bondage for the Vedānta no less than the desire for performance. For Vedāntins, ethics must be established on the metaphysical foundation which does not deny the former but simply enriches it. The framework of reference requires a different perspective according to which renunciation has emerged not merely as a 'theory' but as a religio-philosophical way of life.

Regarding the question of the world and its delusory status which has attracted a good deal of attention, my answer is quite simple. Renunciation as an adjunct to consciousness does not either deny the world or doubt the existence of the world but simply modifies or radically changes our view of the world. In other words, only the naive view of the world is abandoned as a reality independently of *Brahman* and in doing so it does not abandon the world. There is no question of shifting the world from being something to being nothing as it is impossible even according to Vedāntic metaphysics. What is to be shifted is the attitude regarding the world and all the activities associated with it. This means that the man is involved with the world even before the dawn of *Jñāna* and after the dawn of it but the way he was involved and is involved is different. In the state of *ajñāna* his involvement reflected a sense of 'I-ness' (*ahamkāra*). In the state of *Jñāna*, his involvement is meaningless in the sense that his 'I-ness' is meaningless. The realization that *ahamkāra* is meaningless adds a full dimension of meaning to the world which it never lacked but appeared to be forgotten becanse of *ajñāna*. With the fall of 'I-ness' his involvement with the world on the basis of 'I-ness' falls to the ground but it does not remain in nothingness. The whole process is simultaneously attendant on the realization of Reality which transforms the nature of man to such an extent that it can be regarded as his re-birth. It is this relentless search of meaning that the Vedāntins try to discover through renunciation which has been linked with self-knowledge. Put simply, once *ahaṁkāra* is destroyed by *Jñāna*, it is simultaneously accomplished by a further extension of consciousness within which the renunciant establishes his true identity. At this stage the individual as well as the world is sanctified on the basis of its radical extension within the general scheme of Reality. What was so far artificial becomes spontaneous. This is perhaps a far greater gain than the loss of so-called individuality and the world. The life of activism, thus derived, becomes an expression of spiritual order which takes precedence over all petty considerations. The attitude of a renunciant is not of a simple spectator watching a show. He participates in the human drama with a personal detachment. To the extent, he is attached, to that extent he is precluded from participation. Renunciation therefore is a device in the interest of efficient and genuine participation.

In concluding this enquiry, I would like to make a few observations on some of the new perspectives from which the phenomenon of renunciation has been looked at in contemporary philosophical thought in India. Here what is important to note is that according to my interpretation, all these perspectives are fundamentally rooted in the structure of *Jñāna* towards the dawn of which they had the seeker (*sādhaka*) through the fulfilment of his obligations in a unique way, viz. renunciatory way. This point is of the greatest importance for the social life as it rests on controlling and overcoming anxieties and conflicts of life. Some of the reformation movements within the social framework of renunciation have been quite forceful and beneficial. They harnessed the traditional ideal of renunciation to the requirements and purposes of modern society. Renunciation served as a potential for this worldly activism and cultural transformation. Men with their spiritual concerns might be supposed to manifest no interest in mundane activities. Yet far from this, these *Saṁnyāsins* succeeded in building organizations and religious institutions which played an important role in the modernization of India. Inspirations for such tasks come to them from renunciation which they found equally efficacious for individual salvation, as well as salvation of the people of which they were representatives. The task they set to examine were social issues, interpersonal relations, growth of the individual personality and creativity, a sense of unity, self-esteem and the cultivation and preservation of a unique sense of identity in terms of Indian values and meanings. In the light of this, it is easy to see why Vivekananda, Swami Rama Tirtha, Mahatma Gandhi, Tagore were such successful innovators acceptable to India.

Renunciation in its philosophical setting was strengthened by some of the modern philosophers in terms of self-knowledge. In respect of the self-knowledge, the doctrine of renunciation provides a clear unitary perspective. Unlike asceticism, pure and simple, renunciation is not by any means unrelated to thought. It is constantly fed and sustained by the understanding of the nature of consciousness. The contemporary philosophy occupied with such problems reflects a tendency of thought which I call the philosophical theory of renunciation. It may be regarded to be a theoretical understanding of renunciation though in the final analysis it cannot be distinguished from the former. They are held as distinct only in a theoretical sense.

In the contemporary Indian philosophical thought on the subject of the world and renunciation B.G. Tilak has attracted a good deal of attention. He complains against Śaṁkara that he explains away the life of activism by assigning it a secondary status for the purification of mind (*citta-śuddhi*). We have partly answered to his objection but here it might be added that Tilak forgets the division between the *Vividiṣā-Saṁnyāsa* (renunciation of the seeker) and *Vidvat-Saṁnyāsa* (renunciation of the enlightened) and also between ethical and metaphysical which constantly occupied the mind of the Advaitins. This aspect of the problem which has found explicit expression in the contemporary Indian thought is what I call the activistic theory of renunciation. This again is a part of the Vedānta and not the whole of it.

In the light of what has been said here, one may say, that renunciation provides one of the possible ways to social welfare but not the only way. Acceptance or rejection of any position is governed to a large extent by the values one is willing to embrace and there is hardly any controversy over this question. In other words, men committed to different set of values, may not hold renunciation as a universally acceptable valid way. We are not denying the possibility of such tendencies of thought. What we are denying is the possibility of any system of broader commitment which is not at the same time sustained and pervaded by an urgent inculcation of the spirit of renunciation. It would be wrong to think that the Vedānta denied any positive ideal of life. It simply provided a metaphysical urge for a radical extension of such an ideal. The real problem for the Advaitins does not lie in acceptance or denial of action; it does not interest a philosopher to deny what common sense assumes. The Advaitins' task is to provide an explanation which significantly lies in the transforming aspect of action by *Jñāna*. The same pattern of thought is equally true with regard to the world. Renunciation consists essentially in transforming the nature of man and the universe, a tranformation whose accomplishment consists in manifesting or letting the true nature of them emerge to the surface. The unbroken continuity of this tradition until today speaks for itself.

Victoria University, Wellington, Newzealand

8

THE SPIRITUAL LIFE AS ETHICAL SENSITIVITY

W. E. Stein Kraus

It is reported that Hermann Goering once said: "When I hear the word 'spirit', I get my revolver ready." And there are leaders in the world today who agree, asserting that power grows out of the barrel of a gun or arguing that the only way to deal with opponents is by threats of physical power. Thus we find a sickening continuance of the arms race and unquestioning trust in material might. It is not popular to talk about things of the spirit or the spiritual life, especially in the West. This is so not only because logic-chopping analysts can readily find flaws in the meaning of the word itself, but also because an acquisitive and decaying civilization characteristically provides little chance for spiritual culture. It is easy to deny what one has no awareness of and to decree that it is meaningless. Some philosophers today have argued against "private language" and have ridiculed "the ghost on the machine."

Reticence to discuss the spiritual life also comes about because there has been so much elusive mystery associated with those who speaks of it. Moreover, those who allegedly practice it have given the impression of otherworldliness and have refrained from opposing wrong in high places. John Dewey once remarked: "While the saints are introspecting, burly sinners run the world."

But the testimony of the ages and the witness of our own time will not allow a reflective person to ignore the idea of the spiritual life. It has been prized and sought for by generations of persons. It has usually been viewed as a phase of religious experience though this need not be. In its broadest sense, we may say that the spiritual life is one which seeks and cultivates those values which are uniquely human. It is what Socrates called "human excellence". Accordingly, the pursuit of truth, wisdom, artistic creativity and moral character as well as an attitude of reverence may constitute a spiritual life. Even thinkers with Marxist orientation have been willing to talk of spiritual values in this broader sense.[1]

Now while one may view the spiritual life in a broad way, as E.S. Brightman does in his fine book, *The Spiritual Life*,[2] I wish in this paper to focus on the two basic directions the spiritual life has taken historically and argue for an interpretation which has wide applicability and promise, yet is not limited by sectarian loyalties. If we concede that the spiritual life is desirable, is it possible to have a view of it which does not require a metaphysic or which does not slip in theological doctrines in disguised fashion ? Though we must initially admit that there are overlappings and variations in types, we can notice two basic tendencies. The first is inner directed; the second is outer directed. These two tendencies are found in almost all of the religions of the world as well as among those who repudiate religion.

I. In the most general sense, the inner directed form of the spiritual life aims at some mental state that is rewarding in and for itself. These states are variously interpreted depending on one's metaphysic. Religious thinkers may see such a state as union with God. Secular minds, say the classical Epicurean, seek ataraxia or mental serenity. Persons like Nietzsche try for intellectual or aesthetic solace. Obviously there are differences in kind and degree but the aim is uniformly inward and subjective.

To attain their goal, persons have engaged in various techniques and disciplines and have laid down prescriptions. The non religious try to overcome unconscious fears, nervous habits, and background limitations. They remove themselves from practical problems, as Santayana did, avoiding marriage and social responsibility in a thirst after solitary fulfilment. Religious views insist that the spiritual life cannot be attained without discipline, though there are Western views which speak of sudden radical conversions as an initial step.

The disciplines necessary vary almost as much as the theological interpretations which accompany them. Sometimes the interpretation informs the experience. Hindus do not ordinarily understand their heightened mystical experiences as union with Christ and Christians do not regard their high moments of inner joy as fellowship with Krishna. The disciplines have much to do with an assumed mind-body dualism. Since the body and its appetites are viewed as hindrances to spirituality, we can notice many types of discipline and abstinence. "The ascetic foundation", writes Evelyn Underhill, "in one form or another, is the only enduring foundation of a sane contemplative life."[3]

There are different forms of bodily control. Very common are prescriptions about food and drink, sleep, physical exercise and sex. Some adopt special bodily postures and breath control, the implied view being that once the body is properly disciplined, the spirit is free to soar to its goal. A few, like the Darwishes and some Tantrists, use their bodies actively as ways to induce desired mental states. Extremists like the Christian flagellants and certain Shiite Moslems injure their bodies purposively for their goal. Some others starve themselves to death. A few, like Abelard, emasculate themselves for their soul's sake. There is a disconcerting history of aberration here.

Many seekers after inner states engage in significant mental disciplines too, not only ritual prayers and chants, but meditative exercises and techniques of high-powered concentration. In some cases such practices take years to develop and must be learned under supervision. There are "spiritual ladders" to climb, like the one found in *Theologia Germanica*. From the first step of Purification, one moves to Enlightenment, and lastly Union. In short, there must be, as Gerald Heard states it in his book title, *Training for the Life of the Spirit*.[4]

Now the justification for such preparation is that it makes possible the highest state an individual can attain. Some say it is a "foretaste of eternal blessedness", others that it yields complete self-realization, or provides us with a chance for "extinction without remainder, or salvation, or supreme bliss.

In spite of such high claims, some criticisms may be made:
1. The inner type of spiritual life demands much time and hence tends to be exclusivistic. Ordinary people cannot engage in long hours of meditation or secular intellectual cultivation. Consequently, it is open only to a privileged few who must then rely on others for their practical needs. 2. Such

privilege makes for a divisive class consciousness. Those who do not have the time for supernormal experiences are led to think that their type of life, however sincere, will always be second best. Celibates with spiritual prowess presumably lead better lives than productive householders. Unusual rationalizations are presented to justify this dualism. Karma is one of them. Or, it is claimed that mankind needs select persons to explore the spiritual life unhindered. Again, it is argued that there must be some privileged saints set apart from normal humanity to pursue spiritual goals so can they help lesser humans by means of their super-abundance of accumulated merit. But this double-standard is question begging. 3. Critics also say that sheer inwardness may lead to psychological aberration because one withdraws into escapist phantasy. Mounier notes :

> Excessive rumination dissipates us, too much interiorization leads to over-subtlety, and too much self-solicitude however spiritual, can engender an egocentricity that grows like a psychic cancer.[5]

4. The inner emphasis may also divert one from moral issues with the consequence that things in the everyday world get worse rather than better. Walter Rauschenbusch observes: "None can tell what a place this earth would be if all the force that has been spent in spiritual gymnastics had been put into fighting wrong."[6] And Gandhiji, who believed in the essential unity of mankind said: "I do not believe that an individual may gain spirituality and those that surround him suffer."[7] We are well aware of the ancient Greeks who sought intellectual and aesthetic culture and cared nothing about the poor, the downtrodden or slaves. Bowne once warned that the contemplative life "loses itself in quietistic indifference to the work of the world...in which all moral quality and moral strenuousness disappear altogether."[8]

Now such criticisms do not vacate this first view of the spiritual life. But they point out its classical difficulties and lead us to examine the other type.

II. The outer-directed spiritual life is one which seeks expanded ethical sensitivity. It is interested in the welfare of others, not in its own fulfilling experiences. The thrust is ethical. Gandhiji said: "I use the adjective moral as synonymous with spiritual,[9] "and one of his mentors, John Ruskin wrote, "One act of service is better than seventy years of prayer."

Genuine ethical sensitivity is no mere acquiescence in a series of moral prohibitions. It is not much easier to nurture than inward meditation for it requires commitment and vivid social imagination. Buddhists have pointed out how our intellectual resistance works against our recognition of the pervasiveness of suffering. "Know that all suffering is your concern, O mortal," cries Lanza del Vasto.[10] It takes effort to advance one's concern from his immediate neighbours to the wider community and thence to the world. One must become, as Dom Helder Camara says, "an expert in the art of discovering the good in every person."[11] More than that, he must essay to discover and root out the causes and conditions which produce human suffering and injustice. He must seek to transform inhuman structures that leave two thirds of humanity in a sub-human condition. He must become sensitized to those forces that stifle human development. He will become aware of the obsessions nations have with their own importance and with the techniques for killing,—which they dub "military power". He will oppose and repudiate such things for he sees himself as a champion of humanity not a chauvinist patriot.

Ethical sensitivity may also extend to other than human creatures, illustrating what Schewitzer called "reverence for life" and what the Jains call *ahiṁsa*. As such sensitivity expands, genuinely spiritual persons come to identify themselves with the most unfortunate, as Gandhi did with the Harijans. They are willing to endure suffering for the sake of others though they do not seek it for its own sake. They may engage in fasts, overt compaigns of non-violent resistance against evil structures as Martin Luther King did in the United States and as Denilo Dolci does in Sicily today. Yet they maintain a responsiveness toward those they oppose as well. The hardest thing they have to do, as Camara says, is "to create awareness in the privileged."[12]

I submit that this type of the spiritual life is a means to human nobility which is open to all and is not hindered by sectarian divisions. It is characterized by decision, not by a state of mind. Though difficult, it does not take years of quiet discipline or esoteric study. It requires rather earnest decision, study, and creative imagination. It is open to all. Furthermore, it offers some hope for mankind because it sets about working on substantive problems instead of seeking otherworldly realities or state of bliss. While it has a place for those inclined to inwardness, it judges all inward claims by moral results. Moreover, it can be a source of international unity too especially among those outside of religious traditions who yet favour developing their human responsiveness. Thus it can make for a concept of world community which gives the lie divisive nationalistic or ideological nonsense.

The most persuasive support for this mode of the spiritual life that it is not mere theory. It is a manner of life which we have seen illustrated in the true heroes of the human race in the past in all lands. What is more, we have paradigm cases in our own century. The list is not long, but each name becomes an argument in itself. Toyohiko Kagawa of Japan, Albert Schweitzer of Germany and Africa, Dom Helder Camara of Brazil, Albert Luthuli of South Africa, Leo Baeck and Abraham Heschel of the Jewish tradition, Lanza del Vasto of France, Martin Luther King and Dorothy Day of the United States, Danilo Dolci of Italy, and Gandhiji and Vinoba Bhave of India.

NOTES

1. At the World Congress of Philosophy in Varna, Bulgaria in 1973, Lubomir Dramaliev of Bulgaria read a paper entitled : "The Place and Role of Morality in the System of Spiritual Values." (See Abstract No. 39 in *Proceedings*).

2. New York : Abingdon, 1942. Brightman discusses spirit as personal, social, divine, developing, and as free.

3. Evelyn Underhill, *Practical Mysticism* (N.Y. : Dutton, 1915), p. 66.

4. Gerald Heard, *Training for the life of the Spirit*, (N.Y. : Harper & Bros., 1042). Heard treats some of the popular criticisms of the inner spiritual life but seems to insist on a metaphysics. "The ethic which does not depend on a Cosmology is untrue; the Cosmology which does not result in an Ethic, a life of deduced action, is meaningless." (pp. 19f)

5. Emmanuel Mounier, *Personalism* (Notre Dame, Indians; Notre; Dame Univ. Press., 1252), p. 42. Robert Ornstein [in his recent *The Psychology of Consciousness*(N.Y. : Viking Press, 1972) notes that obsessive indulgence in spiritual exercises "may lead to a permanent withdrawal from life, a regression from and a devaluation of intellectuality." p. 105. But see Akhilananda's *Hindu Psychology* (N.Y. : Harpers, 1946) Chapter X for counter criticisms.

6. Walter Rauschenbusch, *The Righteousness of the Kingdom*, ed. Stackhouse, (N.Y. : Abingdon Press, 1968), p. 108. Edward Conze remarks that Zen Buddhism cultivated a moral indifference that enabled it to fall into the demands of Japanese militarism. (*Buddhism : Its Essence and Development*, N.Y. : Harper Torchbook, 1959, p. 204).

7. In N.K. Bose, *Selections from Gandhi* (Ahmedabad : Navajivan Publ. House, 1948), p. 27.

8. Borden P. Bowne *The Christian Life* (N.Y.: Eaton and Mains, 1899), p. 127.

9. Gandhi, *op. cit.*, p. 73. Lanza Dal Vasto writes: "If you want to lead a holy life, first try to be honest." (*Principles and Precepts of the Return to the Obvious*, N.Y. : Schocken, 1974, p. 11).

10. Lanza Del Vasto, *op. cit.*, p. 275.

11. Dom Helder Camara, *The Desert is Fertile* (Maryknoll, N.Y.: Orbis Books, 1974), p. 21f.

12. *Ibid.*, p. 37.

State University College Oswego, New York, U.S.A.

SCIENCE, RELIGION AND MAN

Santosh C. Sengupta

There has been a persistent movement which emphasises the similarity between Science and Religion to the extent of assimilating the one to the other in respect of aim and approach. The motivation to the movement which is associated with the scientists and the theologians alike is the avoidance of what may be called the dichotomy in experience which disturbs the religious faith of the former and the sense of reliance of the latter on science in view of its impact and prestige. I may refer in this connection to the important papers of Prof. Charles A. Coulson and Prof. Harold K. Schilling. Prof. Schilling's one principal contention is that the method of religion is as much empirical as that of science. As it will be evident the thesis of assimilation which attributes to religion what distinctively pertains to science and vice versa is self-defeating for a number of reasons, one being is that the supposed identical predications are exposed to ambiguity i.e. they have different meanings in different contexts. For instance, the 'personal element' as attributed to science does not have the same meaning as 'personal character' of religion. Similarly the 'experience' which used in the context of religion has a meaning different from its usage in the context of science. I shall try to show in this paper that (a) there is an essential distinction between science and religion in respect of subject-matter and method; (b) there is no dichotomy between the two distinct disciplines. In exposition of my two-fold thesis I shall concentrate on two modes of enquiry into the nature of man which science and religion represent.

There is a clear distinction between science and religion in respect of the method that is employed, the distinction being correlative to the difference in the nature of what the two disciplines enquire into. Now a question may arise : can we legitimately talk of *the* method of science or of religion ? The other way of formulating the question is : are there not sciences and correspondingly different methods that these employ ? Does not this apply to religion which is as much plural as science? The obvious reply to the first question is that the different or the plural sciences claim commonness which is reflected in the modes of approach or the methods that are employed. This commonness legitimatises the characterisation of what may be called *the* method of science or *the* scientific method. The case is that what we call *the* method of science is a complex mixture of certain components. What varies is the proportion of such mixture i.e. the emphasis on this or that component in the combination of such components. To put it symbolically, if the components are X, Y, Z, the combination of X and Y is more emphasised in one science than in the other. What is true of science applies to religion. As it will be evident in the course of discussion one can legitimately talk of *the* method of religion. The method of religion is characterised by complexity. What is variable is the proportion of the complex mixture of the components of the method.

I shall now discuss briefly the nature of the method of science. The question that we have to ask first is : what does Science enquire into ? or what is its subject-matter ? The obvious answer to the question is that science enquires into the nature of phenomenon. Corresponding to plural phenomena which, broadly speaking, are matter, life, mind and society are different sciences which may be characterised as physical, biological, psychological and social. Now the method of investigation which the sciences follow is a complex. The complex consists of two components which are (a) observational and (b) theoretical. The second component admits of division into (a^1) conceptualisation; (b^1) prediction and (c^1) theory-construction. What is significant and this is typical of the method of sciences, is that (a) i.e. the first element (observational) determines (b) and its sub-elements (a^1, b^1 and c^1). It is equally important to note that the different elements of the complex which the method of science is, are inter-related. To take up (a) i.e. the observational element. It is patent that science relies on the method of observation and experiment. (As experiment is a species of observation the first element has been characterised as observational.) Observation is essentially sense-experience and as such essentially external in character. What we call internal experience is directed to what is external. The correlative to sense-experience is datum or fact. The datum is of different types. What is common and essential to these types or what constitutes the giveness or the facticity is externality which is another name for its identifiability as a public object in relation to which the subject concerned has an attitude of a spectator. The data which are presented are numerous and, therefore, a selection of what needs to be investigated by the subject concerned is essential to observational process. It is significant to note that the selection itself is objective as it does not reflect the investigator's personal interest or preference and is a determination of the nature of the object of enquiry. The nature of scientific enquiry is such that the selective observational process which involves analysis into simples be conducted with strict accuracy and exactitude. This is possible through the employment of apparatus or the tools and the theoretical exercise as indicated in the subcomponents of the second principal constituent of the method of science. The data which are observed or recorded need to be understood or communicated through concepts. The concepts have usage in what may be called the language of science. The language is an ordering of concepts and the statements about their relation. The concepts are of different levels. A concept on the higher level is more general than the one on the lower level. The greater generality involves abstractness which is sought with a view to attaining greater understanding of the sense-manifold which means that the abstractness admits of essential reference to what is observed. Now the statements about the relation between concepts which are of general nature are laws and this brings us to the second element of the theoretical component of the scientific method. Science is not just a record of observation-statements. It seeks the formulation of statements of general nature which is another name for predicting or anticipating the future behavior of what is observed. The formulation of general statements i.e. laws is basic to scientific procedure. The mere record of the past or the present occurrences is not science. 'Given similar situations X will behave in a similar way' is the invariable form of genuine scientific assertions. The motivation to the law-formulating function is three-fold : (a) the extension of truth-claim about what is recorded or observed to future cases. This amounts to claiming universality for what the investigator finds to be the case on the basis of the reliance on the uniformity of nature, (b) the explanation of the individual cases through their subsumption under some general statements; (c) the determination or the control of the objects of investigation. The motivation is in evidence in the formulation of the different types of laws of science like physical, biological and of human behaviour. There is no denying that greater reliability can be claimed for laws of the first category than for the laws belonging to other categories. But the point is that the sciences of human phenomena aim at the attainment of the precision and the reliability that can be claimed for physical laws. The laws are intelligible in what may be called a deterministic framework the basis whereof is the principle of causality. This does not mean that the claimed status of universality of laws can be raised to that of logical necessity. The rationalists' attempt at elevating laws to logical principles involves the paradox of emptying the former of observational content which amounts to their denial. The point is that laws are distinguished by their reference to observables. The regularity view of scientific laws as upheld by Hume and others rightly concentrates on this reference. But it, and herein lies its error, emphasises it to the extent of denying the universal character of such laws. That is why the logicians like W.E. Johnson and G.H. Von Wright admit the non-logical necessity of scientific laws. They are necessary so far as they set limits to what is possible as actual fact. Now the question is : how are the laws to be explained ? This again brings us to theory-construction which is an important constituent of scientific method. A theory is viewed as a conceptualised system in the light of which the law-formulating operation of science can be explained. That is, theories are to laws what laws are to facts. A theory, it follows, is much more general than a law (reference may be made to the distinction between the atomic theory and the law of gravitation). One point of distinction between the two is that the former, unlike the latter, contains terms and concepts which apparently are not reducible to what is observable. The question, therefore, arises : how can then there be a connection between theories and scientific laws? The answer is that the connection can be established through rules of correspondence. The rules provide for the relatedness of the theoretical concepts to what is observable. The theory-construction involves the use of models. symbols and analogies. The non-positivistic or the rationalistic approach to science dissociates theoretical construction from empirical reference. The concepts of a theory are viewed as apriori constructs i.e. those which are intelligible in complete independence of what is observed to be existing. There are some who talk of the intellectual enjoyment derived from the contemplation of such dissociated constructs. M. Polyani, for instance, in his book entitled *The Study of Man* likens the enjoyment to the one that a mathematician has. The non-positivists' dissociation of theory-construction from observation is self-defeating so far as it frustrates the very aim of the construction which is one of providing the rationale of experimental laws. Such aim can be fulfilled through the essential relatedness of theoretical concepts to empirical facts. It is further claimed that it is possible to go beyond the fact of relatedness and to visualise conditions under which what appears as unobservable can be observed. That is why, a distinction is made between real and imaginary theoretical concepts ('Red star' and 'wave function' are real concepts, 'ideal gas' and 'frictionless motion' are imaginary). The construction of theoretical entities is relative to present resources. The point is that with the development of the resources conditions can be determined under which what appears as unobservable can be exposed to public inspection. This is not reductionism as it does not consider theoretical concepts as superfluous and admits distinction between such concepts and observation-statements. The brief discussion on the status of theoretical entities bears out that the theoretical or the constructive component of the method of science is under the control of observable. Now this control limits the scope of scientific method and of science itself. In fact what science has achieved or can achieve is because of its limits. It is this limit that legitimises the characterisation of the method of Science as empirical, objective and externalistic. What Science enquires into presents itself as an object considered as external to the enquiring subject. The objectification involves externalisation. It is wrong to restrict the scope of externalistic attitude to what is material. It is claimed that human phenomena at least in certain aspects can be treated as objects and are explorable in external attitude. Such attitude requires that the subject concerned has the role of a spectator or detached observer. That is why it is said that the Scientists' language is spectator language. To have the role of a spectator means that he has to approach the object impersonally i.e. in a way that his relation to the object qua cogniser cannot make any difference to it. That is, his role as a cogniser is such that the object can show itself as it is. There are certain scientists who challenge this on the ground that the scientific method does not require that an investigator's approach to the object of enquiry be impersonal. There is an essential personal element in the scientific approach. It is urged that the role of an impersonal spectator is not possible. Polyani and the current exponents of the thesis of assimilation (Coulson, Schilling etc.) uphold the personal character of scientific knowledge on three grounds: (a) the intense interest of the scientist in his enquiry and the object; (b) the selection of the areas of investigation in the light of the interest; (c) the unifying character of the apprehension that is sought. (The reason is offered by Polyani). It may be observed that none of the three grounds can justify the claim to the supposed personal character of scientific knowledge unless the 'personal' in this context is understood in a loose sense which can only be vacuous. To explain. The scientists' interest in his pursuit does not require of him a living participation or involvement in the object which a personal approach demands. The meaning of the participation or the involvement is that what is explored admits of natural connection with the subject concerned. This connection is mutual. Subject-wise it means the appreciation of or the reverence for the object concerned. (The attitude of reverence is typical of spiritual apprehension or realisation). The connectedness has also its effects on the living of the subject concerned. This means that the participation-situation has a practicality. That is, the 'personal' and the 'practical' interpenetrate. It is patent that the typical scientific enterprise cannot claim the characteristics of participation-situation. The object that the scientist investigates qua enquirer is so viewed that it does not admit of connectedness with him. For instance, one cannot have an attitude of appreciation to the object of investigation as it is in evidence in the aesthetic situation. M. Polyani attributes an aesthetic attitude to a scientist qua enquirer. He goes to the extent of saying that the problems or theories can be beautiful to a scientist. All that can be said is that the usage of 'beautiful' in such context is loose and misplaced. Besides, the practical consequence of the participation situation is not at all in evidence in a scientific enterprise. What a scientist seeks can be completely fulfilled without having a transforming effect on the way of his life or the person that he is. Schilling's reference to the transforming character of science is misleading to the extent that it is not essential to scientific enquiry that it should have transforming character. The other two grounds on which scientific operation is considered as personal are not tenable. The fact that the scientists' area of enquiry is selected by his interest and purpose does not by itself make any difference to the nature of the activity and involves a connection between the subject and the object that the participation-situation requires. Polyani's advanced reason for the thesis of the personal character of scientific knowledge is not acceptable as the unification which is on the cognitive level with which science is concerned is admissible on the basis of the impersonal and the external attitude of the investigation. Now the object to which the investigator has an impersonal attitude is public. The 'public' means that to which similar persons under similar circumstances have an access. This is possible if the statements about the object are verifiable and if the tool of verification is sense-experience or observation. The way of sense-experience is that what it reveals to one under certain circumstances discloses it to others under similar circumstances. There is no doubt that in certain cases the senses deceive. But the point is that the possible deception is in abnormal or exceptional cases. It is important to note that in such cases we do not have legitimate or proper sense-experience. That this is so is confirmed by inter-subjective testing. The case for inter-subjective testing or for corroboration of observation-statements arises only in cases of doubt about the veracity of the latter. Now the proper sense-experience is one which the normal subject has in normal situations. What is significant is that the criterion for the normalcy of the subject or to situation is the proper response to the determination of the external object. That is, the external object being what it is we have sense-experience of certain sort and not vice versa and this requires that the tool of verification be external experience which observation is. Thus there is a correlation between the public character of an externalised object and sense-verification and between sense-verification and the adoption of the impersonal attitude of a spectator. The method on which science relies operates within a framework limited by the range of observable and that is so because of the restrictedness in respect of the subject-matter and the aim of scientific enquiry. What is characteristic of religion or the method that it follows is what may be called the transcendence of the limitedness and this brings us to the next section.

The method of religion is correlated to what it enquires into. It can be stated without fear of controversy that what religion primarily enquires into is that which is not a being or phenomenon which science investigates but it is the Being. The Being, the infinite, or God is not merely the ground of all that is but is also the ultimate goal of human seeking. Man and nature are viewed in relatedness to the infinite Being. There are faiths, it is true, which claim to be religions and yet deny the infinite. But the point is that these are exceptions. There is no doubt that the general agreement is on the infinite-centredness of religion. What is significant is that this agreement conforms to the nature of what may be called the religious situation. I have tried to show in my paper entitled 'The essence of Religion' how the religious situation requires that the infinite or God be central to religious agency. Now the infinite is the transcendent. What is significant is that the transcendent, the beyond, is that in which man is essentially involved. The religious situation is such that the beyond is the depth of the human self. It is in the realisation of the infinite that the seeking human being attains what he is in essence and a sense of total fulfilment which otherwise is not possible. This means that man's essence which is his authentic selfhood is beyond his ordinary existence. It follows that religion unlike science is not impersonal and that the language cannot be spectator language. Now the infinite in which man is essentially involved cannot, in view of its transcendent nature, be apprehended in the way the nature of the phenomena which sciences investigate, is determined. It is beyond the observable which limits the framework within which science operates. In fact, it is in the attitude of the transcendence of the framework that one can approach the infinite. The method of religion can be rightly characterised as one of transcendence. There is no denying that the method of religion has an essential experiential character. But this cannot be employed as an evidence for the thesis of assimilation as experience in the context of religion is essentially different from that on which science draws. Experience which can provide a clue to the nature of the infinite—the Supreme Reality—is non-sensible. We cannot even think of the conditions under which it can have sensible character. It shares the immediacy or the directness or ordinary experience on which science draws but it transcends the latter's sensible character. That is why it is legitimate to characterise it as transcendental. Donald D. Evans characterises it as depth-experience. The transcendental or the depth-experience. has various forms. What is common to these is the non-observational character. The way of transcendental experience is such that the Real to which it is directed cannot be established through arguments basing themselves on the ordinary experience of the world. The experience of ordinary phenomena cannot by itself be premise for the reasoning to God. Any such reasoning derives its rationale from a leap which the ordinary rules cannot justify. The moral of the breakdown of the proofs of the existence of God on which natural theology can draw is that an attempt at establishing the existence of the infinite on the basis of the ordinary experience of the world is self-defeating. The method of religion, as it is in the case of the method of science, has theoretical element. The transcendental or the depth-experience can be understood and communicated (even the mystics cannot avoid the understanding and the communication of what they call ineffable experience) through concepts as employed in language which can be called religious language. The concepts which are used in religious language are of different levels. The higher level concepts have a greater unifying character than the lower level ones. It is evident that the concept of the highest level is that of God or the infinite. The concepts and the statements thereof admit (this is in accordance with the norm of language) of linkage. Underlying this linkage is the system of principles which provides a rationale of the concepts and the statements and of their connectedness. Two of such principles as stated negatively are ; (a) What is empirical is not the ultimate : (b) What is material is not the supreme Reality. The law-formulating function which is essential to science is not possible in a religious enquiry for a number of reasons. One principal reason is that the observed uniformity which makes prediction possible is not possible in case of a religious enterprise. In such enterprise we can indicate the correlations on different levels but statements of such correlations cannot have the status of laws. For instance, statements about the relation between attainment of the object of religion of human fulfilment for which the religious believers claim universality cannot have the observational support which can assure the reliability which makes prediction possible. Models, symbols, and analogies have a more important place in religious language than they have in scientific language in view of the mystery-character of the Supreme Reality. The symbolisation has a two-fold function : (a) demytholisation as it has been attempted by Bultmann and others; (b) Serving as pointers to the unfathomable nature of what is supremely real. The symbols admit of gradation the criterion whereof is the level of approximation to the Real. It is evident that the method of religion like that of Science has experiential and conceptual elements. But the experiential and the conceptual elements do not have as it has been shown the same signification as the elements or the constituents of the scientific method have. The languages of science and religion have some common concepts. But the point is that the concepts have different usages in two languages. The difference in the procedures which the two disciplines adopt corresponds to the difference in the nature of the object of enquiry. In one case (i.e. science) the object of investigation is public to which the subject concerned has an attitude of a spectator while in the other case (i.e. religion) what is enquired into is not public in the sense as indicated and which is explorable in transcendental attitude. What is explored is that in which the subject concerned participates or is involved. This involvement has ontic grounding to the extent that the infinite, being what it is, an approach to the same through a process of involvement or participation therein is possible. This involvement which indicates the practicability of religion is not, as it has been noticed, essential to science. Some exponents of the thesis of assimilation maintain that science is as much practical as religion and in this connection they refer to the transforming effects of both the disciplines. It may be observed that science as applied has practicality. To repeat, the important point which is ignored is that it is not essential to science that it should admit of application to the fulfilment of practical needs. The situation is different in case of religion. The involvement in the infinite which is the goal of one's seeking has a transforming effect on living. In fact the motivation to the involvement is the hope for a liberating process which is ethical in character. The ethical process which is one of regulation of the human will is an extensive exercise. The exercise has two forms—one negative and the other positive. The negative form consists in overcoming twofold natural way i.e. the way of pleasure and ego and the positive form is one of the cultivation of the altruistic sentiments like love, benevolence etc. The natural connection between the spiritual and the ethical dimension of human existence is grounded in the unlimited goodness of the infinite Being, the Supreme goal of the striving for liberation. The spiritual process is one of continual hope for self-realisation. Faith in the infinite or God and hope for liberation interpenetrate.

I have so far tried to focus on the areas of discrimination between Science and Religion. Now the questions arise : Are the two distinct disciplines really separate? Cannot they be related ? The questions are indeed pressing or urgent as in the satisfactory answer thereto one can resolve a conflict-situation. The human situation requires that science and religion be related that man can overcome the predicament of dichotomy in experience. This is so because as in the words of A.N. Whitehead 'Science and Religion are the strongest general forces which influence man'. It is the same man who is a part of nature and the total evolutionary process and subject to the laws of nature and is capable of transcendence to the infinite or God. It is the same creature who carries on experiments in the laboratory for the understanding of phenomena and offers prayer to God in the Church for liberation. If science and Religion, the two spheres of human enterprise, cannot be related, man will be divided against himself and be in a conflict-situation to which one who has a split-personality is exposed. I shall try to establish that the two can be related and that the human need for overcoming the possible conflict-situation can be fulfilled. This will be shown by way of indication of possible correlation between the scientific and the religious understanding of man. It may be pointed out that one necessary condition of determining the correlation is to demarcate clearly between the two types of understanding both in respect of the sphere of investigation and the modes of approach thereto. It is also necessary to determine the limits of the application of the methods that are employed. In the absence of two-fold determination the conflict between the two types of understanding of man and the resultant existential predicament of dichotomy as indicated are inevitable. An exploration of the nature of the two types of understanding of man involves an enquiry into the nature of man. Space forbids an extensive treatment of the nature and the status of man. I shall make a few general observations on the nature of man. It is relevant to point out at the outset that man can be studied in relation to the total process of which he is a part. The existentialist' investigation of the highest creature in dissociation from the process of evolution in protest against the scientific or the objective treatment of man is a misrepresentation of the human situation. Man emerges as a complex or multi-dimensional creature. The complexity of man is of such proportion that he appears a paradox. The complexification which makes the emergence of man possible corresponds to a proportionately higher level of organisation and this is as Teilhard de Chardin tries to show in the celebrated work entitled *The phenomenon of Man* in accordance with the principle of evolution itself. The complexification which is in evidence in the process of evolution reaches such a stage that a new creature with distinctness or uniqueness emerges. The emergence of man, it may be pointed out, represents proportionately greater novelty than it is in evidence in the appearance of other evolutes. Now the question arises: 'Wherein is man really different from other creatures'? The answer is that it is the two-fold capacity for reflection and freedom that constitutes the differentia of man. Man alone is capable of reflection. Reflection is mental activity of turning towards itself, which means the power of thinking that one thinks, or of knowing that one knows. Teilhard de Chardin shows how hominisation begins with what he calls nosphere. Reflection as a cognitive act is meaning-discerning. It follows that man qua reflected creature can discern meaning. This operation is extensive as there are different spheres of meaning. The capacity for this important operation is no doubt a very unique feature of man. But it is wrong to limit the differentia of man to this capacity or power. The other capacity is one for freedom which has a direct bearing on the human will in its decision-making operations, and is equally essential to man. That is, man is both a reflective and free creature. What is significant is that the two-fold power reflects a basic capacity which may be characterised as one for transcendence. Strictly speaking, man's real differentia consists in his capacity for transcendence. Transcendence, as involved in reflective activity, is on the cognitive plane and as such, as it has been pointed out, it is meaning-discerning. It (transcendence) as indicated in the act of freedom is meaning-conferring. The meaning-conferring operation like the meaning-discerning function can be on different levels. 'Transcendence' needs to the distinguished from 'transcendent' (there are some who wrongly identify 'transcendent' with 'transcendence'.) The act which transcendence is, is one of going beyond what is given. It is a thrust to what is beyond what he finds himself in. The genesis of the transcendence or the thrust is the felt discontent with the given. The discontent which provides phenomenological clue to the meaning of man is to be distinguished from despair. In fact man's hope lies in his dissatisfaction. The human discontent is on different levels and there is a correspondence between the gradation of discontent and that of transcendence. Corresponding to the deeper level of discontent is the higher level of transcendence. Thus man is a discontended and transcendented being. In other words, we can say that he is a meaning-discerning and meaning-fulfilling creature. The criterion for the gradation of the levels of human being is the degree of the fulfilment of meaning which transcendence makes possible. There is a connection between the meaning-fulfilment and the ascent of man. The extent of the fulfilment is proportionate to the degree of development of human existence. Thus there is correlation between (a) the level of discontent and that of transcendence, (b) the level of transcendence and that of meaningfulness and the sphere of meaningfulness and that of the development of man. Broadly speaking, the different levels of the complex creature that man is are : (a) physico-biological (b) mental (c) ethical and (d) spiritual. Each of these is intelligible in the context of the relation to the other and has a social character which varies from one case to other. It is claimed that on the spiritual level of man which religion primarily enquires into complete self-fulfilment is possible. It is relevant to point out that the ascent of man does not mean that the higher place of his existence can bypass or negate the lower one. The human situation is that the lower level is fulfilled in the higher one. Man—the mental or the thinking being—is one who has a body and subject to biological laws. Similarly the moral or the spiritual man has to satisfy certain needs for the sake of living itself. This is so because of the basic structure of human existence which is constituted of inherent limitedness of finitude. Man's having a body and being in a spatio-temporal world represents limiting or, in the words of Karl Jaspers, boundary-situations which man can no more overcome than he can jump out of his skin. Man's ascent to the higher level means freedom from the dominant influence of the lower one which means that it is not negated but employed as a means to the fulfilment of the need of the higher plane. The movement or the ascent to the spiritual or the highest plane of existence means the employment of the lower levels biological, mental and ethical to the attainment of complete self-fulfilment which as religion claims is possible through divine realisation. It follows that the opposite movement i.e. descent from the higher to the lower plane of human existence means an inversion of means-end relationship. One who is on the biological plane thinks, does good acts and prays to God. But the point is that the living is the dominant concern. The ends as relative to the higher levels are used as means to to the furtherance of living.

It is evident from the brief discussion on the nature of man that he is discontented, transcendental and everfulfilling being. Now the question is, how can science understand the complex creature, the supposed crown of creation? Now an answer to this question is possible if we keep in view a distinction which is often ignored between the legitimate and the non-legitimate application of the method of science. The latter is an extension of the method in question to the spheres to which it does not apply and this is another name for dogmatism, to which the scientific study of man is exposed. We have a typical example of this dogmatism in Skinner's defence of what he calls Science of behaviour. The claim is that man's autonomy as expressed in his supposed freedom and dignity is a myth. Man is as much malleable as a natural phenomenon and exposable to observables. The uniqueness of man as manifested in what is called the higher level is reducible to a function of a natural agency. The behaviourists' account of man and the naturalistic treatments of the ethical and the spiritual levels of man are the results of the illegitimate extension of the method of science. The legitimate application of this method, therefore, has to limit itself to an investigation of the facts about man which are really amenable to the objective method. The point of this delimitation is to avoid reductionistic treatment of man which involves the denial of his uniqueness and his resultant abolition. Such facts particularly concern the physio-biological level of man, his mental behaviour (which is not the same as mind), his relatedness of an external nature which is another name for sociality. It is in the light of the framework within which the method of science operates that such facts can be studied. To come to 'physio-biological fact. By 'physico-biologicai fact' I mean man's bodily existence having a physical basis and being situated in a spatio-temporal world determined by the principle of causality. Now the way the human body functions in response to the external stimuli is exposable to observation made possible through instruments and that prediction can be made about its functions on the basis of the observed uniformity and causal relationship. The increasing advance of medical science has its source in the reliability of the predictions. The connection between a drug and its effect on the human organism is a case in point. The determining influence of the physical enviroment on the function of the human organism admits of an objective treatment. Now the agency which makes the operation of the organism possible and its interaction with the physical environment cannot be attributed to the human or the divine will. For instance, the function of the circulatory system cannot be attributed to the function of the human or the divine will. There is no doubt that there is a connection between the mind and its behaviour. Such behaviour admits of objective treatment and undoubtedly helps the understanding of the mind of man. The advance in the determination of the conditions under which the behavioral study is possible is indeed impressive. Similarly the sociological facts can be determined in a way which is natural to a scientific study. The extensive researches of what are called Social Sciences have yielded knowledge of the nature and of the development or evolution of social relationships. Now the important point is that man is more than the facts —physio-biological, psychological (as understood in the sense of behaviour) and sociological. Man has a body but is not the body. What is distinctively mental is not mere behaviour. There is a depth of human relationship which is beyond external communication. If man is reduced to the facts which are accessible to the objective method he ceases to be unique. Man's uniqueness, as it has been already noted is fully disclosed in a sphere in which he can attain complete fullness of meaning in his existence and this is possible on the spiritual place and this brings us to the next section in which we shall throw light on the nature of religious understanding of man.

Religion understands man in a way which is essentially different that which science adopts. This is so because man is viewed in the context of dimension which cannot be objectively determined. This dimension consists in the directedness of man to the infinite or God in which he seeks complete realisation. This is, as it has been already observed, transcendence on the highest level. Transcendence, as it has been noticed, is rooted in discontent and that there is a correlation between the levels of discontent and the planes of transcendence. Discontent which motivates transcendence to the spiritual plane is deeper and more comprehensive than it is in evidence on the moral plane so far as it is not with the natural way of man but with the whole of human existence. This expresses itself in the sense of finitude or basic limitedness. Corresponding to this discontent is the thrust or the transcendence to the infinite, the supremely Real. Underlying this discontent (which is to be distinguished from despair) and the corresponding transcendence is the hope for the realisation of the infinite which is another name for liberation. The liberation, it is claimed again can constitute complete self-fulfilment and the corresponding bliss or happiness. Thus the spiritual situation of man represents a correlation between (a) discontent and transcendence, (b) transcendence and fulfilment, and fulfilment and bliss. The situation is infinite-centred and it is in the light of this that religion understands man. What is significant is that the other levels of man to which reference has been made as viewed in the light of this situation acquire a meaning which is not otherwise possible. For instance, the mental and the moral life of man are not to be understood in terms of psychological and ethical concepts respectively but as means to the fulfilment of the end which spirituality seeks. Now the fulfilment has two aspects (a) cognitive and (b) practical. In the first aspect it is in the nature of disclosure, of what the self is. In the second aspect it is freedom which is correlated to the transforming function of the human will. It is evident that the situation cannot be objectivity determined as the transcendence that is involved is a thrust from observable to the transcendent. The transcendental or the depth-experience which is a clue to the nature of the transcendent is characterised by its essential distinction from sense-experience. This means that the infinite cannot by nature of the case be a public object. Besides, the movement to the infinite viewed existentially is a process of self-unfolding and as such it can be viewed inwardly. The inward approach to the movement to the infinite is all the more necessary as the infinite is that in which the subject concerned is essentially involved. This inward or non-objective approach does not involve the reduction of spirituality to subjective exercise. It may be observed in this connection that the way religion understands man cannot be stated in naturalistic terms. The naturalistic accounts of religion in terms of psychological and social concepts as associated with Feuerbach and Durkheim respectively are misleading to the extent that they misrepresent what may be called the religious situation. Now the non-objective method that religion employs is appropriate so far as it limits itself to the exploration of the situation as indicated. But it cannot be extended to the understanding of facts about man (facts which man cannot bypass). Such facts, as I have tried to show, can be determined only objectively. The point is that we have to demarcate the spheres which science and religion study. That is how we can avoid the conflict between the two (science and religion) and relate the two different types of understanding of man and this brings us to the concluding section of the paper.

The modes of the understanding of man which Science and Religion admit of relatedness as the two approaches to the distinct spheres of the complex creature are different.

There is a case for conflict only when in the emphasis on the similarity between Science and Religion the two-fold distinction is ignored and one is assimilated to the other. The paradoxical situation is that the upholders of what I have called the thesis of assimilation in their overzeal to avoid a conflict between the two modes of enquiry affirm a position which provides for a conflict-situation. The point is that the spheres of the scientific and the religious understanding of man are such that they by nature of the case admit of different treatments. In one case the sphere is one of facts and in the other case the realm is one of comprehensive meaning. We have seen that the two spheres can be apprehended in the objective attitude and the attitude of transcendence (which is inward) respectively. The conflict arises only in the case of illegitimate application of the methods concerned which the exponents of the thesis of assimilation cannot guard against and this results in dogmatism to which both Science and Religion are exposed. Science's exposure to dogmatism is reflected in the naturalistic and the reductionists accounts of man the typical of which is behaviourism or environmentalism. The excess of religion is reflected in its lapse into supernaturalism i.e. the position which represents the denial of the attribution of natural occurrences to natural agencies. We have the vestige of supernaturalism in the postulation of the need for divine intervention for regular occurrences like mind-body relationship or for the correction of the breakdown of natural operations. The point is that we have to avoid the illegitimate claim of either type in order that we can determine the way of relating science and religion. What is significant is that the distincts which the two represent do not exclude each other. We have noticed that the lower sphere or level cannot be negated by the higher one (This is evident from the nature of development of man). Rather the lower level conditions the higher one. The man in the highest of spirituality is the creature who lives and is situated in the physical environment. In fact the living conditions the supreme exercise in transcendence. It is relevant to state in this connection that the lower level conditions the higher one but does not confer meaning thereupon. Rather than the former derives its significance from its relatedness to the latter. That is, the conditioning operation is different from the meaning-conferring function. We can illustrate this by way of an analogy from the authentic field. The aesthetic appreciation of a scene involves perception. One has to perceive in order that he can appreciate. Perceiving, therefore, conditions aesthetic appreciation but does not confer meaning thereupon. It may be observed in this connection that the analogy is not appropriate as in the case under investigation the natural realm has its source in God—God being the ground of all that is. The other way of putting the objection is, is it not that the occurrences which are attributed to natural agencies have source in God. This type of objection involves an important issue which for want of space cannot be discussed here. My general remark is that we cannot look for the answer in certain directions. One, which is typical of the existentialist approach dissociates God nature and views the former in the realm of human selfhood. The other associated with Whitehead—and from Process-theologians is that which distributes the agency over God and natural causes. My positive observation is that following Aquinas we can look for the answer in the direction in which it is possible to affirm that God is the ground of nature and yet grants the possibility of the operation of natural occurrences in terms of natural causes in a manner that God is the ground of man and yet provides for his freedom. I shall develop this observation in another paper.

Visva-Bharati, Santiniketan

RELIGION, SCIENCE AND MAN

L. K.Aravkar

The world has witnessed the wonderful achievements of science and technology in recent times and will, I am sure, continue to see their still more surprising victories. It is really very difficult even to imagine the shape of things to come. Man is completely dazzled by the discoveries and inventions of science and the victories and achievements of technology. In spite of this progress in these fields man was not satisfied, could not become happy and began to think again and proceeded to discover and explore other areas in search of happiness. Science is the architect of the modern world and the modern civilization is described as the technological civilization. But somehow or other, it appears that man is not happy with it though it has come to stay. Swami Ranganathananda observes (Eternal Values for a changing Society, p. 350)

'Man in this technological civilization is feeling inwardly impoverished and empty in an environment of wealth, power, and pleasure; he is full of tension and sorrow, doubt and uncertainty, all the time. Juvenile delinquency, drunkenness, suicide, and a variety of other maladies are ever on the increase. Why ? Because man is not inwardly satisfied; he is smitten with ennui and boredom arising from the limitations of his sense-bound Weltanschauung'.

This is the situation in which man is placed in the technological civilization. Man is therefore compelled to think of the gravity of the situation which has been brought about in recent times. Naturally this subject is getting more and more important to man in the modern world. There is enough evidence to show that there are many representative thinkers in the twentieth century who are having a new live of thinking and making a new approach to solve the problems arising out of this situation.

Before appreciating the new approach, the new line of

thinking or the new way of understanding, it is necessary that one should be aware of the general nature and character of science. Science, it is usually accepted, deals only with the appearances of things and not with the reality behind these appearances. According to some of the modern physicists, what science has revealed of the world is only the outer aspect or the external nature of things. Science deals mainly and essentially with phenomena revealed by the senses or by instruments and appliances which increase the range and improve the quality of sense-perception. 'Science restricts itself to the understanding of the observable part of the universe and to controlling its energies for the use of man.' It deals with the vast world of the not-self aspect of man. The real subject of the positive sciences is 'Man the Known,' 'the exterior of things,' 'or' the without of things.' To express the idea in terms of Indian Philosophy, it can be said that science gives us knowledge of the 'Kṣetra' (not-self) ; science is the study of the objective field.

Now, the question is about the attitude of Science. The attitude of science towards the objective world is usually described as the Western approach and it is embodied in what is known as the scientific frame of mind. Karl Pearson says:

'The classification of facts, the recognition of their sequence and relative significanc, is the function of science, and the habit of formimg a judgement upon these facts unbiased by personal feeling is the characteristic of what may be termed the scientific frame of mind.' (Grammar of Science, p. 6)

Some of the characteristics of the new era such as the reflective analysis, spirit of criticism, revolt against authority and tradition, demand for freedom in thought clearly indicate the spirit of scientific inquiry. The driving force behind the unique achievement of science is this spirit of free inquiry. Criticism is the very essence of science. In science our attitude is critical and not dogmatic. Swami Ranganathananda describes this spirit of inquiry in the following words (Ibid, p. 610)

'The mind that questions, and questions with a serious intent and purpose, and tests and verifies the answers it gets, has a dynamic quality about it which enables it to forge ahead in the world of thought and things. In so forging ahead, it disturbs the wayside calm of untested dogmas and comfortable beliefs. Science is verified knowledge. The explosive character of modern scientific thought is the product of the impact of a rapid succession of verified knowledge against an intractable fund of dogmas, assumptions, and untested beliefs. The history of science in recent centuries is thus the history of the triumph of the spirit of free inquiry over mere opinion, prejudice, and dogma.'

The earnest passion for truth, the keen spirit of free inquiry and the critical method of investigation enabled science to acquire high position, prestige and authority. And because of the dazzling progress of physical sciences, some of the scientists were led to believe that scientific knowledge is the only knowledge and that any knowledge outside the fields of the physical sciences could not be called scientific. It might be termed individual opinion, personal belief or private faith but could not be given the status of knowledge. Science is characterized as the disinterested search for truth. It is further argued that science is neutral so far as its application or utilization is concerned. And this has added to its prestige and authority.

Let us now attend to religion. What is religion? What is the spirit of religion? What is the meaning of religion? Religion deals with the reality behind the appearances. It deals with the universe revealed not by the senses but by the spirit. It is mainly and essentially concerned with the unobservable universe. It deals with the 'self' aspect of man. The true subject of religion is 'Man the unknown,' 'the interior of things,' or 'the within of things' 'It gives us knowledge of 'Kṣetrajña' (self). According to the Upaniṣads, there are two categories of knowledge—aparā Vidyā and parā Vidyā. Aparā Vidyā is the ordinary knowledge of the world of experience which is revealed through the senses. This is scientific knowledge, the knowledge which 'gives' us only knowledge of structural form and not knowledge of content,' in the language of Eddington. Parā Vidyā is the superme knowledge or most excellent knowledge which is usually discribed as wisdom. This is the 'knowledge of which we understand that imperishable reality behind this world of change, the imperishable content of this perishable structural form that we see as the universe. Religion gives us this supreme knowledge. It deals with that which is changeless in this world of change. It seeks to understand and realize the eternal, changeless Reality hidden in our experience of the world of change. It is the science of the beyond. It is the science of the Infinite beyond the finite. It deals with the super-sensual world. 'What lies beyond the sense level may be termed super-sensual but not super-natural, and may form a valid field of study by a science equipped with methods and techniques relevant to that special field.' (Ibid, p. 660). This is the scope of religion. Swami Vivekananda says :

'Beyond (waking) consciousness is where the bold search; (waking) consciousness is bound by the senses. Beyond that, beyond the senses, men must go, in order to arrive at truths of the spiritual world, and there are even now persons who succeed in going beyond the bonds of the senses. These are called riṣs (sages), because they come face to face with spiritual truths.' (The Complete Works, Vol. III, p. 253).

Religion is a matter of experience. The test of religion is 'anubhūti, 'realization.' The Atman is to be seen,' says the Bṛhadaraṇyaka Upaniṣad (ii iv. 5). Religion is the awakening of the spiritual hunger and naturally it involves man's unending struggle to satisfy that hunger. Spirituality is the core of religion and it can be realized through the different 'Sādhanas'' spiritual practices. The meaning and scope of religion have been embodied by Swami Vivekananda in the following well-known statement (Complete Works, Vol I, p. 257) :

'Each soul is potentially divine. The goal is to manifest this Divinity within by controlling nature, external and internal. Do this either by work or worship, or psychic control, or philosophy—by one, or more, or all of these—and be free. This is the whole religion. Doctrines or dogmas or rituals or books or temples or forms are but secondary details.'

Religion is not a particular dogma, or a creed, or a sect, or a belief, or a conformity. It is universal in character because it teaches universal toleration and universal acceptance. Different forms of religion are nothing but the different pathways leading to the same goal. Swami Vivekananda says :

'To him all the religions, from the lowest fetishism to the highest absolutism, mean so many attempts of the human soul to grasp and realize the Infinite, each determined by the conditions of its birth and association and each of these marks a stage of progress; and every soul is a young eagle soaring higher and higher, gathering more and more strength till it reaches the glorious sun.' (Complete Works, Vol I p. 15).

It has already been stated above that religion is a matter of experience and religious experience is everywhere the same. While pleading for a scientific approach to religion and pointing out its unversal character Swami Vivekananda further says :

'Experience is the only source of knowledge. In the world, religion is the only science where there is no surety, because it is not taught as a science of experience. This should not be. There is always, however, a small group of men who teach religion from experience. They are called mystics, and these mystics in every religion speak the same tongue and teach the same truth.'

'This is the real science of religion. As mathematics in every part of the world does not differ, so the mystics do not differ. They are all similarly constituted and similarly situated. Their experience is the same; and this becomes law.' (Ibid., Vol. VI, p. 81).

What we have said so far is just enough to enable any person to frame a fairly clear idea about the nature, character, meaning and scope of both science and religion. Now the question is about the nature of relation between science and religion. Is there any conflict or opposition between science and religion? Is science really an enemy of religion? Is religion really an enemy of science? If so, in what sense? We must turn our attention now to the consideration of these problems.

Even a little reflection will, I believe, be sufficient to indicate that all this creation of problems is entirely due to sheer misunderstanding and confusion in thought regarding the nature and scope of investigations in these two spheres, science and religion. Because of marvellous successes and wonderful achievements in the field of investigations in the physical universe some of the scientists were tempted to advocate the view that the physical universe is the only universe, that is the only reality and that there is nothing beyond. Here they committed an error of omission in not recognizing the beyond. These scientists could not understand the limitations of their investigations. But some of the eminent scientists and great thinkers in this modern age have tried to avoid this error by recognizing and emphasizing the possibility of 'the world beyond' or 'the world within.'

The universe was a great mystery to the primitive man; it has not ceased to be so not only for the civilized man but also for the great scientists in the modern age. Scientists like Sir James Jeans presenting the scientific view of the universe describe the universe as 'the Mysterious Universe.' They treat nature as profoundly mysterious and feel that they have only scratched the outer surface of nature and that they are yet far away from the heart of the universe. Sir James Jeans says:

'Physical science set out to study a world of matter and radiation, and finds that it cannot describe or picture the nature of either, even to itself. Photons, electrons, and protons have become about as meaningless to the physicist as x, y, z, are to a child on its first day of learning algebra. The most we hope for at the moment is to discover ways of manipulating x, y, z, without knowing what they are, with the result that the advance of knowledge is at present reduced to what Einstein has described as extracting one incomprehensible from another incomprehensible.' (The New Background of Science, p. 68)

We thus see that the physical universe is a great mystery even to the scientists in the modern world. We are still more surprised when we come to man because man has become a still greater mystery in the whole universe. Sir Arthur Eddington observes:

'And yet, in regard to the nature of things, this knowledge is only an empty shell—a form of symbols. It is knowledge of structural form, and not knowledge of content. All through the physical world runs that unknown content which must surely be the stuff of our consciousness. Here is a hint of aspects deep within the world of physics, and yet unattainable by the methods of physics. And, moreover, we have found that where science has progressed the farthest, the mind has but regained from nature that which the mind has put into nature.

'We have found a strange footprint on the shores of the unknown.' (Space Time and Gravitation, p. 200)

Einstein recognized the mystery of man when he said:' Science can denature plutonium; but it cannot denature the evil in the heart of man.'

Regarding Einstein's contributions to modern scientific thought, Lincoln Barnett says:

'In the evolution of scientific thought, one fact has become impressively clear: there is no mystery of the physical world which does not point to a mystery beyond itself. All highroads of the intellect, all byways of theory and conjecture, lead ultimately to an abyss that human ingenuity can never span...The further he extends his horizons, the more vividly he recognizes the fact that, as the physicist Niels Bohr puts it,' "We are both spectators and actors in the great drama of existence." Man is thus his own greatest mystery. He comprehends but little of his organic processes and even less of his unique capacity to perceive the world around him, to reason and to dream. Least of all does he understand his noblest and most mysterious faculty: the ability to transcend himself and perceive himself in the act of perception. (The Universe and Dr. Einstein, p. 126)

While attempting to explore the mystery of man on the part of modern science, the eminent paleontologist, Pere Teilhard de Chardin says:

'The time has come to realize that an interpretation of the universe—even positivist one—remains unsatisfying unless it covers the interior as well as the exterior of things; mind as well as matter. The true physics is that which will, one day, achieve the inclusion of man, in his wholeness in a coherent picture of the world.

Chardin asks : 'Up to now has science ever troubled to look at the world other than from without?' And then he further says :

'In the eyes of the physicist, nothing exists legitimately, at least up to now except the without of things. The same intellectual attitude is still permissible in....Finally, it breaks down completely with man, in whom the existence of a within can no longer be evaded, because it is the object of a direct intuition and the substance of all knowledge.'

It will thus be sufficiently clear that the eminent scientists and great thinkers in the modern age are coming to realize more and more that there is the within, the beyond, the different order of being or the other plane of existence unattainable by science and are not willing to uphold the view that the physical universe is the only universe and the scientific knowledge is the only knowledge and the method of positive sciences is the only method of investigation. This is a great truth that should be realized more and more. When science recognizes the fact about its distinct subject-matter and its specific method of investigation it will no more remain an enemy of religion. Similarly, when religion functions within its specified area with its own apparatus it shall never be an enemy of science. The conflict between science and religion arises when the limit is transcended and the dogmatic attitude is developed. In his lecture on 'Religion and Science,' Swami Vivekananda says :

'Religion deals with the truths of the metaphysical world just as chemistry and the other natural sciences deal with the truths of the physical world. The book one must read to learn chemistry is the book of nature. The book from which to learn religion is your own mind and heart. The sage is often ignorant of physical science because he reads the wrong book—the book within; and the scientist is too often ignorant of religion, because he too reads the wrong book—the book without' (Ibid, Vol VI, p. 81)

Science develops hostility to religion when it becomes identified with the pre-established creeds and sects, or when it turns into a body of untested beliefs and dogmas, or when it remains a permanent conformity. This has happened in the history of Europe where religion has often positively functioned as an 'enemy' of science. Fortunately, this has not taken place here in India. Because of our cultural tradition which is characterised by the spirit of free inquiry and universal acceptance and toleration, India could always remain very sympathetic and hospitable to the scientific thought. Never was India apathetic and hostile to the scientific spirit. Our national attitude has always been quite helpful and conducive to the development of science. And so, India has never seen that form of opposition between science and religion.

Really speaking, there is no reason why there should be any opposition between science and religion. Dogmatism in any form is dangerons to both science and religion. What is needed to-day, much more than before, is the synthesis of science and religion. While expounding Swami Vivekananda's synthesis of science and religion, Swami Ranganathananda says :

'The study of the one alone does not exhaust the whole range of experience. Also, the study of the one from the standpoint of the other will not lead to satisfactory results. But the study of the one in the light of the conclusions from the study of the other is helpful and relevant.' (Eternal Values for a Changing Society, p. 337).

Science alone is not enough, nor is religion sufficient by itself. If science is taken away from society, what remains is sheer primitivism. And if religion is taken away from society, what remains is simple barbarism. The wisdom lies in avoiding both—sheer primitivism as well as simple barbarism. Science can create healthy external environment for man while religion can create a healthy internal environment for him. And man, thus taking the help from both science and religion, can hope to achieve his total fulfilment. Man needs the services of science as science can create the conditions for his happiness. But at the same time, he wants to safeguard himself against its possible misuse and abuse. Again, the creation of conditions for happiness is not the creation of happiness itself. And man is in search of happiness. If any increase of scientific knowledge is going to lead to the increase of sorrow, it is very difficult to maintain that it is knowledge.

It is ignorance or spiritual blindness. Man must not put himself into this predicament. The combination of science and religion is thus necessary for the happiness of man. R.A. Millikan says :

'It seems to me that the two great pillars upon which all human well-being and human progress rest are first, the spirit of religion, and second, the spirit of science—or knowledge. Neither can attain its largest effectiveness without support from the other. To promote the latter, we have universities and research institutions. But the supreme opportunity for everyone with no exception lies in the first. (Autobiography)

The modern world needs the synthesis of science and religion. This will enable man to construct the synthetic view of the universe. Both science and religion must work in their respective spheres with the spirit of harmonious cooperation for the sake of humanity. Humanity has a claim on both—science and religion. As remarked by Aldous Huxley, modern technological civilization produces intelligent fool while ancient civilization produces the wise fool; but what the world needs is the production of the intelligent wise. And this can be achieved only through the synthesis of science and religion which is the very condition for the total fulfilment of man.

Ruia College, Bombay

11

RELIGION AND SCIENCE AS DEFINITIONS OF HUMANITY

Howard L. Parsons

The human being derives its definition from both its ideas and its interactive, transactional practice toward others and non-human world. To define, to be defined, is to make definite, to delimit. The human being is impelled to define its self because it is born relatively unformed, plastic, and capable of development—because it is an infant dependent on its dialectical relations with others and the world for survival and the actualizing of its potentialities. For both species and individual person, such practice is initially directed to satisfying the survival needs (hunger, thirst, safety, etc.) and then the suprasurvival needs that distinguish humankind from other species, e.g., the needs for linguistic communication, cognition, aesthetic appreciation, etc. Such needs appear to have a physiological basis but are elicited and formed through the regnant cultural patterns of social practice determining infant personality. Thus, while cultures differ widely as to specified patterns of social practice, they display certain common patterns because the phychologies of psychosomatic individuals are similar, their survival and suprasurvival needs are similar, their social interactions are similar, and their social techniques of interacting with the non-social worlds to fulfill their needs are similar.

Practical definition in the evolution of humankind has preceded conceptual definition and has normally provided the prior basis and ultimate test for conceptual definition. Concepts had to shape and direct practice or become meaningless, while practice had to yield to the guidance of concepts or become brute habit. Unlike other animals, the human animal conceives, turns concepts into impractical fantasies, and fructifies and transforms its practice with concepts.

The physiology of *Homo sapiens* is at least ·25 million years old and perhaps much older, and the genus *Homo* goes back perhaps four million years.[1] The invention of stone tools, fire (accompanied by the routing of game, cooking, and the hearth), and intimate social life (based on dimorphic sexuality and infantile dependency) profoundly shaped the living practice of primitive human beings. In two million years the brain of *Homo erectus*, our immediate ancestor, had doubled in size. Social speech and conceptual thought were created. Thus members of the human species began to reflect on their social practice and shaped it more deliberately and efficiently. Hypothetical alternative plans of practice emerged. Conceptual definition more and more mingled with, affected, and were modified by practice. The human line diverged from the non-human, acquiring definition.

The earliest archeological evidence of a human being's conceptual definition of itself dates from Neanderthal times some 75,000 years ago.[2] The cave burials of these people, which included animals, implements, offerings, weapons and the use of red ochre on the bodies (in simulation of life), suggest a tender concern for the dead and a belief in a continued afterlife.[3] Their concept of "totemic cohesion in space and time"[4] gave definition to the family, group, and clan. This totemic concept and the belief attending the dead have been called "religious," but we should be careful to understand the concrete phenomenon

Paleolithic people defined themselves as both dependent on the invisible powers transcending and pervading nature (powers similar to *anima* and *mana*) and as actively unified with the objects and processes of nature (the totemic plant, animal, or insect) necessary to the economy.[5] The human person and group were conceived to be dependent on both nature and these invisible powers but also capable of manipulating them for their own ends through sympathetic magic. Paleolithic practice displayed a concern with man's appeasement and control of both the unknown, invisible order presumed to be behind the things of this life, and the things themselves. Its symbolism and ritual reflected and rainforced the Paleolithic economy of hunting, fishing, and food-gathering. In it nature and its invisible forces were conceived to be both harsh and benign, alien and friendly, and the human attitude toward nature was both hostile and open, accommodating and manipulative. In the midst of the dark and inscrutable forces of the storm and wind, the lightning and thunder, the deep forest and wild animals, primitive people were conscious of their own power to hunt, to cooperate, and to survive. Fate loomed large, but the power and freedom of human society asserted themselves. Paleolithic practice contained, in uneasy dialectical unity, the germinal attitudes later to be differentiated as "religion" and "science": the attitude that human beings, in dependence and receptivity, are defined by an unknown order; and the attitude that, in independence and activity, they define themselves in relation to a known nature.

The Neolithic economy (c. 6000-3000 B. C. in many parts of the world), a food-producing revolution through the cultivation of crops and the domestication and breeding of animals, issued in a new orientation. The need of people to relate their practice in a fruitful way to the soil and other elements gave rise to a passionate concern to relate themselves rightly to the forces of fertility in nature. The need to know the propitious times for plowing, planting, and harvesting brought forth specialists who studied the movements of the moon and stars and measured the length of the sun's shadow cast by a stick. Deities were conceived to preside over parts of nature and man's agrarian and flock-tending activities, childbirth, war, etc. Impersonal magico-religious amulets and figurines with amplified reproductive organs expressed this concern with fertility.[6] External forces, seen and unseen, were conceived to define human life; but such forces were known to be ordered, and hence were subject to human definition, scrutiny, and increasing control.

Advanced Neolithic society was a transition from Paleolithic communal production and consumption to the developed class societies of the urban period. The surplus food and time of Neolithic society made possible the private appropriation of social wealth. Hence the old totemic unitary and "universal" view of nature and human society and the primitive

Neolithic fertility orientation were displaced by individualized, semi-personal gods who corresponded to the wealthy ruling chiefs in particular regions. The rise of such gods marks the first clear differentiation of religion.

At the start of the urban revolution, c. 3500 B. C., the external forces conceived to define human life and had become specific and personalized. The Sumerians had nearly 2000 deities, each controlling a special aspect of nature. The gods presumed to rule over various city-states were united in an assembly, counterparts of the kings of the city-states, appointed by the gods as stewards to assure the obedience and service of the subjects in "the cosmos as state."[7] In the Egyptian regal cosmology the pharaoh was conceived to be the incarnation of the sun god Horus. Human beings were anxious, uncertain, and dependent; but now it was not nature with which they had to cope directly, but that which was simultaneously source and appeaser of their dependency, the god-king.

Paleolithic people felt at one with their world through the linkage of the totem. Though the things of nature stood over against them, they were convinced they might command them to do so as they wished. The words, rite, and appropriate condition of the performer of the spell and rite[8] conferred on them power over the mysterious and "sacred,"[9] bringing them into the unity of practice with it. Magic thus symbolized their ambivalent relation to nature wherein its transcendent power was perceived alongside their natural power over it. This was crude naturalism.

But urban society, by reason of its underlying class structure, defined man as dual: it emphasized the transcendent in nature and society and de-emphasized man's power over it. It separated nature from heaven, body from soul, survival from fulfilment ("salvation," *mokṣa*). The collectively producing and consuming clan was broken up into private owners division of labour, and the rule of the few over the many. The totemic animal, once a natural expression and symbol of clan unity, became an incarnate god linking man to the divine. Its sacrifice, supervised by specialized priests, would, according to myth, restore the person's ruptured relation with transcendent being, and would, in fact, keep that person obedient to secular powers. Totemic potency, previously uniting individual, society, and nature, now was concentrated in the supernatural power of the gods, the magnified mirror images of urban potentates, with whom the images were often merged in popular imagination.

Urban religion retained, in suppressed form, the humanistic element in totemic religion, i.e., the unity of individual, society, and nature. This element was always in antagonism with the dualistic, alienated element, sometimes openly, sometimes covertly. The new tools, weapons, and implements of the Iron Age of the first millennium B. C. sharpened this antagonism by democratizing power and ideas. The result was prophetic souls, most of them laymen, critical and innovative: some writers of the Upanishads, Lokayata thinkers, Zarathustra, the Ionians, Gautama Buddha, Mahavira, the Jewish prophets, Confucius, Lao-tzu, Jesus, etc.[10] These prophets demanded the humanizing of established religion or the founding of new ways of living. Their successes were limited by the class nature of ancient slave societies, the inadequate class understanding of the prophets, and the unreadiness of the masses; and their concepts were eventually coopted and corrupted by the establishment.

While the forms of urban class religion have changed through 5500 years of human history, its dualistic definition of man has persisted as a reinforcement for the underlying class structure. Religion has greately declined—though not completely disappeared—in socialist societies. In advanced and hence declining class societies, like the U. S. A., the recent themes of "the death of God" and "the end of ideology" are the conceptual side of the deepening vacuity of state monopoly capitalism. The advanced morbidity and disintegration of capitalism can no longer sustain the benign directive myths of transcendent religion, which heretofore has been "the heart of a heartless world."[11] Capitalist mythology is supplied not by religion but by cinema, radio, press, advertizers, and political speech writers. This mythology is still fantasy, but it is secular, pluralized transient, and increasingly less credible. The failure of religion under capitalism to provide a meaningful, widespread definition of man is one of the many signs of capitalism's breakdown.

Broadly conceived, science is much older than religion. Hominids several million years ago made and used tools. Early Paleolithic people probably had the lever and inclined plane, and late Paleolithic people had axes, knives, saws, spokeshaves and scrapers of chipped stone, mallets, awls and piercing tools, ivory needles, spears, and harpoons. Their bows stored energy and their spear-throwers employed the principle of the lever.[12] Primitive people were at least proto-scientific, insofar as they made and used tools for changing and controlling their environment in accordance with preconceived ends.

In the absence of instincts, such activity is essential to survival. Science began in Paleolithic hunting and gathering practice, in magic, in the effort of human beings to control their world to satisfy survival needs. Scientific activity implicitly defines the human being as a tool-making, tool-using, cognitive, controlling being. In this definition man's dependency on the environment is subordinated. Religion reverses this definition of man. But in Paleolithic society control of and dependency on nature were united. Its members were aware of a "hidden order" of nature. Later religion proclaimed this and often mystified it. Science tried to understand and use it.

Human civilization means cities, and cities were made possible by important developments (5000-3000 B. C.) in the application of science; artificial irrigation using canals and ditches; the plow; the harnessing of animal motive-power; the sailboat; wheeled vehicles; orchard-husbandry; fermentation; the production and use of copper; bricks; the arch; glazing; and the seal.[13] Scientific modes of production and distribution through developed tools and machines gave rise to the production of surplus food, surplus time, and agglomerated population. Thus science has freed people from Stone Age subservient dependency on nature, only to deliver them, in class society, into the hands of slave labor, self labor, and wage labor.

In some of the Orient and West science has passed through four stages : the empirical observations, measurements, and records of Egypt and Mesopotamia; the self-conscious rationalism of the Greeks; the medieval period, dominated by Islam; and the modern period from the 15th century onward.[14] This last stage, while facilitated by the transmission of Islamic and prior science thorugh translation of texts, started and grew because the new economy of capitalism demanded enterprize and experiment in dealing with the world, and because, later, experiment and theory fused.[15] For 500 years Western science and capitalism have been closely linked. Today more than half the scientists in the U.S.A. work for the military-industrial-government complex. They contribute to an imperialist system that in the past becade has spent 150 billion to devastate the land and people of Indochina and that helps, with other foreigners, to extract 30 per cent of the net national product from India.[16] Thus much of science has been a partner in defining man not only as a tool-using being but as an exploiting and exploited being, as an inflicter and victim of genocide and ecological contamination. Such modern science, though claiming to be naturalistic, has reinstituted a dualism akin to class religions. In 1637 Descartes, a paradigmatic modern scientist, defined human beings as "maitres et possesseurs de la nature,"[17] exalting human mind over non-human matter. Such dualism violates both the theory and practice, the ontology and ethics, of ecological naturalism, and is cause and result of capitalist dualism. If one objects that "true science" serves human welfare, one must consistently assent to the possibility that "true religion" also does. In class society each becomes dehumanized. If religion is often a spiritual opiate, science is often a material lackey of an inhuman system.

In religion humanity has been defined as split between this natural world and another, as dependent on that other world, and as finding its fulfillment by rightly relating itself to that world. In thus relating itself, it has been guided by myth rather than knowledge. In science humanity has been defined as controlling its own life in nature through tools, as independent in the determination of its own destiny and values, and as concerned primarily with survival. The error in religion is a false claim: for the community of inquirers no compelling evidence today indicates a realm of reality, for man or the world, beyond the continuum of matter/energy which characterizes the present epoch of our universe. The error in science is a narrow-minded claim : humanity is more than a tool-using controller of nature (it poeticizes, it plays, it enjoys, it dreams) ; and nature sets limits to that control.[18] The truth in religion is the recognition (in mythic form) of man's dependency on a suprahuman order and the assertion that to be fulfilled humanity must relate itself rightly to that order. This dependency and its vital and supravital importance to humanity has been confirmed by science's discovery of universal gravitation, the ubiquitous electromagnetic and nuclear forces of the atom, the evolution of the physical universe, the creativity of the genes, biological evolution, human evolution including human history, and the ecological system and subsystems of our planet. The truth in science is that humanity can know the orders of the natural world and by experiment and practice with respect to them can guide itself into a more effective survival.

People of science are properly critical of religion because of its frequently diffused and unwarranted claims to achieve fulfillment ; whereas people of religion answer that in its control of nature to satisfy specific survival needs, science has often been diverted into the satisfaction of spurious needs and into a disregard of the generic fulfillment of human beings. In the history of the human species, the Paleolithic dependent-independent attitude and the dependency of class religion functioned to facilitate adjustment to communal and class economies respectively. Science, from the time of large-scale big game hunting, broke through this static adjustment. It voraciously bit into nature, and the more food it exacted, the more hungry mouths arose to feed, and the more food was demanded. As Marx observed, the prime impulse behind this productive system from the beginning of class society was not human need but private greed, not rational plan but individual aggrandizement.

How can science meet this criticism? It cannot, so long as it remains the hireling of a ruling class which dominates science in its own interests rather than serving the generic interests of humankind as a whole. A generic and creative definition of man, including a study of the conditions that facilitate and frustrate his fulfillment, will elude science so long as it serves the special interests of ruling class power. But this has been the chief occupation of science for most of human history.

Since 1917 an experiment has been going on to test whether in classless societies sciences can be used as a means to define in theory and practice the fulfillment of human beings.[19] Scientific socialism presupposes that bodily survival is basic to and included in human fulfillment. The record is quite clear that socialist societies have built a firm base for human existence by securing the satisfaction of survival needs and have gone some distance toward meeting the distinctively human needs for communication, social belonging, respect, recreation, creativity, knowledge, beauty, etc. If it is objected that they have stressed the economic order, the answer is that they have done so out of the necessities of poverty and defense. If all societies were socialized, all the energies of human beings (much of which is now devoted to national military defense) could be devoted to the all-important experiment of discovering our true human definition. For now our nature must remain largely unknown to us, an open question, so long as survival is not seen as prior and prerequisite to fulfillment, and so long both science and religion are diverted from survival and fulfillment tasks by class society and the costly arms race between class and classless societies.

Religions of the world have offered alternative dreams of human fulfillment and ways of living to achieve them. The sciences have developed vast powers of material control over human beings and nature. Both religion and science have a long heritage in the history of *Homo sapiens*. Each has contributed to a genuinely humanistic definition of humanity, more concrete and more important than both. Both will lose if humankind is destroyed, slowly by deepening poverty and ecological disorder, quickly by genocidal global war. Both will gain if humankind survives, and both, in that saved world, can contribute to a fuller, richer definition of mankind. To secure that world, with its opportunity to create humanity in the full glory of its promise, people of both religion and science must contribute to the reduction and cessation of the arms race, to the alleviation of poverty, and to an eventual socialized humanity.

University of Bridgeport, U.S.A.

NOTES

1. *Scienctific American*, Vol. 213, No. 6 (December, 1974), p. 64.
2. John E. Pfeiffer, *The Emergence of Man*. New York: Harper and Row, 1969, p. 434.
3. Gertrude Rachel Levy, *The Gate of Horn*. London: Faber and Faber, 1963, p. 6.
4. *Ibid.*, p. 65.
5. Gordon Childe, *What Happened in History*. New York : Penguin, 1942, pp. 38-40.
6. Robert M. Adams, Jr., "Origin and Spread of Village Agriculture in the Old World," in "Archeology" *Encyclopedia Britannica*, Vol. 2. Chicago : William Benton, 1959, p. 246.
7. H. and H.A. Frankfort, John A. Wilson, Thorkild Jacobsen *Before Philosophy. The Intellectual Adventure of Ancient Man*. Harmondsworth: Penguin, 1949, chs. 5-6.
8. Raymond William Firth, "Magic," *Encyclopedia Britannica*, Vol. 14. Chicago: William Benton, 1959, pp. 623-625.
9. Robert Ranulph Marett, "Primitive Religion," *Encyclopedia Britannica*, Vol. 19, p. 105.
10. By the definition here, the Buddha like Mahavira was not "religious," insofar as he called on persons to rely on themselves for salvation. See Nolan Pliny Jacobson, *Buddhism* : *The Religion of Analysis*. New York : Humanities Press, 1965. For the naturalistic strain in Indian philosophy and religion, see Dale Riepe, *The Naturalistic Tradition in Indian Thought*. Seattle: University of Washington, 1961. Also Debiprasad Chattopadhyaya, *Indian Philosophy. A Popular Introduction*. Delhi : People's Publishing House, 1964.
11. Karl Marx, "Contribution to the Critique of Hegel's Philosophy of Right," in K. Marx and F. Engels, *On Religion*. Moscow : Foreign Languages, 1958, p. 42.
12. Samuel Lilley, *Men, Machines and History*. New York: International, 1966, p. 3.
13. V. Gordon Childe, *Man Makes Himself*. New York : New American Library of World Literature, 1951, p. 180.
14. George Sarton, *The History of Science and the New Humanism*. George Braziller, 1956, pp, 100-101. For the distinctive development of science in China, see Joseph Needham, *Science and Civilisation in China*, Vols. I-V. Cambridge : Cambridge University, 1954-1975.
15. Alfred North Whitehead, *Science and the Modern World*. New York : Macmillan, 1925, ch. 1.
16. Hamza Alavi, "Imperialism Old and New," *The Socialist*

Register, eds. Ralph Miliband and John Serville. New York : Monthly Review. 1964.

17. *Discourse on Method*, Part VI. For a detailed history of Western attitudes and activities toward nature, see Clarence J. Glacken, *Traces on the Rhodian Shore. Nature and Culture in Western Thought From Ancient Times to the End of the Eighteenth Century*. Berkeley : University of California, 1967.

18. Marx remarked that "Franklin's definition of man, as a tool-making animal, is characteristic of Yankeedom." *Capital, A Critical Analysis of Capitalist Production*; Vol. I. Moscow : Foreign Languages, n. d.' p. 326, footnote 4.

19. J.D. Bernal, *Science in History*, Vol. 4 : The Social Sciences : Conclusion. London : G.A. Watts, 1954, passim. M.V. Keldysh, M.D. Millionshchikov, and P.N. Fedoseev, eds., *Science in the U.S.S.R.: To the 50th Anniversary of the Formation of the Union of Soviet Socialist Republics 1922-1972*. Moscow : Progress, 1972.

SOME PHILOSOPHICAL IMPLICATIONS OF MODERN PHYSICAL SCIENCE

J. R. Puri

Recent investigations into the constitution and the nature of Matter have radically changed our conception of the physical world. The traditional view originated from the ancient Greek Atomists more than two thousand years ago. They believed that the material universe was ultimately constituted of an infinte number of infinitely small particles, which they called atoms. The term is derived from two Greek words meaning that which cannot be cut. The atoms were considered as homogeneous, invisible and indivisible entities.

It was the science of Chemistry which ushered in the modern period in the search for the ultimate units of matter. Reflective thought and hypothesis, controlled by observation and experiment, revealed ninety-two ultimate elements, which comprised all material things. The instruments have revealed that the same elements were found in the sun and other heavenly bodies. It was further learnt that the chemical elements combine in certain definite proportion which could be explained only on the supposition that they are composed of discrete particles. It was Dalton, the early 19th Century chemist who revived, the atomic theory of the ancient Greeks. Since Dalton's time the atomic theory has been universally accepted and perfected.

It is, however, through modern physics, that the marvellous story of the atom has been unfolded. Of all the brilliant triumphs of the 19th and the 20th Century science, the discovery of the electric nature of the atom is perhaps the most startling.

The atoms, exist, but what are they exactly like? What are they made of? The individual atoms of silver or gold do not have the properties we associate with silver and gold.

There are, it is believed, ninety-two elements and ninety-two different kinds of atoms ? But, wherein lies the difference between these different kinds of atoms ; The atom, which was earlier believed to be a simple, unanalyzable unit—uncreated and indestructible—has now been found to be a complex structure made up of smaller units. And, the difference between these units lies not in their quality, but in their number, arrangement and motions. The units themselves are identical in all the atoms.

What are these units and how many kinds of them are there ? Surprisingly, no final answer to this question can yet be given, notwithstanding brilliant recent researches into the constitution of matter. The deeper the inquiry goes, the more mysterious becomes the structure of the atom.

Niels Böhr had given a theory of the constitution and an actual model of it, which seemed to settle the matter finally. It was the beauty and the simplicity of the model, which contributed to the acceptance of his theory. Physicists, however, have now become very cautious about atomic models. They are more inclined to the view that the structure of the atom can be elucidated only mathematically.

According to Böhr's theory, the ultimate elements of an atom are electrical charges, a positive charge called the proton and a negative one called the electron. Each atom has a positive nucleus encircled by one or more negative electrons. The larger the number of electrons, the greater the speed with which they revolve round the nucleus.

This model of Niels Böhr has been called "the miniature solar system" model inasmuch as the nucleus or the proton corresponds to the sun and the electrons to the planets revolving round it. One significant fact to be noted is the amazing emptiness of the world, whether it be the emptiness of cosmic space or the emptiness of the atom.

The above analysis leads us to the conclusion that the atomic world consists of positive and negative charges of electricity. But, what are these things? What is electricity? Physicists are unable to answer this question ? They do not know what it *is*, but only what it *does*. It is a name which is given to certain peculiar forms of energy. If we further ask what energy is, we are told that it is the potentiality of doing. It is not being, but *process*. Things *are* what they do. We cannot know what energy is, we can only know what mathematical ratios prevail in its manifestations.

Such was the picture of the atom prior to the year 1930. Researches which began about this time have revealed other elementary constituents of the atom besides protons and electrons. There is the neutron which is described as a particle having neither a positive nor a negative charge. And, then, there is the position which is an electron having not a negative but a positive charge. Thus, the constituents of the atom increased from two to four. Recent investigations have suggested some more of them.

Here it is important to realize that materialism has lost all significance for Philosophy in its traditional sense. The material universe is no longer the substantial, tangible, objective thing we had always taken it to be. Matter has thinned away into a completely spectral thing that it has now become. At best, we could say that the world is made up of energy, which is the ultimate "stuff" of which the atom is constituted. Patrick has suggested that the term "materialism" 'should now be changed into "dynamism". For, this name would be more characteristic 'of our preceptible world.

We have arrived at our conclusions more or less from the standpoint of the chemist. The Physicist asserts that it is not the whole story of the material world. There is still the "universe of light"—the world of radiation—to be explained. We are constantly being bombarded by rays of many kinds. The light rays are the best known of these certain nerve centres in the brain and certain highly specialized nerve endings of the eye make us aware of these rays as light. Besides these, there are the heat rays, the long wireless rays, the short X-rays and the newly discovered interesting cosmic rays. All these forms of radiant energy differ from protons and electrons in that they are travellers. They travel through space at the same rate. They differ only in their wave-lengths.

Previous to the nineteenth century the corpuscular theory of light had been generally accepted. Little corpuscles or particles were supposed to travel thorugh space. In the 19th century this theory was discarded and replaced by the undulatory theory of light. Light was conceived as a form of wave-motion. It travelled through space as the waves of water travel across the sea. Strangely enough, in the 20th century, the corpuscular theory has been revived. No doubt, light rays behave like waves, but in certain respects they also behave like particles. Now, a theory of radiant energy must be made to fit these facts. No perfect unification has yet been made. Light has wave properties and these wave properties seem to be the tools which the mathematician needs to tell him where the light particles will be. The corpuscular character of light has given rise to the Quantom theory. Light behaves like a stream of particles or quanta. These droplets, bullet, darts or wave packets have atomic character besides showing a wave character. Light energy travels through space in the form of bundles. These light units are called photones. This applies also to other forms of energy. Energy is, therefore, atomic as are also matter and electricity. And, yet, light rays also behave like waves. The electrons, for instance, are both particles and waves. This has led to a most confusing situation. Eddington has given a solution of the dilemma, but it is only a verbal solution. He has given the name "Wavicle" to the electron, as it manifests the character both of the wave and of the particle.

Experiments on the behaviour of electrons as waves and particles have revealed a new and very interesting principle called the Principle of Uncertainty. It is also called the Heisenberg principle of indeterminacy. It has a striking hypothesis to offer for the reconciliation between |Physics and Ethics.

The strange character of this new principle lies in destroying the universal validity of the law of causation and its consequent determinism on which science itself is supposed to depend. According to this principle, Causation does not hold true in the world of the atom. The electron has been found to jump about in an erratic and unpredictable manner from one orbit to another within the atom. The old laws of mechanics on which science has been based for centuries entirely fail us in the microphysical world. This gives us the uneasy feeling that the foundations of science are cracking up.

The principle of uncertainty, however, has been interpreted in two ways. The exponents of the orthodox viewpoint interpret the principle in terms of the incapacity of man to confirm the old laws of mechanics in the infinitesimal world of the atom. It is necessary to have the medium of light in order to see. But, light is heavier than the electron which is to be seen. So, the very act of observation disturbs the movement of the electron. Consequently, the velocity and the position of the electron can never be determined simultaneously. On the other hand, Heisenbreg and others of his way of thinking believe that there is genuine indeterminism or spontaneity in the world of the atom.

We may sum up our account by saying that not only has our conception of the physical world undergone a revolutionary change, but equally so has our undertanding of the laws which govern it. Matter has ceased to be the solid, tangible entity that it used to be. It is no longer a substance, but a mere spectre. The notion of substance has been replaced by the notion of behaviour. This has led many eminent scientists to become idealists or at least to be idealistically inclined— and to give up the traditional realistic standpoint. Simultaneously, has the realization dawned upon them that the laws which operate in the atomic world are radically different if not diametrically opposed from those which apply to the macrocosm. The world is being ruled by the law of indeterminism or freedom rather than by the law of causation. The Causal law has been dethroned from its high pedestal of absolute truth to one or statistical applicability.

Punjabi University, Patiala

13
RELIGION, SCIENCE AND MAN
Tu Li

I

It seems that in both traditions—oriental and occidental, there is such a saying: "Man is incurably religious," or "Man by nature is a religious being." If we understand "religious" here from a general cultural point of view, this description of man is acceptable. For it not only can describe the cultural activity of man in ancient and medieval times but also that of the modern and contemporary centuries. Religious activity is a phenomenon common to ancient or medieval people as well as to modern or contemporary men. If we understand the cultural life of man from this point of view, we cannot accept Auguste Comte's classification of the human history, without qualification, into three different stages—theological, metaphysical, and positive. Since religious activity is not only still essential to man's life in modern times, but people still appeal to religious interpretation for certain problems faced by them nowadays. We cannot have a clear-cut classification of the human history as Auguste Comte did. Man is a child of God at all times.

But though based on man's religious activity we can claim that man is a child of God at all times, we are not allowed to be limited to this aspect and blind to the other aspects of man. For man is also a rational animal. From the development of man's rational activity, he is never fixed to any kind of life. He is in progress both theoretically and practically. From the rational aspect of man or from the aspect of scientific activity of man, Comte's classification of the history of humanity is not without foundation. As we know there is also such a saying that religious understanding of man and his world is replaced by philosophical or scientific understanding. The rise of philosophy or science is due to the advancement of man's knowledge either in philosophy or in science. This refers to the rise of ancient Greek philosophy as well as to that of Western modern philosophy.

I do not want to challenge this kind of interpretation of the rise of philosophy or science here. But based on the fact that "man is incurably religious," or that the phenomenon of religious activity is common to every century, the saying that religious understanding is replaced by philosophical or scientific understanding is one-sided. Owing to the continuity and prevalence of religious activity nowadays, we cannot accept that religious understanding is really replaced by science. It co-exists with the latter.

The assertion of the co-existence of religious activity and that of science is accepted by this paper. So what the paper proposes to discuss in the following pages are: (1) a general description of the situations of these two activities; (2) their relations in the past; and (3) what can be or should be their relations.

II

It is not my intention and I am also not allowed to give a discussion in detail of the origin of religion and that of science here. With reference to the above understanding what I propose to point out is that there are problems inherently concerning man which cannot be dealt with by science. For they are problems unobjectifiable. We can feel that we are faced by them, and try to regard them as problems of knowledge. But actually they are non cognitive and are beyond the field of knowledge. This kind of problem is co-extensive with the existence of man. For when man begins to exist he is faced with it, and he cannot avoid it during his lifetime. With the rise of different kinds of human cultures and the development of different stages of human history, it has been presented in different forms, called by different names, and dealt with by different ways. But its character is obvious. It cannot be understood objectively. It is always beyond and above man's cognition, though it is intimately related with man. It was treated either as a religious problem in ancient and medieval ages and also in modern times. It is still regarded as a religious problem, or metaphysical problem, or philosophical problem, or existential problem at the present time. The different terms used in different periods and by different philosophers might confuse the central meaning of this problem, but in comparison with the problem of science its character is clear, and that it is a problem felt, not cognized, is also obvious.

The problem of sciences opposing and paralleling to that of religion in history, can be dealt with by man. It is objectifiable. We cannot only feel that there is such a kind of problem facing us, but also can recognize what kind of problem it is within the field of knowledge. We can set up scientific rules in terms of which we do objective research. So scientific knowledge is recognised by man as a product of man's co-operative activity of reason and experience. In terms of this recognition, the development of man's activity as a rational animal is clear. With the result of modern achievement in science, nobody would doubt that man is a rational animal. Science is useful to man and there are a lot of problems which are dealt with by science. In contrary to religious feeling, it is regarded as a kind of orderly systematical, and cognitive understanding.

III

The distinction of religious problem from that of science in the West is a result of the advancement of modern thought. For in the past, the problem of religion and that of science were not distinctively recognized. Man's nature in respect to the aspect of "religious" and that of "rational" was not clearly distinguished. Sometimes man was regarded as a religious being or only as a child of God. On this occasion, man was unable or did not like to make a distinction between the problem of religion and that of science. All activities of man were treated as different aspects of his religious pursuits. Sometimes man was regarded as a pure rational being or metaphysical being, and man's problems were understood in some asserted metaphysical categories. Religion was rationalized. It was asserted that God's existence could be proved either ontologically, or cosmologically, or epistemologically. All man's problems could be solved in terms of speculative thinking. Sometimes man was regarded as a natural animal. In this regard, man's attention was concentrated on the problem of science. Not only was a supernatural problem regarded as nonsensical, and thus meaningless, but any problem which cannot be classified into the field of science was rejected from the field of philosophy. Religious thought though not openly denied was neither properly recognized, nor was its importance to man's life and its co-existence with that of science adequately admitted. The concept of scienticism was once advocated.

Roughly speaking, in the Western tradition, it was not until the rise of modern thought, that is after the development of the continental rationalism and the British empiricism, and the criticism of Kant's philosophy that the first two situations mentioned above were clarified. As to the third situation, it prevailed once in current Western thought, and is still insisted on by some contemporary thinkers.

Although the third type of idea in respect to the problem of science and that of religion is still insisted on by some contemporary philosopher, as a result of the development of modern thought, the distinction between religion and science, or that man is not only a rational being or natural animal but also incurably religious, is recognized. This recognition is based on a good ground which would not be shaken by any advancement of human knowledge.

As to the assertion that the distinction between religion and science as a result of the advancement of modern thought, some people might have different ideas, and think that it is not so difficult to recognize the difference between religion and science. For even in ancient times religious problems were already distinguished from that of science. For example, two thousand three hundred years ago some Confucians asserted that religious practice is mainly based on man's unbearable emotion which is different from the problem of knowledge. Man cannot bear to think that his lovable friends, or his parents are finished or are extinguished when they die. He does not know whether or not there are immortal souls or a ghost-spirited world; these are beyond his knowledge. But since he cannot bear to think that they are not, which is forbidden by his emotion, religious things appear in man's imagination. According to these Confucians, not only is ancestor-worship interpreted in this way, other religious practices can be done in the same way.

Man is not only a rational being, but he is not limited to think what he can understand. He is concerned with what he cannot understand. He cannot understand the situation before he was born and what will happen to him after his death. These are beyond the two ends of his life. So the problem of the existence of a supernatural world or the other-world are thought about not only by primitive people but also by most civilized men. In general most people regardless of which century they belong to have a kind of religious belief. Based on their unbearable emotion, they believe that that there is not only one world, one life; they cannot bear to think that all is finished which a man dies, and his death is a kind of extinction like grass, a tree, or a dog.

In general the above understanding is correct. But what I want to point out here is the difference between "recognized" and "distinctively recognized" or "clearly distinguished". Though the distinction between religion and science was recognized or felt by people in the past, making clear of this kind of distinction is a result of the advancement of modern thought. It was not until the achievement of modern thought, the limitation os science made clear. When man has a clear idea of the problem of science religious problems are clarified at the same time.

People in the past only felt or roughly recognized the difference between religious problems and those of science but could not make it clear. Why was this so ? Generally it can be explained in terms of the following two confusions. First, they could not have a clear understanding of the different characteristics of these two kinds of problems and thought that either one can be subsumed by the other; second, they could not have a clear idea of them so one is not clearly distinguished from the other. Let us have a simple description of these two confusions.

The first confusion is clearly indicated by the history of the development of religious thought and that of science, or the conflict between them, in Western history.

As we know, in ancient Greece, at first religious belief was regarded as a kind of superstition, then was subsumed into the field of philosophy which is dealt with by reason. Instead of believing that there is a ghost-spirited world waiting for us when we die, Plato asserted an ideal world by which man transcends this sensible world which is changeable and unstable. As to Aristotle, theology and metaphysics are not two different subjects. God is not an object which cannot be understood. He is an object of contemplation. According to the Hebrew-Judea tradition, the Hebrew-Judea God is an object of belief. He is supernatural and cannot be grasped and understood by reason. But as a result of the mutual influence of Hebrew and Greek thoughts, Hebrew-Judea God is partly rationalized. The medieval theologians not only insisted that the existence of God can be proved by our reason but also asserted that nothing in God is unreasonable, though sometimes they said that man's reason is finite, God's wisdom is infinite. We cannot understand God completely with our reason, and want our reason to subserve faith which is based on revelation. Compared with medieval theologians, modern philosophers are more liberal in respect to the problem of theology. Most religious dogmas are rejected or neglected by them. But they still accept the idea that the existence of God can be proved by reason, and nothing in God is unreasonable. It was not until Kant that the traditional argument of God's existence is rejected. The combination of the idea of God inherited from the Greek tradition and the idea of Hebrew-Judea God is separated. In this regard, philosophers after Kant in general are followers of Kant. Nobody wants to prove the existence of God only in terms of theoretical reasoning again. A new approach to God thus becomes a problem in contemporary philosophy. The difference between religion and philosophy or science is given a further consideration.

The second confusion is that though as pointed out before the religious problem referred to man is based on a different ground and can be asserted distinctively from that of science, yet in order to express this problem properly, a lot of religious subordinate problems are introduced which cannot be dealt with only by religious concern but should be interpreted on the ground of scientific understanding. In general, these problems came up in accordance with their different historical or cultural backgrounds. With reference to the comparative study of religions, we know that the difference of religious subordinate problems between the different great religions is great. But generally, it can be classified into two aspects, theoretical and practical. In the theoretical aspect, in order to set forth the fundamental idea of a certain religious belief, a set of theory in connection with the fundamental idea is set up. This set of theory is concerned with ethical, political, economical, cosmological or ontological problems. We know that as a matter of fact there are no religions in this world which have nothing to do with these mentioned problems. So every religion has its own interpretation of them. In the practical aspect, in order to connect the fundamental idea with the practical life, some kind of religious way of life is established. This includes the different kinds of [ceremonies, the different styles of clothes, architecture, and so on. Since the subordinate problems are intimately connected with scientific knowledge and dealt with by it, the relations between the fundamental problem and that of subordination is not unchangeable. Along with the development of scientific knowledge the mentioned relation got its reformation again and again. This is why there are religious reformations or improvements in human history. Though religious institutions or theologies are revised with the aid of the development of knowledge, we cannot say that religious problems can be replaced by that of science. As pointed out before, they are two different kinds of problems. Though in practice they are influenced by each other, we cannot substitute one for the other. But to our regret, the difference between the fundamental religious problem and that of subordination in the past is not properly recognized.

IV

If what have clarified—the distinction between religion

and science—is acceptable, and the description of the relation between them in the past is correct, then what can be or should be their relations in respect to human life seem obvious. First, religion and science both must be asserted as inedpendent problems related to man, and neither one of them can be asserted to take the place of the other. Second, in addition to the assertion of religion and science as two independent problems we have to make clear the distinction between the subordinate problems and that of fundamentality of religion. As pointed before, the subordinate problems are dealt with by science. They are developed with the advancement of science. So they are not asserted apriori nor being accepted as unchangeable. It is impossible for me to give a description in detail of the development of the subordinate problems in man's religious activity here. What I want to point out is that this development in man's religious activity is very important in respect to man's religious life. And as a result of this development, some kind of superstition has been discarded or modified, some kind of religious doctrine goes along with this modification, and the way of religious practice thus has been improved.

As pointed out before, the fundamental problem of religion is beyond man's knowledge. It cannot be dealt with by science. Since it is beyond man's knowledge, it transcends the activity of practical life. In order to be connected with the latter, it must be supported by the work functioned by subordinate problems. If the subordinate problems are developed with the advancement of science, though the fundamental problem of religion does not get changed along with them (indeed it is unchangeable) yet since its subordinate problems are defined, religious activity as a whole has got its refinement along with the development of human knowledge.

With reference to the above discussion, we can see that the knowledge of science not only should not be regarded as conflicting with the problem of of religion, but it is helpful in getting rid of some kind of superstition, adopting some kind of religious doctrinal refinement, and reorganization of religious institutions. It is also useful to man in settling some kind of his complicated religious feeling and softening some kind of religious tenacity due to ignorance. And in terms of this settlement or softening he can avoid indulging himself in superstitious prejudice on the one hand, and prevent himself from hurting his unbearable emotion which is a part of his nature and which should be treated properly on the other.

  The Chinese University of Hong Kong, Hong Kong.

MAN IN RELATION TO SCIENCE, RELIGION AND PHILOSOPHY

Y. Masih

Philosophy a priori : There is a holistic tendency in each man by virtue of which a philosopher is prompted to think about the whole world as touching his whole being. This was first realized by Plato. According to Plato, the aim of education is to make a man complete and a whole being. For this reason Plato included Geometry for mental culture, Gymnastics for building the body and Music for elevating the soul. On the metaphysical plane the Idea of the Good for Plato, and the Prime Mover for Aristotle serve as the holistic principle which orders and regulates the activities of all beings constituting the entire universe. In addition to this, for Aristotle each form is the hormic drive in each thing by virtue of which it tends to attain its ultimate essence as its final end.

In modern times it was Hans Adolf Eduard Driesch who has given an empirical confirmation of the presence of this holistic drive in each organism. By studying embryo-genetic processes, Driesch came to the conclusion that each organism functions in accordance with 'whole-making' causality. Of course, Driesch went beyond his empirical theory and posited the presence of a supra-individual wholeness. But keeping to the empirical stand, it can be said that in recent years the organismic theorists of personality in psychology have strengthened the doctrine of biological hormism. Kurt Goldstein, Andras Angyal, Abraham Maslow, Prestcott Lecky, Carl Rogers and C. G. Jung have shown that there is a centring tendency in the unitary formation of the personality, which is projected in the form of one's 'symbolic self'. Further, Jung and Goldstein emphasize the role of adjustive processes within the organism itself in the service of the drive towards self-realization. But apart from this kind of 'autonomy', there is also 'homonomy' by virtue of which the individual is prompted to expand and enrich his personality by drawing upon the common fund of human heritage of age-old values. This homonomous activity of an individual in relation to the whole inter-personal environment has been termed by Andras Angyal as biospheric. Therefore, we can say that philosophy is sustained by a biospheric homonomy. And this has been well brought out by Jung's theory of individuation.

According to Jung, each man tends to become his whole being. In the first half of his life, he consciously adjusts himself to the outer world by developing a satisfactory 'persona', and in the second half he adjusts himself to his Unconscious by successfully passing through the stages of *Shadow*, *Anima-Animus*, *Mana-Personality* and *Mandala Experience*. Emboldened by the empirical theory of biological and psychological holism, philosophers, notably J. C. Smuts, F. H. Bradley, Bernard Bosanquet and others have amplified this doctrine into the key-concept of their systems. In his book *Holism and Evolution* (1926), Smuts holds that there is some whole-making factor in the universe. In the world of matter this holistic tendency is imperfect, but this is more fully visible in life, mind and persons. The holistic tendency, according to Smuts is most marked in the spiritual values of love, beauty, goodness and so on. Unlike the views of Driesch and more resembling the theory of Henri Bergson, the 'holistic tendency' of Smuts is ateleological cosmic principle.

In the same way Bosanquet tells that there is a spirit of totality which infects each thing by virtue of which it transcends itself in the direction of the Absolute which is an all-inclusive Reality. To my thinking, the 'natural disposition' at the basis of philosophizing, according to Kant, and, 'the instinct' of Bradley can be assimilated to the above-mentioned holistic tendency. And the presence of this drive in each man accounts for the doctrine of *philosophia perennis* or philosophy *a priori*. In religious philosophy this holistic drive has been variously termed. In Indian system the tendency of *Arhatva* (Jainism), or *Sattva* (Sāṁkhya) tendency for regaining the former state of perfection may be assimilated to the above-mentioned doctrine of holism. It is because of this primordial urge to regain the lost state of perfection each inquirer is prompted to think for himself. According to Plato, there is the state of *reminiscence* which prompts each man to regain his former state of pure Being. This platonic view was put thus by St. Augustine in his Christian theology.

"Thou hast created us for thyself, and our heart knows no rest until it may repose in thee."

Later on, Samuel Alexander, emending Spinoza's doctrine of *conatus*, has advanced the view that there is a *nisus* in each man towards deity. Even atheistic Satre holds that each man tends to become God.

Man is the proper subject-matter of Philosophy : If there be a holistic drive in each man, and once this drive becomes active, man can hardly refrain from asking questions about his nature and ultimate destiny.

Koham kastvam kuta āyàtaḥ?
(Who am I ? Who art thou ? From whence all this ?)
In the same manner, Kant outlined the following three enquiries as the real problems of philosophy proper.

What can I know ?
What I ought to do ?
What may I hope ?

Naturally the self-questioning man turns to himself as his ultimate concern.

Man ! know thyself (Ātmānam viddhi) Socrates seeing this Delphic oracle was aroused from his philosophical slumber, and, in like manner many Indian seekers after Truth have been roused from their complacency by the inner voice of *Ātmānam Viddhi*. Philosophers, both in India and the West have realized that this is the hardest of all problems to solve.[1] Nachiketā, standing in dread before the god of Death could realize that self-perfection or immortality is the real goal of philosophizing.

Yenāham̐ nāmṛtā syām̐ kimaham̐ tena kuryām

But what is the nature of this philosophical knowing which bestows immortality on the knower ? This knowing is not impersonal, objective and scientific knowing. This does not consist in mere intellectual gymnastics. This is transforming or soul-making realization. Here knowing and becoming are one and the same process : Brahmavid brahmaiva bhavati,— ——Guru and Govinda are non-different. For Socrates virtue (process of becoming good) is knowledge and nobody does wrong knowingly. Hence, the task of philosophical knowing is not merely *understanding* the world, but one of changing man and the world, which is constituted by the projection of man. It consists in evoking *bodhi* or viewing the world in right perspectives (samyagdarśana). Here thoughts are not divorced from passions, but draw upon the energies of passions, without which nothing great can be accomplished in the world. Philosophical thoughts have wings and they effect things. In other words, the language of philosophy is mythic, symbolical, evocative and edifying even though this language is constitnted of opparently ordinary abstract concepts. However, idealists remind us that their concepts are concrete and holistic. Philosophical terms can never be fully conceptualized. They are metaphorical, analogical and mythic, cipherical (Jaspers) and symbolical (Jung). Hence, the demand for precision in language is bound to end in failure. Even Wittgenstein had to take recourse to what can be shown, but cannot be said.

The function of philosophy therefore is integrative and holistic by virtue of which the loose ends of competing desires in man are welded together in one organic wholeness. The integrated man is a *wise* man who sees things in changed perspectives, opening up new dimensions of sensibility and widening intellectual horizon, beckoning man towards newer vision by establishing fresh tables of commandments. This shows that man has no fixed essence. He is not a finished being. Giovanni Pico della Mirandola (1463-94) puts the following words in the mouth of God addressing man :

> "A limited nature in other creatures is confined within the laws written down by us. In conformity with thy free judgment, in whose hands I have placed thee, thou art confined by no bounds and thou wilt fix limits of nature for thyself......Thou, like a judge appointed for being honourable, art the moulder and maker of thyself: thou mayst sculpt thyself into whatsoever shape thou dost prefer."[2]

Search for the authentic man : The history of the western philosophy may be viewed as a persistent investigation into the nature and destiny of man. This attempt has resulted in man's awareness of himself as the creator of things and values. At the initial stage this awareness was fraught with the dangers of solipsism, scepticism and even nihilism. For instance the maxim of *homo mensura* of the sophists did emphasize the creative role of man, because man was declared to be the measure of all things, of perceptual objects and values. However, the sophists interpreted perception too subjectively, throwing knowledge into scepticism, and showed the danger of the relativity of all values. It was Socrates who brought philosophy from the heavens to the Earth, and tried to introduce objectivity and universality of ethical values by conceptualizing them. Values are the ideals of man in accordance with which he shapes himself. As man has no fixed essence, so no ideal can be objective, irrespective of his willing and creating it. This awareness has been slow to dawn and even now is most imperfectly realized. For this reason Socrates, in spite of his constant endeavour, could not precisely establish any definition of justice, truth and goodness. Attempts of the Stoics to deduce moral values from cosmic reason failed likewise. Christian theologians, struggling successfully against gnosticism, tried to deduce the universality of all values from their objective realisation in God. It took a long time and that also very haltingly to realise that every talk about God is also at the same time a talk about man. This was clearly understood by Hegel.

"Man knows about God only insofar as God knows about himself in man: this knowledge is self-consciousness of God, but this knowledge is at the same time God's knowledge of man, and this God's knowledge of man is man's knowledge of God; the spirit of man knowing God is only God's own-spirit"[3]

Science as the projection of man : Science itself has arisen from the religious concern of man. In the west it arose from the Biblical myth itself. According to the book of Genesis, God created the world and endowed it with his laws. Hence, the world became the manifestation of God.

"The heavens declare the glory of God: and the firmament sheweth his handywork. Day unto day uttereth speech, and night unto night sheweth knowledge. There is no speech nor language, where their voice is not heard" (Ps. 19: 1-3)

Again,

"Because that which may be known of God is manifest.

> For the invisible things of him from the creation of the world are clearly seen, being understood by the things that are made, even his eternal power and Godhead;......" (Rom 1: 19-20)

Therefore, knowing the secrets of nature means understanding the ways of God to man, for nature is the language of God in which He communicates to man, according to Berkeley[4]. But this nature can be best understood if thought is completely de-mythologised, rendered wholly impersonal and object-oriented. In this scientific thinking man is seen in I-It relationship, in the language of Martin Buber. However, this creation of science and the determining of what is to count as scientific truth follows from the decision of man himself in his task of becoming a whole and established in a world constituted of his own projections. Man creates science and determines what is and what is not to count as scientific truth. This blik-theory of R. M. Hare has its root in the preganant statement of Kant.

> 'Understanding maketh nature out of the materials it does not make'.

Man no doubt creates laws, but in contrast with the relativity and subjectivism involved in the maxim of *Homo Mensura*, Kant holds that the laws have objectivity because they follow from the *a priori* concepts and forms of sensibility. These *a priori* modes are operative and effective for all men. Hence, that alone is to count for scientific truth which is public for all men.

> 'A dream which all dream together and must dream, is not a dream but reality'[5].

Therefore, for Kant, that alone is to count for knowledge which is universal and necessary for all men. In the same way for Kant that alone is to count for ethical duty which can be legislated universally for all human beings. For Kant therefore, an authentic man is the universal man. This universalizing element was further elaborated by Hegel. For Hegel that alone is real which can be conceptualized and that alone is ethical which conforms to the norms of the people and the State. The conceptual nature of the reality has been greatly elaborated by idealists like Josiah Royce, F. H. Bradley, B. Bosanquet, A. Seth Pringle-Pattison and many others. In their various and varied expositions, they have shown that history, culture and ethico-religious values are the progressive and gradual unfolding and realization of the potentialities of the Absolute Spirit. But Sören Kierkegaard, the contemporary of Hegel, saw that by conceptualising our experiences, particulars are lost in the universal : the decision and responsibility of individual men are lost in collective norms and actions. However, according to Kierkegaard, the authentic individuality when he decides for a course of action in relation to the competing concerns of life, with responsibility which is attended with risk and anxiety. Since the time of Kierkegaard, existential movement has been powerfully supported by Nietzsche, Heidegger, Jaspers, Sarte and many others. However, the doctrine of unique individuality in existentialism is free from solipsism, subjectivism and consequent scepticism. Here the individual is said to be embedded in the world and society. Each particular thing or ordinary experience, for example, a table or chair, is perceived as such by an individual by virtue of his belonging to a certain cultural world-view. Hence, an individual has his being in-the-world. In like manner, language and values are highly social and all activities are carried on in a societal set-up. Here an individual has his being with others. The individual whilst remaining a 'pulse-beat' of the social milieu, does not lose his unique individuality. But if we emphasize unique individuality at the expense of societal relationship, then man becomes an unreal abstraction. On the other hand, if the societal relationship be fully spelt out, then the individual becomes an element in Marxist humanism (Sartre) or sociological phenomena (Heidegger). So once again as a result of existential logic of discourse, individual men are swallowed up in man, crowd, mass and 'they'. What is the conclusion from this highly paradoxical situation ?

The significance of philosophy and religion : As soon as a construction is built up, going beyond the limitations of the earlier systems, a fresh wave of intellectual unrest sets in. Dust settles down on the newer systems. No system can ever be final. The urge to be the whole, felt as the deity-hood of S. Alexander or the urge of becoming God (Sartre) can never be realized. The unfinished man[6] can never escape from his underlying urge to become a whole and a god. Man by now has become aware of many 'transcendental illusions', which he creates as a result of his holistic drive to become a finished whole; but he cannot live without some such illusory constructions. Philosophers have been likened by Kant to sailors who have smelt the sea. They are aware of the raging storms and lurking icebergs beneath the sea. They are certain of shipwreck. But they cannot help unfurling the sail of the ship: because they *are* the sailors. Are these illusory attempts meaningless and absurd? To my thinking the main task of philosophy is to make man aware of the tension within him, which Hegel has termed 'the portentous power of the negative'. The germs of unrest follow from the opposing forces of life and death (Freud) or Being and non-Being. Man cannot help being caught up in dialectical puzzles. This situation impels him to find ever newer systheses. But alas ! there can be no resting place. Constant and recurring failures in philosophy remind us of the story of Sisiphus These recurrent failures have the sole task of deepening the consciousness of man, by opening up newer and newer dimensions of experience along divergent routes, and, of compelling man to transcend the intellectual horizon of man's scientific grasp and conceptual precision. The dialectics of percepts and concepts, particulars and universals, thinking and feeling, individual and society, science and religion theism and atheism, value and facts etc., have not been solved and can never be satisfactorily solved. These failures are not due to linguistic confusions: the controversies are not due to imperfect methodology nor due to confused analysis of concepts and contexts. Yet there is hardly any failure which has not given birth to newer insights. Philosophers of the contemporary times have certainly gone much beyond ancient cosmogonies in ontology, beyond magic, ritualism and even traditional religion in theology, and narrow nationalism, colonialism and imperialism in social philosophy. Philosophy does not consist in establishing any objective, impersonal and conceptual conclusion so much, as it consists in struggling against the bewitchment of intellect by stupefying arguments. Each time old puzzles have been dissolved by proper analysis, fresh gains have been registered. Protests by Bacon and Descartes against vain search for 'forms' and 'essences' of medieval philosophy called forth the need of better methodology. The search for an adequate methodology gave birth to the geometrical method of Spinoza, the psychological empiricism of Locke, Berkeley and Hume, and finally gave way to philosophical analysis and phenomenological method. However, it was Kant who could clearly discern the scientific impossibility of Rational Psychology, Cosmology and Theology. In his own way Kant established the truth that man is the creator of science, ethics and religion. But man's creation has validity, according to Kant, when his creation admits of being universalized. Hegel and the Hegelians concluded from this that man is the creator of publicly acceptable science, ethics and religion. The synthetic and synoptic world-view of the idealists has given us a good deal of illumination. But the individual was lost, merged and dissipated in the Absolute. At this stage existentialism was most welcome with its insistence on individual's dignity and freedom. In the same way the demand of precision and clarification of concepts involved in philosophical construction, specially concerning mind-body relationship, other persons and ethical reasoning has removed much confusion. But language has been created by man for manipulating things and communicating with others. Through his dialogues with things and persons man reaches his depth as creative agency. As a creative force man projects his experiences in the form of science, social values and ethical norms. This creative process has within it the principle of negation by virtue of which all that cannot stand up the measure of growing knowledge and wider perspectives of values, gets negated. At one time man created God and entrusted to Him human destiny. Even now a great many people cannot do without God. However, in the wake of science and technology, secularism has emerged. And secularism has made the traditional belief in a personal God obsolete. Man has come of age, in the words of Pastor Bonhoeffer.

> "So our coming of age forces us to a true recognition of our situation *vis-a-vis* God. God is teaching us that we must live as men who can get along very well without him. The God who is with us is the God who forsakes us"[7]

Man has, as a result of God's death announced by Nietzsche,[8] become a superman endowed with full freedom and responsibility and the risk involved in the use of this creative decision, for himself which also means for everyone else. The sense of the risk is so great that it maddens him. But man could not have remained forever in his infantile paradise. Man lives through the sweat of his brow and his labours. However, it is better to be a dissatisfied and restless Socrates than to be a complacent placid cow in the meadows. Man has to be awakened to the realisation of himself as an unfinished being, a determiner of his own destiny, which is bound to be attended with much anguish and anxiety. This is neither cynicism, nor pessimism, but education to reality.

Ranchi University, Ranchi

REFERENCES

1. *Laws* 11: 923a; *Phaedrus* 230a, *Philebus* 48c, PLATO, ed. E. Hamilton H. Cairns (Bollingen series, Princeton)
2. Oration on the dignity of man, Tr. A. Robert Caponigri, Chicogo 1856, pp. 4-5
3. C. Friedrich, *Hegel*, A modern Library Book, 1945, p. XXXV
4. *Divine Visual Language* from SELECTIONS FROM BERKELEY, by A.C. Fraser
5. R. Falkenberg, History of modern philosophy, p. 350
6. *Symposium*, Plato, Ibid. 190-192
7. *Letters and papess from prison*, Fontana books, p. 122
8. W. Kaufmann, *Nietzsche*, Vintage Books, 1968, p. 97

PHILOSOPHY, RELIGION AND TRUTH

P. B. Vidyarthi

I. *Philosophy as the Impulse for Synoptic Vision*

Despite the vigorous attempts on the part of Wittgensteinians and Carnapians, who have brought into currency the view of philosophy whose function is nothing except the clarification of language and for which the only true body of knowledge is the knowledge which consists of the propositions of science thus making a clean sweep of all such eternal problems as have been the concern of traditional philosophy, that Platonic conception of it to consist "in seeing things together", that is to say, in having a synoptic view of all sorts of experiences that man comes to have in his confrontation with the world may rightly be taken to be a more reasonable and more adequate one seeing that it is more human and more comprehensive and rooted in experience than any other account of it which reduces it to a mere formal activity having hardly any connection with the pressing needs of man. It is clear, the view of philosophy which treats it to be only an exercise in the analysis of language has emerged from a false and inadequate assessment of science itself for even science, like philosophy, is after all an interpretation of experience, though unlike the latter it restricts itself only to limited fragments of it and refuses to embrace the whole of it whereas what human experience in its true character is, can be known to us only if we look at it in its totality and keep off from the fashionable tendency to pronounce judgment on the nature of the whole by concentrating on parts isolated or abstracted from it; for it is possible that we may not even get a true perspective of what the parts are if they are disconnected from that, in association with which or as integral aspects of which alone can they be intelligible. It is no doubt true that the rise of empiricism in recent philosophy has been due to the great strides science has made in the material world of man and this has contributed in no small measure to the subordination of philosophy itself to science: for according to the fashionable view of it science has been regarded as completely exhaustive of all the dimensions of man so that there is no longer any aspect or feature of human nature that can be said to stretch beyond the frontiers of scientific thinking. But such a conception of philosophy is only a caricature of it and has not a true representation of its nature and function. Philosophy, which cannot be understood except as an interpretation of human experience as a whole cannot be supposed to be based on what is true of only a part of it.

The unusual persistence in the habit of setting up scientific knowledge as the unquestionable model for and a determinant of knowledge in philosophy is as ludicrous and absurd to say that "the son who was begotten by his father was also progenitor of his father, or that the horse's shoes which have been hammered by the blacksmith on the anvil were also the anterior and superior power that brought the blacksmith into being." (W. P. Paterson, *The Nature of Religion*, p. 374, Hodder and Stoughton, Limited, London, 1925). The positivist, or for the matter of that, the scientist makes the mistake of treating knowledge in science which is only a part or a fragment of or an abstraction from the totality of human experience, as coextensive with the entire range of knowledge as such. Human knowledge with all its diversity of contents and multiple areas and dimensions is the presupposition of scientific knowledge itself which therefore cannot supply us with a sovereign and unquestionable standard for the interpretation and evaluation of human experience in all its ranges. That many of our philosophically-minded scientists like Alfred North Whitehead are not tired of reminding us of the dangers accompanying such a point of view, to human civilization is now a commonplace of philosophical criticism. "A civilization", says Whitehead, "which cannot burst through its current abstractions is doomed to sterility after a very limited period of progress. An active school of philosophy is quite as important for the locomotion of ideas, as is an active school of railway engineers for the locomotion of fuel." (*Science and the Modern World*, Menton Edition, p. 58). "Abstractions have their own advantages (clear cut definite things and clear-cut definite relations and deductions of a variety of conclusions respecting the relationships between these abstract entities.) The advantage of confining attentions to a definite group of abstractions, is that you confine your thoughts to clear-cut definite things, with clear-cut definite relations. Accordingly, if you have a logical head, you can deduce a variety of conclusions respecting relationships between these entities. Furthermore, if the abstractions are well-founded, that is to say, if they do not abstract from everything that is important in experience, the scientific which confines itself to these abstractions will arrive at a variety of important truths relating to our experience of Nature." (Ibid, p. 58). In spite of such repeated reminders issued by philosophically-minded scientists, it is tragic, rather ironical to find philosophers themselves indulging not only in vicious abstractions but in making them represent the concrete facts of human life and experience. Such a procedure of thinking is evidently responsible for the disrepute into which philosophy has fallen because it is being progressively severed from the pressing problems of our social existence with the drastic consequence that the social utility of philosophy as a discipline has now become a matter of questionable and dubious value. It may be said without any exaggeration with Albert Schweitzer that philosophers themselves are in no small measure responsible for the fall of standards in civilization. "So little did philosophy philosophize about civilization that she did not even notice that she herself and the age along with her were losing more and more of it. In the hour of peril the watchman who ought to have us awake was himself asleep, and the result was that we put up no flight at all on behalf of our civilization. (*The Decay and Restoration of Civilization*, p. 24, George Allen & Unwin paperbacks, London, 1961). Logical positivism or what we may call logical empiricism, which in its incipient stages started with its emphasis on the appeal to experience in its *verificational theory of meaning*, has now altogether abdicated its pretence to fidelity or loyalty to experience and has lapsed into a completely formal activity in the logical atomism of Russell and Wittgenstein which sounds a veritable death-knell not only to empiricism on the foundations of which they built up their philosophy but has even resurrected the outworn doctrine of nominalism to which Hegel's idealism is a standing challenge' exposing its rottenness by teaching us that in a nominalistic world, we can know nothing and there can be no solid rock on which even our common experience can rest, let alone all higher interests of our moral and spiritual life. "Mr. Russell's effort to reduce the world to logical form and bare empirical particulars is in the end self-defeating. The formal and the empirical elements will not remain apart on Mr. Russell's terms. His bare empirical we saw long ago to be a myth. His docking and trimming destroy its empirical character. It becomes after all and against his intention virtually nothing but a class-member, and particulars which are nothing but class-members are themselves an element of logical form. We need not, however, press this point, for the fate which awaits logical atomism is perfectly plain. The study of pure logic becomes the function of the mathematician, and what we used to call Nature is reduced to logical constructions which are at once philosophical and scientific. In other words, as natural science progresses philosophy must go on vanishing into it, until it becomes obvious that the analytical philosopher has argued himself out of a job." (G.R.G. Mure *Retreat from Truth*, p. 133, Blackwell, Oxford, 1958). Philosophers are certainly uncommon people in obstinately refusing to learn from past mistakes, and as Berkeley said, they throw dust into their own eyes and complain that they do not see. As Berkeley himself said, "philosophers are not infrequently indebted to their own preconceptions for being ignorant of what everybody else knows perfectly well."

Indeed, of all the sciences and disciplines it is philosophy alone that can claim to be nearest to human interests and by the very nature of the case, therefore, it is bound to be anthropocentric if at all it has to jusify its pledge to account for all those provinces of knowledge in which all his interests are revealed and safeguarded. The need of philosophy, therefore is forced upon man. To ask, therefore, why man requires philosophy is to ask why man is what he is and why human experience is what it is. In other words, it is the most palpable fact about man that it is he who stands at the centre of all his experiences in which all the levels of reality are indisputably unified. It is true that physics inquires into the nature and constitution of matter: biology into the functions of life and psychology into the nature and character of mind: but that in man they are all unified can hardly be gainsaid. Everyman in the different moments of his experience descends to these levels and cannot but ask a question about them because his very existence is characterised by the form which is due exclusively to their co-existence. Hence the demand for philosophy as a synoptic view of all the levels of reality and of all the experiences corresponding to them and above all, which may offer unity in outlook and attitude is not a rhetorical one or of merely an academic interest. Hence howsoever much the sciences may multiply and knowledge by specialization may grow, the need for a *thinking consideration of all things* cannot be dispensed with. In our day, we have, because of too much stress laid on analysis and specialization many accounts of man, many conflicting conceptions of human nature. Biologists, psychologists, sociologists, economists, politicians, eugenists, preachers have all of them mutually contradictory notions and conceptions of man: the enquirer is bewildered and he pauses to discriminate between them and sort things out. This is the need of the present-day civilization. The confusion and chaos of society is verily the product of unsorted knowledge. It is philosophy that alone fulfils this need of synthesis, of looking at things as a whole, of furnishing in other words a synthetic and systematic scheme of all the principles of knowledge and reality. Man, unless he elects to vegetate upon the sense pleasures has no other alternative than to become a philosopher. The ordinary man is not at all confused and bewildered when he passes from one point of view to another, from the material level of his being to the biological and the psychological. He does not experience these transitions from one level of reality and experience to another and does not therefore feel any necessity of a synopsis. But when sometimes his expectations are frustrated, he becomes critical and meditative and begins to reflect upon the many sides of his being. All the levels of reality that are manifested in his being are brought to a single focus and he cannot but evolve a standpoint which seeks to do justice to all his experiences, namely, the physical, the vitalistic, the moral, the aesthetic, religious and so on.

The urge, therefore, for synopsis is something inborn and

intrinsic to human nature and cannot therefore be dispensed with. Hence without explaining the higher experiences such as the moral, the religious and the aesthetic and so forth, philosophy cannot justify its claim to its existence alongside of other provinces of knowledge. Since it is in man that all these experiences take place and are also perfectly unified, the curiosity as to what the nature of the real must be so that his usual transition from one level of experience to another is possible, is inevitable. The demand for philosophy as a synoptic view of all the data that experience supplies, is not a sentimental one but arises from the multi-dimensional nature of human experience itself. The positivist view, therefore, that there are no philosophical problems, that what claim to be propositions are no propositions at all and that all true propositions are the propositions that constitute the corpus of scientific knowledge must be grossly mistaken. Hence science which abstracts a great deal from human experience cannot be "synoptic" and cannot consequently be a substitute for philosophy which seeks to transcend its abstract points of vew.

II. Place of Religion in the totality of Human Experience

Of all the experiences that arise as a result of man's confrontation with reality, religious experience, which engrosses his whole personality and accounts for his ultimate attitude of thought, feeling and will to the universe, is the most important because it is all-inclusive in nature "Religious insight is hospitable to all the modes of knowledge and experience, gathers them into itself and transfigures them. This, as we shall see, applies to myth as much as to metaphysics. Religious knowledge is not poetry or its enjoyment, but it is vastly deepened by the experience of poetry: so, although religion is certainly not identical with myth, the full apprehension of the images of myth and the gathering up of them into a deeper religious understanding, is a part of religious growth. Again, religious knowledge is not identical with metaphysics: but the metaphysical contribution is indispensable and must be assimilated into religious insight. This is true of analogy also. There is no adequate analogy for the being of God: yet knowledge of God is mediated by analogies drawn from fundamental human experiences, which transforms, extends and deepens them. We can only apprehend the meanings which lie beyond some particular level of language or experience by first absorbing to the full what they have to give. Religion is something like an organism accepting food (of an amazing variety) assimilating and transforming it into its own ongoing life." (Louis Arnaud Roid, *Ways of Knowledge and Experience*, p. 117, Gorge Allen & Unwin Ltd., London, 1961). In other words, religion is the summed up product of all his experience. It is the ultimate attitude of thought, feeling and will built up by him in consequence of his contact with the universe. Like philosophy, religion also is *synoptic* because a man's religion is based upon the basic presuppositions of his experience. Like philosophy religion also is concerned with ultimate questions. But religion differs from philosophy in considering these ultimate questions in their direct bearings upon the nature of man and his destiny. Religion is not merely the discovery of certain truths pertaining to the nature and constitution of the universe and his place in it but also the determination to live in accordance with these principles.

We must here clear up certain confusions that have sprung up in our minds as to the true genius and nature of religion. Religion has something distinctive of its own. But we are so accustomed to identify it with any and everything we like that it hardly ever comes to mean anything precise and definite and have a fixed connotation. At the present time, we hear such a thing as *religionless Christianity*. Many identify religion with a mere *blik* or a commitment or what we call a policy of action. For some, it is nothing more than a getting serious about a business. For some people atheism is not incompatible with religion. The well-known psychologist and philosopher William James identifies religion with the process of bringing out the potentialities of the subconscious. God is only another name of the subconscious. Without entering upon a detailed discussion of the worth of such theories, we may add here that religion is primarily and exclusively the consciousness of God and the reference of all values to Him as the Supreme or the Absolute Value. In its essential meaning, religion is the consciousness of a Being who is not only the source of all things and beings of the universe but is in reference to man that which embraces all his life, integrates his whole being and harmonises all his conflicting impulses, emotions and passions by supplying a central focus and gives unity and direction to it and turns the drift of his ordinary course of conduct from the transitory and the ephemeral to the eternal and the permanent, from the particular to the universal and from the finite to the Infinite. Religious consciousness is the unfaltering conviction that all our finite experience presupposes and is grounded in and rests upon the Supreme Spiritual Principle which encompasses and pervades all the contents of his finite personality and transcends all the varied manifestations and expressions of it.

Any attempt, therefore, to identify religion with our secular interests, to restrict it to purely human dimensions or to assimilate it to any endeavour directed to mere secular comforts must stand self condemned: for it is in its very transcendence of all secular consciousness and all secular interests and values the transvaluation of all values that its true genius consists. Unlike the secular consciousness that is little troubled about any principle of unity behind the scene of plurality and difference that it treats to be final, religious consciousness rises to the conception of the eternal and the infinite, which in the first instance we are apt to define as that which the finite is not—the very opposite of the finite. Religious consciousness, that is to say, is the very subversion of our ordinary consciousness beginning where it ends and ending where it begins, affirming that which it denies and denying what it affirms and setting store upon that as most valuable and real which for it must be most trivial and the temptiest of all abstractions. In the absence, therefore, of the consciousness of God, the ultimate source and goal of all existence with whom our relations are of very close and intimate character, there can be no religion at all in the true sense of the term. Everything else is either peripheral to religion or a mere caricature of it, for it must always be borne in mind that religion implies as its presupposition and basis a certain system of metaphysical beliefs and cannot therefore be pulled down to secular and earthly dimensions. Religion involves an element of belief by which is meant that it impels a certain conviction about the nature and existence of the Supreme Reality, a theory of knowledge which tells us that we cannot know it in the way we know all other facts of the world and a graduated scheme of ascent to the supreme goal of human existence which is the vision of the Deity. Any statement therefore as to the truth of religion or for the matter of that religious truth has reference to the philosophy or metaphysic behind religious consciousness for it cannot be gainsaid that even though in the first instance, our knowledge of God is unconscious and not the result of clear and conscious reflection, it is nevertheless there and however faint and feeble it may be, we never miss it in all the forms of the movements of our conscious life.

III. Factual Basis of Religious Assertions

Under the corrosive impact of the rise of linguistic empiricism and an utterly false view of the nature of knowledge, and verification which scientists themselves are reluctant to endorse the question as to the credibility and authenticity of religious experience has very often been raised. While religious experience is an autonomous activity of the human mind involving no doubt the exercise of all its cognitive, affective and volitional faculties the standard of its truth is supposed to be the same as that adopted in empirical science. Knowledge in religion is doubtless not of an *I-It* but definitely of *I-Thou* kind. All the same the cognitive element in religion cannot be disputed for religion itself in the result of an interpretation of the universe and of man's place in it. "As a self-conscious and rationally-thinking being," says Tielo, "man necessarily brings his lot and his life into relations with causes that are outside him, or powers that are above him. This was the origin of religion: for as soon as he conceived of such a power he felt the practical need of placing himself in relations with it." (Quoted in W. P. Paterson, *The Nature of Religion*, p. 307). Religion is rooted in the very rational nature and constitution of the human mind although it is not merely rational but informs and permeates the emotional and volitional sides also of the human mind. Just because man's religion is the product of his cognitive and interpretative powers and is consequently expressed in a system of statements or propositions, it claims to be true and unless the testimony of human experience altogether shatters its credentials, its title to be the true representation of reality cannot be contested.

As the consciousness of God is not an arbitrary or a fanciful product of vague and empty imagination but is rather the very basis or ground of the intelligibility of human experience and of the world, it would not be proper, as the positivists allege, that religion has no factual basis and that it is merely evocative or at best an expression of a certain emotional attitude. It is true that this defence of religion is an old one and it is redundant to advance the already familiar arguments in favour of the truth of religious statements. But human thought moves in a circle and in the absence of a historical perspective pertaining to the evolution of human thought, philosophers are prone to raise the same kind of questions without being familiar with the answers that may have already been given. Nevertheless those who object to the credibility of the religious assertions should ask themselves not whether the answers are familiar but whether they are convincing and if they are so whether their doctrines which are incompatible with them can themselves be true. We seldom make any attempt to analyse and understand our experience but when we have an occasion to do so, and inquire into the conditions which render it possible, we are forced to admit that all that we know is known only as a part in one experience, the experience of the world as a whole as one system, such a unity being the presupposition of the knowledge both of the world and of ourselves. For the nominalist, it is difficult to understand that the given world is an intelligible one and is the manifestation and expression of continuity and self-consistency and testifies to the existence of one spiritual principle underlying all the differences of its forms. But our knowledge of the universe being what it is and there being the evidence in it of the presence of a transcendent spiritual principle behind all its phenomena and events, the existence of God cannot be said to be merely a postulate or a regulative principle or a working hypothesis. Belief in God is the affirmation of the existence of a principle of unity in the universe akin to the human ego, the centre of self-consciousness in terms of which we affirm the existence of our own personal self. The universe is to God what the objects of knowledge are to the human ego. Religious assertions, therefore, have a factual basis seeing that they make it certain once and for all that were there in fact, no God, no spiritual principle of unity behind or immanent in the world, it would not have been intelligible to us nor would have its knowledge ever been possible.

IV. Religious Truth

Religious truth differs from scientific or mere cognitive truth in that it is existential in nature. It is not impersonal but rather personal in nature. A kind of knowledge that involves the entire personality of man cannot be likened to the scientific knowledge which is perceptual or inferential. Śaṅkara in his commentary on the Brahmasūtra has already warned us that 'Scripture does not intend to demonstrate the existence of Brahman in the manner of the ordinary facts of the world.' (Na hi śāstraṁ brahma idantayā pratipipādayiṣati). The Upaniṣad tells us that *Brahman is rasa* (*Taittirīya Upaniṣad*, II. 7) There can be no demonstrative proof of that which is the basis of all knowledge and all proof. Religious truth is existential truth. The object of religious belief does not stand the same footing as the familiar physical facts of our ordinary experience. Religious truth cannot be discovered or known indirectly or by demonstration or proof. By having some one tell anybody the right words no one can expect to know God. The only answer that can be given is "Try it and find it out for yourself." It is truth which can only be discovered or reached by the practice of religion. The Upaniṣad tells us that:

> Him who is hard to see, entered into the hidden,
> set in the secret place (of the heart), dwelling in the depth, primeval
> by considering him as God, through the Yoga-study of what pertains to self,

The wise man leaves joy and sorrow behind (Kaṭha Upaniṣad, II. 12)

"To be religious," says, H. D. Lewis, "is not to be in a strange state where true and false do not matter or where the laws of thought are annulled. It is to apprehend a 'beyond' which thought cannot reach but which thought itself requires as its completion." (*Prospect for Metaphysics*, pp. 225-6, ed., by Ian Ramsey, George Allen & Unwin Ltd., London, 1961). "The point that must needs to be stressed is the quite radical character of the difference between the idea of God and any other idea we may entertain. It is not just, that it is nonempirical. Many ideas might be that, mathematics or certain *a priori* principles perhaps, or some non-natural quality in ethics, but we do claim at any rate to be able to indicate fairly satisfactorily what these ideas mean. There may be no strictly factual exemplification of them, and in the case of the alleged non-natural quality of goodness, no analysis of any sort may be possible. But there is nonetheless much which may be said: we may indicate what sort of things have a non-natural quality, we may draw contests between it and other properties, for example physical ones or mathematical or causal ones. We may make it fairly clear what this property is not, and when we have, in these and kindred ways, induced in others the apprehension of this property, or helped them to realize that they have been apprehending it all the time, we know that it is some one thing or type of thing that they have before their minds, and we do not doubt that they grasp this something in its true nature or as it really is in itself. They may not be able to describe it, except obliquely in terms of its concomitants and so forth. But they know what it is like, and there are certain things at any rate with which there is not the slightest likelihood of their confusing it." (*Ibid.* p. 207) Religious statements and religious truths are unique in that they refer to some kind of experience which no ordinary emotion or sensation can describe. "How can we know that it is not possible to be aware of the existence of God otherwise than by inference or by sense-experience? The claim is not that people have some peculiar kind of sensation or emotion when they are aware of God or that they are entitled to infer the existence of God from this peculiar feeling, which would surely be a weak inference, but that they have some kind of experience not adequately describable as mere sensation or emotion which makes them realize the presence of God." (A. C. Ewing, *Non-Linguistic Philosophy*, p 233, George Allen & Unwin Ltd., London, 1968)

V. Summing Up

The fact that discerning minds of the present century warn us of the futility of the thinking of some of best thinkers of today which does not cross the borders of mere linguistic debates completely cut off from the practical concerns of human life, is doubtless a call to all of us doing philosophy to take care in the matter of adventures of outthought that we make some tangible contribution to the growing world diviliation. This is an enormous responsibility for philosophers who can effectively discharge it only by a return to the traditional moorings. Our civilization is in need of a stable outlook towards the world which will shape and mould the warring impulses of individuals and nations. In such a critical time only the traditional notion of philosophy as the "thinking consideration of all things" can be surest guide to us. In the framework of such an outlook, religion will prove to be the anodyn of all the ills from which we suffer. Religion which is a genuine revelation of the nature of Reality can alone be the practical guide to the troubled mankind of today. All modern criticisms of the cognitive value of religious experience arise from a false view of the nature of science, religion and man.

Ranchi University, Ranchi

16
TO SPEAK CLEARLY
K. K. Banerjee

I

We shall assume that the distinction between speaking and speaking clearly is unreal, and so either we can speak clearly, or we cannot speak. We shall also assume that in philosophy either we can speak in ordinary language, grooming it as and when necessary, or we cannot speak. And, we shall argue the following propositions :

1. A fiction cannot be spoken of, as it has no nature of its own and so cannot be either identified or differentiated.

2. A fact can be spoken of, as it has a nature of its own, can be identified and differentiated, and has categorial and sub-categorial properties besides the unique properties that bestow it its facthood, and the properties that cut across categorial distinctions.

3. To speak clearly is to make use of a categorial scheme.

4. Ordinary language has the scheme as its structure, and so though an analysis of it gives us a clue to the scheme it has structured, to identify the categories and also to detect the category-mistakes we cannot depend on it alone.

5. What we require besides ordinary language to get the categories, and what may be said to evidence them, or to be their source, is, what the Indian logicians termed, *anubhava*, which may be roughly translated, by borrowing an expression from Stout, as noetic sentience, and *lokayātrā* which may be similarly translated as common sense, or on-goings of everyday life[1].

II
A fiction cannot be spoken of

'Sky-lotus', 'rabbit's horn' and words or expressions like them are regarded as symbols for fictions. Such words are a bit queer. We do not ordinarily use them in predicative sentences, affirmative or negative, and this is not without a significance of its own. Thus, a sentence is a grammatical fact, but what figures in it as a subject, or as a predicate, has an epistemological character as well. Thus viewed the predicate gives a determination to the subject, and distinguishes or differentiates it. But a fiction-symbol does not either determine or differentiate. So no useful purpose is served by using a fiction-symbol as a predicate or a predicate-factor. For the same reason it is not used as a subject or a subject-factor. In short, a fiction-symbol does not determine or distinguish, and what it purports to symbolise has no nature to be identified or distinguished.

But this is not the case with a fact. It has a nature of its own. It has, as the Vaiśeṣikas put it, *astitā*[2] is-ness. This is-ness should be distinguished from both *sattā*, existence, and *bhāvatva*, being. 'Being' may roughly be defined as the property of an object of yes-consciousness. But there are objects of yes-consciousness which have this property but do not cease to be. Only the objects that cease to be, and others which do not cease to be but are objects of the same category or categories—the categorial distinction among objects being not a function of occurring or ceasing to occur—have existence as their property[3]. It is a class-property, simple and unanalysable, and may be present in more than one object. Being is not a class-property, for a class-property is an object of yes-consciousness, and if it were a class-property inhering in a class-property that would have been a case of a universal of universal, and the harmful consequence of infinite regress would have been the result. But though not a class-property, it is also simple and unanalysable, and is more comprehensive than existence and is a property of more than one object. But is-ness is not such a property. The is-ness that one object has is not the is-ness that another object has[4]. When a sky-flower is said to be a fiction what precisely is meant is that it has no is-ness, or a property that it alone has. So it may be said to have every property (except is-ness, or a property like it) as well as no property. This is not the case with a fact. It is definite, has a nature of its own, and can be identified and differentiated[5].

III

Every fact can be clearly spoken of

Every fact has is-ness. This may be treated as a definition of a fact in that what has no is-ness or a property like it cannot have any property, so cannot be a fact, cannot be defined, and some definitions give us the use of a word or an expression.[6] Now, if a fact had this property or properties of this type only, it would be unique, and as unspeakable as a fiction is. So though is-ness bestows it its facthood, it does not ensure its speakability. To be spoken of it should have other properties as well. And we should now make an attempt to see what they are, or what sort of properties they are.

So, we may consider the case of a table which is definite, or a fact, and can be spoken of. When we say that an object is a table we distinguish it from what is not a table. That is, we identify it as a member of the class of all tables, and distinguish it from what is a member of a co-ordinate class. And, if classification be not arbitrary, all the members of the class of all tables have a common property, that is, a property that is a property of every member of this class, and is not a property of any member of a co-ordinate class. It is table-ness, a simple and unanalysable property, given to noetic sentience and in terms of it we distinguish a table from a chair, or from any object that is a member of a co-ordinate class.

But, do we or can we always identify and distinguish an object in terms of such a property? Let us see. Thus, we may distinguish one table from another table, and we do this after taking into account qualities like colour, shape, size, texture etc. of the two tables. So we may say that a quality may also help us to distinguish. But such a statement would be inadequate. For, two tables may be exceedingly alike in qualities, and then a quality would not be of any help. Again, if the two tables have different qualities, when one is brown and the other is black, we think that we distinguish them in terms of the different colours they have, but actually we distinguish in terms of some simple property or properties. That is, we have to identify the two colours and distinguish them, and this we do in terms of the simple properties, viz. brown-ness and blackness. Besides, the brown colour of this table may be exceedingly similar to the brown colour of another object—another table, or a cricket ball—and we distinguish them in terms of the objects they qualify. So, there are occasions when we distinguish one quality from another quality in terms of the objects they qualify, and quality does not provide us with the criterion of identification and differentiation we are in search of.

It may be suggested that space or the positions that the tables occupy may help us in distinguishing them. But that would not be a happy suggestion. For, such space cannot be the space a geometrician studies, or a physicist speaks of. It should be what a layman understands as space. That is, to a layman what accounts for the use of expressions like 'near', 'to the left of', 'eastwards' etc. is space. It is a partless, ubiquitous and imperceptible thing.[7] It is not what is immediately given to us. The points, or the so-called parts of space are ideal divisions of it, and if it be not confused with extension, the question of dividing it, and that too infinitely, does not arise. Besides, the points of space are identified in terms of the objects that are said to occupy them, and so the objects are to be identified independently of them. This is borne out by re-identification, or re-cognition. When an object is recognised at a place different from the place where it was cognised, and recognition is expressed as 'this is that object', 'this' stands for the object in the place where it is recognised, and 'that' for the object at the place where it was cognised, and though the two places differ, the difference between 'this', and 'that' is ignored, and the object is regarded as the same identical object, and to account for this we require something that is not separable from the object, or is an inseparable property of the object. The Vaiśeṣikas thought that when an object is a compound object—and such an object is always categorially a substance[8]—it is distinguished from another compound object in terms of its constituent parts, and so when an object is simple, or indivisible, and categorially a substance, it is distinguished from another simple substance of the same class and having similar qualities and actions in terms of an ultimate differentium[9] which is self-differentiating. We need not consider if by introducing something self-differentiating they did not cut the Gordian knot, or begged the issue. We would be content with the observation that a compound object like a table may be more happily distinguished from another exceedingly similar table in terms of its parts than in terms of positions in space, and shall consider the question if a table is not distinguished from table-ness, or from its brown colour or objects of that type in a way that differs from the way it is distinguished from another table, or a chair, and for that, any object like paper, or a pencil, or a broomstick.

We think that the question should be answered affirmatively. A table is not distinguished from table-ness, or a colour in the same way as it is distinguished from a chair, or a soffa. The class of all chairs is a co-ordinate class of all tables. This is not the case with the class of all browns. Neither is the class of all browns either super-ordinate or sub-ordinate to the class of all tables. Besides, though its colour occasionally distinguishes a table from another table, it is also distinguished from another exceedingly similar colour in terms of the table of which it is a quality. Similarly with table-ness. Now, the objects that may be members of co-ordinate classes (or sets), or members of classes (or sets) that may be arranged by way of super-ordination, or sub-ordination may be said to be in or under the same tree; and objects of one tree are distinguished in a different way from objects of a different tree, and may be said to be categorially different—a categorial property being the property which is the property of all the members of the most comprehensive class (or set) of the tree, other than the properties of 'being an object', 'being', and 'existence'. That is, 'being an object' is not a categorial property in that it does not differentiate, and the objects having it cannot be given the tree-type arrangement. Similarly, 'being' is a property that every positive fact has, and though it differentiates the objects having it, they cannot be arranged in the way spoken above. This is true also of 'existence'. But properties like 'being a substance', 'being a quality' etc. are not of this sort. And they are the categorial properties.

Thus, a property like 'is-ness' that confers uniqueness to a fact and enables it to have or not to have some other properties is of no help in clear speaking. Similarly, a property like 'being' that may be a property of objects of many trees does not mark off objects in the way required for clear speaking.

A category, or a categorial property does it. They help us to identify objects in a broad way. They are the 'ultimate predicates', to use an Aristotelian term, and all predications in terms of them are 'essential predications'. Anyway, when we say that an object is a substance, or a quality, and so on, we in a broad way identify it, and we make the identification more specific when we ascribe the sub-categorial, less comprehensive properties—the least comprehensive such property being the property to which the narrower or the less comprehensive property is is-ness or a property like it.

IV

To speak clearly is to make use of a categorial scheme

From what has been said above it would be obvious that to speak clearly we should use a categorial scheme, and we need not dwell on this point any more. We may now ask the question if when we use categories we speak of facts as they are or as they are known. In other words, if the categorial and sub-categorial properties are the contributions of imagination or understanding, then when to speak clearly we use categories, we do not speak of the facts as they are but as they are known. This is a well-known doctrine, and we cannot discuss it fully. We would only say a few words against it, and also a few words in support of the contrary doctrine that we endorse.

Thus, against the doctrine we would say that it is difficult to understand how one may distinguish the two kinds of unspeakables, viz. the fictions and the facts as they are. A fiction is without a nature of its own, and a fact, it ought to be said, has a nature, but its nature is not categorial. That is, in our mode of speaking, a fact as it is has is-ness, but no other property. But there is hardly any reason for distinguishing between properties in this way. That the other properties are comprehensive i.e. may be properties of more than one object is not puzzling, if a property be not understood on the model of a quality. So also the distinction between what has a property and the property is not unintelligible if we do not try to understand what has a property as something to be understood as something with a property but without it. And the question on the relation between them presents difficulties if relations are treated as terms, or if it is not seen that the fundamental relation is one in which the nature of either of the relata may function as a relation. Besides, the facts as they are is distinguished from facts as they are known, and if this is sought to be accounted for in terms of having or not having categorial properties, the account would be self-defeating in that even if 'having a categorial property' be treated as a property, it will not distinguish, and besides 'not having a categorial property' will be a property, different from a property like 'is-ness' and co-ordinate with 'having a categorial property', and so will be either a categorial property, or a more comprehensive, super-categorial property like 'being'.

It may be argued that our mode of speaking is misleading us, and is at the root of the above considerations which are or look like sophistries. But the argument would be a lame one. For, our mode of speaking has for its basis common sense, or the on-goings of everyday life. Thus, a sub-categorial property like table-ness, if a property of the object, and not an imposition, ensures that classification is not arbitrary, and so an object is a member of a class not because we are pleased to make it its member, but because it demands or coerces us to recognise it as such. To deny this, or to hold that classification is always arbitrary is to deny the distinction between the world of facts and the world of fancy, and this makes the on-goings of everyday life impossible. Besides, noetic sentience evidences the reality or the non-impositional character of these properties.

Another point, a technical one in Indian logic, may be mentioned. To hold that properties other than is-ness and its like are constructions of imagination is to hold also that every inference is positive-contrapositive[10]. But a careful analysis of inference shows that only in the case of purely contrapositive inference, the fact-implicate may figure as the qualificand of an inferential judgment, and the relation between acontrapositive application and the inferential judgment consequent upon it differ radically from the relation between a positive application and the inferential judgment consequent upon it, and the difference is so radical that the causal character of the two types of application has to be separately stated, that is cannot be assimilated and expressed in a single formula[11]. Indeed, the relation of implication flowing from smoke to fire is different from the relation of implication flowing from absence of fire to absence of smoke. From 'p implies q' we may by transposition obtain 'not-q implies not-p'. But this is to educe. And no such eduction or transposition is permissible when the factual implicative relation (FIR), or the inductive relation is asserted from the nature of the case on positive instances only, or on negative instances only: and it is questionable if without being exceedingly artificial one definition of FIR may cover two types of FIR.

V

Categories and Ordinary language

On the basis of what we have said we may assert that the categories are embedded in ordinary language, or that an analysis of ordinary language gives us a clue to the categories involved in speaking. So, it is only natural that many philosophers with interest in the question of categories have given considerable attention to language, and we have neither the requisite scholarship nor space at our disposal to subject the outcomes of these efforts in this paper. We would only spell out our qualms about any theory of categories based on a consideration of language only. Thus, we may ask if such a theory would be based on a consideration of uncombined expressions or words, or on a consideration of combined expressions or sentences. When it is based on a consideration of the first type it may provide us with ultimate predicates. But if the ultimate predicates be the predicates generalised, then they are all that may in final analysis be said of an individual. This implies that only individuals may figure as subjects. Whether it is reasonable to hold this from a strictly logical point of view, we do not know. But undoubtedly from the epistemological point of view this cannot be maintained. It also implies that the categorial distinctions are not absolute in the sense required for clear speaking. Thus, an individual table may be said to be a substance, a member of the class of all tables, brown and so on. But when we say that a table is member of the class of all tables we do not distinguish it from another substance, say a chair, in the same way as we distinguish it from table-ness, or from its colour etc. In other words, 'being a substance', 'being a quality' etc. are, as we have argued before, properties of all the members of the co-ordinate and comprehensive classes (or sets), and so what has one such property cannot have another such property. But the table of categories provided by Aristotle, and based on a consideration of uncombined expressions, when interpreted in the above manner, denies this, and so cannot be very helpful in clear speaking. Possibly this was the reason for his scholastic followers for converting his theory of categories into a theory of ultimate types of namable objects. But then such a theory cannot be based on a consideration of language merely. We should seek the help of experience. It would have been very unfortunate if language were not adequate for experience. But then it cannot decide if it is adequate. An extra-linguistic criterion is necessary. Besides, a theory of categories when based on a consideration of uncombined expressions cannot do justice to the objects of no-consciousness. 'No', 'not' and similar words when uncombined do not give any clue to the kind of objects they stand for. When combined with words, but not made parts of a sentence, they can convey only something indefinite, or otherness. This defect may be partly remedied when we base our theory of categories on a consideration of sentences. But then also we do not do full justice to the objects of a no-consciousness. The subject of negative facts is too large to be discussed here. We should only observe that a negative fact satisfies all the conditions for being called a fact that a positive fact satisfies. It has is-ness, is definite, distinguishes and can be distinguished. Besides, we cannot say that a no-consciousness can be reduced to a yes-consciousness, or that it denies or declares to be false what a corresponding yes-consciousness asserts, or that it is non-intentional. And a no-consciousness shows a negative fact as abiding in a locus, and a consideration of an ordinary predicative sentence cannot bring this out. Indeed, the only kind of negative fact on which it may throw some light is, what the Nyāya logicians call, mutual absence. If we consider sentences only we should deny constant absence, and we cannot do it.[12]

Again, when we base our theory of categories on a consideration of sentences, we should ask the question if the sentences are to be considered as expressions of some knowledge or judgment, or just as they are. If we adopt the first course, we perilously approach a theory of categories of the Kantian type the consequence of which is that we can talk clearly of facts as they are known and not as they are. But we have already argued that this is not a satisfactory position to hold. But if we adopt the second course, we seem to claim that la nguage unaided by experience can lay down its criterion of adequacy. And we have already argued that this is a very tall claim on the nature of language and it cannot be met. In substantiation of it we may refer to the criterion of absurdity on which Prof. Ryle relied heavily to identify the categories or the category-mistakes, and to the opinion of competent thinkers that he was not successful. We may also add that even if he were successful, the claim would have appeared plausible but not counter-intuitive.

VI

Noetic Sentience and Categories

Though categories are embedded in language and language may provide us with clues about categories, yet if not aided by noetic sentience, language cannot be of any help. Noetic sentience is experience uncorrupted by obscure and artificial metaphysical views, and is at the basis of the on-goings of everyday life. What is given to it is never a bare particular, but particulars with properties that may be arranged hierarchically in respect of their comprehensiveness. We have argued before in what way the on-goings of everyday life justify us in holding that a class-property like table-ness is a property of the object, and so not an imposition, and that this is true of every categorial or sub-categorial property. We have also argued that is-ness or a property like it is not a property of a fiction, and so no categorial or sub-categorial property is also a property of it. But this is not the case with a fact. A fact is definite. It would not have been definite if it had no is-ness. But it would not be adequately definite if it had it only and not the categorial and sub-categorial properties. And if it is not adequately definite it is hardly definite. That is, there is no opposition between is-ness and the comprehensive properties. 'Not having is-ness' does not imply 'having comprehensive properties' and vice versa; otherwise a fiction would have either is-ness or some comprehensive property. Similarly 'having is-ness' does not imply 'not having comprehensive properties' and vice versa. For, a comprehensive property is referred, not to a fiction but to a fact which on receiving it as a predicate does not cease to be a fact. Besides, we may affirm or deny any comprehensive property of a fiction. But we cannot do this with a fact. We affirm or deny some comprehensive properties of some facts, and the distinction between affirmative and negative judgments is not arbitrary, but based on the nature of facts. So what has is-ness, has some comprehensive properties and has not some others. 'Having is-ness' does not imply 'not having any comprehensive property'. Every fact has is-ness and one or other categorial property or properties, and can be clearly spoken of.

Notes and References

1. The Nyāya-Vaiśeṣika philosophers hold that *vācyatā* or namability (speakability) is an unnegatable property, *kevalānvyidharma*. They also formulate a theory of categories. There is a connection between the two. But they do not work out the connection. This paper attempts to do it as a Nyāya-Vaiśeṣika philosopher would have done if asked to do it, and it has done this from the standpoint of a speaker. But then it is not just a paper on Nyāya-Vaiśeṣika philosophy, but on a philosophical question.

2. '*astitā*' as used by Praśastapāda has been interpreted differently by different writers on him, and we have followed Śrīdhara and Jagadiśa.

3. *dhvaṁsakāraṇatāvacchedakatayā sattājatisiddeḥ* : This way of constructing *sattā* has some limitations, but they may be overcome by suitable insertions.

4. *Ubhayavṛittidharma* : Tarkācārya K. on Bhāṣāratnam, Cal. 1936 p 63.

5. In fables, myths, stories etc. we seem to talk clearly on fictions. But actually we do not. For, whereas a sentence like 'A tiger tore him to pieces' yields knowledge, a sentence like 'A dragon tore him to pieces' does not. In the first case, 'tiger' figures as the qualificand, *viśeṣya*, and its state or condition of being a qualificand, *viśeṣyatā* is limited, *avacchinna*, by the limiting property, *avacchedakadharma*, 'tigerness', a simple and unanalysable property given to noetic sentience. But in the second case no such qualificand-ness limiting property is available. 'Dragon-ness' is not given to

noetic sentience, nor is it a cause-ness limitor, *kāraṇatāvacchedaka*, or an effect-ness limitor, *kāryatāvacchedaka*. And there cannot be any knowledge if qualificandness is not limited. Somilarly, barring the case of sensations, qualificandness should be described by qualifier-ness, *prakārata*. In the first, 'tearing him to pieces' figures as the qualifier-ness and it describes the qualificand-ness residing in tiger, as it permits itself to be described. But in the second case, it does not describe, for the so-called qualificandness residing in 'a dragon' does permit itself to be described.

6. A definition, so the Indian logicians think, serves either of the two purposes. viz. *vyavahāra* and *vyāvṛtti*. The first gives the use of a word or expression, and the second states how the definiendum is to be differentiated. 'What has earth-ness, is earth' illustrates the first type, and 'What has smell, is earth' illustrates the second type. It is the orthodox view that the types are irreducibly different. But it should be mentioned that even the first type of definition is not stipulative or nominal. It is real as it is given in terms of the property which every definiendum has. The definition of fact, given in the paper, is of the first type. A definition of the second type is not available. For, a fiction does not differentiate. Besides the word 'fiction' is not a fiction. And so a definition of the first type for both 'fiction' and 'fact' may be given.

7. The Nyāya-Vaiśeṣika account of *dik* when read between the lines is an account of a layman's use of such expressions, or of the experiences at their back.

8. Rightly viewed, the question of distinguishing is the question of distinguishing what is categorially a substance. A quality or an action is distinguished in terms of the substance of which it is a quality or an action. A class-property or its analogue distinguishes that of which it is a property from that of which it is not a property. But it may be given to us only as the property of the object of which it is a property. So, all problem of distinguishing is in ultimate analysis a problem of distinguishing between substances.

9. *viśeṣa*.

10. *anvayi-vyatireki*. We have adapted some expressions of Mill and Johnson translated *vyāpti*, as factual implicative relation, FIR, or as inductive relation, *sādhya* as fact-implicate, *hetu* as fact-implicans, *parāmarśa* as application or applicative judgment, *anumiti* as inferential judgment. And following Stcherbatsky *anvayi* as purely positive, *vyatireki* as purely contra-positive, and *anvayi-vyatireki* as positive-contrapositive. And following Ingalls *viśeṣya* as qualificand, *viśeṣyatā* as qualificandness, *prakāra* as qualifier, *prakāratā* as qualifierness, *avacchedakadharma* as limitor. And throughout the paper we have used the term property as the English equivalent of *dharma*, and knowledge as, that of *jñāna*.

11. Pakṣatā : Jagadīśa, Chowkhamba edition, pp-117-18 Śabdaśaktiprakāśikā : Jagadīśa : Calcutta edition, p 5

12. *anyonyābhāva*; mutual absence; *atyantābhāva*, constant absence

Jadavpur University, Calcutta

LANGUAGE, THOUGHT AND REALITY
SOME ASPECTS OF INDIAN THOUGHT

R. R. Dravid

A good deal of philosophising in India has been concerned with questions relating to the nature of language and its relation to reality. A host of problems is raised concerning the ontological and epistemological status of language, its conventionality, its competence to express reality and so on. The answers given to these problems by the various systems are varied and conflicting. They are primarily determined by the metaphysical stand-point that a system adopts. Almost all types of views—Absolutism, Pluralism, Empiricism, Transcendentalism, Realism and Nominalism—are represented in Indian thought. It is not possible for me to consider in this brief paper all the important aspects of the problem concerning language and its relation to reality as found in Indian Philosophy. I, therefore, propose to confine myself to two questions: (i) Is language conventional? and (ii) Does language reveal reality, or hide or distort it? Needless to say that my discussion of these questions would be strictly within the confines of Indian Philosophy.

I

The question whether language is conventional or not is hotly debated by the Nyāya, the Mīmāṁsā and the school of Grammar. The Nyāya represents the conventionalist view of language. Language, in its view, is constituted with words which are but combination of syllables (*varṇas*). Words signify objects and this signification may be by way of denotation (*abhidhā*) or implication (*lakṣaṇā*). Every word has a meaning which is essentially a relation between itself and the object it refers to. This relation is not natural but is established by convention. The way in which we learn the meaning of words confirms this view. It is through public usage, instructions, dictionaries and gestures that we come to know the meaning of words. The older Nyāya believed that the convention that such and such a word should mean such and such an object was established by God (*Īśvarasaṅketaḥ Śaktiḥ*). This view is justified on the ground that scriptural language, which is the source of the language that we use, cannot be conceived to have human origin. Its originator must be God. The later Nyāya however widens the scope of language. With the growth of knowledge new words signifying new meanings come into being. Language cannot be restricted to the words found in scriptures. Thus words come to possess meanings by human convention also (*icchāmātram śaktiḥ*). This view is clearly empiricistic and closer to common sense.

The non-conventionalist view of language is represented by the Mīmāmsā and the school of Grammar. Both of them maintain that the relation between a word and its meaning is natural, not created by convention, and therefore necessary and eternal. The view of non-eternality of the word and the conventionality of meaning, according to them, springs from a confusion between the word and the overt sound manifesting it. In each significant word there are two elements : One is the word itself and the other is the sound (*dhvani*) manifesting it. The cognition of the word is preceded by the appearance of sounds. But to identify the word with overt physical sounds is to confuse entities of two different orders. Sounds manifest the word but the conveyance of meaning is the function of the word not of sounds. If the word is identified with the complex of sounds produced by a speaker, there would be no common word. Each complex of sounds would be unique and there would be no common comprehension of meaning. It is a fact of experience that a word may be uttered by different persons at different times and places, but it is recognised as *the same* in spite of the differences. This points to the oneness and eternal nature of the word. Bhartṛhari establishes the point by distinguishing between word-form (*śabdākṛti*) and the particular word (*śabda*). A word is a word-form and is the same throughout particular occurrences of it. It is the word-form that this is meaningful. If this is denied, common understanding of language and intelligibility of verbal communication would be impossible.

Both the Mīmāṁsā and the school of Grammar, however, recognise the role of convention in language in some sense. The Mīmāṁsā admits that instructions regarding the meaning of words by one who is familiar with them is necessary for learning language. But meaning of words itself is not established either by divine or by human convention. The Grammarian recognises the role of convention in another way. Prior to convention a word is not related to any specific meaning. All words are naturally related to all meanings. What the convention maker does is to restrict their meanings to specific class of objects and not to give meaning to them. The relation of word and meaning is *apauruṣeya*, that is, not dependent on either divine or human convention. What is produced by convention is the specific usage of words with reference to specific objects. Thus language as such is not conventional though the specific usage or application of words for our practical purposes may depend on convention.

It is clear from the above account that the clash between the conventionalist and the non-conventionalist is a conflict of two philosophical stand-points. The Nyāya with its empiricistic bias identifies the word with overt sounds produced through vocal organs and refuses to recognise at ranscendental entity called *Śabda* which is said to be manifested by the sound. The most crucial point made by the non-conventionalist is that if the word is identified with the sound produced by vocal organ, the recognition of *sameness* in spite of the difference of time, place and persons would be inexplicable. The Nyāya might meet the objection by maintaining that the said recognition becomes possible because every word has an element of unity as it belongs to some particular class. When a word, say 'cow', is heard we recognise that it is of the *same class* as the word 'cow' spoken or heard in the past. Thus there is no necessity of postulating the word over and above the sound manifesting it. The non-conventionalist would however be not satisfied with this explanation. He would point out that we recognise the words to be *the same* and not to be of the *some kind*. It is a case of individual identity and not that of identity of a class. So the Nyāya explanation is logically untenable. There is however a more serious objection against the conventionalist view of language made by the non-conventionalist.

It is that convention itself presupposes language. Convention would not be possible unless words are used and understood by persons participating in the convention. Thus to make language dependent on convention would involve circularity. The Nyāya invocation of God also does not solve the problem. It is inconceivable how could God communicate his conventions without making use of speech to persons who did not know any language. Thus an absolute beginning of language is logically untenable.

II

Now to turn to the second question, viz. does language reveal reality, or hide or distort it ? On this question also Indian systems are widely divided. The Nyāya-Vaiśeṣika holds that whatever is real is knowable and speakable. Not only language reveals reality, but also there is no reality whatsoever which is not expressible by language. Things are *padārthas*, the meanings of words. Categories of reality such as substance, quality, relation, universal etc. are derived from the categories of language. The Nyāya-Vaiśeṣika believes that there is total correspondence between language and reality; from the structure of language in which our judgments are expressed we could validly infer the structure of reality. For most of its ontological categoriest he Nyāya-Vaiśeṣika adduces only linguistic usage (*vyavahāra*) as the proof. The Mīmāṁsā would also agree with the Nyāya so far as the question of the competence of language to express reality is concerned, although there is some divergence in their ontology.

The Buddhist on the contrary holds a view diametrically opposed to the view stated above. Language does not reveal the real; it rather presents a distorted view of it. Words are intimately related to concepts; the two originate in each other and cover the same field. All concepts are relative, because they are intelligible only in contrast with their opposites. So also all words express their meanings only in contrast with their opposite meanings. This shows that the import of words is negative. Words appear to assert a positive meaning but actually they deny the contrary meaning. Pure affirmation is the function of sense-apprehension; judgments which are products of thought only negate. Thus words do not convey the knowledge of any real positive entity as their meaning; they convey only the negation of the opposite meaning. The Buddhist distinguishes between two kinds of knowledge— direct and indirect. The former is pure sense apprehension of the real and the latter is judgment expressed in language. The whole function of judgment is to represent as unity what involves spatial, temporal and qualitative differences. Words therefore signify thought-constructions or universals which are relative and negative. This is what is conventionally established as the meaning of words. If words convey the knowledge of reality, then on hearing the word 'fire' one must have the sensation of heat. That is, verbal cognition should be as lively and vivid as sense cognition. This being not the case, the former cannot be regarded as the cognition of the real. The Buddhist however does not deny the utility of language altogether. There are, according to him, two orders of reality— ultimate and empirical. Language though incompetent to reveal the former is fully competent and helpful in the field of empirical reality. In fact it is necessary for conducting our practical life.

A completely different evaluation of language is presented by the Grammarian. Language not only reveals reality, it is reality. Things, according to Bhartṛhari, are ultimately of the nature of the word because they are apprehended as identical with it in all our cognitions. It is through the eye of the word that all the diversity of understanding is perceived. It is the word which sees the object, it is the word which speaks of it, it is the word which reveals the object which was lying hidden. Even an existent is no better than non-existent as long as it does not come within the perview of verbal usage. And even a totally non-existent thing like 'hare's horn' when brought to the mind in verbal discourse appears as if possessing reality. Bhartṛhari denies that there is any knowledge worth the name which is free from words. Even the so-called indeterminate apprehension is not an exception. The word seed is present in it in unmanifested form and hence no verbal expression takes place. When the word-seed is awakened and its powers are manifested in the form of expressive words restricted to specific meanings, the stage of determinate knowledge is reached. Only at this stage the object acquires a definite shape and comes within the range of clear cognition. It becomes capable of being designated as such and such and can really be said to be known. The same is true of our thoughts also. It is only thought as expressed in words that can be understood and communicated. Language is not an accidental or dispensable associate of thought. There is no thought without word and no word without thought. Word and thought grow together. They represent the efforts of our consciousness to comprehend and express reality. Thus all experience and thought being possible only through words, the word, Bhartṛhari declares, is the ultimate reality.

It is clear from the above account of rival views concerning language and its function that the answer to the question: 'does language reveal reality?' is not simple. It depends on the conception of reality one holds. The Nyāya-Vaiśeṣika conceives the real as nameable and, therefore, language, according to it, faithfully reveals reality. The Buddhist, on the contrary distinguishes two orders of reality—ultimate and empirical. The ultimate by definition is beyond thought and language. So language in an attempt to express it presents a distorted view of it, although it is quite at home with empirical reality. The Grammarians on the other hand, conceive speech ($Vāk$) itself as the ultimate reality. It appears as words and objects denoted by them. The distinction of words and objects is only empirical, it is convenient fiction. Ultimately language and reality are non-different. Thus it appears that there cannot be an agreed view of language and its relation to reality, for it varies with the metaphysical stand-point one holds. This may prompt us to abandon the metaphysical approach and confine ourselves to the logical definition and classification of terms employed in a philosophical discourse. Even so, it seems hard to ignore the demand to distinguish and make explicit the metaphysical assumptions underlying the discourse. Therefore it seems natural to ask the question regarding the competence of language to reveal reality. We thus pass from logical questions of definition and classification of terms to metalogical questions concerning the function of language and its relation to reality. This seems to be inevitable, for logical differences are rooted in metaphysical differences and they are brought to the surface when any philosophical discourse is carried on. I cannot venture to deny that an evaluation of language and its functions completely free from metaphysical considerations is possible. But I do not see how it is possible. At least in Indian philosophy such an evaluation of language does not exist.

Banaras Hindu University, Varanasi

18

HEIDEGGER ON LANGUAGE
(The Role of the Poet and the Thinker)

Thomas A. Fay

Since the Hölderlin lectures of 1936 the importance of the language-question in the thought of Heidegger has become increasingly apparent. He was, to be sure, very much interested in the problem of language and its relation to logos from the very beginning of his "way". In the early writings, however, this concern remained largely in the background. In *Sein und Zeit* for example the treatment of logos is situated within what is for Heidegger at that time a larger question—the nature of phenomenology. The question of language is, of course, treated in Sz[1] but it does not seem to show the crucial importance that it will have later on. It is only when we come to his later writings that the thought which had been germinating since the beginning of his philosophic activity comes to full fruition. In the later Heidegger the language-question is seen as part of a larger issue, that of technicity (*Technik*). The spirit of technicity is itself the result of basic disorientation of man toward Being. The Faustian stance of man toward Being in which he views Being and Beings as things to be controlled and manipulated for his advantage has caused such diverse phenomena as the despoliation of the earth, the age of atomic bombs, the standardization of man, and in terms of language, mass communications media, thought machines and electronic brains. All of these phenomena have conspired to destroy man's "World" (*Welt*, in the Heideggerian sense of the term) and to produce an environment in which man cannot live as *man*. For this reason Heidegger wishes to attack what he views as the root cause of all of this, rather than merely treating surface symptoms. As he sees it, this root cause is man's relation to Being. (*das Sein*).[2] The mode of thought which has characterized the Western tradition since Plato has been that of metaphysics and this metaphysics itself has been characterized by re-presentative thought (*das vor-stellende Denken*) which re-presents (*vor-stellen*) Being (*das Sein*) as a being (*das Seiende*). This metaphysical thought which re-presents Being and treats it as a being led inevitably to technicity with its characteristic posture of control and manipulation of beings. It is for this reason, too, that Heidegger speaks of the necessity of "overcoming" Western metaphysics.

But how is Western metaphysics and its characteristic mode of thought (*das vor-stellende Denken*) to be overcome? It will be overcome through the work of the thinker and the poet, since for both thinking is not the re-presenting (*vor-stellen*) of beings but rather a receptive attunement to Being. For Heidegger this has meant emphasizing the role of the poet, since the poet, by the very nature of the case, is not a controller and manipulator of Being or beings, but rather one who has received Being's revelation and clothed it in words. Thus, in effect, Western metaphysics will have been overcome when man dwells poetically. This is simply to say that when man dwells poetically a change in his relation to Being will have taken place.

From this it can be seen that the basic thrust of Heidegger's thought concerning language is a humanistic one, although not a humanism in the sense of a new philosophical anthropology, a designation which he has steadfastly rejected as simply treating surface phenomena. Heidegger, then, is attempting a radical transformation in man's relation to Being, since it is the metaphysical posture toward Being which has produced the spirit of technicity with all of its baneful consequences. Thus Western metaphysics must be overcome. Since language as logos is so intimately tied to Being, a change in our relation to Being must, of necessity, involve a change in our relation to language, logos.

But what is the relationship of language, Being and logos, as Heidegger sees it? Logos, according to Heidegger, is Being in its collectedness; it allows Being to appear, lie forth in openness and be manifest. It gathers in the mighty and overpowering surge of Being, and holds it in openness in human language, logos. Language itself is founded on Being's logos, i.e. Being's intrinsic drive toward self-revelation and disclosure. Yet language is an all too defenseless prey which readily falls victim to its special enemies—mere glibness, banality, idle chatter (*Gerede*), and babbling.[3] Thus the "house of Being" (*das*

Haus des Seins)[4] stands in need of guardians[5] who will care for it through solicitude for language and thought. The poet, then, and the thinker[6] are both needed if the house of Being, language, which is man's only appropriate dwelling, his world, is to be truly fashioned into a suitable place for him to abide. The poet is, indeed a "house-friend" as Heidegger calls him in the Hebel work, since by his labors he is especially dedicated to the building of Being's house.

> But we can observe both that the poetic character of human abiding needs the poet, and the manner in which it needs him. For the poet is a friend in a sublime and encompassing sense, that is, he is a friend to the house which is the world. We can look toward that to which Johann Peter Hebel was pointing when he thought of the poet as a house-friend who brings to language the house which is the world as the dwelling place for man.[7]

By the poet's experience which comes to words in great poetry, the world is always seen in its pristine freshness as though for the first time.

> The poet gathers together the world in his saying... in which the world appears as though it were seen for the first time.[8]

The surge of the sea, the chiaroscuro of the sun and shade in the snow-covered forest in the early light of a winter morning, the sun turning the sparkling drops of rain on a budding tree in springtime into diamonds, all of these, and indeed all beings, are seen with the freshness of original experience. This experience is then captured in word and song which preserves Being's original multifarious and variegated self-revelations, and safeguards them from the flatness, the triteness, the banality, to which daily usage so readily exposes them. As Heidegger sees it, it is precisely this relationship to language, that of *using* it, which causes and constitutes its commonplaceness. The poet and the thinker *serve* language; language is not *used* to serve their purpose. It is this relation to language alone which will preserve it from the emptying process which daily *usage* inflicts upon it.

Both the poet and the thinker, then, grasp Being in its primordial emergence and revelation and express this experience in word, and by their care for language they both administer to Being's openness, build a dwelling place, a world, which alone can be an appropriate dwelling place for man. But although there is a marked affinity between the poet and the thinker, since they both are closely attuned to Being, and since Being's revelation is grasped by both in authentic thought, still their manner of expressing Being in language is not the same. They dwell, both of them, on twin mountain peaks, but peaks which are nonetheless separated.

Out of long-guarded silence and solicitude for the clarification of the place which has been cleared by this comes the saying of the thinker. Of a like origin is the naming of the poet. Because, however, likeness can only be likeness if there is also difference, poetry and thought find their purest affinity in their care for words, and yet the two are at the same time completely distinct as to their essences. The thinker speaks Being. The poet names the holy.[9]

This view of the intimate union of Being, thinking, and language, is as far removed as possible from the philosophic stance which sees Being as the representation (*Vor-stellung*) of the subject man, the world as an object (*Gegen-stand*) over against him which he represents, and language as a tool of his communication. This latter point of orientation, which has as its starting point the apotheosis of man as the measure of all things, Being included, which conceives of the universe as homocentric, which establishes man and his power of reason as master over Being and beings, following the ineluctable drive of its own internal logic, must inevitably issue in *der Wille zur Macht* and *Übermench*,[10] the despoliation of the earth, and the creation of a world which is no longer an appropriate dwelling place for man.

At this point in human cultural history the importance of what Heidegger is saying concerning language can scarcely be overestimated. What he is advocating is no less than a radical transformation of man's relationship to language. This radical change is necessary because the present relationship of man to language is yet another manifestation of the metaphysical stance, that is, re-presentative thought which approaches the world in terms of manipulation, control and exploitation. This metaphysical posture has spawned the spirit of technicity with all of its baneful consequences, i.e. the standardization of man, the age of atomic bombs and world wars, the despoliation of the earth, as well as the many devastating dangers which imperil our world and which we now subsume under the title of ecology. Because man's relation to his world has been one of *use* and exploitation, his world has been devastated. What Heidegger calls "poetic dwelling" is the diametric opposite of this way of relating to world. The poet, and the thinker, do not relate to language and the world in terms of use and exploitation. Rather, their relationship to language and world are the exact opposite of this. The poet is used by language, it is language which speaks, not the poet—"Die Sprache spricht.."[12] He is merely the spokesman for Being. The reason why Heidegger stresses this so heavily is because he wishes to change completely man's relationship to Being, first of all, and consequently to world and language. As Heidegger sees it, language *is* man's world—"Nur wo Sprache da ist Welt". Therefore if the relationship of man to language can be changed, his world will also be changed. Heidegger stresses the role of the poet because the poetic way of relating to language is the diametric opposite of the metaphysical approach, characterized as it is by use and manipulation. When the concept of language which sees the poetic as the foundation has been established, it will also have as its fruit "poetic dwelling". Just as the poetic is the exact opposite of the metaphysical approach to language, so also is poetic dwelling the opposite of the spirit of technicity as this latter confronts our world. If the spirit of technicity has produced a world in which man's very survival *as man* is threatened, then, it would seem, the philosophy of language of Martin Heidegger which suggests a radically different approach to Being, World and Language may be well worth serious consideration.

St. John'i University, Jamaica, New York

NOTES

1. *Sein und Zeit* (10th ed.; Tübingen: Niemeyer, 1963), pp. 160-170.
2. In this paper we shall translate *das Sein* as "Being" with a capital "B" and *das Seinde* as "being" with a lower case "b".

3. *Einführung in die Metaphysik* (3rd ed.; Tübingen : Niemeyer, 1966) pp. 132, 141-142.
4. *Uber den Humanismus* (Frankfurt a. M. : Klostermann, 1947), pp. 21-22. Hereafter, HB.
5. HB, p. 5.
6. *Hebel der Hausfreund* (2nd ed.,; Pfullingen: Neske, 1958), p. 25. Hereafter, HH.
7. HH, P. 25.
8. *Was its Metaphysik* (7th ed.; Frankfurt a.M. : Klostermann, 1949), pp. 50-51.
9. *Was heisst Denken* (Tübingen : Niemeyer, 1961), pp. 24-29, 63-70.
10. *Vortrage und Aufsatze* (Pfullingen : Neske, 1954), p. 73.
11. *Unterwegs zur Sprache* (Pfullingen: Neske, 1959), pp. 12, 13, 14, 16, 19, 20, 28, 30, 32, 32, 254, 255, 262, 263, 265, *et passim.*

19

EPISTEMOLOGICAL LANGUAGE VIS-A-VIS 'KNOWN OBJECT'

K. Bagchi

I

The aim of this paper is to enquire into the distinctive sort of language, if any, that is needed for Epistemology in order that it may, as it does, speak of 'known' object. Is it the same thing to say that 'X is known' as it is to say that 'X is brown', 'Y is round', 'Z is elliptical' and so on? Doubtless, there are many for whom there just *is* no 'known' object (KO) other than a brown object or a rectangular object etc. etc., i.e. object which exists in *rerum natura* and *might not as will be known*, object which may be called as subject-neutral object (SNO). It is the latter which, it will be said, is 'known' : to speak of a 'known' object is not to speak of any other *kind* of object,—it is to speak of the subject-neutral object with its features, characters, aspects, position, magnitude etc etc. Now, it is not intended to say in this paper that 'KO' and 'SNO' are two *kinds of objects*. Nor is it intended to say that 'KO' *cannot*, whereas 'SNO' *can be*, spoken of, if 'of' in 'speaking of' suggests the distinction between speaking and *what* is being spoken : as little does one speak *of* 'SNO' as one speaks of 'KO'. Making temporary allowance for 'of' (in 'speaking of'), we may say that 'speaking of SNO' amounts to using language in a certain sort of way. It is using language to *report*, e.g., that the object is brown, that it is rectangular etc. etc. Our issue is : *in saying 'X is known' do we use the reporting sort of language* ?

II

There are epistemologists of the idealistic school who find the distinction of epistemological language from reporting language to lie in, what may be loosely described at this stage, a sort of reflective tale. Indeed, that tell-tale word 'reflection' would be viewed by these epistemologists as the *pivot* round which the distinction of epistemological language from reporting or informative language centres. According to this line of thought, to understand a 'known' object *as* a 'known' object is to understand it subjectively. It is not to know the object from a point of view in which the fact of its being 'known' does not appear to matter at all. What such 'knowing' consists in, or whether it should be understood as 'knowing' at all *as* 'knowing' is understood in common parlance may appear in the sequel: but this little is clear even at this stage that, to understand the 'known' object is *not* to understand it from the point of view of a detached onlooker. It is, i.e., not to understand the 'known' object as what is, *merely as a matter of fact*, 'known', such that the fact of its being known might not matter to it at all but simply consists in discovering some features of the object by analytic attention. On the contrary, to understand an object as 'known' is to conceive it to be object *for* a subject: this, however, is not to echo the trite commonsense that when something is known, it has a knower. For to view the object as 'known' is not to view it as having characters etc. which *might not as well be known*, characters which might be described as objective, i.e., non-subjective. So our problem, "What is it to understand an object as 'known' ?" cannot be solved by putting forward an empirical thesis, i.e., by pointing to a case or an *instance* in which a knower knows an object. And, again, it cannot be said that the present problem is otiose : that what we have been calling 'known' object is nothing but the object which is, e.g., brown, rectangular etc., i.e., object with characters etc. which exist in *rerum natura* and might be *left unknown*. Such reduction of the understanding of 'known' object into statements regarding its characters etc. is not justifiable : there does remain an *irreducible surd* in the 'known' object,—which is just the *apparent* character or adjective, viz., 'known'. Nor can it be said that to know an object as 'known' is to know some *truth* about it, e.g., 'the object is brown', 'it is rectangular' etc., etc.

III

The idealistic theory may, however, be sought to be countered by a theory the basic strain of which might be that epistemology is by no means confined to the 'informative'—'Subjective' alternatives. Reflection, it may be said, is neither informative nor subjective. Or, to be precise, it is as little subjective as it is informative. In it we are, of course, aware of a 'known' object, but then to speak of a 'known object' is not the special prerogative of idealistic epistemologists. There are non-idealists too who are as good epistemologists as the idealists. Now, what, according to the non-idealist epistemologists, are we aware of when we speak of the 'known' object ? It is a *proposition*. Thus, e.g., 'X is known' articulates our reflective awareness of the propositions, such as, *that X is brown, that X is rectangular, that X is elliptical* and so on. In other words, while in 'X is brown' we predicate brown of X, in 'X is known' we do not make any predication : What we do in saying 'X is known' is to speak of a *proposition*.

So much about the 'proposition'—theory (if it may be so called) of Reflection for the present : *for the present*, because another theory of epistemological reflection needs be considered together with the 'proposition'—theory as their presuppositions are the same : so that the gamut of our contention may emerge on the basis of a joint review of these two theories.

What is that other theory ? This may be called the 'introspection' theory. According to this theory, reflection does not consist in anything more than, i.e., it does not involve anything other than a turning of consciousness towards itself. The form of reflection may be expressed or articulated as 'I know that I know' in which 'that I know' appears to be a fact to 'I know'.

Aside from the joint consideration of the two foregoing theories, a remark can be made immediately against the 'introspection' theory in particular. The form in which reflection is articulated, viz., 'I know that I know' gives the appearance of a knower turning its attention to i.e., a knower introspecting upon, its knowledge of object. But then, the contingent fact of a knower or a psychological being turning its gaze upon an object has no place in the kind of issue we are considering. As already noted, from the idealistic point of view, the present issue ought not to be taken as relating to a knower's knowing an object which it (i.e., the knower in question) *might not as well know*. The issue is clearly marked off from an empirical issue in this that here we are concerned with understanding 'object' to *be* 'what is known'. 'Reflection', then, cannot be taken to be a variant of introspection.

Taking both the 'proposition'—theory and the 'introspection'—theory together, we find that both these theories are equally disappointing. The question of questions is : in saying 'X is known' do we say the same sort of thing as we do when we say 'X is round' ? That is, do we *use language* in the same sort of way on both these occasions ? *Is 'X', in short, subject of predication in 'X is known'* ? This, we think, is the crux of the issue.

In both these theories, it is assumed that about 'X' a judgment is made and it is *then*, i.e. in reflection known. The 'proposition'—theory tells us that 'X is known' supervenes upon 'X is brown'. It assumes that 'X' is first judged and *then* the judgment about 'X' is attended to : it is such reflective attention that is articulated in 'X is known'. So in this theory there is an indirect route, through 'X is known', to 'X' as a subject of predication, to 'X is brown' etc. The 'introspection' = theory tells us that reflection is the consciousness of the consciousness of object. It assumes that consciousness of an object is an event in time, a matter of historical fact : the object first *comes to be* known and *then* there is reflection into the knowledge of object. So in this theory too, as in the earlier one, 'X is known' would assign to 'X' the same sort of status which it has in 'X is brown'. Of course, the point of both these theories is not a historical point about the object being first known and then reflectively attended to : this does not make the object a subject of predication. What makes it so is a particular way of knowing it. How does this theory yield 'X is known' ? To see how it does, we have to look at one vital point in the theory, viz. consciousness is always *of* : it asserts what is *other than* it. In the introspective theory, the difference between 'consciousness' (in consciousness of consciousness) and 'consciousness' (in consciousness of object) is not of much moment. Apart from the fact that they are two different pieces of consciousness occurring at two different points of time and having two different kinds of objects, there is no difference between those two pieces of consciousness insofar as the manner of asserting their objects is concerned : both the pieces of consciousness are 'of....' That is, in terms of the 'introspection'—theory, 'X' in 'X is known' is asserted in the same sort of way as 'X' in 'X is brown'. The consequence of this theory, thus, is that 'X' is a subject of predication,—a presupposition which it shares with the proposition-theory.

We have then to ask ourselves : Is 'X' the subject of predication ? But what is the subject of a predication ? In trying to answer the latter question, we shall see the emergence of one thing which epistemology has not so far taken note of, viz. ,the relation of consciousness to language. Of course, 'relation of consciousness to language' is rather a naive way of expressing the intentions of epistemology. The issue comes into bold belief when we state it thus : in 'X is known', how does consciousness view 'X' ? Is 'X' viewed by consciousness as distinct from itself ? Is 'X', in other words, 'spoken of', i.e., understood (by consciousness) as distinct from its speaking of 'X' ? According as the manner of its speaking of a content is viewed by consciousness from the point of view of itself, it becomes the subject of predication or does not become so. 'Becoming', however, is not to be taken in the sense of becoming in time: it may be taken in the Kantian sense of constituting. And if 'constituting' too cannot rid ourselves of the lurking prejudice that it is another name for 'becoming' and that (therefore) using it in place of 'becoming' does not improve matters a whit more, we can say that a content becomes or does not become the subject of predication according as consciousness views it and expresses its attitude to it in a mode of using language.

So a content known in consciousness, when it is known *as* 'asserted as distinct' from the consciousness of it, i.e., when the knowledge of it is in the *form* of assertion of something as distinct from the asserting act, is a subject of predication. To revert to our example, 'X' in 'X is known' would be subject of predication *according to the linguistic form in which consciousness views it*. What is that linguistic form ? It is 'spoken of' or 'asserted as distinct', If 'X' is *viewed* by consciousness *as* 'spoken of' or 'asserted *as* distnict', it would be subject of predication in 'X is known'.

Formulating the central issue in these terms, what answer can we expect from the idealist and what from the non-idealist?

The answer from the idealist's side would be that X in 'X is known' is *not* viewed by consciousness as 'spoken of': whereas that it *is* so viewed would be insisted upon by the non-idealist.

What is the reason for this difference? That is, the non-idealist *cannot* give a *negative* answer (like the idealist) because he cannot find *any context* in which what is known is *not* understood as distinct from the speaking of it. On the contrary, according to him, in every content in which 'X is known' is said, 'X' is understood as distinct from the speaking of it.

This (i.e., the alleged distinctness of 'X') would be just what the idealist would not accept. And here he would be *relying on consciousness*. Whether a content is 'spoken of' or not 'spoken of' is to be determined purely on the evidence of consciousness. It is, *consciousness which is to determine the linguistic form of a content*. The point of the idealistic theory is precisely that 'X' is nothing apart from the knowledge of it. To say this is not to put forward any factual or empirical thesis that 'X' is nothing apart from the *fact* of its being known in a certain spatio-temporal context. It is indeed empirically impossible to find any instance of an item of nature which depends upon the *quite accidental fact* of its being 'known': clearly, the idealistic epistemologist does not want to fly in the face of facts and concoct his cherished theory. When he says 'X is known', *he does not intend it to be taken as any judgment at all*. For him 'X' that is known is the knowledge of it.

It is, therefore, necessary to establish this point, viz., that 'X' *is* the knowledge of it. Here it is that the idealist at last comes to grips with the issue.

Apparently, the idealist pursues a hopeless task: for, in so far as 'knowledge' is understood in ordinary parlance, nothing that 'knowledge' is *of* can fulfil the idealist's requirement. So, in the context of what is required of 'X', 'knowledge' cannot be taken in its usual parlance. That is, in 'X is known', 'knowledge' is not to be taken in the ordinary sense of being 'of. . . .' what is one to do, the non-idealist would wonder, with such moth-eaten piece of knowledge?

A context, however, *is* available in which the idealist requirement can be fulfilled. It is the context of *self-consciousness*. Self-consciousness is the name of consciousness being, i.e., being the same as consciousness of it. Self-consciousness, however, is not expressible even in the form of an analytic judgment like, " 'Consciousness' is 'Consciousness of consciousness' ": For 'consciousness' *need not assert that* it is 'consciousness of consciousness',—'assertion', logically speaking, being about what is other than consciousness : it *need not* because there is no *doubt* that perhaps it *may not be* 'consciousness of consciousness'. There is, in fact, no doubt *to counter which* 'consciousness is conscious of consciousness' is formulated as an analytic proposition. That is to say, " 'consciousness' is 'consciousness of consciousness' " is not an anatic proposition *because* the contradictory of it *would* be contradictory: its supposed contradictory is not even assertible—it would be an example of "infructuous thinking". Consciousness, which asserts, cannot *itself* be an assertible, i.e., subject of predication.

A two-fold point emerges out of the foregoing analysis of 'consciousness of consciousness'. The first point relates to consciousness itself. It is this : *consciousness is not assertible, no content of judgment*. The second point is of wider importance. It is about the application of the first point, viz., 'consciousness is not assertible' to the task of clearing up our understanding of 'X' or 'KO'. It is this : '*X*' *is consciousness itself.* That is, 'X' is *not* viewed by consciousness as an *assertible*, as distinct from the speaking of it (by consciousness) : on the contrary, it *is* viewed as 'not distinct from the speaking of it', as the speaking consciousness, as 'I', as 'incarnated' in speaking which is *not* 'speaking of....' as a contingent fact or happening. Through the consciousness of 'KO' what comes out is that 'objectivity' as the mode of reference is, after all, subjects or consciousness' form of 'spoken-of-ness', is 'not-I' in relation to 'I' or speaking consciousness : that is to say, 'being spoken of' or assertibility can be form of consciousness only in so far as consciousness is incarnated in speaking. Consciousness of the 'KO', then, is consciousness of consciousness' form of objective reference. It is the consciousness of consciousness' objectivity through language.

Indeed, apart from language-use on the part of consciousness, there is no distinction between 'assertible' and 'non-assertible' contents. Whatever epistemological contents may be, this little is clear by now that, apart from modes of language-use on the part of consciousness, distinction between epistemological and non-epistemological contents cannot be drawn. The distinction of epistemological contents from non-epistemological contents ultimately boils down to *linguistic distinction within consciousness*. For, only insofar as consciousness is articulated in speaking can it 'speak of', i.e., assert any content, make it 'assertible' : it, in other words, utilises speech-forms to make objective reference. Consciousness of 'KO', then, is consciousness of consciousness' form of objective reference. Actually, consciousness objective reference is just the other side of its incarnation in speaking : consciousness *forms* itself or *articulates* itself in speaking and thereby provides for objective reference, for 'speaking of' a content. Consciousness of KO, in short, is consciousness of 'objectivity', the form of all discourse. Epistemology deals with this form but then it is not a mere linguistic study inasmuch as the forms of discourse are evidenced and elaborated in consciousness. Epistemology may, then, be viewed as *phenomenology of language* rooted as it is in the consciousness of consciousness' objectivity through language.

Reverting to our initial question as to the sort of discourse in which epistemology is rooted, we can say that epistemology *does not speak in reportive or informative language*. So far, epistemology stands on a different footing from objective sciences. for 'objectivity' of which Epistemology speaks is not any *object*, any assertible content. On the contrary, 'objectivity' is understood *only through speaking*-which is conciousness' *being* what eonsciousness is of. And therefore 'objectivity' is not formulable in judgment. Supposing that it *could be* so formulated, the judgment would be something like, 'The known object is known', where the subject is not understood as what the predicate is not : on the contrary, the subject is understood *only through the predicate*. So the subject and the predicate are not logical subject and logical predicate, and the judgment is only *apparently* a judgment of which the (apparent) subject is understood only through speaking.

Lest this 'only through speaking' should *not* be misunderstood as just a contingent affair, lest 'speaking' should *not* be misconstrued as though it amounted to some sort of magical creation (!) of the 'known object', we should understand it as *consciousness' being 'I'* : it is in consciousness' being 'I' that language owes its origin. 'I' is not just a word : outside the dictionary, there is something more to the word than the mere use of it by *any* speaker, something more than what Russell called 'the biography of the speaker', something which is *being 'I'*, when, as now: so much is being said to distinguish between the 'surface' and the 'depth' of language, it may not be too late in the day to turn this distinction in the service of Epistemology and ask ourselves 'where lies the novelty of Epistemology to which Kant's insight groped ? and return the answer that Epistemology is novel inasmuch as it is rooted in the consciousness of consciousness' incarnation in language, i.e., in 'I'. "In the beginning was the Word". Thus is Kantianism revived with a Chomskyan rim about it, thus does philology capitulate to Epistemology.

The upshot of our contentions is then, two-fold. *First*, in trying to find a language for epistemological discourse, we come to the conclusion that epistemology is phenomenology of language. That is, it views language from the point of the subject's mode of using language in order that something may be object of discourse: in short, it views language from the point of view of speaking consciousness. *Secondly*, epistemological statements cannot be treated as just statements of fact. They are statements about 'knowledge' or 'consciousness': of course, these statements have puzzled many who have tried to understand whether or not there *is* any distinction between them and statements of fact. On the one hand, we have philosophers who maintain that those statements are just like statements of fact : no philosophically interesting theme emerges out of the consideration of those statements. On the other hand, philosophers who *have* found something interesting in those statements are impressed by, what we may call, *two faces of those statements*. They could not, of course, explain clearly just what this (alleged) double-faced-ness is. For us, it is as good as fact that epistemology is expressible *in* statements as it is that those statements *embody* some thesis about 'consciousness' or 'knowledge'. For us, i.e., it is as good a fact that statements about 'consciousness' or 'knowledge' can be fixed upon, attended to, viewed from a distance by an onlooker—just as statements of facts can be attended to—as it is that 'consciousness' or 'knowledge' *expresses itself* in language. For us, once again, it is as good a fact that a statement about 'consciousness' or 'knowledge' can be made to, and understood by a *hearer* as it is a fact that a speaker, i.e., *speaking consciousness expresses itself* in those statements. It is this two-pronged fact, viz., of consciousness' objectivity in language that is most interesting in a philosophical or phenomenological study of language: and epistemology is based upon the *phenomenological distinction between speaker and hearer.*

The hearer, of course, understands them, i.e., the statements made by the speaker: but then he understands them as reflective statements, i.e., as statements in which the speaker's consciousness is 'incarnate'. So what sort of understanding is it ? It is the understanding of incarnation, understanding by the hearer of a statement which he *would have made* if he were speaker, not, of course, as the utterer of the verbal sounds produced by the speaker for whom he is the hearer but as expressing himself. So 'speaker' is phenomenologically 'consciousness as expressing itself' and the distinction of roles between speaker and hearer is at bottom a phenomenological distinction, distinction between consciousness of incarnation and that of 'meaning'. If we do not introduce this phenomenological distinction between speaker and hearer, the epistemoloical statements would come to be considered from the hearer's point of view and then their distinctiveness would be lost. 'Know'-statements, then, are understood only from the point of view of the speaker and not, as statements in science or common parlance from that of the hearer. Epistemological language, then,—

(i) involves the distinction between speaker and hearer, and

(ii) is used for a purpose which is not up till now recognised,—i.e., not for 'speaking of' anything but for 'incarnating' the consciousness of the subject as speaker, for using language as the very form of consciousness.

Of course, the distinction between speaker and hearer is not *uniquely* a phenomenological distinction. There may be non-phenomenological distinction between them too. *Phenomenologically*, speaker is 'consciousness *expressing itself*,' and hearer is *possible speaker*: whereas, *non-phenomenologically*, the hearer, in fact, expresses the same thing *as and when* the speaker expresses it,—what to speak of the hearer's being a 'possible' speaker, i.e., taking the role of speaker at any future point of time. That is to say, in the case of the phenomenological distinction between speaker and hearer, their use of identical expressions is conditional upon the hearer's obliterating his role: whereas in the case of the non-phenomenological distinction between them, their use of identical expressions does not require the hearer's obliterating his role. And why? That is, why is it that in the one case, in using the same sort of expression or expressions as the speaker, the hearer *does not change* his role, whereas, in the other case, to use the same sort of expression or expressions, the hearer *has to change* his role? Because, phenomenologically speaking, what is central to the distinction between the roles of speaker and hearer is *not* the fact of hteir using or not using identical expressions but the fact of their using or not using expressions *to express oneself*. It is only from the point of view of using expressions to express oneself that we can phenomenologically distinguish between speaker and hearer: in the phenomenological framework, the hearer is hearer *because he does not express himself. His role is defined, though negatively, in terms of the speaker's use of language*. But in the non-phenomenological framework, he may use the same expression as the speaker : upon the speaker's saying "The wind blew the leaves off the trees", the hearer might say the very same thing. The case is not, however, the same when, upon the speaker's saying "I am running temperature" the hearer too (in all sincerity) uses the same expression. The fact is, he *does not say the very same thing*. He says about himself, expresses himself and uses language to that end, being *now* the speaker himself (in the phenomenological sense).

Now, what does all this point up to? It is this, that *the non-phenomenological framework is not demanding upon the hearer*: for it does not involve the use of language in expressing the user himself. The hearer, in non-phenomenological context, is just *listener* and is not (negatively) defined with reference to the speaker as in the phenomenological framework. So the mere fact of using the same expression does not turn the hearer into a speaker in a phenomenological context: indeed, the speciality of such contexts may, admittedly, be sought to be disputed by pointing out that as much here as in the non-phenomenological context the hearer comes to use the same language. Thus, e.g., the speaker's expression "The wind blew the leaves off the trees" may be used by the hearer who *then* becomes the speaker *just as* the expression, "The wind blew the leaves off the trees" may be used by the hearer. Now, if these two instances are not taken to be indicative of any difference between the *two cases*, the reply will be that the failure to do so amounts to the failure to see that it is not using expressions but using expressions to express the user that makes the user a speaker in a phenomenological context: while, using expressions to—what we have earlier called—'speak *of*' something makes the user a speaker in a non-phenomenological context. There is, therefore, a difference between these two contexts : in the phenomenological context, language is used to express the speaker whereas in the non-phenomenological context, it is used to 'speak *of*', i.e., to indicate something distinct from the speaking consciousness of it.

In connection with the discussion of epistemological statements, we can see that linguistic forms are to be understood from the point of view of consciousness. Insofar as the 'hearer' (in the phenomenological sense) understands the speaker, he imaginatively adopts the forms employed by the speaker. And it is here that espistemology goes as much beyond logic as it goes beyond natural science. For epistemology does not rest content with understanding the linguistic forms of our discourse by themselves. There is a characteristic difference between the logician's understanding of the forms and the epistemologist's understanding of the same. The logician understands them *from a distance*, i.e., from the point of view of what we have called 'hearer' in the non-phenomenological context. Of course, the logician may insist that there is no more in understanding the forms than listing them, determining their place in a system and—what precisely is the core of such understanding (according to him)—understanding the logic or the principle in terms of which the statements in a logical system are understood : that is to say, according to the logician, *nothing more* is involved in understanding logical forms than just understanding the statements as constructed and arranged according to a pattern or principle. And the logician may scoff at the suggestion that understanding logic is *something more* than understanding the statements *as* having been made according to a principle. From our point of view, however, the forms of logic cannot be viewed in such a neutral manner : they cannot, i.e., be understood in a way *as if* their discovery were just accidental to the understanding. In spite of all that the logician says about the understanding of logical forms or about the *mode* of understanding them, the over-riding consideration remains whether the statements—forms of which are discovered in logic—are made from the speaker's or the hearer's point of view. As made from the speaker's point of view, they are *understood* from the point of view of the 'hearer' in the phenomenological sense, from the point of view of the possible 'I'. Thus to recall what we have said about the characteristic way of understanding epistemological statements, we can point out that the person who understands the person who expresses himself, as it were, reason within himself : if I were the speaker, I would have expressed myself in that linguistic form. The hearer understands the 'know'-statements uttered by the speaker by imagining himself to be adopting those forms in having to express himself.

And, turning to statements made from the hearer's point of view, we can say that they are to be understood as just statements *not* made from the speaker's point of view.

There is, therefore, a characteristic difference between logic and phenomenology in respect of the apprehension of the 'forms'. From the phenomenological point of view, 'Forms' are nothing if not apprehended subjectively. And the three forms of such subjective apprehension of 'forms' are (1) apprehension from the viewpoint of the speaker, (2) that from the viewpoint of the possible 'I' and (3) that from the viewpoint of what is *not* even a possible 'I', what *is* 'listener' as we have called. Anything more than this suggestion of just a formal outline of this phenomenological distinction between 'speaker', 'hearer' and 'listener' would fall outside the scope of this present enquiry.

What then, does Epistemology say about the 'known object'? The answer is that whether a content is 'object' of knowing depends upon the consideration, namely, whether it is understood by consciousness as 'spoken of' in relation to it, as constituted by its 'spoken' of' form : it is its 'spoken-of-ness', so to say, in relation to consciousness that constitutes the objectivity of 'object'. The 'spoken of' object is what Epistemology starts from. Thus there is no transcendent or metaphysical object in Epistemology, i.e, when we talk in the subjective language, when we understand the object as what consciousness realises itself as *its* form. From the epistemological point of view "the transcendent object is simply meaningless and metaphysic is the quest of a chimera".* What is not understood as 'speakable' in relation to consciousness cannot be object.

Visva-Bharati

* Professor Krishnachandra Bhattacharya,: *Studies in Philosophy*, Vol. II, p. 30 (Calcutta 1958)

20

CAN ONE PARTICIPATE IN THE VEDĀNTIC GNOSIS (JÑĀNA) THROUGH THOUGHT ALONE ?
A modern question raised in the light of the word, śabda.

J. G. Arapura

Why this question?

It must be clearly stated that the thrust of the question "Can one participate in the Vedāntic gnosis through thought alone?" lies in the word 'alone'. Otherwise, that is without that word, it would be plainly absurd to ask it, for who can ever deny the utmost importance to thought given in the Vedānta ? Further exposition of the word 'alone' will be made shortly. But first about 'participation'. In clarifying this word, however, one can do no better than quote what Martin Heidegger says:

> The Latin word *participium* is the translation of the Greek *Metoxn*. The taking part of something in something is called *Metexely*. This word is fundamental to Plato's thinking. It designates the participation of any given being in that through which it—say this table—shows its face and form (in Greek *LSED* or *EISOS*) as this being. In this appearance it is in present being, it *is*. The idea is the face whereby a given something shows its form, looks at us, and thus appears, for instance, as this table. In this form the thing looks at us.
> Now Plato designates the relation of a given being to its idea as participation. But this participation of the one, the being, in the other, the Being, already *presupposes* that the duality of being and Being does exist.
> (*What is called Thinking?* Religious Perspectives, translation, 1968, p. 222: cf. Was Heisst Denken? Tübingen, 1961, pp. 134-5.)

Heidegger further stipulates that this has determined "the style of all Western-European philosophy. (However, we do not have to accept his pontifical and very arbitrary assertion, "and there is no other, neither a Chinese nor an Indian philosophy".)

Now, to pursue the concept of participation of thought by itself in the Vedāntic gnosis we may adopt the style of duality between gnosis (as Being, with a capital 'B') and thinking, individual thinking (as being, with a lower case 'b'), and inquire as to how the one can show itself in the other. Here we do not have to define gnosis because it comes fully expressed in the tradition of the Vedānta, in the Word, (primarily, śabda, śruti and the dependent words). But thinking is problematical, especially as we wish to put the illustrative-demonstrative and dialectical reasoning of the tradition in abeyance.

One cannot question the self-sufficiency and all-completeness of gnosis in the Vedānta tradition itself. Clearly our "thinking" is not directed towards that notion in the form of a critical inquiry. What the question really means is whether it is possible, and if so how, for thinking by itself to participate in gnosis without having to adopt the traditional ways of realizing Vedāntic gnosis, which are : (1) study of the *darśana* through the traditional methods of exegesis and argumentation, and (2) mystical practice leading to unitive experience, *anubhava*. (The two need not be mutually exclusive, but can be really complementary). Doubtlessly also, one is nevertheless free to adopt them without the least prejudice to the independence of thinking as a way. That too must be recognized.

It may at this point be made crystal clear that the question as to thinking and its ontological dimension, as having reference to modern man (whoever he is) is being asked by using some of the things one has learnt (however imperfectly so) from Martin Heidegger's writings. As applied to the Vedāntic gnosis the thinking and its "new" ontological dimension are visualized in terms of the question of the certainty of knowledge; but the certainty is bifurcated into certainty of the *ground*— to which thinking returns—as against certainty of the *goal* of knowledge. This distinction is seen to be important, as the possibility of pursuing our question will hinge on it.

Why should we accept a modern Western expression of philosophy for an essentially Eastern enquiry ? This is a big question. The reason for our doing it here is not because it is fashionable or convenient or because we do not know any other way. Rather, it is the knowledge that all of us, Easterners and Westerners alike, are united in what is most essential about human thought today. We are bound together in our *inabilities*, although we may be separated in our respective abilities. The historic mission of Western philosophy, as we see it from an undivided perspective, whatever else Heidegger might say about the nature of that mission, is the fact that it is that philosophy in its relentless unwinding towards the existential ground, particularly in its more recent developments, including what Heidegger himself has contributed, that has brought to us the knowledge of our common inability and our *need* to start all over again. In this need of ours we must not cheaply exchange our respective "abilities" or superficially foist one upon the other. The discovery of our common inability is what we have to start from. Our inability might be our incapability to think. (Heidegger makes a distinction between our ability and our capability—if we say we are *able* are we also capable?) However, our incapability to think is what we should think about, but as no other path is open to us we must come out thinking of that too. We are all together indebted to those who have articulated this fundamental truth.

The masters of Western philosophy have called into question those particular abilities of Western thought which have grasped and detained many of the inside practitioners and many superficial outside imitators. Heidegger's observation of how Logic has become Logistics is much to the point as a leading example.

In our start from the knowledge of our common inability, we move towards a new ability. But this movement must always attend to the inability itself. The new ability must be called *the holy* insofar as the holy, as Heidegger rightly says, is what is not yet. The new ability, therefore, is also not yet.

Now, the addition of the word 'alone' expresses the character of the question, and thereby, even ahead of the nature of the question, the nature of the questioner is revealed. The questioner is the typical heir to the uncertainties of modern man, although by no means is he the official sceptic. In fact, he may even be one who has gone beyond the bounds of erstwhile scepticism, possessing a new openness to some of those grounds for certainty so harshly ridiculed by the proponents of scepticism. However, by the very dominance of the word 'thought' in the question it is clear that he is by no means identical with the person who turns to one of the many novel forms of pseudo-mysticism apparently of Eastern origin in his naive quest for certainty. Such prospects did not have to be rejected by him because he never had and never would have, given *thought* to such things. For one cannot give thought to what is not even on the outside to-be-thought.

The questioner is heir to the deep uncertainties of modern man, but insofar as he can turn to thinking and especially to thinking of what is to-be-thought, he must divide, by reason of the internal constraint of thinking as well as what is to-be-thought, certainty as ground from certainty as goal. He can participate in certainty as ground while eschewing certainty as goal. This distinction being allowed, certainty and uncertainty, as also knownness and unknownness, can co-exist, and thinking itself receives their co-existence as one of its essential dimensions.

Thinking is being on the way or *underway* as one might say. But in order to be underway one must start from the ground of certainty, but instead of turning the ground into the goal, it must return to the ground in order ever to set out and be firmly and assuredly on the way.

Thinking is not means to an end: neither can it make it an end in itself. Nothing results from thinking, neither knowledge nor action: no purpose, no programme or resolution. If any of these results from thinking it would become a means to an end. And again, very emphatically, it must never be also its own end. For it is always being on the way. But what it is on the way *to* is governed by uncertainty. Nevertheless, it is saved from despair and futility by returning to the ground ever and anon. It is, therefore, a task never to be finished.

Which is it that modern man can tolerate more easily : the certainty as ground without a corresponding goal, or the goal of certainty without a corresponding ground? In purely Indian terms, which of the two : the ground of Being, *Sat*, even if it did not hold—merely hypothetically speaking—the promise of realizable *Nirvāṇa*, or the promise of *Nirvāṇa* by itself not grounded in *Sat* ? One must not expect an answer to this question at once. And surely at this point it is not intended to be a new way of carrying on the polemics between the Vedānta and Buddhism. But it is more important, now, to turn to the clarification of the word 'tolerate', tolerate in the sense in which a patient tolerates a medicine that is good for him. What modern man *does* tolerate is one thing, what he *ought to* is another. What is it that decides the 'ought to' ? It is nothing other than the call to think. However, it turns out, as Heidegger lays down in his lectures published under the title, *What is Called Thinking* ? (*Was Heisst Denken* ?), and exegetes through the lectures ? *Most thought-provoking in our thought-provoking time is that we are still not thinking.* For instance, and supremely, "the essence of technology" which ought to concern us in our thought does not yet do so. The change the technological age has brought about is a change in the being of modern man. The dominance of the machine is not the cause of it but the result. (Cf. *What is called Thinking* ? p. 24).

But where do we start in assessing the change in modern man's being ? Not by what he actually thinks (or thinks he thinks) but by what he neglects to think, by studying his failure to heed what calls him to think. So the prospect is still not negative. However, modern man does not heed the call which the change in his own being that modernity has brought about makes. This is a paradoxical situation. In the light of this we see that contrary to expectation, most modern men respond enthusiastically to the multifarious offers, nowadays abundant, of pseudo-*Nirvāṇas* and pseudo-salvations as long as they have the appearance of the sanctity of revolution and wear the garb of intellectual (or spiritual) validity.

While the concept of modernity as affecting man's being is to be taken seriously, the Vedāntist knows that it should not be taken more seriously than it deserves, and therefore not in any absolute sense. No doubt he is protected by *satkārya-vāda*, which tells him that all Becoming had been hidden in Being and, therefore, is nothing but a manifestation, but he must not be insulated by it from exposure to the knowledge that the infinitive 'to be' (*bhū*) is beyond the three tenses and yet as the womb of time expresses itself first and foremost in the present. (Is it also accident that all conjugations of verbs come after the infinitive ?) Heidegger also calls attention to the infinitive form (Cf. *What is Called Thinking* ? p. 217).

The "change" in being affecting modern man, even if it is seen in the light of *satkārya-vāda*, must still be taken seriously enough as the call of Being to thought 'now'. *To be* is, therefore, the impingement of Being upon man calling upon him to refuse postponement of thinking, in other words to think *now*. Outside the framework of 'now', thinking is not thinking.

The story of philosophy as it is written in its history does not always express the pathway of thinking. On the contrary, often it is the story of the techniques and devices for unthinking postponement of thinking. Thinking postponed is thinking avoided or evaded.

Towards Thinking according to the Vedānta

It is true that in obedience to the call to thinking that modern man faces, a way has to be found whereby he can participate in the gnosis of Vedānta from certainty as ground alone. And thinking has to be open-ended towards the goal. But, between this possibility of open-ended thinking which would now be permitted under certainty as ground as it is in Vedānta and the thinking which Heidegger seems to outline or rather which unfolds itself in his writings, there is a divergence not to be ignored insofar as, although the latter allows no other end, he appears to say that thinking can be its own end. The last seems to belong to the very substance of the new ontology he unveils. But let it be understood that he does not do this in any but the gravest fashion. In fact, the dynamite hidden in his extremely difficult writings may not be readily noticed.

In the Greek philosophical tradition, emanating from Parmanides, thinking is inseparable from Being. (In the Vedānta tradition it is nevertheless gnosis, not thinking, that is identical with Being, but more of this later). According to traditional understanding of this, thought is regarded as the extension of Being. But by means of radical exegesis of certain sayings of Parmanides, Heidegger revolutionaizes this concept of their belonging together. Let us attend to Heidegger's interpretation of two of these Greek sayings. First, usually translated : "One should both say and think that Being is." Heidegger translates it thus : "Useful is : letting-lie-before-us and so (the) taking-to-heart too : being : to be", (*What is Called Thinking*? p. 217). [The German original : Es brauchet : das Vorliegenlassen und so (das) Im-die-Act-nehmen auch : Seindes : sein, *Was Heisst Denken*? p. 161).

Second, usually translated : "For it is the same thing to think and to be." Heidegger translates it thus : "for the same : taking to heart is also presence of what is present" (*What is Called Thinking*? p. 241). (The German original : das nämlich Selbe in-die-Achtnehmen ist so auch Anwesen des Anwesenden, text above cited, p. 147].

Heidegger replaces "being" and "to be" with the less accustomed ones "present" and "to be present", which are acceptable enough. Certainly the "presence of what is present" is what modern man in particular must heed but fails to heed. But insofar as this condition of need to heed and failure to heed does seem to become itself the further call to thinking (and as an infinite progress must obviously be avoided), is it not possible that at this point in Heidegger's thought thinking becomes an end in itself and that from which Being itself comes to man? In other words, are we not faced with a situation at least as far as man is concerned (and in Heidegger's thought there is no one else who is concerned with Being), the traditional formula, "thought is the extension of Being" is all but replaced by the new formula, "Being is the extension of thought"?

It is true that there are no express indications anywhere in Heidegger's writings, as far as one can understand, where thought itself has been turned into the new ability, though certainly nowhere into the old ability that dominated Kant's and particularly Hegel's writings. But it is important to notice this subtle shift. Thought is still a waiting, a receptivity. But waiting for what? And receptivity to what? One does not find the answers to these too readily. Are there not implications, even suggestions, that thought is the waiting for itself, receptivity to itself, especially in view of the privation of any other way for Being to meet man and for man to meet Being? No doubt *ΛΕΥΕLV* and *VOELV* are to be held unseparated in this yet. waiting and this receiving. No doubt the holy, is what is not yet. But is not this proposition in a sense turned around so that we can say in effect that what is not yet is the holy and it is *here* in that it is here *in the thinking*? Is Heidegger perhaps making traditional ontology stand on its head? (Excuse the crudeness of this expression). These are, no doubt, big questions and one must not rush to give answers to them even if one were an expert in Heidegger's thought (to being which the present speaker at least does not lay the vaguest claim). But it is well within our competence to ask them. To put them in question form is enough for us in order to note the possible points of departure for the Vedāntist (and one would think for the Platonist).

It is obvious that for Heidegger thought is not the Master that it is in Hegel's absolutism. Neither is it the slave like the *jinn* in Aladdin's lamp, held in servitude to do man's bidding that it clearly appears to be in *the hands* of the practitioners of logistics and technical reason (the Indian counter-part of whom being the Naiyāyikas). It is not even held by Heidegger as the ground of reflection leading to *methods* that it is in Descartes and even in Husserl. It is neither master nor servant, nevertheless it possesses an inner sovereignty over itself, held in silence, in the waiting and in the receiving. In the light of this, thought is not all that humble for Heidegger. Thought is good for nothing. It makes nothing, neither politics nor science, nor even knowledge. But it seems to make one thing, poetry of a particular kind, or a poetic existence (the way to *let be*) which is what enables the thinker to be the thinker. We can understand this novel consummation only in one way, that is by seeing it as the directing of the forward movement of thinking in such a way that it turns upon itself. In other words, thinking becomes its own goal.

In contradistinction to this position, for the Vedāntist it is gnosis, as it is concretely articulated in concrete words (like *tat tvam asi*) which moves thinking, not necessarily in the sense of the goal [of uncertainty] but rather in the sense of the ground [of certainty]. The forward motion here is not directed in such a way that thinking turns upon itself making for poetry and poetic existence perhaps, but keeps on being forward motion, although the proviso applicable to modern man of forward motion ever refreshing itself on the ground [of certainty] allowing uncertainty of goal to still prevail must be maintained. Parenthetically, unarrested forward motion keeping on being that might well be regarded as one of the ways of understanding what is sometimes called religion.

Thinking in the Vedānta is neither proud nor humble. It is neither master nor servant. For thought here there is neither exaltation or abasement. It is rather union with gnosis and in a distant sense aspiration for union with Being. But gnosis and Being are (along with Bliss or *ānanda*) one and the same by definition. But the union with Being as such is not the immediate concern of thought; rather it is one of the things it must hold in the realm of the goal as an uncertainty, in order that it may participate in gnosis now, which it can do only by turning gnosis itself into the problematic of the most serious kind, that is to say, into the greatest question of all. That way gnosis becomes the surest foundation for thinking, and modern thinking requires foundations more than authority. The words through which gnosis reveals itself (like *tat tvam asi, ahaṁ brhmāsmi*) form the foundation for thinking, upon the basis of which modern man can now prosecute thinking and seek meanings for life.

Thought participates in gnosis through the union, but the union is like the union of shadow to substance. In this sense thought is an image, But this union is not a temporary union of convenience, eventually to be dissolved, rather it is a self-fulfilling one for thought.

It seems to be decidedly possible that the great works of the Vedānta allows for this kind of participation in gnosis through thought, although clearly they never envisage participation through thought *alone*. As was explained in the beginning the "alone" only stipulates a condition which permits a modern man's entry into gnosis. Hearing (*śravaṇa*) is followed by two degrees of participation through thought, namely *manana* and *nididhyāsana*.

There, however, seem to be suggestions—at least as commonly understood—that participation through thought alone is impossible. (But this is the case only if thought is understood to be independent of the word and to be the result of the initiative of reason). Śaṅkara at the beginning of *Pāda* 2 of *Adhyāya* II of this *Brahma Sūtra Bhāṣya* states that, although his purpose in writing the work is to propound the meanings of the Vedānta passages (which of themselves communicate the gnosis) and not to establish or demolish any views whatsoever, unlike the sciences of reasoning (*tarkaśāstras*), by mere arguments (*kevala yukti*), he has now to use the method of these sciences in order to refute the *darśanas* such as the *Sāṅkhya* which rest on that method. He further states that the special virtue of this method is that the refutation of these *darśanas* is being accomplished without appeal to the Vedic words. Put in another way he means that the *logic* or *tarka* or *yukti* nevertheless contains enough Logos to be of use in refuting what is not of the Logos. And he further recognizes the existence of a logic blessed by the Vedic word (*śrutyanugṛhīta tarka, Brahma Sūtra Bhāṣya*, II.1.12), that is to say where Logos is positively operative as a guide to gnosis.

Surely thinking is not, for Śaṅkara, mere argumentation. And *tarkaśāstra* is only good for refuting what is *not* gnosis. Clearly we cannot get a direct answer from Śaṅkara to the question as to whether one can participate in the gnosis through thought alone, even if it were something more blessed than the *tarka* blessed by the Vedic word.

We can only search for indirect answers, which mightg ive us grounds for existential guesses now. This we shall do briefly.

The word *tarka* is from the root *tark*, meaning to conjecture, guess, suspect, infer, try to discover or ascertain, reason or speculate about, to reflect, to think of, to recollect, have in one's mind, intend (as the *Mahābhārata* and the *Bhāgavata* have) The *Kaṭha Upaniṣad*, I.2.9 even treats it as baseless thought, *naiṣā tarkeṇa matirāpaneyā* (Not by *tarka* is this knowledge attainable). But in the *Maitrī Upaniṣad* VI. 18 and 20 it has a very different meaning. It is listed, in 18, as one of the *ṣaḍaṅgas* (six members of yoga, as clearly part of deeper thinking. In 20, it is even stated that Brahman is seen through *tarka*.

In this context at least the verbal connection between *tarka* as one of the members of yoga and *yukti* becomes an intriguing problem. *Yukti* and *yoga* are but different nouns from the same root *yuj*, meaning to unite, to yoke together, to fit. In *yoga* there is the connotation of the uniting of the mind (*citta*) with the things themselves. What is *yukti* union with? One might say with the logical connections, with the conclusion, by way of fitting perceptions and their inner logic together. The stress is not on the process itself but on the immediacy of the relation between the unperceived object and the perception, a rendering transparent, a manifesting of the incontestible, innate relation. The *Gauḍapāda Kārikā* 4.25 clearly regards *yukti* as a *darśana* (seeing). The same work in 3.23 compounds it in the from of *yukti-yuktam* (united by *yukti*, or rather united by union). There are enough suggestions that union between gnosis and thought is possible and very much in accord with the Vedānta.

We must come further down to *anumāna*, the leading *pramāṇa* (method, if we may call it), which has become the special province of the *Naiyāyikas*, We must ignore the enormous technical matters connected with it. Let us also remember *upamāna*. *Anumāna*, usually translated as inference, and *upamāna*, usually translated as comparison, come from the same verbal root, *mā* or *mī* (*mīyate*) meaning to measure (from which *māyā* also comes). *Anumāna* is a kind of measuring after and *upamāna* is a kind of subsidiary measuring or a type of analogical thinking. In the *Maitrī Upaniṣad* we have the sole instance of the word *anumīyate* (verbal form of *anumāna*) appearing in the Vedic literature. Here we are told that the Atman bears himself in two ways, as the *Prāṇa* (Life, Breath) and as the Sun. The *Prāṇa* is the inner self and the Sun is the outer self. Each of these selves measures itself by the course of the other. Measuring too is a kind of union, so that the Sun is seen as the EIDOS of the inner self. Thought, similarly, could very well be the EIDOS of gnosis.

In sum, the question which forms the title of this brief discourse need not be answered. The question itself will suffice if it is allowed to live by being asked. Here we shall apply one of the many lessons that Heidegger teaches : questions pertaining to thinking are not to be answered, but are only to be asked. In the asking they live and thereby thinking itself lives.

McMaster University Canada

CONSCIOUSNESS—THE VEDĀNTIC PREDICAMENT

Debabrata Sinha

'Consciousness' is one of those commonplace expressions which could prove to be philosophically most intriguing. The expression presents a wide range of variation in connotation across the different areas of philosophical discipline—such as, theory of knowledge, philosophical psychology, metaphysics. Thus at one end of its notional range we find that, for example, which can be described in positive terms as some function with reference to the central nervous system (more conspicuously, the brain). At the other end, perhaps, would stand the metaphysical principle of Reality or Being, identified with what is generally referred to as 'Spirit'. It is more often in the context of the latter pole that the typical Indian concept of *Cit* or *Caitanya* occurs— preeminently in Advaita Vedānta. The Advaitic formulation of Reality as *Sat-Cit-Ānanda* seems to the present paradigm of consciousness being promoted to the order of metaphysical reality par excellence.

So far as the Western tradition goes, the orientation of the concept is found to take a very definite turn in philosophical discourse since Descartes. Taking off from the Cartesian definition of the soul or mind as 'res cogitans' (i.e., conscious or cogitative substance), consciousness has generally come to mean what is essential to the mental or the individual mind. And of course, the necessary implication of its distinction from the essence of the bodily and the material is there. This has consequently led to the common acceptance of the expression as a 'blanket term' more or less, used to mean indefinitely whatever is referred to the individual's mind or experience (in its inner aspect).

Coming to the Indian (and more specifically, the Vedāntic tradition, however, the usually (uncritically) accepted rendering of the Sanskrit expression *Cit* by 'Consciousness' is likely to give rise to basic difficulties and puzzlements for the interpretive understanding of contemporary mind. It is not the problem of mere language translation—the implications in view are much too deep. It is essentially the problem of confronting, from a different perspective which is the current one, a key notion (not a mere expression), with the totality of its contextual meaning and insight, and of translating it in terms of the idiom of contemporary thinking and language habit.

It is true that the genuine import and essence of what *Cit* stands for in the Advaitic scheme is sought to be conveyed more appropriately by ostensibly qualifying 'consciousness' as 'pure' (obviously, it seems, for want of any further appropriate expression). Even then, would that substantially improve our understanding of the whole conception in its own terms ? In posing this question, in some of its principal ramifications, I propose to consider what would appear to be predicament(s) confronting a modern mind in its attempt to understand the key Vedāntic notion in the context of a critique of experience.

The Advaita Vedānta thesis of *Ātman* as *Cit*—i.e., self as pure consciousness, to adopt the accepted mode of translation—presents the unique model of subject principle, which is substantive (not attributive—not a *guṇa*), yet unobjective (*aviṣaya*): which is indeterminate (*nirviśeṣa*) in its core, yet self-evidencing (*svaprakāśa*): which is itself evidencing-witnessing (*sākṣībhūta*), and yet not to be equated with the empirical consciousness of the individual (*jīva*) altogether. Now as to all these characterizations and descriptions of the Advaitic *Cit*, the model that comes out can hardly be brought in line with the traditional model in Western philosophical psychology—i.e., consciousness essentially as 'mental'—nor with the accepted epistemological model in broad—i.e., consciousness necessarily referring to the epistemic object concerned.

It is generally accepted as a truism that 'consciousness' can operate as a meaningful expression primarily in the context of two mutually related situations. (a) Mind, its functions and states—strictly speaking, the subject-matter of the natural science of psychology. Taken apart from the mental context, it would be asked, what remains of consciousness ? (b) The context of the individual : Consciousness is necessarily to be understood with reference to an individual, at whatever level individuality be conceived of—whether at the level of bodily-physical existence, or at the level of mental being, or at the ethico-social level of person, and finally, the supposed metaphysical level of soul or self (as in the Western tradition at large). Thus the generally accepted mode of viewing consciousness is to represent it as mental and as pertaining to the individual—in other words, never outside the context of the individual's mind or mental framework.

Now coming to the Advaitic thesis of *Cit* (*qua Ātman*), the very two features of mentality and individuality are held in suspense in the final conception. No doubt *cit* is primarily envisaged in and through mental states, as the supposed essence behind all that is mental: yet it is not to be treated as equivalent to (or as the general name for) whatever is mental. In other words, it is not to be defined in psychological terms. Be it *antaḥkaraṇa*, i.e., the psychic organ, or *antaḥkaraṇa-vṛtti*, i.e., the modalisations of *antaḥkaraṇa*, whether outer or inner—with none of them, strictly speaking, is consciousness to be wholly identified. (Of course, *cit*, it is said, does get actually involved in the mental complex, without, however, losing its ideal integrity of essence in the least). Secondly, as the Vedāntic position goes, *Cit* is not to be exhausted within the context of the individual (*jīva*). Thus the essential nature and status of consciousness cannot be defined by *jīva*, although the category of *jīva* itself is in a way defined in the light of *Cit* as the foundational essence (compare the definition in *Vedānta-Paribhāṣā* of *jīva* as *antaḥkaraṇa-viśiṣṭa-caitanya*.[1]

In view of the Vedāntic thesis stated above, the question would now arise as to how *cit* is to be comprehended in its own terms—particularly if the psychological as well as the epistemological frame of reference, strictly speaking, do not exhaust the Vedāntic universe of discourse. Of course, it can be said, *cit* is a metaphysical concept through and through—to be envisaged neither in psychological nor in epistemological terms.

---

1. As the theme has been more exhaustively worked out by the author in his book, *The Idealist Standpoint: A Study in the Vedāntic Metaphysics of Experience*, we do not show here separately the gounds for positing *Cit* as *the* essence of subjectivity. I would rather concentrate on the problematic leading from that position and attempt to meet the situation by introducing a fresh clue towards an overall understanding of the same.

True, it is incorporated in the very conception of Being (*Sat*), as Vedānta holds it—both *cit* and *sat* formally standing all possible contradictions. In view of such metaphysical equation, however, our question would be : is there involved here a theory of reality conceived *a priori*—a theory which could possibly be derived from certain *a priori* postulates ? In this context it may generally be observed that metaphysical apriorism can hardly be traced within the frame—work of Vedānta as well as other Indian systems generally.

The latter point can be further borne out if we keep in view one basic feature characterizing the original drive of Vedāntic thought—namely, its being essentially experience-oriented. In fact, the system would lose its central drive if not oriented to deeper intuitive insights. In that sense the legitimate and satisfactory mode of defining the Advaita view of reality [should rather be a *phenomenological* one, proceeding by way of a first-hand critique of experience. For a closer understanding of *cit*, of all notions, a broadly phenomenological approach might be particularly relevant, if we care to fix the notion in the light of in-depth analysis of experience, without bringing in any ostensive metaphysical presupposition or postulates as such.[2]

To translate in *phenomenological* terms, the Vedāntic *Cit* would be closely approximated by the concept of 'transcendental consciousness' or 'transcendental subjectivity' as in Husserlian Phenomenology. Like the latter, the former also is approached in subject-ward attitude, on suspension of the natural objective attitude, and sought to be posited as the presuppositional background of all our experiencing. In its conception of consciousness as pure subjectivity, as 'the region of purified experience', the phenomenological standpoint certainly comes close to the Advaitic conception of *cit* as pure unobjective consciousness, which is the constant, self-evidencing (*svaprakāśa*), transcendental background of the individual's experience-manifold—what is typically brought into shape by the category of *Sākṣin*. It is not our concern in this paper to work out the phenomenological implications of the Advaitic critique of

2. The 'phenomenological' procedure here need not mean that it would strictly follow the Husserlian model—which is, however, the conspicuous methodological program in this direction. What I propose in this context is a first hand analysis and critique of experience, without necessarily bringing in any metaphysical presuppositions and theories as such.

experience, centred around the pivotal notion of *cit* in the shape of self-evidencing witnessing consciousness (*svaprakāśa-sākṣicaitanya*). Nor is it our business here to point out just now how the concluding position of Advaita Vedānta would depart from the strictly phenomenological one. It may only briefly be observed at this stage that while in phenomenology as an allegedly self-complete philosophy, consciousness remains, on final analysis, "the phenomenological residuum", the theoretical-functional presupposition for the essence-wise analysis of experience-contents, the Vedantic *cit* is much more than a bare theoretical presupposition—it is *existentially* real.

Proceeding from the phenomenological perspective, if we now turn to the doctrine of *Cit* in its own original terms, we would confront certain innerly paradoxical situations. We define and discuss below some of these questions.

A. Phenomenologically understood, *cit* proves to be the very essence of subjectivity or the subjective, which is meant to be grasped in steps of subjectivization, through gradual 'dissociation' (For 'deconditioning) from the objective and and object-ward attitude. The paradigm point of departure for subject-ward reflection or reflective analysis would be provided by the notion of 'I' or I-hood (*ahaṃkāra*). But the question is : if *cit*, the essence of subjectivity, be approached in subjective attitude, how could it be envisaged in the long run as the over-subjective over-individual principle ? On the Vedāntic terms of reference, even the notion of *sākṣin*, though it stands as the transcendental subject, at the terminal point, so to say, of subjectivity-individuality, is yet sought to be transcended in favour of Brahman (or *Ātman qua Brahman*), the metaphysical Reality.

B. Can Consciousness, in its ideal purity of essence, be understood at all in a wholly de-personalized language? This question is closely linked up with the first, and would formulate itself in the form of a further question. If *Cit* be posited as *the* essence behind the complex of what we call 'person' or 'personality', in what way, then, would *Cit* be related to the latter ? To pose the question in another way, if *cit* is to be approached entirely in the subject-ward attitude of inwardization, then how can it at all prove, in the long run, to be an over-personal principle? It seems, again, to pose a paradox.

Referring, in this context, to the orientation of the problem within the framework of Husserlian Phenomenology itself, the question would take on a very definite shape as to how to bridge between the transcendental sphere of consciousness and the empirical sphere of human ego (or what Husserl refers to as "I-man"). Consequently arises the "praradox of human subjectivity"—a typical predicament in the strictly phenomenological procedure. The being, that is subject *for* the world, is at the same time the being, that is object *in* the world. Subjectivity in the form of object in the world and the same in relation (or reference) to the world—that poses the theoretical problem. As Husserl states directly, "each man carries in himself a transcendental I"—a position which seems to come close to the notion of *Sākṣin*. But the so-called 'transcendental ego or subject' would remain, on Husserl's own admission, in the long run "anonymous" in relation to the factual ego.[3]

C. A further question—and one that pertains to the basic attitude in Vedānta—would be in respect of the over-all *cognitive* (*jñāna-*) model of Advaita. Is *Cit* necessarily to be understood—and exclusively—in the *cognitive* context, as Advaita obviously claims to adopt it right from the Upaniṣads? To pose the question in a sceptical strain : why is there an exclusive preference for the cognitive model over a possible *non-cognitive* mode of approach to Reality—whether in terms of emotive (*bhakti*) or of conative (*karma*) frame of reference? Why, in other words, should it be imperative to accept *jñāna* as the only frame of reference in terms of which the whole doctrine of *Cit* could be meaningful?

In attempting to meet the questions formulated above I propose to introduce a line of understanding which might provide an answer to all of them—entailing a fresh understanding of the central drive of Vedānta to the whole human question.

Let us turn to the two key Vedāntic concepts in respect of *cit*, viz., *Pratyagātman* and *Sākṣin*. The former means the inner-

---

3. The problem is discussed in close details, with exclusive reference to Phenomenological philosophy, in author's book, *Studies in Phenomenology*, ("Phaenomenologica", Nijhoff, The Hague), Ch. V.

most self, evidently distinguished from the apparent self in its empirico-psychological complex centred around the body. Śaṁkara uses the Upaniṣadic expression *Pratyagātman* (Cf. *Kaṭha Up.* II-.1) in his *Adhyāsa-bhāṣya*, to mark out the unambiguous subject in the situation of false identification (*tādātmya-adhyāsa*) between 'I' and non-'I', consciousness and non-consciousness (*acit*). The original conception of *Pratyagātman* as the inward self (that is inwardized) seems to be pushed by Vācaspati Miśra (in his *Bhāmatī*) towards an epistemological orientation. The immediate 'certitude' is said to be pertaining to the inner self—in contradistinction from the bodily-vital complex, which has always an element of mediacy and dubitability about it. The key to such epistemological overtone, developed subsequently, could apparently be derived from the underlying strain in Śaṁkara's exposition towards holding up, within an implicitly epistemological model, the transcendental status of consciousness as self-certifying, evidencing background of mental states.[4]

As for the *Sākṣin* concept, it represents the positive idea of transcendental evidencing subject behind the complex of successive mental states. While the *Pratyagātman* concept points to the positively inner dimension of the individual, the subject, the *Sākṣin* concept emphasizes rather the presuppositional ('transcendental') character with reference to the epistemological-psychological functions and processes.

Now, in view of these formulations, the question that emerges can be put straightway thus : Why can the essence behind 'I' not be denoted by 'I' ? This situation seems to be, on the face of it, no doubt a paradoxical one. Indeed the Vedāntic position with regard to the final transition from *Sākṣin* (or *Sākṣicaitanya*) to Brahman seems to frustrate our attempt to categorize, in usual terms, the exact ontological status of the former. At best such status is sought to be spelt out with reference to two orders of reality—the metaphysical *per se* and the empirical (or perhaps, phenomenological). Having its place, so to say, intermediate between *Brahman* and *Jīva*, *Sākṣin*, though metaphysically of the very nature of Brahman, nevertheless presents

4. The concept of *Svaprakāśatva*, i.e., self-evidencing character, in post-Śaṁkara Vedānta (Cf. *Citsukhī*) thrusts this direction in an express form.

itself as involved in the empirical individual with his associational complex.[5]

In trying to review the situation afresh, without conforming to a set metaphysical framework as such, we have to consider the Vedāntic approach (right from the Upaniṣhads) in its own terms. Through a progressive deepening of the inward attitude, the quest for Ātman evidently consummated in a point of view which is maintained to be beyond the subject-object polarity. The ideal terminal point of progressive subjectivization, obtained co-ordinately through gradual withdrawal from the barely objective attitude (committed to outer, phenomenal reality), has often been negatively characterized in Advaita literature as 'unobjective' (*aviṣaya*), 'non-it' (*anidam*) i.e., that which cannot be denoted as 'this',—non-entitative (*avastu*), and so on. Yet to define that ideal stage categorically in terms of subjectivity would again mean the intrusion of the primary epistemological framework of subject-object dichotomy.

As the original Upaniṣhadic position goes, the Ātman-model would not evidently admit of any strict subject-object dichotomy in the final analysis.[6] No doubt Śaṅkara starts in *Adhyāsabhāṣya* with a statement of a dichotomy which is at least implicitly that of subject and object (in the form of what is meant by 'I' and what is meant by 'you'). Such distinguishment, however, as Śaṁkara himself observes subsequently, would have meaningfulness only on the relative level of ordinary human experience. The negative situation is stressed by Śaṁkara in another way by stating that *avidyā* is the matrix on which the usual subject-object distinction prevails, the necessary condition for all our cognitive practice (*pramāṇa* and *vyavahāra*) in actual life.

This brings us again to that ideal stage of consciousness losing its ostensive character of a differentiated individual

---

5. Cf. *Paramārthato brahmatvepi pratibhāsataḥ sākṣiṇah saṁsārī antarabhāva eva*, Jñānaghana, *Tattvaśuddhi*, Ch. 35

N.B. The concept of *Sākṣin*, however, comes to stand pre-eminently for the category of epistemological-transcendental subject, distinguished from the empirical cogniser (*pramātā*)—i.e., as the constant evidencing background presupposed by *antaḥkaraṇa-vṛtti*.

6. Cf. *Bṛhadāraṇyaka Upaniṣad*, IV. v. 15 : "Yatra tu asya sarvam ātmaiva abhūt tat kena kaṁ paśyet kena kam vijānīyāt vijñātāram are kena vijānīyāt".

subject—only to gain its deepest integral essence. The accepted epistemological model presumably proves to be inadequate and inappropriate in defining the situation. The latter could rather be grasped in *existential* terms—that is, as an inner involvement of the subject at its deepest level of being, in the so-called objective reality. In the light of this approach, the object is not just posited in its *cognitive* context—that is, as the object to which knowledge (and knower) has self-transcending reference as the 'other'. Rather the object would come into view so far as one's inner being gets involved in it, and the latter is of direct interest or concern for the subject—not a theoretic interest, but a deeper life-interest. In the Upaniṣadic-Vedāntic scheme of thought and culture, such interest is finally to be traced to the basic concern for *Mokṣa*—a drive which has been variously described as the intense longing for *Amṛtam* (Cf., e.g., *Bṛhadāraṇyaka Upaniṣad*, II in. etc.) or for *Mokṣa*—what Śaṁkara refers to as *Mumukṣutvam*.

Our line of understanding the Vedāntic theme of Consciousness as the paradigm of existential situation might as well provide the possible clue in regard to the third question concerning the *cognitive* (*jñāna*) model. The original *jñāna*-drive of the Upanishads was directly taken over by Śaṅkara in his emphasis on *Jñāna* as leading to liberation (*mokṣa*), overcoming *ajñāna*. But the way this *jñāna* approach tends to develop in Śaṁkara's and particularly in post-Śaṁkarite Vedānta, the cognitivity-model seems to be more and more over-emphasized. In the Upaniṣadic inquiry after Ātman, to 'know' does have a deeper import than what the 'knowledge-of-object' situation strictly implies. It pertains not to the cognitive faculty alone but implies the total being of man integrally involved in search of the central meaning and essence of his self. At this stage we might recall, although in a widely apart context, the words of Nietzsche "Behind your thoughts and feelings, my brother, there stands a mighty ruler, an unknown sage—whose name is self."[7] And the model behind Nietzsche's thrust towards the higher self is admittedly non-cognitive (will-oriented) rather than an exclusively cognitive one.

The Upaniṣadic expressions for 'knowing' in the sense of the highest life-ideal of enlightenment (*jñāna* or *vidyā*) lost

7. F. Nietzsche, *Thus Spoke Zarathustra*, **First Part**

subsequently much of its original meaningfulness in the Vedānta system. In place of the original ideal of integral existential illumination, involving the total being of man—cognitive as well as volitive-emotive,—the cognitive model seemed to be gradually adopted in the strict context of 'knowledge-of-object'. The paradigm of integral experience, where the subject, in its innermost fulfilment, is supposed to 'lose' itself in the heart of the universe, gave place to an intellectualised model, more or less, since Śaṁkara. In the light of the former alone, rather than the latter, could such apparently paradoxical statement assume meaningfulness : "One who knows Brahman becomes Brahman itself."[8] Such 'knowing' would not naturally be equivalent to knowing in the strict sense—it would be nothing short of an integral sense of harmony with all existence (*Sarvam*) gained at the innermost depth of one's being.

Viewed in the light of the foregoing observations, the situation about the relationship between *ātman* and *jīva* or the individual with the bodily-mental complex, would be paradoxical only in appearance rather than in essence. That would be so only when *ātman* is sought to be represented purely in conceptual terms, on the model of our experience of things and objects. The proper understanding of *ātman* would be that of an order or dimension other than that of empirical-psychological and entitative facts. In this sense *ātman* does not stand for *another* reality besides body, senses, mind etc., nor is it a mere extension of the spatio-temporally existent reality. It would rather prove to be the inner dimension of within the individual being—as much different from the empirical-psychological order as involved in the same.

On the other hand, the true import of the Vedāntic *Cit* cannot properly be translated in phenomenological terms. Thus, though functionally 'transcedental' in reference to experience-manifold, it cannot be reduced to the hypothetical status of 'phenomenological residuum'. For a phenomenological philosopher (Husserl or even Sartre), the theme of 'consciousness', in effect, proves to be the functional range of experience within which the subject-object (or subjectivity-objectivity) polarity

---

8. *Muṇḍaka Upaniṣad*, III, u. 9

operates. For the Upaniṣadic-Vedāntic model, on the other hand, consciousness presents itself, on ultimate analysis, as the innermost *existential* core of the human individual—the foundational-existence-stratum, in which the inner dimension of man is actualized.

From the perspective of such inner dimension alone could an integration of the inner and the outer be (existentially) effected in and through the depth of human experience. Ideally envisaged, this could also resolve the inner-outer dichotomy, or that between the individual self and nature or the universe around—not in conceptual nor in epistemological-psychological nor in theoretico-metaphysical terms, but in existential terms. Perhaps this approach to the notion of *cit* (qua *ātman*) could furnish the perspective proper in which a clue might be found towards a post-modern understanding of the Upaniṣadic mind working behind such statements as "Brahmavid brahmaiva bhavati".

Brock Univ.
St. Catherines, Ontario
Canada.

22
ARE THERE LOGICALLY UNANSWERABLE QUESTIONS?

Mihirvikash Chakravarti

There indeed are many questions in our discourse to which it is impossible for us to know the right answers, purely because of certain empirical reasons, *e.g.* the laws governing the mind that is to know, those about the objects that are to be known, and so on. Likewise, nobody would deny that there are countless questions whose answers we are not in a position to know just on account of this or that technical reason, *e.g.* lack of suitable equipments, etc. But are there, in the like manner, also instances of questions, where it is impossible for us to know the right answers because of the very laws of logic? That is, are there *logically unanswerable questions*?

Insofar as it seems to suit some of his basic commitments in philosophy, Moritz Schlick proceeds to answer this question sharply in the negative. Schlick says:

> I am advocating that there are many questions which it is empirically impossible to answer, but not a single real question for which it would be logically impossible to find a solution.[1]
> ..a question which is unanswerable in principle can have no meaning.[2]

The position happens to bear closely on a number of fundamental philosophical problems as also on certain historical matters about philosophy. All that we have mentioned elsewhere.[3] Besides, it goes to contradict what appears in our eyes to be a very significant logical point about the nature of questions. The point, which also has been worked out by us in a different context, is briefly that the word 'unanswerable', as much as its opposite 'answerable', describes the logical value of meaningful questions *only*, so that a question which is meaningless is to be called merely meaningless, neither answerable nor unanswerable.

For these reasons, the position, quite rightly we think, has come to assume a good deal of importance for us. Therefore, in what follows we have undertaken to examine it.

1. On what, let us enquire, is the position, namely, that *there are no logically unanswerable questions*, logically grounded? As we understand, the ground is only a theory which says that the *meaning of a question consists in the ways of finding its answer*.

This theory will remind one at once of another, namely, its counterpart as regards the indicative sentences which, as everybody knows, purports to equate the meaning of an indicative sentence with the method of its verification. The two theories, as they spring from the same source, do have some family resemblance between them. That is msot natural. Yet neither perhaps can be viewed as a mere variant or corollary of the other : their disanalogies are too salient to permit that. And this makes one thing clear, namely, that whatever has been said by philosophers—a lot indeed—about the latter in course of the last few decades cannot be indiscriminately passed on to the former to subserve the same purpose. As far as is known to us, till now the theory about the meaning of questions has remained virtually eclipsed by that about the meaning of indicative sentences. The former has never known anything of that limelight which has been lavishly enjoyed by its sister.

For this historical reason, combining with its obvious bearing on a philosophical issue of fundamental importance, the theory, we think, merits serious and thorough consideration. Unfortunately, that however is not going to become any part of our present preoccupation. We do not plan to enquire into the validity or otherwise of the theory. Our strategy in executing the proposed examination of the position in question will not be to repudiate the theory but only to show that the position does not follow from it.

2. How, really, from the theory

(1) that the meaning of a question consists in the ways of knowing its answer

does Schlick proceed to deduce his conclusion

(2) that there is no question to which it is logically impossible to know the answer?

This is by no means explicit. Let us therefore look into the anatomy of the procedure to find out the hidden link between (1) and (2), if there is any. And this, we think, may well begin with an analysis and comparison of the two.

One thing seems quite clear. (1) and (2) both of them involve a common presupposition. It is : every question must have an answer. The presupposition, if we may say so, has the standing of an axiom. So, nobody, we suppose, will ever think of calling its validity in question. 'Having an answer' constitutes undoubted the core of the notion of a question, and so no word or combination of words will count as a question, unless this basic requirement is not fulfilled by it.

2.1. What, however, is of particular significance to us here is not the presupposition which is innocuous, but some additional propositions involved in (1) and (2). They are respectively the following :

(3) There *must always be ways* for knowing the answer to a question.

(4) The answer *must* be logically knowable.

There may of course be other propositions too. But these two are most fundamental. Anyway, in the light of the two propositions, we are perhaps in a position to restate the matter in a bit more precise form. That is, we may say that the inference from (1) to (2) is ultimately an inference from (3) to (4).

To consider (3). Is it really true that there *must always* be ways for knowing the answer to a question ? It, certainly, would be so, if (4), *i.e.* that the answer must be logically knowable, were true. For, if you admit that the answer is logically knowable, then, by that only, you admit further that there must be ways for knowing it : the former entails the latter and would make no sense without it.

But are we, in this way, entitled logically to look for a justification of (3) by reference to (4) ? True, by itself, there might not be anything wrong in this procedure; but in the present setting, it would turn out to be totally inadmissible. (4) can, by no means, work as the logical ground of (3), because in the inference under consideration, it is (3) which has been made the logical ground of (4).

But can there be any other method of proving (3) ? We don't know. To be candid, we have in mind certain very serious doubts about its validity, though, for the present, that need not bother us at all. We can very well afford to take its truth for granted. And we shall do it for the present. That is not going to cause any damage to our purpose. As a matter of fact, it is not our business here to ascertain whether or not (3) is true. Nor is it whether or not (3) follows from (4). It is rather the converse of that. That is to say, what we propose to do is just to examine whether or not (4) can be said to follow from (3).

1.1 Considered entirely by itself, (3) is, by no means, adequate for yielding (4). And the reason, which is quite simple, is that its logical content is far less than that of the latter. It is true that the notion of *there being some way for knowing the answer* is included in that of the *answer being logically knowable*. We have already mentioned this. Yet to cover the whole of what the latter, *i.e.* (4), means, the former, *i.e.* (3), must have to combine, as we understand, with at least two more propositions which, needless to mention, must in turn be themselves true. The two propositions are:

(5) That the *ways of knowing the answer* must themselves be logically knowable.

(6) That, besides, it must be logically possible to follow the ways.

2.2. (5) and (6), then, are to play a decisive role. They must hold good; otherwise, there will be nothing to show that there is a link between (3) and (4) and therefore, a genuine ground for one to pass from the former to the latter.

So, the problem is whether there really is anything to make it certain:

(7) that it would be logically possible to *know the ways* in which the answer to a question is to be known:

and (8) that it would be logically possible, further, to *follow the ways* (so that the answer might become known to one).

It appears a bit strange that neither Schlick nor any of his compatriots is quite alive to these problems in the way one might expect them to be. Schlick's treatment of the matter is in fact too perfunctory to be capable of yielding any clear-cut answer. Nonetheless, there are certain clues which, we suppose, may be followed by us, not unsafely perhaps, to find out the kind of solution he seems to have in mind.

The clues happen to inhere in Schlick's treatment of the concept of *logical possibility*. The particular point in the treatment which interests us is that he seems to equate *logical possibility* with possibility of another kind, namely, the *possibility to describe*. In Schlick's language :

I call a fact or process 'logically possible', if it can be described....[5]

Which means, according to Schlick, whatever is *describable* is logically possible , that is to say, it is *describability* which is to distinguish what is logically possible from what is not so.

2.3. Let us turn now to the "ways" or 'prescriptions" for knowing the answer. They are describable, and from that it is straightway concluded that they are logically possible. But what is it that is to provide us with an assurance on the two further points which are more important, namely : (*a*) that it is logically possible to *know the ways or prescriptions*, and (*b*) that it is logically possible to *follow* them.

Schlick's solution, if we have understood him rightly, is pretty simple. If we may say so, it consists just in a certain readjustment being made by him in the meaning of the phrase 'logical possibility', when it is to be used to characterize the 'prescriptions' or 'ways' of knowing the answer. That is, he appears to have liberalized its meaning and incorporated both (*a*) and (*b*) . The latter *directly*: and the former *indirectly* through the latter, in the sense that (*b*) presupposes (*a*) and, that way, entails it. This interpretation of Schlick's position, we hope, will not be incorrect. In our opinion, it is substantially corroborated by the following lines which we quote from Schlick:

> It may be empirically impossible to follow those prescriptions (like travelling around the moon), but it cannot be logically impossible (to follow them). For what is logically impossible (to follow) cannot even be described....[6]

Anyway, the notion of *describability*, or that of *logical possibility* as meaning mere describability, as one can see, has been introduced for a crucial use by Schlick. It is basically and entirely on it that rests his explanation of how it becomes logically possible to *know* and to *follow* the *ways* or *prescriptions*, for knowing the answer to a question. But the question is : Does it do its job ?

Describability may indeed be a condition for the logical possibility in question. Even a necessary one. But is it sufficient ? Our answer : No, it isn't. Merely that they are describable is far inadequate to establish that it must be logically possible to *know* or to *follow* the ways or prescriptions. For, as we shall now explain, certain more conditions, which are not covered by describability, will have to be fulfilled for that purpose. Kant knew of this. But Schlick is not Kant : he says nothing on the point.

Consider what it is for the 'way' or 'description' to be describable (or logically possible in that sense), according to Schlick (and his colleagues). As far as we understand, merely that the prescriptive sentence in which the way or prescription is stated accords with the rules of 'logical grammar' *i.e.* the rules describing the circumstances of its use.

It is obvious that, just as a *thing* is not the same as the *knowing of it*, so the *way or prescription for knowing the answer* is not also the same as the *knowing of the way or prescription for knowing the answer*. From this it follows that the describability of the former and that of the latter are not to mean the same thing. The two stand for two different problems, so that what answers the first does not *ipso facto* answer the second.

What, then, is going to tell us whether or not the *knowing of the way or prescription for knowing the answer* is describable ? We must ascertain this. Can we say : Consideration of whether or not the sentence describing our *knowledge-claim about the way or prescription for knowing the answer* obey the rules which state the circumstances of its use ? Well, in that case, there will be the question : What, precisely, is to be said to constitute these circumstances ? There is no ready answer. One thing however seems certain. It is that the circumstances cannot be said to consist just in those which are described by the rules of the use of the prescriptive sentence itself. As far as we can see, the *only* things in which they can be supposed to consist are perhaps those circumstances which are embodied by the rules that define the *logical conditions of knowing*, *e.g.* those in which the *way* or *prescription for knowing the answer* can itself become an object of knowledge, those of the knowing mind that is to know it, *etc.* But these are none embraced by the particular sense which Schlick is prepared to assign to 'describability'. Nor, also, can they be accounted for in the light of it in some other way.

In saying all this, we might appear to one—not unjustly—to be viewing the matter through the eyes of Kant. That seems quite true. But in that case, we must admit that Kantianism on this particular point is inescapable for us.

3. To wind up our argument so far.

There is nothing in Schlick which might be said to confirm (7) and (8) and, for that matter, naturally, (5) and (6), (*i.e.* that the *ways of knowing the answer* must themselves be logically knowable, *and* that it must be logically possible to *follow the* ways).

This shows that there is no link between (3) and (4) (*i.e.* that there *must be ways* for knowing the answer to a question, *and* that the answer *must* be logically knowable): so that (4) does not follow from (3).

And from this, it finally follows that there is nothing of the required kind of continuity between (1) and (2), (namely, that the meaning of a question consists in the *way of knowing its answer*, *and* that there is no question to which it is logically impossible to know the right answer), which could have justified Schlick in deducing the latter from the former.

4. One additional point about Schlick. It is obvious that 'being known', 'being knowable', *etc.*, can none of them be said in any sense to form parts of the kind of logical entities which become related as answers to questions : the latter are *logically independent*[7] of the former. Why, then, must answers have to be *necessarily knowable* in any way whatever? There is no logical foundation for the idea—not at least one which we are able to see. But in that case, how may we account for Schlick being so intensely obsessed with it? Can it possibly be linked up with the kind of empiricism to which he happens to have generously subscribed? We do not definitely know. However, history will tell a story which may not be altogether irrelevant on this point. The story is that the empiricists, despite conscious effort on their part, have not always been able to keep themselves at a secure distance from the philosophy which goes

with the name of Berkeley. And Schlick, if we are allowed to so suppose, might have become just an example in this empiricist tradition. The suspicion may not prove true, but it may not be prudent to dismiss it as well.

5. So, it is possible that there are logically unanswerable questions, questions to which it would be logically impossible to know the answers. In fact, such questions do exist actually in our discourse. Many, many of them. We do not know whether there is more than one place to find them, or what, exactly, *all* of such places are: though we know for certain at least of one. It is, we would say, metaphysics. Questions of metaphysics, we maintain, are logically unanswerable—I mean all of them.

But will it, for us, mean that, *as a body of questions*, metaphysics, as is said by many, is meaningless? No, not at all. For, as we have already said, the word 'unanswerable' (also answerable) can be predicated in its primary logical sense *only* of questions which are meaningful; and so metaphysical questions, in being logically unanswerable, will have to be called meaningful merely for that reason alone, if not for any other. In fact, to say that metaphysical *questions* are meaningless would make no sense: that this nonsense could linger in philosophy for a few decades in the past is entirely on account of a highly mistaken equation from which it arises, I mean the equation of the concept of *unanswerability* and that *meaninglessness*.

However, considered merely *as a body of answers*, metaphysics, in our opinion, will have to be called meaningless. For, verily, there cannot be any sense in speaking of knowing, or in making an attempt to know, the answers to certain questions, when the answers are logically unknowable for us.

But what to say about metaphysics as such? Is it to be called meaningful or meaningless? Well, that, we think, will depend ultimately on how we view the *logical role* of a question, our ways of dealing with it.

Our usual way of dealing with a question, when we face it, is to find an answer to it. This means that yielding answer is the most common logical role performed by a question. It is no doubt the most important role too. Now, if this answer-yielding were the *only* logical role which we were in a position to assign to questions, then, obviously, metaphysics as occupied with logically unanswerable questions could be disbanded unequivocally as meaningless.

But must we confine a question's significance to that of begetting answers. Can't we attribute to it some more logical functions which also would be equally significant? This indeed is the crucial point.

It is now a matter of common knowledge in philosophy that an indicative may have more roles in our thought than that of conveying information to us. Can't we, extending this analogy of the indicative to a question, afford to look upon its role as more than that of a mere answer-yielder? This is a possibility which, we think, is definitely worth exploring: although, right now, we are not in a position to engage ourselves with that exploration or with the many problems which it is likely to trigger off. Anyway, pending the exploration is done, the only course of action which would be justified for us to follow is to suspend our judgment on whether metaphysics as such is to be called meaningful or meaningless.

North Bengal University
Distt. Darjeeling

References

1. "Unanswerable Questions?", reprinted in *Philosophy in the Twentieth Century*, vol. 3, ed. W. Barrett and H.D. Aiken, Random House, New York, p. 25.
2. *Ibid.*, p. 26
3. The author's "The Concept of Unanswerable Question" (unpublished).
4. The author's "Towards a Theory of or the Classification of Questions", IIAS, Simla, 1971.
5. "Verification and Experience", reprinted in *Philosophy in the Twentieth Century*, vol. 3, ed., W. Barrett and H.D. Aiken, Random House, New York, p. 36.
5. "Verification and Experience", reprinted in *Philosophy in the Twentieth Century*, vol. 3, ed., W. Barrett and H.D. Aiken, Random House, New York, p. 36.
6. "Unanswerable Questions?", the same volume, p. 26.
7. The notion is employed in the Russellean and Moorean sense.

ANOTHER LOOK AT BUDDHA-HUME "CONNECTION"

Bina Gupta

Attempts to discuss parallels between David Hume's philosophy and Gautama Buddha's philosophy have become very popular for scholars in the East and in the West. Although it might seem far-fetched to some philosophers, there do exist certain similarities between Buddhism and certain aspects of Hume's philosophy. In this study I propose to discuss : (1) parallel between Hume's philosophy and Buddhist philosophy; (2) the question of whether or not Buddha influenced Hume: and (3) the contrasts between Buddha and Hume. My discussion will evaluate the thesis of Nolan Pliny Jacobson,[1] who holds that Hume was influenced by Buddha insofar as Buddhist philosophy was carried to the West by way of Chinese cultural traditions, and Edward Conze,[2] who sees no real parallel between the two. It is my intention to show that the Buddhist conception of the self is more intricate than the Humean conception, and that this is due to the viewpoints on perception adopted by each of these men. I am going to restrict my remarks on Buddhist philosophy to Buddha as he is interpreted in the Theravāda tradition.[3]

Accepting the empirical theory of the origin of knowledge, Hume deprives the concept of substance of all rational justification. He holds that we know only our impressions and so we have no right to assert the reality of substance. Thus, he rejected Locke's "unknown substance" and Berkely's "spiritual substance." Similarly, Gautama Buddha denies the existence of any permanent substance. Everything, for example, perceptions, feelings, objects are in a state of flux and belief in a substance is nothing but an illusion. T.R.V. Murti puts it, "Denial of substance is the foundation of Buddhism down the ages."[4]

So, Buddhists argue that there is no soul or self in the sense of a permanent entity (*anāttā*). Self is made of five *kandhas* (sanskrit: *skandhas*), which are impermanent and cannot give rise to a permanent entity called self. As Lakshmi Narasu observes, according to the Buddhists : "That which is called the Ego, which says 'I am', is merely an aggregate of *skandhas*, a complex of sensations, ideas, thoughts, emotions and volitions."[5]

Here we have a striking similarity with Hume. Hume also observes :

> "For my part when I enter most intimately into what I call *myself*, I always stumble on some particular perception or other, of heat or cold, light or shade, love or hatred, pain or pleasure. I never can catch *myself* at any time without a perception, and never can observe anything but the perception."[6]

Thus, for Hume as well as for Buddhists there is no thinker, but only thought, no perceiver but only perception.

Thus far we have seen some of the similarities between the views of Hume and Buddha on substance, and self. It seems appropriate to consider to what degree, if any, Hume was influenced by Buddha. Are the parallels between the two "real"? Different philosophers have taken different positions on this issue.

Edward Conze, in his article, "Spurious Parallels to Buddhist Philosophy," maintains that any parallels between Hume and Buddhist Philosophy are superficial. "Spurious paralleles", he holds, are those parallels which "often originate from a wish to find affinities with philosophers recognized and admired by the exponents of current academic philosophy, and intend to make Buddhist thinkers interesting and respectable by current Western standards."[7] He agrees that there is a parallel between Hume's and Buddha's concept of the self, since both reject the notion of a permanent self. But as they have different purposes, the parallel is "merely deceptive."[8] He says : "A negative proposition derives its true meaning from what it is directed against, and its message entirely depends, therefore, on its context. In different contexts two identical negative statements may, therefore, have nothing in common,"[9] because negative statements which are merely destructive of another point of view derive their meaning in connection with what they are negating. Humean and Buddhist philosophy lead in opposite directions. Hume "reduced selfhood to the level of the subpersonal," and "the Buddhist doctrine of *anāttā*—invites us to search for the super-personal."[10] And since these two philosophies have different goals and purposes, he claims that the parallels which we find in the two are deceptive.

Nolan Pliny Jacobson, in his article, "The Possibility of Oriental Influence in Hume's Philosophy," on the other hand, maintains that Hume's ideas to a large extent were borrowed from Buddha *via* China. Jacobson holds that Pierre Bayle was not only a vehicle of Oriental thought, but also a major influence on Hume's thoughts and ideas. Hume's central ideas, particularly his treatment of causality, God, substance, and self, were shaped by Bayle. Hume read Bayle when he was writing the *Treatise*. Bayle was very much impressed by the "tolerance of the Chinese emperor for Jesuit missions."[11] There was a craze for Chinese art culture in European markets at that time. Jacobson writes that:

> Oriental influences were so much a part of the intellectual climate in which Hume moved that neither he nor anyone of comparable prominence in the debate of the time could have formulated his thoughts apart from these influences. Asia played a dominant role in the thinking of the eighteenth century, especially in that thinking which had the longest future to play in the secularization of modern life; it played a prominent role in the shaping of Hume's thought, particularly in his working over of the notions of causality, substance, the role of reason in religion, and the enduring, ever-identical self.[12]

Therefore he concludes that Hume had to be influenced by Oriental thought.

To sum up: we have, on the one hand, the view of Conze who maintains that there is no real parallel between Humean and Buddhist philosophy, and on the other hand, we have Jacobson's view that Hume was greatly influenced by Buddha.[13]

There is bias in Conze's article. His view that there is no real parallel between the two seems to be based on the thesis that there is a very little hope for interchange between East and

West in philosophy. As a matter of fact, he is convinced that the time has come to abandon the quest for parallels between thinking in the East and in the West.[14] The fact that Hume's and Buddha's philosophies lead in opposite directions does not make the parallels "spurious," as Conze claims. It appears that Conze forgot that there is an affirmative aspect of every negation, and so in spite of the differences the parallels between the two cannot be denied. Simply because two parties happen to develop their central idea in obviously different directions, this, in itself, need not imply that the central idea is, *ipso facto*, dissimilar. In fact, there might well be genuine similarity in the idea selected as points of departure for philosophic inquiry. The point I am trying to make is that Hume and Buddha have a real similarity so far as their conceptions of self are concerned, although they have different purposes, and reach different conclusions.

Jacobson's position, also seems to be far-fetched. If one puts his position into logical form, we get the following premises and conclusion :

Bayle was influenced by Oriental thought.

Hume was influenced by Bayle.

Therefore, Hume was influenced by Oriental thought.

While Jacobson's logic appears sound on the surface, his use of "influence" is perhaps questionable. Clearly there are cases in which one can be said to be "influenced" by another and yet the specific area of influence be, at least, ambiguous. Jacobson's thesis has speculative weight, but it is lacking in historical and intellectual weight. Hume never mentioned Buddha in his writings and so there is no direct evidence that Hume was influenced by Buddha.

We can safely conclude that, due to the lack of evidence, we cannot say to what degree Hume was influenced by Buddha or if he was at all influenced by him. In view of the fact that the attitudes and goals of Buddhism are so different from Hume's, Jacobson's thesis that Hume borrowed his ideas from the Buddha seems to be improbable.

I do not intend to suggest that there are only similarities between the two philosophies. There are major differences between the two and I agree with Jacobson that "differences certainly outweigh the similarities."[15] Having dealt with the similarities, we will proceed to look at the major differences between Humean and Buddhist philosophy.

The chief aim of Buddha was to free people from sorrows and delusions of life. Life in this world is full of suffering (*duḥkha*). All human beings in this world need to be saved from suffering and released from suffering which can be possible only through *nibbana* (sanskrit: *nirvāṇa*). Buddha did not stop by telling about life as *duḥkha*, but in the Second Noble truth pointed out the cause of *duḥkha* and in the third and fourth showed that there can be a cessation of the *duḥkha* and the way by which one reaches the cessation of *dukkha*. *Duḥkha* depends on some conditions, if those conditions cease, *duḥkha* ceases also. Thus, Buddha as a teacher and physician diagnosed the disease but did not stop with the diagnosis: he went further and also provided the cure.

Hume, on the other hand, was not bothered by the suffering in the world, and we do not find in him any concept comparable to the Buddhist concept of *nibbāṇa*. Hume's aim was to analyze different ways of knowing and to discover the principles which would meet the most critical examination.[16] He wrote that he hoped he could contribute something to the advancement of knowledge by expounding on some particulars which could give a new turn to the speculation of philosophers, as well as pointing out to them "more distinctly those subjects, where alone they can expect assurance and conviction. Human Nature is the only science of man."[17]

Even with their similarity about the conception of self, their different purposes are obvious. Since Hume rejects all concepts which are not based on sensory experience, he necessarily rejects the view of self as substance: "When I enter most intimately into what I call *myself*, I always stumble on some particular perception or the other......I never can catch *myself* at any time without a perception and can never observe anything but the perception."[18] This observation raises some very important problems. The question immediately is: If we can only observe perceptions, how can we know about the "observer," the "self"? Hume cannot say that these perceptions inhere in some substantial subject as the qualities do because he rejects the notion of substance.

If perceptions do not inhere in any substratum, it might

be said that the factor which integrates the particular perceptions in the self is some kind of relation. But Hume rejects both the relation of identity and the relation of cause and effect. He rejects the former, because it is self-contradictory. Identity refers to two things which two are different, and not identical.[19] He rejects the view that there is a necessary connection between cause and effect, as we only observe one event following the other, we never observe any connection between the two.[20] Therefore, the only conclusion to be inferred is that the self is just a collection of different percepions, "which succeed each other with an inconceivable rapidity, and are in a perpetual flux or movement......They are the successive perceptions only, that constitute the mind."[21]

Buddhism, on the other hand, holds that everything is impermanent (*anicca*). There is nothing in experience which is not impermanent but change. Unchanging substance exists only in thought and not in reality. *Anicca* or impermanence is a cyclic process. The law of change passes through the phases of birth, growth, decay, and death. And as everything is impermanent there is no such thing as a self which is permanent and endures through the changes. The very search for self is wrong, and all false doctrines and notions arise out of this misconception. The belief in a permanent self causes attachement to it, and that, in turn, brings craving for pleasure. Impermanent *Kandhas* cannot give rise to a permanent "self." Search for permanence in this impermanent world is the cause of our sorrow. And as self is nothing but a flow of these impermanent *Kandhas*, there is all the more reason that we should try to avoid it.

Although Hume's conception of the self resembles Buddha's conception of the self, the latter's conception goes further than the former's by explaining the continuity of seemingly separate perceptions. Buddha in essence has a way ofa voiding Hume's dilemma in this case. He maintains that self is nothing but a stream of consciousness (*dhammas*). These *dhammas* are arranged in an intellectual hierarchy starting from the sensual states of consciousness and progressing to the ultimate goal which is *nibbāna*. These *dhammas* in themselves are not static but are regarded as "events" or "processes." Each *dhamma* rises from the preceding perception, develops and then passes its links to the succeeding perception. Every phase of perception has within itself the potentialities of its predecessor. So, *dhammas* are not only parts of the process but the process at the same time. With the help of the above analysis, the Buddhists explain continuity in the conception of the self as a stream of consciousness. Hume's self, on the other hand, stands out "loose and separate", without any connection between parts of the selves. Hume simply could not find a way to ground the notion of self : "But all my hopes vanish, when I come to explain the principles, that unite our successive perceptions in our thought or consciousness. I cannot discover any theory, which gives me satisfaction on this head."[22] And then he explains in the next paragraph : "In short there are two principles, which I cannot render consistent: nor is it in my power to renounce either of them, viz. *that all our distinct perceptions are distinct existences, and that the mind never perceives any real connection among distinct existence.*"[23] He concluded: "For my part, I must plead the privilege of a sceptic, and confess, that this difficulty is too hard for my understanding. I pretend not, however, to pronounce it absolutely insuperable."[24] And here the matter rests.

Thus, Hume wrote what he merely "thought". More encompassing, however, is the contribution of Buddha. Buddha not only "thought" what he preached, but also he had a "belief" in *nibbāṇa*. He not only conveyed belief in *nibbāṇa* but also he displayed in feeling and action the meaning of that consummate religious perspective. Hume wrote about the theory of knowledge; Buddha talked about a way of life. Hume's empiricism implies the task of conforming to the standards of knowledge; Buddha clarified the ethical dimension of one's way of life. The similarities which we find between the two are really remarkable; and the contrasts which we see between the two make the similarities all the more remarkable.

Missourie University
Columbia U.S.A.

FOOTNOTES

1. Nolan Pliny Jacobson, "The Possibility of Oriental Influence in Hume's Philosophy," *Philosophy East and West* XIX (Jan. 1969), pp. 17-37.
2. Edward Conze, "Spurious Parallels to Buddhist Philosophy, *Philosophy East and West* XIII (July, 1963), pp. 114-115.

3. Theravāda Buddhism emphasizes that the teachings and thoughts of the historical Buddha. The account of Buddhism we are concerned with in this study is based on the original teachings of Buddha. Buddha wrote no books, and all his instructions were oral instructions. Whatever knowledge we possess about Buddha depends on *Tripiṭakas* or the "Three Baskets" which comprise Buddha's views as recorded by his intimate disciples. There is no doubt that the *Tripiṭakas* or the "Three Baskets" which comprise Buddha's views as recorded by his intimate disciples. There is no doubt that the *Tripiṭakas* are the earliest and most authentic accounts of Buddha's teaching which are available now, and they are the Canon of the Theravāda Buddhist.

4. T.R.V. Murti, *The Central Philosophy of Buddhism*, (London: George Allen and Unwin Ltd., 1960), pp. 26-27.

5. Lakshmi Narasu, *The Essence of Buddhism*, (Bombay: Thacker and Co., Ltd., 1948), p. 218

6. Hume, *A Treatise of Human Nature*, edited with an analytical index by L. A. Selby-Bigge (Oxford: at the Clarendon Press, 1888), p. 252.

7. Conze, "Spurious Parallels to Buddhist Philosophy," p. 105.

8. *Ibid.*, 106.

9. *Ibid.*, 113.

10. *Ibid*, 114.

11. Nolan Pliny Jacobson, "The Possibility of Oriental Influence in Hume's Philosophy," p. 35.

12. *Ibid.*, 36-37.

13. Jacobson maintains that when Hume came to France to write the *Treatise*, Europe had been under the influence of Oriental culture for three centuries. He states: "China by this time had become a repository for all major ideas of the entire continent of Asia, and far too much coalescence of Hindu, Buddhist and Chinese philosophy had occurred over the centuries to permit any dissociation for our purposes here between the influence of Chinese thought, on the one hand, and the influence of Buddhist and other Indian ideas, on the other." *Ibid.*, 28.

14. Conze, "Spurious Parallels to Buddhist Philosophy," 105.

15. Jacobson, "The Possibility of Oriental Influence in Hume's Philosophy," p. 23.

16. Hume, *Treatise*, p. 272.

17. *Ibid.*, p. 272.

18. *Ibid.*, p. 252.

19. *Ibid.*, p. 200.

20. David Hume, *An Inquiry Concerning Human Understainding*, ed. C. W. Hendel (New York: The Library of Liberal Arts Press, Inc., 1955), p. 74.

21. Hume, *Treatise*, pp. 252-53.

22. *Ibid.*, pp. 635-36.

23. *Ibid.*, p. 636.

24. *Ibid.*, p. 636.

AUROBINDO* AND WHITEHEAD :* A QUEST FOR GENERAL IDEAS

A. K. Sarkar

In this paper an attempt will be made to compare some aspects of thoughts of two twentieth century philosophers, one of the East and the other of the West. The expressions, East and West, have been used in a broad sense to indicate two cultural poles of the World.

Both Aurobindo and Whitehead became prominent in the early decades of the twentieth century and both became interested in reassessing their respective philosophic attitudes and pursuits. Here an attempt will be made to clarify their philosophic methods, which are comparable in their respective stands in depth psychology, yet show the uniqueness of the two cultural histories of mankind. Both develop an evolutionary scheme, one from a transcendental and the other from a non-sensuous background: to both perceptual experiences,—presentational situations or ideas—are not simple forms, but surface results of deep and complex, many-dimensional, pervasive, relative and connected processes. Both, therefore, comment on and try to reform earlier philosophical methods, which they think, tend to be too restrictive and closed. Aurobindo and Whitehead are interesting studies in comparison.

Aurobindo, born of Indian parents, was brought up and educated in England. As a professor of English in one of the Indian Universities, he was fascinated by the cultural history of India and read deeply the philosophical deliberations of the ancient Vedas, Upaniṣads, Bhagavadgītā and Buddhism, and also of the Indian philosophical systems, different theistic and mystic cults as *Tantras*, some of which evolved towards extreme complexities integrating many novel elements, indigenous and foreign, to suit the temper and vissicitudes of the times. The experiential contrasts between the apparent and the transcendent developed in all these modes of deliberations, struck Aurobindo as an intriguing problem in Indian thought. In his *The Life Divine*[1], Aurobindo reviews the past cultural traditions of India, and suggests from a higher symbolic perspective as well as by practical yogic methods, how the apparent and the transcendent can be integrated. This paper will be broadly based on Aurobindo's *The Life Divine*, and Whitehead's *The Adventures of Ideas*[2], where Whitehead brings into focus the main trends of Western philosophy as he sees them and formulates his own.

In the study of Indian philosophy Aurobindo notices how the glimpse of the transcendental is obtained in the meditative pursuits of the Vedic seers when they shift their minds through polytheism, monotheism and philosophic monism to the pervasive features. The hymns (*Mantras*) of the *Ṛg Veda* were supplemented by the practical philosophy of activity and rituals (*Brāhmaṇas*) of the Yajur Veda, which were, again, subjected to the symbolic and philosophic processes (*Āraṇyakas*) and *Upaniṣads*) of the *Sāma* and *Atharva Vedas*. The new interpretation of the *Mantras* and *Brāhmaṇas* evolved towards the transcendent orders of experience with higher dialectical schemes of the *Upaniṣads*—the philosophic sections of the *Vedas*. The real then was viewed as something deeply immediate, neither sensuous nor conceptual, but a self-shining unrestricted pervasive process. In the *Māṇḍūkya* Upaniṣad, for example, it is explained how this transcendent order of experience is immanent in, yet different from, the three transient apparent orders of experience, e.g. (i) the *ignorance* of deep-sleep (ii) the subjective constructions of the dream, and (iii) subjective-objective processes of waking. After this great discovery of a transcendental order of experience (*Turīya*) which is not cancelled even in the ignorance of deep-sleep, the Upanisadic thinkers ventured to conclude that it is not even cancelled by the process of death, which is only a perishing of bodily process and vital-mental processes on the surface; the dispositional mental processes (*saṁskāras*) the psychic attitudes (*vāsanās*)—the cores which control the surface modes—continue beyond bodily death and account for the bodily processes in a new form. This discovery of a process of such depth and pervassiveness in Indian philosophy, fascinates Aurobindo, for, this cancels all anthromorphic attitudes resting merely on the sensuous waking orders of experience.

Aurobindo appreciates the evolution of Indian thought, the discovery of the transcendent-immanent process that gives worth and continuity to otherwise discrete appearances or states, but he also wonders how the transcendent and the apparent are linked, and how to understand the transcendent beyond the apparent. In the Upaniṣadic stage, it is indicated that an individual can attain transcendent experience through meditation or discriminative knowledge which dispels the duality of appearance and reality. In the Bhagavadgītā, there is an indication of an objective personality (kṣetrajña), who from a transcendent background (kṣetra) controls and redirects socio-political-moral situation in periods of crises. The *Gītā* (Bhagavadgītā) indicates that religious-moral-social processes, in all apparent spheres, could be corrected from a transcendent aspect: it also points out that an individual from his socio-cultural-moral situation can be operative in unison with the transcendental process by practising detached activity, which is doing his duties without any immediate interest or motive. This detached activity (niṣkāma-karma) is a step to go beyond one's limited subjectivity.

With cues from the Upaniṣads and the *Gītā*, with insightful readings in later philosophies, and with his own yogic meditations, Aurobindo proposes that philosophy has to be both meditatively oriented and practically directed. He interprets that the transcendental Upanṣadic processes of consciousness-existence-bliss (sat-cit-ānanda) are not merely pervasive meditative situations, but involve a dynamic transcendent process of Supermind. Aurobindo conceived of the Supermind somewhat differently from the emergent-operative personality of the Bhagavadgītā. It is 'Super' because it is beyond the subject-object dichotomy of ordinary mind and therefore comprehended only through meditation. The idea is, that, there is not only a relativity of silent existential base (of *Turīya*, *Ātman* or *Śiva*) and the energetic process of a divine personality (kṣetrajña or śakti), but there is in Supermind a reaching and rescuing of the matter restricted to inconscience and ignorance. Unlike Gītā's transcendent-personality that emerges in times of distress, Aurobindo's Supermind is continuously operative as a process of involution (descent) and evolution (ascent) in a dual character, along with the transcendent and the apparent-empirical. Aurobindo is not likely to agree with the non-dualist Śaṁkara if Śaṁkara interprets the presented objective—practical order of experience as a mere lapse (Māyā) from the transcendent-meditative situation. He accepts the transcendent-meditative, affirmative negative contrasts of the Upaniṣadic-Buddhist-Vedāntic currents but avoids their restrictions in either transcendent or immanent aspects, in terms of "either or" or in terms of "neither nor." The Buddhist thought, in its evolution, had suggested that the operative processes of compassionate Bodhisattvas help aspiring and disciplined souls; Aurobindo's Supermind does the same function, with a further extension, reaching the lowest material or imperfect processes. Aurobindo, of course, acknowledges all possible orders of experience from the lowest to the highest, but his stress is on the integral vision of the spiritual goal; he says, "a veil of insensibility of matter hides the universal conscious-force that works within it......" and holds out hope for "the passage from the evolution in the Ignorance to a greater evolution in the knowledge......" (*The Life Divine*, pp. 734-735). For mankind, the evolution is towards spiritualism and peace.[3]

In the background of Western culture, Whitehead's general ideas follow an almost similar course of evolution. The writer thinks that Whitehead's reflections specially in his *Adventures of Ideas*, take on a meditative-theoretic turn, when he reviews the past abstract conceptual and empirical trends before Hegel, and restricted reactionary empirical modes in post-Hegelian thought. In developing this discipline, Whitehead does not bifurcate between the processes of nature and processes of mind (awareness), that emerge in cosmic process. He, therefore, cancels all dualist modes that had become dominant since Descartes. He draws attention to the complex processes that are involved in an apparently simple perceptual act. Behind the presented universe (presentational immediacy in Whitehead's phrase), there is a basic non-sensuous cosmic-causal process (causal efficacy). Hence a simple and positive analysis of the presented universe is discouraged by Whitehead. His is a symbolic analysis of the positivist analytic-synthetic scheme of the Hegelian or pre-Hegelian philosophical deliberations. His philosophic method is symbolical understanding of the general ideas and mingling of logical processes, and her eshapes the philosophical traditions by his four principal interpretative schemes, which are spatio-temporal processes, eternal objects, God and Creativity. Each of the principles is many-dimensional and not conceived from a linear mode. The spatio-temporal process is not a restricted process fostering a specific hypothesis; it is a general idea or an experiential process inextricably associated with the eternal objects as signifying possibilities. The two orders, cosmic and psychic in togetherness, in turn, can be understood from another cosmic-psychic possibility, which is Creativity. If the preceding stages from spatio-temporality to God are in any sense restricted, the Creativity belongs to an unrestricted order to account for a further order of process in different dimensions. All these principles, being note xclusively conceptual or empirical, are both formal and non-formal; they are only symbolical approaches to the understanding of many-dimensional experiential processes. It is natural, therefore, that Whitehead is critical of the medieval scholastic Christian theological belief in God as a final principle, and of the Absolute of the modern thinkers to the stage of Hegal. To Whitehead, there is no such thing or situation as "simply located" or as an ultimate. Each presented situation is dual. It is a background and possibility. It is perishing in one aspect and persistent in another; it is immanent yet transcendent, immediate yet ultimate—a "both and." It is for this reason, none of the principles of Whitehead, is ultimate or one, there is an 'other' in each. In other words, he advocates a "process-philosophy" akin to the Chinese or the Indians, abandoning the "fact philosophy" or entity consciousness of the Europeans or West Asians[4]. Whitehead, therefore, has no difficulty in utilizing the four abovementioned cosmic-psychic principles as varied grounds for elaborating multi-dimensional cosmic-psychic pursuits of truth, beauty, art, adventure and peace. In developing his final pursuit to *peace* beyond other pursuits, in many-dimensional spheres, Whitehead's language is meditatively oriented in a deep Buddhist sense. He says: "As soon as high consciousness is reached, the enjoyment of existence is entwined with pain, frustration, loss, tragedy. Amid the passing of so much beauty, so much heroism, so much daring, peace is then the intuition of permanence. It keeps vivid the sensitiveness to the tragedy.. each tragedy is the disclosure of an ideal—what might have been, and was not; what can be...." (*Adventures of Ideas*, p. 286). Whitehead's language in this context of *peace* is not "a superficial play of discursive ideas," but a deep metaphysical insight in the feeling-aspect, expressing a "motive interest of the spirit," in its project towards a "unity of adventure" and a "world loyalty" (Ibid, p. 295-6).

In this paper Whitehead's attitudinal trends are intepreted in terms of general ideas, in cosmic-psychic, meditative-intellectual spheres, and it can be seen that Whitehead's broad generalization is as comprehensive as Aurobindo's[5]. Both Aurobindo and Whitehead wrote volumes to give expression to their general and symbolical ideas. Without going into confusing details, this paper attempts to show that both these thinkers had intuitive insights to see the complexity involved in an experiential situation in its various dimensions, and in its involutions and evolutions. As any theory restricts this protean involvement of a presented situation, Aurobindo and Whitehead look for "general ideas" to give expression to an integral vision. Each is rooted in his respective cultural background, yet a deeper investigation shows their close affinity. Each furnishes a hope for spiritual evolution of a living and changing personality.

California State University
Hayward. (U.S.A.)

SELECT REFERENCES

* 1872-1950
* 1869-1947

(1) Sri Aurobindo Ashrama, Pandicherry, India, First Edition 1955; India Library Society, N. Y. 1965, Third Edition; Specially Chpts. II-III (The Two Negations), Chpts. IX-XII (On Transcendent Triads: Existence-Consciousness-Bliss), Chpts. XIV-XVIII and XXVII-XXVIII (For Supermind), Chpt. XXVIII (For Overmind) and Chpts. XXVII-XXVII-XXVIII (For The Gnostic Being and The Life Divine).

(2) The Macmillian and Co., 1933, The Free Press, N. Y. 1967 (Paperback Edition), chiefly Parts III-IV.

(3) For details of Indian Philosophy, vide S. Radhakrishnan : *Indian Philosophy* in two volumes, George Allen and Unwin, London, 1923 (First Edition); Humanities Press, N. Y. 1969, and also: S. Radhakrishnan and C. Moore: *A Source Book in Indian Philosophy*, Princeton University Press, Princeton, New Jersey, 1967 (Sixth Printing).

(4) Whitehead: *Process and Reality*, The MacMillan Co. 1929, The Free Press, N. Y. 1969 (Paperback Edition), Chiefly Preface, Chpt. I., Part V, Chpt II (God And The World)

(5) For details about Whitehead's philosophy, vide the present writer's *Whitehead's Four Principles From West-East Perspectives* (Bharati Bhawan, Patna, India, 1974 and *An Outline of Whitehead's Philosophy* (Arthur H. Stockwell Ltd., London, 1940).

LANGUAGE, THOUGHT, REALITY

Thomas J. Sheehan

(*I*) The very nature of this congress, entitled "Indian World Philosophy Conference," prompts two introductory questions: (1) Is it possible to speak of a "world dialogue" that is not merely a Westernizing monologue? (2) Can such a world dialogue be properly speaking "philosophical?"

First question: In 1935 Edmund Husserl[1] spoke of Europe in its spiritual-intellectual form as the teleological goal of all mankind. He said: "Whereas we (Europeans), if we understand ourselves properly, would never Indianize ourselves, "there is in us" something unique..that is recognized in us by all other human groups" and which "becomes a motive for them to Europeanize themselves...." On that basis it would seem that a *dialogue* between Western and Eastern traditions would not be possible—rather, only a Europeanizing monologue. But if we seek a *world* dialogue in which the participants retain the uniqueness of their traditions and the outcome is not apriori determined, then we must ask what this element of "world" is. I take it that the word "world" in the title of this conference does not stand for a "given" (*gegeben*) already achieved but for a task yet to be accomplished (=*aufgegeben*). By "world" we do not mean the simple collection of all peoples or nations or even all philosophical traditions, but rather the unifying horizon that *could* bring us together and *could* hold us in a community of discourse and action—presumably a world that is not yet actualized and that we are here to seek. Is this unifying horizon best expressed as "the infinite goals of reason" and the "purely theoretical attitude" that Husserl finds articulated in science and philosophy as "unconditioned truth"? Is the unifying principle of a possible world dialogue

---

1. Cf. *Die Krisis der europaische Wissenschaften...*, S. 314 et seq.

the extension *of the European teleology* of "reason" to all peoples ? If so, it seems that we cannot speak of a "world dialogue" between East and West, but only of some form of a vehicle for Europeanization of the world, indeed, some form of Western "intellectual imperialism."

Second question : But if a real "world dialogue" is possible, can its focus be, properly speaking, "philosophical" ? There are two problems here, one dealing with the *nature* of philosophy, the other with its *present situation*.

(1) From the outset, by the choice of this word "philosophy," the focus would seem to be oriented to Western models. "Philosophy" (*philosophia*) has its home in the West, in Greece, and it developes under properly Western conditions through the Middle Ages into modern and postmodern times. To say this, however, is not to deny that India and China and Japan have indeed developed parallel spiritual efforts at comprehending the nature of all-encompassing reality. However, my remarks mean to emphasize that the bases as well as the goals of these two traditions, East and West, may well be radically different, that therefore we must not presume from the beginning that Western *philosophia* and Eastern wisdom are the same, (any more than we can unquestioningly accept in the West the medieval synthesis of Greek *philosophia* and Judeo-Christian faith). What then is "Eastern philosophy" ?

(2) A further complication lies in the fact that Western philosophy in the present situation seems to be at its *end*, whether one takes that in a Comtean sense (the full development of the positive sciences from out of and beyond philosophy) or the Marxist sense (Thesis XIII against Feuerbach) or the Heideggerian sense (the end of metaphysics, the task of *der andere Anfang*). If it is true that more and more the positive sciences or the all-encompassing union of theory and practice are becoming the heirs of what once was the domain of philosophy in the West, then it is incumbent upon participants in a "world philosophy conference" to ask *what was* the philosophy that has come to its end and *what might philosophy be* if it it were to learn from Eastern thought and to serve as a focus for a world dialogue. Is it the epistemological grounding of the positive sciences, a theory of science ? or the logical analysis of language ? or the

rational grounding for natural theologies? or historical materialism? What then is Western philosophy?

In summary: If there is to be a world philosophical dialogue, then all parties must stand firmly within their own traditions (East *as* East, West *as* West) and resist the facile and superficial syntheses offered by Europeanization on the one hand and Western pop-culture's "turn to the East" on the other. Further and most important: As one stands within one's own tradition, one must raise anew and radically the question: What is "philosophy"?

(*II.*) In approaching the above question from within the Western tradition, I begin with a thesis (which I can only *state* here): The West is dominated by its Greek origins even when it would deny them. We might speak of a philosophical analogue to what Freud called "the slow return of the repressed." Both the theologized philosophy of the Middle Ages and the various anthropological and transcendental turns of modern and post-modern philosophy are dominated by the Greek philosophy that, in one way or another, they deny. (Christianity: philosophia *ancilla* fidei: Marx: "Die Philosophen haben die Welt nur verschieden *interpretiert*...."; Nietzsche: transvaluation of Platonism). To recognize this fact is to see the direction of an answer to the question "What is 'philosophy'?" as lying in a *recollection* of that "repressed content" (Greek philosophy) that continues to function in, indeed to drive, modern philosophy and anti-philosophy. In what follows I will make an attempt at such a recollection under the rubric "Language, Thought, Reality" by interpreting these three words in the original Greek. Obviously what is at stake here is not romantic antiquarianism or Hellenic philology, but a search for the West *as West* in the interest of asking about the possibility of a world philosophical dialogue.

The three words, "language, thought, reality" name all that is essential at the basis of Western thought. If we translate them back into Greek, we have: language—logos, thought—nous, and reality=? The problem of finding a Greek word for "reality" is not accidental, but rather summarizes the whole problem inherent in the development of Western philosophy. It becomes the crucial question for the following remarks.

(i) *Reality* : The linguistic ambivalence of this word in English can serve as a fruitful entry into the problem. The English "reality" contains two meanings : (1) *that which* is real (*id quod est reale*) and (2) *that whereby* something is real (*id quo aliquid est reale*). (We dispense with the Latin distinction between *realitas* and *actualitas* insofar as this distinction between *essentia* and *existentia* is a *derivative* problem vis-à-vis Greek ontology). In the second instance, reality means "realness"—the norm or criterion whereby something is taken as real or rejected as unreal, that is : the state or condition that accounts for a real thing *as* real. If we translate this problematic into Greek, it becomes the question of (*ousia*), the "beingness" that characterizes a being as a being. The distinction between *a real being* and *that whereby it is real* (=realness) is absolutely crucial to the Western philosophical project. If philosophy has any birthright, it consists in man's need to raise ever anew the question about the realness of the real. The urgency of this question as well as the precise focus of it becomes clear as soon as one notices the *fundamental changes* that the concept of realness undergoes in the history of the West. Each change effects fundamental changes in what man takes for real beings Philosophy's mandate is to make realness questionable in its very meaning. In order to raise anew the question "What is the sense or meaning of realness as such?" I will take the word "reality" in the phrase "language, thought, reality" and make it into a heuristic divice, naming the "unknown X" in the following sentences : "Reality is that which thought thinks when it thinks philosophically. Reality is that which language speaks when it speaks philosophically." Not only does this make reality questionable again, it also points to the horizon (language, thought) within which alone the question might be answered.

(ii) *Nous/noein* : One of the earliest appearances of the word "noein" in Western philosophical discourse occurs in Parmenides' Fragment 3. Here the concept "reality" is decisively raised as a question, not only because we are at astounded what this "sameness" might be between Being and thinking, but especially the question as to *what* reality is is to be worked out in conjunction with the question of human perception in the broadest sense ("noein"). In this turn to "noein" is born that unique form of spirituality called philosophy, whose subjectmatter is this unique correlation between realness and thinking. The very essence of thinking consists in the fact that *only* in thinking does realness appear. This is *not* to say that without thinking there are no things, rather it says that the *question* of what it is that makes up the *realness* of what is real occurs only with the essence of man as "noein". With the emergence of "noein" there appears for the first time the question of the *meaning* of what there is. With man comes the possible question, "Is this real ? If so, by what criterion ?" With man there appears the event of $KPI\Im IS$, $KPIVEIV$ the fundamental distinction between the real and the unreal on the basis of the distinction between things and their realness. Realness and thinking are "the same"—i.e., belong together—in the sense that realness as an issue appears only when "noein" appears.

We have moved from "reality" back to the arena where alone the meaning of reality can be raised as a question : "noein". In turn, the meaning of "noein" can be clarified by moving back to the third word in the triad : "logos/legein."

(*iii*) *Legein* : The experience of "logos" was so preeminently a part of Greek life that they defined the essence of human nature in terms of "logos" : man is the living being that has "logos". The Latin translation of the Greek phrase as *homo animal rationale*, "man, the rational animal" stands at some remove from the original Greek meaning. In early Greek (e.g., Homer) the word $\Upsilon E \mathcal{J} EIV$ means "to collect," "to gather"—but not just "to bunch together" but rather to collect in such a way that the *collecta* are related to each other, distinguished and articulated. Hence "legein" indicates a collecting that, by relating the collected to each other, reveals them, brings them to meaning. Although of itself this shows no relation to "speech" or "reason", when the word "logos" came to mean "discourse" or "talk" it was this element of collection-revelation that persisted as the meaning of "logos" the living being that has speech, i.e., that collects the beings of the world into a *unity of sense* whereby they are *revealed* as what they are. This *bringing to sense* is simultaneously a bringing *out of un-sense*, metaphorically, a bringing out of "unseenness" into "sight" :

aletheia. The essence of "logos" is to bring beings out into revealedness ("aletheia") and that means: into availability to man. With "aletheia" we meet *the* fundamental notion that underlies the whole problematic of Western philosophy. "Aletheia" as the revealedness of beings to man *is definitive for "ousia" as the realness of the real*. The changing modes of revealedness determine the changing modes of availability of beings to man. Philosophy in all its systematic transformations in the West is grounded in the question, "Is this real ? If so, in terms of what criterion ?" Philosophy is the question of the real *as real*, i.e., the real in terms of its realness, and the history of philosophy is the history of the transformations of the criterion whereby things are adjudged real or not. Each such transformation has made beings available (revealed) to man in different ways, thereby bringing about different "worlds of meaning" or "epochs." If today one speaks of the "end" of philosophy, it is presumably in the sense of the *fulfillment* of philosophy. That is, the question about the criterion that decides what beings are real has presumptively been decided "once for all" : The realness of beings is their *complete availability to man*. In today's "technological" world, which functions under the rubric of "the humanization of nature", nature as the totality of what is has become raw material available to be appropriated and dominated by man for his project of the rationalization of nature. Thereupon enter the positive sciences and their attendant techniques for the domination of the real. If philosophy has any role left, it is that of epistemological reflection on the sciences or the theoretical justification of human praxis.

(*III*) We have attempted to answer the question "What is philosophy ?" by reading "language, thought, reality" in the original Greek sense of philosophical problematic. What have we gained thereby for answering the question, "Is a world philosophical dialogue possible ?"

Can a "fulfilled" Western philosophy, as we have described it' serve as the focus for a world philosophical dialogue that would resist "Europeanization" and preserve its nature as pluralistic? To me, it seems not. But at the point where Western philosophy reaches its end, i.e, fulfillment in the complete availability of the real, a new insight becomes possible for the first time. In all the transformations in the criterion for deciding what is real, the focus has always been on the meaning and availability *of the real*. It has not been on the meaning of *realness as such*, that is, apart from the various forms it takes. If indeed one wants to think a *post*-philosophical thought that is more than just the *last stage* of philosophy (= technology), then one must ask *beyond* and *behind* realness as complete availability, one must ask "Why (i.e., how, whence, in terms of what) is realness at all?" To ask this question is to have stepped *out* of Western philosophy and to inquire into the unity that governs all the transformations that have made the epochs of meaning of Western history. This would mean asking : If realness and revealedness (*ousia, aletheia*) are what possibilize beings as beings, what possibilizes realness and revealedness ? If "logos" is the act of bringing out of un-sense to sense, what of this un-sense to which "logos" is related but over which it does not dispose ? To be sure, this un-sense concerns man, yet without entering the framework of "complete availability." Hence it stands beyond the last stage of Western philosophy with its "imperialistic" tendencies of rationalization; perhaps it even ccmes from earlier than the first stages of Western thought among the Greeks.

I suggest that *if* we would seek to dialogue across East-West lines without predetermining that the unifying horizon of our discussion be that particular form of spirituality called Western reason, *then* we should take as our unifying horizon the *question* that Western philosophy has never raised, much less answered : the question is not about the real as real, but about *realness itself as such*.

Loyala University of
Chicago at Rome,
Rome (Itala)

REFLECTIVE INQUIRY AND LANGUAGE

Lewis E. Hahn

For the contextualist language is critically important in our thinking and our interactions with our world, and nowhere is this fact more evident than in problem solving activity. If we think of reflective inquiry as problem solving, language plays a focal role for human problem solvers throughout this process: and the more difficult the problem, the more important is the role of language. The pattern for this activity as outlined in Dewey's analysis of reflective thinking starts with the appearance of a problem, moves through observation and analysis to clarify and define it, sets forth ways of solving the problem, develops deductively the implications of the proposed solutions, and finally tries out the more promising hypotheses.

In a problematic situation we need to formulate the precise nature of the problem or difficulty, the possible solutions for it, and the consequences of one proposed hypothesis as contrasted with those of another. Through language we can anticipate possible dangers and formulate ways of dealing with them before they are physically present. Knowing what will probably occur if steps are not taken to prevent a specified eventuality, we can change or avoid a possible occurrence. Language thus makes possible prediction and control.

Language is a primary means of making inferences—of using knowledge we already have to gain further knowledge. Because we can formulate alternative sets of consequences, we can weigh them critically and act on the basis of considered consequences instead of having to respond in unreflective haste. In effect an experiment in terms of ideas may guide our conduct, obviate certain risks of overt experimentation, and enable us finally to try out only the more promising possible courses of action.

Language makes possible distinguishing between legitimate and illegitimate inferences and, further stating the principles which must be observed if thinking is to achieve trustworthy conclusions. Determining the implications of a proposition, passing from the truth of one statement to the truth or falsity of another, ascertaining whether two statements say the same thing, are consistent, contradict one another, or what, and the like all depend on language. And these logical operations are crucially important for problem solving.

Verification of a state of affairs is also dependent on language. What we verify is whether or not a given statement accurately describes a situation. In looking to experience to check on the truth or falsity of a specific descriptive statement, we look to experience as modified, formed, or constituted by prior linguistic conditioning.

What we perceive is linguistically conditioned in a host of ways, as an example or so may readily show. Although words may function in other ways than to refer to things (for example, connectives) and the fact that we have a word which appears to refer to something does not mean that there is always a corresponding thing, nonetheless it is true that our range of sensory discriminations is greater in areas in which we have a richer vocabulary. For example, we tend to make far more discriminations in colors than in feelings, moods, or emotions, and it would appear to be no accident that our color vocabulary is far more extensive than our set of words for feelings or emotions. Although we have hundreds of terms for colors, the best we can do in referring to some feelings is to speak of the mood or feeling evoked by this or that piano piece of Chopin. Within a given area such as color, moreover, those whose working vocabulary is slight are likely to make fewer discriminations than those with a richer vocabulary. The kinds of distinctions made in field after field seem to be correlated with our linguistic facility or range.

We confidently expect that what we see, hear, and do will be affected by directives to watch or listen for this, that, or the other: and from earliest childhood words help form our patterns of expectation and observation.

Presupposed in all we have said about language as an instrument for problem solving is the notion that language is a social product. It is communication through the use of symbols; and ideas or meanings, conceptions and theories thinking and knowing, depend on it. It occurs in a culture, and a basic part of our acculturation depends on language. Our language, of course, antedates any given speaker. We learn to speak and think in terms of the social structure of our language. Fluency in our mother tongue makes us members of a linguistic community, a membership we retain in significant measure even if geographically separated from other members of our community. As members of a linguistic community we are pervasively influenced by our language and culture and are not solitary, self-sufficient egos possessed of an antecedent stock of ideas which we have only to name or articulate.

On this view as developed by Mead, Dewey, and Royce we do not first think out ideas and put them in words. The relation between language and thinking is far more intimate than that. Reflection is not a prior condition of communication but a concomitant of it, indeed, a form of it. It is a kind of converse in which, through a process of role-taking, questions are posed and responses made, now in one role, then in another, and so on.

In terms of this general outlook we may escape certain of the difficulties which have beset modern Western Philosophy since Descartes and Locke : difficulties of how to get beyond a solitary thinker and his ideas to a real external world. This view reverses the procedure which professed to discover an indubitably existing ego or mind at the center of the universe and then struggled to reach an external world of other persons and things. For G. H. Mead we distinguish between myself and others in a social matrix; and the distinction may be drawn some-what differently, depending on the problem; but in any event, the others are not simply derivative and my self primary.

If, in accordance with one later version of the Cartesian problem, everything I find and anything I think of turns out to be by that very fact one of my ideas, what, then, the new view of Mead and Dewey ? In terms of it what is one to say of the central ego ? Perhaps first we should note that this problem does not arise on their view. From their outlook it seems clear that this ego, once posited, no matter how isolated it is geographically from its neighbours, is a social one. Its deliberations are formulated in language. The social structure of language, moreover, as a Cassirer or Heidegger might readily show, carries with it something of the culture which gave rise to it. And the allegedly solitary thinker or ego raises his questions in a highly social context. Without language they could not be raised at all.

That we interact with our environment and solve a never ending succession of problems and that language helps us find our way about in our world, all this seems clear enough; but if we raise questions concerning language and the structure of thinking and ones concerning language and reality or the extralinguistic setting of reflective inquiry two important limitations of our thinking become evident : (1) All of the thinking with which we are concerned in problem solving is expressed in language, and there is always the possibility that our thinking may be influenced by the symbols in which it is expressed. We may mistake accidents of grammar for logical inference, or we may call a thing or group names instead of merely using symbols to describe it. We may think that because we have a name (say, "chance") there must be an objective referent for it. (2) Our thinking about a problem is always conditioned by beliefs and systems of interpretation—social, psychologial, linguistic, etc.—already accepted. And we may be more concerned to make the system look good than to get at the relevant facts. These limitations correspond roughly to Bacon's Idols of the Market Place (or Forum) and Idols of the Theatre.

Various philosophers apparently have thought that we could overcome these limitations to a degree by setting up a kind of dialogue with nature or by discerning in nature the same logical forms to be found in language. Bacon spoke of putting questions to nature instead of simply waiting to observe what happens. Heidegger, Merleau-Ponty, and others have sought through an interrogation of being to allow the basic facts to show themselves forth. And the Wittgenstein of the *Tractatus* attempted to exhibit the logical syntax or grammar of the universe.

For various problems distinguishing between language and thought, thought and reality, language and reality, may be both necessary and proper; but a comparison between language and the extralinguistic involves greater complications than may at first appear. If we try to make a sharp separation between language and its referents, we find ourselves using language to formulate the distinction. To talk about the extralinguistic we must begin with language, and there is the possibility that the structure of these referents is imposed by our manner of speaking.

Many contemporary philosophers are convinced that the classic accounts of the nature of reality in certain important respects tell us more about the structure of our language than about the structure of the world. What Aristotle spoke of as laws of being and the Neo-Hegelians treated as laws of thought, they argue may be more properly viewed as rules of language. In speaking of the structure of language and the structure of the world, however, it may be well to remember that it is not as if we could set side by side language and the extra-linguistic real world utterly free from prior linguistic conditioning and to a point by point comparison. Whatever we may hold, concerning the extralinguistic will be expressed in sentences. The structure of our language, moreover, may be due at least as much to the requirements of our inference-making process as to the antecedent structure of the extralinguistic.

Language, it seems safe to say, provides an important part of the structure of our thinking; and much of what we see or experience comes to us in terms of the structure of our language. Perhaps the best evidence we have of the usefulness or adequacy of our language in dealing with our world may come from our continued success in solving problems.

Southern Illinois University
at Carbondale,
U.S.A.

THE UNCONVENTIONAL CHARACTER OF MYTHICAL-SYMBOLIC LANGUAGE

Caterina N. Conio

The founder of the modern philosophy of language is rightly considered the Italian philosopher Giambattista Vico,[1] both for what he wrote about the origin of language and about myth as an original expression of human consciousness. In the second book of *La scienza nuova*[2] Vico tells how he supposes language and letters (i.e. written language) were born out of the necessity of communicating among men and between different nations. Language is thus considered a natural and spontaneous effort of mankind meant to establish links and develop trade. But the practical purpose of language does not, of course, exhaust its meaning and its value. Poetical language constitutes a particular and unconventional aspect of human culture and arises out of human spirit in a supra-historical sphere, in "a process", as E. Cassirer pointed out, which consciousness can perhaps resist at certain moments, but which, as a whole, it cannot impede, much less annul".[3]

The language of mythology, as Romantic German Philosophy and particularly W.F. Schelling demonstrated,[4] has a distinctive reality of its own both subjectively and objectively insofar as it overcomes the dicothomy of epistemological dualism.

Mythical language is highly symbolic and distinguishes itself from other sorts of symbols, or signs, such as those which are employed in science or in figurative arts. It is therefore necessary to make a distinction between various sorts of symbols without

---

1. The pioneering achievement of G.B. Vico (1688-1744) was recognised by many contemporary philosophers, as for ex., E Cassirer in his book *The Philosophy of Symbolic Forms* (New Haven 1955) vol. II, Introduction pp. 3 ff.
2. *La scienza nuova seconda* (ed. 1744) Bari, Laterza, 1967 (3 ed).
3. E. Cassire, op, cit. vol. II p. 6.
4. F.W. Schelling, *Einleitung in die Philosophie der Mythologie* (ed. Schroeter) *Werke*, Vol. VI, Muenchen, 1928.

forgetting that some of them have a polivalency and a richness liable to undergo different interpretations.

The mythical world discloses in fact a lot of relationships which, however, are not reducible either to the laws of pure reason or to historical and empirical categories, but have, on the contrary a structural form of our independent character.

Among the many symbols of mythical language we would choose today some of a particularly significant kind and of a most spontaneous nature. Let us recall, for example, what Plato said about divination and *enigma*, in *Timaeus*[5] "It belongs to a man when in his right mind to recollect and ponder both the things spoken in dream or waking vision by the divining and inspired nature, and all the visionary forms that were seen, and by means of reasoning to discern about them all wherein they are significant and for whom they portend evil or good in the future, the past or the present"....It seems therefore that there is need of interpreters of those mysterious voices called *enigmas*, as well as of any sort of myths. What Plato wants to say here, and in various other famous passages of his Dialogues, is that the symbolic world of dreams, myths and "mysterious voices" is not in contrast with reason, but, on the contrary, stimulates reason to find out suitable interpretations.

Enigma means a sort of puzzle, and sometimes, a word or a group of words having no meaning in ordinary language, and therefore totally unconventional. Why then should such words be interpreted at all and not dismissed as meaningless? Before answering this question, let us proceed a little further. If I am allowed to use a parallel, I would recall what in Indian tradition is called a *mantra*, and particularly those *mantras* used in Āgamic or Tantric texts denoting a totality, the divine world, creation and so on. Syllables like *Omkāra* or *mantras* like Sauḥ, Hrīm etc[6] assume a *definite* meaning only if they are interpreted by *gurus* of the particular schools they belong to, and in that case they constitute clear examples of metaphysical insight.

It may thus be said that what is a puzzle for ordinary man and what is intuited by inspired people needs to be interpreted,

---

5. *Timaeus* 71 C and 72 A.
6. See for instance, *Tantrāloka* of Abhinavagupta, Chapter XXX

but not by anybody: the interpreter must be a reasonable man
who is endowed with a particular insight and has undergone
a special initiation. For, a *mantra* and an *enigma* (in the Platonic sense)—and we may also speak of other symbols and
myths—belong to a field which surpasses the ordinary needs
for communication. But, it may be argued how can such
words denoting metaphysical reality, or referring to meanings
not immediately graspable given a *reliable* significance? If
it is not mere reason which has to decide about their meaning,
what is the criterion of judgment? Religious tradition both in
the West (Greece, and, later on, Christianity) and in the East
has its own interpreters of what is called "revealed language",
or "inspired Word" and it is precisely within this realm that the
hermeneutic work takes place : a work which demands not only
a long training and special insight, but also a continuous
rethinking of human problems as well as a connection with
philosophical inquiry.

Philosophy, it may be said, springs from the "enigmatic"
world of myto-poetical language, and although it deals with
questions and problems of different kinds (such as methodological problems of scientific language, of ethics and politics),
it also has to keep on striving with the hermeneutic of religious
language.

The symbolic language of mythological consciousness
expresses precisely the most profound concern of philosophy
and is its *primary language*, a sort of monologue in a kind of dialogue of universal consciousness with itself and within itself,
meant to comprehend and illuminate its own depths, dissipating
the darkness of unconsciousness.

But one more important question, at this point, may be
raised about the meaning of myto-political language, and about
enigmas : why is such a mythical language, arising within what
we have called a universal consciousness, so mysterious and not
so easily understandable? The answer to this question may,
of course, be different according to the different traditions :
Indian tradition will introduce the concept of avidyā, or māyā
or some other category as cause of "obscuration" and delusion;
whereas Christian tradition will speak of "original sin" and
its consequences for mankind. In another way, analytical
psychology would say that only gradually will the limited

human consciousness "rescue" its unity and its universality, and precisely for this purpose it will need again and again to be guided on the long path of interiority by those who are enlightened.

2. A further problem regards the internal differences between the various symbols of mythical lanugage, insofar as we cannot straightaway equate those words which somehow have a meaning understandable by everybody (although with different shades of meaning, like: God, or Brahman, or Paradise, Brahmaloka, Walhalla and so on) and words of oracles, or *mantras* which, immediately and without explanation, do not convey any meaning. The difference is, in my opinion, less important than we may think, because what is relevant here is not how familiar or unfamiliar a word may be, or how many people understand it, but the fact that such a word is not related to ordinary or material life, and is not meant only for communication, but deals with a reality whose existence and significance have to be discovered by inner experience. One would perhaps object that such an experience has first to be had at least by those people who have taught mythical language. In fact the ṛṣi, or prophets, or authors of religious poems did have this experience, which, in any case, is *not merely private*, but belongs to mankind at large insofar as it can be taught to anybody who wants to hear about and learn it, and what truth can be "proved" or "verified" through the latter's personal experience itself, although not in the same degree or in the same way and at the same time by everybody.

Mythical language deals therefore with *truth*, even if this truth, when formulated in philosophical or theological categories, may appear differently articulated and, sometimes, inexplicably paradoxical. But a plurality of philosophies should not disconcert and make people doubtful or sceptical. We all know how reason can be entangled in logical fallacies, in new problems arising out of old knowledge. The human mind will always have to overcome obstacles, or *problemata* (which in Greek means, originally, obstacles). Only myth seems to give a certain peace to consciousness, a sort of shelter, as it were, a motherly womb, a point of reference. In fact myth, properly understood, (i.e. not as mere fancy, or arbitrary invention of a foolish mind) is a source of peace and delight, and, on the other hand, a stimulating force promoting human philosophising.

Let us take again, for example, the symbol of Oṃkāra. How can it become meaningful for universal philosophy and universal consciousness? No doubt this syllable *stands for* an intuition, a revelation and means the primary Word, vāk, out of which any other word and meaning, and therefore, any *being*, has come. This primary Word equates *sound*, *meaning* and *reality*, without any gap and need of any bridge. It is the intuition of absolute consciousness. But this word demands to be further analyzed and qualified in its articulations. Therefore Indian tradition has speculated on Oṁkāra and keeps on meditating on it, guided by many useful philosophical treatises.

And what is unconventional about this word? Indian tradition would answer that it is not humanly invented, but that it is a divine word heard by ṛṣis. It is a word which cannot be translated. At most, it would find its counterpart in other religious traditions, in revealed divine names (as for example, *mutatis mutandis*, the divine tetralem of Jewish tradition) or could be equated with visual symbols of the absolute which we find in art and which recur in spontaneous symbolisation, in unconscious drawing, in dreams etc. In this sense one would say that a word symbolising the abosolute is a sort of *natural* (i.e. neither conventional nor arbitrary) word: natural amounts to saying *connatural*, interchangeable with an exclamation of wonder and joy, with an intuition or a realization of God, in fulness of conscious knowledge. Such Word or symbol is thus immutable in meaning, although it may graphically and verbally variate. Being unconventional, this *mantra* could find equivalent words only if these are also *uncommon* symbols, rooted in "enigmatic" language and signifying the same transcendental experience.

3. What we have been saying up to now does not refer in any way to the origin of language as such in the onomatopoeic sense, as several scholars have suggested among whom our G. B. Vico. If we somehow accept his scheme of three sorts of languages—namely, language of the gods, language o heroes and language of men—it is only with reference, to (a) mythical-religious language (b) epic language (c) practical and scientific language. All the three are, each in its own way,

symbolical, as E. Cassirer pointed out, but to a different degree. As far as the first language is concerned, we think that it may rightly be called 'divine' not only because it regards the divine world, but because it expresses the starting-point and the end at which mankind aims: i.e. its cosmic integration or its 'divinization'.

Any sort of mythical language raises man above the common world. Heidegger would even say that any poetry reveals Being better, perhaps, than conceptual philosophy (at least traditional western philosophy). And we may agree with him in saying that the common significance of words assumes, in poetry, a stronger meaning, and becomes full of suggestions, of insight and musical power.[7] Paradoxically, even those who cannot understand each and every word of a poem can appreciate it musicality and have, sometimes, a sort of ecstatic feeling in which enthusiastic experience and religious sentiment are mingled together.

The contemporary concern with the formal aspects of language developed in the field of Linguistics seems to have diminished the particular significance of poetical and mythical language as a means of intuitive knowledge, of contemplation and even of mystical insight in Being. But since today the different branches of philosophy are linking hands, feeling the necessity of mutual help and understanding structural analysis in theoretical Linguistics is aiding also general philosophy with many interesting contributions *so that language*[8] be rightly considered, primarily, as an instrument of speculative thought.

The most recent development Semiotic has helped philosophy to overcome the old problems of idealism, realism or the so-called critical realism[9] by showing that existence

---

7. See, for instance *Unterwegs zur Sprache*, Guenther Verlag, 1959 where Heidegger criticises Aristotle's conception of language, and also the work of Wilhelm von Humboldt, developing the traditional idea of language. For Heidegger, language is essentially *Dichten, Denken* und *Denken*.

8. See, for instance L. Heilmann, *Corso di linguistica teorica*, Milano, 1971, p. 81, who points out the connotative process of language which cannot be formalised as scientific or ordinary language.

9. See, for instance L. Hielmslev, I *fondamenti della teoria del linguaggio*, (Italian translation of G C. Lepschy) Torino, Einaudi, 1968 and F. Rossi-Landi, *Semiotica e Ideologia* Milano, Bompiani, 1972, especially pp. 81 ff.

is relative to the linguistic universe in which it is predicated, and that this epistemological relation to reality belongs to each linguistic universe. Any inference regarding existence of non-perceived objects is grounded in language and in its significance. Word, as sign (or symbol), is in itself a synthesis of *signans* and *signatum*, as European Semiotic has already pointed out since Fernand De Sassure and, in a different way (more akin to idealism), Ernest Cassirer. Semiotic is a preparation to Logic—for which I mean inferential Logic—and Metaphysics which in its turn is grounded on Logic.

But, moreover, Semiotic has made a great contribution to aesthetics and to poetry—both in formal sense and in the pregnant allusive sense . This method is now applied, in Italy, to the teaching of poetry starting from primary schools.

Coming back to our main point, i.e. to mythical and poetical language , it is now easier to see how deeply this language penetrates the human mind, from childhood up to old age. The sensitiveness of children, of the so-called "primitive people" and of theologian poets (as G. B. Vico used to call those who first composed poetry) shows how art, religion and philosophy are linked together. Our G. B. Vico did not know, at his time, about the *Vedas*; had he known them he would have classed them among the most beautiful religious poems of the world. much less did he of course, know about Indian theories of language: namely the philosophy of language (such as Bhartṛhari's), Metaphysics and Mysticism of Language (such as that of Kashmiri Śaivism)—theories about which are so well-known in India, and from which Western Philosophy of language has much to learn. There is, anyhow, a point of convergence between G. B. Vico and Eastern Philosophy (or better Theology of Language) namely poetical Metaphysics or, conversely metaphysical Poetry. "Poetical wisdom is neither rational nor abstract, but strongly felt and imagined.[10] Such a poetry was conatural to the first men (but we know that according to Vico, human history is cyclical and "old times" or creative metaphysical Wisdom may recur again and again, after periods

---

10. "Adunque la sapienza poetica, che fu la prima sapienza della gentilita dovette incominciare da una metafisica, non ragionata ed astratta qualee questa or degli addottrinati, ma sentita ed imaginata".; (*Scienza Nuova*, libro secondo, Sezione I, Cap. I.)

of decandence represented by social and intellectual disintegration). It was born out of wonder and astonishment and became the mother of philosophical thinking.

In our times, which seem to be, in many respects, a period of moral and also philosophical decadence (with some exceptions) at least in the West, intuition seems to diminish and creative religious poetry has almost totally disappeared. Now, what G. B. Vico said about the cyclic return—which does not mean absolute determinism in history but rather a cyclic return of attitudes —is true, we may expect a new "age of the gods", arising perhaps—as we do hope and believe—from a new encounter between East and West, with a new flowering of religious language, or, at least, to begin with, with a new revaluation of old wisdom books and mythological poetry.

We shall not have, obviously, to go back to the origins of mankind, because a return does not exclude progress and cannot be a mere repetition; on the contrary, science and philosophy will coexist with a renewal of poetry and religion, in the West as in the East, after demythologising only false myths—such as the myth of technological progress, utopical politics, racism and so on. The language of such ideologies resembles, but not quite, true mythological language, because it is a sort of borrowing from and transposing original myths—buried in the unconscious realm, and re-emerging in a sort of pathological way, which constitutes a danger for mankind. And we all know how difficult it is to get rid of such diseases...

The best therapy—if I am allowed to use such a word in a sense contrary to that of the therapeutic method of analytical philosophy—against the maladies of sceptical reason, false myths and so on, is a fresh usage of mythological language, knowing that, being symbolical, it contains in a "condensed" manner, so to say, highly metaphysical and theological truths. Such a language demands a new "innocence"—not a naiveness—but a *trust* both in intuition and in reason, in imagination and symbolic creativity: which is as G. B. Vico said, the only true "creation" allowed to man by the divine Providence.

Catholic University
Milan, Italy

STATEMENTS ABOUT THE FUTURE AND THE LAW OF EXCLUDED MIDDLE

D. Y. Deshpande

One of the problems which have come down to us from antiquity is the problem of future contingents, and it was first considered and dealt with by Aristotle in his treatise *De Interpretatione*, Chapter IX. Unfortunately Aristotle's solution of the problem is not as clear as one could wish, and scholars have been divided about the correct interpretation of it. I cannot claim to be an Aristotelian scholar, and so shall content myself with presenting some of the divergent views and suggesting some considerations which might help the discussion of the subject.

I

Aristotle raises the problem in the course of his treatment of contradictory pairs of statements. He introduces the idea of an *antiphasis*, which is a pair of propositions in which the same predicate is in one affirmed and in the other denied of the same subject, and goes on to say that given an antiphasis about the past or present, the affirmative proposition must be true or false, and similarly for the negative. But for what is singular and future it is not like this. He says: "For if all propositions, whether positive or negative, are either true or false, then if one man affirms that an event of a given character will take place and another denies it, it is plain that the statement of one of them will correspond with reality and that of the other will not."[1] But if this be so, then "nothing is or takes place fortuitously, either in the present or in the future, and there are no real alternatives; everything takes place of necessity and is fixed."[2] There would in that case be "no need to deliberate or to take trouble, on the supposition that if we should adopt a certain course, a certain result would follow, while, if we did not, the result would not follow"³ But "we see that both deliberation and action are causative with regard to the future, and that, to speak more generally, in those things which are not continuously actual there is a potentiality in either direction. Such things may either be or not be; events also therefore may either take place or not take place. ..It is therefore plain that it is not of necessity that everything is or takes place; but in some instances there are real alternatives, in which case the affirmation is no more true and no more false than the denial"

What is Aristotle's solution of the problem? To give the solution in his own words: "Now that which is must needs be when it is, and that which is not must needs not be when it is not. Yet it cannot be said without qualification that all existence and non-existence is the outcome of necessity. For there is a difference between saying that that which is, when it is, must needs be, and simply saying that all that is must needs be, and similarly in the case of that which is not....Everything must either be or not be, whether in the present or in the future, but it is not always possible to distinguish and state determinately which of these alternatives must necessarily come about.

"Let me illustrate. A sea-fight must either take place tomorrow or not, but it is not necessary that it should take place tomorrow, neither is it necessary that it should not take place, yet it is necessary that it either should or should not take place tomorrow. Since propositions correspond with facts, it is evident that when in future events there is a real alternative, and a potentiality in contrary directions the corresponding affirmation and denial have the same character."⁵,

II

Scholars differ in their interpretation of this passage. There are mainly two views. The first and the oldest view is that Aristotle held that propositions about future contingents are neither true nor false, and that the Law of Excluded Middle (LEM) does not apply to them. This view was supposed to be Aristotle's by the Stoics and the Epicureans alike in antiquity, and in recent times by J. Lukasiewicz and A. N. Prior who have developed a three-valued logic on its basis.

The medieval philosophers however understood Aristotle

to have held a different view. According to this interpretation Aristotle does not hold that future contingent propositions are neither true nor false. On the contrary he actually held that all propositions are either true or false (i.e. the LEM applies to all propositions without exception). But he draws a distinction between what Rescher describes as "collective necessitation" and "distributive necessitation",[6] and holds that whereas collective necessitation applies to all propositions (including future contingents), distributive necessitation does not apply to future contingents. This is the distinction between "N (p V-p)" and "Np V N-p" (where "N" represents "it is necessary that"). Aristotle's doctrine, according to this view, is not that future contingents lack a truth-status (true or false), but they lack a necessitation status (necessarily true or necessarily false), or as the medievals put it, that they are not determinately true or determinately false.

There can be little doubt that this second interpretation has much to be said in its favour, certainly much more than the first interpretation, for Aristotle certainly holds that "p V-p" is true of all propositions, i.e. that the LEM applies to all propositions including those about future contingents. Towards the close of chapter IX of *De Interpretatione* Aristotle says: "This is the case with regard to that which is not always existent or not always non-existent. One of the two propositions in such instances must be true and the other false, but we cannot say determinately that this or that is false, but must leave the alternative undecided."[7]

III

I shall now proceed to amplify and comment on the argument summarised above.

Aristotle obviously assumes the following division of propositions:
1. Non-temporal or timeless propositions: e.g. "Two and two are four".
2. Sempiternal or omnitemporal propositions: e.g. "The moon goes round the earth".
3. Tensed propositions of three kinds :

3a. About the past: e.g. "The Battle of Waterloo was fought in 1815".
3b. About the present: e.g. "A sea-battle is being fought today".
3c. About the future : e.g. "A sea-battle will be fought tomorrow".

Now Aristotle's problem concerns neither propositions of the first kind, nor those of the second kind. It is about one species of the third kind, viz 3c. In class 3, Aristotle finds a distinction between propositions about the past and the present on the one hand, and those about the future on the other. The distinction is simply that the former are necessary in some sense of the word "necessary", whereas the latter are not, in that sense, necessary, but contingent. It is clear that Aristotle uses the words "necessary" and "contingent" here in a sense which is distinct from the senses familiar to us. That he does not have *logical* necessity, in mind is clear from the fact that all tensed statements are logically contingent, whereas he holds that some tensed statements are necessary and some (i.e. those about the future) are contingent. Another sense of necessity familiar to us is *factual* or *causal* necessity. It is true that it is a debated question whether *all* events are causally determined. The determinists hold that all events are causally determined, while the indeterminists hold that some, viz men's volitions, are not causally determined. But whichever view we adopt on the question, there is no distinction between a past and a future event. If all events are causally determined, then not only past events, but future events also would be factually necessary. If, on the other hand, some events are not causally determined, then too not only future events, but past events also would be contingent. But Aristotle seems to hold that an event which is a future contingency becomes a past or a present necessity after it takes place. So it is clear that Aristotle does not have causal necessity in mind when he says that an event which takes place or has taken place is necessary, but an event which is future is contingent. It would appear that in calling what is or what has taken place "necessary" Aristotle has in mind merely the irrevocability or the unalterability of a past or a present event. A future event, since it has not yet happened, is not beyond recall, and may be called contingent.

Of course it is not enough for an event to be a future contingency that it be future; it is also required that it be contingent in the causal sense. A causally determined event is necessary (in the sense of being irrevocable) even when it is future. It is necessary, for example, that an eclipse of the sun will take place on a certain day, because it is causally determined. Thus Aristotle means by a future contingency an event which is not only (causally) contingent, but also future. Of a causally determined event it is necessary that it is going to take place; but of a causally contingent event it is necessary only that either it or its absence will take place, but it is not necessary that it will take place, nor necessary that it will not take place. But even such an event when it happens or has happened is necessary in a third sense, viz that of being irrevocable or beyond recall.

IV

Having made clear what Aristotle meant by a future contingent, we can now pass on to expound the further stages of his argument. He says that if the law that of two contradictory propositions one is true and the other false were to be held as applying universally, then we are caught in the meshes of determinism. If we suppose the above law to be applicable to singular statements relating to the future, then we are required to conclude that there is nothing contingent, everything happens of necessity. Let us take the following example: "There will be a sea-battle tomorrow," and let us suppose that this statement is either true, or if not true, then false. Now if the statement is true, then there is bound to be a sea-battle tomorrow; for if there is not, then the proposition would not be true. Again if the statement is false, then there cannot be a sea-battle tomorrow, again for the same reason. Thus if we hold, that a statement predicating something future about an individual must be either true or false, determinism seems inescapable.

Now Aristotle is convinced that everything does not take place of necessity, that deliberation and choice have causative force with regard to what is future. How then does he avoid the deterministic conclusion? On the one hand, he maintains that the LEM applies to future contingents no less than to past and present ones. On the other hand, he denies that the proposition "There will be a sea-battle tomorrow" is either (determinately) true or (determinately) false. This is possible only if the LEM is interpreted non-truth-functionally. The LEM on this interpretation says merely that if p is false then -p is true, and if -p is false then p is true, without implying that one of them is true and the other false. This would be an interpretation which allows us to maintain "Either p or -p" to be necessarily true, without our having to grant a determinate truth-value to either disjunct. And this is probably the view which Aristotle maintains in *De Interpretatione*.

V

I shall now pass on to the criticisms made of the position adopted by Aristotle.

First there is the criticism that it is meaningless to take up the position attributed to Aristotle in the last paragraph of the last section, viz that "Either p or -p" (non-truth-functional) may be true without "P V -p" (truth-functional) being true. It is held that "Either p or - p" is a truth-function which is true and that it is fantastic to suggest the contrary. Certainly the idea of a disjunction being true without either of its components being true seems bizarre. But if it is required by facts it must be accepted. After all not all logic is truth-functional. It is well-known that counterfactual conditionals cannot be dealt with in a truth-functional logic. And the same is true of modal logic. So there is no reason to suppose that the idea of a non-truth-functional Law of Excluded Middle is ruled out.

Another objection which has been widely levelled against Aristotle is that his conception of temporalised truth-values is opposed to the standard practice in modern logic. Aristotle's treatment requires that a proposition which is at first neither (determinately) true nor (determinately) false, later acquires a (determinate) truth-value. But this goes against the standard practice of treating truth or falsity as eternal or timeless. As Quine observes: "Logical analysis is facilitated by requiring that each statement be true once and for all and false once and for all".[8] But it may be objected that this timeless conception of truth might fit the timeless propositions and even the omnitemporal ones; but how will it fit propositions relating to past, present or future times? According to Quine "this can be effected by rendering verbs tenseless and then resorting to explicit chronological descriptions when need arises for distinctions of time. The sentence 'The Nazis will annex Bohemia', uttered as true on May 9, 1936, corresponds to the statement 'the Nazis annex (tense-less) Bohemia after May 9, 1936'; and this statement is true once and for all regardless of date of utterance."[9]

Quine in these observations is not dealing with Aristotle's problem. He is dealing with the distinction between a sentence (which is intrinsically neither true nor false) and a statement (which is definitely either true or false), and points out that owing to the presence of words like "I", "you", "here", "there", "now", "then" etc the same sentence when uttered by one person at one time in one context may express a true statement, whereas uttered by another person at another time in another context may express a false statement. Words like "I", "here", "now" have been called "ego-centric" by Russell, and he includes among them not only "past", "present" and "future", but tenses as well.[10] Now it is certainly proper to wish to reduce sentences which contain ego-centric words and which therefore cannot be said to have a definite truth-value to sentences which contain no such ambiguous words and which therefore have a definite truth value. However this transformation leaves Aristotle's problem untouched as I shall now proceed to show.

Aristotle's problem is not that there are sentences which when uttered in one situation make a true statement and when uttered in another situation make a false statement. It is that statements about the future do not seem to have any (determinate) truth value, whereas statements about the same events when they have happened acquire truth value. There is nothing ambiguous about the sentence "There will be a sea-battle tomorrow". It is true that this sentence might be uttered on different days to refer to different "tomorrows". So let us specify the day on which the statement is made. Let us say "There will be a sea-battle tomorrow, today being 20th June 1975". Now this is a perfectly unambiguous sentence and yet Aristotle would hold that it expresses nothing which is either (determinately) true or (determinately) false, because it is about a future contingent. It is true that Quine's recommended rendering of "There will be a sea-battle tomorrow" will be different. It will be "There is (tenseless) a sea-battle one day after 20th June 1975". But this leaves out an important part of the original statement, viz. that the battle in question is future, that the statement is a forecast. It is then clear that Quine's way of rendering a tensed statement is of no avail to meet Aristotle's problem.

VI

Of course Quine will dispute Aristotle's view that before an event takes place any statement about it has no determinate truth value. But what are the grounds on which Aristotle's claim is contested? We have already seen that Aristotle was driven to his conclusion by the realisation that if a singular statement about the future is supposed to be either (determinately) true or (determinately) false, then we cannot escape determinism. If in spite of this untoward conclusion, the hypothesis is to be maintained, there must be strong grounds in its support. What are these grounds?

Unfortunately, as far as I can see, there are hardly any grounds of any kind: there is only prejudice against taking time seriously. It is an old prejudice going back to the time when it was customary to regard time as unreal and an appearance. It is not of course customary now to regard time as an unreal appearance of a timeless reality; still the old prejudices die hard, and it appears today in the form of the view that past, present and future are subjective and only earlier and later are objective features of time. Objective time is regarded as consisting of an infinite series of events bearing to one another the relation of earlier than (or its converse later than), and distinctions of pastness, presentness and futurity are thought of as introduced by a thin field of presentness moving across events from earlier to later, giving us our experience of happening or becoming. What we call future is spread out endlessly ahead of the present, just as what is past is spread out beginninglessly behind the present. Since the mere fact that a past event is no longer happening does not imply that there is no past, or that the past is not real, so the mere fact that a future event has not yet happened does not imply that there is no future, or that the future is not real. Thus all events are all there, at once, so to speak, spread out like points of space, and related to one another by the timeless relations of earlier than, simultaneous with and later than. These relations are *timeless* because what is once earlier than (or simultaneous with or later than) something is so for ever. By contrast pastness, presentness and futurity are changing determinations: everything that is present was once future and will become past.

If, following C. D. Broad, we use the expression "A-characteristics" to stand for the determinations of pastness, presentness and futurity, and the expression "B-relations" for the relations of earlier than, simultaneous with and later than, the above theory can be briefly stated as one which holds B-relations to be objective features of time and A-characteristics to be subjective features which can be analysed in terms of B-relations. Russell who calls "past", "present" and "future" ego-centric words, suggests the following analysis of the notions for which those words stand. Taking "this" as the basic ego-centric word, he says that other ego-centric words can be defined in terms of it. "E is present" is to be analysed as "E is (tenseless) simultaneous with this", "E is past" as "E is (tenseless) earlier than this", and "E is future" as "E is (tenseless) later than this". "This" is, according to Russell a proper name for a sense-datum experienced by the speaker at the time of utterance. Thus A-characteristics can be eliminated with the help of B-relations.

But can they? I am afraid that an affirmative answer to this question is hasty and based on a superficial consideration of the subject. A second closer look reveals the fact that A-characteristics are not reducible to B-relations at all, and that on the contrary there can be no B-relations without A-characteristics. The subject is a large one and cannot be tackled here. I have dealt with it elsewhere and to these the reader is referred.[1] Here I shall content myself with a brief summary.

Let us examine briefly the reduction of A-characteristics to B-relations recommended by Russell. He says that "E is present" is reducible to "E is simultaneous with this" where "this" is a proper name for a sense-datum experienced by the speaker at the time he utters the sentence. But why should simultaneity with a sense-datum experienced by the speaker at the time of utterance make E present? Is it not because the sense-datum of which one is aware at any time is present absolutely and what is simultaneous with what is present, is also present? The sense-datum whose proper name is "this" is to be a sense-datum which is being experienced, not remembered or otherwise thought of, because though remembering and thinking, like perceiving, take place in the present, their objects, unlike those of perception, are not present. Otherwise a sense datum which one remembers could have done equally well. Presentness cannot be reduced to simultaneity a sense-datum which is being experienced, because the sense-datum which is being experienced is present at the time it is experinced absolutely and without being required to be simultaneous with another sense-datum which is experienced.

The fact of the matter is that (to put the matter dogmatically) to be present is merely to happen, or occur, or take place. To be past is to be no longer happening, and to be future is to be yet to happen. So far from A-characteristics being definable in terms of B-relations, the latter themselves require the former for their definition. Thus "A is earlier than B" simply means "When A is present B is future and when B is present A is past".

Not much should be made of the fact that B-relations hold timelessly. What is once earlier than anything, it is said, is for ever earlier. Certainly, but note the proviso: "What is once earlier. And how can anything be earlier than anything else until both events have happened, i.e. are present. Suppose A is earlier than B. Then this means that when A was present B was future, and when B was present A was past. Thus not until both A and B happen can one of them be earlier than the other. It is thus impossible for two events to be related by a B-relation wihout first acquiring A-characteristics. And therefore the picture of time as an infinity of events ranged as earlier and later, but without the characteristics of pastness, presentness or futurity is delusive.

I said above that there is hardly any reason except a prejudice in support of the picture of world drawn in terms of B-relations alone. Consider for example, what Russell says: "......let us observe that no ego-centric particulars occur in the language of physics. Physics views space-time impartially, as God might be supposed to view it; there is not, as in perception, a region which is specially warm and intimate and bright, surrounded in all directions by gradually growing darkness.. There can be no question that the non-mental world can be fully described without the use of ego-centric words."[11] Similar remarks can be quoted from a number of other writers. I have already argued that "past", "present" and "future" are not ego-centric words, nor are the determinations for which they stand in any way subjective. It seems to me perfectly obvious that even in a non-mental world events will go on happening: if so there would be past, present and future in such a world too.

It would then appear that Aristotle was quite justified in thinking that future contingents raised a problem for us, and his solution is still worth our consideration.

Vidarbha Mahavidyalaya
Amravati

1. Aristotle, *De Interpretatione*, Chapter IX 18a 34-39. Translated by E. M. Edghill, *YThe Works of Aristotle*, W. D. Ross, ed.
2. Op. Cit. 18a 5-8.
3. Op. Cit. 18b 32-35.
4. 19a 7-20.
5. Op, Cit. 19a 22-34.
6. Nicholas Rescher, "Truth and Necessity in Temporal Perspective" in *The Philosophy of Time*, ed. Richard M. Gale, Pp. 183-220.
7. Op. cit. 19a 35-39
8. *Elementary Logic*, P. 6
9. *Loc. cit.*
10. *An Inquiry into Meaning and Truth*, P. 102 (Pelican edition).
11. "Professor Ayer on the Past", *Mind*, Jan, 1956; "McTaggart on Time", *Journal of the Philosophical Association*, July. October 1955; "The Alleged Unreality of Time", *Proceedings of the Indian Philosophical Congress*, 1956.
12. *Loc. cit.*

TARKA AS CONTRAFACTUAL CONDITIONAL

V. K. Bharadwaja

Some recent logicians have identified the notion of *tarka* with either hypothetical argument[1] or reductio ad absurdum argument.[2] Outside the Hindu Nyāya, there are to be found at least two different conceptions of *tarka*. I mean the Jaina[3] and the Buddhist[4] conceptions. But I am not concerned with them here in this paper. Here I am concerned with a recent position[5] on the analysis of *tarka* which seeks to identify this notion with the notion of implication or more strictly with deducibility or entailment. The advocates of this position, in general, do not seem to make any differentiations between these notions of implication, deducibility, and entailment. However whenever they wish to delineate the structure of *tarka* they wish it to be so construed that it satisfies, at least intuitively at the truth-functional level, the rules of modus ponens (If p, then q, and p, therefore q), modus tollens (If p, then q, and not q, therefore not p), and contraposition $[(p \supset q) - (\sim q \supset \sim p)]$. To make their position clearer consider the following piece of inference as it is traditionally formulated :—

(A) (1) There is fire on the mountain
    (2) Because there is smoke on it
    (3) Where there is smoke there is fire as in the kitchen
    (4) There is smoke (caused by fire) on the mountain
    (5) Therefore, there is fire on the mountain.

In this inference, (1) is the thesis to be shown to be supported by the relevant evidence available in (2). But (2) cannot be said to be the evidence unless there is a covering law (3) applied to the case in question as it is done in (4). The covering law (3) is not acceptable to the Nyāya thinker unless there is available an observable instance of the causal relation expressed in the law. The interesting question whether a paradigm case must be produced in every case of inference remains a much disputed question.[6]

The theory of *tarka* I am considering identifies *tarka* with the form or structure of (3) in (A), construing (3) as a proposition of the 'If p, then q' form. My submission is that this construal of (3) is a mistake. (3) is an unrestricted empirical generalization, and its logical character cannot be correctly shown unless it is quantificationally analysed. A quantificational rendering of the proposition will be as follows:

At every place P if there is smoke at P, then there is fire at P. Abbreviating "x is smoke", by 'Sx', "x is fire", by 'Fx' and "x is at y" by "Axy", symbolically the proposition stands as follows:

$$(x) \{Px. [(\exists y) \ (Sy. \ Ayx) \supset (\exists z) \ (Fz. \ Azx)]\}.$$

Quantificationally analysed, as I have shown above, (3) which is a covering law presents a picture quite at variance with the one presented by the logicians who seek to render (3) truth-functionally. My analysis is further supported by the Sanskrit rendering[7] of (3) as *Yatra dhūmastatrāgniḥ*, where there is smoke there is fire, which is a statement of cause-effect relation between fire and smoke: or *Yatra vahnir-nāsti tetra dhūmopi nāsti* where there is no fire there is no smoke either which is a statement of the relation of nonexistence of fire with the nonexistence of smoke.

Besides the fact that the logicians have misconstrued a general proposition as a truth-functional one, they also have misidentified *tarka* which is of the form 'If such and such were not the case, then such and such would not have been the case,' *Yadi vahnir na syāttarhi dhūmo'pi na syāditi*, If there were no fire there would not have been smoke on the mountain, a contrafactual conditional with a generalized conditional which is of the form 'For all values of x, x is P and if there is y at P which is S then there is z at P which is F. *Yatra dhūmas-tatrāgnih*, Wherever there is smoke is fire there. It is an extremely difficult question whether it is possible to give an adequate analysis of the contrafactual conditionals in terms of generalized conditionals expressing cause-effect relations;[8] but this much at least is clear that in no case can the notion of a contrafactual be identified with the notion of a generalized conditional.

The Nyāya logician traditionally defines *tarka*[9] as *Vyāpyāropeṇa vyāpakāropas-tarkaḥ* and illustrates it by saying

Yadi vahnir na syāttarhi dhūmo'pi na syāditi.

To explain : Suppose the opponent does not accept the argument (A) above, and has doubt (saṃśaya) about the inference of there being fire on the mountain. The doubt can be removed[10] by telling him 'Had there been no fire on the mountain, there would have been no smoke on it (*tarka*). But, it is a matter of observation that there, in fact, is smoke on the mountain. It follows therefore, granting the generalization (*vyāpti*), that there must be fire on the mountain.' In this reasoning *tarka* and *vyāpti* both have been used, *tarka* a contrafactual and *vyāpti* a generalized conditional. The two have not been conflated with each other. The Nyāya logician has kept them apart with utmost logical care.

Universiy of Delhi

NOTES AND REFERENCES :

1. Chatterjee, Satischandra, *The Nyāya Theory of Knowledge*, Calcutta. Pp. 43-48.
2. Athalya, Y.V., and Bodas, M.R., *Tarka Saṁgraha of Annambhaṭṭa*, Poona. Pp. 356-358.
3. Bhargava, Dayananda, *Jaina Tarka Bhāṣā* of Yaśovijaya Gaṇi, Delhi 1973, P. 10.
4. See a statement of the Buddhist position in the *Jaina Tarka Bhāṣā*, p 11.
5. Barlingay S. S., *A Modern Introduction to Indian Logic*, Delhi- pp. 119-128.
6. Vidyabhusana, S. C., *A History of Indian Logic*, Delhi, 1971.
7. As in (1) above.
8. Goodman, Nelson, 'The problem of Counterfactual conditions'. *Journal of Philosophy*, vol. 44 (1947), pp 113-128.
9. As in (1) above.
10. Visvanatha Pancanana, *Bhāṣā Pariccheda*, Calcutta, p 10. *Tarkaḥ k vacicchaṅkānivartakaḥ.*

COMMON SENSE AND PHILOSOPHICAL PARADOX

Shashi Bharadwaja

Moore, throughout his arguments, has treated philosophers' statements like "Material things are not real", "Space is not real", "Time is not real", "The other selves are not real" *on par* with factual statements. For him, both the philosopher and the ordinary man are operating within the same conceptual framework. They are using the same ordinary language that we all speak.

On this, Moore's critics have often accused him of misunderstanding and therefore misrepresenting what the paradoxical philosopher is actually doing when, for instance, he denies the existence of material things, space, time and other selves. They point out that Moore's defence of Common Sense is based on this misunderstanding and misrepresentation of the philosopher's job.

2. The critics' arguments is many-faceted. (i) One line of their argument is that the expression "Common Sense" as it is ordinarily used in English language, is not at all applicable to beliefs. Hence, there can be no such thing as beliefs of Common Sense.[1] Hence, Moore's attempt to defend Common Sense is misplaced and misguided. (ii) Another line of the critics' argument allows for the existence of Common Sense beliefs, but argues that such beliefs do not need any defence, what to speak of a philosophic defence. For, as soon as we understand a belief of Common Sense we know that it is true. The basic assumption of this line of argument is that Common Sense is not a philosophical position.[2] (iii) A third line of argument which Moore's critics take is this : Granting that Common Sense is a philosophical position, it has validity only within its own linguistic or conceptual framework peculiar to it. On this view, the paradoxical philosopher has one such framework and Common Sense another. Assertions made in the one need not be false in the other, such that there

is no conflict between the two.³ And, if this is so, Moore's defence of Common Sense misfires, so far as the paradoxical philosopher is concerned. (iva) A fourth line of the critics' argument gives due recognition to the apparent success which Moore's defence of Common Sense has achieved. But, it argues that if he has been successful and if his arguments have proved to be effective against the paradoxical philosopher, it has been possible not because he defended Common Sense, but only because he defended Ordinary Language, though he mistakenly thought that he was defending Common Sense, while really defending Ordinary Language.⁴ The underlying assumption of this line of argument is that Moore was doing something quite different from what he thought he was doing, and this assumption is aimed at explaining the apparent success of his criticism against the paradoxical philosopher. (ivb) Following the same line of argument, sometimes the critics have arrived at a different conclusion suggesting that in apparently defending Common Sense, Moore really was making linguistic recomendations⁵ as to how language ought to be used. I propose to discuss in the present paper only the third line of the critics' argument.

3. Moore's critics have offered two major arguments with a view to showing that the Common Sense world-view and the paradoxical philosopher's theses, for instance, Bradley's thesis that Time is unreal, simply cannot compete with each other. And, therefore, they assert that Moore's defence of Common Sense against the paradoxical philosopher is misguided and uncalled for. *One* of their arguments is that the paradoxical philosopher's theses are not contingent statements, whatever else they might be; while the Common Sense position is constituted of contingent statements only. Misunderstanding the nature of the paradoxical philosopher's assertions Moore misrepresents them as contingent statements. And, insofar as the two positions are not of the same logical order, they do not and logically cannot compete or clash with each other.

The *second* of their arguments is that Common Sense and the paradoxical philosopher are making assertions within two different conceptual or linguistic frameworks. They offer us two different and logically consistent conceptual systems in which general descriptions about the world are given. Assertions made within 'the system of common sense' are true or false relative to the system, and those made within the metaphysician's system, are true or false in the one will be said to be true or false in the other. Moore misunderstands and therefore misrepresents the paradoxical philosopher's assertions by taking them as *internal* to the system of Common Sense, and consequently, judging them as true or false by the criteria of Common Sense.[6]

4. Let us begin with the second of the critics' arguments. To be able to discuss it, it is important to clarify Carnap's distinction between the internal and the external questions.[7] According to Carnap, "questions of the existence of certain entities of the new kind *within the framework*", are called *internal questions*: and "questions concerning the existence or reality *of the system of entities as a whole*" are called *external questions*.[8] The answers to the internal questions "may be found either by purely logical methods or by empirical methods depending upon whether the framework is a logical or a factual one".[9] Questions like 'Is there a white piece of paper on my desk?', or, Did Jawahar Lal Nehru die on May 27, 1964?', for example, are "to be answered by empirical investigation. Results of observations in the case of internal questions are evaluated according to certain rules as confirming or disconfirming evidenced for possible answers."[10] In other words, internal questions are asked and answered within a given linguistic or conceptual framework, and also there are appropriate criteria for accepting or rejecting the answers given. In cases in which there is doubt, the framework provided for relevant tests to be applied for removing the doubt. In the system of Common Sense, thus, it is internally decidable whether there are tables, chairs, and centaurs in the world. In the first two cases the answer will be in the affirmative; in the third case it will be in the negative. The external questions, on the other hand, are questions about the framework itself. Such questions are "raised neither by the man in the street nor by scientists, but only by philosophers".[11] The question, for example, whether there are material objects, or whether Space and Time are real, are external questions, on this view.

Now, the critics' argument is that if one treated metaphysical questions as internal to the conceptual system of Common Sense, then in that case, one would be misunderstanding and therefore misrepresenting the philosopher's actual practice in the course of which naturally he makes such assertions as "Material things are not real, what is real are only sense-data", or "Space and Time are not real, what is real is only Brahman." Moore makes this mistake, they declare. He treats these external questions as if they were internal to the framework of Common Sense. To misrepresent the philosopher thus, Ayer points out, would not explain what the philosopher is really doing. For this, he suggests, we need to look at his actual procedure to study the way in which he comes by his pradoxical conclusions.[12] The philosopher's actual procedure is that he arrives at his conclusions by reasoning and argument.[13] He does not adduce any empirical evidence for his paradoxical theses, like "Material objects, Time, Space, and other selves are not real". The reasoning that he offers in support of his conclusions generally takes the following two forms: One, it shows that the category in question is not ultimate,[14] and then the philosopher seeks to find out what really is ultimate. The second form of his reasoning is to show that a certain given concept is defective, and then he searches for that which is free from all defects.[15]

One may ask: How does the philosopher know that a certain concept or category is not ultimate? What criteria does he use for deciding this? How are we to understand what he he is meaning? It seems to me that the question 'what is ultimate?' cannot be answered intelligibly or adequately unless a prior question about the criteria of ultimacy, or what one wants to do with a certain concept or category has already been answered in some intelligible sense. Furthermore, the concept of ultimacy is a relative concept: what is ultimate for one may not be so for the other.[16] Similarly with the concept 'defective'. What are the philosopher's criteria for characterizing it defective? How does he answer the question about its relativity? All these questions need to be answered fully if the philosopher has any likelihood of being understood. From the point of view of Common Sense, however, as Ayer says, it is not clear "How can there be any hope of disqualifying a concept of which it is obvious that we make successful use? If it is a plain matter of fact that a concept has empirical application, then how can one think that it is radically defective, that it is meaningless or contradictory ? Surely, the metaphysician can proceed only by shutting his eyes to what the knows to be true".

The philosophers whom Moore is criticising do not appear to give any satisfactory answers to these questions. Nor do their 'improved' or 'ultimate' concepts fare any better than those which they term defective and which they deny, are ultimate. On the contrary, the concepts and categories of Common Sense which Moore employs, for instance, the concepts of material things, Space, Time, and other minds, do have effective application in providing a general description of the world as a whole. Above all, these are the concepts and categories which are presupposed by us both in the ordinary life and in the special sciences as well. They are the necessary conditions of ordinary existence.

5. Our discussion so far, on the paradoxical philosopher's procedure shows that his conclusions are neither intelligible nor acceptable to Common Sense, apart from the fact that they are arrived at by logically corrupt reasoning and argument involving the validity of an impossible thesis, namely that it is possible for a concept both to be self-contradictory and yet have empirical application. Now, if I am right in this thinking, then certain important consequences follow from our analysis :

(1) If the paradoxical philosopher is offering us an alternative framework for giving general descriptions about the world, then his alternative is not acceptable; because it is based on bad logic and also because it involves us in inconsistency with what we know to be true with absolute certainty. Furthermore, the paradoxical alternative is not at all viable, and as Ayer points out, "it is hard to see how there could be any intelligible description of the world which did not include the category of time".

(2) If the praradoxical philosopher is thought to be offering criticism of the framework of Common Sense, then (as we have shown above) his criticism, far from being valid, is not even intelligible to us; for he fails to give any criteria by means of which we should be able to understand him.

(3) And, finally, nor are the two frameworks—those of the Common Sense and of the paradoxical philosopher's—consis-

tent with each other. For, one says, 'Material objects, Space, Time, and other selves are real', and the other says 'They are not.' The paradoxical philosopher's case becomes all the more weakened when he fails to provide us with any basis to ascertain if the two assertions belong to two different levels of discourse, so that there is no inconsistency between them. He leaves it an open option for us to take his assertions, as Moore understands them, as pure and simple factual descriptions about the world.

In the preceding argument, we have been speaking of the intelligibility of the paradoxical philosopher's statements. Now supposing that he really offers us a viable linguistic framework for giving general descriptions about the world we live in. It is perfectly reasonable for us to ask : How can we understand them? My answer is that if at all we understand them we do so within the framework of Common Sense, as Moore conceives it. If the paradoxical philosopher makes any assertions about the world, the natural way which seems to be available to us for understanding them is that we use the concepts and categories of Common Sense. This is in fact what Moore does. He sees clearly that these concepts and categories are presupposed by us human mortals both in the ordinary life and in the special sciences as well, and also that to deny them inevitably lands us in contradictions. He therefore tries to understand the paradoxical philosopher within the conceptual framework of Common Sense. He knows no other way. It is possible that this is his commitment to the Common Sense world-view.

At this point of the argument, the critics will be quick to point out that it is because of this commitment of his that Moore misunderstands and misrepresents the paradoxical philosopher. He treats his questions as if they arose within the scope of Common Sense. To this, Moore would reply that this is how we can, if at all, understand him. His fundamental reason for this is that the ordinary men and the paradoxical philosopher both operate within the same conceptual framework of Common Sense. It is impossible for the philosopher to make himself intelligible by going outside this framework.[19]

6. Consider now critic's argument that Moore has mis-

understood the nature of the paradoxical philosopher's assertions and therefore he has misrepresented them as if they were contingently true, like the statements of Common Sense. What these critics are emphasising is that the paradoxical assertions really are not contingent, empirical, statements. By mistaking them to be empirical assertions, Moore has misrepresented the philosopher. What sort of assertions they are, on this question, however, there is wide disagreement among the critics.

Why do these critics think that the paradoxical philosopher is not making empirical statements? Part of the explanation is that they believe that philosophers and scientists are not doing the same kind of job. Their enquiries are different. While scientists are engaged in empirical or mathematical investigations, philosophers are occupied with something different, a kind of nonempirical, nonmathematical enquiry. A typical difference between them is this, that when the scientist makes a statement about facts he also makes certain empirical evidence relevant to its truth or falsity; but when a philosopher asserts something about the world, he may refuse to make any kind of empirical evidence relevant to the truth or falsity of his assertion. His statement would be neither established nor refuted on the basis of empirical evidence. He may continue to hold, like Bradley for example, the philosophical position that Space is not real, Time is not real, and yet, at the same time continue to believe in the world as we ordinary human mortals do, taking the reality of Space and Time as a presupposition of all our behaviour in the day to day life.

A part of explanation why these critics think that philosophical statements are not contingent is that there is wide disagreement on the question of the nature of a philosophical thesis, or what philosophy is. Moore conceives philosophy to be one thing—analysis and descriptions of the world as a whole; while the critics take it to be another thing—purely analysis and nothing else. Moore thus holds, with good conscience of course, that Common Sense constituting of contingently true statements giving general descriptions of the world, certainly, is a philosophical position; while the critics would deny this.

I do not think that Moore misunderstands and therefore

misrepresents the philosopher whom he is attacking. He clearly recognises that "some philosophers have so used the expression "material thing" that there is no contradiction in saying "there are human hands, but there are no material things".[20] He adds: "But I think it is also the case that *some* philosophers have used "material thing" in such a sense that from "there are no material things" there does follow "there are no human hands", and it was only of *this* usage of "there are no material things", that I meant to say that the propositions thus expressed by these words can be proved false"[21] by holding up one's hands and saying "This is a material thing".[22] Remarking on John Wisdom's reference to Wittgenstein's statement that "those philosophers who have denied the existence of matter have not wished to deny that under my trousers, I wear pants", he says: "If by this Wittgenstein meant that no philosophers who have even denied the existence of matter have ever wished to deny that pants exist, I think the statement is simply false. Some philosophers, at all events *sometimes* have meant to deny this: they have meant to assert that no such proposition as that pants exist is true; and it was only against *this* assertion that I supposed my proof to be a proof".[23]

Again, in his *Reply* to Alice Ambrose's criticism that he misrepresented the paradoxical philosopher by mistaking his statement "there are no material objects" to be an empirical statement, Moore says "there are external objects" may really be an empirical statement. It seems to me that my statement, that there are, certainly *is* empirical. Why should it not be the case that from his false non-empirical statement that "there are external objects" is self-contradictory, the philosopher invalidly infers the empirical statement "there are no external objects".[24] He adds: ,'this seems to me to be what has actually happened; and that therefore, philosophers who say "there are no external objects" are making a false empirical statement".[25]

From this, it follows that Moore is not saying that *every* philosophical thesis is a contingent statement. He is saying that only some philosophical theses are contingent statements, particularly those that are contrary to, or contradictory of

Common Sense and entail consequences which are incompatible with it. Above all, his own Common Sense propositions belong to the class of contingently true propositions. Thus, in regarding some of the philosophical theses as contingent statement, Moore, to my mind, has neither misunderstood nor misrepresented the paradoxical philosopher. The philosophical position which asserts such "monstrous" propositions as "Material things are not real", "Space is not real", "Time is not real", "The other selves are not real" does compete and clash with what we all with certainty know to be true, namely the propositions of Common Sense. For these considerations, I think, Moore's defence of Common Sense is not uncalled for.

University of Delhi

NOTES AND REFERENCES

1. See Mohanty, J.N., "On Moore's Defence of Common Sense", in the *Indian Journal of Philosophy*, Vol. II, No. 4, August 1960; pp. 44-49. Malcolm, N., "George Edward Moore", in his *Knowledge and Certainty*, 1963; pp. 163-86; Malcolm, N., "Review of White's book", *Mind*, Vol. 69, 1960; pp. 92-98.

2. Mohanty, J.N., op. cit., pp. 40-49. Malcolm, N., "Review of White's book", *Mind*, 1960;pp. 92-98.

3. For a critical discussion of this position, see Ayer, A.J., *Metaphysics and Common Sense*, London, 1969, Chapter V. Grave, S.A., *The Scottish Philosophy of Common Sense*, Oxford, 1960, Chapters III and IV.

4. Malcolm, N., "Moore and Ordinary Language", in *The Philosophy of G.E. Moore*. 1942; pp. 343. Malcolm, N., "Review of White's book", *Mind*, 1960; pp. 92-98.

5. See Lazerowitz, M., "Moore's Paradox" in *The Philosophy of G.E, Moore*. Lazerowitz, M., "Moore and Linguistic Philosophy", in *G.E. Moore Essays in Retrospect*, London, 1970. Ambrose, Alice, "Moore's Proof of an External World" in *The Philosophy of G.E. Moore*.

6. Ayer, A.J., op. cit., p 71.

7. Carnap, R., "Empiricism, Semantics and Ontology" in his *Meaning and Necessity*, 1956. See also Ayer, A.J., op. cit., Chapters IV and V.

8. Carnap, R., op. cit.,p. 206.

9. Ibid, p. 206.

10. Ibid, p. 207.

11. Ibid, 207.

12. Ayer, A.J., op. cit., p. 72.

13. Ayer, A.J., op. cit., p.72 See Lazerowitz, M., "Moore's Paradox" in the *Philosophy of G.E. Moore*.
14. Ayer, A.J., op. cit., p. 72.
15. Ibid, p. 73.
16. Cf. Wittgenstein, L., *Philosophical Investigations*, 3rd edition; para 47.
17. Ayer, A.J., op. cit., p.74.
18. Ibid, pp. 80-80.
19. Ibid, p. 81.
20. Moore's Reply, p. 669.
21. Ibid, p. 670.
22. Ibid, p. 669.
23. Ibid, p. 670.
24. Ibid, p. 672.
25. Ibid, p. 673.
26. Moore's Autobiography, pp. 13-14.

KNOWLEDGE PREDICATES

B.S.Sanyal

In this paper I have tried to map out the span of knowledge predicates.

1. *Epistemic Words.* Such a predicate may be defined as a word which is used in the epistemic sense : this is a circular and obscure definition, but good enough to begin with. The words which are frequently used in this sense are 'know', 'believe', 'doubt', 'true', 'experience', 'apprehension', 'proof', 'cognition', and so on. The same words may also be used in the nonepistemic senses. For example, in the sentence 'That's a knowing hat', 'knowing' means stylish. The same word is used in the epistemic sense in the sentences 'Everybody knows that the earth is round' and 'I don't believe in God but know that God exists'.

The epistemic sense may be blended with varying shades, varying as things known vary, such as events past, present or future, objects near or distant, object-object relations, other minds, self, God, subject-object relations, subject-subject relations, truth-values of propositions, logical values of arguments, and so on. But these do not lead to Rylean zeugmas or category mistakes; for example, 'We know that there exist both bodies and minds' is not a condensed zeugma, not to speak of its being a category mistake. Neither do these varying shades affect the peculiarly epistemic character of knowledge predicates, which is always there in the epistemic sense or use, whatever view one may hold about the definability of the knowledge predicates or about definition itself: for the simple reason that otherwise there would be no such discipline as an investigation into knowledge expressions.

In commonsense and scientific discourses, we can make or do with pairs, such as 'unknown' and 'known', 'unknowable' and 'knowable', 'true' and 'false', and so on; but in formal logic and philosophy, we need the four words 'unknowable', 'knowable' 'completely knowable' and 'not completely knowable'. This foursome agrees with other sets of four such as: 'meaningless', 'meaningful'; 'true' and 'false'; 'impossible, possible'; 'necessary' and 'not necessary'; and so on.

2. *Epistemic Sentences.* By an epistemic sentence we may now mean a sentence in which an epistemic word is used. Epistemic sentences of the elementary kind may use the four predicates either in the monadic or the dyadic form: thus 'this is unknowable, knowable, fully knowable, or not fully knowable' is enquivalent to 'one cannot, can, cannot but, can but need not, know this'. By symbolizing 'one knows this' as 'kxy' and 'necessary' as 'N', we have the full expressions of the four predicates as 'N (—Kxy)', '—N(—Kxy)', 'N(Kxy)' and '—N(Kxy)' respectively. Each is a tertiary second order monadic predicate, of which the parameter is a primary or secondary first order dyadic predicate.

There has been a lot of philosophizing with nonelementary epistemic sentences such as 'X knows that p' or 'I know she will be late' or 'Jones knows she would be late': especially to find out whether such sentences are descriptive or nondescriptive (especially performative) in character. As a result several metatheories of knowledge have emerged in bold relief, as in the case of truth or morality.

3. *Epistemic Arguments.* An argument that contains at least one epistemic sentence is an epistemic argument. In a standardised systematic argument of this kind, the conclusion is a sentence of the singular kind such as 'This is known or knowable or..'; the minor premise is an experiential sentence such as 'This is bodily sensed, sensually preceived, perceptually conceived, conceptually reasoned, rationally judged, judgingly acted, or actively realized'; and the major premise is a criterion sentence such as 'A fact p is said to be known if p is bodily sensed, sensually perceived, perceptually conceived,..'

4. *Epistemic Theories.* By an epistemic theory or theory of knowledge, we mean a set of arguments backing an M-sentence i.e. a metadescription of knowing, a C-sentence i.e. a statement of criterion of knowledge, or a D-sentence i.e. the definition of 'know'. The M-sentence has the structure

'If K, then M' : if a fact is said to be knowledge, then its knowability has a certain nonepistemic characteristic or a set of such characteristics. The C-sentence has the structure 'If C, then K' : if such and such conditions (necessary but not sufficient) are fulfilled by a fact, then it can be said to be knowable. The D-sentence has the structure 'K if D' : a fact is said to be knowable, if and only if such and such (necessary and sufficient) conditions are fulfilled.

For examples, 'I *know* is like *I promise*' is an M-sentence; 'If a fact p is perceptually experienced, then it is conceptually knowable' is a C-sentence; and the nearest instance of a D-sentence is : 'A fact p is said to be known if it is experienced in the corresponding mode.'

4.1. *Open and Closed Theories.* An open or non-fixational theory of knowledge recognizes all M, C, and incomplete D, —sentences as such respectively, and then proposes a comprehensive D-sentence. A closed or fixational theory proposes an M-sentence or a C-sentence or an incomplete D-sentence as *the* D-sentence i.e. as giving the best view of knowledge.

4.2. *Metatheories and Normative Theories.* A theory that presents an M-sentence about knowledge may be called a metaepistemic theory; a normative theory of knowledge presents a C—, or a D—, sentence. For examples, phenomenalism (which makes it impossible to use the words 'true' and 'knowledge') is a metatheory of knowledge; wheras realism which processes experience as a criterion of knowledge is a normative theory.

The question 'What is knowledge?' is preceded by the question : 'Is the word knowledge meaningful at all?'; and this latter question is answered in the form of many metatheories of knowledge. These range from extreme noncognitivism to extreme cognitivism and may be analogically called a spectrum, so that a natural synthesis gives a light-like unity.

The answers are nihilism(which says that 'K' is utterly meaningless), moderate nihilism (which says that 'K' is redundant or expendable), nondescriptivism ('K' is an interjection, mere expression of feeling or wish, a performance, speech-act or illocutionary act), naive subjectivism (a state of mind), relativism ('K' is only sociologically meaningful, it has only pragmatic use); intuitionism (it is meaningful logically but indefinable) and extreme cognitivism (it is logically definable). The last has several variants : prelogical naturalism, ordinary linguism, scientism, formal logicalism, metaphysicalism, religionism and mysticism according as 'know' is said to be meaningful in the respective languages.

The nihilists call the knowledge predicate meaningless since it is obviously equivocal, and when it is made univocal it remains vague and unanalysable. 'I know' being only a claim to knowledge, the claim may or may not be justifiable, and there is no knowing whether it is justified, because the second knowing again is to be justified as a claim thus leading to an infinite regress. The other major kind of nihilism is what may be called phenomenalism, phenomenologism and phenomenologism in which the questions of truth and hence of knowledge are dissolved by way of solipsism of one kind or another.

The prescriptivists may call 'know' only in the psychological conative and emotive senses, and not in the cognitive sense. When I say that I know there is a tree outside, all that I mean is that I would like to say that there is a tree outside. I have just a certain feeling or wish (or simply decide to assert) that a certain state of affairs obtains. Another version of nondescriptivism is the performist theory. 'I know' is like 'I promise' or 'I do' or 'I warn' or 'I name' or 'I take': 'I know' is not making a statement about self to the effect that I was "in some special state, or undertaking some special performance, but saying these words, engaging in the performance." (Jonathan Harrison : Knowing and Promising : KNOWLEDGE AND BELIEF, p.126) In short, 'know' is a speech act or illocutionary act. ('It is interesting to note Harrison's objection that the two verbs are not similar. Someone who promises what he does not perform has nevertheless promised (and failed to keep, or broken, the promise), whereas someone who says he knows something which is false cannot have known. Furthermore, someone saying 'I promise..' is thereby promising, wheras someone saying 'I promising, whereas someone saying 'I know..' is not thereby knowing but simply claiming that he knows, and the criterion for judging this claim is that of truth. So the classical philosophers' question about the conditions for justifying the claim remains answerable.)

The naive subjectivists hold the view that the word 'know' is meaningful only in the descriptive-psychological sense, and that it is logically meaningless. They maintain that when someone says 'I know that the tree is tall', he would not mean anything by knowledge except a state of mind, which may or may not occasion the knowledge, or which another man may not have when he knows, or which may be the genus or the differentia of an epistemic situation. Here again it is possible to wonder whether someone must be in a unique state of mind when it is true of him that he knows that p. "It is difficult to see what the state of any human individual's mind, whatever it might be, could have to do with the truth of such statement as The sun is bigger than Jupiter or The Pterodactyl is extinct." (ibid.,p.7 : Intro. by A.Phillips Griffiths).

According to the relatives, the meaning of 'know' differs from culture to culture : there is no universally accepted notion corresponding to the word. For example, in a science-dominated society, knowledge is restricted to verifiability by way of organic sensation, sense perception, perceptual conception and conceptual reasoning; whereas in a mysticism-dominated culture, knowledge is not so restricted : it spans all these modes of experience and knowledge and further ones such as reasoned judgement, judged action and acted realization.

The intuitionists would call the predicate meaningful, not merely in the psychologically or sociologically subjective sense, but in the logically objective sense; that is to say, in their view, the word can be made univocal. When a word is used in the epistemic sense, the sense is unique; but the definition of the word is not possible : its intension is too simple to be analysable and its extension too homogeneous to be discernible in parts and aspects.

The extreme cognitivists, who may be called rationalists, agree with the intuitionists in calling 'K' univocal; but at the same time they call it definable, because in their view it has a complex structure : $N\ (Kxy)$; the tertiary predicate 'N' stands for the differentia; and the dictum 'Kxy' 'for the genus. The structure of its definition is given by a biconditional of 'Kp' and 'Dp : its funstion is to lay bare the epistemic and the ontic contents of K.

Once rationalism is accepted we try to define 'know' : the resulting C-sentences and unsuccessful D-sentences make normative theories of knowledge :

4.3 Latitudinal and Longitudinal Theories.

4.3.1. Latitudinal Theories. Every theory proposes its core affirmation in the language or thought of any one of the following modes of experience and knowledge : prelogical natural, commonsense, scientific, formal logical, metaphysical, religious and mystical. These give several standpoints varying as knowledge or experience varies from full unconsciousness to full consciousness through bodily sensation, sense perception, perceptual conception, conceptual reasoning, reasoned judgement, judged action, and acted realization. These theories may also be called standpoints as well as theories in levels, or matter theories. These can be logically arranged as follows, although historically these might have arisen in different chronological order or some of them might have appeared and developed simultaneously.

	Theory	Knowledge viewed as
1.	prelogical naturalism	bodily sensation
2.	empiricism	sense perception
3.	scientism	perceptual conception
4.	logicalism	conceptual reasoning
5.	metaphysicalism	reasoned judgement
6.	religionism	judged action
7.	mysticism	acted realization

The metaepistemic theories here can be summarily stated as : 'K' is meaningful in the language of prelogical experience, commonsense, science, formal logic, metaphysics, religion and mysticism. And the normative epistemic theories can be given in the form of fixational D-sentences as follows : Of all facts p, p is said to be knowable, if it is verifiable by way of bodily sensation, sense perception, perceptual conception, and so on. The last one, viz. the mystical Dt-senence can be regarded as *the* D-sentence (provided we don't forget the transcendental aspect of the absolute); in its longitudinal formulation, it should be sociolinguistic, rationalistic and idealistic.

4.3.2. *Longitudinal Theories*. Each closed theory proposes a C-sentence, an M-sentence or a D-sentence as the D-sentence. And each has followed either the extensional (material) mode, the intensional (conceptual) mode, or the expressional (linguistic) mode of analysis. In these modes, the subject is respectively related to the object-in-reality, object-in-consciousness, and object-in-symbols; and in each mode the relating can be done in three ways : the way of correspondence, by which the subject forbears imposing itself on the object; the way of solipsism, by which the subject imposes itself on the object overwhelmingly; and the way of coherence, in which the balance is reached between imposition and aloofness.

Thus arise nine generic theories of the longitudinal kind : these may also be called viewpoints, theories in perspectives, or method theories. These may be logically arranged as appended, although historically these might have arisen in a different chronological order or some of them might have appeared and existed and developed simultaneously.

	Theory	Core Affirmation	and Its kind
1.	realism	extensionalistic	C—sentence
2.	phenomenalism	...	M—sentence
3.	idealism	...	D—sentence
4.	empiricism	intensionalistic	C—sentence
5.	phenomenologism	...	M—sentence
6.	rationalism	...	D—sentence
7.	psycholinguism	expressionalistic	C—sentence
8.	phenomenolinguism	...	M—sentence
9.	sociolinguism	...	D—sentence

These may be formulated as follows :

1. realism : If a fact p is experienced as an object-in-reality, then p is said to be known (C).

2. phenomenalism : If a fact p is called known, then, p

is just experienced (but not known) as an object-in-reality (M)

3. idealism : A fact p is said to be known if p is experienced as an object-in-reality (D)

(It may be noted that in idealism, knowledge and experience are looked upon as correlatives : when bodily sensation is experience, sensation is knowledge; when sensation is experience, perception is knowledge; when perception is experience, conception is knowledge; when conception is experience, reasoning is knowledge; when reasoning is experience, judgement is knowledge; when judgement is experience, action is knowledge; when action is experience, realization is knowledge).

4. empiricism : If a fact p is experienced as an object-in-consciousness, then p is said to be known (C)

5. phenomenologism : If a fact p is called known, then p is just experienced (but not known) as an object-in conciousness (M)

6. rationalism : A fact p is said to be known if p is experienced as an object-in-consciousness (D)

7. psycholinguism : If a fact p is experienced as an object-in-symbols, then p is said to be known (C)

8. phenomenolinguism : If a fact p is called known, then it is just experienced (but not known) as an object-in-symbols (M)

9. sociolinguism : A fact p is said to be known if p is experienced as an object-in-symbols (D)

In the first set (1,2,3), 3 is the synthesis of (1,2); in the second set (4,5,6), 6 is the synthesis of (4,5), and in the third set (7,8,9), 9 is the synthesis of (7,8). And the members of the set (3,6,9) are isomorphic (and equivalent if we ignore the difference in mode of analysis); otherwise a synthesis of the three called idealistic rationalistic sociolinguistic can be presented as the best view.

5. *Conclusion.* Knowledge is one; but theories of knowledge are many. There can however be one theory of knowledge, or we should say there can be only one open and non-fixational theory, although there can be many fixational and closed ones.

The one and nonfixational theory arises as a logically graded spectrum of affiirmations in different theories based on different standpoints and viewpoints, none of which by itself is acceptable in toto; in other words, as a spectrum of affirmations yielded by different standpoints none of which is recommended as the one and only one fixed point and thus none of which is allowed to yield a closed theory. An attempt can thus be made to make it the most comprehensive yet non-fixational.

Secondly, in spite of this attempt, some lacunae are bound to be there; so, we keep our theory open. This is how our theory becomes the true theory in the sense of the best theory though in an open manner, open to further refinement.

This is not system building in the bad sense, because the different stands and views here become systems in the bad sense only when taken severally as the best; and we are considering them all and collecting only their positive points.

North Bengal University.

SEEING AND TASTING AFTER-IMAGES*

S. Chandra

The suspicion about the status of sense-data has led some philosophers to be suspicious about the status of after-images. Thus Norman Malcolm questions, "What would it mean to get a better view of my after-image? I cannot even try to "observe" an after-image "more accurately".[1] In his discussion on "After-Images" C. E. Burlingame has gone a step further. After-Images, according to him, are not only *like* sensations, they *are* sensations—bodily sensations. "We rub our eyes when we have them".[2] Therefore it seems to him "curious that we don't commonly speak of after-images as "being in one's eye"."[3] Burlingame's assimilation of after-images to sensations is also a strategic move against sense-data. Sense-data are introduced, according to him, by assimilating "seeing tables, colours etc., to after-images".[4] Once it is shown about after-images that "one does not see (taste) them, one has them", in the sense in which one has one's pains, there will remain no ground for the introduction of sense-data in terms of after-images.[5] For, "there is little desire to introduce them (sense-data) into the discussion of pain."[6] In this article I have tried to unravel the reasons which led Burlingame to the sort of view he holds about after-images. Malcolm's view does not succeed in doing much injury to after-images. In spite of all his doubts about their character, Malcolm does not deny the possibility of

---

*I am grateful to Professor Gilbert Ryle for helpful comments on the original draft of this article. The final draft of this article has been prepared at the Indian Institute of Advanced Study, Simla.

1. *Knowledge And Certainty*, p. 80
2. *Mind*, July 1972, p. 444.
3. Ibid. p. 444.
4. Ibid. p. 443.
5. Ibid. p. 443.
6. Ibid. p. 444. The expression 'sense-data' occurring within the brackets in this quotation is mine.

seeing them. What he denies is simply the possibility of seeing an after-image "more accurately" or "seeing it twice".[1]

Consider the following situation. One gazes at a four-pointed star shape (Malcolm's example) and then transfers his gaze to the white wall to obtain its after-image. On being asked to describe the items of his visual experience he says, I see a grey splodge (Ryle's term for the after-image), a fly to, the right of the splodge and a red dot to its left. The fly and the red dot were already there, the grey splodge is the only fresh entry on the wall. If Burlingame's suggestion is accepted then it is wrong to say that one sees the grey splodge, but quite right to say that one sees the fly and the red dot on the wall. His thinking on this issue is not very unlike the thinking of a sense-datum philosopher. Since one sees the grey splodge on the wall, and one also sees the fly on the wall, therefore, argues a sense-datum philosopher, the grey splodge and the fly both belong to the same class, the class of objects seen—*directly* seen—sense-data. The fly has also been converted into a fresh entry (an image) on the wall. For further justification the fly seen on the wall is compared with a fly seen in a dream or some kind of hallucination. Burlingame starts with the other end of the thought. Since the grey splodge is a fresh entry on the wall, it is unlike the fly which was already there on the wall. Before settling down between the fly and the red dot, the grey splodge passed over (through) the fly without hitting or in any way disturbing the fly. Therefore, the grey splodge cannot be the same sort of object as a fly. From which it follows that if one sees the fly one cannot see the grey splodge. To obtain justification for his view Burlingame compares seeing after-images with having pains in one's body. He is not saying that there are no such objects as after-images. He is simply saying that they are not the sort of objects that could be seen, because they are not the same sorts of objects as flies and pennies. A sense-datum philosopher argues: Like mode of detection, therefore like objects. Burlingame argues: Unlike objects,

---

7. I have attempted to show the possibility of seeing the same afterimage twice in my article "Scepticism, Identity and Interrupted Existence". The *Indian Philosophical Quarterly*, Jan. 1975, has published this article in an abridged form.

therefore unlike modes of detection. You cannot detect a pain by seeing, chewing or biting it, for a pain is not the same sort of object as a piece of bread. But Burlingame's argument is as misleading as the argument of the sense-datum philosopher. With Burlingame's argument one should also be debarred from seeing *shadows*, *rainbows* and *mirror-images* (Austin's variety), for none of them is like a fly.

Burlingame hopes to smuggle after-images into the category of sensations because he thinks that "there is no "neat" category of sensations"[1] But it is sufficiently "neat" that something on the wall (a fly, a red dot, a grey splodge) may produce sensations in me (my body), but sensations themselves are not those items that are found on the wall as are flies, red dots and after-images. Suppose one considers it just a contingent fact that his sensations are restricted to his body. He proposes to see, like Armstrong, whether he could feel sensations in his wrist watch or the walls of his room.[2] For the sake of argument let us grant that he succeeds in his project. Does his success in feeling sensations *in* the wall support Burlingame's view? It does not. Not because the sensations, in this situation, are felt *in* the wall rather than *on* it, but because Burlingame is not questioning the restriction of sensations to one's body. He is not interested in increasing the stock of items decorating the wall—a sensation to be added to the fly and the red dot. Rather he is interested in rubbing out some items from the wall. The grey splodge is to be rubbed out from the wall, for if it is allowed to occupy a position on the wall then it cannot be found *in* one's eye. One thing cannot exist at the same time in two different places. Burlingame's argument amounts to saying that if an after-image is like a sensation then it is not the sort of object that is to be found along with a fly on the wall. It is a sort of object that is to be found along with a pain in one's body. And this argument is quite weak. For a sensation is not whereas an after-image is a sort of thing which has a certain colour, shape and size. If an after-image is a sensation then it should be deprived of its colour, shape and size. As Hamlyn points out about an after-image, "treated as a

1. Mind, July 1972, p. 444.
2. See D. M. Armstrong's book *Bodily Sensations*, p. 48.

sensation it makes no sense to say that it has a size at all".[1] Hamlyn's analysis holds good for the grey colour and the four pointed shape of the after-image in question.[2]

Perhaps the cases of after-images seen with closed eyes might have led Burlingame to think that after-images are sensations. But the fact that after-images could equally be seen with closed eyes simply shows that after-images are unlike flies, shadows and mirror-images. There is no implication that one cannot see them or that seeing after-images is the same thing as having a sensation. If I continue to see the grey splodge after I have closed my eyes, then the splodge is certainly not on the wall. Where is then? Could t be in the eye? But the grey splodge could certainly not be in the eye in the sense in which a dust-particle is in the eye (physical sense of "in"). It could not be in the eye even in the sense in which a pain is in one's leg or a sensation of numbness in one's toe. When Burlingame considers an after-image to be in the eye, he is using "in" in its phenomenological sense. But the right phenomenological description of an after-image is not that it is *in* one's eye, it is *in front of* one's eye. And it is because an after-image is in front of one's eyes that it continues to retain a colour, a shape and a size. A physical sensation to which Burlingame assimilates after-images, could not be in front of one's eye, it must be in one's eye. Medicines are prescribed and doctors are consulted for curing and suppressing sensations. But it is unheard of that one goes to the doctor for curing the malady of having after-images, for having after-images is not any physical malady. Of course, this is not to deny that certain temporary physiological disturbances, dazzle effects, accompany seeing an after-image, but seeing an after-image is not the same thing as having those physiological disturbances.

One may, however, argue that it makes sense to say about a fly but not about a grey splodge (after-image) that one has *detected, spotted, observed* or *caught sight of*.[3] I could have spotted something on the wall only when it was already there on the wall before I spotted it. But the grey splodge, if it is really

---

1. D. W. Hamlyn, "The Visual Field And Perception" *Aristotelian Society*, Supplementary Vol. XXXI, 1957, p. 118.
2. *ibid.* pp. 115-118.
3. Ryle's suggestion to consider the argument.

an after-image, was not there on the wall before I spotted it, so I could not have spotted it. This argument merely distinguishes a grey splodge from such an object as a fly. A fly could be whereas a grey splodge could not be the accusative of such verbs as 'to spot', 'to detect' and 'to observe' etc. But it fails to show that a grey splodge could not be the accusative of the verb 'to see'. Suppose following Burlingame one does not allow the grey splodge to be the accusative of the verb 'to see', rather it is the accusative of the verb 'to have'. One does not *see* the grey splodge, one *has* it. But where does one have it? To say that I have the grey splodge in my *visual field* or in my *sight* etc., is simply way of saying that I see it.

Ryle's analogy of *seeing* with *winning* and his theory of predication are two other factors which seem to have influenced Burlingame's treatment of after-images. One could *see* an after-image only if one could *look at* it. One could *win* a game only if one plays it. But, as Malcolm points out, there is no sense in saying that I might *look away* from my after-image and, therefore, no sense in saying that I look at it".[1] Transition from Malcolm's to Burlingame's view is easy. If you fail to look at an after-image, you also fail to see it, for seeing is at end of the process of looking at. You cannot achieve the end without undergoing the process. However, Ryle's analogy of games fails to prohibit seeing after-images, and therefore, there is no necessity of taking the further step of assimilating after-images to sensations. It is a fact that people win games by playing them in a proper fashion. But it is also a fact that sometimes games are won without playing them—having a walk-over. Seeing an after-image is a case of winning a game by having a walk-over. Of course, if no games are won by playing them in a proper fashion, no walk-overs could be granted. But this simply means that seeing after-images is impossible if people do not ever see objects in a proper fashion, i.e., by looking at them and scrutinizing them from a close distance. When you see flies, shadows and mirror-images generally you win your game playing it in a proper fashion. So there is nothing wrong in granting walk-overs to after-images. Of course, it is not only the after-images which are found without looking or searching for them. I found the coin in my pocket without searching for

1. *Knowledge And Certainty*, p. 78.

it. I heard the thunder without trying to listen (trying to hear) it. I saw the lightning without looking for it.[1] So an after-image cannot be distinguished from other sorts of objects simply on the ground that seeing an after-image is the case of an unearned success.

Ryle's theory of predication also fails to prohibit us from seeing after-images. For one can say about a fly no less than about an after-image that is it has a certain colour, is in front of one's eyes, is on the wall etc. Of course, not all questions that are raised about a fly could be raised about an after-image. But this is because a fly is unlike an after-image. The fact that certain subjects are proper subjects of visual predicates does not prohibit them from having their individual differences. A fly is unlike its shodow and its mirror-image. And all of them are unlike after-images and rainbows. One can have a better view of a fly or its shadow by coming closer to it, but one cannot do so with after-images and rainbows. Both after-images and rainbows maintain distance from you.

Perhaps the popular, though muddled, distinction between 'sensation' ad 'after-sensation' found in the text-books of psychology may be one of the reasons for Burlingame's refusal to see after-images. If an after-image is identical with an after-sensation, as is maintained in these books, then it makes no sense to say that one sees an after-image, for it makes no sense to say that one sees an after-sensation. One could, of course, be said to have an after-image, for it makes quite good sense to say that one has an after-sensation. But an after-image is not identical, numerically identical, with an after-sensation, though it may involve such sensation. If having a sensation fails to prohibit one from seeing a four-pointed star (physical object), how could having an after-sensation prohibit one from seeing a grey splodge (after-image) ? For to have an after-sensation is either to have a sensation—retain the same sensation which one had when one saw the physical four-pointed star,—or else to have the ghost (impression) of a sensation—ghost of the same sensation which one had when one saw the physical four-pointed star. But be it a sensation or its ghost, its existence is only a causally necessary condition for seeing the grey splodge as is

2. I owe these examples to Ryle.

the existence of a sensation only a causally necessary condition for seeing the four-pointed star. Seeing the grey splodge is no more reducible to having the ghost of a sensation than seeing the four-pointed star is reducible to having a sensation.

Consider now Burlingame's Comparison of 'seeing' with 'tasting'. He says: "Still tasting the wine after the sip has been swallowed?" One *tastes* the wine, but *has* the *taste* of it afterwards. One *sees* the bright light, but *has* the *image* afterwards. One may *still taste* the wine, but *tasting* it is different. One may *still see* the light, but *seeing* the light is different. One can still taste, but not taste an after-taste, *simpliciter*. The same with 'see' ".[1] Burlingame wants to distinguish seeing an object from having its after-image on the pattern of taste and after-taste. But his distinction between taste and after-taste is questionable. He denies that one could *taste* an after-taste. True. One cannot taste an after-taste. But could one *taste* a taste? One can *taste* the wine but not its taste or its after-taste. And the fact that one fails to taste either a taste or an after-taste has some tendency to show that taste and after-taste are like one another, and unlike the wine (object of taste) or the after-images of wine (objects of after-taste) which occur when after-taste occurs.

Burlingame's distinction between seeing an object and having its after-image does not correspond to the pattern of his distinction between taste and after-taste. Though he converts 'still taste' into 'after-taste', he fails to do the same with 'still see'. But if Burlingame, or for that reason *any* speaker of English language, is consistent in his conversion of terms, then following the pattern of 'still taste' he should convert 'still see' into 'after-see' or 'after-seeing'.[2] The visual distinction which is to correspond to the distinction between taste and after-taste should be seeing and after-seeing. The fact that there is no such term as 'after-seeing' in our ordinary language is no reason why it should not be introduced for philosophical purposes. The distinction between seeing and after-seeing is not so awkward as it may appear at first sight: this distinction involves

---

1. Mind, July 1972, p. 443
2. The term 'after-sight' because of its prevalent associations does not perform the required job.

interesting consequences. One of its consequences is the elimination of the possibility of introducing sense-data in terms of after-images. When our subject is gazing at a four-pointed star shape (physical object), he is *seeing* it. Afterwards when he turns his gaze to obtain the after-image on the wall, his experience could be described as the experience of *after-seeing* the object. The grey splodge is the object of his after-seeing. The discovery of 'after-seeing' is not the discovery of a new mental act hitherto unknown to philosophers. If it is a discovery it is just a verbal discovery, that seeing the grey splodge is to be described as the case of after-seeing, so that seeing the grey splodge may not be confused with seeing a penny or a fly. You can see a penny and afterwards you can see a fly, but seeing the fly in this case is not a matter of after-seeing. It is a contingent truth about objects that are not after-images (a penny, a shadow, a rainbow) that one of them is seen after the other has already been seen. But it is a necessary truth about after-images that they are seen only when other objects partly unlike (unlike in colour especially) have already been seen. Hence there is no scope for sense-data to be introduced in terms of after-images. For sense-data are prior to flies, shadows and mirror-images. But according to the present analysis flies, shadows and mirror-images all belong to the same epistemological level, and their epistemological level is prior to the epistemological level of after-image.[1]

Let us consider in detail the case of after-images associated with taste. It is a fact that philosophers have not made claims as to their success in tasting after-images, perhaps because people use their eyes more frequently than their mouth, and much of the time their mouth is busy in other affairs than the affairs of taste. So the finer distinctions which philosophers succeeded in making about the visual situations they failed to make about the situations of taste. There are no such *eatables* that are described as after-images, therefore the question of *tasting* such eatables does not arise. However, the absurdity in tasting after-images arises on account of the fact that some-

---

1. If one allows an unperceived existence to a fly, one has also to allow such an existence to the shadow or mirror-image of the fly. Therefore, shadows and mirror-images are not sense-data.

times tasting is achieved through such activities as sipping, munching, gulping and chewing etc. Therefore, the question 'Are you tasting after-images?' is easily confused with the question 'Are you sipping or munching after-images?'. One cannot be sipping or munching after-images so one cannot be tasting after-images. But one of the functions of philosophy is to prohibit people from getting confused because of their everyday use of language. Ryle's distinction between the *process* and *achievement* verbs is meant for prohibiting people from getting confused because of their everyday use of language. The fact that he is more attracted by the visual situations does not imply that his technique cannot be extended to the situations of taste. Saying 'taste the wine' means 'try to detect its taste by drinking or sipping it', Saying 'taste the pork-pie' means 'try to detect its taste by eating or munching it'. 'Eating', 'munching', 'drinking' and 'sipping' etc., are process verbs which may or may not succeed in detecting a taste. One is eating only from politeness. One is eating though one is having a cold.[1] These cases are like listening for a sound without success in hearing it, and, looking for something without success in seeing it.

You cannot order to win, you can only order to play. You cannot order to see, you can only order to look for. Similarly you cannot order to taste when 'taste' functions as a success verb, you can only order to eat, to munch, to drink, to sip etc. And if tasting is not confused with eating, munching, drinking etc., then there arises no absurdity in tasting after-images. It is interesting to note that the after-images of taste behave in the same fashion as the after-images of seeing. The four-pointed star with black background is white, but its after-image on the wall is grey. The wine is sweet but its after-image on the tongue is sour. Consider an actual situation of taste (a taste field) and see its implications. Suppose you sipped the sweet wine, and now you are munching a pork-pie. What are the objects of your present taste field? There is no doubt that your present taste field is having a pork-pie as one of its constituents. But your mouth continues to have the taste of wine which you sipped a few moments earlier. The wine

---

1. I owe these examples to Ryle.

(physical object) is, however, not a constituent of your present taste field, it was a constituent of your earlier taste field.[1] What tastes sour to your mouth now is not the wine but its after-image. You have the taste of pork-pie (physical object) and the taste of wine (after-image) at the same time. Your present taste field is having two constituents, a physical object and an after-image. This situation is exactly like the situation when you find a fly (physical object) and a grey splodge (after-image) in the same visual field.[2]

The arguments against tasting after-images are as weak as the arguments against seeing after-images. If I am now tasting two objects, a pork-pie and an after-image of wine, then I am now involved in two different activities (processes), the activities of munching and sipping. But I am now involved only in one activity, munching a pork-pie, therefore, I am now tasting only one object, a pork-pie. But what happened to the the after-image of wine? Has it disappeared from your taste field? If it continues to occupy a position in your taste field then you cannot deny that you are tasting it. Granted that after-images are not the sort of things one could sip or munch, how does it follow that they are not the sort of things one could taste? Neither 'to taste' nor 'to savour' mean the same as 'to sip' or 'to munch' etc. Of course, tasting after-images presupposes tasting wines and pork-pies. But this merely shows that the epistemological level of after-images is different from the epistemological level of wines and pork-pies. This does not prohibit tasting after-images or tasting them at the same time as one is tasing a physical object.

The after-images of taste, like visual after-images, pass both the tests prescribed by Ryle. Since the physical objects like wines and pork-pies generally win their games by playing them in a proper fashion, we can allow the after-images of taste to win their games by granting them walk-overs. But it is not only the after-images which one succeeds in tasting without trying.

1. It is possible that some quantity of wine (a drop or so) remains on my tongue for a long time, therefore, it is the wine itself which is a constituent of my present taste field. But the wine in question is sweet, therefore, what tastes sour is not wine.

2. The argument in question does not mean that the concept of a taest field is exactly analogous to the concept of a visual field.

I tasted the onion (physical object) of the chicken-soup without trying for it. This is just like seeing the lightning without looking for it. (Opposite case—I tried to taste the onion of the onion-soup but I failed on account of my cold). So an after-image cannot be distinguished from a physical object simply on the ground that in having the former one is having an unearned success. Similarly, Ryle's theory of predication fails to disting—guish an after-image from a physical object. For we apply the taste predicates like 'being sweet' and 'being sour' etc., to after-images no less than to physical objects.

Indian Institute of Advanced Study,
Simla

THE PROBLEM OF FOUNDATIONS : HUSSERL

Gopal Chandra Khan

Again and again, the philosophers since ancient times have worked on the problem of foundations. In modern times we find at least three great philosophers, namely, Husserl, Russell and Wittgenstein, who have turned to philosophy, all being confronted with the problem of the foundations of mathematics. The problem of the foundations of mathematics is but an aspect of the problem of the foundations of knowledge and experience in general. Husserl realises that the problem is a hard pressing one and need be solved rather than dissolved. In fact Husserl believes that the European sciences are facing serious crises for not being aware of their own epistemic validity.[1] It is thus that philosophy can render invaluable services to sciences by working out their foundations. But before philosophy can be so serviceable, it will have to be reconstructed on a new base and into the form of a rigorous science. Husserl's phenomenology thus announces the beginning of a new science of philosophy. The thing that is so striking about Husserl's phenomenology is its method. The method, Husserl claims, is distinctly philosophical and is alone capable of raising philosophy to the status of a science, the sort of science it deserves to be.[2]

Before we enter into a discussion about the nature of the method and its bearings on the problem of foundations, we would like to see if the phenomenological method could be the same as the ones followed in sciences. This we should do because, phenomenology claims itself to be a science, even the most rigorous of all sciences. It will again help us realise the peculiar problem facing phenomenology. The rigour of science is due to its regard for evidence. The scientific outlook can be described in terms of 'Occam's razor'. It means that no proposition in science is to be entertained for which no evidence in experience is available. Here we consider two types of sciences—the pure deductive sciences like geometry, logic etc., and the empirical or the natural sciences like physics, astronomy etc.

Mostly the deductive sciences have developed in the form of deductive systems. Every deductive system starts from a number of postulates that are not proved but taken for granted within the system. The other propositions of the system follow from the postulates by virtue of the rules of logic. The mode of inference employed here may be called demonstrative inference. In a demonstrative inference the conclusion follows from the premise or the premises necessarily so that given the premise or the premises true the conclusion cannot but be true. The premise or the premises from which the conclusion follows may therefore be regarded as supplying the 'basis' or the 'evidence' for the truth of its conclusion. They are therefore, the postulates which serve as the ultimate basis for the truth of the propositions of a deductive system. But what about the truth of the postulates? The truth of the postulates cannot be determined in the same way in which the truth of the other propositions of the system are determined. So if we are permitted to question the truth of the postulates of a system we will have to go in search after their foundations elsewhere than the system. It may be that the truths of the postulates are so obvious that only simple intuitions are required to establish their validity. But the fact that we can have alternative deductive systems having equally sound logical character in which the postulates are not so obvious or even which go to the contrary lead to the conclusion that a deductive system is not founded in experience at any stage; it is just a deductive machinery and the validity of the system depends upon its internal consistency. This is one conception of logical and mathematical truth which by no means is easily acceptable. For, the consistency of the deductive system itself cannot be proved within the system. Moreover, the basic incompleteness of the sufficiently strong deductive systems (Godel's thesis—1931) point to the fact that there are many truths of mathematics and logic which cannot be formally demonstrated. They are known otherwise. Again, mathematics and logic find their important applications in reality. We always look upon these systems which can be applied in natural sciences. From a consideration of all these things we see that the question of the foundation of logic and mathematics comes in and also that either logic or mathematics is unable to answer the question regarding its own foundations.

Let us now try to follow the methodology of the empirical sciences. Our empirical knowledge may be regarded as built up by means of non-demonstrative reasonings. Here the matters of facts given in sense experience are regarded as supplying the basis or the evidence for the truth of its conclusions. The conclusions of such reasonings are of the nature of hypotheses which go beyond the evidences of experience. Since the conclusions go beyond the evidences of experience, the evidences can never confirm the hypotheses directly. For this science employs an indirect method which may be characterised as the 'hypothetico-deductive method'[4] The scientific method essentially consists in (a) framing hypotheses, either instantial or non-instantial; (b) deducing consequences either with or without combination of other facts; (c) testing the consequences in accordance with observable facts and (d) finally, confirming the hypotheses by right of factual consistencies. The act of verification leads to the predication of similar natural phenomena. The term theory stands for such a confirmed hypothesis along with its power of predication. In fact, any hypothesis may later be proved false. In this way it is also possible to speak of rival theories and rival hypotheses. For example, there were the corpuscular and the wave theories of light both of which were highly credible. Any particular hypothesis is taken in science in order to explain certain facts or phenomena and is accepted until some conflicting fact is discovered. However, when some conflicting fact is discovered it does not mean that the hypothesis is to be discarded; it only means that some modifications are needed. Thus the Newtonian law of gravitation is supplemented or replaced by the Einstenian law of relativity in order to cover some new facts discovered afterwards. But Newton's law of gravitation still holds good for relatively small bodies that move not too fast and are not too small. It is clear therefore that the law of science works within a limited 'horizon of expectation'[5] When the horizon gets expanded due to the discovery of new and new facts the theory or the law in question stands in need of either modification or replacement. It is this horizon that determines the total perspective under which observations in science are made. In scientific procedure hypotheses precede observations and not conversely.[6] Progress in science consists in construction of new and new hypotheses and new and new 'horizon of expectations'.

From the foregoing discussion on the methodology of the empirical sciences it is clear that the world of science is a world of construction. It is far away from the world of lived experience. Kant is of opinion that science has been able to make wonderful progress only because of its methodology. The success of science is due to its ability to question and to force nature to answer its questions. Husserl, on the other hand, points out that the methodology of the science is the source of both its strength and weakness. The original world upon which the superstructure of science is based is ever inaccessible to science. As a result the status of science and scientific knowledge remains unclarified and unfounded. The understanding of nature due to science is theoretical and is susceptible to questioning. It is for this that science stands in need of another science to work out its foundation. The new science will go in search after the original world upon which the superstructure of science is based and thereby supplying it with its foundations, The problem of foundation is not only a problem peculiar to science, it is also the problem of our every day experience. In our everyday experience we use so many concepts borrowed from past heritage, from science and from other cultural fields. So the naivety of experience is not available in our common experience also. It is the special concern of the science of philosophy to work out foundations of scientific as well as pre-scientific knowledge.

Phenomenology considers itself a science. Like that of other sciences it also pays its due regard for evidences. But the evidences to be counted in phenomenology should neither be of the nature of postulates, nor of matters of facts, for, none of them are capable of verifying the foundational propositions which demand absolute verifications. The evidences, according to Husserl, will be of the nature that they can be seen right and when they are seen the impossibility of their being otherwise is also seen. Such evidences will verify the foundational propositions directly and absolutely. Both these two concepts of direct verification and absolute verifications are, however, foreign to the perspective of science; for science verification is either demonstration or indirect verification by right of factual consistency.

Phenomenological method, then we see, involves the concepts of direct verification and absolute verification. In order that such verifications can be achieved it requires evidences as are absolute. But where can such evidences be found ? Such evidences cannot be found in the realm of nature, for nature is characterised by contingency and facticity. Husserl shares the conviction of Descartes that consciousness constitutes a separate region of being and that things can be grasped with absolute certainty in the field of consciousness. In relation to nature consciousness is transcendental and nature is transcendent to it. That means consciousness is what remains even when we think away nature from it. It is in this field of consciousness that absolute evidences can be found. However, consciousness by its very nature is opposed to facts. So the things appear in consciousness in their 'essential regards'. The essences are what are called by Husserl 'phenomena'. The essences being absolute and unconditioned are universally valid. They are therefore, the 'essences' or the 'phenomena' that can serve as absolute evidences needed for anything demanding absolute verifications. Phenomenology thus hopes to solve the problem of foundations by unravelling the phenomena of the respective field of study in consciousness.

Husserl's phenomenology, as we see, undergoes certain stages of development.[7] Starting with the conviction that foundations can be found nowhere than in the side of the subject Husserl goes on to explore the field of consciousness and in the process discovers three successive grounds namely, the essences, the transcendental ego, and the life-word (lebenswelt). In the first stage[8], Husserl discovers that there are certain acts of consciousness which are intentional in character. Intentionality is that characteristic of consciousness whereby consciousness is 'consciousness of..' At this moment I may be perceiving a table. The actual table is there outside. In my consciousness the table is in the form of 'experience of the table', the 'perceptum qua perceptum', This is also the meaning of the perceived table for my consciousness. The table-sense is not in the existent table but is in my consciousness. The way the 'table-sense' is related to my consciousness is 'intentionality'. Husserl is of opinion that what we call essences or universals are pure and simple intentions of consciousness. There is however, no necessary commitment as to the ontological status of the intentional essences; they are precisely the 'phenomena'. The phenomena are grasped in intuitions preceding any judgment and in the mode of apodictic certainty. With the discovery of the intentional essences Husserl finds a solution to the problem of the foundations of mathematics and logic. 'The problem becomes for him the problem of reconciling the objective validity of logic and mathematics with the subjective processes of thinking. Husserl points out that the objects of logic and mathematics are not what logicism or psychologism would suggest. They are not found in or are abstracted from factual reality. Yet if they are found to be infallibly given they must be given apriori and are grasped in intellectual intuitions (categorical intuitions).

In the next stage of development[10] Husserl's phenomenology follows the course of transcendental phenomenology. Husserl now comes to see his problem from a wider perspective; it is the problem of the foundations of reason itself which gives to science and experience in general their meaning. Husserl now realises more clearly that consciousness is not anything of the world; it is what remains even when the existing world is taken out of consideration.[11] That means consciousness is transcendental in character. Consciousness is also transcendental in Kant's sense. For Kant anything is transcendental which is concerned with the apriori conditions of the possibility of knowledge and experience. For Husserl consciousness constitutes the transcendental ground wherein can be found the ultimate clarification and justification of all knowledge and experience. Husserl however, flatly rejects the Kantian thesis that consciousness is an empty form and that it can be perceived only in connection with the object transcendent to it. Consciousness, according to Husserl, is of such nature that it can never remain unperceived[2]. But normally consciousness is perceived in connection with the objects transcendent to it and that is due to consciousness' involvement with the world. In all of my conscious acts I am concerned with the world. As a result my consciousness assumes the forms of the objects of the world. But I can get out of the world and reach the heart of my pure consciousness and see consciousness in its original set up. The famous phenomenological reduction through epoche introduced in philosophy by Husserl is an aid to this process.

The word epoche is a greek term which means suspension of judgment. Phenomenological reduction through epoche consists in neutralising our belief concerning the existence of the world. This we do by suspending all judgments concerning existence. Phenomenological reduction is a twofold movement; it is a moving away from the natural world and a moving towards transcendental consciousness. By reduction consciousness' involvement with the natural world is disrupted. Consequently, a new field is opened up—the field of transcendental consciousness. All phenomenological 'seeing' take place within this field, 'seeking' being an immanent perception. In immanent perception the object belongs to the same stream of consciousness as perception itself. As a result every immanent perception necessarily guarantees the existence of the object; it is the source of authority and apodicticity.[13] Now the first thing that thus guarantees itself is the intentional structure of consciousness. The full intentional structure presents itself to be 'ego-cogito-cogitatum'[4]. Consciousness comprises itself in a series of acts. For each act there is the same ego that is conscious of its object. Reduction has placed under bracket all of consciousness' reference to the transcendent and the existent. Naturally the things that consciousness discloses before itself are only its intentions. The international objects are what

Husserl calls 'phenomena'. A close and detailed examinations of these phenomena further disclose that the phenomena are both presented and constituted in the acts of consciousness. The sense 'I' or the 'ego' as the identical subject is also subjectively constituted in these acts. While constitution becomes the project phenomenology turns out to be egology. In this way phenomenology in its search for foundations leads to the discovery of the 'transcendental ego' as the radical source of apodicticity which gives to science and reason in general their meaning.[15]

The Husserlian move towards foundations in consciousness is in line with the cartesian move towards new beginning in the self certitude of the ego but with different intentions and different outcomes. Descartes is after ratifying the world; Husserl is after disclosing the meaning of the world which finally may or may not ratify the sciences. The cartesian move is a horizontal move from the dubitable part of the natural world to the indubitable part of it.[16] As a result Descartes fails to grasp the ego in its transcendental significance. Descartes' identification of the ego with the human soul and the realm of consciousness with the psychological domain defeats Descartes' intention of radicalism. According to Descartes the ego is grasped in such a way that it permits to draw inferences as to the existence of the world. But Descartes' ego neither guarantees the existence of the world nor does explain its meaning. It is ultimately God's veracity that establishes the existence of the world. Unlike Descartes Husserl does not doubt the existence of the world. He simply withdraws from it and stays exclusively within the immanent data of consciousness which partake in the apodicticity of the ego. Thus the Husserlian move is a vertical one—from the natural world including me as a psychophysical being, to the transcendental ego which contains and constitutes the world.[17] The ego which is disclosed by epoche proves to be when rightly understood the 'transcendental ego'. The transcendental ego goes beyond the world and yet constitutes and confers meaning to the world.

In the last years of his phenomenological career[18] Husserl is concerned with the more specific problem of the foundations of science and culture. The ground proves to be nothing other than the 'life-world' or the 'lebenswelt'. The 'life-world' is the world of common experience; it is what remains when the world of science is reduced. The lebenswelt, according to Husserl, has been superseded by the world of science which passes for reality. But the world of science is the world of construction; it is inaccessible to direct and immediate perceptual experience. The lebenswelt on the other hand, presents itself in immediate perceptual experience. There it appears to be the common ground for all of us, in which we live and grow, in which we discover ourselves as mundane existents and in which we enter into co-operation and collaboration with each other. All theoretical truth—logical, mathematical, and scientific finds its ultimate validation and justification in evidences in the lebenswelt, the lebenswelt however, enters into the scope of phenomenological analysis when a second reduction is performed with regard to it and is rendered phenomenon in individuals' consciousness. The phenomenal content of the lebenswelt is thereby found to be intersubjectively constituted on the transcendental level. Husserl arrives at the notion of transcendental inter-subjectivity by finding the 'senses' of the others as 'alter egos' being constituted in one's individual consciousness. That means the individual ego still remains the subject with regard to the world even though it is foreshadowed in the background of the lebenswelt.

In appreciation we can say that the Husserlian move towards foundation in consciousness is an important philosophical move though it is too much to claim that Husserl has been able to reach the ultimate ground in transcendental ego-consciousness or even in the more concrete ground of the life-world. Husserl's phenomenology has left unaccounted the existence of the concrete-world. To say that the world has its intentional existence is not to explain the rationale of its existence. Heidegger, in particular, realised the short comings of Husserlian phenomenological analysis and he initiated a move towards 'Being' which according to him constitutes the 'foundation of all foundations'. Again, the world that is meaningful to us is an intersubjective world. By finding the sense of the 'others' getting being constituted in one's transcendental ego-consciousness Husserl has sought to preserve the primacy of the ego and the intersubjectivity of the world but till to the last analysis the tension between subjectivity and intersubjectivity is evident in Husserl. In this regard Sartre's analysis of consciousness as non-egological better explains the meaning of 'I' and 'others' in connection with the world.[20] Despite all its short comings the Husserlian move towards foundations in self-consciousness is a salutary move. It has at least opened up new directions in the analysis of consciousness. It points out that self-analysis can be more fruitful to science and philosophy if carried on in the perspective of foundations. More penetrating phenomenological observations may lead to the discovery of some other structures of consciousness and some other foundational grounds but individual's consciousness provides the right access to it. The conscious field is still to be explored and the foundations are yet to be found.

Burdwan University, Burdwan

REFERENCES

1. Gurwitsch : The Last work of Edmund Husserl : P.P.R. XVI—1956 Opening Section.
2. See Husserl's Preface to the English edition of 'Ideas' trans. B Gibson, London.
3. Richard Jeffry : Formal Logic : Its Scope and Limits. Ch. 10. Undecidability. Incompleteness (McGraw-Hill Book Company 1967).
4. J. Wisdom : Foundations of Inference in Natural Sciences P 46, London.
5. Ibid. P.44.
6. B.Russell : Human knowledge : Its Scope and Limits, P.65, P.201.
7: Cf. Marvin Farlur : Edmund Husserl and the Background of Philosophy. P.P.R.,Vol.I (1940-41) P 1—20.
8. Refers to Husserl's phenomenology represented by 'Logical Investigation' first edition (1900—1901).
9. M.Farber : The Function of Phenomenological Analysis P.P.R. Vol.I P.432.
10. Phenomenology represented by 'Logical Investigations' (Second edition) 1913, 'Ideas' (1913), Article 'Phenomenology' in Britanica (14th) ed.).

11. E. Husserl : Ideas Eng. Trans. B. Gibson. P. 113.
12. Ibid. P. 141.
13. Ibid. P. 124.
14. Ibid. P. 172.
15. Cartesian Meditation (Eng. Trans. D, Cairns), Sec. 28.
16. Jean Mark Laporte, S.J. Husserl's Critique of Descartes P.P.R. Vol. XXIII. (March, 1963) P. 339.
17. Ibid. P. 340.
18. Phenomenology represented by Husserl's last work : The Crisis of Eurpoean Sciences and Philosophy : An Introduction to Transcendental Phenomenology.
19. M. Heidegger : Being and Time. Eng. Trans. Macquarrie & Robinson (London) P.31.
20. A. Gurwitsch : A Non Egological Conception of Consciousness. P.P.R. Vol.I (1940-41) P. 325—345.

EDUCATION AND HUMAN DEVELOPMENT

Chand Mal Sharma,

The off-spring born to man is a human animal and not a human person. If he has to behave characteristically as a human being, he must be educated. The word education here is being used in a wide and non-formal sense, which is its true sense, considering the unanimously acknowledged aim of education. In its wide sense, the process of education is coterminus with socialisation and accultarisation process. In this sense, education is the necessary pre-condition for humanisation of the human animal. Wolf-children (children who were carried away from their human homes by wolves in early infancy and who were brought up in the jungles in wild environment) were found utterly wanting in characteristic human patterns of behaviour. Moreover, they were found to be incapable of learning what is typical human behaviour when efforts were made to educate them after reclaiming them. These studies have almost conclusively shown that human development is not a biological process but a bio-social process which requires existence of human environment as a condition sine qua non.

There is another sense of human development. In this other sense, human development means the fullest development of human personality, that is to say, a harmonious growth of various desirable traits pertaining to the cognitive, the affective and the conative mental faculties. The role of education in human development in the second sense is, indeed, immense. What is traditionally known as liberal education endeavours to promote human development in this sense. Thus the liberal education aims at intellectual, emotional and moral development of human person. It seeks to attain this aim by facilitating the cultivation of moderation, temperance, self-restraint and respect for fellow human beings.

The aim of educating for human development should be distinguished from the aim of education for attaining scholarship. Education for scholarship has the restricted objective of the growth of cognitive faculties of the person which does not lead ipso facto to the development of affective and conative faculties. The Universities and other higher centres of learning aim primarily at the cognitive or intellectual development of the individual. The comprehensive aim of education which consists in harmonious development of personality, is sought to be achieved at the school level. If education is taken in non-formal and wider sense it is a continuous and an unending process brought to halt only by biological degeneration. If one can meaningfully speak of essence of man, it is his educability. The capacity of man for education and development is immeasurable. What truly is the fullest development of human personality which education should aim at achieving is a question to which various answers have been given. The different answers have been given from the standpoints of different philosophers of education; their value can be assessed only by the critical evaluation of the philosophies of education in which they are embedded.

University of Rajasthan

CAN HUMAN NATURE BE CHANGED THROUGH THE EDUCATION PROCESS?
—The Confucian View—

Tsung I Dow

Whether or not human nature can be changed through education may remain debatable. Confucians may be excessive in stressing morality in education, but China seems presently to be continuing in this direction. Education in the Confucian perspective is the sole instrument for transforming and elevating man from the animal level to the level of Chun Tzu, the ideal man in whom Confucius rested his hope for final prevailing of the universal peace (Ta Tung). In three important passages he set forth the fundamental principles for attaining this goal. The first sentence of the *Analects* starts with "learning with constant practice is happiness." The opening statement of "Hsueh Chi" of the *Book of Ritual Records* (Li Chi) says that "the only way to establish customs and conventions for habitual observance of the rules of propriety is to mould and transform their characters through education." And the *Great Learning* defines its way (Tao) as follows: "To illustrate the illustrious virtues, to renovate people, and to rest in the utmost goodness."

Why did Confucius place such high value upon education? Because he firmly believed that mind is the master of body and action. Therefore, "one can cultivate his person by rectifying the mind." How can the mind be rectified? By extending knowledge to the utmost. He said:

"Things have their root and their branches. Affairs have their end and their beginning To know what is first and what is last will lead near to what is taught in the *Great Learning*.

"The ancients who wished to illustrate illustrious virtue throughout the world, first brought peace and order to their own states. Wishing to bring peace and order to their states, they first regulated their families. Wishing to regulate their families, they first cultivated their persons. Wishing to cultivate their persons, they first rectified their minds. Wishing to rectify their minds, they first sought to be sincere in their thoughts. Wishing to be sincere in their thoughts, they first extended to the utmost their knowledge. Such extension of knowledge lay in the investigation of things.

From the Son of Heaven down to the mass of the people, all must consider the cultivation of the person the root of everything besides."

Skepticism over the Confucian optimism naturally arises. Was he unrealistic? Can human nature be changed to meet the Confucian expectation? Confucius once said that "the gap between the most intelligent and the most stupid cannot be bridged" and that "man is born with uprightness." Ambiguities such as these abound in the sayings of Confucius. As Tzu Kung complained that "we can hear our master's views on culture and its manifestation" but we cannot hear his views on human nature and the way of heaven." Though Confucious may have been able to dodge this question, his followers had to face the issues. Their historical debates fill the pages of the history of Confucian philosophy.

2

What is human nature? What does it mean to say that man is by nature good? *The Doctrine of the Mean* (Chung Yung) speaks as follows: "What heaven imparts to man is called human nature. To follow our nature is to follow the Tao. Cultivating the Tao is called education." The goodness of human nature is hereby implied. Although *Chung Yung* was often translated as the *Mean*, "Chung" refers to what is central, and "Yung" refers to what is harmonious, in its universality. Together it suggests that there is harmony in human nature, a harmony that underlies our moral character and prevails throughout the universe. Upholding this tradition Mencius refuted the theory of Kao Tzu that human nature is neutral between good and evil. He asserted that "man's nature is as naturally good as water flows naturally downward." "If man does evil, it is not the fault of his endowment." For the feelings of commiseration, shame, propriety, and a sense of right and wrong are found in all men. Mencius argued further that "if we let people follow their feelings they will be able to do good." They have the innate knowledge (Liang Chih) and capacity (Liang Nung) to know and to do what is good. In this respect Mencius concluded "everything is complete within us."

Questions, however, persist. If man by nature can know and do what is good, education would seem unnecessary. Responding to this doubt, Mencius asserted that although man's nature is originally good, its natural goodness is lost without education. "Originally we have the four beginnings with us, except that when we do not think of them, they will be lost." As Confucius said: "Hold it fast, and it remains with you; let it go and you lose it." "Man differs from beasts very little;" "Man possesses a moral nature.: For Jen (humanity) is man's mind, and righteousness (I) is man's path; how lamentable it is to neglect the path and not pursue it, to lose this mind and not know how to retrieve it." "The difference between a superior man (Chun Tzu) and an ordinary man is that the former is able to preserve the mind and knows how to retrieve it when lost." "When one loses his chickens and dogs, one tries to retrieve them. How then can one not retrieve the lost mind?" Therefore, Mencius declared that "the great end of learning is nothing but to retrieve the lost mind."

While the advance of the theory of the four beginnings by Mencius perhaps put the Confucian doctrine of innate goodness of human nature on a solid psychological ground, his theory of retrieving the lost mind is singled out by Hsun Tzu as not reflecting the reality of mind. For Mencius himself had admitted that "the reasoning process is the master of mind," dictating man's reaction to sense stimuli so that man acts according to what he considers to be good and avoids what he considers to be bad. Therefore, Hsun Tzu maintained that "it is evident that nature of man is evil" because it is self-seeking and "that his goodness is acquired" because it is the result of education or conditioning. He said that "mind is like a piece of white cloth (tabula rasa), whether it becomes yellow or blue depends on how to dye it." In the chapter on the "Evilness of Human nature" in *Hsun Tzu*, he argued:

"The nature of man is evil; his goodness is the result of his activity. Man's inborn nature is to seek gain..envious and hates others..and possesses the desires of ear and eye....To follow man's nature and feelings will inevitably result in strife and rapacity combined with rebellion and disorder, and end in violence. Therefore, there must be the civilizing influence of teachers and laws and the guidance of propriety..What is in man and cannot be learned is his nature. What is in him and can be learned through education is what can be achieved through discipline.

Some one may ask: "If man's nature is evil, whence come propriety and righteousness? I answer that all propriety and righteousness are results of the activity of sages and not originally produced from man's nature. The potter pounds the clay and makes the vessel.."

Apparently Hsun Tzu contradicted Mencius on the goodness of human nature. However, both recognized the role of education in elevating man from the level of beast to the level of civility, and for that matter Hsun Tzu even placed higher value on education than Mencius. Moreover, both agreed that the nature of something whether good or bad, cannot be changed without changing the thing itself but the potential of perfectibility in man is there whether it can be developed fully from within or without.

After the ascendancy of Confucian ideology as state doctrine via Tung Chung-shu, the views of Hsun Tzu on human nature, under the challenge of Buddhism, gave in to Mencius. The resiliency of Confucian ideology demonstrated its greatest strength in the emergency of the Neo-Confucianism. A new interpretation on human nature was developed which well high abandons Mencius position. The new position is that human nature is originally good but evil arises from the material aspect (Chi) in man which may be impure and unbalanced. The role of education, for the Neo-Confucianists, is to remove the impurities, transform the unbalances, and preserve and insure the fullest development of the original nature. This amounts to a change in the original nature of man.

New-Confucians contended that everything in the universe embodies a law of its own being. This law is Li (Principle). This principle is the unalterable nature of man. According to Chu Hsi, Li is the source of goodness in man and the standard of right or wrong. If one obeys it and preserves it, everything will be right. In the opinion of Ch'eng I, "If one understands it clearly, one will be happy to follow it." Therefore, the principal task for man is to investigate Li to the utmost. It does not matter whether one does it through study, or engaging in human affairs; nor does it matter whether one investigates one thing deductively or many things inductively. With sufficient effort, one will achieve a thorough understanding. When that is done, one will see the distinction between right and wrong. Chu Hsi said: "The nature of all men is good, and yet there are those who are good from their birth and those who are evil from their birth. This is because of the difference in material force (Chi) with which they are endowed. .The objective of learning is to transform this material endowment."

It is a consensus among all Neo-Confucians, whether they are Ch'eng-Chu followers or Lu-Wangs, that man's nature is good, and cannot or need not be changed. But some aspects of man's nature, such as temperamant and dispositions (Chi Chih) can obscure the original goodness and must be moulded through education. When sufficient effort has been made to remove the obstacles from the mind, goodness will reveal itself. And when nature is cultivated to the fullest, one will act according to his inner dictation of goodness—the full manifestation of Li in his nature. To Neo-Confucians, the foundation of goodness is Jen. There we meet the Confucian virtues of love, compassion, and the like which permeate all human relationships. This is why Chu Hsi announced that Jen, conceived as a sort of sympathetic feeling toward the object, is a prerequisite for cognition because one must become receptive to knowledge before anything can be learned. Thus cultivation of person by rectifying the mind, and rectifying the mind by extension of knowledge, became the cornerstone of the Confucian theory of education. Clearly for them, the primary objective of education is character-moulding. Knowledge is its means. For the cultivation of persons, they expound the doctrine in the *Book of Changes* to maintain a balance between seriousness and righteousness. The former means concentration on one thing; the latter means the sense of right and wrong and the understanding of the correct way to do things. For the extension of knowledge they were critical of the prevalent habit of memorization, devotion to literary studies and flowery composition, but exhorted the virtues of thinking, doubting and probing and examining the principle of things so that one can get at the essentials, and achieve something new every day and advance every day. Finally all must be put into practice. According to Wang Yung-ming, "the attainment of knowledge is the beginning of learning, while practicing knowledge with effort is its end." Otherwise, all effort is in vain.

3

Since practice as the criterion of true knowledge is a Confucian contention, the characteristics of Confucian education in moral-building or the growth of man were fully reflected in its practice. A few important facts may illustrate the point.

First, good citizenship was the focus of Confucian curriculum. Although Confucius himself included music, archery, horsemanship, mathematics, and writing along with the rules of conduct in his curriculum, he also asserted that the purpose of teaching music was not for the sake of art or aesthetic value but for harmonizing mind and emotion. To Confucians, teaching knowledge apart from the cultivation of moral character would amount to training a thief to steal or strengthening a wretch in conceiving evil, thereby doing greater injuries to the world. During Mencius' time a certain P'ang Meng learned archery of E. When he had acquired completely all the science of E, he thought that in all the empire only E was superior to himself, and so he murdered E. Mencius blamed E for causing his own death because, Mencius argued, "If E had taught morality to P'ang, P'ang wouldn't have done that to him." Anyone who studied Chu Hsi's curriculum for his White Deer Grotto Academy would sense the urgency of this Confucian spirit.

Secondly, individual tutorship and personal exemplification were considered to be the most effective means for teaching. Confucius maintained an intimate relationship with his students and taught them according to their aptitudes, backgrounds and intelligence levels, etc. When he died, some of the students camped near his tomb for three years and left. In the chapter "On Studies" (Hsueh Chi) of the *Book of Ritual Records* (Li Chi) we are told that "when the solemn teacher wins respect, then respect for the Tao of teaching will be established; once respect for the Tao of teaching is established, people will begin to appreciate education." Often a teache'sr name was inscribed on the ancestor tablet in a Confucian home. For they contended that "parents give us life but teachers help us to become a man." When the Ming Confucian, Fang Hsiao-ju, infuriated the emperor, Chu Ti of the Yung Lo reign, for refusing to accept his legitimacy and went to gallows, eight hundred students of Fang went together.

Thirdly, education is a life long process. Confucius said: "At fifteen, I had my mind bent on learning. At thirty, I stood firm. At forty, I had no doubts. At fifty, I knew the decrees of heaven. At sixty, my ear was an obedient organ for the reception of truth. At seventy, I could follow that my heart desired, without transgressing what was right." Hsun Tzu asserted in the "Encouraging of Learning" that "learning continues until death and only then it does cease." For character moulding, the basic objective of Confucian education cannot be confined to school campus alone. Confucius said that "when I walk along with two others, they may serve me as my teachers. I will select their good qualities and follow them, their bad qualities and avoid them."

Fourth, Confucius and Mencius believed in the inseparability of education and politics. In the opinion of Confucius one of the attributes of Jen is "to establish others as one establishes himself" (Li-chi Li-jen) For that purpose Confucius instructed that "when educated, one must serve in the government." (Hsueh erh yu tse shih) and government must be served by the most virtuous and qualified men. For "one only sought knowledge and goodness for himself, the masses will not be affected. The masses cannot be transformed unless and until the government succeeded to standardize and institutionalize morality through its power." Thus education is the first order of politics," Confucius argued. Hsun Tzu defined education as "making use of good to lead others," The theoretical justification of the Chinese examination system lies right here.

Mencius went further than Confucius by proclaiming that to govern means to educate—to provide and insure people a right livelihood so that they will be able to cultivate propriety and righteousness." "If not," he said: "they will only try to save themselves from death; what leisure have they to proceed to what is good." That is why "in bad years, youth often abandon themselves to evil."

4

Finally Mencius placed that if an animal trainer in a circus can make lions to perform for the audience, there is no reason why man cannot be made to do better and live in peace than lions. (Jen erh pu ju chihshou hu?)

Florida Atlantic university, U.S.A.

36

SRI AUROBINDO ON EDUCATION AND HUMAN DEVELOPMENT

Pramod Kumar Koyal

Sri Aurobindo is one of the master minds of the present age. The rare versatility of his genius, the rich exuberance of his creativity and the synthetic comprehensiveness of his outlook are simply astounding. He has written on different branches of human knowledge with unsurpassed skill and profound insight. We shall, however, confine ourselves here only to an exposition of his views on education and human development.

Education, believes Sri Aurobindo, is a very important method of human development, but its true nature cannot be understood properly unless one tries to know the metaphysical background in which it is rooted. Viewed in this light, Sri Aurobindo's concept of education can be grasped only in relation to his concept of metaphysics, that is, the nature of Reality, Society and Man conceived by him.

Sri Aurobindo presents an integral Metaphysics, an integral weltanschauung, which does not reject any aspect of the Reality, but synthesises and integrates all aspects of the Supreme Truth. It maintains that the Transcendent, the Universal and the Individual are three indispensable aspects of the self-same Reality—Saccidānanda. The world is a playground of both Śiva and Śakti and the goal of creation is to become perfect like God, manifest Him in all aspects of life and fulfil His purpose in the world. In fact, the establishment of Kingdom of Heaven upon earth is the true aim of all human pursuits and education is no exception to it. Hence, the aim of education, according to Sri Aurobindo, is the realisation of divine perfection of man and society. Sri Aurobindo, thus, presents on the basis of his integral metaphysics an integral view of education, which synthesises the ideals of the East with the findings of the West.

The true basis of education, argues Sri Aurobindo, is the study of the human mind, infant, adolescent and adult. He is firmly convinced that any system of education, which is founded on theories of academic perfection but which ignores the instrument of study is more likely to impair intellectual growth than to produce a perfect and perfectly equipped mind. The reason behind this is that the educationist has, "to do, not with dead material like the artist or sculptor, but with an infinitely subtle and sensitive organism. He cannot shape an educational masterpiece out of human wood or stone ; he has to work in the elusive substance of mind and respect the limits imposed by the fragile human body."

The integral system of education propounded by Sri Aurobindo is based on three fundamental principles. First, the child should be allowed to know and develop by himself, while the teacher should only guide and help. Explaining the essence of this principle, Sri Aurobindo remarks, "The first principle of true teaching is that nothing can be taught. The teacher is not an instructor or task-master, he is a helper and guide. His business is to suggest and not to impose. He does not actually train the pupil's mind, he only shows him how to perfect his instruments of knowledge and helps and encourages him in the process. He does not impart knowledge to him, he shows him how to acquire knowledge for himself. He does not call forth the knowledge that is within ; he only shows him where it lies and how it can be habituated to rise to the surface." Sri Aurobindo rejects the contention that this principle could be applied only to the teaching of adolescent and adult minds and not to the teaching of children, because in his opinion there is only one sound principle of good teaching, which holds good for all— irrespective of age or sex. As a matter of fact, difference of age only serves to diminish or increase the amount of help and guidance necessary, it does not change its nature.

The second principle of integral education is that the education must suit the particular qualities, capacities, ideas and virtues etc., of the educated. To quote the inspiring words of

Sri Aurobindo, "The second principle is that the mind has to be consulted in its own growth. The idea of hammering the child into the shape desired by the parent or teacher is a barbarous and ignorant superstition. It is he himself who must be induced to expand in accordance with his own nature. There can be no greater error than for the parent to arrange beforehand that his son shall develop particular qualities, capacities, ideas, virtues, or be prepared for a pre-arranged career. To force the nature to abandon its own dharma is to do it permanent harm, mutilate its growth and deface its perfection. It is a selfish tyranny over a human soul and a wound to the Nation, which loses the benefit of the best that a man could have given it and is forced to accept instead something imperfect and artificial, second-rate, perfunctory and common." Sri Aurobindo has firm conviction that every one has in him something divine, something his own, a chance of perfection and strength in however small a field, which God offers him to take or refuse. The main task is to find it, develop it and use it. Hence, the chief aim of education should be to help the evolving soul to draw out that in itself which is best and make it perfect for a nobler use.

The third principle of integral education is to work from the near to the far, from that which is to that which shall be. The basis of a man's nature, according to Sri Aurobindo, is almost always, in addition to his soul's past, his heredity, his surroundings, his nationality and his country ; they mould him very powerfully and, therefore, from that we must begin. As Sri Aurobindo elaborates, "A free and natural growth is the condition of genuine development. There are souls which naturally revolt from their surroundings and seem to belong to another age and clime. Let them be free to follow their bent ; but the majority languish, become empty, become artificial, if artificially moulded into an alien form. It is God's arrangement that they should belong to a particular nation, age, society, that they should be children of the past, possessors of the present, creators of the future. The past is our foundation, the present our material, the future our aim and summit. Each must have its due and natural place in a National System of Education."

The instrument of education, according to Sri Aurobindo, in antaḥkaraṇa, which consists of four layers—citta, manas, buddhi and supramental faculties. Our education, in fact, should satisfy all these faculties. In this context, Sri Aurobindo lays great stress on moral and religious education. Moral education should be imparted by transformation of emotions, saṁskāras and svabhāva. It should be taught by example and suggestion and not merely by text books. Similarly, religious education should be imparted not only through books but also by different kinds of religious disciplines and practices, sādhanās.

Education, argues Sri Aurobindo, should not be piecemeal or by snippets, but it should be both simultaneous and successive. He suggests that teaching should start at seven or eight years of age. Another important point is that education should be imparted through one's mother-tongue. Once the child attains mastery of his mother-tongue, he should be imparted training of the senses, which means that senses should be improved by practice and the obstructions of the senses, nerves and manas should be removed. In addition, mental faculties should also be trained by using a particular faculty in mastering a particular subject. The pupil should be directed by the teacher to concentrate first on things and then on words and ideas. Memory and imagination should also be improved. Judgement should be trained by self-confidence, comparison and contrast. Moreover, one should cultivate a fine sense of words. The logical powers of the mind should be trained and improved by practice and not merely by formal teaching of logic. Again, a perfect education includes as an indispensable element physical culture, which aspires after perfection of body. Sports, marches, drill, games and, finally, Brahmacharya, are the essential features of physical culture.

The scheme of perfect education, however, according to Sri Aurobindo, is neither complete nor satifactory without yoga. It is undoubtedly yoga which leads man to realise the aim of true education, namely, self-education and divine perfection of man, society and the universe. Yoga, Sri Aurobindo is convinced, is the most important and potent method of human development. Yama, Niyama, Āsana and Prāṇāyāma can certainly help students in concentration. The importance of yoga in the field of education can well be appreciated, if we take into consideration the fact that merely imparting physical and mental training is not the goal of education. Its aim, on the other hand, is to lead individual and society towards the goal of perfection. In this process a stage comes when school education becomes inadequate and then the need of Yoga becomes imperative.

It may be pointed out here that the yoga, which makes human education complete and perfect, should not, in the opinion of Sri Aurobindo, be confused with any of the traditional systems of Yoga. By the term 'Yoga', Sri Aurobindo means always Integral Yoga, the essence of which may be expressed thus. If 'Yoga' literally means union, Integral Yoga is essentially man's conscious union and active co-operation with the Mother or the dynamic divine. The aim of Integral Yoga is integral union with the Infinite, and the technique of Integral Yoga is conscious co-operation with the integral consciousness of the Infinite. Against the traditional systems of yoga, which breathe more or less the spirit of world and life-negation, the Integral yoga of Sri Aurobindo maintains that the supreme goal of life is not merely the attainment of mukti or transcendental freedom, but also bhukti or free participation in the creative joy of the Spirit. It pleads for the synthesis of Śuddhi, Siddhi, Mukti and Bhukti and reveals the technique of actualising glorious ideals of Divine Transformation of the entire embodied existence, earthly immortality and conquest of death, collective liberation and perfection of the whole humanity, and Divine Life upon earth. Such glorious ideals, emphatically declares Sri Aurobindo, can be attained not by mere school-education, but by sincere and constant practice of the discipline of Integral yoga.

To sum up, it becomes quite obvious from the foregoing brief discussion of Sri Aurobindo's philosophy of education, that he has established a unique and marvellous synthesis between the important truths inherent in the Indian and

Western, ancient and modern systems of education. In this scheme of education, the development of every aspect of human life—physical, mental, spiritual and religious—has been sought. Since Sri Aurobindo regards the attainment of the goal of divine perfection impossible without the development of the social aspect of man, therefore in his theory of education the development of individual powers, capacities and virtues has been emphasised along with that of social qualities. Today, when the thinkers and teachers are facing numerous serious problems in the field of education, the philosophy of education put forth by Sri Aurobindo can provide a great help in finding out the main causes and solutions of these problems. Like other fields of human knowledge, in the field of education also Sri Aurobindo has undertaken the search for truth with great comprehensiveness and depth and has thrown new light on the problem of education and human development. And, hence, the concept of education presented by Sri Aurobindo, which expounds the principles of true education and reveals the technique of integral development and growth of personality, is highly relevant not only for the contemporary Indian educational philosophers, but also for the educationists of the whole world.

Government Post Graduate
College, Mandsaur
(M.P.)

37

PHILOSOPHY AND EDUCATION FOR DEVELOPMENT

J. de Marneffe

When the organizers of the Indian Philosophical Congress opened a Section on "Education and Human Development" for this Golden Jubilee Session of the Congress, they surely wanted us to examine what Philosophy can contribute to both education and development. But when they specified that we should deal with *human* development, they appeared to indicate that the topics to be studied are not those linked with 'development' in the now commonly used sense of "industrialization," but with those topics linked with the liberal and humanistic formation of man, in contrast with his technological training.

My submission is that today human development inevitably implies industrialization. The consideration of education for human development would then have to include this aspect of the matter too. I think also, however, that human development goes far beyond industrialization, though it must always remain linked with it. We shall explore also the implication of this fact. We shall thus try to find out what philosophy can contribute to these two aspects of human development and what place philosophy should get in an education geared to this total human development.

Development Includes Industrialization

In the vocabulary of the mass media of today, the word 'development' has come to mean 'industrialization'. When the mass media speak of 'developing countries', it is not to suggest that these countries are not civilized, or do not have a culture. Their culture, in fact, might be superior to the one of the so-called 'developed countries'. The phrase 'developing countries' is used just to say that these countries do not have the same industrial equipment as the development countries have.

There have been recently, among the youth, movements which rebelled against the trend towards industrialization. There have been philosophers who opposed it. Herbert Marcuse, for instance, wrote a book on the *One-Dimensional Man*[1] and denounced the baleful results of advanced industrialization. According to him, the progress of industry leads to a totalitarianism which represses the vital needs of its subjects and dulls their minds into the wilful acceptance of such tyranny. Not being sure that the present or coming generations will be able to see where their genuine good lies, he understands that we should at least respect those who give their life to the "Great Refusal".

Is it for the Economists alone to argue the modern man cannot live without advanced industrialization or has Philosophy its say in the matter? The level at which Marcuse raised the discussion, implies that the answer must come from both sides. The economists may point out that the present world population and its foreseeable increase requires a fairly advanced industrialization, if the vital needs of that population have to be satisfied. But the basic outlook on life, on the respective value of poverty, sufficiency and wealth must be supplied by philosophy. Marcuse has well argued that once we are engaged in a system like the one of the industrialized countries, there is a great difficulty not only to change it or check it, but even to pass correct judgment on it. While the developing countries tend eagerly towards industrialization, are they going to pursue it as an absolute good or as a good which must remain relative to the other requirements of human development? Philosophy should help man to decide if he should say 'No' to that development or a 'Yes' which knows the dangers and the risks.

The question is not an easy one? Philosophers have dwelt upon it again and again. We have, for instance, the criticisms which Gabriel Marcel has levelled against the technological age and the uneasiness it sets us in. Must his criticisms be declared pessimistic or are they just the right warnings which must awake our generation to the dangers it is in? We can hardly go back to the easy optimistic views of the last century which considered that science and industry would progress continually and that their progress would infallibly ensure man's happiness. The use in the past and the still pending threat of the atomic weapons would surely make us pause and think. The dilemma is clear: either we neglect industrialization, and men will die of hunger, or we go ahead with it and, sooner or later we are likely to perish in an atomic holocaust. Only an increase of wisdom can show us the way out between the two threatening disasters. Personally, I feel a simple 'No' to industrialisation is wrong. We must say 'Yes' to industry; we must say 'No' to its excesses and one-sidedness. We must advance towards a synthesis of effort and caution, in hope.

Human Development beyond Industrialization

Industrialization itself is a mere equipment, however required it is for men to survive, numerous as they are today. Industrialization, ecologically husbanded, should ultimately improve man's health and comfort. From it also man can obtain greater opportunity for employment. Work after all should be the chief intermediary for the distribution of wealth.

But beyond the benefits of industrialization, the human sciences put more and more into evidence the wealth of other advantages available to man for his fulfilment and happiness. Elementary introspection had always told man what made him happy. But the recent psychological and social enquiries have revealed the ways in which man's psychological development is linked with the experience of his youth, with the types of persons he met, with the events he went through. Anthropology has peered into the past of mankind and still explores its present to find out the springs of culture. Beyond the analyses of recent Existentialism, the recent trend of Structuralism goes deeper and deeper into the hidden mechanism of our thoughts, feelings and powers of expression. Language itself is submitted to an ever more rigorous analysis.

The increase of knowledge in all these fields helps us to realize the possibilities of man's fuller development. However when we try to use this knowledge, we discover that, besides repealing new aspects and possibilities of human development this knowledge puts also into doubt things which we thought were since long secure and unquestionable. What is morality? What is religion? Studies on culture have revealed a certain ethical relativism. Analyses of religious languages have put into evidence their far from literal meanings.

Again, here, philosophy is called to play a crucial role. What is the ultimate nature of that 'man' whom we want to develop? Has any aspect of his nature to be given a priority over the other? What is he in regard to society? Just a part of it or its very *raison detre*, the very justification of its being? What are the foundations of morality and religion. What is the status of the values which are said to be the very bearings of human existence: Truth, Goodness and Beauty.

A human development which looks beyond industrialization cannot find its ultimate norms in the human sciences alone, if these do not include a philosophical reflection. Obviously, to fulfil this role with regard to development, philosophy must not just be an ideology, a standpoint uncritically adopted and forced upon the minds of all through propaganda. It must seek the truth critically. But it is not enough to criticize. Philosophy must also try to build some constructive outlook within the framework of which one can develop a wisdom for action. Thus the philosophy which is called for, should be essentially discernment, knowledge and wisdom.

Education for Development

Development is not reached by a few people having formed for themselves a vision of things in their unity and ultimate value. It is not attained by a few people knowing the more recent scientific discoveries. Development is a collective effort which needs to be carried on through a succession of generations. Hence it must assure its own maintenance and constant renewal through that complex process which we call Education.

Education, first, suggests formal schooling, teaching or training and, secondarily, the knowledge, ability, etc. thus developed. But, at present, there is a whole trend to broaden the concept of education and to make it cover all forms of learning, within or without the school, in youth or during the whole of one's life.

A study of education for development presupposes a study of the philosophy of education. George K. Kneller of the University of California, in his *Introduction to the Philosophy of Education*, points out that "we cannot criticize existing educational policies or suggest new ones without considering such general philosophical problems as (a) the nature of good life, to which education should lead (b) the nature of man himself, because it is man we are educating; (c) the nature of society, because education is a social process; and (d) the nature of ultimate reality which all knowledge seeks to penetrate." He thus concludes rightly that "Educational philosophy, then, involves among other things the application of formal philosophy to the field of education."[3]

Once more, philosophy is called in, as for development, to supply the framework within which education itself must be set. Kneller, in the same book, shows how different types of philosophies such as Idealism, Realism and Pragmatism, are at the basis of various philosophies of education, such as 'Perennialism', 'Progressivism' and 'Reconstructionism'. It would take us too long to go into the detail of his analysis, but it is interesting because it illustrates well the relevance of philosophy here also.

A more concrete approach to the question of education and especially of education for development is supplied by the recent report prepared for the UNESCO by an international team of scholars, under the chairmanship of Edgar Faure, former Prime Minister and former Minister of Education in France. The report of this commission, presented in 1972, has a significant title : *Learning to Be* : *The World of Education Today and Tomorrow*.[4] The burden of their conclusion is that today and tomorrow, more than ever, education is not just teaching and instructing, but helping people to learn, and not to learn just in schools but in so many other ways now available to us through the mass media. Though the report insists, on the need of imparting skills, especially for modern industrial development, it emphasizes, again and again, that the total human development is the one which should ultimately be aimed at.

Though the explicit reference to Gabriel Marcel is not made, it is his distinction between 'being' and having' which is used in the title of the book to focus the attention on what ultimately counts for man. It is not just what he *has*, but what he *is*. Education, then, does not reach its aim, unless, besides helping people to learn things, it helps them to learn how to learn, so that education can be a life concern. And, furthermore, education is not complete, unless it helps people to improve what they are rather than what they have. *Aprendre à etre*, "*Learning to Be*" is really the aim of education and of total development.

The same ideal inspires the outlook of the recently much spoken of educationist, Ivan D. Illich. He wants also that man, and what he *is*, should be the centre of perspective of all education. In a vein somewhat similar to the one of Herbert Marcuse, who took a negative attitude to industrialization, Ivan Illich takes a negative attitude to schooling. In his book *Deschooling Society*,[5] he claims that the putting together of instruction and its certification, as it is done in the whole system of schools and in the certificate requirements for jobs, does harm to learning and true education. Another illusion on which school rests, he says, "is that most learning is the result of teaching."[6] There are so many other ways of learning, such as experience, reading, group discussion, etc,..., that teaching and especially compulsory submission to schooling should be discontinued. The suggestion is linked with an attack on the type of society which is thus created, a society of consumption and of institutionalized access to it, on the basis of certificates issued by teaching institutions at all the levels of education.

Such an extreme position as the one of Illich did not fail to provoke strong reactions. Another book, with the title *After Deschooling, What?*[7], offers further essays of Ivan Illich and of some of his supporters and opponents. In the last group we have Herbert Gintis of Harvard University. His essay has for title : *Toward a Political Economy of Education* : *A Radical critique of Ivan Illich's Deschooling Society*."[8] The burden of his criticism rests on the view that the whole matter is more complex than Illich has made it. Gintis points to Illich's failure to see that man does not have an essence preceding all social experience and condition. I would add : if the present social set-up is taken into consideration, we see, for one thing, in the light of what we said earlier, that, today more than ever, the needed industrialization requires schooling and that individual cannot on a large scale be left completely on their own in matter of education, without the human race itself, large as it is, courting chaos and starvation on a large scale.

If Illich's solution of Deschooling is not acceptable, the point of his exhortation to personal initiative and voluntary collaboration in order to acquire a more human education should not be lost. It is the same point as was made by the report to the UNESCO. This personal effort for education is felt as the great need everywhere today.

The Place of Philosophy in Education and Development.

If philosophy is so required to justify development and set it in its proper perspective, one would think that philosophy should be a favoured subject in the complete curriculum of education. But, in fact, in many places, it receives the treatment which Kant lamented had become the lot of Metaphysics: "Time was, he wrote, when she was the *queen* of all sciences; and if we take the will for the deed, she certainly deserves, so far as regards the high importance of her object-matter, this title of honour. Now, it is the fashion of the time to heap contempt and scorn upon her; and the matron mourns, forlorn and forlorn and forsaken..."[9]

I know that we must not generalize. There are centres where philosophy is still studied quite earnestly. Even the last number of *Radical Philosophy* reports from London in a review of books on "Philosophy in China", that at present, "almost everyone in China studies philosophy"[10]

In India, in spite of a long philosophical tradition, philosophy is studied by a small minority of scholars and students. Undergraduates in Arts are made to study formal logic, even in some places, symbolic logic. Should not all future graduates, in view of their being expected to take responsible posts in the country, be rather made to study some philosophy of values?

Industrialization is helped by science and advanced science requires a philosophy of science. Economic and social progress requires a knowledge of the human sciences and these call for a philosophy of man. Corruption and malpractice defeat our progress in development. Should not students be acquainted at least with what have been throughout the ages the efforts made to establish the foundation of morality? While the religious traditions are shaken by a modernist crisis, while the social and family ties are relaxed, there is a real vacuum which is created concerning morality. If we do not want to have recourse to a State enforced morality, how should this vacuum be filled if not by conviction arising from personal effort of discernment? The views of others may help us here; at least the chance of having access to them should be given through the system of education. We find ourselves still threatened by communalistic religious conflicts. Should not a knowledge *about* religion and religions be given to all, even though, in secular countries, State Schools are not allowed to teach religion to their students? This last distinction between "education about religions" and "religious education" is made, to favour the former, by the *Report of the Education Commission* (1964-66); *Education and National Development*.[11]

I know that it is extremely difficult, in some countries, and particularly in India, to bring everywhere a change in the curriculum, because the authority on matters of education is divided in as many centres as there are States in the country and independent Universities in the States.[12] What is left to be done, then, is to create an awareness, a consensus regarding needs and the ways of satisfying them. It should be the result of such Congress as ours to create this awareness and to foster this consensus.

In the present need for industrialization, in the present yearning for total human development, philosophy is not just something peripheral, something we can dispense with. As the compass is not what moves the ship but what directs it, so also in the world of today, philosophy may not be able to bring about development, but it can guide it. That is why it is very much wanted.

Institute of Philosophy and Religion, Poona

REFERENCES

1. *Studies in the Ideology of Advanced Industrial Society*, Boston, Beacon Press, 1964; 7th Printing 1968.
2. New York, John Wiley and Sons, 2nd ed. 1971, p,5.
3. *Ibid.*
4. Delhi, Sterling, 1973, xlix, 313 pp.
5. London, Calder and Boyars, 1971.
6. *Op.cit.*, p.12.
7. Edited by A. Gartner, C.Greer, add F. Riessman; New York, Harper and Row, Perennial Library, 1973.
8. *Ibid.*, pp.29-76.
9. *Critique of Pure Reason*, Preface to the First Ed. London, Dent, 1934,p.1.
10. Spring 1975, n.10, p.33.
11. Ministry of Education, Government of India, r966, p.20
12. M.V. Mathur : "Tasks of Universities in India", in S.D. Kertes (Ed.): *The Task of Universities in a Changing World*, Notre Dame, Univ. of N.D. Press, 1971, pp.40-4758.

THE PROCESS OF UNIVERSALIZATION IN POETIC CREATION

Nagendra

How and why does the general reader find pleasure in the experiences of particular man and women in a poem or a drama? This is one of the most ancient and valuable possessions of humanity and no sooner had man started thinking about the problems of life, than the one question which should have exercised his mind at the very outset must be this : How are we concerned with Rāma and Duṣyanta? When a vast span of time and space divides us from them, how do we identify ourselves with their sorrows and joys? A convincing answer was found in the theory of universalization in poetic creation.

The germs of this theory can be found in Bharata's Nātyaśāstra itself—composed about two thousand years ago and a more positive evidence of at least a preliminary knowledge of the theory was available in Aristotle's Poetics.

These evidences only prove that the theorists have been conscious of the problem from the earliest times. The first systematic thesis was, however, propounded by the Sanskrit theorist Bhaṭṭanāyaka about a thousand years back near about the 9th century A.D. His relevent quotation in this behalf runs as follows :"....the basic sentiment which is converted into *Rasa* or aesthetic experience as a result of the process of universalization affected by *Bhāvakatva*[1] is made exteremely enjoyable to the reader by the third function (of the poetic language)—namely *Bhojakatva*.[2] *Bhāvakatva* is the second function of poetic language characterized by the absence of flaws and presence of poetic qualities as well as figures of speech and is endowed with a capacity for turning the particulars of poetry into universal forms and purging the sensibility of the reader or the spectator of personal infatuations.

An analysis of this quotation leads to the following conclusions.
   (i) The particulars in a poem viz. the particular objects of emotion and their manifestations etc. are converted into universals.
   (ii) This process is the essence of creative activity.
   (iii) It is rendered possible by the poetic qualities and figures of speech etc., i.e., by the imaginative use of language.
   (iv) As a result of this process the basic sentiment also is ultimately universalized and thereby converted into aesthetic bliss.
   (v) Universalization takes place before aesthetic enjoyment—actually this is the process which renders poetic material enjoyable by divesting the particulars of their peculiar characteristics bound by time and space.

Bhaṭṭanāyāka's junior contemporary—the great Abhinavagupta—made a few modifications and re-stated the thesis as follow :

"During the process of poetic experience, wherein the object ceases to be an individual and the subject does not appear to be real, the sentiment itself is freed from the limitations of time and space i.e. as a result of the universalization of the subject and the object, the sentiment itself becomes impersonal and universal."

The gist of it is that our emotional experiences cause pleasure and pain so long as our ego is involved in them, but during poetic creation they are impersonalized and thereby get purged of the sensous elements. Thus, the essence of the process is the universalization of the sentiment.

In the light of this modification, a later theorist Govinda Thākkur, (15th cent. A.D.) one of the commentators of Kāvyaprakāśa, has presented the thesis in clear-cut terms :—

"Bhāvakatva means universalization. This process imparts a universal form to the particular subject and object as also to the sentiment. In the case of the former, universalization means the portrayal of individuals like Sītā etc. in universal forms—as beautiful damsels ; whereas in the latter i.e. in the case of the sentiments and their external manifestations, it means freedom from particular relationships."

(K.P. Nirnaya Sagara Press, p. 66)

According to this interpretation, all the components of a poem : viz. the object, the subject, the stimulus and the external manifestations as also the basic sentiment along with its accessory transient feelings undergo the process of universalization.

This formula was accepted in general by most of the critics except for two, namely, Viśvanātha (14 cent.) and Jagannātha (17th cent.) whose interpretations are slightly different. Normally Viśvanātha also believes in the universalization of all the components, but he has laid greater emphasis on the identification of the reader with the subject.

Panditarāja Jagannātha has also, in his own way, laid the main emphasis on the reader's identification with the subject. Formally he has rejected the theory of universalization, but the rejection is only academic ; for in practice what he has done is just a substitution of the technical term. In the light of his own philosophical convictions, he has explained the process as 'an error of feeling'.

The glorious tradition of Indian Poetics broke down after Panditarāja and there was little activity in this branch of literature in any of the Indian languages except Hindi. But in Hindi also, the poet-theorists dealt only with the lighter aspects of poetic art with the result that along with all other basic problems the present topic, viz. the theory of universalization was also utterly neglected till after about three centuries the great Hindi critic Ācārya Rāmacandra Śukla revived it in his monumental essay which was published in 1933. According to him 'Unless the object of an emotion is depicted in such a way that it becomes a common object of the same emotion for every sensitive reader, it fails to acquire in full the capacity to evoke proper aesthetic response. This is described as the process of universalization in Indian Poetics."

The topic was discussed by some later critics as well, but they could hardly make any substantial contribution.

Four Basic Issues

From the above discussion the followsng points emerge :

(i) The process of universalization affects all the items of the aesthetic material viz. subject, object, external manifestations, accessory feelings, and the basic sentiment. This happens in succession which is, of course, imperceptible ; the universalization of the subject, object etc. takes place earlier and that of the basic sentiment follows immediately as an inevitable consequence.

This is Bhaṭṭanāyāka's point of view in which the subjective and the objective attitudes are properly balanced.

(ii) Although originally the subject and the object etc. are universalized resulting in the universalization of the basic sentiment, yet the essence of the process is the liberation of the reader's sensibility in which all the distinctions finally disappear.

That is the view of Abhinavagupta whose approach is basically subjective.

(iii) The third point of view is presented by Viśvanātha who accepts the principle of the universalization of all the components, but highlights the reader's identification with the subject. According to him the reader whose sensibility is sublimated during the process identifies himself even with supernatural characters and shares their extraordinary experiences.

(iv) According to Ācārya Śukla, the pivot is the object (Ālambana) or its objective qualities. The poet describes the object in such an effective manner that, even though retaining its identity, it evokes the same emotion in the reader as is experienced or expressed by the subject in the poem. Ācārya Śukla also believes in the universalization of the sentiment but his emphasis is on the object or its qualities.

An Evaluation

Which of these is the corrrect version? Wherein does universalization actually take place? That is the crux of the matter and unless it is properly resolved the real meaning and significance of this principle will not be clear.

In the context of a poem, there are obviously two entities: the poem or the art-object and respondent. The poem consists of subject, object, stimuli, external manifestations and ancillary feelings, and the respondent is the reader. In the opinion of Bhaṭṭanāyaka, all the components of the art-object are universalized and consequently the basic sentiment of the respondent as well. That's the original thesis, but, before we examine this, it would be more in order to consider the amendments.

Indentification with subject: In the process of universalization, all the components including the subject are covered : the universalization of the subject also is an integral parts of the process. But there is a difference between the universalization of the subject and the identification of the respondent with the subject. Whereas in the former process, the subject sheds off its special characteristics and is converted into a common human being, in the latter the reader identifies himself with the special character of the subject. Thr term 'subject' here is very vague and identification with the subject in every case is neither possible nor desirable. This character may be thoroughly repugnant to the reader or his plight may be miserable in which the reader would not like to place himself.

Therefore, the theory of 'identification with the subjects' untenable. Identification is not an independent and self-sufficient activity, it is a part of the general process.

The universalization of the object or its essential qualities:—

The rationale of this view is that although the object of emotion in a poem makes a particular and concrete impresion on the mind of reader, yet, by virtue of his or her essential qualities which have the same appeal for all, this object evokes almost the same feeling in the heart of the entire reader community. Thus, it is the object, or, to be more correct, his essential qualities which are basically universalized. The major objection to this view is that it will delimit the range of the poetic objects and only the traditional attitude will prevail i.e. some of the characters like Rāma will always be the subject of pleasant emotions and others like Rāvaṇa would be permanently associated with unpleasant emotions: thus the aesthetic appreciation will be invariably controlled by moral conventions.

Universalization of the reader's experience: The universalization of the reader's experience or the liberation of his sensibility is the basic as well as the culminating point in the process of aesthetic appreciation. But it is an effect—as a result of the universalization of the subject and the object etc, the sensibility of the responsive reader is liberated from all personal involvements. This interpretation also cannot stand the test, because in the final analysis the liberation of sensibility cannot be differentiated from the composure of the spirit saṁvidviśrānti—which converges on the experience of the 'aesthetic bliss' (i.e. Rasa) itself. Thus, the liberation of the reader's sensibility is not the cause of universalization but its effect.

The universalization all the items :

In this way, all the amendments proposed by later theorists have fallen and we are left with the original proposition of Bhaṭṭanāyaka the universalization of all the components. For example, in the context of the famous scene from Rāmacaritamānasa, *where Rāma and Sītā meet for the first time in King Janakaś garden* the subject Rāma, the object Sita, the stimuli i.e. the romantic environments on the one hand and 'the celestial grace' of Sītā on the other, Rāma's gestures and his immediate reactions of joy, hesitation and self-assurance—all are universalized. In other words, the situation as a whole appears not as a particular event bound by time and space, but as a universalized phenomenon with the result that the sentiment evoked thereby in the heart of the reader transcends all personal associations and is universalized. This poetic situation, however, is an inanimate object; its appeal lies in its essential meaning which the poet wants to communicate. And, what is it that the poet wants to communicate except his own experience—not the personal experience, but the artistic experience, the creative experience or the experience of recreating an emotive response through imagination? This is the poetic meaning which on the one hand embodies the poet's artistic emotion and on the other evokes a similar emotion in the respondent. The whole poetic situation or texture is the concrete form or image of this experience.

In conclusion, therefore, one can safely assert that it is the poet's experience which is universalized. When a person is able to communicate his experience in such a way as to evoke a similar experience in everybody, he has, we would say, the capacity for universalization. Each one of us is able to feel and also to express himself to a certain extent; but everybody is not capable of universalizing his experience; and that is why, in spite of his ability to feel and express, everybody is not a poet. A poet is one who is able to universalize his experience.

University of Delhi

WITTGENSTEIN ON PUZZLEMENT & EXPLANATION IN AESTHETICS

V.P. Sharma

In, what might be called, the aesthetic situation, we are in the presence of a work of art, to which we might respond in a variety of ways. We might talk or behave or gesture in all kinds of ways to express our appreciation, puzzlements, discomforts, delights, or some other kinds of profound impression that great works of art often make on us. Is there anything here that needs to be explained, and what would that explanation be like ? According to Wittgenstein, one can appreciate a work of art in all kinds of ways, the linguistic response being only one of them. For example, I can show my appreciation of Mozart by going to Mozart concerts very often, just as I can show my unhappiness with Wagner by giving away all of my Wagner records to some one hung up on the late nineteenth century jungleful of romantic noises. If you show your liking or disgust by behaving in certain ways, your behaviour does not invite any explanation, if only because no one has asked for it. But now imagine some one expressing his puzzlement or discomfort or delight through language and saying things like "Why do the opening bars of Beethoven's Fifth have a peculiar impression on me ?" or "Why does any kind of rock music make me feel so uncomfortable ?" Obviously some kind of explanation is being asked for here. I shall first briefly explore Wittgenstein's thinking on this question and then suggest some criticisms. Let me say quickly that my account of Wittgenstein's thinking in this area is based on two sources: Cyril Barrett's *Wittgenstein : Lectures and Conversations on Aesthetics, Psychology ond Religious Belief* and the remarkable record of Wittgenstein's 1930-33 lectures that Prof. Moore has left us in *Mind* LXIII, 1954 and LXIV, 1955.

Aesthetic Puzzlements, Discomforts, etc. Wittgenstein thinks that aesthetic puzzlements and discomforts are more correctly understood as directed to the work of art than as caused by it. "There is a 'why' to aesthetic discomfort", he says, "not a cause to it."[2] We allow ourselves into this cause and effect way of talking through the misleading analogy with pain and the cause of pain. To take one of Wittgenstein's examples, when I, looking at a door which is out of proportion to the rest of the building, express my aesthetic discomfort by saying "Too high!", "Too high!" is directed to that door, not caused by that door. Another example: When I am afraid of John, my fear is directed to him, but need not be caused by him. Also, the expression of discomfort or puzzlement need not involve the knowledge of its cause.

Explanation in Aesthetics. This means, says Wittgenstein, that a 'way' question in aesthetics (which is incidentally one of the many ways of expressing aesthetic discomforts or puzzlements) is not a question inviting a causal explanation in the psychological-physiological sense of certain sounds causing certain changes in the listener's brain and, through them, causing him to say "Why do these bars have a peculiar impression on me?". Apart from the unavailability of such a detailed scientifically established explanation, Wittgenstein says that even if some scientist could, at some time in the future, provide it, the aesthetic puzzlement might still not be banished.[3] Therefore, "why do these bars have a peculiar impression on me?" must be calling for an altogether different kind of explanation. What kind? Wittgenstein's answer is as follows: To explain aesthetics (or to give reasons in aesthetics) is to do criticism, not to give a causal explanation. And you do criticism when you give further appropriate, detailed, significant and interesting descriptions of the work under consideration, often against the background of descriptions of works of a different kind. You do criticism when you dramatise the distinguishing features of a work through carefully arranged samples of works of different kinds; when you show how the work is put together, and what happens, for example, when certain important chords in a Beethoven piano sonata are changed, and what happens when they are put back. You do this, says Wittgenstein, to get someone to see what you see and thereby end his puzzlement or discomfort. Explanation, analysis, giving reasons in aesthetics, is a kind of practical pragmatic affair to get someone to see something, and, hopefully, to end disagreement because criticism is partly persuasive. It is analogous to what happens in the court room where you clear up the circumstances of the action and thereby appeal to the jury.[4]

The Criterion for Correct Explanation. Imagine someone saying to Wittgenstein: "If aesthetic explanation is not causal, we can never know it is correct." Since we are interested in correct not incorrect explanations, the question arises: "What in Wittgenstein's view is to count as a correct explanation? His answer is very interesting and provocative: An explanation in aesthetics isn't really an explanation unless it is accepted by the other person[5]. It is somewhat analogous to explanation in psycho-analysis, where the whole point of explanation is to get the patient to accept it, so that he is cured of whatever was bothering him. Until that happens nothing that the psycho-analyst might say would count as an explanation. If I were guessing what the chairman of this session has in mind right now, what could be a better criterion for the correctness of my guess than his acceptance of my guess. Something like this is true of aesthetics and psycho-analysis: there are no independent checks to the correctness of explanation, i.e. independent of the other person's agreement and acceptance.

So far I have given you, partly in my own words, Wittgenstein's thoughts on puzzlement and explanation in aesthetics, and I must confess that I am very much fascinated by the originality and the sparkling freshness of a good part of his approach to aesthetics. But not every thing; so I turn to some critical comments.

I

First let us take his distinction between 'something being caused by X' and 'something being directed to X'. There is obviously such a distinction as our examples have shown, and the question now is whether it applies to the aesthetic situation exactly the way Wittgenstein thinks it does.

Wittgenstein's own example, through which he shapes his distinction, has to do with someone feeling discomfort at the sight of a door that is out of proportion to the rest of the building and expressing discomfort by saying "Too high!" According to him the correct thing to say about his discomfort is that it is directed to something out there, not that it is caused by something out there. Also, it would be misleading and incorrect for the person to say that he knows its cause or that his discomfort has a cause. It seems to me that the situation described by his example should permit us to say *both* that his discomfort is directed to that door and that he is aware of the cause of that discomfort. "Too high!" one might say is on the one hand the beginning of criticism (I say only the beginning); on the other hand, it is an expression of discomfort. Insofar as saying "Too high" is doing criticism, in the sense that you are pointing out what is aesthetically wrong with that door, the utterance can be properly said to be directed to the door or the entire building. But insofar as the utterance "Too high" is an expression of discomfort (which incidentally could have been expressed through some other utterance, or through some appropriate gesture or other kind of behavior) it is devoid of any critical dimension and, therefore, cannot ordinarily be said to be directed to anything. Discomforts and puzzlements are, and are felt as caused, while criticisms are directed at something out there. As an expression of discomfort, therefore, "Too high!" is very likely accompanied by the speaker's awareness of its being caused by something and followed by a desire to discover that cause, if only because discomforts and puzzlements are experiences we would all like to get out of. So I am aware of the cause of my discomfort in the sense that I am aware of the likelihood of discomfort disappearing if the door were lowered. This does not mean—and Wittgenstein is right in pointing this out—that there are two things going on in my mind, feeling discomfort and knowing its cause. The point is that as soon as I am aware of whatever my utterance "Too high!" is directed to, I am aware of the cause of my discomfort expressed by the same utterance. To Wittgenstein's objection that saying I know the cause makes it look "as if I had analyzed the feelings (as I analyze the feeling of hearing my own voice and, at the same time, rubbing my hands), which of course I haven't done" I am tempted to give a somewhat Wittgensteinian answer : "It need not look because it doesn't"[6]. Also if, as Wittegenstein himself says, " 'Too high !' is a reaction analogous to my taking my hand away from a hot plate"[7], why is it misleading to say that I know the cause of that uncomfortable movement of my hand ? Reading Wittgenstein's *Lectures on Aesthetics*, it is difficult not to get the impression that he is overly fascinated by the mechanical model of causal connection, in which context causal explanation consists in tracing a mechanism. What causes the bicycle wheel to move ? You trace the mechanism. Since there is no such mechanism to be traced between my discomfort and disproportionate door, Wittgenstein doesn't want us to bring the cause and effect language into aesthetics.

II

Finally I turn to an examination of Wittgenstein's thinking on the question "What is to count as a correct explanation in aesthetics?" or "What is the criterion for correct explanation?". And here I find lot of tension in his thinking insofar as he gives me the impression of alternating between three positions scattered over his 1930-33 and 1938 lectures referred to earlier.

(1) The first one, that the criterion for the correctness of explanation is that the person to whom it is offered accepts it, I have already given you in the earlier part of my paper. I developed it more fully because I thought that Wittgenstein made the strongest case for it in his 1938 *Lectures*, and also because it strikes me as a very fresh and original approach.

(2) But at other times, again in his 1938 *Lectures*, he also approaches the question of the criterion for correct explanation from the side of the traditional rules governing both critical practice and artistic creation; so much so that the correct explanation begins to look more and more a function of the observance of traditional rules, like rules of harmony and counterpoint, etc. Let me quote him :

> "In the case of the word "correct" you have a variety of related cases. There is first the case in which you learn the rules. The cutter learns how long a coat is to be, how wide the sleeve must be, etc. He learns rules—he is drilled—as in music you are drilled in harmony and counterpoint".[8]

If you wonder what this business of suits and cutters has to do with aesthetics, let me remind you that Wittgenstein is against the drawing of hard and fast boundaries between paintings and symphonies on the one hand and other objects that we usually don't consider aesthetically interesting. The same goes for the usual dichotomy between aesthetic experience and other life experiences. That the difference between the two is only a difference of degree, not of kind, can be shown by arranging intermediate cases (object or experiences) between the two extremes.

Again, after making the distinction between the mechanical interpretation of a rule and the development of a feeling for the rule, he continues; "If I hadn't learnt the rules, I wouldn't be able to make the aesthetic judgment. In learning the rules, you get a more and more refined judgment."[9] Wittgenstein cannot make up his mind about whether the rules are relative to a culture or whether one can speak of standards in a cross-cultural sense. On the one hand he says that "to describe a set of aesthetic rules fully means really to describe the culture of a period:[10] on the other, speculating about his theory of decline in standards—which he says gets its meaning from the examples he could give—he makes the remark that "deterioration applies to a tiny bit of that I may know."[11] I understand his "tiny bit of knowledge" to mean his knowledge of something being aesthetically right or wrong that is not culture bound, somewhat similar to the right kind of bass in a musical performance.

So, to come back to our question, to the extent Wittgenstein is tempted to define the correctness of aesthetic explanations—which, we are told, are nothing more than further descriptions of the work of art—in terms of the rules of a tradition, of a particular culture-game if you please, he has to give up his first definition of the correctness of explanation in terms of its acceptance by the person who is puzzled.

(3) The third answer to the question of the criterion for correct explanation in aesthetics comes out of Prof. G.E. Moore's record of Wittgenstein's 1930-33 lectures. There Wittgenstein clearly gives us the impression of relating correctness and rightness with the sound judgments of a man of taste, who is either above rules or does not rely on them. According to Prof. Moore, Wittgenstein is reported to have dramatised the view that every case of rightness or correctness in art has an individual shape in the sense that no mechanical application of traditional rules could help you discover that. At the same time, though uniquely individual, this particular case of rightness can be shown and conveyed to others. He argues that if we say, e.g., of a bass that "it is too heavy; it moves to much" we are not saying that "if it moved less it would be more agreeable to me; that on the contrary, that it should be quieter is an end in itself. What we are trying to do is to bring the bass nearer to an ideal though we haven't the ideal before us that we are copying."[12] It would not be inappropriate to understand the discovery of any individual shape of rightness or correctness in art in terms of the metaphor of clicking when, e.g., the bass is brought down to the right level. Wittgenstein himself plays with this metaphor many times in his 1938 lectures. It chicks in the sense that you are satisfied with it as if you had said to yourself "yes that is it." It is clear from the above quotation that the phrase "bringing the bass nearer to an ideal" describes the connoissure's search for the ideal rightness of *this* particular case in *these* particular circumstances, not anything as general as a rule that could be applied to other cases. The absence of any ideal that one could copy and apply to many cases draws our attention to the severe limitations of any set of traditional rules.

Now if every case of rightness has an individual shape, which is identified by a man of taste, and where the rules are no help, then Wittgenstein's other two attempts to define the rightness or correctness of aesthetic explanation exclusively in terms of the traditional rules or in terms of the acceptance of the explanation by the person who is puzzled go by the board. This tension in his thinking between three different answers cannot be and is not resolved. He must give up any two of the three positions. It is idle to speculate on which of these positions he would be least inclined to give up.

University of California

REFERENCES

1. Barrett, Cyril. (Ed) *L. Wittgenstein, Lectures & Conversation, on Aesthetics, psychology & Religious Belief*, Berkeley & Los Angeles: University of California Press, 1966, pp. 14-15.
2. Barrett, p.14.
3. Barrett, p.20 & G.E. Moore, Wittgenstein's Lectures in 1930-33, *Mind*, LXIV (1955): p. 18.
4. *Mind*, LXIV (1955), p.19.
5. Barrett, pp. 1821.
6. Barrett, p.14.
7. Barrett, p.14.
8. Barrett, p.5.
9. Barrett, p.5.
10. Barrett, p.8, footnote 3.
11. Barrett, p.1o.
12. *Mind*, LXIV (1955), p.18.

OF FAMILY RESEMBLANCES AND AESTHETIC DISCOURSE

N.J. Mantafakis

The ensuing analysis examines the view that in a descriptive sense it is impossible to specify the necessary and sufficient conditions for saying that something is a work of art. This thesis, as expounded by Weitz, Kennick, and others, has recently encountered criticism which misses the substance of the way it relies upon aspects of Wittgenstein's later thought. A review of the literature ever since Weitz' pioneering work suggests a need for surveying the manner by which Weitz adopts Wittgenstein's insights for his own designs. Hopefully what can be shown is that the view under investigation is far from acceptable, since the basic philosophical presuppositions upon which it is founded, that is, family resemblances and the open concept, neither necessarily nor provisionally suggest the conclusions which Weitz' supporters and critics alike find unavoidable. For the Wittgensteinian influence which is the foundation of this theory is itself remarkably unclear, making its unreflecting adaptation yield the production of less than tenable conclusions. Even in most recent discussions dealing with the definition of art, the nature and significance of Wittgenstein's thought upon Weitz is accepted as is, without careful consideration of its very tenability.

The analysis is presented in three sections. First, an exposition of Weitz' position and the effectiveness of Mandlebaum's criticism of it. Secondly, an examination of Weitz' position from the viewpoint of the notion of family resemblance, and whether the latter is as clear a notion as some suppose. Finally, a view of aesthetic discourse which looks beyond Weitz' attempt by seeing such discourse as a phenomenum immanent in the very *practice* of a particular language, which cannot be meaningfully spoken of in terms of family resemblances or apart from the particular language it manifests itself in.

I

Weitz proceeds on the observation that though works of art have certain specifiable characteristics in common, there is no single characteristic or set of characteristics which all works of art possess. Hence one can speak of certain resemblances between works of art, but not about so-called "essential" characteristics *all* such objects have. The similarities between instances of art are seen as family resemblances, referred to by Wittgenstein when attempting to illustrate the nonessentialistic nature of ordinary discourse. At this juncture one must note that the idea of family resemblance is considered by Wittgenstein in contexts which involve the use of language. Weitz, however, often expounds his position by weaving in and out of contexts which involve either art objects *themselves*, or the *speaking about* such objects[2]. Hence where Weitz speaks of family resemblances, one must keep in mind that he is considering how such resemblances are manifested in both contexts. Thus just as various art objects may exhibit certain similar characteristics, without their all sharing any one single characteristic, so also various instances of talk about art exhibit family resemblances as well. However, in Weitz' view it is futile to search for essential properties for all such objects or modes of discourse, as aestheticians since Aristotle have attempted[3].

The persistent difficulty is seen by Weitz as being both epistemological and logical. For he is interested in exploring the grammar of the word art, as it is influenced directly by the variety of objects which are recognized or referred to when the word is employed. Aestheticians have failed to realize that the sense of discourse involving art is never predictable, in that the "expansive" and "adventurous" nature of art itself defies an essentialistic definition, and points to the inescapable "wide-open texture" of art as a concept. Thus the logic or "grammar" of the word art, or of aesthetic discourse generally, cannot be something which can be formalized for all possible cases. Rather, one can only notice the resemblances between different cases in which the word "art" is being used.[4]

Consequently, when it comes to deciding whether or not something new is to be called art, one must either extend or totally alter the prevalent meaning (use) of the word. This is why when aestheticians are called upon to defend their definition and uses of the term, they cannot appeal to clear and direct evidence to justify their pervasive claims. For there will always be the possibility of including some new and different thing to all that which has been covered by the term before. Being that there always is an exception, their theories of art's meaning, or what art refers to, can never be open to objective proof. On the other hand, where these theories are interpreted to be a priori true (in an analytical sense), conflict invariably arises as to whether such theories conform with the everyday use of discourse. At most Weitz would view this approach to theory construction in aesthetic as the setting forth of arbitrary definitions of what art is supposed to encompass. Generally, theories of art stem from theorists seeking to answer the question "What is art?" instead of trying to answer the more realistic question "How is the word "art" used?" The latter involves studying the workings of discourse with respect to the word's use. The farmer has been taken as implying (however erroneously) a single answer, or one which is essentialistic in nature.[5]

In understanding Weitz' view one must see it as distinct from issues involving the nature of aesthetic qualities, e.g. whether they are affective or directive. For Weitz does not deal with the phenomenology of aesthetics, but with the logic of aesthetic discourse. Keeping in mind as well that Weitz is developing his position by applying Wittgenstein's insights into the workings of language, one must consider what he has to say on a linguistic level of analysis.[6] Thus the issue one is faced with when considering the adequacy of Weitz' view is whether or not his conception of aesthetic discourse is in fact correct. For he does not cocentrate specifically upon the problem of how to conceive of aesthetic objects as such, but how they are to be spoken about. Even in contexts where he considers objects of art in themselves, he views them as given. Clearly, the questions which supposedly concerned Wittgenstein in *Lectures and Conversations* were matters which did not have a direct influence upon the presentation of Weitz' viewpoint. Rather, he is more directly influenced by the Wittgenstein of the *Philosophical Investigations*, who views language as a collection of games one plays with words. For Weitz then, aesthetic discourse is a particular kind of language game, whose rules are uniquely flexible, and open to an apparently endless variety of transformations.

Weitz' thesis of course has received amplification by a number of writers. To mention but a few, W.E. Kennick observes that aestheticians in doing art criticism have erroneously assumed that they must apply or work with universal standards of analysis. Their assumption is that art is basically a monolithic subject for analysis, wherein its variety does not come to influence the standards of criticism one brings to it.[7] Again, Weitz' argumentation is seen as underlying Beryl Lake's criticism of Croce's theory of art. Lake observes that Croce must assume, in defining art as "intuitive knowledge," that his definition is a priori true (in an analytical sense), since Croce cannot empirically illustrate what he means by intuitive knowledge. On the other hand, if it is taken to be an a priori statement, it surely does not reflect how the term is widely used. For other aestheticians use the term differentally, making the latter an arbitrary definition at best. Similarly, W.B. Gallie employs Weitz' line of attack to criticize essentialists for presupposing that in order to define art, they must know what it is *in essence*. Gallie prefers a much more experimental approach to the problem, so as to determine how art manifests itself in different ways, and then to proceed to more rigorously define art as a concept.[8]

Alternatively, opposition to Weitz' position centers mainly on how it is based upon Wittgenstein's notion of family resemblance. Mandlebaum, borrowing from Helen Harvey, argues that to say works of art or uses of the term "art" exhibit family resemblances, but that there is no single characteristic or set of characteristics which all works of art have in common, really does not clarify the situation. For the similarities which are at issue here do not in themselves manifest *genetic* resemblances. Surely there can be accidental resemblances between things which have absolutely no genuine bond between them, and hence they cannot be said to have a "family" resemblance. Mandlebaum argues the sense of saying that art objects, or different instances of aesthetic discourse, exhibit a family resemblance, and that for this reason one uses the word "art" to refer to them. One does not know which way to go with the idea of family resemblance in this situation. Does it imply inherent relationship or accidental appearances? Weitz failure to face this question gives him no right to speak in terms of a "logic" for the word "art". If one is dealing with genetic relationships here, where are the criteria for determining that there are genetic similarities to consider?[9]

Mandlebaum, however, is all too eager to claim that when Wittgenstein spoke of family resemblances he meant genetic relationships, in a biological sense. Scrutiny reveals that this is hardly defensible. When speaking of resemblances Wittgenstein repeatedly asks us to look for and "see" these resemblances in the very use of language. This is not a matter of specifying genetic linkage, but of simply noticing the function of discourse. On the resemblances between language games, Wittgenstein makes the following observation:[10]

> "Don't say: 'there must be something common, or they would not be called 'games'—but *look* and *see* whether there is anything common to *all*, but similarities, relationships, and a whole series of them at that. To repeat: don't think, but look:—"

Quite clearly, in his criticism Mandlebaum seems to be concentrating only upon similarities manifested in family resemblances, to the point of interpreting these similarities as genetic identities, and thus misconstruing Wittgenstein. His emphasis upon how they must somehow reflect a family tie amongst various exemplars of games, uggests that Mandlebaum views these resemblances as designating essentialistic properties. This they cannot be. For by saying that family resemblance involves the exhibition of similarities, etc.,

Wittgenstein does not mean to say that because of this things exhibiting a family resemblance to each other cannot be totally unlike each other in many other ways. Such differences are also part of all that is involved in the notion of family resemblance. Wittgenstein's very directive above for *not* thinking but rather looking for these resemblances indicates that one should not approach them with any preconception concerning their inherent nature (e.g. genetic linkage), but merely to observe *that* they are present.

On the other hand, Mandlebaum's interpretation of resemblances misses an essential point of development in Wittgenstein's thought, namely the latter has moved away from an essentialistic conception of language as exposited in the *Tractatus*. In fact the very notion of noticing a resemblance between various language games is percipitated by Wittgenstein's recoiling from his earlier conception of ordinary discourse as a structure of atomic propositions, whose logical nature constituted the essence of such discourse.[11] How incongruous is it then to argue that family resemblances must in some way reflect genetic linkages? Most recently, W.G. Bywater has emphasized the fact that Weitz and Kennick adopt Wittgenstein's notion of family resemblance since they, like Wittgenstein, are reacting to closed systems, which in their case are the a priori theories in aesthetics.[12]

Mandlebaum's second main argument against Weitz seems equally inadequate. The former argues that Weitz has not provided any evidence by which to demonstrate how the formal requirements necessary for arriving at any theory are *logically incompatible* with the concomitant requirement that however conceived, art objects must be said to exhibit an inherent novelty and creativity.[13] Here it is hard to see what sort of evidence would satisfy Mandlebaum on this point, other than what Weitz and others have already pointed to. For if he is challenging the view that aesthetic expression necessarily of itself alters any established conception of art, then Mandlebaum has overlooked both the *fact* of novelty and creativity in such expressions, and one's manner of talking about it. Basically, supporters of Weitz' view rely upon the evidence that aesthetic expression invariably involves controversy prior to recognition (which is usually a matter of saying whether some particular object can fit into some accepted view of art), and artists themselves seem to hold as a primary objective an intentional departure from traditional modes of expression. Hence, on an empirical level, Weitz argues that works of art do not seem to follow a pre-established path, which will predetermine how these objects will manifest themselves. Consequently, this spontaneous nature of art is reflected in the way one comes to speak about it. For example, one finds that manifestations of art engender the use of descriptive terms like "novel," "revolutionary," "creative," etc. which are antonyms of terms connected with the attempt to define, e.g. "determine," "establish," "circumscribe," etc.[14] Essentially, Weitz is saying that defining is an activity which by its very requirements cannot formalize the ever-changing subject matter of art. Apart from pointing to the very puzzling fact of trying to define art, it is difficult to fathom what Mandlebaum would accept as proof for the impasse Weitz has recognized. Since Mandlebaum does not really question the way Weitz sets up the problem, the logical impossibility the latter points out seems unavoidable.

II

Thus Weitz' thesis is not reduced to paralytic inaction by the thrust of Mandlebaum's argumentation. However, Weitz is vulnerable on some of the points the former concentrates upon, though for significantly different reasons. In reviewing Weitz' position it is convenient to consider it from different vantage points. First, it is fruitful to consider 'how he treats aesthetic objects in relation to games. Secondly the acceptability of his conception of aesthetic discourse is open to dispute, because of certain deficiencies in Wittgenstein's own conception of family resemblance. Thirdly, a theme permeating the whole of Weitz' position—namely that one can preceive how the variety manifested in works of art themselves influences the diversity in talk about aesthetic objects, leaves a great deal unexplained. Perhaps this latter point in itself provides most dramatic evidence for the shortcomings of Weitz' view.

First, however, it is appropriate to consider how Weitz

employs the notion of games so as to call attention to the fact that art objects and aesthetic discourse seem to reflect the same traits exhibited by games. For such an investigation touches upon Weitz' fundamental conception of aesthetic objects. Interestingly, Weitz observes that one comes to see that an activity is like some familiar one called a "game", yet one also realizes that it is apparently impossible to unequivocally define what games are. Similarly, one comes to see how a work is like some other creation, which is recognized as "art," but one also realizes that it is impossible to arrive at a definition of art. Hence there are two points of similarity between games and art, which are reflected in discourse concerning them. On the one hand, games and art each constitute collections of things which exemplify family resemblances within each collection. On the other hand, it seems apparently impossible to define what kinds of things should constitute these collections. In view of this, Weitz argues in a way which strongly suggests that weatever Wittgenstein had to say about games and their various resemblances can be freely applied to discourse about art.[15]

Significantly, Wittgenstein himself did not make definite the above crucial association between games and art. Perhaps he realized basic differences between these two areas. Focussing upon these differences reveals the really fragile connection between these two thinkers. For instance, essentially, games are activities, which require that one or more persons *do* something. Art, on the other hand, deals largely with objects, specifiable entities considered in terms of the spatial temporal characteristics they exhibit. Moreover, the activity which a game involves, that is the participation or the playing, *is* the game. However, the activity which is involved by art, insofar as say the appraising of such objects is concerned, is surely something after the fact of having the object. Nor can it be said that the making of such objects is the activity to which the word "art" refers to, since the exact way of creating such objects is often unknown to the beholder. Even in the cases of poems and novels, the reader is presenting to himself through his own reading of the material the object, that is, the theme or the story the author endeavours to convey through his writing. It may be objected that symphonies, plays, etc. all involve performance, and this is the activity which art refers to. Such argumentation is equally untenable, however. For in cases requiring performance by actors etc. one is really concerned with the *effect* of what they are doing, that is, the space-time event beheld by the audience. It is not the acting as a personal inner feeling within the actor which is observable here, but the projected appearance of the acting as an externalized spatial event. The latter again is an object in the sense that it is understood and criticized in relation to how its various facets integrate over a span of time and space to form a consistent objective whole. Hence the observation that games refer to activities, but art apparently exclusively deals with objects, is a point which does not distort the way in which this distinction seems to underlie ordinary discourse about such matters.

It may be pressed that art objects also involve activities, insofar as they intimately involve the perceptual acts of seeing, hearing, etc. which come to constitute or make possible the aesthetic experience. This, however, is hardly persuasive since it calls attention to the most fundamental prerequisites of all experience, and thus does not inforce anything but the basic fact that one must have a reasonably conscious mind in order for there to be *any* awareness. The latter of itself does not justify the conclusion that conceptually art is somehow like games. Even where one was to put forth the view that aesthetic qualities are affective, and thus become manifest by the interplay of sense stimulation and perceptual activity, one still cannot claim that art and games are thus on an equal par, both involving activity. For the affective qualities result from an inner and therefore subjective reaction, whereas the activity a game involves is the public and therefore objective participation of one or more individuals. Hence though it can be said in a very general sense that some sort of activity is involved at particular stages in both cases, it is still not the same sort of activity. Furthermore, the so-called affective qualities which come to constitute aesthetic experience are still qualities *of* something, however that something or object is completely manifested to the perceiver. Hence it appears that one cannot escape referring to art as some thing, though constructed of interrelated aesthetic qualities, whereas games *are* activities.

If the above can be accepted as a substantial basis for distinguishing between games and art, then a second major divergence between these two areas emerges. For games, as activities, invariably seem to involve rule-directed behavior, whereas this is not the case with objects of art. However simple a game may be, the person(s) participating must adhere to some pre-established guidelines so as to achieve the goal, win, etc. Indeed, the way in which one determines whether or not an activity should be recognized as a game of somekind is to see whether or not it conforms to some rules of action, however simple or complex they may be. In short, the determination of whether or not a rule is being followed becomes an important criterion for saying if an activity is or is not a game. There is no rule, however, which when followed or violated allows one to say that such and such is or is not a work of art. Even in cases where a critic speaks of the "correctness" in a certain style of say architecture or painting, one must not interpret such statements as dealing with rules or normative standards for the generation of art. As F.J. Coleman recently pointed out, considerations dealing with the correctness of certain style invariably involve determining whether or not a certain aspect of an artistic creation properly relates to the whole work in a certain way.[16] However, this is not a matter concerning a rule for creating art, but involves the homogeneity of a particular work in relation to some established way of making such objects. Correctness of style is then a notion which comes into play where one endeavors to *recreate* art in some way, and thus involves a kind of indirect reference to already existent aesthetic objects. Hence the idea of the rule directed activity which animates games, as contrasted to the absence of such controlled activity in the case of art objects, appears to hold up to careful scrutiny.

Moreover, the differences between games and art are reflected in the reasons one has for their respective definitions. Significantly, one expects that a definition for games should enable one identify such activity as uniquely different from other kinds of activity, as say surgery or farming. Furthermore, it is expected that however it turns out a definition of games should enable one to distinguish such activity from random or haphazard activity.[17] The definition of games then provides a means of making a selective and accurate identification. In defining art, however, the purpose of the definition is not only to identify the object as of a particular sort, but also to point out that the object is valued, which in turn becomes a standard or criterion by which to compare other similar objects. For whether it is a justified practice or not, objects of art once recognized as such acquire an honorific status, which projects them as in some sense exemplars of what art *should* be.[18] Yet, though an activity is defined as a game, that particular game does not necessarily itself become a model by which to identify other games. Hence there is room for saying that definition for art is more demanding, insofar as it should also be able to explain why the object is somehow special. This added requirement is not evident in the case of a definition for games.

In view of the above, it is highly tenuous to argue that art, as considered in ordinary discourse, is like or similar to games. Yet Weitz does proceed on the assumption that both exhibit a similarity, so that the apparent open-texturedness of art is justifiable *since* games are open-textured. At crucial junctures in their arguments, Weitz and his supporters claim that there is an analogous relationship between games and art.[19] Moreover, when Wittgenstein attempted to explain the workings of language he alludes to the games within language in a metaphorical way to show how certain forms of communication are like the playing of a game. Yet Wittgenstein does not say that there is a precise similarity between games and linguistic forms of life.[20] In articulating his theory, however, Weitz is interpreting Wittgenstein's allusion to games and language activity analogically, and thus he presupposes an exact relationship between games and art or discourse about art. The evident differences indicated above between these two underscore that at best their relationship cannot be analogical, but perhaps metaphorical.

If one were to allow the view that art is like games only in a metaphorical sense, then a basic rewording of Weitz' thesis must be undertaken. For it is art *in terms of* the language which is appropriate to it which is said to be akin to the playing of a game. There is an awkwardness in not seeing that art in itself cannot be compared to an activity, as if both were the same sort of thing. As it has been pointed out, art refers to various things or entities which are considered in terms of their total integration. Conversely, games are activities in which one or more take part in. The two cannot be treated in the same way, without their differences coming into consideration. Apparently, it seems more appropriate to say that aesthetic discourse is in some metaphorical sense somewhat like the playing of a game. In this re-presentation of Weitz' view at least one is comparing two activities, rather than an object (work of art) and an activity (the playing of a game). Thus as a form of activity, discourse about art is seen as an open-textured phenomenon, which defies any general definition. This restricts Weitz' manner of speaking indescriminately in contexts involving art objects *per se*, and discourse about such objects. However, this does not distort Weitz' position, since he had others who subscribe to his view argue that aesthetic discourse is a particular kind of linguistic activity, which one comes to recognize through familiarity with the language one uses. Having thus reduced Weitz' viewpoint to a more intelligible version, it is appropriate to consider how he can justify the so-called "recognition" of aesthetic discourse as such.

The question here can be put simply yet forcibly as follows: how does one come to recognize linguistic forms of life as those which are peculiar to art? Clearly Weitz and his followers wish to escape the allusion to any sort of stable reference points, i.e. criteria, which would justify the recognition of such forms of life.[21] For criteria of even a provisional sort would bring them closer to the essentialism they are seeking to repudiate. Surely to say that such and such characteristics are the objective grounds for aesthetic discourse is to move towards the establishment of necessary and sufficient conditions for such discourse. Yet this is the dead end Weitzs see as the undefensible presupposition of all aesthetic theorizing. On the other hand, Weitz cannot go in the direction of maintaining that aesthetic discourse functions in the same way as emotive discourse, as perhaps the word "pain" functions in ordinary discourse. Surely his earlier rejection of the emotivist theory in aesthetics would prohibit his claiming that the word "art" works in the same way to replace some private experience, known only to the perceiving subject. More recently, though commenting upon a latter manuscript not actually authored by Wittgenstein (*Lectures and Conversations*), F.J. Coleman also disowns as too simplistic the possibility that one can interpret aesthetic discourse solely upon an emotive level of analysis.[22] Again the logical consequence of the emotivist interpretation would be that one cannot really know any public sense of the word "art". Yet Weitz and others speak of the meaning of this term as something which is exemplified by various cases of linguistic use. However, whatever the nature of its meaning, "art" is not allowed criteria of recognition. Understandably, to allow such criteria would incur undercutting the thesis of the "adventurous" and "expansive" nature of art. Thus one is faced with the internal contradiction by saying that the logic of the word "art" is recognizable in different language games, yet the ever-changing meaning of "art" itself prohibits the possibility of establishing criteria for the recognition of its meaning.

The difficulties surrounding the exegesis of how aesthetic discourse involves a particular kind of language activity are inherited by Weitz through his uncritical acceptance of Wittgenstein's notion of family resemblance. For, where he talks of the application of general terms, Wittgenstein asks us to look for and see the resemblances in its use, and cautions us not to insist that there *must* be a resemblance. Yet what is this resemblance? Does it result from pointing to specifiable denotata, or is it manifested through the intercrossings of various language games themselves. In his article "Something Common," Robert J. Richman points to the difficulties of the notion of family resemblance as expounded by Wittgenstein in the *Investigations*, and his insights can be applied to the present discussion with telling results.[23]

Richman states that in seeing the limitations of the notion of family resemblance one must keep the following two issues distinct. First, the question of whether or not general univocal terms are meaningful because they allude to "something common" between them is itself an ambiguous question, since what is going to count as the "something common" is difficult to explicate. Secondly, the preceding question is an issue separate from the fact that certain general terms are purposefully ambiguous.[24] This is to say that certain general terms like "warm" or "bald" are used in ways which presuppose that they are not going to be used to refer to certain precise phenomena, but rather to degrees of the appearance of certain things.[25] It can be safely said that aesthetic discourse is not purposefully ambiguous, since one usually presupposes he knows what sort of things *should* be covered by its terms. For even Weitz argues that there is a logic to aesthetic discourse, and hence it is not inherently ambiguous. Thus the second issue Richman points to does not pertain to the present analysis.

The first point Richman brings out concerning the nature of the meaning of univocal general terms is actually the central issue which undermines the notion of family resemblance, and thus proves useful to the discussion at hand. Richman observes that the Wittgensteinian point that family resemblance is a phenomenon one sees in the use of language is difficult to explain. For, is such resemblance the result of the interweaving of certain properties of linguistic activity, or does it arise from a direct reference to particular *denotata*? The latter kind of answer would open up the possibility of introducing subsistent entities which are *the* "meaning" of general univocal terms. Wittgenstein, however, seeks to present an alternative to this essentialistic conception of meaning, so as to distinguish general terms from simple terms, such as 'red.' In doing this he introduces the notion of family resemblance to suggest an alternative to strict denotative meaning. His remedy, however, is not very useful since there is no clear way of explaining what constitutes family resemblance. This is to say that since such resemblance is not tied down to any reference point, one cannot specify the kind of things (the "something common") which would satisfy saying that there is such a resemblance. Even holding that the intercrossings of usages as the meaning for general terms is inadequate, since one would still not be able to specify the precise points of interdiction on pain of advocating a referential basis of meaning. Furthermore, if one were to attempt strengthening the notion of family resemblance by arguing that *any* sequence of the denotata of some general term say T would come to constitute the something common making possible the family resemblance which is the meaning of T, then still one cannot continue to maintain a clear distinction between the nature of the meaning of T and that of a simple term of say S. For one could always point to the quite obvious relationship of "being next to" which both respective denotata of T and S exhibit, and then argue in a way suggesting that T and S are alike in the nature of their meaning.[26]

Richman's interest is of course directed towards showing the weakness of the notion of family resemblance, and how on Wittgensteinian terms it cannot defend an important distinction between the meaning of simple and complex terms. Yet Richman's insights pertain to Weitz' conception of the role of family resemblance in aesthetic discourse. For where the latter speaks of the recognition of family resemblance, which makes aesthetic discourse somehow unique, the meaning of such "recognition" is problematic. It clearly cannot involve a reference to devotata, since Richman's analysis shows that family resemblance cannot, as a particular type of meaning, involve specific reference points. Hence what is one to look for where he turns to the specific family resemblance which determines that one is dealing with aesthetic discourse? The question here has no answer because it fails to achieve a meaningful interrogative. For since the notion of family resemblance does not involve referring to anything, and since also connotatively family resemblance as a notion does not seem to unambiguously connote anything, one is really unable to claim that he identifies any consistent set of linguistic phenomena as *the* family resemblances which aesthetic discourse exemplifies.

Pursuing Richman's analysis indicates that if one were to argue that family resemblance is somehow directly the result of the intercrossings of usages, then it is in essence abstracted from various forms of linguistic life. Indeed, where Wittgenstein admonishes the reader not to insist that there are resemblances, but to look for the possibility of such a resemblance, he appears to suggest that the resemblance itself is somehow inferred by the language user in the special way the discourse proceeds. Yet if the resemblance peculiar to aesthetic discourse is in any way inferred, then it should be open to some sort of exemplification, and if not then it is somehow intuited. Yet to allow for demonstration would bring him closer to some sort of essentialism. Alternatively, to say that such resemblance is somehow intuitive, i.e. private, makes the fact of intersubjective communication in aesthetics difficult if not impossible to explain. Thus Weitz' allusion to the notion of family resemblance forces him either to a form of essentialism, which he desires to avoid, or to an intuitionism which renders impossible any explanation of such discourse. Towards the end Weitz speaks of peculiar "criteria of recognition" for discourse dealing with the arts, though these criteria are taken to be neither necessary nor sufficient. Yet what kind of criteria can the latter be? He alludes to them as bundles of properties which are somehow the excuse for applying a descriptive use of the word "art". Yet these properties, conditions, etc. seem to suggest stable reference points, though Weitz would deny that they must be present in order to recognize something as art. The ambiguity here has not been seen by recent analysts.

The thrust of Richman's analysis also has interesting implications for the manner in which Weitz argues, weaving as he does in and out of contexts involving art objects and aesthetic discourse itself, taken metalinguistically. As it has been shown, Weitz apparently believes that somehow the very variety of art works becomes reflected in talk about art, and possibly contributes to the open-texturedness of the latter. Yet if such discourse is somehow intimately connected with the physical phenomena it deals with, then these phenomena become criteria or sources of explication for the use of the terms which concerns such discourse. However this alternative cannot be admitted since it again leads towards stable criteria of reference, which is a form of essentialism. This not only suggests that one cannot argue in terms which intercross contexts dealing with art objects and contexts involving discourse about such objects, but a basic Weitzian presupposition that art objects somehow influence the open-texturedness of aesthetic discourse becomes less tenable. The nature of the connectedness between the two contexts of art object and aesthetic discourse cannot be consistently confirmed without tying down the notion of family resemblance in aesthetic discourse to some sort of reference.

Perhaps most striking is the point that according to Richman one cannot really specify where there is *no* family resemblance. This is to say that even if one were able to specify in some way that some modes of linguistic behaviour exhibit a family resemblance, the notion of family resemblance because of its inherent opacity, does not in itself provide any internal means by which to say that there is no family resemblance with respect to other modes of linguistic activity. The ramifications for what has been said about aesthetic discourse thus far are quite significant. For one can point to nothing in the so-called "logic" of aesthetic discourse which would explicitly exclude saying that such and such linguistic activity is not aesthetic discourse. Here one may ask what sort of "logic" can this be which provides no internal means of expressing contradiction? Without a means of saying that something is not aesthetic discourse, Weitz cannot defend his general thesis that there is a particular kind of dicourse which *is* aesthetic discourse.

The line of criticism suggested above differs from Mandlebaum's in that: (1) it concentrates upon a distinction between games (as activities) and art objects, and (2) it suggests a serious problem in explaining how one comes to *recognize* a particular kind of discourse as aesthetic discourse. Neither Weitz nor Mandlebaum care to even consider the implications of these two points, and both presuppose that they can speak of aesthetic discourse interchangeably with aesthetic objects, with the latter somehow influencing aesthetic discourse Though Mandlebaum alludes to Richman's article, the former misses the depth of implication in Richman's work, concentrating instead on a too literal interpretation of the notion of "family resemblance". Both Mandlebaum and Weitz fail to see when and how the conjuring trick of the fact of aesthetic discourse has taken place. As it has been repeatedly brought out above, to recognise discourse dealing with art presupposes that one already has criteria for the application of the term. This means that one already has some knowledge of such discourse or language of art. Yet how does this knowledge by recognition come about? One seems to be here in the same position as that described by Wittgenstein himself, where he says that language, like a spider's web, dissolves at the very touch of explication. Hence to even suggest that aesthetic discourse is a special kind of discourse since it reflects in its many forms a particular pattern, or resemblance, is to assume already that one knows what such discourse is supposed to be. How else can the pattern be recognized? Thus the delicate *fact* of language is torn by the crude requirements of recognition implicit in the very articulation of the notion of family resemblance.

III

Some attempt should be made perhaps to pursue the question concerning how discourse about art does come about. In doing so it is interesting to return to Wittgenstein once more, specifically to his last known manuscript: *On Certainty*, for some illuminating insights. In the latter he endeavours to clarify some basic issues involving the problem of knowing the problem of knowledge. In a passage where he considers the implications of G.E. Moore's view comcerning how it can be said that one knows matters of immediate experience, Wittgenstein observes that to say that one knows some statement to be true implies that one can produce "compelling" reasons to bring to bear so as to prove that it is true.[28] This insight has interesting ramifications when applied to issues of how one comes to recognize aesthetic discourse. Hence, how can one say that it is *known* that some sort of linguistic behaviour is aesthetic discourse? What sort of compelling reasons can be brought forth to *prove* what is supposed to be known? Weitz and those who subscribe to his view would surely insist that some sort of proof should be forthcoming before one can accept any account of one's knowing that something is aesthetic discourse. Proof for these analysts would be, as has been repeatedly stated, some allusion to family resemblences. Yet apart from the lucidity of the latter notion, the new difficulty here is to make sense of the very attempt at *proving* the knowing that something is aesthetic discourse. The latter seems to defy justification by any sort of proof, because it is a form of linguistic behaviour whose certainty one learns *alone with*, in conjunction with, the very learning of a natural language.

It seems more accurate to say that one believes some particular linguistic behaviour is aesthetic discourse. Belief here is taken in a Percean sense, involving action based upon success in a given context of language use.[29] Its certainty arises from the very practice of language, rather than from proving that aesthetic discourse must somehow correspond to certain exterior facts in the spatio-temporal world. One might say that aesthetic discourse is an aspect of the spontaneous development of a culture's language, and thus cannot be *proven*, as if some claim were open to constant doubt and always must be verified by appealing to evidence. To ask for such varification is to miss its significance, insofar as this is *not* a matter of there being offered a choice of say either the acceptance of a general definition someone suggests, or adopting some vocalized mode of speech. Rather, aesthetic discourse is a form of linguistic life which is inseparable from one's actual success in communicating in a culture.

To speak of aesthetic discourse in terms involving one's believing entails *pragmatico-semantical* considerations. This is to say that the belief here is by somone who, on the basis of prior success in his use of language in some contexts, believes that the same mode of language will work (i.e. communicate) on a further occasion. Thus the language will work (i.e. communicate) on a future occasion. Thus the language user is related to the language behaviour he employs from the viewpoint of its success or its being true for communicating in a given context. There is an added flexibilty in this approach towards analysing aesthetic discourse. For if factors within the believer's environment bring about a change so that new or innovative manifestations of language use are required to speak about new phenomena in art, then the language user must adopt such new modes of discourse so as to communicate about aesthetic objects. Hence one can say that as an environment undergoes transformations, the aesthetic discourse operative within it also undergoes change. However, older manifestations of this kind of discourse are not inaccurate or somehow false examples of aesthetic discourse. Rather, the latter once served a purpose, whereas they can no longer serve that purpose again due to the environmental changes. There is not a question of proving one mode of aesthetic discourse is true, whereas another is false. In essence there is no ideal form of aesthetic communication. Apparently, what one has here is a question of what happens to work, for someone, at some particular time, in a certain context.

There is a profound difference between the view expressed above, and Weitz' view involving the recognition of family resemblances. For recognition in the latter view entails the notion of acceptance. This is to say that where Weitz requires that one recognizes the peculiar resemblances exhibited by cases of aesthetic discourse, he is supposing that there are patterns in discourse, which one can accept as indicative of a particular kind of language activity. Thus the idea of recognition, in its involvement of acceptance, also implies alluding to proof, or "compelling reasons," to justify the act of accepting. However, the aesthetic discourse being accepted is viewed by the acceptor *inscriptionally*, that is, the specific linguistic form of life is taken as a syntactic phenomenum, or a sequence of syntactically concatenated and verbalized expressions. Thus in Weitz' view, the language user is related to the language he is supposed to recognize as aesthetic discourse from the perspective of a *pragmatico-syntactical* relation. Thus the act of recognition, with its implicit notion of acceptance, does not have the language user employing any linguistic expression. Most likely, the reason for considering aesthetic discourse in such a syntactical manner is due to Weitz' strict adaptation of Wittgenstein's idea of *looking for* family resemblances. Apparently, the notion of looking entails "looking at", which turns the phenomenum of aesthetic discourse into something which is *to be* observed, rather than an activity which one gradually learns about through his practice of the language.

In essence Weitz and his followers are saying that so variable is the pattern of aesthetic discourse, that no essentialist theory thus far is flexible enough to explain it. Their approach then sees aesthetic discourse from the outside, as *de facto* present. The latter is different from the approach which considers the belief factor which is operative in the very practice of such discourse.

Moreover, generally it may be said that a fundamental reason as to why aestheticians have had difficulties in presenting their positions, whether essentialist or of any other variety, is because they endeavour to find a single theory to cover many different objects, originating in various cultures, at different times. Even Weitz, in his criticism of other theories of aesthetic discourse, finds fault because they are not complete enough to cover *constant* exceptions. Hence he proposes that one observe language in aesthetic contexts so as to achieve a freedom from exceptions manifested by the very variety of art. However, particularity evidently should be preserved in any account of discourse about art. Art critics tend to seek out similarities between art objects, rather than considering the place these kinds of objects have in different cultures. For Example, one often finds them assuming that because say an Egyptian mirror is found in an art museum, it is a kind of art along with other art objects. Hence they seek to discover points of congruence between it and other forms of aesthetic expression. Their approach, however, misses the individuality of the object, the cultural contexts from which it arose, and the entire linguistic form of life which was sensitive to it.[30]

One can only suggest in a peripheral manner the kind of factors which enter into the question when discourse about the arts is considered in terms of the beliefs which underlie its success as communication. Evidently, the complexity of the task would take this investigation beyond its intended bounds of indicating the shortcomings of Weitz' general position. One major point, however, suffices to underscore the point of departure between Weitz and the proposed alternative. This is to say that the latter by-passes questions dealing with the justification of recognizing patterns of aesthetic discourse. Rather, it raises the question of why one believes that the discourse he engages in with respect to certain objects will function to communicate with other people. The very thrust of this kind of question will necessitate the introduction of cases in the past where it has worked, as well as the specification of the reason why it would not or does not work to communicate. The factors which contribute to the development of these beliefs may be quite varied, since the reasons animating the believing may very well range over a wide area of anthropological factors. There is no presupposing here of what aesthetic discourse is, or what it should be. Rather, the issue becomes why some particular form of communication succeeds.

The emphasis upon noting the particularities within aesthetic communication does not preclude that general statements cannot be made about such discourse. Apparently, the shared fact that *human* communication is operative in diverse *human* environments will manifest points of similarity in the way in which different people talk about art objects. The latter, however, should not become the paramount factor which somehow comes to be the key point of analysis in understanding the nature of aesthetic discourse.

University of Cleaveland, Ohio, U.S.A.

FOOT NOTES

1. Wladyslaw Tatarkiewicz, "What is Art? The Problem of Definition Today," also: *British Journal of Aesthetics*, 11, (1971), 146-147. T.J. Diffey, "Essentialism and the Definition of Art," *British Journal of Aesthetics*. 13, (1973), 105-106.

2. Morris Weitz, "The Role of Theory in Aesthetics," *Journal of Aesthetics and Art Criticism*, 15, (1956), 30-31. (Evident shifting from talk about aesthetic discourse to talk of aesthetic objects themselves is seen in the way Weitz goes from considering the logic of the word "art" p. 30, to considering the open texture of art objects p. 31.)

3. Ibid., p. 30.
4. Ibid., p. 32.
5. Ibid., p. 33.
6. Ibid., p. 30.

7. William E. Kennick, "Does Traditional Aesthetics Rest on A Mistake," *Mind*, 67, (1958), 319-320.
8. William Elton, ed. *Aesthetics and Language*, (Oxford, 1967), 104-105, and 23-24.
9. Maurice Mandelbaum, "Family Resemblances and Generalization Concerning the Arts," *American Philosophical Quarterly*,2, (1965), 221, also see T.J. Diffey, Op. Cit., 105.
10. Ludwig Wittgenstein, *Philosophical Investigations*, (Macmillan, 1970), 31 e, para. 66.
11. David Pears, *Ludwig Wittgenstein*, (The Viking Press, 1970), 73-75.
12. William G. Bywater, "Who's in the Warehouse Now?", *Journal of Aesthetics and Art Criticism*, (Summer, 1972), 524-525.
13. Maurice Mandelbaum, Op. Cit., 226.
14. Morris Weitz, Op. Cit., 30, *also* D.W. Peetz, "The Autonomy of Aesthetics," *British Journal of Aesthetics*, 8, (1968), 177-178.
15. Morris Weitz, Op. Cit. 31.
16. Francis J. Coleman, "A Critical Examination of Wittgenstein's Aesthetics," *American Philosophical Quarterly*, 5, (1968), 259.
17. William E. Kennick, Op. Cit., 320-321.
18. John Dewey, *The Philosophy of John Dewey*, Volume II., John J.McDermott, editor, (G.P. Putnam's Sons, 1973), 529.
19. Morris Weitz, Op. Cit., 31.
20: Ludwig Wittgenstein, *Philosophical Investigations*, (Macmillan, 1970), 6e-7e.
21. William Kennick, 322-323.
22. Francis J. Coleman, "A Critical Examination of Wittgenstein's Aesthetics," 260.
23. Robert J.Richman, "Something Common," *The Journal of Philosophy*, LIX, (1962).
24. Ibid., 821.
25. Ibid., 824.
26. Ibid., 827-828.
27. Ibid., 828-829.
28. Ludwig Wittgenstein, *On Certainty*, (Harper and Row, 1972), G.E.M. Auscomb, and G.H. VonWright editors, 32e-34e.
29. Charles S. Peirce, "The Fixation of Belief," in *Pragmatic Philosophy*, (Doubleday, 1966), Amelie Rorty, editor, 7-9.
30. Paul Ziff, "The Task of Defining a Work of Art," in *Contemporary Studies in Aesthetics*, Francis J.Coleman, editor, (McGraw-Hill, 1968), 108.
(The position developed here differs from Ziff's, insofar as it concentrates upon the *beliefs* which underlie this particular kind of discourse, rather than the often incalculable consequences of aesthesic discourse.)

AN ANALYTICAL NOTE ON ABANINDRANATH'S AESTHETICS

S.K. Nandi

A careful scrutiny of the aesthetic ideas found in Abanindranath's writings would reveal that the concept of 'mimesis' as understood by Abanindranath is the pivotal concept in his aesthetics. 'Mimesis' may mean 'representation, resemblance and/or relativism'. Resemblance may constitute a necessary condition for pictorial representation. Again, the question may be posed as to what are the conditions which must obtain for it to be said that A represents B. The immediate (and of course most naive) response is : A represents B if and only if A appreciably resembles B. This, however, is rejected on the grounds that :

1. Resemblance, unlike representation is reflexive (meaning that I resemble myself considerably, but represent myself rarely).
2. Resemblance, unlike representation, is symmetric (meaning that if a painting resembles an orange, the orange resembles the painting, but in no ordinary way represents it) ;
3. Resemblance frequently occurs with no hint of representation (as is found among birds of a feather).

So resemblance is obviously not sufficient for representation. But perhaps it is a necessary condition, if accompanied by a further restriction. Goodman treats it to one such conjunct—that object A be a painting—which fails on the grounds that a painting of Marlborough castle happens to resemble all other paintings in more ways than it does the Castle : which then does it represent, and why ? Thus we reach the crux of the problem. We may incidentally turn to Goodman's very poignant observation[1] in point :

1. See Nelson's Goodman's book, Languages of Art, New York, 1968 p. 5.

"The plain fact is that a picture, to represent an object, must be a symbol for it, stand for it, refer to it; and that no degree of resemblance is sufficient to establish the requisite relationship of reference. Nor is resemblance necessary for reference; almost anything may stand for anything else". A picture that represents—like a passage that describes—an object refers to and, more particularly denotes it. Denotation is the core of representation and is independent of resemblance.

But it is common knowledge that some representations are more realistic than others. What, if the above is the case, can our criteria of realism possibly be, or are we deluding ourselves, or belying our own confusion, in even thinking in terms of realistic representation. Yes, we are deluding ourselves, if we think that realism has anything to do with resemblance per se. But on our new interpretation we can call a realistic representation a familiar representation, with familiarity defined in terms of 'the system of representation standard for a culture or a person at a given time.'

This line of argument would leave us with :

a) Realism is relative, relative to the prevailing system.

b) Denotation may well be purely arbitrary—it is decidedly not founded on any relationship of resemblance, but rests, rather, upon convention.

c) As a result, representation is contingent—whether A represents B depends on whether A consists of symbols which are understood as denotative of B.

As a tail piece to this interesting introduction to the discussion on hand we may suggest that denotation, representation and realism are responsive to relativistic interpretations whereas resemblance is forced into a predominantly essentialistic mould.

Abanindranath catches up with this idea of the 'essentialistic mould'. The essence of nature is spiritual in content. The infinite peeps through the finite and the vision of the artist transcends finitude. The infinity of suggestiveness (Vyañjana) again outgrows the 'essentialistic mould' and that is why Abanindranath's paintings were not 'natural' although most of them represented the 'nature gestalt'. When 'nature gestalt' is transformed into 'art gestalt' it picks up Vyañjana. It is not there in nature. This element of Vyañjana or Lāvaṇya in art, as understood by Abanindranath precludes the applicability of the denotation or representation. Concept in the same sense to a 'bed' or to the picture of the bed (in the Platonic sense). Picture of Y as done by an Artist is something more than Y as he appears to the most sensitive eye of camera. If painting and picture (as done by a camera) were identical, the concept of representation or denotation might have worked. But the concept of Vyañjana introduces a qualitative change in the concept, it is not fully denoted by 'representation or denotation' concept. Relativism may work if the 'essentialistic mould' of nature is taken to be spiritual in essence. The essence of the bed and the painting of the bed if similar, the painting might be considered relative to the bed in nature for our understanding and comprehension. Bed is referent for the painting of the bed and the differential between the two was Vyañjana or Lāvaṇya. If one insists on the representation concept as explaining the relation between nature and art, art would represent nature only in the generic sense as 'man' represents animal. This representation is notional and not actually based on sense experience. Representation, if traced to intuition in the cocean sense, may take us close to what Abanindranath thought in point. Intuition is an amalgam of the actual and the possible. This idea of the possible in art gives a qualitative difference to the art world. That is how art corrects nature. The exact techno-craft through which this correction is effected is unknown. Abnindranath quotes the Tantras to say that the flight of the artist from the domain of nature to the realm of art is comparable to the flight of a bird from one tree to another and it leaves no trace of its flight in the blue sky. The flight line is untraceable. That gives art an esoteric character. That is how Rabindranath Tagore came to conclude that art was Māyā. If the ultimate determinant (art in this case) is indeterminable, it becomes obvious that the concept of representation, denotation, and relativism will fail to work. That is what has happened in the aesthetics of Abanindranath Tagore.

Nature as a point of reference in all art work does not work in the world of aesthetics. Tagore's insistence on the concept of 'Niyatikṛtaniyamarahita' as applied to art and aesthetics precludes reference to the objective world to determine the reality to talk of art being representative of nature. Art can neither be said to resemble, represent or denote nature, in any of its aspects, as nature is unknown and unknowable. The nature is my 'private nature', it is the private nature of the artist as well. When Tagore quotes "Tarubar raser hutase dahe", he describes a withering tree. His way of seeing the withering tree makes his private world blossom forth into a fascinating world of art. This art (Śilpa) is Ānanda. To put it differently this Ānanda as objectified in a particular reference, is the object of art. The joy of the artist being immeasureable at every stage, is indeterminate. This indeterminateness again negates the possibility of art being representative of nature. To represent means to determine and negation is concomitant to this determination.

It would be quite pertinent if we take into account some of the poignant statements of Abanindranath in point.

(a) Man-made tinsals—the elephant, the utensils, clothings and draperies, the golden wares and horse-drawn chariots—copy the 'Deva-śilpa' i.e. nature. So they are not art. They are all ectypes of the divine prototype. In doing them, God has all the glory; man has nothing but the status of a copyist (Silper anadhikara, Bagiswari lectures p. 5)

(b) Man came at long last. He lamented over the one way traffic—as he received unilaterally from the bounties of nature. He had nothing to offer ? His grim determination to give something ultimately gave back to nature what nature could not possibly aspire to produce (Silper Adhikara, Bagiswari Lectures p. 221).

(c) Therefore we may conclude that as we find our own images on the looking glass beautiful, so we may as well call the images beautiful that agreeably reflect on the mirrors of our mind (Saundaryer Sandhāna, Bagiswari Lectures p. 72).

(d) Imagination and memory—they are the eternal handmaids of fine arts. Existential world is fixed and determined : the world of imagination is a world of subsistence and hence it is limitless. Existential world is static. In man's creative activity in art and literature, in knowledge and science, imagination has the pride of place and realism comes next. This is the logical order in all creative activities. Imagination works best in man and in imaginary pursuits man's physical and mental powers get their full fruition (Antara-Bahira, Bagiswari Lectures pp. 107 and 109).

(e) Artistic forms are not imitated from nature nor are they images of natural forms : They are 'Svayaṁrūpa i.e. they represent themselves (Ruper māna O parimāṇa : Bagiswari Lectures p. 316).

The lines as quoted above from Abanindranath Tagore's famous Bagiswari Lectures point to the following:—

I. Negation of copy theory.

II. Art is an improvement upon nature.

III. Coherence and agreement are the guiding principles of aesthetic determination.

IV. Art creates and imagination is the creative faculty ; Private nature is there to be referred to as a referent. Memory links up the art-work with the referent. Imagination is paramount in all forms of creative activity.

V. Art-forms are sui generis ; they are not dependent on some outer forms for their origination. They are Svayaṁrūpa. Art activity is free activity.

The 'essentialistic mould' concept as propounded earlier may, in some measure, hold ground. Nature is just a distant referent. Coherence with our private knowledge of nature may be taken to be just a good or bad guide for knowing what has been painted or made on stone. Resemblance, close or remote is of no consequence. Imagination makes art what it is, the determinant principle being coherence. Nature does not always cohere. That is why we come across grotesque forms in nature. Art has coherence, even in inconsistencies. That is how comic art is born. That is how a Wordsworth regains his lost faith in the 'beautiful Yarrow' by rediscovering the lost sense of coherence within his own mind. This sense of coherence and agreement may indirectly refer to nature but it has no effective guidance from that quarter. The denotation of a 'bed in nature' and the denotation of a 'painted bed' are quite different. Bed in nature is handicapped by the cross matter of which it is made. The painter's bed is made by imagination and it has limitless flexibility. The painted bed rejects all the imperfections inherent in the 'natural bed suffers from utilitarian considerations. The painted bed is free from such utilitarian bias.

When Tagore enunciates the principle of imagination in art and propounds the idea of 'Svayaṁrūpa' in art, we see the 'possible'. The idea of the 'probable' in Crocean aesthetics guaranteed artist's freedom. Tagore assured the artist of his full freedom by giving imagination the paramount importance. He held memory to be of some importance and this means that nature as made in memory was there as a referent to the world of art. The art was neither a symbol of nature nor of the Infinite. Had it been a symbol, art would have lost its 'Svayaṁrūpa', its self-subsistent character. The myth that art was a symbol of nature or of the super-natural has been given a decent burial by Tagore. The utilitarian bias, the legacy from the west and from the east as well, could not make any headway in Abanindranath's aesthetics and it is evident in his enunciation of Līlāvāda in art. His implied rejection of the play theory is also pertinent in this context. To put it negatively:

    I. Tagore believed in the non-functional character of art.

    II. According to him, art was non-representational.

    III. Art did neither present nor represent nature.

    IV. Art was not subservient to any end extraneous to its nature.

V. Art did not belong to the natural world, as it was enlivened with 'Lāvaṇya'.

These negative enunciations somewhat determine and make precise Tagore's position. We know that all determination is negation and to put the truth conversely : all negation is determination. If so, the above-quoted negative statements would help make the Tagorite position clear to some extent.

University of Calcutta.

—ooo—